IMAGES OF WOMEN
IN LITERATURE

IMAGES OF WOMEN IN LITERATURE

FOURTH EDITION

MARY ANNE FERGUSON

University of Massachusetts, Boston

HOUGHTON MIFFLIN COMPANY   Boston

Dallas   Geneva, Illinois   Lawrenceville, New Jersey   Palo Alto

Cover art: Gabriele Münter. *Thinking*. 1917. Städtische Galeria im Lenbachhaus, Munich.

Printed in the U.S.A.
Library of Congress Catalog Card Number: 85-80772
ISBN: 0-395-36908-8

ABCDEFGHIJ-H-898765

CONTENTS

•────────────────────•

CONTENTS

vi

PREFACE

The fourth edition of this anthology consists of seventy-two works that illustrate traditional images of women and also reflect the changes in those images brought about by the women's movement and current serious scholarship about women. In addition to sixty-four works complete in themselves—thirty-two short stories, three plays, and twenty-nine poems—this edition includes, for the first time, eight excerpts from diaries and letters by women; along with one short story, these works constitute a new section, Part III, "Self-Images."

Part I, "Traditional Images of Women," exemplifies the major images of women associated with their biological roles—wife, mother, sex object, woman on a pedestal, and women without men. Although these images are stereotypes associated with the culture out of which they arose, each work shows how the stereotype limits the humanity of the characters and hints at ways to transcend such limitations. Both male and female authors show women characters caught in their roles, but their exemplification is a critique of the culture that reduces human beings to role-playing.

The images in Part II, "Woman Becoming," illuminate the processes by which women seek to transcend their ascribed roles. That most of these works are by contemporary authors is an indication of the relationship of literature to life: since women's roles in society are broadening, their images reflect that fact and also record the pain and anger that accompany such change.

Part III, "Self-Images," shows how some women in the past and some doubly caught by race and economic class as well as by gender have perceived themselves. Especially significant is the stress the diarists have placed on their spiritual and moral development, topics seldom treated in other literature with the immediacy of these self-revelations. These works also tie literature closely to psychologists', historians', and anthropologists' current research into and theories about women's real lives.

All of these works require careful reading to perceive that they do in fact move beyond mere description of roles. Plot and characterization, tone and imagery, genre convention, and above all, the voice of the narrator need to be scrutinized and discussed in order to discern the ways in which the works move beyond stereotypes. This kind of scrutiny is appropriate for introductions to literature as well as for more advanced literary courses. The inclusion of important male authors allows for comparisons of materials within the anthology; but the fact that most of the authors are women allows for ample comparison of styles and perspectives among women writers themselves. Extensive introductions, the biographical notes, and an annotated bibliography—this time of literary works and criticism only—provide ample critical background for readers; they also invite research and the formation of independent judgments. Students and teachers alike will want not only to read literary critiques of a work or an author but also to explore the entire *oeuvre* of an author as a basis for criticism. Other possibilities for research include investigating the lives of some of the authors and characters (for example, former slave Harriet Tubman), the variety of literary approaches available for evaluating works, and the mythological background some of the works evoke (such as Olga Broumas's poem "Artemis" and Martha Collins's "Homecoming").

The variety of styles and genres invites students to write not only about the works but also in imitation of them. This is especially true of the diaries and letters included in Part III, "Self-Images." Each selection includes a comment about the value to the writer of her writing activity, and most express the difficulty the authors found in writing. These selections are very accessible and encouraging to beginning writers, and especially to women writers, whom research has shown to be especially lacking in the self-confidence needed for an assertive, even declarative style. The intimacy of these personal narratives should encourage students to probe their own beliefs and examine their assumptions—and therefore to write more meaningfully.

To keep pace with the momentum of recent changes in women's roles and attitudes and with the increased volume of publication by women writers, this edition includes many new authors as well as a few forgotten ones recently rediscovered. It also offers new perceptions of images, especially of mothers and daughters and women without men. Users of previous editions will miss some excellent works that had to be dropped in order to reflect the current reality about women. Most of the works eliminated are now readily available elsewhere. Students and teachers will undoubtedly want to read longer works not included here; one profitable augmentation is to choose works by authors who have written successfully in more than one genre, such as Alice Walker, Emily Brontë, and Erica Jong, who are competent as both poets and novelists. Another effective augmentation is to read a novel and criticism of it that is representative of several schools, including feminist. This anthology serves as a core for adaptations to many different uses.

By the time one has published a fourth edition, the list of contributors to the complex process of cutting and adding, of determining new emphases, has grown very long. In attending scholarly conventions and poetry readings, in reading avidly the new works of my old authors and trying to keep up with the new, I am indebted to the general discussion of feminist literary theory and practice. My perspective was widened to include diaries and letters by the reading I did to develop a new course (Pioneer Women and Men: the Myth and the Reality); time off for this reading was supported by the National Endowment for the Humanities. Margarita Stearns, Deborah Rosenthal, and Julia Robbins, graduate students at the University of Massachusetts, Boston, did research for the new selections and for the biographical and bibliographical notes; a former student, Marianne Harding, suggested Bradbury's "I Sing the Body Electric!"; and a colleague, Professor Marc Prou, translated the Haitian Creole in Zora Neale Hurston's "Erzulie Freida." Professor Carol Kessler of the Pennsylvania State University sent me a copy of Charlotte Perkins Gilman's "Three Women," and Professor Claire Keyes of Salem State College suggested Denise Levertov's "Living Alone." Many other users of the anthology, both faculty and students, have shared their reactions with me and influenced my decisions. Among them are the following: Teri Bardash, Suffolk County Community College (New York); Patricia M. Bellace, Lord Fairfax Community College (Virginia); Janet Bickel, Mercer County Community College (New Jersey); Julie R. Brickley, University of Wisconsin at Green Bay; Ruth A. Cameron, Eastern Nazarene College (Massachusetts); Curtis Dahl, Wheaton College (Massachusetts); Marcia Dalbey, University of Missouri at St. Louis; Janay Downing, Regis College (Massachusetts); Theresa Enroth, American River College (California); Julie Fay, East Carolina University; Lucy M. Freibert, University of Louisville; Suzanne Gossett, Loyola University (Illinois); Andrea Green, Union County College (New Jersey); Michelle Hoffnung, Quinnipiac College (Connecticut); Barbara A. Kathe, Saint Joseph College (Connecticut); Janet Kauffman, Jackson Community College (Mississippi); Kathleen Gregory Klein, Indiana University at Indianapolis; Jerry Lincecum, Austin College (Texas); Annette M. Lopez, University of Maine at Presque Isle; Marilou B. McLaughlin, State University College at Cortland (New York); Toni McNaron, University of Minnesota; Peggy McIntosh, Wellesley Center for Research on Women; Iely Burkhead Mohamed, Jackson State University (Mississippi); Linda Pannill, University of Kentucky; Lois W. Parker, Southwestern University (Texas); Virginia T. Pond, Catonsville Community College (Maryland); Roberta Rubenstein, American University (Washington, D.C.); Margaret Schramm, Hartwick College (New York); Jo C. Searles, Pennsylvania State University at Altoona; Edna L. Steeves, University of Rhode Island; Alice L. Swensen, University of Northern Iowa; Dorothea Walker, Nassau Community College (New York); David Wee, St. Olaf College (Minnesota); Lynn F. Williams, Emerson College (Massachusetts); and Elizabeth Williamson, Howard Community College (Maryland).

As always, I am grateful to Tillie Olsen and my three daughters for encouragement and advice.

M.A.F.

IMAGES OF WOMEN
IN LITERATURE

INTRODUCTION

Previous editions of this book (1973, 1977, 1981) discussed a riddle
about the identity of the surgeon for a young man injured in an automobile
accident in which his father was killed. The surgeon called to the scene
looked at the patient and said, "I can't operate; this is my son." One would
think that today everyone would know that the surgeon was the boy's
mother. Yet recent trials of the riddle show that though some teenagers
could get the answer immediately, their parents often could not.

The continuing capacity of this riddle to puzzle shows how hard
it is to change our perceptions, even when they are contradicted by
facts. Research by Professor Mary Roth Walsh for her book, *Doctors
Wanted, No Women Need Apply: Sexual Barriers in the Medical Profession, 1835–1975*, indicates that the number of women medical students has
increased by 700 percent since 1959. In 1985, half of all women doctors
are under thirty-five; very few practice surgery, the most prestigious and
lucrative of medical specialties. And even though today about one-third of
all medical students are women, most people still think of doctors as male.
Although teenagers are somewhat more aware of the reality than adults
are, the comparative rarity of women doctors before 1959 still determines
public perceptions in 1985. Such a lag between experience and perception
means that in this time of great change our images of women are confused
and contradictory. Adjectives used by sociologists to describe real women
and by literary critics to describe their reflections—or models—in literature
include such baffling pairs of opposites as passive-aggressive, intuitive-logical,
possessive–self-sacrificing, materialistic-spiritual, frigid-lustful. The only
common factor among these contradictory descriptions is that they all use
the same standard of measurement: the characteristics of men are the
norm and those of women are subsidiary.

Women are thought to be passive when compared to men, who assume
the initiative in sex, in business, and in politics; passivity has a lower
value because assertiveness is needed for success, and it is men who succeed.
Aggressive women who succeed in male spheres are judged to be unfeminine

and unnatural. When women are considered intelligent, their kind of intelligence, their mysterious intuition, is equated with flightiness and fuzzy thinking; male logicality is the norm few women achieve. The other opposing pairs of characteristics are extremes both of which are applicable to women; the norm is a happy medium reached by men. Possessiveness in men is associated with protectiveness and responsibility, in women with narrowness and selfishness; self-sacrifice in men is marveled at, in women taken for granted. Women are seen paradoxically as highly materialistic and as devout and pious; but they carry these traits to undesirable extremes, whereas men exemplify admirable restraint by not allowing their religion to influence their business ethics. A woman may be less or more desirous of sex than a man; either frigidity or lust in a woman is a negative characteristic because the male appetite is the norm. Because of the conflicts among these images, women are bewildered about their identity: they feel damned if they do and damned if they don't.

Even for physical measurements the male is accepted as the standard: women are smaller, weaker, digitally more adept, and capable of longer periods of continuous effort than men. Smallness and weakness are signs of inferiority, even in situations where size and strength are irrelevant. Moreover, so universal is the association of masculinity with superiority that women's "good" qualities make them suitable for inferior positions: their skilled fingers and ability to withstand monotony fit them admirably for menial jobs in industry and business and for the unpaid job of housewife.

As Simone de Beauvoir has said, the image of women has been that of the second sex, the Other for man. This view has emphasized sexual differences instead of human similarities, to women's disadvantage. Even when exalted as a model of purity and generosity, woman has been considered strange and mysterious—superhuman or supermale. The adjectives used to describe woman make it apparent that she is not the equal of man: she may be supernatural, she may be childlike—she is both more and less than man. This sexist and reductive image of women has prevailed in myth and literature for so long that it seems inevitable and true in spite of the obvious logical impossibilities.

Illogical images resist change because of their basis in the emotions. A beautiful woman is despised, even feared, if she uses her "weapons" of tongue and sex to diminish a man's sense of worth. Though she may no longer be condemned to death as a witch because of her mysterious power, she may be ostracized by shame or ridicule. Yet a beautiful woman who uses her power benignly is worshipped as a goddess, exalted as the muse of poetry and music, propitiated as man's mediator and comfort. Such differing views may even be applied to the same woman or image; the difference in the image is in the eye of the beholder.

How have such images come to prevail both in life and in literature? If we try to understand what happens when a single individual forms an image of a particular woman, we begin to comprehend the process at work in history and in literature. Imagine that you are looking through a family album. You stop at a picture of your mother holding you in her arms the day she brought you home from the hospital. Is that slender girl in the too-short skirt really the same person as the matronly woman sitting beside you now? Which one do you see when you think the word *mother?*

Your image of your mother may be kaleidoscopic, a merging of past memories and present reality. You may see her primarily as she used to be, obscuring the present because the changes in her remind you of your own mortality. A deep need to think well of your mother in order to bolster your own self-esteem may transmute your image of an actually cold, selfish woman into a warm, loving one. Conversely, a need to avoid facing your own faults may reverse this process and turn your image of an ordinary, well-meaning person into a monster of greed and selfishness. Your vision of your mother is shaped by your own self-image and by your dreams for the future. If you are ambitious to become a doctor, say, you may credit your mother's tenderness with giving you the desire to serve humanity, but if you cannot stand the sight of blood and must change your goal, you will blame her squeamishness. Your sex too, according to Freud, influences your attitude toward your mother: if you are male, you may see your father as a rival; if you are female, you will see your mother as a threat to your relationship with your father. Our images of others may be a good deal more subjective than objective. Our pictures of the external world must fit our own pattern of memory, desire, and dream. When we look out, we look into a mirror.

Furthermore, to a degree we are only now realizing, each person's images of others are colored by the ideas of society as a whole, of family and peers, and of the nation and the times. In a time and place in which women are expected to stay home and care for children, the image of a mother who does not is tarnished. She herself is likely to feel guilty no matter how valid her reason for absenting herself and no matter how many other women do not fulfill society's expectations. In spite of the fact that more than 50 percent of all women in this country go out of their homes to work, the notion persists that most women are to "stay in their place," the home. Women's own deep agreement with this image, according to behavioral psychologists and sociobiologists, is based on biological conditioning as well as on cultural expectations. Regardless of their origin, such images are closely tied to emotions and thus are very subject to distortion, like images in the mirrors at carnivals. Trying to conform to such blurred images causes great emotional stress.

The rigidity of such images is reflected in the word used to describe them, *stereotypes,* a term taken by sociologists from printing, where it refers to metal plates used to make exact copies. Stereotypes of people differ in one major way from metal ones: they need not duplicate the pattern exactly. As long as some aspects of the stereotype are present, the observer supplies the others from previous experience. Such patterns are called *prejudices;* they provoke judgment before full knowledge is possible. To the pattern "beautiful and blonde," the observer adds "dumb," whether it applies to the specific person or not. A wife or mother, expected to be happy in putting others first, cannot have selfish goals. To win social approval, the beautiful blonde may use her intelligence to play dumb; women who assert their individuality may be laughed at or attacked unless they suppress it. Thus the stereotypes that shape our personalities are even more rigid than metal ones. The configuration of characteristics is held together by mental patterns harder to escape than factory-formed ones; the mind so quickly fills in the blanks that individual differences are not perceived. A person who deliberately departs from a socially approved stereotype by adopting a new role—developing a new life style—may pay a heavy cost in guilt, alienation, or psychosis; tendencies toward schizophrenia may be aggravated by the person's sense of divided self. Women's emotional disorders often stem from the stress of stereotypical thinking.

According to some psychologists, certain stereotypes are particularly strong because under them lie patterns called *archetypes,* which are the basis of all human experience. They are the images of myths, stories told in every society to impose order upon and interpret the chaotic and mysterious aspects of experience. Jungian psychology teaches that our image of mother, for example, stems from deep within our minds in the realm of the *collective unconscious,* where images common to all people and perhaps also to animals are found. These images are too deeply embedded to be available to any individual's conscious mind, but they find expression through symbol and art. Figures in myths and art are powerful because they correspond to the images in the collective unconscious.

Sociologists who do not share Jung's theories about the genetic and universal structure of the psyche nonetheless testify that the stereotypes based on archetypes, grounded in emotion, are strong; they represent our desires and fears about our nature and the structure of the world. A myth of creation must explain both our presence in the world (our beginning) and our knowledge of death (our ending). The images of good and evil embodied in the Great Mother, so widespread among primitive societies, reflect not only our love for the giver of life but also our fear of the inescapable death that the gift brings with it. Such images strongly resist modification by facts and logic and are often fortified by religion, which inevitably involves a large measure of myth.

One peculiarity of the images of women throughout history is that social stereotypes have been reinforced by archetypes. Another way of putting this would be to say that in every age woman has been seen primarily in her biological, primordial role as the mysterious source of life. Women have been viewed as mother, wife, mistress, sex object—their roles in relationship to men. Of course, men also are viewed in their biological roles, but not to the same degree as women; men are neither defined by nor limited to these roles. Cave drawings that show men casting spears or running after a boar also show women pregnant, their secondary sexual characteristics grossly exaggerated so that they seem all bosom, belly, and butt. Man has been defined by his relationship to the outside world—to nature, to society, indeed, to God—whereas woman has been defined in relationship to man. The word *defined* means "having a limit around," "fenced in." Women have been fenced into a small place in the world.

Because women's biological restriction is assumed to have existed forever, the tendency is to believe that it is part of the nature of things, that it is innate; because it has "always" been thus, it must ever be. It is upon this assumption that the dangers of departing from their biological roles have been impressed upon women. Perhaps more than anyone else, Sigmund Freud in our own century reinforced the idea that an unwillingness to accept fully her biological role was the cause of woman's hysteria, neurosis, and psychosis; if women are to be healthy, they should remain "natural." Though scholars have pointed out Freud's bias because of his place in history and though his theories have been modified by Karen Horney and others, Freud's analysis of women's assertiveness as based on "penis envy" has remained in the popular mind and underlies many literary images.

The Stereotypes in Literature

The study of literature does not proceed in a vacuum. Our understanding and evaluation of literary images must have a basis in what history, psychology, sociology, anthropology, and other disciplines—as well as our own experience—tell us about reality. Literary history and theory tell us something about the process by which literature is related to other interpretations of the world. Literature both reflects and helps create our views of reality; it puts us in touch with our deepest feelings, with our prerational knowledge of the world. It is through their preservation in works of art that we know what the stereotypes and archetypes have been and are; in turn, knowing the images influences not only our view of the world and ourselves but also our behavior. In Dante's *Inferno,* the famous lovers Paolo and Francesca tell of reading about those famous lovers Launcelot and Guenevere when they yield to the passion that leads to their damnation. It was largely from reading romances that Emma in Flaubert's *Madame Bovary* (1856) got the dreams that drove her to dissatisfaction, adultery, and suicide. Today serious literature is absorbed and adapted by the popular media so rapidly and effectively that the distinction between imaginary characters and real people has become blurred in the minds of many readers and viewers. Advertising images of impossibly slender women contribute not only to the huge diet industry but also to the incidence of anorexia nervosa, a psychological condition that causes young women to starve themselves to death. Stereotypical images are often destructive.

In literary criticism the word *stereotype* is usually a pejorative one; it has been traditionally felt that only fully developed, "round" characters are aesthetically valid. Yet there are legitimate uses of stereotypes in literature. A flat character may serve as a contrast or foil to a more rounded one; character types used in comedy and satire make readers who recognize them feel superior and hence in a position to laugh. Recent writers have deliberately created static characters to represent what they feel to be the inhumanity of our times. Furthermore, behind any rounded character must lie a recognizable human type with which readers may identify. Literature presents specific characters in concrete circumstances; we measure literary success by the individuality, complexity, and even ambiguity of characters. But readers must be able to extract from the specifics a generalization, an observation about human beings, which they see as relevant to other specific situations—especially their own. The problem with images of women in literature is that they are largely male representations. According to Tillie Olsen in *Silences,* of writers who have been recognized as significant in our time, only one out of twelve has been a woman. It is not surprising, then, that female characters have been most often presented as stereotypes, serving as foils, motivators, barriers, rewards, and comforters to males who actively pursue adventure and their own identities. From a male perspective, the central and most desirable characteristic of female characters has been their passivity.

Traditional Stereotypes

The Mother Images of women in literature have always been ambivalent; for every biological role there has been both a negative and a positive view. In the Biblical creation myth, Eve, the mother of us all, is the temptress who brought sin and death into the world. But the Virgin Mary, passively acted on by the Holy Ghost, pondering in her heart the experience of her Son, is the Queen of Heaven, the Mother of God and, through Him, of us all. Eve could be tolerated as a necessary evil; Mary was worshipped as a model for all womankind. In Greek mythology, Pandora, sent to earth by the gods to marry and establish the human race, brings with her a magic box or vial; opening it, she releases not only all evil but the greatest gift humankind can have—hope. Both Eve and Pandora act in defiance of divine law. If they had passively obeyed (experienced the world vicariously, as Mary did), humanity would have been spared the particular kind of life known as human. In both myths, except for the action of a woman humans would have been godlike. Because of woman, we are condemned to be mortal; we must die. Yet all of us in our early years see our mothers as bringers of life, nurturers, sources of pleasure and comfort. We soon learn that mother also takes away pleasure; she says no, and we blame her for denying satisfaction, no matter what her reasons may be. The role of mother is ambiguous. Myths about woman's dual nature are attempts to explain primordial reactions to her double role as the giver of life and death, of pleasure and pain.

The Wife Both in myth and in life the roles of mother and wife overlap; the difficulty even a husband has in separating the roles in his mind is reflected in the common American custom of a man's referring to his wife as "Mother." A wife performs many of the functions of the mother; both her children and her husband require her attentions as cook and nurse. But when she extends to her husband her motherly role of disciplinarian, scolding, nagging, or withholding her services, her husband reacts as negatively as a child. For him the very qualities desirable in a good mother—firmness, decisiveness, ability to organize time—seem undesirable in a wife. A submissive wife, happy to be supportive and to "stay in her place," is the ideal; a dominating wife is ridiculed or hated.

Woman on a Pedestal Outside of marriage, a beautiful woman may be exalted; her beauty makes her seem superhuman and exonerates men who fall victim to her power. Frequently the effect of the seductress is disastrous. In the *Iliad,* Helen of Troy's decision to run away with Alexandros (Paris) brought death to thousands of men, the destruction of Troy, and the enslavement of the Trojan women. Though objectively Alexandros' weakness and disregard of the mores might seem to have been equally at fault, it was Helen's face "that launched a thousand ships and burnt the topless towers of Ilium" in Marlowe's *Dr. Faustus* (1588). Similarly, Guenevere, married to King Arthur, caused her lover Launcelot to betray his king and start a civil war. Both Malory (fifteenth century) and Tennyson (nineteenth century) put the blame squarely on Guenevere for seducing the noble Launcelot.

Yet other beautiful women are seen as ennobling to men who loved them: Dante is led through Purgatory by the vision and guidance of Beatrice; Petrarch worships Laura even though he can never possess her. Perhaps it is significant that both Beatrice and Laura, in life apparently happy as the wives of other men, are exalted by the poets more after death than before; inconvenient facts must not interfere with mythical roles. The lack of children among the goddesslike heroines of romance can be ascribed only to literary convenience, the fictitiousness of their roles. Yet it is this unrealistic image that most powerfully shapes images of women today. Not only in courtship but also within marriage, the obligation to be beautiful and to use one's powers beneficently is woman's heritage from the view first established in the fantasies of twelfth-century courtly love romances.

The Sex Object and Sexual Politics In another biological role the woman is the opposite of the all-powerful woman on a pedestal: the sex object is man's prey, the fulfiller of man's sexual needs, a receptacle for his passions. Once she fulfills this role and becomes a fallen woman, she may be callously discarded; even the sexual revolution has not overcome adherence to a double standard in sexual mores.

It is impossible to consider women as sex objects without discussing what Kate Millett has called "sexual politics," the system by which men have kept women subordinate. It is their usefulness to men that has determined women's value in society. Virgins have been valued not only because of youth, possible beauty, and freedom from venereal disease, but also because they could become wives and mothers whose children's legitimacy could not be questioned; through their offspring, property could be lawfully transferred. Virgins have been exalted not only because of myths about their special powers over beasts like the unicorn, but also because of their value as commodities. As late as the eighteenth century Dr. Samuel Johnson remarked about chastity: "Upon that all the property in the world depends." The primitive practice of the bride-price, the careful negotiation of dowry, and the vesting of all property rights in the husband are aspects of the economics of marriage. Until the late nineteenth century and in many parts of the world even today, economic and social considerations have been the primary basis of marriage. For both men and women marriage has been a way of obtaining comfort and status as well as sexual service. But this avenue was closed to women who lost their virtue; their disgrace meant living somehow on the fringes of society as servant or governess, seamstress or washerwoman, "kept woman" or prostitute—or it could result in being stoned to death. Sexual politics has kept women (whether married or not) as men's dependents, often literally their chattel, properly to be kept locked into a chastity belt—as rigid as any stereotype can be.

Women Without Men The roles we have considered so far—those of mother, wife, mistress, and sex object—have received more literary treatment than any others, though women have appeared frequently as daughters, sisters, grandmothers, and aunts in drama, fiction, and poetry. An examination of their images would show just as much ambivalence as in women's more frequent roles (those more explicitly connected with sex). Yet throughout history many women have not been wives or mothers or sex objects; many have been single. Unlike the other stereotypes, the image of the single woman has not been at all ambivalent; with very few exceptions the old maid—a single woman beyond the marriageable age of, say, thirty— has been either pitied or ridiculed in literature. The exception is the nun, admired for giving herself to a supernatural cause as bride of the church. But a single woman who remains in society is seen as queer, frequently thin and emaciated to symbolize withdrawal from life, prim, highly conventional, excessively curious, and quarrelsome. Seldom does she function as a main character; normally she acts in a subordinate role reflecting her marginal position in society. Earlier centuries used to give single women the title of "mistress" or "madame" after they had passed the age of consent; the title "miss" is an ironically apt reflection of the opinion that they have missed out on living. The label "old maid" is always pejorative in our society.

Other single women historically have been viewed as marginal in society. Widows and divorcées, assumed to be on the lookout for new mates, are often viewed fearfully as predators both by men and by wives. The children of such women undergo emotional turmoil if their fathers are usurped, yet experience guilt if they themselves do not fill their mothers' emotional needs. In the past widowhood represented freedom from the eternal cycle of childbearing; yet the need for a male "protector" usually led to a new marriage, and the widow's freedom was as short as the interlude between marriage and the first child. Our modern knowledge of contraception and the possibility of abortion allow a new freedom: the decision to marry or remain single may be based on personal desires instead of on social necessity.

In every age women have lived together in pairs. Until recently such unions were assumed to be asexual, and the partners in the "Boston marriage" were regarded with many of the same pejorative attitudes as held about single women. Even today lesbian couples are viewed by many as deviant, especially if they are mothers. Despite such attitudes, lesbians have "come out" and have been expressing their feelings in writing.

So far we have considered stereotypes closely related to woman's biological role as man's mate; she has been defined according to her assumption or nonassumption of this role. But there are other stereotypes less closely related to biology.

The Young Girl Even though the young unmarried girl experiences the major biological events of a woman's life—the onset of menstruation and the development of secondary sex characteristics—she has traditionally been viewed as asexual, as a pure symbol exalted like the woman on a pedestal. A young girl is viewed as silly, flirtatious, concerned with the externals of sexual attractiveness, such as cosmetics and clothes, but without any serious sexual desires. Her years of development are seen as if she were asleep; like Sleeping Beauty of the fairy tale, only identification with a male will make her a real person. Though the fairy story uses a kiss as the means of awakening, it is rape that serves as a girl's rite of passage into adulthood in archetypal myths like that of Persephone. All the other elements of a human being's maturation are ignored—the establishment of metabolic rates that make one a morning or night person, the determination of body size and shape, decisions about religion and philosophy of life, intellectual interests. Indeed, in Freudian terms women are viewed as cases of arrested development; because they do not fully separate from their mothers, their characters as adult individuals are considered inferior to men's. Recent research indicates a pattern of development different from and later than men's; the continued closeness to their mothers that extends into early middle age probably accounts for women's traditional skills in and concern for interpersonal relationships. Expectation of a need to reject their mothers because of the prevalence of Freudian attitudes may be the cause of the much-publicized tension between mothers and daughters, a tension that often is absent. Persephone continued to love her mother Demeter; both were sad that they had to be separated but both accepted their adult roles. The Persephone myth reflects the reality that adulthood involves loss as well as gain. The Greek myth of Psyche, who was the beloved of Eros (Cupid in Roman myth), shows a young woman establishing her individuality; the name Psyche means "soul" or "spirit." Women do have an inner development that makes them fully human.

The Educated Woman   Whether married or single, young or old, a learned woman has usually been suspect and the butt of ridicule in literature. Particularly mocking is the picture Byron gives in *Don Juan* (1819) of Donna Inez, who flaunts her little Latin and even less Greek and henpecks her husband. One does not know whether Byron despises her more for her learning or her domination, but he sees them as part of the same pattern. Even now the stereotype of a highly educated woman is of an unattractive female in sturdy oxfords and tailored suit. When Germaine Greer, a professor at Warwick University in England and author of *The Female Eunuch* (1971), appeared in television interviews in this country, reviewers invariably expressed amazement at her attractiveness. Beginning in puberty, American girls become afraid of success in school, hiding their learning as much as possible or deliberately failing. Though they make better grades than men, their success is usually dismissed as superficial, not goal-directed, or insignificant because it is not in important areas such as math and science. Even women do not expect high intellectual achievement from other women. Asked to grade the performance of scholars, a group of college women rated as inferior articles ostensibly written by women but rated the same articles as superior when men's names were attached to them. Perhaps this tendency accounts for the fact that many successful women downgrade women in general; these women see themselves as successful *and* feminine but use the stereotype when they view other women.

The Lady   Another stereotype, dependent more on social class than on biology, is that of the *grande dame,* or lady. Special rules for her behavior were prescribed by rigid social systems including that of the antebellum South in this country. A gentlewoman truly gentle, such as Melanie in *Gone with the Wind* (1936), has been a part of the romantic exaltation of women; but D. H. Lawrence's view in *Lady Chatterley's Lover* (1926) that *gentillesse* diverts women from their true role as sexual creatures has prevailed in modern literature. Lady Chatterley realized that her place in life was not presiding at a tea table but being serviced by her gardener; since the sexual liberation of the 1920s, ladies have removed themselves from their pedestals. But popular images of clubwomen, idle rich women playing at social work, pampered wives who "entertain" but do not work, show that the stereotype is still alive.

Images in This Anthology

Part I of this anthology includes examples of the five images of women most closely related to their biological roles: the wife, the mother, woman on a pedestal, the sex object, and woman without man. Although a stereotype underlies all the examples of each image, not a single work stops with merely describing the stereotype; all go beyond to show the complexity of the role both for the woman and for those associated with her. Through irony and satire, through description of women's self-perception, through overt expression of anger, authors—both male and female—expose the wastefulness of stereotypical thinking and its cost to individuals and society. Some works reveal the mythic base that reinforces the stereotype; others use stark realism to explode the myth. Through a variety of perspectives, the selections cumulatively document the tenacity of the stereotypes. The effect of reading these works, especially for women, is likely to be anger and depression.

Writers, especially since the beginning of the current women's movement, have been trying to find ways not only to counter these universal stereotypes and the negative emotions they evoke but to create new images. Part II of this anthology, "Woman Becoming," shows women in the process of changing, of breaking out of the old rigid patterns. Women writers are finding support for their deepest perceptions in the work of women scholars; readers recognize themselves in the new images. In Part III, new in this edition, self-images expressed in diaries and letters reveal, even more than fiction and poetry, women's true nature, their concern for education, for religion, for self-development. These selections show that the new images not only reflect current reality but also have their roots in women's private writings.

The nature of the new images is symbolized by the existence of Professor Walsh's book on women doctors, published by a prestigious university press. Like the women's movement as Betty Friedan perceived it in 1980, women's studies in the late 1970s reached a "second stage." Perceptions about women have moved from the realm of cocktail party jokes into that of serious scholarship. Today several extensive bibliographies document the explosion in research about women; they also reveal the interdisciplinary nature of women's studies and the difficulty of mastering the field. In order to survive in the academic world, feminist scholars must usually establish themselves within a traditional discipline. They must investigate, even attack, the principles of the discipline they choose to enter before the feminist perspective can begin to affect the mainstream research and teaching within that discipline; at the same time they must acquire insights and methodological strategies from feminist colleagues in other disciplines. They must also be in touch with new information about women's lives and with new interpretations of old data. A literary critic needs knowledge from psychologists and sociologists to evaluate a woman writer's description of adolescent trauma or mother-daughter interaction; women writers learn from literary historians that they have a female tradition of imagery, attitudes, style. Professor Walsh, for example, though writing about history and medicine, is a psychologist. Without the work of social historians and without her understanding of women's desires and motives, she would not have had the fresh insight to ask the right questions about previous medical historians' assumption that there have been no women physicians to speak of.

The need for exchange of information caused by the interdisciplinary nature of women's studies resulted in the formation in 1978 of the National Women's Studies Association, which publishes a national newsletter and holds national conventions annually. The organization recognizes the need for communication among women working for feminist education and social change on all levels; its members are trying to create a structure to achieve egalitarian goals by egalitarian means. Such structure has few models in our society where hierarchy and credentials are the framework for institutions, academic and otherwise. Feminist educators find that the learning style of the women's movement and of the early days of women's studies—group interaction of peers—leads to trustworthy knowledge. They have found that such devices as admitting their ignorance, sharing their insights and questions with peers, involving students actively in real research, passing around syllabi and bibliographies, and team-teaching lead to the demystification of research as a prerogative of the initiated, to the use of the language of everyday life to communicate new knowledge, and to critiques of established disciplines.

In every field feminist scholars are showing the inadequacy of previous research, which has failed to ask appropriate questions about women because of the predominantly male frame of reference. For example, Dr. Mary Jane Sherfey shows that scientists have done more research on male hormones than on female hormones largely because they have assumed that hormonal imbalance is "normal" for women. Dr. Sherfey also puts into perspective a fact long known to biologists: that the human fetus is initially female; this fact should preclude the attitude that male development must be the basis for comparison. In anthropology recent studies of extant hunter-gatherer societies have contradicted the earlier conclusion that in primitive societies hunting by males was the main source of food. Archaeology had discovered only the stone tools used by hunters; observation of extant societies reveals that probably two-thirds of the food consumed in such societies is gathered by women using sticks and leather pouches, which perish with the society. To rediscover women who lived during historical times has required new techniques also. After raising the question of why half the human race has rarely been mentioned in history books, feminist historians have turned to methods found useful in the study of other groups previously considered insignificant. They are re-examining archives with new questions in mind, using demographic techniques to deduce individual and group history from statistics, focusing on social units such as the family instead of on political and military figures, and using biography and personal records as a resource to recreate the past. A new encyclopedia, *Notable American Women,* documents the lives of women active in politics, business, religion, the abolitionist movement, and the fight for women's rights, and of women writers, artists, philosophers—all deserving fame in their own right. Discovering that we as women have foremothers who achieved in the public sphere gives us a basis for countering the argument that women *should* function only in their biological roles because they always have. Knowledge of women's past achievements gives us a sense of continuity and a basis for perceiving women as agents, as actors in history, rather than as an undifferentiated passive mass.

Recovering their history and finding role models of women who have been achievers is an important step for women in overcoming their characteristic low self-esteem, an attitude that causes them to undervalue other women as well as themselves. Important psychological research about women's views of their own incompetence has led scholars Rosalind Barnett and Grace Baruch not only to reinterpret previous research but to suggest ways of changing the socialization of women and men so that their perceptions will accord with the facts of women's competence. In *Beyond Sugar and Spice: How Women Learn to Grow, Learn, and Thrive* (1979), Barnett and Baruch make practical suggestions for helping children perceive women as autonomous beings. They suggest that seeing parents work both at home and away on an equal basis can begin to change perceptions within the family. Professor Dorothy Dinnerstein feels that even more basic parental sharing of infant care is necessary not only for equality and happiness but for the very survival of the race. Women activists are working for institutional change that will support the concept of gender equality. They point out that society's refusal to help parents care for children by such adaptations as flexible work schedules, for example, perpetuates the myth that only biological mothers are capable of child care. Mothering—or parenting—is a learned skill; research indicates that men as well as women are able to acquire it, though probably not all people want to. Though current research makes it clear that there are significant sex differences in behavior and capacity, the research also indicates that there is as wide a variance among members of the same sex as between the sexes. Gender does not determine individual limits. Because of centuries of acculturation, it is clear, however, that women today have special sensitivity to the emotional dimension of human behavior. Psychiatrist Jean Baker Miller suggests that perceiving the value of this sensitivity will not only enable women to overcome their low self-esteem but will aid society in overcoming the sense of alienation and despair that dominates current attitudes.

Recent feminist literary research has resulted in new concepts important to the study of images of women in literature. In the 1970s, studies of almost every country and period as well as of many individual authors documented the predominance of negative—or at best, not affirmative— images of women in literature by men. The fact that American fiction as late as the 1960s portrayed women as negatively as any medieval text illustrates literature's continuing function of conserving tradition. But recent research shows the falsity of assuming that women have had no alternative but to write according to the dominant male modes. Professor Elaine Showalter sees the interrelationships among nineteenth-century women writers in Britain as a subculture with its own style and concerns. Professor Emily Stipes Watts shows that American women poets shared common imagery, treatment of myth, attitudes toward marriage, nature, and God, which differ from those of American male writers and of English women writers. Professor Nina Baym has shown the traditional dichotomy between the fair good heroine and the dark bad one in American literature to be an oversimplification. In hundreds of nineteenth-century novels written by women for women, she has found a focus on strong young women who achieve both psychic and economic independence by venturing out into the world, much as young men did. The traditional ending of these stories with the heroine's marriage, corresponding to the reality of life for most nineteenth-century women, has obscured the degree of autonomy achieved by the heroines. The "happy ending" no doubt helps account for the continued popularity of heroic romances today, in spite of their silence about "afterwards." But these heroines can serve as better role models than the seduced and abandoned victims that dominate male American fiction.

Other scholars are resurrecting and reassessing previously unknown or long-forgotten works. Diaries and letters by black women discovered in manuscript in libraries have been edited and published. We now know of their experiences as slaves and of their search to define personal freedom and to find dignity through religion. Recent studies both by historians such as Jacqueline Jones and by literary critics such as Mary Helen Washington emphasize that the preservation of family life was the guiding motivation for black women who were slaves; the sense of community as an ideal of blacks is expressed in the works of many black writers, perhaps most vividly in those of Toni Morrison. Massive publishing ventures have made us aware of the numerous works yet to be recovered. A new encyclopedia of biography and criticism, *Guide to American Women Writers,* is a valuable tool for recovering our heritage. A series selected by Elizabeth Hardwick for the Arno Press makes available again eighteen forgotten but important nineteenth-century American novels by women. Already some rediscovered works of feminist literature have achieved the status of classics: one thinks of such treasures as Agnes Smedley's *Daughter of Earth,* Harriet Arnow's *The Dollmaker,* Christina Stead's *The Man Who Loved Children,* Zora Neale Hurston's *Their Eyes Were Watching God.*

Literary critics are also explaining why such works by women have been so consistently ignored. They disappeared for the same reason women doctors, according to Professor Walsh, disappeared in the 1880s: they were ignored or rejected by institutionalized male superiority. Professor Frank Kermode, a prominent literary critic, points out that the past century's professionalization of the teaching and criticism of literature has resulted in the establishment of a literary canon considered as sacred as the canon of books of the Bible, and as fiercely protected against change. Not only the canon of works to be studied but the methods of interpretation are being determined by professionals—usually academic—who have been, historically, white males. Incursions by "outsiders," the uninitiated such as women and blacks, are thought to lower the standards set by literary critics; when they are considered at all, their works are dismissed with condescension or scorn as minor and crude.

The fact that such judgments are often based on sex discrimination or what Mary Ellman has called "phallic criticism" and that they persist into the 1980s may be demonstrated by the critical response to two authors separated by more than a century. Carol Ohman has shown that many critics' acclaim for Emily Brontë's *Wuthering Heights,* published in 1847 under the pseudonym Ellis Bell, changed to pejorative when the author's female identity was disclosed. Recently, after James Tiptree, Jr., received three coveted prizes for science fiction, a male critic introduced a collection of Tiptree's short stories with high praise for the masterly masculine style that set them above all others in this field dominated by male writers. Later, in the introduction to another collection, Ursula Le Guin revealed that Tiptree is in fact Alice Sheldon. Whatever virtues her style may have, they are not based on gender. Whether her reputation will survive this disclosure remains to be seen. But the equation of excellent with masculine is clear.

For feminist literary theorists, many developments in literary theory during the 1970s and 1980s seem to offer support for new evaluation of differences between male and female writers. The rejection of the so-called New Criticism, which dominated attitudes toward literature from the 1930s through the 1960s, paralleled the development of many new theories, which are today being hotly debated. The New Criticism evaluated literature primarily according to standards of unity and perfection of form, the "integrity" of the individual work; it minimized, even repudiated, the perspective of biographical, psychological, historical, and social context. Achievement and recognition of literary perfection were closely tied to working within the tradition under which the various literary forms had been established—historically by male writers. Whether imitating or rebelling against tradition, artists were expected to have deep awareness of its specifications. The prejudice against women inherent in these attitudes was epitomized as late as 1959 by a male critic of Emily Dickinson who suggested that the phrase "woman poet" was a contradiction in terms.

Reactions against the New Criticism have been various. So-called structuralist criticism derived techniques from anthropology, especially from the belief of Claude Lévi-Strauss that there are universal narrative structures among primitive peoples. Structuralist literary critics have had to work against the accusation that, in searching for universal structures, they reduce all literature to its underlying bases; and feminist anthropologists have pointed out the need to correct Lévi-Strauss's data by gathering stories from female informants. Feminist critics have shown that certain literary forms, such as autobiography and the *Bildungsroman,* differ according to the gender of the writer; discovery of such differences leads to new definitions of the forms themselves and undermines the assumption that male equals universal.

In the last ten years a new approach, known as poststructuralist or deconstructionist, has emphasized the literary text itself as an unstable concept subject to endless variations according to critical insights brought to it. This view tends to downgrade authors (and their gender) while exalting criticism as a supreme literary performance. Since these views derive largely from French critics, who use French literature as a point of departure, many American critics reject their validity. But feminist critics, both French and American, are using some concepts from this perspective to examine fundamental differences between women's and men's writing. Following the psychoanalytical approach of Jacques Lacan, they are finding that the female body is a determinant of female language and thus of women's literary expression. Focusing as it does on defining gender differences, this school of criticism also undermines assumptions about the universality of male norms.

Another important critical perspective, also based on psychological insights, is reader-response theory, which emphasizes the role of readers in "creating" texts. Since women have been avid readers—especially since the nineteenth century—this approach would seem to lead to valuing women's responses; it should help explain why the immensely popular women writers of the nineteenth century both in America and England have been ignored by critics or at best passed over with faint praise as anomalous phenomena. But the frame of reference of most critics of this school has largely been male writings; they seem to define "readers" as clones of themselves, not only highly learned and versed in the male literary tradition but sharing male rites of passage. Recently, feminist critics have made use of some of the tenets of this school in a way that furnishes a basis for a new concept of the role of literature in a democracy. Instead of dismissing such works as *Uncle Tom's Cabin* and *Gone with the Wind* as inferior because they appealed so greatly to readers, Jane Tompkins has shown that their appeal was based on feminine insights about basic human attitudes toward social ills. Harriet Beecher Stowe showed that Christian love could not condone slavery; in her fictionalized version of the only war Americans have experienced on their own land, Margaret Mitchell showed the tragedy of loss and poverty, which was well understood by American readers who had just been through the Great Depression. Tompkins makes clear that it is the appeal to basic human attitudes that explains the worldwide best-selling status of these two books.

Tompkins has also written about the advantage Nathaniel Hawthorne had, because of his network of male critics, over the mid-nineteenth-century best-selling writer Susan Warner, who had no such support. In *The Resisting Reader,* Judith Fetterly has shown why such acclaimed writers as Hawthorne and Melville have been rejected by women readers who cannot accept the negative images of women or their total absence in the works of these "classic" writers.

In their monumental study of nineteenth-century women writers—mostly British—Sandra Gilbert and Susan Gubar discovered that these writers resisted their exclusion from the mainstream. The relationship among male writers has been explained as stemming from the necessity that "sons" rebel against their "fathers," their literary predecessors; Professor Harold Bloom identified Milton as the point of departure for male writers. Gilbert and Gubar show that women writers could find no place for themselves in this line of descent; they could feel only deep ambivalence about themselves as both writers and women. Their feelings were expressed in their works through consistent images of enclosure, suffocation, starvation, madness, death; fantasies of escape and freedom appeared comparatively rarely. But the novel *Jane Eyre* and the poems of Emily Dickinson transcend the problems of self-identity of their writers. It is clear that many women writers in the twentieth century have emphasized survival, not destruction, as Blanche Gelfant has pointed out in *Women Writing in America: Voices in Collage*. And Lee Edwards in *Psyche as Hero* has shown that the myth of Psyche underlies many important novels by women, works in which a strong woman hero determines her own destiny and shares her happy ending by helping to form a harmonious community.

Though traditional images of women persist in works by both men and women, a whole body of literature that may be labeled *feminist* has been appearing since the 1970s. This new literature shows fully human women characters who, like men, are in some sense self-aware and autonomous; who fail or succeed for the same reasons men do—limitation by circumstances (poverty, poor health, ignorance), by the actions of others, by narrow societal roles, by lack of energy or insight; who assume responsibility for their own acts and are thus capable of heroism and of tragedy. By showing ways in which women experience the world differently than men, feminist writers expand our knowledge of human nature. New works explore the dynamics of mother-daughter relationships, of friendship among women as a major aspect of their socialization, of sexual unions between women as valid and enriching human experiences. They establish links with women of the past and women of different classes and races; they invite women to find, by developing a sense of community with other women, ways of evaluating themselves positively. Searching for language and forms in which to express their insights, feminist writers are creating new images that not only reflect but reveal to women their own reality. Anyone reading the works in this book will see changing, growing, fully human beings—women becoming.

PART
I

TRADITIONAL IMAGES OF WOMEN

The Wife

The earliest meaning of the word *wife,* not only in English but in many other related languages, was "woman," a general term to denote a person of the female sex. But as early as the ninth century the word had narrowed to mean primarily "a woman joined to a man by marriage, a married woman." This etymological shift is a meaningful parallel to the history of women's position in a society in which men are dominant: under patriarchy women came to be valued less as persons in their own right than as role-players; their relationships to men became their very definition. How well they played their roles, in the judgment of males, determined their value in society. A woman who lives happily and submissively with her husband is the ideal; one who rebels—especially if she does so successfully—is both feared and abhorred. Most writers have focused on one of these two poles in their images of women; but occasionally in the past, and more often in the twentieth century, writers have represented a wife as primarily a woman, a female person who experiences the role of wife sometimes with joy, sometimes with ambivalence, and sometimes with despair and anger. The selections in this section reveal the variety of images of the wife.

As early as the fourteenth century, Chaucer embodied the ideal wife, who submits first to her father, then to the husband whose name she must take, in the image of Griselde in *The Canterbury Tales.* The daughter of a serf, Griselde is honored when chosen by a nobleman as his bride, endures without complaint his depriving her of her children and replacing her with a new wife, and continues to be kind and loving to all regardless of her personal status. Although even the pilgrims who heard this tale in Chaucer's poem knew it was only an ideal, this image has persisted in literature and in life because it is an easy solution to the problem of dominance in a hierarchically organized society. Its ambiguity in a democracy—officially acknowledged only in 1918, when women won the vote in this country—accounts for the guilt and anger in contemporary society as the reality of women's human need for self-development becomes impossible to deny.

Chaucer's fictional audience in *The Canterbury Tales* heard the story of Griselde from a priest, an otherworldly idealist. Audiences today, who receive the ideal with all the trappings of realism, may be less skeptical than Chaucer's readers, more willing to accept the ideal without being reminded of the actual person behind it. In "Death in the Woods," Sherwood Anderson's fictional audience for the tragic death of old Mrs. Grimes includes a young boy, now grown, for whom seeing Mrs. Grimes's dead body in the snow was an initiation into the mystery of sex; as an adult narrator, he tries to tell of this experience so as to share with the reader his sense of this initiation as a mystic experience that shaped his life. In order to foreground the mysticism, Anderson tells in quick narrative summary the story of the male brutality that dominated Mrs. Grimes's life. Throughout the story, as in Chaucer's tale of Griselde, there is no hint of Mrs. Grimes's inner feelings. The reader is allowed to *see* her stoically nurturing animals, children, and men and is thus invited to admire her, even to be somewhat in awe of such selflessness. Anderson does evoke a sense of awe paralleling that in the myth of the suffering servant, of which the story of Jesus is a version. But he does so by making this story the narrator's, not that of Mrs. Grimes. She is a symbol, not a real human being.

Similarly, Sally Benson lets us see only a little of the feelings of her "Little Woman"; she focuses on the husband's early enchantment and growing disillusionment as Penny, the wife, plays her role to the hilt. The reader sees the limitation of Penny's self-imposed confinement to home and husband and is encouraged to see her willingness as a sign of her insignificance as a person and to sympathize with her husband, for whom her total dependence is becoming burdensome. Readers are not likely to understand that Penny's role-playing must stem from lifelong conditioning but are likely to think of her as little in mind and spirit as well as body.

In a story that was enormously popular in the nineteenth century, "The Angel over the Right Shoulder," Elizabeth Stuart Phelps validates her heroine's resumption of wifehood after an abortive rebellion by ascribing it to religious beliefs. Such reasoning carries weight even now. Phelps is very modern in focusing on the interruptions of Mrs. James's "private" time by apparently legitimate claims on her time and attention, on the discontinuity in a woman's life that prevents serious work, especially intellectual work; even with what her husband considers his full cooperation and approval, she cannot find time for study. She buries her anger, but one wonders how long she can pay such a price for her Christian faith, the price of abandoning her right to self-development, of having a self aside from her roles. The price she pays is parallel to that symbolically represented in Ruth Whitman's poem "Cutting the Jewish Bride's Hair." This act represents the bride's willingness to assume the role of wife and mother, to subordinate her beauty, and sexuality, to this role. These two works— Phelps's lightly, perhaps, but Whitman's with strong irony and anger— reveal the support lent by religion to the subservience of women. The daily prayer of Jewish men—"I thank God I was not born a woman"—probably could be repeated with heartfelt emotion by most males in our society. May Swenson's poem "Women" expresses visually as well as verbally the traditional attitude that women should be "the gladdest things" in the world because they restore men's egos by being "sweetlipped / sturdy / and smiling."

Women who do not happily assume their roles but rebel or protest have been viewed angrily as ones who, in Ruth Whitman's words, "shift the balance of the universe," who upset not just their husbands but the entire economic and political system. The negative image has as long a tradition as the ideal.

As the submissive wife corresponds to the "good" mother, the dominating wife corresponds to the "terrible" mother. In the past the shrewish wife has often been viewed as comic and could be laughed at as a necessary evil: the medieval stock character Mrs. Noah, who rants and raves as she orders her husband around; Chaucer's Wife of Bath, who brags about her manipulation of five husbands; Shakespeare's Kate, who has to be tamed by her husband. But women with strong wills, such as Lady Macbeth and Cleopatra, were often the source of tragedy. Sometimes just by being beautiful a wife could unman her husband and cause his disgrace, as in the French romance about Erèc and Enide. Though we laugh at James Thurber's bossy Mrs. Mitty in "The Secret Life of Walter Mitty," a selfish, destructive alcoholic like Martha in Edward Albee's *Who's Afraid of Virginia Woolf?* is perceived as realistic. Unlike the submissive wife and the mother about whom some ambiguous attitudes remain, the dominating wife is usually perceived with unrelieved hostility and anger. Thurber's famous cartoon of the little man about to be swallowed by the monstrous matriarch ruling his house seems true to life in a society that tends to ascribe a dominant role in every relationship.

Violence and death are the effects of an unnatural woman, one who dominates men. In Eugene O'Neill's play *Before Breakfast,* Mrs. Rowland dominates the scene so forcefully that we do not even see her husband, toward whom she directs her tirade of abuse and threats. She taunts him for his dependence on her and makes it clear she will never let him pursue his own happiness. Margaret Macomber in Ernest Hemingway's "The Short Happy Life of Francis Macomber" not only deprives her husband of his courage and virility but (it is strongly implied) may have been his executioner to prevent him from assuming the dominant role in their marriage. The effects of female dominance are unrelievedly disastrous. The main cause of this dominance, from a male perspective, is an unnatural lack of womanly qualities. The slovenly and prematurely old Mrs. Rowland is an alcoholic who drinks before breakfast to gain the courage to search for evidence of her husband's infidelity; an unnatural woman, she enjoys her "triumphal malignity" as a witch might. From the perspective of Wilson, the hunting guide, Margaret Macomber is typical of American women, whom he sees as "the hardest in the world; the hardest, the cruelest, the most predatory and the most attractive." Wilson sees Mrs. Macomber as her husband's murderer and intends to blackmail her.

For these stories it is especially important to recognize the significance of the persona from whose perspective the story is told. As readers, we need not be limited to the attitudes of the narrative voice but can use our own experience with life and reading to go beyond the narrator's view. Since O'Neill's work is a play, we are free to judge the scenes without a narrator as guide; subtly, the play builds on our expectations, on public stereotypes. Objectively, we can have little doubt about Mrs. Rowland's bitchiness. But her horror when she sees the full effect of her threats suggests that she did not intend anything as extreme as driving her husband to suicide. From a feminist perspective we may believe that the husband's insistence on his right to nourish his genius at her expense led to her alcoholism and rage. We know that a person who is abusive has usually been abused. Though Mrs. Rowland is given no visible redeeming qualities, it is not reasonable to suppose she is evil incarnate, as the play suggests. Similarly, in Hemingway's story we need not accept as totally reliable the view of the hunting guide, to whom the Macombers are foreigners. Our own experience of American women can help us generalize more reliably than Wilson can, though of course it is sobering to realize that anyone perceives American women so negatively. We can at least wonder about Margaret's motivation for shooting; she may indeed have tried to save her husband, as she claims. We can question Wilson's motivation for accusing her so quickly. In any case, Hemingway invites the reader to focus on questions about Francis Macomber, not Margaret. Was he happy at all? When? By choosing Wilson as the central consciousness, Hemingway limits our information for assessing Margaret.

O'Neill, Hemingway, and Benson prevent sympathy with the female characters by foregrounding male perceptions. When a writer focuses on a female character and her inner feelings about the necessity of role-playing, readers react differently. Though we may think Mrs. James in Phelps's story foolish for giving up so easily in her attempt to study, we can certainly share her annoyance at the constant trivial interruptions that prevent it; Phelps paints a very realistic picture of the dailiness of life at home for most housewives, especially those with young children. Alice Cary, a younger contemporary of Phelps, was bolder in her poem "The Bridal Veil," overtly stating a bride's ambivalence about embarking on her new role. The bride enunciates the terms on which she will continue to be a wife, warning that she is not an ideal stereotype but is made of "common earth, common dew." As a human being, she must inevitably grow and change and will not stay with her husband unless, guided by love for her, he also continues to develop. She will remain ever ready to flee, at least in spirit, though in body she will be "turf at . . . [his] feet." Cary's declaration of independence seems like whistling in the dark from the perspective of Phelps's story, in which even a devoted husband cannot enable his wife to escape her role limitations; perhaps the fact that Cary (and her sister) remained single and earned a living by writing is an indication that she knew Phelps to be telling the truth.

In the last three stories in this section, the difficulties of escaping role limitations are spelled out for twentieth-century characters. Jane Augustine's story "Secretive" exposes the battered-woman syndrome and its most horrifying aspect—the victim's willingness to blame herself. This story should make any reader hesitant to see any wife's activities as trivial; behind the consumer, the alcoholic, the volunteer, or the hard-working executive may be a nameless role-player whose anger, kept secret, eats her alive. Now, in the 1980s, we know that many such secrets are kept by women in all walks of life, and we also know how difficult it is to change not only their situations but their internal view of themselves as deserving punishment or the stoicism that is their only front. Mrs. Grimes, Mrs. James, the Jewish bride, Alice Cary's bride—any of these wives might have become the narrator of such a secret.

The stories by Ann Beattie and Jean Thompson show how difficult it is to change the traditional role even under circumstances that seem to invite change. Like Cary's bride, Beattie's heroine asserts her right to freedom, specifically to spend every "Tuesday Night" alone, without ex-husband or present husband or child. But she faces the common human dilemma of how to use her freedom; having all her life lacked a personal goal outside of her wife-mother role, she aimlessly fritters away her time. We can see that she lacks any sense of sacrifice or success, such as sanctioned the same role for Phelps's Mrs. James; we can also wonder whether her freedom as woman will compensate for her husband's effect on their daughter, whom he is subtly influencing to become like Penny Loomis, a happy "little woman." Will Beattie's wife—significantly, unnamed—if divorced a second time, have any consolation? Beattie's picture is bleak; neither wifehood nor freedom seems to offer much hope.

The effort by both partners to make a marriage work is epitomized in Jean Thompson's "Driving to Oregon," an ironic return to the hopeful days of the westward movement. An interracial couple meets with disapproval from parents and most other people they know in a small town in the Midwest, represented repulsively as having "ulcers in brick" and "graceless new enterprise" in the suburbs; it is a place "where the sight of big black Bert and his skinny white wife often stops traffic." Her pregnancy and the glowing picture of Oregon painted by friends who have visited the state and brought back brochures make the couple decide to follow the American dream and leave behind "the families, the friends, the lifetime of habit." But, like many other pioneers, they learn that the habits and attitudes of home await them in the West as well. Thompson leaves her characters with some hope; they are not stereotypes but individuals, each with a history that explains their love for one another. But the pattern of restriction and reduction in others' views of them makes race, like sex, a deterrent to human growth. Changing such patterns is beyond individual effort, but the characters' determination leaves us hoping for a beginning, at least, of change.

LITTLE WOMAN

by

SALLY BENSON

(1900–1948)

Sally Benson began her career as a journalist and ended it writing movie scripts. Two collections of her short stories, Junior Miss *(1941) and* Meet Me in St. Louis *(1942), depict female adolescent rites of passage. Both became popular in dramatized and film versions that somewhat distorted their insights. More than one hundred of her short stories appeared in* The New Yorker.

Penny Loomis liked to look back to the day when Ralph had first seen her. It was the day she had first seen Ralph, too, but she didn't think of that. She remembered only the delighted, incredulous look in Ralph's eyes when he caught sight of her sitting in the large chair in the Matsons' living room. In the short skirts and long waists of ten years ago, she had seemed just like a doll. Later in the evening he had told her so. "I can't get over you!" he exclaimed. "You're so tiny!"

"Oh, I know! And I hate it!" she answered. "It's dreadful, really! About clothes, I mean. Why, I wear size eleven!"

"You could look taller," Louise Matson said. "Naturally, those flat-heeled shoes make you look awfully little. If you *wanted* to look taller, you could wear high heels."

Penny Loomis had surveyed her strapped, patent-leather shoes thoughtfully and then her eyes had rested for a rather long instant on Louise's substantial Size 7 brocade slippers. "It's all very well for you to talk," she replied ruefully. "Your feet are a decent size, not disgraceful little Chinese feet like mine. You have nice, *big* feet."

Taking her home that night, Ralph had commented on Louise's attitude. "She was just trying to be catty," he said. "And you were swell about it. You may be little, but you aren't *small*!"

There was nothing to it after that first evening. It was as though Ralph never knew what hit him. There were three months of being engaged, of dancing night after night, attracting attention because Ralph was so tall—over six feet—and she was so tiny. He was enchanted with her daintiness and made jokes about it. "Now where," he would ask, looking over her head and pretending he couldn't see her, "did I put that woman I had with me?"

Everybody would laugh, especially Penny. "Big silly!" she would say. "Take me home!"

Everything she did pleased and amazed him. When, the Christmas before they were married, she presented him with a scarf she had knitted, he was genuinely overwhelmed. "I don't believe it," he said, smoothing it over and over with his hands. "You're not big enough to hold the needles."

He made so much fuss about the scarf at home that his mother, who had knitted scarves, sweaters, and socks for him all his life, was inclined to be bitter. "You act as though she'd knitted that scarf with her feet," she said acidly. "And by the way, I put those golf stockings I just finished for you in your bottom bureau drawer."

His enchantment lasted long after they were married. It amused him to see her childish, round-toed shoes lying on the floor, to see her diminutive dresses hanging in the closet. Their house was full of company, too, those first months, men mostly, who marvelled with Ralph at the sight of Penny in an apron actually being able to get dinner, carrying platters of food almost bigger than she was.

They had no children, which was a pity, as Penny had fancied the idea of herself surrounded by tall, stalwart sons, but she had Ralph to flutter over and take care of. She made few friends and was content in their small apartment. Once Ralph asked her why she didn't go out more. "Do you good," he said, "to get out and play bridge or something in the afternoon. Why don't you look up Louise? You and she used to be pretty good friends."

Penny replied scornfully. Women were all right, she supposed. But she hated bridge, really. It was such a silly game. And she felt so funny going out with Louise, who was so tall. They looked ridiculous walking together.

Ralph had laughed at that. "Say, listen," he said, "I'm taller than Louise."

"You are a man," she answered. "Men are supposed to be big."

She looked so little and so pretty that Ralph agreed with her. "Louise is kind of a horse," he said.

They spent their vacations in Canada, where Ralph liked to fish. And Penny, dressed enchantingly in boys' denim trousers, checked shirt, and felt hat, lounged against cushions in the canoe while he paddled. She would scream a little, hiding her head, as he took the fish off the hooks. When they walked, Ralph carried her over the rough spots and took her arm up the hills, so that finally, although he insisted she was no trouble, he took to fishing nearer the Lodge.

Sometimes he was surprised at the number of things a man who was married to a little thing like Penny had to think of. There was the question of theatre tickets, for instance; he had to make an effort to get seats in the first row so that Penny wouldn't have to crane her neck or sit on her coat to see the stage; he must also remember to shorten his steps when they walked together or Penny got tired and out of breath; things must be left where Penny could reach them without having to stand on a chair.

Once he had spoken to her about it. "Gosh," he said "it is kind of tough to be as little as you are! I never thought how it must be for you, not being able to do things that other people do."

The instant the words were out of his mouth, he knew he had said the wrong thing. "I'd like to know what I can't do that other women can!" she told him indignantly. "I think I manage to keep busy!"

He had to admit she did keep busy. In fact, she was never still. She was as busy, he thought, as a canary in a cage, fluttering, picking, keeping up an incessant chirping. "Sure you keep busy," he said. "Busy as a bird."

When they had been married almost ten years, he went on a business trip to Chicago. The thought of being left all alone frightened Penny and she made a great deal of it. He must put a chain lock on the front door and write down where he would be every night so that she could call him in case anything happened. Her anxious fluttering depressed him, and his depression lasted until he was safely on the train and seated in the warm, noisy dining car.

His second night in Chicago, the man he had come to see, a Mr. Merrick, asked him out to dinner. Mrs. Merrick went with them. She was a plain-looking woman, a little too stout, but there was something pleasing in the monotony of her solid brown hair that had no disturbing highlights, in her soft, friendly brown eyes, and her uninteresting brown felt hat. She had the appearance of a woman who had contemplatively set aside all personal vanity and turned to other things.

Ralph was surprised to find himself having a rather hilarious evening with them, and delighted to learn that Mr. Merrick had about decided to go back to New York with him and wind up their business for good and all. "And take me," Mrs. Merrick said.

"Oh, sure, take you," Mr. Merrick agreed.

And Ralph had added, "You bet!"

That night at the hotel, he wrote to Penny. It was a long, enthusiastic letter, and he wrote everything he could think of to please her. "They asked all about you," he wrote. "And I told them you were no bigger than a minute and as pretty as a picture. So we'll take them to dinner, when I get back, which should be about Friday. I'll wire exactly when. I miss you."

As he wrote "I miss you," he stopped and put his pen down on the desk. It struck him that he hadn't missed Penny at all, while she—well, he supposed that she was rattling around in the apartment not knowing what to do with herself. It occurred to him that she ought to have something to do, something better than fussing around with things at home. Not that he wanted her to work, he thought. Penny was far too helpless and little to be able to cope with a job. His heart softened when he remembered their evenings together with Penny curled up on his lap as he sat in the big chair, talking to him a mile a minute in her rather high, clear voice. He was ashamed of the many times he had wished she would read more, and recalled one dreadful evening when he had looked up from his paper at the sound of her nervous wandering about the room to say, "For the love of Pete, *light,* can't you?"

Thinking of these things and of the fine evening he had had with the Merricks, he picked up his pen again and underlined "I miss you."

The trip back to New York with the Merricks was great, but Penny was not at the station to meet him. "Unless we've missed her," he said gaily. "She's so darned little, she's easy to miss."

He assured the Merricks that he would just dash home, change his clothes, pick up Penny, and meet them at their hotel.

Penny was waiting for him at home. She was almost hysterically glad to see him, and he noticed that the house was shining and spotless, with fresh flowers in the vases and a wood fire burning in the grate. She was already dressed for the evening in a pale-pink taffeta dress with many ruffles, and stubby satin shoes tied with large bows. She wore a ribbon around her hair, and in the shaded lights of the living room she looked very young. It was only when she followed him to the bathroom to talk to him while he shaved that he noticed her more closely; the line of her mouth, always too thin, looked set and unhappy; the skin on her face looked drawn; and there was more than a sprinkling of gray in her black hair. The pink taffeta dress looked suddenly absurd on her, and he wished that she had worn something more suitable, something more her age. Why, Penny must be thirty-five!

She was curious about the Merricks, she said. "I never heard you make so much fuss over any two people in my life. What's she like?"

"Mrs. Merrick?" he asked, struggling with his stiff white shirt. "Oh, she's darned nice."

"Oh, I *know* that," Penny answered impatiently. "I know you think she's nice. What does she look like? Is she pretty?"

"No," he told her. "You couldn't call her pretty."

"Well, is she big, little, fat, thin?"

"She's not little," he said. "Why, she'd make two of you."

This seemed to satisfy her and she asked no more about the Merricks.

At the hotel they were told that Mr. and Mrs. Merrick were waiting for them in the main dining room. Walking through the lobby and down the long corridor, Penny was pleasantly conscious of the stir they created. She even shortened her steps a little, so that she appeared to be keeping up with Ralph by tripping at his side.

Mrs. Merrick's first words to her were what she expected. "Why, you're tiny!"

Penny laughed sweetly and looked up at Ralph. "Yes, isn't it silly?" she said. "I must look perfectly absurd beside Ralph, who is so enormous."

Mrs. Merrick's eyes took in every detail of Penny, her dress, her shoes, and the ribbon around her hair, and then she said, in almost the exact words that Louise had used so many years ago, "Do you know, with heels you'd look much taller. Why, you must be five feet one or so, and with good, high heels you'd look three inches taller. That would make you five feet four, which is a nice height. A great many movie actresses are five feet four."

Penny laughed again, but she flushed slightly.

"Now, Nellie," Mr. Merrick said, "don't go to making people over the first minute you see them. Maybe Mrs. Loomis *likes* to look small."

"Nonsense!" Mrs. Merrick exclaimed heartily. "No one wants to look like a midget! That is, no one wants to look *too* different. I know I was awfully tall for my age when I was about fifteen and I felt terribly about it. I was a sight, I can tell you."

And you're a sight now, Penny thought furiously. She chose a seat next to Mrs. Merrick and during dinner she rested her small, thin hand next to Mrs. Merrick's large, square one. She picked at her food daintily and exclaimed pleasantly when the other woman ordered ice cream with chocolate sauce for dessert. "Not that I wouldn't love it, but I just haven't *room*," she said.

Later, when the music started, she was surprised to see Ralph spring eagerly to his feet and ask Mrs. Merrick to dance.

"I haven't danced much lately," he said. "But let's go!"

He put one arm around Mrs. Merrick's waist and they started off. It was pleasant to have her face so near his own, to feel her soft, straight hair brush his forehead. She wore a dark-brown velvet dress, not very new and not very smart, but she had dignity and she moved smoothly with him across the dance floor. Over her shoulder he saw Penny dancing with Mr. Merrick. She was looking up into his face and talking brightly and animatedly. Mr. Merrick was bending down to catch what she was saying, smiling a frozen sort of smile, but he didn't look very happy.

The rest of the evening was not especially successful. Ralph tried in vain to recapture the spirit of hilarity he had felt with the Merricks in Chicago. But there was a sort of uneasiness in the air, even though Penny showed them several match tricks.

He was a little relieved, as they said good night, to learn that the Merricks had bought theatre tickets for the following evening and were leaving the day after for Chicago.

All the way home, Ralph sat in one corner of the taxi watching Penny as she talked. Her head was bent slightly to one side in the birdlike way she affected, and the white street lights flashing through the window were not kind to her. As he looked at her, she seemed to grow smaller and smaller until there was nothing much left of her but a pink taffeta dress and a pink ribbon. It had started to rain and the drops on the glass cast black dots on the pink taffeta dress, and he had the impression that it, too, might eventually disappear.

He did not notice that the cab had stopped in front of their apartment until Penny's voice gaily brought him back to earth. It was habit that made him pick her up and carry her across the wet, slippery pavement. And for such a little woman, she felt surprisingly heavy in his arms.

DEATH IN THE WOODS

by

SHERWOOD ANDERSON

(1876–1941)

Sherwood Anderson is an important American novelist and short story writer. In Winesburg, Ohio *and other short story collections he probed beneath the surface of small-town life, often focusing on sexual frustration as the cause of wasted lives. In "Perhaps Women" (1931), an essay on the evils of industrialization, he wrote about women as men's hope of salvation in a technological society.*

•————————————————•

I

She was an old woman and lived on a farm near the town in which I lived. All country and small-town people have seen such old women, but no one knows much about them. Such an old woman comes into town driving an old wornout horse or she comes afoot carrying a basket. She may own a few hens and have eggs to sell. She brings them in a basket and takes them to a grocer. There she trades them in. She gets some salt pork and some beans. Then she gets a pound or two of sugar and some flour.

Afterwards she goes to the butcher's and asks for some dog-meat. She may spend ten or fifteen cents, but when she does she asks for something. Formerly the butchers gave liver to any one who wanted to carry it away. In our family we were always having it. Once one of my brothers got a whole cow's liver at the slaughter-house near the fairgrounds in our town. We had it until we were sick of it. It never cost a cent. I have hated the thought of it ever since.

The old farm woman got some liver and a soup-bone. She never visited with any one, and as soon as she got what she wanted she lit out for home. It made quite a load for such an old body. No one gave her a lift. People drive right down a road and never notice an old woman like that.

There was such an old woman who used to come into town past our house one Summer and Fall when I was a young boy and was sick with what was called inflammatory rheumatism. She went home later carrying a heavy pack on her back. Two or three large gaunt-looking dogs followed at her heels.

The old woman was nothing special. She was one of the nameless ones that hardly any one knows, but she got into my thoughts. I have just suddenly now, after all these years, remembered her and what happened. It is a story. Her name was Grimes, and she lived with her husband and son in a small unpainted house on the bank of a small creek four miles from town.

The husband and son were a tough lot. Although the son was but twenty-one, he had already served a term in jail. It was whispered about that the woman's husband stole horses and ran them off to some other county. Now and then, when a horse turned up missing, the man had also disappeared. No one ever caught him. Once, when I was loafing at Tom Whitehead's livery-barn, the man came there and sat on the bench in front. Two or three other men were there, but no one spoke to him. He sat for a few minutes and then got up and went away. When he was leaving he turned around and stared at the men. There was a look of defiance in his eyes. "Well, I have tried to be friendly. You don't want to talk to me. It has been so wherever I have gone in this town. If, some day, one of your fine horses turns up missing, well, then what?" He did not say anything actually. "I'd like to bust one of you on the jaw," was about what his eyes said. I remember how the look in his eyes made me shiver.

The old man belonged to a family that had had money once. His name was Jake Grimes. It all comes back clearly now. His father, John Grimes, had owned a sawmill when the country was new, and had made money. Then he got to drinking and running after women. When he died there wasn't much left.

Jake blew in the rest. Pretty soon there wasn't any more lumber to cut and his land was nearly all gone.

He got his wife off a German farmer, for whom he went to work one June day in the wheat harvest. She was a young thing then and scared to death. You see, the farmer was up to something with the girl—she was, I think, a bound girl and his wife had her suspicions. She took it out on the girl when the man wasn't around. Then, when the wife had to go off to town for supplies, the farmer got after her. She told young Jake that nothing really ever happened, but he didn't know whether to believe it or not.

He got her pretty easy himself, the first time he was out with her. He wouldn't have married her if the German farmer hadn't tried to tell him where to get off. He got her to go riding with him in his buggy one night when he was threshing on the place, and then he came for her the next Sunday night.

She managed to get out of the house without her employer's seeing, but when she was getting into the buggy he showed up. It was almost dark, and he just popped up suddenly at the horse's head. He grabbed the horse by the bridle and Jake got out his buggy-whip.

They had it out all right! The German was a tough one. Maybe he didn't care whether his wife knew or not. Jake hit him over the face and shoulders with the buggy-whip, but the horse got to acting up and he had to get out.

Then the two men went for it. The girl didn't see it. The horse started to run away and went nearly a mile down the road before the girl got him stopped. Then she managed to tie him to a tree beside the road. (I wonder how I know all this. It must have stuck in my mind from small-town tales when I was a boy.) Jake found her there after he got through with the German. She was huddled up in the buggy seat, crying, scared to death. She told Jake a lot of stuff, how the German had tried to get her, how he chased her once into the barn, how another time, when they happened to be alone in the house together, he tore her dress open clear down the front. The German, she said, might have got her that time if he hadn't heard his old woman drive in at the gate. She had been off to town for supplies. Well, she would be putting the horse in the barn. The German managed to sneak off to the fields without his wife seeing. He told the girl he would kill her if she told. What could she do? She told a lie about ripping her dress in the barn when she was feeding the stock. I remember now that she was a bound girl and did not know where her father and mother were. Maybe she did not have any father. You know what I mean.

Such bound children were often enough cruelly treated. They were children who had no parents, slaves really. There were very few orphan homes then. They were legally bound into some home. It was a matter of pure luck how it came out.

2

She married Jake and had a son and daughter, but the daughter died.

Then she settled down to feed stock. That was her job. At the German's place she had cooked the food for the German and his wife. The wife was a strong woman with big hips and worked most of the time in the fields with her husband. She fed them and fed the cows in the barn, fed the pigs, the horses and the chickens. Every moment of every day, as a young girl, was spent feeding something.

Then she married Jake Grimes and he had to be fed. She was a slight thing, and when she had been married for three or four years, and after the two children were born, her slender shoulders became stooped.

Jake always had a lot of big dogs around the house, that stood near the unused sawmill near the creek. He was always trading horses when he wasn't stealing something and had a lot of poor bony ones about. Also he kept three or four pigs and a cow. They were all pastured in the few acres left of the Grimes place and Jake did little enough work.

He went into debt for a threshing outfit and ran it for several years, but it did not pay. People did not trust him. They were afraid he would steal the grain at night. He had to go a long way off to get work and it cost too much to get there. In the Winter he hunted and cut a little firewood, to be sold in some nearby town. When the son grew up he was just like the father. They got drunk together. If there wasn't anything to eat in the house when they came home the old man gave his old woman a cut over the head. She had a few chickens of her own and had to kill one of them in a hurry. When they were all killed she wouldn't have any eggs to sell when she went to town, and then what would she do?

She had to scheme all her life about getting things fed, getting the pigs fed so they would grow fat and could be butchered in the Fall. When they were butchered her husband took most of the meat off to town and sold it. If he did not do it first the boy did. They fought sometimes and when they fought the old woman stood aside trembling.

She had got the habit of silence anyway—that was fixed. Sometimes, when she began to look old—she wasn't forty yet—and when the husband and son were both off, trading horses or drinking or hunting or stealing, she went around the house and the barnyard muttering to herself.

How was she going to get everything fed?—that was her problem. The dogs had to be fed. There wasn't enough hay in the barn for the horses and the cow. If she didn't feed the chickens how could they lay eggs? Without eggs to sell how could she get things in town, things she had to have to keep the life of the farm going? Thank heaven, she did not have to feed her husband—in a certain way. That hadn't lasted long after their marriage and after the babies came. Where he went on his long trips she did not know. Sometimes he was gone from home for weeks, and after the boy grew up they went off together.

They left everything at home for her to manage and she had no money. She knew no one. No one ever talked to her in town. When it was Winter she had to gather sticks of wood for her fire, had to try to keep the stock fed with very little grain.

The stock in the barn cried to her hungrily, the dogs followed her about. In the Winter the hens laid few enough eggs. They huddled in the corners of the barn and she kept watching them. If a hen lays an egg in the barn in the Winter and you don't find it, it freezes and breaks.

One day in Winter the old woman went off to town with a few eggs and the dogs followed her. She did not get started until nearly three o'clock and the snow was heavy. She hadn't been feeling very well for several days and so she went muttering along, scantily clad, her shoulders stooped. She had an old grain bag in which she carried her eggs, tucked away down in the bottom. There weren't many of them, but in Winter the price of eggs is up. She would get a little meat in exchange for the eggs, some salt pork, a little sugar, and some coffee perhaps. It might be the butcher would give her a piece of liver.

When she had got to town and was trading in her eggs the dogs lay by the door outside. She did pretty well, got the things she needed, more than she had hoped. Then she went to the butcher and he gave her some liver and some dog-meat.

It was the first time any one had spoken to her in a friendly way for a long time. The butcher was alone in his shop when she came in and was annoyed by the thought of such a sick-looking old woman out on such a day. It was bitter cold and the snow, that had let up during the afternoon, was falling again. The butcher said something about her husband and her son, swore at them, and the old woman stared at him, a look of mild surprise in her eyes as he talked. He said that if either the husband or the son were going to get any of the liver or the heavy bones with scraps of meat hanging to them that he had put into the grain bag, he'd see him starve first.

Starve, eh? Well, things had to be fed. Men had to be fed, and horses that weren't any good but maybe could be traded off, and the poor thin cow that hadn't given any milk for three months.

Horses, cows, pigs, dogs, men.

3

The old woman had to get back before darkness came if she could. The dogs followed at her heels, sniffing at the heavy grain bag she had fastened on her back. When she got to the edge of town she stopped by a fence and tied the bag on her back with a piece of rope she had carried in her dress-pocket for just that purpose. It was hard when she had to crawl over fences and once she fell over and landed in the snow. The dogs went frisking about. She had to struggle to get to her feet again, but she made it. The point of climbing over the fences was that there was a short cut over a hill and through a woods. She might have gone around by the road, but it was a mile farther that way. She was afraid she couldn't make it. And then, besides, the stock had to be fed. There was a little hay left and a little corn. Perhaps her husband and son would bring some home when they came. They had driven off in the only buggy the Grimes family had, a rickety thing, a rickety horse hitched to the buggy, two other rickety horses led by halters. They were going to trade horses, get a little money if they could. They might come home drunk. It would be well to have something in the house when they came back.

The son had an affair on with a woman at the county seat, fifteen miles away. She was a rough enough woman, a tough one. Once, in the Summer, the son had brought her to the house. Both she and the son had been drinking. Jake Grimes was away and the son and his woman ordered the old woman about like a servant. She didn't mind much; she was used to it.

Whatever happened she never said anything. That was her way of getting along. She had managed that way when she was a young girl at the German's and ever since she had married Jake. That time her son brought his woman to the house they stayed all night, sleeping together just as though they were married. It hadn't shocked the old woman, not much. She had got past being shocked early in life.

With the pack on her back she went painfully along across an open field, wading in the deep snow, and got into the woods.

There was a path, but it was hard to follow. Just beyond the top of the hill, where the woods was thickest, there was a small clearing. Had some one once thought of building a house there? The clearing was as large as a building lot in town, large enough for a house and a garden. The path ran along the side of the clearing, and when she got there the old woman sat down to rest at the foot of a tree.

It was a foolish thing to do. When she got herself placed, the pack against the tree's trunk, it was nice, but what about getting up again? She worried about that for a moment and then quietly closed her eyes.

She must have slept for a time. When you are about so cold you can't get any colder. The afternoon grew a little warmer and the snow came thicker than ever. Then after a time the weather cleared. The moon even came out.

There were four Grimes dogs that had followed Mrs. Grimes into town, all tall gaunt fellows. Such men as Jake Grimes and his son always keep just such dogs. They kick and abuse them, but they stay. The Grimes dogs, in order to keep from starving, had to do a lot of foraging for themselves, and they had been at it while the old woman slept with her back to the tree at the side of the clearing. They had been chasing rabbits in the woods and in adjoining fields and in their ranging had picked up three other farm dogs.

After a time all the dogs came back to the clearing. They were excited about something. Such nights, cold and clear and with a moon, do things to dogs. It may be that some old instinct, come down from the time when they were wolves and ranged the woods in packs on Winter nights, comes back into them.

The dogs in the clearing, before the old woman, had caught two or three rabbits and their immediate hunger had been satisfied. They began to play, running in circles in the clearing. Round and round they ran, each dog's nose at the tail of the next dog. In the clearing, under the snow-laden trees and under the wintry moon they made a strange picture, running thus silently, in a circle their running had beaten in the soft snow. The dogs made no sound. They ran around and around in the circle.

It may have been that the old woman saw them doing that before she died. She may have awakened once or twice and looked at the strange sight with dim old eyes.

She wouldn't be very cold now, just drowsy. Life hangs on a long time.

Perhaps the old woman was out of her head. She may have dreamed of her girlhood at the German's, and before that, when she was a child and before her mother lit out and left her.

Her dreams couldn't have been very pleasant. Not many pleasant things had happened to her. Now and then one of the Grimes dogs left the running circle and came to stand before her. The dog thrust his face to her face. His red tongue was hanging out.

The running of the dogs may have been a kind of death ceremony. It may have been that the primitive instinct of the wolf, having been aroused in the dogs by the night and the running, made them somehow, afraid.

"Now we are no longer wolves. We are dogs, the servants of men. Keep alive, man! When man dies we become wolves again." When one of the dogs came to where the old woman sat with her back against the tree and thrust his nose close to her face he seemed satisfied and went back to run with the pack. All the Grimes dogs did it at some time during the evening, before she died. I knew all about it afterward, when I grew to be a man, because once in a woods in Illinois, on another Winter night, I saw a pack of dogs act just like that. The dogs were waiting for me to die as they had waited for the old woman that night when I was a child, but when it happened to me I was a young man and had no intention whatever of dying.

The old woman died softly and quietly. When she was dead and when one of the Grimes dogs had come to her and had found her dead all the dogs stopped running.

They gathered about her.

Well, she was dead now. She had fed the Grimes dogs when she was alive, what about now?

There was the pack on her back, the grain bag containing the piece of salt pork, the liver the butcher had given her, the dog-meat, the soup-bones. The butcher in town, having been suddenly overcome with a feeling of pity, had loaded her grain bag heavily. It had been a big haul for the old woman.

It was a big haul for the dogs now.

4

One of the Grimes dogs sprang suddenly out from among the others and began worrying the pack on the old woman's back. Had the dogs really been wolves that one would have been the leader of the pack. What he did, all the others did.

All of them sank their teeth into the grain bag the old woman had fastened with the ropes to her back.

They dragged the old woman's body out into the open clearing. The worn-out dress was quickly torn from her shoulders. When she was found, a day or two later, the dress had been torn from her body clear to the hips,

SHERWOOD ANDERSON

but the dogs had not touched her body. They had got the meat out of the grain bag, that was all. Her body was frozen stiff when it was found, and the shoulders were so narrow and the body so slight that in death it looked like the body of some charming young girl.

Such things happened in towns of the Middle West, on farms near town, when I was a boy. A hunter out after rabbits found the old woman's body and did not touch it. Something, the beaten round path in the little snow-covered clearing, the silence of the place, the place where the dogs had worried the body trying to pull the grain bag away or tear it open—something startled the man and he hurried off to town.

I was in Main Street with one of my brothers who was town newsboy and who was taking the afternoon papers to the stores. It was almost night.

The hunter came into a grocery and told his story. Then he went into a hardware-shop and into a drugstore. Men began to gather on the sidewalks. Then they started out along the road to the place in the woods.

My brother should have gone on about his business of distributing papers but he didn't. Every one was going to the woods. The undertaker went and the town marshal. Several men got on a dray and rode out to where the path left the road and went into the woods, but the horses weren't very sharply shod and slid about on the slippery roads. They made no better time than those of us who walked.

The town marshal was a large man whose leg had been injured in the Civil War. He carried a heavy cane and limped rapidly along the road. My brother and I followed at his heels, and as we went other men and boys joined the crowd.

It had grown dark by the time we got to where the old woman had left the road but the moon had come out. The marshal was thinking there might have been a murder. He kept asking the hunter questions. The hunter went along with his gun across his shoulders, a dog following at his heels. It isn't often a rabbit hunter has a chance to be so conspicuous. He was taking full advantage of it, leading the procession with the town marshal. "I didn't see any wounds. She was a beautiful young girl. Her face was buried in the snow. No. I didn't know her." As a matter of fact, the hunter had not looked closely at the body. He had been frightened. She might have been murdered and some one might spring out from behind a tree and murder him. In a woods, in the late afternoon, when the trees are all bare and there is white snow on the ground, when all is silent, something creepy steals over the mind and body. If something strange or uncanny has happened in the neighborhood all you think about is getting away from there as fast as you can.

The crowd of men and boys had got to where the old woman had crossed the field and went, following the marshal and the hunter, up the slight incline and into the woods.

My brother and I were silent. He had his bundle of papers in a bag slung across his shoulder. When he got back to town he would have to go on distributing his papers before he went home to supper. If I went along, as he had no doubt already determined I should, we would both be late. Either mother or our older sister would have to warm our supper.

Well, we would have something to tell. A boy did not get such a chance very often. It was lucky we just happened to go into the grocery when the hunter came in. The hunter was a country fellow. Neither of us had ever seen him before.

Now the crowd of men and boys had got to the clearing. Darkness comes quickly on such Winter nights, but the full moon made everything clear. My brother and I stood near the tree, beneath which the old woman had died.

She did not look old, lying there in that light, frozen and still. One of the men turned her over in the snow and I saw everything. My body trembled with some strange mystical feeling and so did my brother's. It might have been the cold.

Neither of us had ever seen a woman's body before. It may have been the snow, clinging to the frozen flesh, that made it look so white and lovely, so like marble. No woman had come with the party from town; but one of the men, he was the town blacksmith, took off his overcoat and spread it over her. Then he gathered her into his arms and started off to town, all the others following silently. At that time no one knew who she was.

5

I had seen everything, had seen the oval in the snow, like a miniature racetrack, where the dogs had run, had seen how the men were mystified, had seen the white bare young-looking shoulders, had heard the whispered comments of the men.

The men were simply mystified. They took the body to the undertaker's, and when the blacksmith, the hunter, the marshal and several others had got inside they closed the door. If father had been there perhaps he could have got in, but we boys couldn't.

I went with my brother to distribute the rest of his papers and when we got home it was my brother who told the story.

I kept silent and went to bed early. It may have been I was not satisfied with the way he told it.

Later, in the town, I must have heard other fragments of the old woman's story. She was recognized the next day and there was an investigation.

The husband and son were found somewhere and brought to town and there was an attempt to connect them with the woman's death, but it did not work. They had perfect enough alibis.

However, the town was against them. They had to get out. Where they went I never heard.

I remember only the picture there in the forest, the men standing about, the naked girlish-looking figure, face down in the snow, the tracks made by the running dogs and the clear cold Winter sky above. White fragments of clouds were drifting across the sky. They went racing across the little open space among the trees.

The scene in the forest had become for me, without my knowing it, the foundation for the real story I am now trying to tell. The fragments, you see, had to be picked up slowly, long afterwards.

Things happened. When I was a young man I worked on the farm of a German. The hired-girl was afraid of her employer. The farmer's wife hated her.

I saw things at that place. Once later, I had a half-uncanny, mystical adventure with dogs in an Illinois forest on a clear, moon-lit Winter night. When I was a schoolboy, and on a Summer day, I went with a boy friend out along a creek some miles from town and came to the house where the old woman had lived. No one had lived in the house since her death. The doors were broken from the hinges; the window lights were all broken. As the boy and I stood in the road outside, two dogs, just roving farm dogs no doubt, came running around the corner of the house. The dogs were tall, gaunt fellows and came down to the fence and glared through at us, standing in the road.

The whole thing, the story of the old woman's death, was to me as I grew older like music heard from far off. The notes had to be picked up slowly one at a time. Something had to be understood.

The woman who died was one destined to feed animal life. Anyway, that is all she ever did. She was feeding animal life before she was born, as a child, as a young woman working on the farm of the German, after she married, when she grew old and when she died. She fed animal life in cows, in chickens, in pigs, in horses, in dogs, in men. Her daughter had died in childhood and with her one son she had no articulate relations. On the night when she died she was hurrying homeward, bearing on her body food for animal life.

She died in the clearing in the woods and even after her death continued feeding animal life.

You see it is likely that, when my brother told the story, that night when we got home and my mother and sister sat listening, I did not think he got the point. He was too young and so was I. A thing so complete has its own beauty.

I shall not try to emphasize the point. I am only explaining why I was dissatisfied then and have been ever since. I speak of that only that you may understand why I have been impelled to try to tell the simple story over again.

THE ANGEL OVER
THE RIGHT SHOULDER

by

ELIZABETH STUART PHELPS

(1815–1852)

*Born in Andover, Massachusetts, Elizabeth Stuart Phelps was the
daughter of a clergyman and later married one. She started writing
stories at ten and started publishing in a religious journal at sixteen.
While living in Boston, she published stories and poems. A novel
based on a journal she kept about her family was a best seller in
1851 and was translated into several languages. Her daughter became
a writer and took her mother's name to try to make up for her
mother's premature death.*

* • ——————————————————— • *

"There! a woman's work is never done," said Mrs. James; "I thought, for
once, I was through; but just look at that lamp, now! it will not burn, and
I must go and spend half an hour over it."

"Don't you wish you had never been married?" said Mr. James, with a
good-natured laugh.

"Yes"—rose to her lips, but was checked by a glance at the group upon
the floor, where her husband was stretched out, and two little urchins
with sparkling eyes and glowing cheeks, were climbing and tumbling over
him, as if they found in this play the very essence of fun.

She did say, "I should like the good, without the evil, if I could have it."

"You have no evils to endure," replied her husband.

"That is just all you gentlemen know about it. What would you think,
if you could not get an uninterrupted half hour to yourself, from morning
till night? I believe you would give up trying to do anything."

"There is no need of that; all you want, is *system*. If you arranged your
work systematically, you would find that you could command your time."

"Well," was the reply, "all I wish is, that you could just follow me
around for one day, and see what I have to do. If you could reduce it all
to system, I think you would show yourself a genius."

When the lamp was trimmed, the conversation was resumed. Mr. James
had employed the "half hour," in meditating on this subject.

"Wife," said he, as she came in, "I have a plan to propose to you, and I wish you to promise me beforehand, that you will accede to it. It is to be an experiment, I acknowledge, but I wish it to have a fair trial. Now to please me, will you promise?"

Mrs. James hesitated. She felt almost sure that his plan would be quite impracticable, for what does a man know of a woman's work? yet she promised.

"Now I wish you," said he, "to set apart two hours of every day for your own private use. Make a point of going to your room and locking yourself in; and also make up your mind to let the work which is not done, go undone, if it must. Spend this time on just those things which will be most profitable to yourself. I shall bind you to your promise for one month— then, if it has proved a total failure, we will devise something else."

"When shall I begin?"

"To-morrow."

The morrow came. Mrs. James had chosen the two hours before dinner as being, on the whole, the most convenient and the least liable to interruption. They dined at one o'clock. She wished to finish her morning work, get dressed for the day, and enter her room at eleven.

Hearty as were her efforts to accomplish this, the hour of eleven found her with her work but half done; yet, true to her promise, she left all, retired to her room and locked the door.

With some interest and hope, she immediately marked out a course of reading and study, for these two precious hours; then, arranging her table, her books, pen and paper, she commenced a schedule of her work with much enthusiasm. Scarcely had she dipped her pen in ink, when she heard the tramping of little feet along the hall, and then a pounding at her door.

"Mamma! mamma! I cannot find my mittens, and Hannah is going to slide without me."

"Go to Amy, my dear; mamma is busy."

"So Amy busy too; she say she can't leave baby."

The child began to cry, still standing close to the fastened door. Mrs. James knew the easiest, and indeed the only way of settling the trouble, was to go herself and hunt up the missing mittens. Then a parley must be held with Frank, to induce him to wait for his sister, and the child's tears must be dried, and little hearts must be all set right before the children went out to play; and so favorable an opportunity must not be suffered to slip, without impressing on young minds the importance of having a "place for everything and everything in its place;" this took time; and when Mrs. James returned to her study, her watch told her that *half* her portion had gone. Quietly resuming her work, she was endeavoring to mend her broken train of thought, when heavier steps were heard in the hall, and the fastened door was once more besieged. Now, Mr. James must be admitted.

"Mary," said he, "cannot you come and sew a string on for me? I do believe there is not a bosom in my drawer in order, and I am in a great hurry. I ought to have been down town an hour ago."

The schedule was thrown aside, the work-basket taken, and Mrs. James followed him. She soon sewed on the tape, but then a button needed fastening—and at last a rip in his glove, was to be mended. As Mrs. James stitched away on the glove, a smile lurked in the corners of her mouth, which her husband observed.

"What are you laughing at?" asked he.

"To think how famously your plan works."

"I declare!" said he, "is this your study hour? I am sorry, but what can a man do? He cannot go down town without a shirt bosom!"

"Certainly not," said his wife, quietly.

When her liege lord was fairly equipped and off, Mrs. James returned to her room. A half an hour yet remained to her, and of this she determined to make the most. But scarcely had she resumed her pen, when there was another disturbance in the entry. Amy had returned from walking out with the baby, and she entered the nursery with him, that she might get him to sleep. Now it happened that the only room in the house which Mrs. James could have to herself with a fire, was the one adjoining the nursery. She had become so accustomed to the ordinary noise of the children, that it did not disturb her; but the very extraordinary noise which master Charley sometimes felt called upon to make, when he was fairly on his back in the cradle, did disturb the unity of her thoughts. The words which she was reading rose and fell with the screams and lulls of the child, and she felt obliged to close her book, until the storm was over. When quiet was restored in the cradle, the children came in from sliding, crying with cold fingers—and just as she was going to them, the dinner-bell rang.

"How did your new plan work this morning?" inquired Mr. James.

"Famously," was the reply, "I read about seventy pages of German, and as many more in French."

"I am sure *I* did not hinder you long."

"No—yours was only one of a dozen interruptions."

"O, well! you must not get discouraged. Nothing succeeds well the first time. Persist in your arrangement, and by and by the family will learn that if they want anything of you, they must wait until after dinner."

"But what can a man do?" replied his wife; "he cannot go down town without a shirt-bosom."

"I was in a bad case," replied Mr. James, "it may not happen again. I am anxious to have you try the month out faithfully, and then we will see what has come of it."

The second day of trial was a stormy one. As the morning was dark, Bridget over-slept, and consequently breakfast was too late by an hour. This lost hour Mrs. James could not recover. When the clock struck eleven, she seemed but to have commenced her morning's work, so much remained to be done. With mind disturbed and spirits depressed, she left her household matters "in the suds," as they were, and punctually retired to her study. She soon found, however, that she could not fix her attention upon any intellectual pursuit. Neglected duties haunted her, like ghosts around the guilty conscience. Perceiving that she was doing nothing with her books, and not wishing to lose the morning wholly, she commenced writing a letter. Bridget interrupted her before she had proceeded far on the first page.

"What, ma'am, shall we have for dinner? No marketing ha'n't come."

"Have some steaks, then."

"We ha'n't got none, ma'am."

"I will send out for some, directly."

Now there was no one to send but Amy, and Mrs. James knew it. With a sigh, she put down her letter and went into the nursery.

"Amy, Mr. James has forgotten our marketing. I should like to have you run over to the provision store, and order some beef-steaks. I will stay with the baby."

Amy was not much pleased to be sent out on this errand. She remarked, that "she must change her dress first."

"Be as quick as possible," said Mrs. James, "for I am particularly engaged at this hour."

Amy neither obeyed, nor disobeyed, but managed to take her own time, without any very deliberate intention to do so. Mrs. James, hoping to get along with a sentence or two, took her German book into the nursery. But this arrangement was not to master Charley's mind. A fig did he care for German, but "the kitties," he must have, whether or no and kitties he would find in that particular book—so he turned its leaves over in great haste. Half of the time on the second day of trial had gone, when Amy returned and Mrs. James with a sigh, left her nursery. Before one o'clock, she was twice called into the kitchen to superintend some important dinner arrangement, and thus it turned out that she did not finish one page of her letter.

On the third morning the sun shone, and Mrs. James rose early, made every provision which she deemed necessary for dinner, and for the comfort of her family; and then, elated by her success, in good spirits, and with good courage, she entered her study precisely at eleven o'clock, and locked her door. Her books were opened, and the challenge given to a hard German lesson. Scarcely had she made the first onset, when the door-bell was heard to ring, and soon Bridget coming nearer and nearer—then tapping at the door.

"Somebodies wants to see you in the parlor, ma'am."

"Tell them I am engaged, Bridget."

"I told 'em you were to-home, ma'am, and they sent up their names, but I ha'n't got 'em, jist."

There was no help for it—Mrs. James must go down to receive her callers. She had to smile when she felt little like it—to be sociable when her thoughts were busy with her task. Her friends made a long call—they had nothing else to do with their time, and when they went, others came. In very unsatisfactory chit-chat, her morning slipped away.

On the next day, Mr. James invited company to tea, and her morning was devoted to preparing for it; she did not enter her study. On the day following, a sick-head-ache confined her to her bed, and on Saturday the care of the baby devolved upon her, as Amy had extra work to do. Thus passed the first week.

True to her promise, Mrs. James patiently persevered for a month, in her efforts to secure for herself this little fragment of her broken time, but with what success, the first week's history can tell. With its close, closed the month of December.

On the last day of the old year, she was so much occupied in her preparations for the morrow's festival, that the last hour of the day was approaching, before she made her good night's call in the nursery. She first went to the crib and looked at the baby. There he lay in his innocence and beauty, fast asleep. She softly stroked his golden hair—she kissed gently his rosy cheek—she pressed the little dimpled hand in hers, and then, carefully drawing the coverlet over it, tucked it in, and stealing yet another kiss—she left him to his peaceful dreams and sat down on her daughter's bed. She also slept sweetly, with her dolly hugged to her bosom. At this her mother smiled, but soon grave thoughts entered her mind, and these deepened into sad ones. She thought of her disappointment and the failure of her plans. To her, not only the past month but the whole past year, seemed to have been one of fruitless effort—all broken and disjointed—even her hours of religious duty had been encroached upon, and disturbed. She had accomplished nothing, that she could see, but to keep her house and family in order, and even this, to her saddened mind, seemed to have been but indifferently done. She was conscious of yearnings for a more earnest life than this. Unsatisfied longings for something which she had not attained, often clouded what, otherwise, would have been a bright day to her; and yet the causes of these feelings seemed to lie in a dim and misty region, which her eye could not penetrate.

What then did she need? To see some *results* from her life's work? To know that a golden cord bound her life-threads together into *unity* of purpose—notwithstanding they seemed, so often, single and broken?

She was quite sure that she felt no desire to shrink from duty, however humble, but she sighed for some comforting assurance of what *was duty*. Her employments, conflicting as they did with her tastes, seemed to her frivolous and useless. It seemed to her that there was some better way of living, which she, from deficiency in energy of character, or of principle, had failed to discover. As she leaned over her child, her tears fell fast upon its young brow.

Most earnestly did she wish, that she could shield that child from the disappointments and mistakes and self-reproach from which the mother was then suffering; that the little one might take up life where she could give it to her—all mended by her own experience. It would have been a comfort to have felt, that in fighting the battle, she had fought for both; yet she knew that so it could not be—that for ourselves must we all learn what are those things which "make for our peace."

The tears were in her eyes, as she gave the good-night to her sleeping daughter—then with soft steps she entered an adjoining room, and there fairly kissed out the old year on another chubby cheek, which nestled among the pillows. At length she sought her own rest.

Soon she found herself in a singular place. She was traversing a vast plain. No trees were visible, save those which skirted the distant horizon, and on their broad tops rested wreaths of golden clouds. Before her was a female, who was journeying towards that region of light. Little children were about her, now in her arms, now running by her side, and as they travelled, she occupied herself in caring for them. She taught them how to place their little feet—she gave them timely warnings of the pit-falls—she gently lifted them over the stumbling-blocks. When they were weary, she soothed them by singing of that brighter land, which she kept ever in view, and towards which she seemed hastening with her little flock. But what was most remarkable was, that, all unknown to her, she was constantly watched by two angels, who reposed on two golden clouds which floated above her. Before each was a golden book, and a pen of gold. One angel, with mild and loving eyes, peered constantly over her right shoulder—another kept as strict watch over her left. Not a deed, not a word, not a look, escaped their notice. When a good deed, word, look, went from her, the angel over the right shoulder with a glad smile, wrote it down in his book; when an evil, however trivial, the angel over the left shoulder recorded it in his book—then with sorrowful eyes followed the pilgrim until he observed penitence for the wrong, upon which he dropped a tear on the record, and blotted it out, and both angels rejoiced.

To the looker-on, it seemed that the traveller did nothing which was worthy of such careful record. Sometimes she did but bathe the weary feet of her little children, but the angel over the *right shoulder*—wrote it down. Sometimes she did but patiently wait to lure back a little truant who had turned his face away from the distant light, but the angel over the *right shoulder*—wrote it down. Sometimes she did but soothe an angry feeling or raise a drooping eye-lid, or kiss away a little grief; but the angel over the right shoulder—*wrote it down.*

Sometimes, her eye was fixed so intently on that golden horizon, and she became so eager to make progress thither, that the little ones, missing her care, did languish or stray. Then it was that the angel over the *left shoulder,* lifted his golden pen, and made the entry, and followed her with sorrowful eyes, until he could blot it out. Sometimes she seemed to advance rapidly, but in her haste the little ones had fallen back, and it was the sorrowing angel who recorded her progress. Sometimes so intent was she to gird up her loins and have her lamp trimmed and burning, that the little children wandered away quite into forbidden paths, and it was the angel over the *left shoulder* who recorded her diligence.

Now the observer as she looked, felt that this was a faithful and true record, and was to be kept to that journey's end. The strong clasps of gold on those golden books, also impressed her with the conviction that, when they were closed, it would only be for a future opening.

Her sympathies were warmly enlisted for the gentle traveller, and with a beating heart she quickened her steps that she might overtake her. She wished to tell her of the angels keeping watch above her—to entreat her to be faithful and patient to the end—for her life's work was all written down—every item of it—and the *results* would be known when those golden books should be unclasped. She wished to beg of her to think no duty trivial which must be done, for over her right shoulder and over her left were recording angels, who would surely take note of all!

Eager to warn the traveller of what she had seen, she touched her. The traveller turned, and she recognized or seemed to recognize *herself.* Startled and alarmed she awoke in tears. The gray light of morning struggled through the half-open shutter, the door was ajar and merry faces were peeping in.

"Wish you a happy new year, mamma,"—"Wish you a *Happy new Year,*"—"a happy noo ear."

She returned the merry greeting most heartily. It seemed to her as if she had entered upon a new existence. She had found her way through the thicket in which she had been entangled, and a light was now about her path. The *Angel over the Right Shoulder* whom she had seen in her dream, would bind up in his golden book her life's work, if it were but well done. He required of her no great deeds, but faithfulness and patience to the end of the race which was set before her. Now she could see plainly enough, that though it was right and important for her to cultivate her own mind and heart, it was equally right and equally important, to meet and perform faithfully all those little household cares and duties on which the comfort and virtue of her family depended; for into these things the angels carefully looked—and these duties and cares acquired a dignity from the strokes of that golden pen—they could not be neglected without danger.

Sad thoughts and sadder misgivings—undefined yearnings and ungratified

ELIZABETH STUART PHELPS

longings seemed to have taken their flight with the Old Year, and it was with fresh resolution and cheerful hope, and a happy heart, she welcomed the *Glad* New Year. The *Angel over the Right Shoulder* would go with her, and if she were found faithful, would strengthen and comfort her to its close.

CUTTING THE JEWISH
BRIDE'S HAIR

by

RUTH WHITMAN

(b. 1922)

Ruth Whitman graduated from Radcliffe College in 1944 with honors in Greek and English. She has published several volumes of translations as well as four volumes of poetry, one of which, Tamsen Donner: A Woman's Journey *(1977), recreates the experience of a pioneer on the Oregon Trail.* Permanent Address *appeared in 1980. A winner of many awards, Ms. Whitman held a grant from the National Endowment for the Arts in 1974–1975. She regularly conducts poetry workshops at the Mary Bunting Institute at Radcliffe.*

It's to possess more than the skin
that those old world Jews
exacted the hair of their brides.
   Good husband, lover of the Torah,
   does the calligraphy of your bride's hair
   interrupt your page?

Before the clownish friction of flesh
creating out of nothing
a mockup of its begetters,
a miraculous puppet of God,
you must first divorce her from her vanity.

She will snip off her pride,
cut back her appetite to be devoured,
she will keep herself well braided,
her love's furniture will not endanger you,
   but this little amputation
   will shift the balance of the universe.

WOMEN

by

MAY SWENSON

(b. 1919)

Born and educated in Utah, May Swenson has written children's books and a play, but she is best known for her poetry. Volumes include To Mix with Time *(1963),* Half Sun Half Sleep *(1967),* Poems to Solve *(1966),* More Poems to Solve *(1971), and* Iconographs *(1970), and* New and Selected Things Taking Place *(1978). She has won many prizes and in 1970 was elected to the National Institute of Arts and Letters.*

•————————————————•

Women	Or they
should be	should be
pedestals	little horses
moving	those wooden
pedestals	sweet
moving	oldfashioned
to the	painted
motions	rocking
of men	horses

the gladdest things in the toyroom

The	feelingly
pegs	and then
of their	unfeelingly
ears	To be
so familiar	joyfully
and dear	ridden
to the trusting	rockingly
fists	ridden until
To be chafed	the restored

THE WIFE

52

egos dismount and the legs stride away

Immobile   willing
 sweetlipped   to be set
  sturdy   into motion
   and smiling   Women
    women   should be
     should always   pedestals
      be waiting   to men

BEFORE BREAKFAST

A Play in One Act

by

EUGENE O'NEILL

(1888–1953)

The first great American dramatist, Eugene O'Neill won the Pulitzer Prize four times and the Nobel Prize in 1936. Author of a number of one-act plays, he is best known for his comedy Ah, Wilderness *and for many great tragedies echoing Greek drama. His master-piece,* Long Day's Journey into Night, *is the story of his own family tragedy and shows the influence of Freudian and other contemporary psychological thought.*

•————————————————•

Characters

MRS. ROWLAND
ALFRED   Her husband (not seen)

Scene

A small room serving both as kitchen and dining room in a flat on Christopher Street, New York City. In the rear, to the right, a door leading to the outer hallway. On the left of the doorway, a sink, and a two-burner gas stove. Over the stove, and extending to the left wall, a wooden closet for dishes, etc. On the left, two windows looking out on a fire escape where several potted plants are dying of neglect. Before the windows, a table covered with oilcloth. Two cane-bottomed chairs are placed by the table. Another stands against the wall to the right of door in rear. In the right wall, rear, a doorway leading into a bedroom. Farther forward, different articles of a man's and a woman's clothing are hung on pegs. A clothes line is strung from the left corner, rear, to the right wall, forward. A man's underclothes are thrown over the line.

It is about eight-thirty in the morning of a fine, sunshiny day in the early fall.

THE WIFE

54

Mrs. Rowland enters from the bedroom, yawning, her hands still busy putting the finishing touches on a slovenly toilet by sticking hairpins into her hair which is bunched up in a drab-colored mass on top of her round head. She is of medium height and inclined to a shapeless stoutness, accentuated by her formless blue dress, shabby and worn. Her face is characterless, with small regular features and eyes of a nondescript blue. There is a pinched expression about her eyes and nose and her weak, spiteful mouth. She is in her early twenties but looks much older.

She comes to the middle of the room and yawns, stretching her arms to their full length. Her drowsy eyes stare about the room with the irritated look of one to whom a long sleep has not been a long rest. She goes wearily to the clothes hanging on the right and takes an apron from a hook. She ties it about her waist, giving vent to an exasperated "damn" when the knot fails to obey her clumsy, fat fingers. Finally gets it tied and goes slowly to the gas stove and lights one burner. She fills the coffee pot at the sink and sets it over the flame. Then slumps down into a chair by the table and puts a hand over her forehead as if she were suffering from headache. Suddenly her face brightens as though she had remembered something, and she casts a quick glance at the dish closet; then looks sharply at the bedroom door and listens intently for a moment or so.

MRS. ROWLAND *(in a low voice)* Alfred! Alfred! *(There is no answer from the next room and she continues suspiciously in a louder tone)* You needn't pretend you're asleep. *(There is no reply to this from the bedroom, and, reassured, she gets up from her chair and tiptoes cautiously to the dish closet. She slowly opens one door, taking great care to make no noise, and slides out, from their hiding place behind the dishes, a bottle of Gordon gin and a glass. In doing so she disturbs the top dish, which rattles a little. At this sound she starts guiltily and looks with sulky defiance at the doorway to the next room)*
(Her voice trembling) Alfred!
(After a pause, during which she listens for any sound, she takes the glass and pours out a large drink and gulps it down; then hastily returns the bottle and glass to their hiding place. She closes the closet door with the same care as she had opened it, and, heaving a great sigh of relief, sinks down into her chair again. The large dose of alcohol she has taken has an almost immediate effect. Her features become more animated, she seems to gather energy, and she looks at the bedroom door with a hard, vindictive smile on her lips. Her eyes glance quickly about the room and are fixed on a man's coat and vest which hang from a hook at right. She moves stealthily over to the open doorway and stands there, out of sight of any one inside, listening for any movement from within)
(Calling in a half-whisper) Alfred!
(Again there is no reply. With a swift movement she takes the coat and vest from the hook and returns with them to her chair. She sits down and

takes the various articles out of each pocket but quickly puts them back again. At last, in the inside pocket of the vest, she finds a letter)
(Looking at the handwriting—slowly to herself) Hmm! I knew it. *(She opens the letter and reads it. At first her expression is one of hatred and rage, but as she goes on to the end it changes to one of triumphant malignity. She remains in deep thought for a moment, staring before her, the letter in her hands, a cruel smile on her lips. Then she puts the letter back in the pocket of the vest, and still careful not to awaken the sleeper, hangs the clothes up again on the same hook, and goes to the bedroom door and looks in)*
(In a loud, shrill voice) Alfred! *(Still louder)* Alfred! *(There is a muffled, yawning groan from the next room)* Don't you think it's about time you got up? Do you want to stay in bed all day? *(Turning around and coming back to her chair)* Not that I've got any doubts about your being lazy enough to stay in bed forever. *(She sits down and looks out of the window, irritably)* Goodness knows what time it is. We haven't even got any way of telling the time since you pawned your watch like a fool. The last valuable thing we had, and you knew it. It's been nothing but pawn, pawn, pawn, with you—anything to put off getting a job, anything to get out of going to work like a man. *(She taps the floor with her foot nervously, biting her lips)*
(After a short pause) Alfred! Get up, do you hear me? I want to make that bed before I go out. I'm sick of having this place in a continual mess on your account. *(With a certain vindictive satisfaction)* Not that we'll be here long unless you manage to get some money some place. Heaven knows I do my part—and more—going out to sew every day while you play the gentleman and loaf around bar rooms with that good-for-nothing lot of artists from the Square.
(A short pause during which she plays nervously with a cup and saucer on the table)
And where are you going to get money, I'd like to know? The rent's due this week and you know what the landlord is. He won't let us stay a minute over our time. You say you *can't* get a job. That's a lie and you know it. You never even look for one. All you do is moon around all day writing silly poetry and stories that no one will buy—and no wonder they won't. I notice I can always get a position, such as it is; and it's only that which keeps us from starving to death.
(Gets up and goes over to the stove—looks into the coffee pot to see if the water is boiling; then comes back and sits down again)
You'll have to get money to-day some place. I can't do it all, and I won't do it all. You've got to come to your senses. You've got to beg, borrow, or steal it somewheres. *(With a contemptuous laugh)* But where, I'd like to know? You're too proud to beg, and you've borrowed the limit, and you haven't the nerve to steal.
(After a pause—getting up angrily) Aren't you up yet, for heaven's sake?

It's just like you to go to sleep again, or pretend to. *(She goes to the bedroom door and looks in)* Oh, you are up. Well, it's about time. You needn't look at me like that. Your airs don't fool me a bit any more. I know you too well—better than you think I do—you and your goings-on. *(Turning away from the door—meaningly)* I know a lot of things, my dear. Never-mind what I know, now. I'll tell you before I go, you needn't worry. *(She comes to the middle of the room and stands there, frowning)*
(Irritably) Hmm! I suppose I might as well get breakfast ready—not that there's anything much to get.
(Questioningly) Unless you have some money? *(She pauses for an answer from the next room which does not come)* Foolish question! *(She gives a short, hard laugh)* I ought to know you better than that by this time. When you left here in such a huff last night I knew what would happen. You can't be trusted for a second. A nice condition you came home in! The fight we had was only an excuse for you to make a beast of yourself. What was the use pawning your watch if all you wanted with the money was to waste it in buying drink?
(Goes over to the dish closet and takes out plates, cups, etc., while she is talking)
Hurry up! It don't take long to get breakfast these days, thanks to you. All we got this morning is bread and butter and coffee; and you wouldn't even have that if it wasn't for me sewing my fingers off. *(She slams the loaf of bread on the table with a bang)*
The bread's stale. I hope you'll like it. *You* don't deserve any better, but I don't see why *I* should suffer.
(Going over to the stove) The coffee'll be ready in a minute, and you needn't expect me to wait for you.
(Suddenly with great anger) What on earth are you doing all this time? *(She goes over to the door and looks in)* Well, you're *almost* dressed at any rate. I expected to find you back in bed. That'd be just like you. How awful you look this morning! For heaven's sake, shave! You're disgusting! You look like a tramp. No wonder no one will give you a job. I don't blame them—when you don't even look half-way decent. *(She goes to the stove)* There's plenty of hot water right here. You've got no excuse. *(Gets a bowl and pours some of the water from the coffee pot into it)* Here. *(He reaches his hand into the room for it. It is a beautiful, sensitive hand with slender, tapering fingers. It trembles and some of the water spills on the floor)*
(Tauntingly) Look at your hand tremble! You'd better give up drinking. You can't stand it. It's just your kind that get the D.T.'s. *That would be* the last straw! *(Looking down at the floor)* Look at the mess you've made of this floor—cigarette butts and ashes all over the place. Why can't you put them on a plate? No, you wouldn't be considerate enough to do that. You never think of me. You don't have to sweep the room and that's all you care about.

EUGENE O'NEILL

57

(Takes the broom and commences to sweep viciously, raising a cloud of dust. From the inner room comes the sound of a razor being stropped) (Sweeping) Hurry up! It must be nearly time for me to go. If I'm late I'm liable to lose my position, and then I couldn't support you any longer. *(As an afterthought she adds sarcastically)* And then you'd have to go to work or something dreadful like that. *(Sweeping under the table)* What I want to know is whether you're going to look for a job to-day or not. You know your family won't help us any more. They've had enough of you, too. *(After a moment's silent sweeping)* I'm about sick of all this life. I've got a good notion to go home, if I wasn't too proud to let them know what a failure you've been—you, the millionaire Rowland's only son, the Harvard graduate, the poet, the catch of the town—Huh! *(With bitterness)* There wouldn't be many of them now envy my catch if they knew the truth. What has our marriage been, I'd like to know? Even before your *millionaire* father died owing every one in the world money, you certainly never wasted any of your time on your wife. I suppose you thought I'd ought to be glad you were *honorable* enough to marry me— after getting me into trouble. You were ashamed of me with your fine friends because my father's only a grocer, that's what you were. At least he's honest, which is more than any one could say about yours. *(She is sweeping steadily toward the door. Leans on her broom for a moment)* You hoped every one'd think you'd been forced to marry me, and pity you, didn't you? You didn't hesitate much about telling me you loved me, and making me believe your lies, before it happened, did you? You made me think you didn't want your father to buy me off as he tried to do. I know better now. I haven't lived with you all this time for nothing. *(Somberly)* It's lucky the poor thing was born dead, after all. What a father you'd have been!

(Is silent, brooding moodily for a moment—then she continues with a sort of savage joy)

But I'm not the only one who's got you to thank for being unhappy. There's one other, at least, and *she* can't hope to marry you now. *(She puts her head into the next room)* How about Helen? *(She starts back from the doorway, half frightened)*

Don't look at me that way! Yes, I read her letter. What about it? I got a right to. I'm your wife. And I know all there is to know, so don't lie. You needn't stare at me so. You can't bully me with your superior airs any longer. Only for me you'd be going without breakfast this very morning. *(She sets the broom back in the corner—whiningly)* You never did have any gratitude for what I've done. *(She comes to the stove and puts the coffee into the pot)* The coffee's ready. I'm not going to wait for you. *(She sits down in her chair again)*

(After a pause—puts her hand to her head—fretfully) My head aches so this morning. It's a shame I've got to go to work in a stuffy room all day in my condition. And I wouldn't if you were half a man. By rights I ought

THE WIFE

58

to be lying on my back instead of you. You know how sick I've been this last year; and yet you object when I take a little something to keep up my spirits. You even didn't want me to take that tonic I got at the drug store. *(With a hard laugh)* I know you'd be glad to have me dead and out of your way; then you'd be free to run after all these silly girls that think you're such a wonderful, misunderstood person—this Helen and the others. *(There is a sharp exclamation of pain from the next room)* *(With satisfaction)* There! I knew you'd cut yourself. It'll be a lesson to you. You know you oughtn't to be running around nights drinking with your nerves in such an awful shape. *(She goes to the door and looks in)* What makes you so pale? What are you staring at yourself in the mirror that way for? For goodness sake, wipe that blood off your face! *(With a shudder)* It's horrible. *(In relieved tones)* There, that's better. I never could stand the sight of blood. *(She shrinks back from the door a little)* You better give up trying and go to a barber shop. Your hand shakes dreadfully. Why do you stare at me like that? *(She turns away from the door)* I'll give you fifteen cents—only promise you won't buy a drink with it. Are you still mad at me about that letter? *(Defiantly)* Well, I had a right to read it. I'm your wife. *(She comes to the chair and sits down again. After a pause)*

I knew all the time you were running around with some one. Your lame excuses about spending the time at the library didn't fool me. Who is this Helen, anyway? One of those artists? Or does she write poetry, too? Her letter sounds that way. I'll bet she told you your things were the best ever, and you believed her, like a fool. Is she young and pretty? I was young and pretty, too, when you fooled me with your fine, poetic talk; but life with you would soon wear anyone down. What I've been through! *(Goes over and takes the coffee off the stove)* Breakfast is ready. *(With a contemptuous glance)* Breakfast! *(Pours out a cup of coffee for herself and puts the pot on the table)* Your coffee'll be cold. What are you doing —still shaving, for heaven's sake? You'd better give it up. One of these mornings you'll give yourself a serious cut. *(She cuts off bread and butters it. During the following speeches she eats and sips her coffee)* I'll have to run as soon as I've finished eating. One of us has got to work. *(Angrily)* Are you going to look for a job to-day or aren't you? I should think some of your fine friends would help you, if they really think you're so much. But I guess they just like to hear you talk. *(Sits in silence for a moment)* I'm sorry for this Helen, whoever she is. Haven't you got any feelings for other people? What will her family say? I see she mentions them in her letter. What is she going to do—have the child—or go to one of those doctors? That's a nice thing. I must say. Where can she get the money? Is she rich? *(She waits for some answer to this volley of questions)* Hmm! You won't tell me anything about her, will you? Much I care. Come to think of it, I'm not so sorry for her, after all. She knew what she was doing. She isn't any schoolgirl, like I was, from the looks of her letter. Does she know you're married? Of course, she must. All your friends know about your unhappy marriage. I know they pity you, but they don't know my side of it. They'd talk different if they did. *(Too busy eating to go on for a second or so)*

This Helen must be a fine one, if she knew you were married. What does she expect, then? That I'll divorce you and let her marry you? Does she think I'm crazy enough for that—after all you've made me go through? I guess not! And you can't get a divorce from me and you know it. No one can say *I've* ever done anything wrong. *(Drinks the last of her cup of coffee)* She deserves to suffer, that's all I can say. I'll tell you what I think; I think your Helen is no better than a common street-walker, that's what I think. *(There is a stifled groan of pain from the next room)*

Did you cut yourself again? Serves you right. Why don't you go to a barber shop when I offer you the money? *(Gets up and takes off her apron)* Well, I've got to run along. *(Peevishly)* This is a fine life for me to be leading! I won't stand for your loafing any longer. *(Something catches her ear and she pauses and listens intently)* There! You've overturned the water all over everything. Don't say you haven't. I can hear it dripping on the floor. *(A vague expression of fear comes over her face)* Alfred! Why don't you answer me?

(She moves slowly toward the room. There is the noise of a chair being overturned and something crashes heavily to the floor. She stands, trembling with fright)

Alfred! Alfred! Answer me! What is it you knocked over? Are you still drunk? *(Unable to stand the tension a second longer she rushes to the door of the bedroom)*

Alfred!

(She stands in the doorway looking down at the floor of the inner room, transfixed with horror. Then she shrieks wildly and runs to the other door, unlocks it and frenziedly pulls it open, and runs shrieking madly into the outer hallway.)

(The curtain falls.)

THE SHORT HAPPY LIFE
OF FRANCIS MACOMBER

by

ERNEST HEMINGWAY

(1899–1961)

Winner of both Pulitzer and Nobel Prizes, Ernest Hemingway has been one of the most important influences in contemporary American fiction. He wrote often about boys and men who were searching for and living by a code of behavior in the masculine world of hunting, fishing, bullfighting, and war. He became an exemplar of the legendary heroes he created and followed his own code by committing suicide when faced with incurable cancer. Collections of his short stories include Men Without Women *(1927) and* Winner Take Nothing *(1933), whose titles are descriptive of his work.*

•———————————————•

It was now lunch time and they were all sitting under the double green fly of the dining tent pretending that nothing had happened.

"Will you have lime juice or lemon squash?" Macomber asked.

"I'll have a gimlet," Robert Wilson told him.

"I'll have a gimlet too. I need something," Macomber's wife said.

"I suppose it's the thing to do," Macomber agreed. "Tell him to make three gimlets."

The mess boy had started them already, lifting the bottles out of the canvas cooling bags that sweated wet in the wind that blew through the trees that shaded the tents.

"What had I ought to give them?" Macomber asked.

"A quid would be plenty," Wilson told him. "You don't want to spoil them."

"Will the headman distribute it?"

"Absolutely."

Francis Macomber had, half an hour before, been carried to his tent from the edge of the camp in triumph on the arms and shoulders of the cook, the personal boys, the skinner and the porters. The gun-bearers had taken no part in the demonstration. When the native boys put him down at the door of his tent, he had shaken all their hands, received their congratulations, and then gone into the tent and sat on the bed until his wife came in. She did not speak to him when she came in and he left the tent at once to wash his face and hands in the portable wash basin outside and go over to the dining tent to sit in a comfortable canvas chair in the breeze and the shade.

"You've got your lion," Robert Wilson said to him, "and a damned fine one too."

Mrs. Macomber looked at Wilson quickly. She was an extremely handsome and well-kept woman of the beauty and social position which had, five years before, commanded five thousand dollars as the price of endorsing, with photographs, a beauty product which she had never used. She had been married to Francis Macomber for eleven years.

"He is a good lion, isn't he?" Macomber said. His wife looked at him now. She looked at both these men as though she had never seen them before.

One, Wilson, the white hunter, she knew she had never truly seen before. He was about middle height with sandy hair, a stubby mustache, a very red face and extremely cold blue eyes with faint white wrinkles at the corners that grooved merrily when he smiled. He smiled at her now and she looked away from his face at the way his shoulders sloped in the loose tunic he wore with the four big cartridges held in loops where the left breast pocket should have been, at his big brown hands, his old slacks, his very dirty boots and back to his red face again. She noticed where the baked red of his face stopped in a white line that marked the circle left by his Stetson hat that hung now from one of the pegs of the tent pole.

"Well, here's to the lion," Robert Wilson said. He smiled at her again and, not smiling, she looked curiously at her husband.

Francis Macomber was very tall, very well built if you did not mind that length of bone, dark, his hair cropped like an oarsman, rather thin-lipped, and was considered handsome. He was dressed in the same sort of safari clothes that Wilson wore except that his were new, he was thirty-five years old, kept himself very fit, was good at court games, had a number of big-game fishing records, and had just shown himself, very publicly, to be a coward.

"Here's to the lion," he said. "I can't ever thank you for what you did."

Margaret, his wife, looked away from him and back to Wilson.

"Let's not talk about the lion," she said.

Wilson looked over at her without smiling and now she smiled at him.

"It's been a very strange day," she said. "Hadn't you ought to put your hat on even under the canvas at noon? You told me that, you know."

"Might put it on," said Wilson.

"You know you have a very red face, Mr. Wilson," she told him and smiled again.

"Drink," said Wilson.

"I don't think so," she said. "Francis drinks a great deal, but his face is never red."

"It's red today," Macomber tried a joke.

"No," said Margaret. "It's mine that's red today. But Mr. Wilson's is always red."

"Must be racial," said Wilson. "I say, you wouldn't like to drop my beauty as a topic, would you?"

"I've just started on it."

"Let's chuck it," said Wilson.

"Conversation is going to be so difficult," Margaret said.

"Don't be silly, Margot," her husband said.

"No difficulty," Wilson said. "Got a damn fine lion."

Margot looked at them both and they saw that she was going to cry. Wilson had seen it coming for a long time and he dreaded it. Macomber was past dreading it.

"I wish it hadn't happened. Oh, I wish it hadn't happened," she said and started for her tent. She made no noise of crying but they could see that her shoulders were shaking under the rose-colored, sun-proofed shirt she wore.

"Women upset," said Wilson to the tall man. "Amounts to nothing. Strain on the nerves and one thing'n another."

"No," said Macomber. "I suppose that I rate that for the rest of my life now."

"Nonsense. Let's have a spot of the giant killer," said Wilson. "Forget the whole thing. Nothing to it anyway."

"We might try," said Macomber. "I won't forget what you did for me though."

"Nothing," said Wilson. "All nonsense."

So they sat there in the shade where the camp was pitched under some wide-topped acacia trees with a boulder-strewn cliff behind them, and a stretch of grass that ran to the bank of a boulder-filled stream in front with forest beyond it, and drank their just-cool lime drinks and avoided one another's eyes while the boys set the table for lunch. Wilson could tell that the boys all knew about it now and when he saw Macomber's personal boy looking curiously at his master while he was putting dishes on the table he snapped at him in Swahili. The boy turned away with his face blank.

"What were you telling him?" Macomber asked.

"Nothing. Told him to look alive or I'd see he got about fifteen of the best."

"What's that? Lashes?"

"It's quite illegal," Wilson said. "You're supposed to fine them."

"Do you still have them whipped?"

"Oh, yes. They could raise a row if they chose to complain. But they don't. They prefer it to the fines."

"How strange!" said Macomber.

"Not strange, really," Wilson said. "Which would you rather do? Take a good birching or lose your pay?"

Then he felt embarrassed at asking it and before Macomber could answer he went on, "We all take a beating every day, you know, one way or another."

This was no better. "Good God," he thought. "I am a diplomat, aren't I?"

"Yes, we take a beating," said Macomber, still not looking at him. "I'm awfully sorry about that lion business. It doesn't have to go any further, does it? I mean no one will hear about it, will they?"

"You mean will I tell it at the Mathaiga Club?" Wilson looked at him now coldly. He had not expected this. So he's a bloody four-letter man as well as a bloody coward, he thought. I rather liked him too until today. But how is one to know about an American?

"No," said Wilson. "I'm a professional hunter. We never talk about our clients. You can be quite easy on that. It's supposed to be bad form to ask us not to talk though."

He had decided now that to break would be much easier. He would eat, then, by himself and could read a book with his meals. They would eat by themselves. He would see them through the safari on a very formal basis—what was it the French called it? Distinguished consideration—and it would be a damn sight easier than having to go through this emotional trash. He'd insult him and make a good clean break. Then he could read a book with his meals and he'd still be drinking their whisky. That was the phrase for it when a safari went bad. You ran into another white hunter and you asked, "How is everything going?" and he answered, "Oh, I'm still drinking their whisky," and you knew everything had gone to pot.

"I'm sorry," Macomber said and looked at him with his American face that would stay adolescent until it became middle-aged, and Wilson noted his crew-cropped hair, fine eyes only faintly shifty, good nose, thin lips and handsome jaw. "I'm sorry I didn't realize that. There are lots of things I don't know."

So what could he do, Wilson thought. He was all ready to break it off quickly and neatly and here the beggar was apologizing after he had just insulted him. He made one more attempt. "Don't worry about me talking," he said. "I have a living to make. You know in Africa no woman ever misses her lion and no white man ever bolts."

"I bolted like a rabbit," Macomber said.

Now what in hell were you going to do about a man who talked like that, Wilson wondered.

Wilson looked at Macomber with his flat, blue, machine-gunner's eyes and the other smiled back at him. He had a pleasant smile if you did not notice how his eyes showed when he was hurt.

"Maybe I can fix it up on buffalo," he said. "We're after them next, aren't we?"

"In the morning if you like," Wilson told him. Perhaps he had been wrong. This was certainly the way to take it. You most certainly could not tell a damned thing about an American. He was all for Macomber again. If you could forget the morning. But, of course, you couldn't. The morning had been about as bad as they come.

"Here comes the Memsahib," he said. She was walking over from her tent looking refreshed and cheerful and quite lovely. She had a very perfect oval face, so perfect that you expected her to be stupid. But she wasn't stupid, Wilson thought, no, not stupid.

"How is the beautiful red-faced Mr. Wilson? Are you feeling better, Francis, my pearl?"

"Oh, much," said Macomber.

"I've dropped the whole thing," she said, sitting down at the table. "What importance is there to whether Francis is any good at killing lions? That's not his trade. That's Mr. Wilson's trade. Mr. Wilson is really very impressive killing anything. You do kill anything, don't you?"

"Oh, anything," said Wilson. "Simply anything." They are, he thought, the hardest in the world; the hardest, the cruelest, the most predatory and the most attractive and their men have softened or gone to pieces nervously as they have hardened. Or is it that they pick men they can handle? They can't know that much at the age they marry, he thought. He was grateful that he had gone through his education on American women before now because this was a very attractive one.

"We're going after buff in the morning," he told her.

"I'm coming," she said.

"No, you're not."

"Oh, yes, I am. Mayn't I, Francis?"

"Why not stay in camp?"

"Not for anything," she said. "I wouldn't miss something like today for anything."

When she left, Wilson was thinking, when she went off to cry, she seemed a hell of a fine woman. She seemed to understand, to realize, to be hurt for him and for herself and to know how things really stood. She is away for twenty minutes and now she is back, simply enamelled in that American female cruelty. They are the damnedest women. Really the damnedest.

"We'll put on another show for you tomorrow," Francis Macomber said.

"You're not coming," Wilson said.

"You're very mistaken," she told him. "And I want *so* to see you perform again. You were lovely this morning. That is if blowing things' heads off is lovely."

"Here's the lunch," said Wilson. "You're very merry, aren't you?"

"Why not? I didn't come out here to be dull."

"Well, it hasn't been dull," Wilson said. He could see the boulders in the river and the high bank beyond with the trees and he remembered the morning.

"Oh, no," she said. "It's been charming. And tomorrow. You don't know how I look forward to tomorrow."

"That's eland he's offering you," Wilson said.

"They're the big cowy things that jump like hares, aren't they?"

"I suppose that describes them," Wilson said.

"It's very good meat," Macomber said.

"Did you shoot it, Francis?" she asked.

"Yes."

"They're not dangerous, are they?"

"Only if they fall on you," Wilson told her.

"I'm so glad."

"Why not let up on the bitchery just a little, Margot," Macomber said, cutting the eland steak and putting some mashed potato, gravy and carrot on the down-turned fork that tined through the piece of meat.

"I suppose I could," she said, "since you put it so prettily."

"Tonight we'll have champagne for the lion," Wilson said. "It's a bit too hot at noon."

"Oh, the lion," Margot said. "I'd forgotten the lion!"

So, Robert Wilson thought to himself, she *is* giving him a ride, isn't she? Or do you suppose that's her idea of putting up a good show? How should a woman act when she discovers her husband is a bloody coward? She's damn cruel but they're all cruel. They govern, of course, and to govern one has to be cruel sometimes. Still, I've seen enough of their damn terrorism.

"Have some more eland," he said to her politely.

That afternoon, late, Wilson and Macomber went out in the motor car with the native driver and the two gun-bearers. Mrs. Macomber stayed in the camp. It was too hot to go out, she said, and she was going with them in the early morning. As they drove off Wilson saw her standing under the big tree, looking pretty rather than beautiful in her faintly rosy khaki, her dark hair drawn back off her forehead and gathered in a knot low on her neck, her face as fresh, he thought, as though she were in England. She waved to them as the car went off through the swale of high grass and curved around through the trees into the small hills of orchard bush.

In the orchard bush they found a herd of impala, and leaving the car they stalked one old ram with long, wide-spread horns and Macomber killed it with a very creditable shot that knocked the buck down at a good two hundred yards and sent the herd off bounding wildly and leaping over one another's backs in long, leg-drawn-up leaps as unbelievable and as floating as those one makes sometimes in dreams.

"That was a good shot," Wilson said. "They're a small target."

"Is it a worth-while head?" Macomber asked.

"It's excellent," Wilson told him. "You shoot like that and you'll have no trouble."

"Do you think we'll find buffalo tomorrow?"

"There's a good chance of it. They feed out early in the morning and with luck we may catch them in the open."

"I'd like to clear away that lion business," Macomber said. "It's not very pleasant to have your wife see you do something like that."

I should think it would be even more unpleasant to do it, Wilson thought, wife or no wife, or to talk about it having done it. But he said, "I wouldn't think about that any more. Any one could be upset by his first lion. That's all over."

But that night after dinner and a whisky and soda by the fire before going to bed, as Francis Macomber lay on his cot with the mosquito bar over him and listened to the night noises it was not all over. It was neither all over nor was it beginning. It was there exactly as it happened with some parts of it indelibly emphasized and he was miserably ashamed at it. But more than shame he felt cold, hollow fear in him. The fear was still there like a cold slimy hollow in all the emptiness where once his confidence had been and it made him feel sick. It was still there with him now.

It had started the night before when he had wakened and heard the lion roaring somewhere up along the river. It was a deep sound and at the end there were sort of coughing grunts that made him seem just outside the tent, and when Francis Macomber woke in the night to hear it he was afraid. He could hear his wife breathing quietly, asleep. There was no one to tell he was afraid, nor to be afraid with him, and, lying alone, he did not know the Somali proverb that says a brave man is always frightened three times by a lion; when he first sees his track, when he first hears him roar and when he first confronts him. Then while they were eating breakfast by lantern light out in the dining tent, before the sun was up, the lion roared again and Francis thought he was just at the edge of camp.

"Sounds like an old-timer," Robert Wilson said, looking up from his kippers and coffee. "Listen to him cough."

"Is he very close?"

"A mile or so up the stream."

"Will we see him?"

"We'll have a look."

"Does his roaring carry that far? It sounds as though he were right in camp."

"Carries a hell of a long way," said Robert Wilson. "It's strange the way it carries. Hope he's a shootable cat. The boys said there was a very big one about here."

"If I get a shot, where should I hit him," Macomber asked, "to stop him?"

"In the shoulders," Wilson said. "In the neck if you can make it. Shoot for bone. Break him down."

"I hope I can place it properly," Macomber said.

"You shoot very well," Wilson told him. "Take your time. Make sure of him. The first one in is the one that counts."

"What range will it be?"

"Can't tell. Lion has something to say about that. Don't shoot unless it's close enough so you can make sure."

"At under a hundred yards?" Macomber asked.

Wilson looked at him quickly.

"Hundred's about right. Might have to take him a bit under. Shouldn't chance a shot at much over that. A hundred's a decent range. You can hit him wherever you want at that. Here comes the Memsahib."

"Good morning," she said. "Are we going after that lion?"

"As soon as you deal with your breakfast," Wilson said. "How are you feeling?"

"Marvelous," she said. "I'm very excited."

"I'll just go and see that everything is ready," Wilson went off. As he left the lion roared again.

"Noisy beggar." Wilson said. "We'll put a stop to that."

"What's the matter, Francis?" his wife asked him.

"Nothing," Macomber said.

"Yes, there is," she said. "What are you upset about?"

"Nothing," he said.

"Tell me," she looked at him. "Don't you feel well?"

"It's that damned roaring," he said. "It's been going on all night, you know."

"Why didn't you wake me," she said. "I'd love to have heard it."

"I've got to kill the damned thing," Macomber said, miserably.

"Well, that's what you're out here for, isn't it?"

"Yes. But I'm nervous. Hearing the thing roar gets on my nerves."

"Well then, as Wilson said, kill him and stop his roaring."

"Yes, darling," said Francis Macomber. "It sounds easy, doesn't it?"

"You're not afraid, are you?"

"Of course not. But I'm nervous from hearing him roar all night."

"You'll kill him marvellously," she said. "I know you will. I'm awfully anxious to see it."

"Finish your breakfast and we'll be starting."

"It's not light yet," she said. "This is a ridiculous hour."

Just then the lion roared in a deep-chested moaning, suddenly gutteral, ascending vibration that seemed to shake the air and ended in a sigh and a heavy, deep-chested grunt.

"He sounds almost here," Macomber's wife said.

"My God," said Macomber. "I hate that damned noise."

"It's very impressive."

"Impressive. It's frightful."

Robert Wilson came up then carrying his short, ugly, shockingly big-bored .505 Gibbs and grinning.

"Come on," he said. "Your gun-bearer has your Springfield and the big gun. Everything's in the car. Have you solids?"

"Yes."

"I'm ready," Mrs. Macomber said.

"Must make him stop that racket," Wilson said. "You get in front. The Memsahib can sit back here with me."

They climbed into the motor car and, in the gray first daylight, moved off up the river through the trees. Macomber opened the breech of his rifle and saw he had metal-cased bullets, shut the bolt and put the rifle on safety. He saw his hand was trembling. He felt in his pocket for more cartridges and moved his fingers over the cartridges in the loops of his tunic front. He turned back to where Wilson sat in the rear seat of the doorless, box-bodied motor car beside his wife, them both grinning with excitement, and Wilson leaned forward and whispered,

"See the birds dropping. Means the old boy has left his kill."

On the far bank of the stream Macomber could see, above the trees, vultures circling and plummeting down.

"Chances are he'll come to drink along here," Wilson whispered. "Before he goes to lay up. Keep an eye out."

They were driving slowly along the high bank of the stream which here cut deeply to its boulder-filled bed, and they wound in and out through big trees as they drove. Macomber was watching the opposite bank when he felt Wilson take hold of his arm. The car stopped.

"There he is," he heard the whisper. "Ahead and to the right. Get out and take him. He's a marvelous lion."

Macomber saw the lion now. He was standing almost broadside, his great head up and turned toward them. The early morning breeze that blew toward them was just stirring his dark mane, and the lion looked huge, silhouetted on the rise of bank in the gray morning light, his shoulders heavy, his barrel of a body bulking smoothly.

"How far is he?" asked Macomber, raising his rifle.

"About seventy-five. Get out and take him."

"Why not shoot from where I am?"

"You don't shoot them from cars," he heard Wilson saying in his ear. "Get out. He's not going to stay there all day."

Macomber stepped out of the curved opening at the side of the front seat, onto the step and down onto the ground. The lion still stood looking majestically and coolly toward this object that his eyes only showed in silhouette, bulking like some super-rhino. There was no man smell carried toward him and he watched the object, moving his great head a little from side to side. Then watching the object, not afraid, but hesitating before going down the bank to drink with such a thing opposite him, he saw a man figure detach itself from it and he turned his heavy head and swung away toward the cover of the trees as he heard a cracking crash and felt the slam of a .30–06 220-grain solid bullet that bit his flank and ripped in sudden hot scalding nausea through his stomach. He trotted, heavy, big-footed, swinging wounded full-bellied, through the trees toward the tall grass and cover, and the crash came again to go past him ripping the air apart. Then it crashed again and he felt the blow as it hit his lower ribs and ripped on through, blood sudden hot and frothy in his mouth, and he galloped toward the high grass where he could crouch and not be seen and make them bring the crashing thing close enough so he could make a rush and get the man that held it.

Macomber had not thought how the lion felt as he got out of the car. He only knew his hands were shaking and as he walked away from the car it was almost impossible for him to make his legs move. They were stiff in the thighs, but he could feel the muscles fluttering. He raised the rifle, sighted on the junction of the lion's head and shoulders and pulled the trigger. Nothing happened though he pulled until he thought his finger would break. Then he knew he had the safety on and as he lowered the rifle to move the safety over he moved another frozen pace forward, and the lion seeing his silhouette now clear of the silhouette of the car, turned and started off at a trot, and, as Macomber fired, he heard a whunk that meant that the bullet was home; but the lion kept on going. Macomber shot again and everyone saw the bullet throw a spout of dirt beyond the trotting lion. He shot again, remembering to lower his aim, and they all heard the bullet hit, and the lion went into a gallop and was in the tall grass before he had the bolt pushed forward.

Macomber stood there feeling sick at his stomach, his hands that held the Springfield still cocked, shaking, and his wife and Robert Wilson were standing by him. Beside him too were the two gun-bearers chattering in Wakamba.

"I hit him," Macomber said. "I hit him twice."

"You gut-shot him and you hit him somewhere forward," Wilson said without enthusiasm. The gun-bearers looked very grave. They were silent now.

"You may have killed him," Wilson went on. "We'll have to wait a while before we go in to find out."

"What do you mean?"

"Let him get sick before we follow him up."

"Oh," said Macomber.

"He's a hell of a fine lion," Wilson said cheerfully. "He's gotten into a bad place though."

"Why is it bad?"

"Can't see him until you're on him."

"Oh," said Macomber.

"Come on," said Wilson. "The Memsahib can stay here in the car. We'll go to have a look at the blood spoor."

"Stay here, Margot," Macomber said to his wife. His mouth was very dry and it was hard for him to talk.

"Why?" she asked.

"Wilson says to."

"We're going to have a look," Wilson said. "You stay here. You can see even better from here."

"All right."

Wilson spoke in Swahili to the driver. He nodded and said, "Yes, Bwana."

Then they went down the steep bank and across the stream, climbing over and around the boulders and up the other bank, pulling up by some projecting roots, and along it until they found where the lion had been trotting when Macomber first shot. There was dark blood on the short grass that the gun-bearers pointed out with grass stems, and that ran away behind the river bank trees.

"What do we do?" asked Macomber.

"Not much choice," said Wilson. "We can't bring the car over. Bank's too steep. We'll let him stiffen up a bit then you and I'll go in and have a look for him."

"Can't we set the grass on fire?" Macomber asked.

"Too green."

"Can't we send beaters?"

Wilson looked at him appraisingly. "Of course we can," he said. "But it's just a touch murderous. You see we know the lion's wounded. You can drive an unwounded lion—he'll move on ahead of a noise—but a wounded lion's going to charge. You can't see him until you're right on him. He'll make himself perfectly flat in cover you wouldn't think would hide a hare. You can't very well send boys in there to that sort of a show. Somebody bound to get mauled."

"What about the gun-bearers?"

"Oh, they'll go with us. It's their *shauri*. You see, they signed on for it. They don't look too happy though, do they?"

"I don't want to go in there," said Macomber. It was out before he knew he'd said it.

"Neither do I," said Wilson very cheerily. "Really no choice though." Then, as an afterthought, he glanced at Macomber and saw suddenly how he was trembling and the pitiful look on his face.

"You don't have to go in, of course," he said. "That's what I'm hired for, you know. That's why I'm so expensive."

"You mean you'd go in by yourself? Why not leave him there?"

Robert Wilson, whose entire occupation had been with the lion and the problem he presented, and who had not been thinking about Macomber except to note that he was rather windy, suddenly felt as though he had opened the wrong door in a hotel and seen something shameful.

"What do you mean?"

"Why not just leave him?"

"You mean pretend to ourselves he hasn't been hit?"

"No. Just drop it."

"It isn't done."

"Why not?"

"For one thing, he's certain to be suffering. For another, some one else might run onto him."

"I see."

"But you don't have to have anything to do with it."

"I'd like to," Macomber said. "I'm just scared, you know."

"I'll go ahead when we go in," Wilson said, "with Kongoni tracking. You keep behind me and a little to one side. Chances are we'll hear him growl. If we see him we'll both shoot. Don't worry about anything. I'll keep you backed up. As a matter of fact, you know, perhaps you'd better not go. It might be much better. Why don't you go over and join the Memsahib while I just get it over with?"

"No, I want to go."

"All right," said Wilson. "But don't go in if you don't want to. This is my *shauri* now, you know."

"I want to go," said Macomber.

They sat under a tree and smoked.

"Want to go back and speak to the Memsahib while we're waiting?" Wilson asked.

"No."

"I'll just step back and tell her to be patient."

"Good," said Macomber. He sat there, sweating under his arms, his mouth dry, his stomach hollow feeling, wanting to find courage to tell Wilson to go on and finish off the lion without him. He could not know that Wilson was furious because he had not noticed the state he was in earlier and sent him back to his wife. While he sat there Wilson came up. "I have your big gun," he said. "Take it. We've given him time, I think. Come on."

Macomber took the big gun and Wilson said:

"Keep behind me and about five yards to the right and do exactly as I tell you." Then he spoke in Swahili to the two gun-bearers who looked the picture of gloom.

"Let's go," he said.

"Could I have a drink of water?" Macomber asked. Wilson spoke to the older gun-bearer, who wore a canteen on his belt, and the man unbuckled, unscrewed the top and handed it to Macomber, who took it noticing how heavy it seemed and how hairy and shoddy the felt covering was in his hand. He raised it to drink and looked ahead at the high grass with the flat-topped trees behind it. A breeze was blowing toward them and the grass rippled gently in the wind. He looked at the gun-bearer and he could see the gun-bearer was suffering too with fear.

Thirty-five yards into the grass the big lion lay flattened out along the ground. His ears were back and his only movement was a slight twitching up and down of his long, black-tufted tail. He had turned at bay as soon as he had reached this cover and he was sick with the wound through his full belly, and weakening with the wound through his lungs that brought a thin foamy red to his mouth each time he breathed. His flanks were wet and hot and flies were on the little openings the solid bullets had made in his tawny hide, and his big yellow eyes, narrowed with hate, looked straight ahead, only blinking when the pain came as he breathed, and his claws dug in the soft baked earth. All of him, pain, sickness, hatred and all of his remaining strength, was tightening into an absolute concentration for a rush. He could hear the men talking and he waited, gathering all of himself into this preparation for a charge as soon as the men would come into the grass. As he heard their voices his tail stiffened to twitch up and down, and, as they came into the edge of the grass, he made a coughing grunt and charged.

Kongoni, the old gun-bearer, in the lead watching the blood spoor, Wilson watching the grass for any movement, his big gun ready, the second gun-bearer looking ahead and listening, Macomber close to Wilson, his rifle cocked, they had just moved into the grass when Macomber heard the blood-choked coughing grunt, and saw the swishing rush in the grass. The next thing he knew he was running; running wildly, in panic in the open, running toward the stream.

He heard the *ca-ra-wong!* of Wilson's big rifle, and again in a second a crashing *carawong!* and turning saw the lion, horrible-looking now, with half his head seeming to be gone, crawling toward Wilson in the edge of the tall grass while the red-faced man worked the bolt on the short ugly rifle and aimed carefully as another blasting *carawong!* came from the muzzle, and the crawling, heavy, yellow bulk of the lion stiffened and the huge, mutilated head slid forward and Macomber, standing by himself in the clearing where he had run, holding a loaded rifle, while two black men and a white man looked back at him in contempt, knew the lion was dead. He came toward Wilson, his tallness all seeming a naked reproach, and Wilson looked at him and said:

"Want to take pictures?"

"No," he said.

That was all any one had said until they reached the motor car. Then Wilson had said:

"Hell of a fine lion. Boys will skin him out. We might as well stay here in the shade."

Macomber's wife had not looked at him nor he at her and he had sat by her in the back seat with Wilson sitting in the front seat. Once he had reached over and taken his wife's hand without looking at her and she had removed her hand from his. Looking across the stream to where the gun-bearers were skinning out the lion he could see that she had been able to see the whole thing. While they sat there his wife had reached forward and put her hand on Wilson's shoulder. He turned and she had leaned forward over the low seat and kissed him on the mouth.

"Oh, I say," said Wilson, going redder than his natural baked color.

"Mr. Robert Wilson," she said. "The beautiful red-faced Mr. Robert Wilson."

Then she sat down beside Macomber again and looked away across the stream to where the lion lay, with uplifted, white-muscled, tendon-marked naked forearms, and white bloating belly, as the black men fleshed away the skin. Finally the gun-bearers brought the skin over, wet and heavy, and climbed in behind with it, rolling it up before they got in, and the motor car started. No one had said anything more until they were back in camp.

That was the story of the lion. Macomber did not know how the lion had felt before he started his rush, nor during it when the unbelievable smash of the .505 with a muzzle velocity of two tons had hit him in the mouth, nor what kept him coming after that, when the second ripping crash had smashed his hind quarters and he had come crawling on toward the crashing, blasting thing that had destroyed him. Wilson knew something about it and only expressed it by saying, "Damned fine lion," but Macomber did not know how Wilson felt about things either. He did not know how his wife felt except that she was through with him.

His wife had been through with him before but it never lasted. He was very wealthy, and would be much wealthier, and he knew she would not leave him ever now. That was one of the few things that he really knew. He knew about that, about motor cycles—that was earliest—about motor cars, about duck-shooting, about fishing, trout, salmon and big-sea, about sex in books, many books, too many books, about all court games, about dogs, not much about horses, about hanging on to his money, about most of the other things his world dealt in, and about his wife not leaving him. His wife had been a great beauty and she was still a great beauty in Africa, but she was not a great enough beauty any more at home to be able to leave him and better herself and she knew it and he knew it. She had missed the chance to leave him and he knew it. If he had been better with women she would probably have started to worry about him getting another new, beautiful wife; but she knew too much about him to worry about him either. Also, he had always had a great tolerance which seemed the nicest thing about him if it were not the most sinister.

All in all they were known as a comparatively happily married couple, one of those whose disruption is often rumored but never occurs, and as the society columnist put it, they were adding more than a spice of *adventure* to their much envied and ever-enduring *Romance* by a *Safari* in what was known as *Darkest Africa* until the Martin Johnsons lighted it on so many silver screens where they were pursuing *Old Simba* the lion, the buffalo, *Tembo* and the elephant and as well collecting specimens for the Museum of Natural History. This same columnist had reported them *on the verge* at least three times in the past and they had been. But they always made it up. They had a sound basis of union. Margot was too beautiful for Macomber to divorce her and Macomber had too much money for Margot ever to leave him.

It was now about three o'clock in the morning and Francis Macomber, who had been asleep a little while after he had stopped thinking about the lion, wakened and then slept again, woke suddenly, frightened in a dream of the bloody-headed lion standing over him, and listening while his heart pounded, he realized that his wife was not in the other cot in the tent. He lay awake with that knowledge for two hours.

At the end of that time his wife came into the tent, lifted her mosquito bar and crawled cozily into bed.

"Where have you been?" Macomber asked in the darkness.

"Hello," she said. "Are you awake?"

"Where have you been?"

"I just went out to get a breath of air."

"You did, like hell."

"What do you want me to say, darling?"

"Where have you been?"

"Out to get a breath of air."

"That's a new name for it. You *are* a bitch."

"Well, you're a coward."

"All right," he said. "What of it?"

"Nothing as far as I'm concerned. But please let's not talk, darling, because I'm very sleepy."

"You think that I'll take anything."

"I know you will, sweet."

"Well, I won't."

"Please, darling, let's not talk. I'm so very sleepy."

"There wasn't going to be any of that. You promised there wouldn't be."

"Well, there is now," she said sweetly.

"You said if we made this trip that there would be none of that. You promised."

"Yes, darling. That's the way I meant it to be. But the trip was spoiled yesterday. We don't have to talk about it, do we?"

"You don't wait long when you have an advantage, do you?"

"Please let's not talk. I'm so sleepy, darling."

"I'm going to talk."

"Don't mind me then because I'm going to sleep." And she did.

At breakfast, there were all three at the table before daylight and Francis Macomber found that, of all the men that he hated, he hated Robert Wilson the most.

"Sleep well?" Wilson asked in his throaty voice, filling a pipe.

"Did you?"

"Topping," the white hunter told him.

You bastard, thought Macomber, you insolent bastard.

So she woke him when she came in, Wilson thought, looking at them both with his flat, cold eyes. Well, why doesn't he keep his wife where she belongs? What does he think I am, a bloody plaster saint? Let him keep her where she belongs. It's his own fault.

"Do you think we'll find buffalo?" Margot asked, pushing away a dish of apricots.

"Chance of it," Wilson said and smiled at her. "Why don't you stay in camp?"

"Not for anything," she told him.

"Why not order her to stay in camp?" Wilson said to Macomber.

"You order her," said Macomber coldly.

"Let's not have any ordering, nor," turning to Macomber, "any silliness, Francis," Margot said quite pleasantly.

"Are you ready to start?" Macomber asked.

"Any time," Wilson told him. "Do you want the Memsahib to go?"

"Does it make any difference whether I do or not?"

The hell with it, thought Robert Wilson. The utter complete hell with it. So this is what it's going to be like. Well, this is what it's going to be like, then.

"Makes no difference," he said.

"You're sure you wouldn't like to stay in camp with her yourself and let me go out and hunt the buffalo?" Macomber asked.

"Can't do that," said Wilson. "Wouldn't talk rot if I were you."

"I'm not talking rot. I'm disgusted."

"Bad word, disgusted."

"Francis, will you please try to speak sensibly?" his wife said.

"I speak too damned sensibly," Macomber said. "Did you ever eat such filthy food?"

"Something wrong with the food?" asked Wilson quietly.

"No more than with everything else."

"I'd pull yourself together, laddybuck," Wilson said very quietly. "There's a boy waits at table that understands a little English."

"The hell with him."

Wilson stood up and puffing on his pipe strolled away, speaking a few words in Swahili to one of the gun-bearers who was standing waiting for him. Macomber and his wife sat on at the table. He was staring at his coffee cup.

"If you make a scene I'll leave you, darling," Margot said quietly.

"No, you won't."

"You can try it and see."

"You won't leave me."

"No," she said. "I won't leave you and you'll behave yourself."

"Behave myself? That's a way to talk. Behave myself."

"Yes. Behave yourself."

"Why don't *you* try behaving?"

"I've tried it so long. So very long."

"I hate that red-faced swine," Macomber said. "I loathe the sight of him."

"He's really *very* nice."

"Oh, *shut up,*" Macomber almost shouted. Just then the car came up and stopped in front of the dining tent and the driver and the two gun-bearers got out. Wilson walked over and looked at the husband and wife sitting there at the table.

"Going shooting?" he asked.

"Yes," said Macomber, standing up. "Yes."

"Better bring a woolly. It will be cool in the car," Wilson said.

"I'll get my leather jacket," Margot said.

"The boy has it," Wilson told her. He climbed into the front with the driver and Francis Macomber and his wife sat, not speaking, in the back seat.

Hope the silly beggar doesn't take a notion to blow the back of my head off, Wilson thought to himself. Women *are* a nuisance on safari.

The car was grinding down to cross the river at a pebbly ford in the gray daylight and then climbed, angling up the steep bank, where Wilson had ordered a way shovelled out the day before so they could reach the parklike wooded rolling country on the far side.

It was a good morning, Wilson thought. There was a heavy dew and as the wheels went through the grass and low bushes he could smell the odor of the crushed fronds. It was an odor like verbena and he liked this early morning smell of the dew, the crushed bracken and the look of the tree trunks showing black through the early morning mist, as the car made its way through the untracked, parklike country. He had put the two in the back seat out of his mind now and was thinking about buffalo. The buffalo that he was after stayed in the daytime in a thick swamp where it was impossible to get a shot, but in the night they fed out into an open stretch of country and if he could come between them and their swamp with the car, Macomber would have a good chance at them in the open. He did not want to hunt buff with Macomber in thick cover. He did not want to hunt buff or anything else with Macomber at all, but he was a professional hunter and he had hunted with some rare ones in his time. If they got buff today there would only be rhino to come and the poor man would have gone through his dangerous game and things might pick up. He'd have nothing more to do with the woman and Macomber would get over that too. He must have gone through plenty of that before by the look of things. Poor beggar. He must have a way of getting over it. Well, it was the poor sod's own bloody fault.

He, Robert Wilson, carried a double size cot on safari to accommodate any windfalls he might receive. He had hunted for a certain clientele, the international, fast, sporting set, where the women did not feel they were getting their money's worth unless they had shared that cot with the white hunter. He despised them when he was away from them although he liked some of them well enough at the time, but he made his living by them; and their standards were his standards as long as they were hiring him.

They were his standards in all except the shooting. He had his own standards about the killing and they could live up to them or get some one else to hunt them. He knew, too, that they all respected him for this. This Macomber was an odd one though. Damned if he wasn't. Now the wife. Well, the wife. Yes, the wife. Hm, the wife. Well he'd dropped all that. He looked around at them. Macomber sat grim and furious. Margot smiled at him. She looked younger today, more innocent and fresher and not so professionally beautiful. What's in her heart God knows, Wilson thought. She hadn't talked much last night. At that it was a pleasure to see her.

The motor car climbed up a slight rise and went on through the trees and then out into a grassy prairie-like opening and kept in the shelter of the trees along the edge, the driver going slowly and Wilson looking carefully out across the prairie and all along its far side. He stopped the car and studied the opening with his field glasses. Then he motioned to the driver to go on and the car moved slowly along, the driver avoiding wart-hog holes and driving around the mud castles ants had built. Then, looking across the opening, Wilson suddenly turned and said,

"By God, there they are!"

And looking where he pointed, while the car jumped forward and Wilson spoke in rapid Swahili to the driver, Macomber saw three huge, black animals looking almost cylindrical in their long heaviness, like big black tank cars, moving at a gallop across the far edge of the open prairie. They moved at a stiff-necked, stiff-bodied gallop and he could see the upswept wide black horns on their heads as they galloped heads out; the heads not moving.

"They're three old bulls," Wilson said. "We'll cut them off before they get to the swamp."

The car was going a wild forty-five miles an hour across the open and as Macomber watched, the buffalo got bigger and bigger until he could see the gray, hairless, scabby look of one huge bull and how his neck was a part of his shoulders and the shiny black of his horns as he galloped a little behind the others that were strung out in that steady plunging gait; and then, the car swaying as though it had just jumped a road, they drew up close and he could see the plunging hugeness of the bull, and the dust in his sparsely haired hide, the wide boss of horn and his outstretched, wide-nostrilled muzzle, and he was raising his rifle when Wilson shouted, "Not from the car, you fool!" and he had no fear, only hatred of Wilson, while the brakes clamped on and the car skidded, plowing sideways to an almost stop and Wilson was out on one side and he on the other, stumbling as his feet hit the still speeding-by of the earth, and then he was shooting at the bull as he moved away, hearing the bullets whunk into him, emptying his rifle at him as he moved steadily away, finally remembering to get his shots forward into the shoulder, and as he fumbled to reload, he saw the bull was down. Down on his knees, his big head tossing, and seeing the other two still galloping he shot at the leader and hit him. He shot again and missed and he heard the *carawonging* roar as Wilson shot and saw the leading bull slide forward onto his nose.

"Get that other," Wilson said. "Now you're shooting."

But the other bull was moving steadily at the same gallop and he missed, throwing a spout of dirt, and Wilson missed and the dust rose in a cloud and Wilson shouted, "Come on. He's too far!" and grabbed his arm and they were in the car again, Macomber and Wilson hanging on the sides and rocketing swayingly over the uneven ground, drawing up on the steady, plunging, heavy-necked, straight-moving gallop of the bull.

They were behind him and Macomber was filling his rifle, dropping shells onto the ground, jamming it, clearing the jam, then they were almost up with the bull when Wilson yelled "Stop," and the car skidded so that it almost swung over and Macomber fell forward onto his feet, slammed his bolt forward and fired as far forward as he could aim into the galloping, rounded black bull, aimed and shot again, then again, then again, and the bullets, all of them hitting, had no effect on the buffalo that he could see. Then Wilson shot, the roar deafening him, and he could see the bull stagger. Macomber shot again, aiming carefully, and down he came, onto his knees.

"All right," Wilson said. "Nice work. That's three."

Macomber felt a drunken elation.

"How many times did you shoot?" he asked.

"Just three," Wilson said. "You killed the first bull. The biggest one. I helped you finish the other two. Afraid they might have got into cover. You had them killed. I was just mopping up a little. You shot damn well."

"Let's go to the car," said Macomber. "I want a drink."

"Got to finish off that buff first," Wilson told him. The buffalo was on his knees and he jerked his head furiously and bellowed in pig-eyed roaring rage as they came toward him.

"Watch he doesn't get up," Wilson said. Then, "Get a little broadside and take him in the neck just behind the ear."

Macomber aimed carefully at the center of the huge, jerking, rage-driven neck and shot. At the shot the head dropped forward.

"That does it," said Wilson. "Got the spine. They're a hell of a looking thing, aren't they?"

ERNEST HEMINGWAY

79

"Let's get the drink," said Macomber. In his life he had never felt so good.

In the car Macomber's wife sat very white faced. "You were marvellous, darling," she said to Macomber. "What a ride."

"Was it rough?" Wilson asked.

"It was frightful. I've never been more frightened in my life."

"Let's all have a drink," Macomber said.

"By all means," said Wilson. "Give it to the Memsahib." She drank the neat whisky from the flask and shuddered a little when she swallowed. She handed the flask to Macomber who handed it to Wilson.

"It was frightfully exciting," she said. "It's given me a dreadful headache. I didn't know you were allowed to shoot them from cars though."

"No one shot from cars," said Wilson coldly.

"I mean chase them from cars."

"Wouldn't ordinarily," Wilson said. "Seemed sporting enough to me though while we were doing it. Taking more chance driving that way across the plain full of holes and one thing and another than hunting on foot. Buffalo could have charged us each time we shot if he liked. Gave him every chance. Wouldn't mention it to any one though. It's illegal if that's what you mean."

"It seemed very unfair to me" Margot said, "chasing those big helpless things in a motor car."

"Did it?" said Wilson.

"What would happen if they heard about it in Nairobi?"

"I'd lose my license for one thing. Other unpleasantnesses," Wilson said, taking a drink from the flask. "I'd be out of business."

"Really?"

"Yes, really."

"Well," said Macomber, and he smiled for the first time all day. "Now she has something on you."

"You have such a pretty way of putting things, Francis," Margot Macomber said. Wilson looked at them both. If a four-letter man marries a five-letter woman, he was thinking, what number of letters would their children be? What he said was, "We lost a gun-bearer. Did you notice it?"

"My God, no," Macomber said.

"Here he comes," Wilson said. "He's all right. He must have fallen off when we left the first bull."

Approaching them was the middle-aged gun-bearer, limping along in his knitted cap, khaki tunic, shorts and rubber sandals, gloomy-faced and disgusted looking. As he came up he called out to Wilson in Swahili and they all saw the change in the white hunter's face.

"What does he say?" asked Margot.

"He says the first bull got up and went into the bush," Wilson said with no expression in his voice.

"Oh," said Macomber blankly.

"Then it's going to be just like the lion," said Margot, full of anticipation.

"It's not going to be a damned bit like the lion," Wilson told her. "Did you want another drink, Macomber?"

"Thanks, yes," Macomber said. He expected the feeling he had had about the lion to come back but it did not. For the first time in his life he really felt wholly without fear. Instead of fear he had a feeling of definite elation.

"We'll go and have a look at the second bull," Wilson said. "I'll tell the driver to put the car in the shade."

"What are you going to do?" asked Margaret Macomber.

"Take a look at the buff," Wilson said.

"I'll come."

"Come along."

The three of them walked over to where the second buffalo bulked blackly in the open, head forward on the grass, the massive horns swung wide.

"He's a very good head," Wilson said. "That's close to a fifty-inch spread."

Macomber was looking at him with delight.

"He's hateful looking," said Margot. "Can't we go into the shade?"

"Of course," Wilson said. "Look," he said to Macomber, and pointed. "See that patch of bush?"

"Yes."

"That's where the first bull went in. The gun-bearer said when he fell off the bull was down. He was watching us helling along and the other two buff galloping. When he looked up there was the bull up and looking at him. Gun-bearer ran like hell and the bull went off slowly into that bush."

"Can we go in after him now?" asked Macomber eagerly.

Wilson looked at him appraisingly. Damned if this isn't a strange one, he thought. Yesterday he's scared sick and today he's a ruddy fire eater.

"No, we'll give him a while."

"Let's please go into the shade," Margot said. Her face was white and she looked ill.

They made their way to the car where it stood under a single, wide-spreading tree and all climbed in.

"Chances are he's dead in there," Wilson remarked. "After a little we'll have a look."

Macomber felt a wild unreasonable happiness that he had never known before.

"By God, that was a chase," he said. "I've never felt any such feeling. Wasn't it marvellous, Margot?"

"I hated it."

"Why?"

"I hated it," she said bitterly. "I loathed it."

"You know I don't think I'd ever be afraid of anything again," Macomber said to Wilson. "Something happened in me after we first saw the buff and started after him. Like a dam bursting. It was pure excitement."

"Cleans out your liver," said Wilson. "Damn funny things happen to people."

Macomber's face was shining. "You know something did happen to me," he said. "I feel absolutely different."

His wife said nothing and eyed him strangely. She was sitting far back in the seat and Macomber was sitting forward talking to Wilson who turned sideways talking over the back of the front seat.

"You know, I'd like to try another lion," Macomber said. "I'm really not afraid of them now. After all, what can they do to you?"

"That's it," said Wilson. "Worst one can do is kill you. How does it go? Shakespeare. Damned good. See if I can remember. Oh, damned good. Used to quote it to myself at one time. Let's see. 'By my troth, I care not; a man can die but once; we owe God a death and let it go which way it will, he that dies this year is quit for the next.' Damned fine, eh?"

He was very embarrassed, having brought out this thing he had lived by, but he had seen men come of age before and it always moved him. It was not a matter of their twenty-first birthday.

It had taken a strange chance of hunting, a sudden precipitation into action without opportunity for worrying beforehand, to bring this about with Macomber, but regardless of how it had happened it had most certainly happened. Look at the beggar now, Wilson thought. It's that some of them stay little boys so long, Wilson thought. Sometimes all their lives. Their figures stay boyish when they're fifty. The great American boy-men. Damned strange people. But he liked this Macomber now. Damned strange fellow. Probably meant the end of cuckoldry too. Well, that would be a damned good thing. Damn good thing. Beggar had probably been afraid all his life. Don't know what started it. But over now. Hadn't had time to be afraid with the buff. That and being angry too. Motor car too. Motor cars made it familiar. Be a damn fire eater now. He'd seen it in the war work the same way. More of a change than any loss of virginity. Fear gone like an operation. Something else grew in its place. Main thing a man had. Made him into a man. Women knew it too. No bloody fear.

From the far corner of the seat Margaret Macomber looked at the two of them. There was no change in Wilson. She saw Wilson as she had seen him the day before when she had first realized what his great talent was. But she saw the change in Francis Macomber now.

"Do you have that feeling of happiness about what's going to happen?" Macomber asked, still exploring his new wealth.

"You're not supposed to mention it," Wilson said, looking in the other's face. "Much more fashionable to say you're scared. Mind you, you'll be scared too, plenty of times."

"But you *have* a feeling of happiness about action to come?"

"Yes," said Wilson. "There's that. Doesn't do to talk too much about all this. Talk the whole thing away. No pleasure in anything if you mouth it up too much."

"You're both talking rot," said Margot. "Just because you've chased some helpless animals in a motor car you talk like heroes."

"Sorry," said Wilson. "I have been gassing too much." She's worried about it already, he thought.

"If you don't know what we're talking about why not keep out of it?" Macomber asked his wife.

"You've gotten awfully brave, awfully suddenly," his wife said contemptuously, but her contempt was not secure. She was afraid of something.

Macomber laughed, a very natural hearty laugh. "You know I *have*," he said. "I really have."

"Isn't it sort of late?" Margot said bitterly. Because she had done the best she could for many years back and the way they were together now was no one person's fault.

"Not for me," said Macomber.

Margot said nothing but sat back in the corner of the seat.

"Do you think we've given him time enough?" Macomber asked Wilson cheerfully.

"We might have a look," Wilson said. "Have you any solids left?"

"The gun-bearer has some."

Wilson called in Swahili and the older gun-bearer, who was skinning out one of the heads, straightened up, pulled a box of solids out of his pocket and brought them over to Macomber, who filled his magazine and put the remaining shells in his pocket.

"You might as well shoot the Springfield," Wilson said. "You're used to it. We'll leave the Mannlicher in the car with the Memsahib. Your gun-bearer can carry your heavy gun. I've this damned cannon. Now let me tell you about them." He had saved this until the last because he did not want to worry Macomber. "When a buff comes he comes with his head high and thrust straight out. The boss of the horns covers any sort of a brain shot. The only shot is straight into the nose. The only other shot is into his chest or, if you're to one side, into the neck or the shoulders. After they've been hit once they take a hell of a lot of killing. Don't try anything fancy. Take the easiest shot there is. They've finished skinning out that head now. Should we get started?"

He called to the gun-bearers, who came up wiping their hands, and the older one got into the back.

"I'll only take Kongoni," Wilson said. "The other can watch to keep the birds away."

As the car moved slowly across the open space toward the island of brushy trees that ran in a tongue of foliage along a dry water course that cut the open swale, Macomber felt his heart pounding and his mouth was dry again, but it was excitement, not fear.

"Here's where he went in," Wilson said. Then to the gun-bearer in Swahili, "Take the blood spoor."

The car was parallel to the patch of bush. Macomber, Wilson and the gun-bearer got down. Macomber, looking back, saw his wife, with the rifle by her side, looking at him. He waved to her and she did not wave back.

The brush was very thick ahead and the ground was dry. The middle-aged gun-bearer was sweating heavily and Wilson had his hat down over his eyes and his red neck showed just ahead of Macomber. Suddenly the gun-bearer said something in Swahili to Wilson and ran forward.

"He's dead in there," Wilson said. "Good work," and he turned to grip Macomber's hand and as they shook hands, grinning at each other, the gun-bearer shouted wildly and they saw him coming out of the bush sideways, fast as a crab, and the bull coming, nose out, mouth tight closed, blood dripping, massive head straight out, coming in a charge, his little pig eyes bloodshot as he looked at them. Wilson, who was ahead, was kneeling shooting, and Macomber, as he fired, unhearing his shot in the roaring of Wilson's gun, saw fragments like slate burst from the huge boss of the horns, and the head jerked, he shot again at the wide nostrils and saw the horns jolt again and fragments fly, and he did not see Wilson now and, aiming carefully, shot again with the buffalo's huge bulk almost on him and his rifle almost level with the on-coming head, nose out, and he could see the little wicked eyes and the head started to lower and he felt a sudden white-hot, blinding flash explode inside his head and that was all he ever felt.

Wilson had ducked to one side to get in a shoulder shot. Macomber had stood solid and shot for the nose, shooting a touch high each time and hitting the heavy horns, splintering and chipping them like hitting a slate roof, and Mrs. Macomber, in the car, had shot at the buffalo with the 6.5 Mannlicher as it seemed about to gore Macomber and had hit her husband about two inches up and a little to one side of the base of his skull.

Francis Macomber lay now, face down, not two yards from where the buffalo lay on his side and his wife knelt over him with Wilson beside her.

"I wouldn't turn him over," Wilson said.

The woman was crying hysterically.

"I'd get back in the car," Wilson said. "Where's the rifle?"

She shook her head, her face contorted. The gun-bearer picked up the rifle.

"Leave it as it is," said Wilson. Then, "Go get Abdulla so that he may witness the manner of the accident."

He knelt down, took a handkerchief from his pocket, and spread it over Francis Macomber's crew-cropped head where it lay. The blood sank into the dry, loose earth.

Wilson stood up and saw the buffalo on his side, his legs out, his thinly-haired belly crawling with ticks. "Hell of a good bull," his brain registered automatically. "A good fifty inches, or better. Better." He called to the driver and told him to spread a blanket over the body and stay by it. Then he walked over to the motor car where the woman sat crying in the corner.

"That was a pretty thing to do," he said in a toneless voice. "He *would* have left you too."

"Stop it," she said.

"Of course it's an accident," he said. "I know that."

"Stop it," she said.

"Don't worry," he said. "There will be a certain amount of unpleasantness but I will have some photographs taken that will be very useful at the inquest. That's the testimony of the gun-bearers and the driver too. You're perfectly all right."

"Stop it," she said.

"There's a hell of a lot to be done," he said. "And I'll have to send a truck off to the lake to wireless for a plane to take the three of us into Nairobi. Why didn't you poison him? That's what they do in England."

"Stop it. Stop it. Stop it," the woman cried.

Wilson looked at her with his flat blue eyes.

"I'm through now," he said. "I was a little angry. I'd begun to like your husband."

"Oh, please stop it," she said. "Please, please stop it."

"That's better," Wilson said. "Please is much better. Now I'll stop."

THE BRIDAL VEIL

by

ALICE CARY

(1820–1871)

*Born on a farm near Cincinnati, Alice Cary and her sister Phoebe
were educated at home. The poems they began to publish as teenagers were widely admired; Edgar Allan Poe considered a lyric by
Alice to be one of the most musically perfect in English. Moving
to New York City in 1850, the sisters earned a living by writing.
Alice Cary's realistic novel* Clovernook *(1852), a best seller, revealed
the cultural deprivation of women. Both sisters worked for women's
suffrage and the abolition of slavery.*

•————————————————————•

We're married, they say, and you think you have won me,—
Well, take this white veil from my head, and look on me:
Here's matter to vex you, and matter to grieve you,
Here's doubt to distrust you, and faith to believe you,—
I am all as you see, common earth, common dew;
Be wary, and mould me to roses, not rue!

Ah! shake out the filmy thing, fold after fold,
And see if you have me to keep and to hold,—
Look close on my heart—see the worst of its sinning—
It is not yours to-day for the yesterday's winning—
The past is not mine—I am too proud to borrow—
You must grow to new heights if I love you to-morrow.

We're married! I'm plighted to hold up your praises,
As the turf at your feet does its handful of daisies;
That way lies my honor,—my pathway of pride,
But, mark you, if greener grass grow either side,
I shall know it, and keeping in body with you,
Shall walk in my spirit with feet on the dew!

THE WIFE
86

We're married! Oh, pray that our love do not fail!
I have wings flattened down and hid under my veil:
They are subtle as light—you can never undo them,
And swift in their flight—you can never pursue them,
And spite of all clasping, and spite of all bands,
I can slip like a shadow, a dream, from your hands.

Nay, call me not cruel, and fear not to take me,
I am yours for my lifetime, to be what you make me,—
To wear my white veil for a sign, or a cover,
As you shall be proven my lord, or my lover;
A cover for peace that is dead, or a token
Of bliss that can never be written or spoken.

SECRETIVE

by

JANE AUGUSTINE

(b. 1931)

Jane Augustine, whose poems have appeared in Ms., Aphra, Chrysalis, Woman Poet: The East, *and many other literary magazines, has had one chapbook of poems,* Lit by the Earth's Dark Blood *(1977), published. A former member of the editorial board of* Aphra *and twice a winner of fellowship-grants in poetry from the New York State Council on the Arts, she is adjunct assistant professor of English at Pratt Institute, Brooklyn, and a member of the faculty of The New School in New York City. She is a graduate of Bryn Mawr College and is finishing a doctorate at the City University of New York.*

If I don't tell someone, I'm not sure what will happen. I'll crack perhaps. I'm not sure I can even tell it to you, my secret friend, although you're utterly safe, the receiver of my thought-words. You're comfortable, sympathetic—as if you were somebody's mother (not mine) or a lady psychiatrist, foreign, a little drab, and as if you were sitting across from me at my kitchen table, nodding yes and asking me unformulated questions to which I have exact and full answers, with explanations.

My secret can't even be written in a journal, if I kept a journal. Even my nonsecrets look bad when written out in words. I'd have to write: "I spent all day Saturday downtown looking for the right lining material for my new coat. The lining almost never shows but I was annoyed by the sleazy taffetas and coarse satins and inadequate moires. The inside matters! I kept saying to myself, searching desperately. Almost everything I saw would do, more or less; I could put up with it if I had to, but nothing was exactly right. The lining should pick up one of the colors of the coat's tweed, I decided, but I didn't know which color. It should be a rich fabric but not stiff or heavy. But woven or knit? Or perhaps a contrasting color . . . ?"

You see how my journal would sound—just a list of absurd concerns that burn up my caring. You would probably agree with him that I'm stupid, if you saw my day-to-day life translated into words that way. Now, as you sit absorbing my thoughts, you're sympathetic. You're aware that there's more to me than just that I get involved with trivial matters not worth caring about. My mind latches onto them and labors over them while my secret lies down inside me escaping my attention. I know it's there, but only a little of it makes itself known to me.

If I kept a journal, I'd be tempted to write about him in it. Don't you think people delude themselves when they think that a journal or diary can be kept private? He'd find it and that would set him off again, no matter what I said. He couldn't bear my looking at him and recording him. And if I hinted at the secret, which of course he knows, he'd really blow up. "Who are you writing this to? How can you make up lies like this? You know that I have nothing to do with it—you, *you* bring it on yourself—"

You see why I can't speak out loud, why I have to send thought-words out to you. You understand the way it came about even if I can't explain it properly. You know my secret is a real secret. It really can't be told without showing me up, showing how I bring it on myself, and whatever I do to enrage him—even though I don't know what that is.

He says that I'm weak, and I try to counteract the weakness with misplaced aggressiveness. He says I try to hide my dependency pretending to be independent, learning to sew and getting a job and all that. I don't know about that; it sounds like doubletalk and yet there may be something in it. He's not stupid, he's well educated, a social worker; he's read a lot about what goes on in people's minds.

Writing the secret down in a journal would be bad enough, but worse would be if I ever dropped a hint to any of our friends, as I sometimes wish I could. But there I'd be, talking against my own husband, a complainer, a bitch—I don't want to be like that. It could be just temporary in him too, something that won't last—and then if word of it spread around . . . But it's awkward. Verna came over today, returning the sheath dress pattern, and I showed her how to insert one of those new invisible zippers. You can't see an opening anywhere; all the seams look stitched up—no sign of how to get in or get out.

Of course she looked at me and asked about it. I showed her how the kitchen cupboard door by the stove springs back sharply enough to blacken an eye. That's not so farfetched; after all, he says I do it to myself. Something in me drives him to uncontrollable outbursts. He was never like this before he married me, he says.

So this is what I need you to tell me: what do I do that I don't see myself doing? It must be huge and obvious and yet I can't see it. I try thinking back over all the times it's happened. The last time (before this) was in December; he added up the bills and came into the kitchen yelling that I'd spent three hundred dollars on the children's clothing in a year and I had to stop being such a goddam irresponsible spendthrift. "If you had to work," he yelled, "you'd understand the value of money—"

Trying to keep him cool, I asked if maybe three hundred dollars wasn't what was spent on all four of us, which wouldn't be too bad on an income of ten thousand dollars. That's when it happened. Luckily my face wasn't involved; I put on a long-sleeved blouse the next day, and went and got a job typing in an insurance company.

This time—last night—it happened because I hired a babysitter all day Saturday while I went downtown shopping for the lining material I never did buy. He exploded: "You hired a goddam babysitter all day for nothing? The girls are out of school on Saturdays, you ought to be with them." Then I said—which I guess was a mistake: "You can think of it this way: I earned the babysitter money." I was horrified when I looked in the mirror this morning and remembered that Verna was coming over.

But what's gone wrong? I thought learning to sew was a good idea, a way to save money and show him I'm not incompetent. But he says with my Vogue patterns and highfalutin ideas I spend more on material than I would on ready-to-wear. How do I know what I would have spent on ready-to-wear? And he says I just got the job so I could manipulate him and his money decisions by saying it's my money. I don't think that's why I got the job, but I recognize that the mind is full of twistings and turnings, and mysterious hidden levels. There's more in it than I can ever know about.

But maybe *you* know more, seeing it from an expert's point of view. You can tell me about what's going on, though I understand that I have to be honest with myself and not block off what's happening even though it frightens me. I've been reading, and I know that the mind is mostly unconscious, that we all repress angry and hateful thoughts and wishes, but at a price. Whenever there's a slip of the tongue, part of the unconscious is revealed. Whenever there's an accident, there's a reason for it from earliest childhood, a sexual or incestuous reason that's too strong to be concealed and too terrible to be revealed.

So there are no accidents. It wouldn't make any difference if the kitchen-cupboard door *had* sprung back on me. Things like that just don't happen unless something is hidden in the unconscious mind. My abnormality had to earn it. After all he's a respected man, a professional. He works hard on his job and coaches the Little League in the park on Saturdays. When I go to watch a game, the parents tell me how good a coach he is, really driving the kids to win and building their character. But not by getting mad at them, just by keeping everything under control. I'm the only one he blows up at. No one else has ever seen him more than annoyed at a pop fly. I'm the *only* one—

Now you know the depth of my problem. If I told anyone what he's done to me, they wouldn't believe me. They'd whisper behind my back that I must be a real nut to say such things. Or they'd say, so fights happen in the best of families, but it takes two to tango. They'd say I was crazy if they saw me like this in my kitchen talking to yes, myself, in the only way that relieves me, as if I were my own understanding woman, my invented doctor who doesn't charge me twenty-five dollars an hour.

She's almost real, this listener that I imagine. I can almost see her, wavy grayish hair and searching eyes, rather stern. She sympathizes but she isn't going to let me get away with anything. I might be imagining myself too, as a woman who's trying hard to live right and do what her husband wants. But all the time there might be a woman in me to whom those words apply which he uses: manipulative, incompetent, secretive. . . .

Can't you give me some other words for myself? Like "conscientious, thoughtful, a hard tryer . . ." But it takes a friend to speak these compliments; I must only be flattering myself. . . .

Yes, of course I know you must remain impartial; you have to tell me the truth even if it's not on my side. So can't you tell me why I worry about trivial things like zippers and linings? Then I can get over being that way. I'm sure that's one thing he hates me for.

There. Self-scrutiny does help. I've discovered something.

But the next discovery is more frightening. This woman isn't just trivial, she's full of senseless anger. Sometimes it sticks in her throat till she nearly chokes to keep it back. A little thing like his saying, "You didn't sew that button on yet." Only a petty person would flare up over a remark like that. Her feelings aren't right. Really good people have the right kind of feelings deep inside; then the rest takes care of itself.

Oh, she has secrets all right. So now she has to make sure that no one sees more of the inside of her, no more black-and-blue coming to the surface. Then at least they can't say she's crazy, though they'd almost be right; crazy from keeping secrets and holding in. But that's the way it's got to be.

They can just say she wanders around in department stores all the time, with nothing but colors and fabrics running through her head. Sleazy taffeta, slippery nylon, inferior rayon. But the coat must be finished; it has to be properly lined.

And the lining must be a contrast to the outside of the coat, which is a soft blurry pinkish-orange tweed, the color of rubbed flesh, mixed in with knobs of scarlet. It's a fitted pattern. Now the inside will be a bright green, bright as a parrot's wing, an acid green knit of some tough synthetic fiber that will hang nicely but give only when give is needed. It'll do to hold the coat together, and will only show for a moment before it's hidden away, buttoned, on the closet hanger.

DRIVING TO OREGON

by

JEAN THOMPSON

(b. 1950)

A prolific writer of short stories, Jean Thompson teaches creative writing at the University of Illinois at Urbana-Champaign. Her stories have been published in many periodicals; one appeared in Best American Short Stories of 1979. *Her first collection,* Gasoline Wars *(1979), is part of the series* Illinois Short Fiction. *Her most recent work is a novel,* The Woman Driver *(1985).*

Friends sent them one of those postcards produced by the same technicians who can make a Kansas Holiday Inn suggest a palmy oasis. This time the process had resulted in overkill. Inflamed, tomato-colored wildflowers were grafted to a background of turquoise lake and emerald pines. One white, cone-shaped mountain rose in a sky so densely blue it resembled the paste-waxed fender of a new car. Bert and Mary Ann Lilly taped the card to the refrigerator. When their friends came back they said:

Pretty? That's not the word. Beautiful. Gorgeous. Better than that. Up in the mountains it's cool even in summer, with all that pine smell. Deer, oh yeah, we saw plenty deer. Down in the valleys are orchards. Apricot, cherry, pear. You can pick wild blackberries. And the rivers. What was that big slow one, the color of a green apple? The Umpqua. The Alsea. Waterfalls. People graze horses along the banks. And we haven't even begun to tell you about the coast.

Bert and Mary Ann smiled at each other with one corner of their mouths sucked in, meaning, Some people have all the luck. Man, said Bert, why wasn't I born there? The only deer I ever seen is Bambi.

Waterfalls, huh? said Mary Ann, and chewed for a moment on one of her lank, light-brown pigtails. I've never even been out of crummy old Illi-*noy*. Except for Indiana.

You been to St. Louis, Bert reminded her.

Oh, excuse me, St. Louis. Yeah I guess I have been around.

Everyone laughed and Bert shook the plastic bag of marijuana, pinched off enough to fill the pipe bowl.

That's another thing, the friends said. In Oregon you get busted with under an ounce, it's like a parking ticket. No shit.

You guys tryin to make it hard on me? asked Bert. Like you got to keep reminding me what's out there? He flung his hand toward the window and it tangled in the curtains.

Out there beyond the aluminum-sided bungalow with its frill of dusty grass: Decatur, Illinois.

Beans. Soybeans.
You get em from the Staley Plant.

Beantown. Staley Soybean, right squat in the middle of the city. The highway arches over it. A panorama of webbed pipes, giant tanks, chimneys throwing dirty blond smoke into the air. Like driving into a huge stinking motor. Now, at harvest time, trucks rock through the streets, spilling hard wrinkled little beans into the gutters. What do they make out of them, shoe polish? Bug killer? Jesus, how can anything that's supposed to be food smell so bad?

Always plenty of cooking oil in the stores.

Now, in August, the big shallow man-made lake is drying up, showing its bottom of yellow mud. The sky is hazy windless blue. A wooly heat clogs the skin.

At night the sidewalks are still hot enough to sting your feet. Downtown, above the squirming pink neon of taverns, rows of black windows. Broken, barred, shuttered, burnt, and empty. Ulcers in the brick.

Honest blight at least makes no pretenses. But farther from the city center, where the town begins to unravel on the prairie, are blocks and blocks of new graceless enterprise. The used car burgers handy pantry discount king liquors. The formica slabs, plate glass and cellophane.

You know what I saw here once, said Mary Ann. A squirrel trying to drag a package of Kraft American Cheese Slices up a tree.

No worse, maybe, than any other small American city. And surely there are blue spring days, shade trees, first snowfalls.

Surely there is some reason we live here. We were born here. We are comfortable with its bland Midwestern sky. Its ugliness has accumulated like rust, stiffening our eyes and hearts. This place.

Where Bert drives an hour to run a machine that bags fertilizer, coming home with bitter white dust worked into his dark skin. Fertilizer to grow more of those damn beans.

Where the land is so flat you could see the curve of the earth, if there were anywhere high enough to view it from.

Where the sight of big black Bert and his skinny white wife often stops traffic. Whose Caucasian citizens, noting Mary Ann's pregnancy, are moved to sociologic commentary: A yellow baby with frizzy red hair, that's what she's got in there. Twice as ugly as a plain old nigger. Can you imagine the two of them—makes your skin crawl, don't it.

Not to mention, just yet, what Mary Ann's family said.

Why can't we, asked Mary Ann that night when they were in bed.

Em-oh-en-ee-wy, said Bert. What's got into you? Why all of a sudden we got to move?

For the baby. Her answer so prompt and positive in the dark room. I hated growing up here, you know I did.

She was silent, biting her lips at old grievances. Bert reached out and let her long hair sift through his fingers. You think it makes a difference, being in one place or another? You think it would have made you happier?

Yes.

Well, said Bert, you know we can't afford it now. He kissed her and rolled over into sleep, glad there was something easy and practical to set against her vehemence. But the third time somebody at work rammed his car, they began to talk seriously about it.

After all, it's a free country. Why can't we? Didn't we find each other? Just think of that. Out of this whole world we found each other. I chose you and you me. If we did that we can do anything.

Bert was the oldest of seven children. He watched his brothers and sisters marry, he stood up at their weddings and baby-sat for their kids. Getting fat and going bald early. Good old Uncle Bert. He could see himself in twenty years, grinning over his chins at their grandchildren. Letting them play pat-a-cake on his bare scalp. It wasn't that he had trouble meeting girls, just that none of them stuck. Then at a concert he met Mary Ann. She came home with him that night and never left.

The next morning he drove her to breakfast. I got something to tell you, he said.

She was bent over her pocketbook, looking for a match. Mm? she said.

Her hair was pulled back in a long smooth tail and her skin was pink from the cold morning. How pretty she looked, this moment before he would lose her. I'm twenty-nine years old, he said.

Here's one, she said. Nope. Empty.

Did you hear me? Bert demanded.

Uh huh. I'm nineteen.

I know that. Don't it worry you? I mean, on top of bein black and practically bald—

Oh hush, said Mary Ann. If it'll make you feel better, I got a glass eye. The right one.

Not the first time he'd crossed, been with a white girl. Not the first time for her either. How come you don't wear platform shoes and crazy hats and lavender britches, she asked him when she'd known him for two days. You are the dowdiest black dude I ever saw.

He told her Us fat guys look like walking potatoes in clothes like that. Lavender britches, good Lord, girl.

I don't like those superpimp clothes anyway, she said. But you ain't fat, really.

THE WIFE

94

Or, meeting his family: Gee, they're pretty nice about you bringing home white tail, aren't they?

They traded the car for a pickup with four-wheel drive. You needed something to get around in those mountains, they decided. Bert worked as much overtime as he could that winter. The wind blew stinging dirt across the flatness. Then chunks of filthy ice formed in the gutters, stayed there for weeks. Skin took on the stale, chafed texture of a root left too long in the ground. This is our last winter here, said Bert and Mary Ann. The mercury huddled at the base of the thermometer like frozen blood and they looked at maps and tourist brochures.

> From the colorful past to the bustling present, the saga of Oregon is marked by immense natural wealth and beauty. Mighty volcanic peaks overlook the lush coastal plain. A temperate climate makes year-round vacationing popular. See miles of rugged coastline, well-supplied with recreational facilities. Unique opportunities for the sportsman exist, from salmon fishing in crystal streams to stalking antelope in the vast grasslands. Follow the historic Oregon Trail. Magnificent timberland, jewel-like lakes, winding rivers—and more!

I bet folks out west are a lot less prejudiced to blacks, Bert told a friend at work. You know, it being sort of the frontier. Less set in their ways.

Probably, said his friend. They've always got the Indians.

Bert asked him what he meant but his friend said nothing, nothing.

In March the baby was born. They named her Dawn. Lookit that complexion, said Mary Ann. Looks like you didn't have nothing to do with her.

Aw she'll get darker. And she's got a little Afro nose. Hey little girl, pretty girl, don't burp at your daddy.

You're gonna have a pony, Mary Ann told her. Just as soon as those fat little legs are long enough. For they had decided they would live in the country and raise horses.

In June they sold everything but the stereo and a box of kitchen things. How easy it was to strip things away. To discover that once you took the pictures curtains rugs and flowerpots, you were still there. None of it bound you. Leave it behind along with the families, the friends, the lifetime of habit. You were as free and light as the dust balls rolling from one empty room to the next. Dizzy with your own recklessness. You pulled yourself loose and could as easily set down again. Nothing out there you couldn't outwork, outwit, outmaneuver, outlast.

Why can't a little caramel-colored girl-child grow up with a pony in Oregon?

Mary Ann raked through closets, sending tangled coat hangers rattling to the floor. She bruised her knees on suitcases, plunged her uncertain hands into heaps of clothes which she folded and refolded, sorted and resorted. What is the matter with you, Bert demanded after she upset the stack of towels again.

She sat down on the floor, right where she'd been standing. I got to see my folks before we go, she said flatly. Bert started to say something. She held up her hand. I know, I know. But I got to. No I won't take Dawn. You ought to know better than to ask.

He waited for her, crooning to the baby as the summer evening poured through the windows. Blue darkness blurred the corners of the room. In them he saw the vague shapes of his dread.

Evil, blind as a root probing rock, always squirming to reach them.

Something would happen. Even now they would find a way to coax, threaten, or force her.

Evil. You raised your hand to ward it off, but the hand fell away, frail as paper burned to ash. A legacy of malice focused on you. Whispers and warnings. Then the snapping of bone, the wet thick tearing of flesh as the darkie nigger coon got it, got it good.

She would not return. He would stand here all night and the darkness would muffle him, drive him mad. Still he fought with his fear and did not turn on a lamp.

When there was one shining rim of sky left in the west, he heard the truck. It choked and dieseled in the driveway. There was just enough light for him to see her small pale face crossing the room toward him. She pressed against him, hard, and only then began crying. Furious deep tears. The baby, out of fright or hunger, joined in. He held them both, sweet weight, heavy comfort.

Petroleum stink. The flat sun fastened to the hood like an ornament. Concrete, did you ever think there was so much of it? Stale, uniform, wearying: I will multiply thy seeds as the stars of the heaven, and as the concrete which is upon the Interstate.

No matter. It could be ignored, like Iowa, endured, like Nebraska. The tires drummed smoothly, the miles accumulated, tangible, finite. In the back of the pickup their belongings were roped together under taut waterproof canvas, checked at every stop. New maps and new eight-track stereo cartridge tapes that they had not yet grown tired of. A pound of reefer hidden under the seat.

Hey, said Mary Ann. I got an idea. We can get off the Interstate in Wyoming—skewering the map with a fingernail—and go up to Grand Teton or Yellowstone. See?

Bert squinted at the pink and green rectangle that was Wyoming. Aw, that's miles and miles out of our way.

No it ain't. Well maybe a little. But if we stay on 80 we have to go south out of our way. Besides, everything looks the same from the Interstate. I want to see mountains so bad.

It was true. The land had become more open, rolling, as they approached Wyoming. Bleached earth covered with scrub. But the prim green signs equalized everything, made it hard to believe they'd driven a thousand miles. So on their third day from home they turned north, drawn by the names on the map: Green Mountains. Antelope Hills. Sweetwater. Owl Creek.

Bert thought, as the land began to climb, We're doing it. Really doing it. Look, he said, pointing to a sign. Open grazing. Damn, they got cattle traipsing all over the road. He was delighted. I could almost enjoy this, huh?

Uh huh, said Mary Ann, shielding the baby's face from the sun. She could almost enjoy it. Except for something that happened the summer after high school graduation. When a fast-moving full-sized Oldsmobile appeared in the path of her girlfriend's MGB in which she was the third passenger, draped over the gear shift.

Not that she remembered much. Sometimes she tried to recall the exploding glass, the somersault they said she made onto the slick black roof of the Olds. Since she could not remember it she could not forget it, and imagined it in a number of different versions.

Seven weeks she was in a coma. When they were fairly certain she would live, they began to rebuild her face. Wired her mouth shut so the synthetic jawbone and porcelain teeth could get to know each other undisturbed. Inserted a precision-made blue eye into her blind socket. Drew the skin of her neck and scalp forward and sanded it down. Replaced the bony structure of her nose with silicone. Even took out the bump I used to have, says Mary Ann. Stitched in eyebrows with black surgical thread and planted them with hair.

Mary Ann's mother: Who paid to have you put back together when you were in twenty-seven pieces? We did, we never gave it a second thought, we did it because you were our little girl. We did that for you, doesn't that count for anything?

On her last check-up, two years after the accident, the doctor agreed to show her photographs that had been taken during the last phases of surgery. In them you could see the welts, new scar tissue, but that wasn't so bad.

There were other photographs he refused to show her.

The sound of squealing brakes no longer frightened her. And little by little she accustomed herself to the feel of a steering wheel sliding back and forth in her hands.

They had, after all, done an excellent job with the plastic surgery.

Dawn had fallen asleep while nursing. Her small greedy mouth formed bubbles of milk as she breathed and her face was wrinkled, fierce, oblivious. Mary Ann studied her, looking as she always did for some sign of herself in this little brown child with the fluffy hair. A pint of white mixed with a gallon of black. She had been blended in. But maybe it was always like this, children could not mirror or repeat you. They went their own way.

JEAN THOMPSON

97

Mary Ann's mother: Go on, heap dirt on our heads. I'm telling everyone who asks, you're adopted. Then when they see you running off to live with the niggers, they'll think you have nigger in you yourself. That'll probably make you happy.

And her father saying Now that's enough, over and over again. Embarrassed eyes that would not meet hers. And she hated him almost as much because he was weak, he would never stand up for her.

So much taken from her. Like the struggle to wake in the white, white room, swimming to the surface of consciousness and pain, then learning she had lost seven whole weeks. Even now, sometimes she woke gasping and numb. *How long had she slept?*

So much taken from her. She saw things flatly, like a child's drawing with everything lined up on the horizon. She learned to make her voice light and careless when she had to, never admitting loss, not letting anything else be taken. Humming, she looked out the window.

Wide pale sky and hills like a rumpled bedsheet. Khaki-colored grass and outcroppings of red rock. An arid, silent landscape whose foreignness excited them. On the horizon, a dark line which they hoped was mountains. The new eight-track stereo cartridge tape sang:

> He-ey, tonight
> Gonna be the night
> Gonna fly right to the sky
> Tonight

> then

> He-ey, *chunk*night
> Gonna *chunk* the night
> Gonna *rechunkrechunkre*
> *Chunkchunk*

Oh shit. The exhaust? Carburetor? Fuel pump? The truck spat and died as Bert eased it to the side of the road. Je-sus, said Bert, and flipped the music off. They waited, Bert until he controlled his anger, Mary Ann until he would tell her what was wrong. Without the singing and the comfortable noise of their motion, the huge hot sky seemed to press down on them. Bert got out and raised the hood. Restarted the engine, but it died in a fit of noise and stinging smoke. Dawn woke up and began to cry.

Great, said Bert. Just great. He thought of the Interstate, the smooth ordered road they could have taken if only she hadn't talked him out of it. Can't you get her quiet, he said. I got to think.

Oh sure, said Mary Ann. I'll just explain that to her.

Bert studied the map. I think we're about nine miles from Crowheart, he said over the screaming.

Neither the distance nor the name seemed to offer much hope. They

THE WIFE

looked out at the dry hills and empty road. We'll wait awhile, said Bert, and if nobody comes I'll start walking.

Walk? You're kidding, that'll take hours. Wait til somebody comes along.

Yeah, you want to spend the night here? Fifteen minutes, that's all I'll give it. He put as much decisiveness as he could into the statement, trying to forget the money he could feel ticking away even as he spoke.

Waiting. And waiting. Mary Ann rocked the baby into quiet; Dawn regarded them both with wide uncertain eyes. Just as Bert was about to look at his watch for the last time, the road behind them produced first noise, then a red glittering pickup with an over-the-cab camper. Well hallelujah, said Bert. He got out to stand on the shoulder with his arm raised. The truck approached, slowed, as if to get a good look at them—they could see a woman's face pressed to the glass, two kids in the back reading comics—then accelerated past.

The sun seemed ready to puncture the metal roof. Maybe they'll at least tell a garage we're out here, said Mary Ann when Bert got back in the truck and slammed the door.

Sure. If there is a garage. And if they have to stop for soda pop anyway. Assholes.

I still say let's wait.

Don't tell me what to do. I got enough problems already.

Well it's my problem too and I've got a say in it.

Well, you're the one who said to take this stupid road, he said, giving in to his impatience. I had enough of your good ideas.

Oh, so it's my fault? Who's the big-shot mechanic who said he could fix anything?

I don't have to listen to this, said Bert, getting out.

Bullshitter, she screamed, as he started down the highway. Go ahead. I won't be here when you get back.

But just then the road came to life again. A slow-moving '63 Chevy, blue-green and battered, rolled toward them, pulled ahead of the truck and stopped. Mary Ann watched Bert run back, lean over the driver's side. Both doors opened and two men, boys really, got out. Oh Christ, said Mary Ann. Indians.

One, the driver, had a barrel chest and squat legs, a sly wide face. His hair was drawn into two braids which grazed his shoulders. The other was thinner, his black hair cut short and ruffled by the wind. Both of them wore jeans and stretched-out T-shirts. She guessed them to be about eighteen. They walked towards the truck and one, the thin one, glanced at her, an indifferent narrow-eyed look.

After a moment Bert opened the door. Come on, they'll give us a ride.

I'm not going anywhere with you. She was crying by now.

Man, he said, you are too much. You know where we are? On an Indian reservation. If you're waiting for the Boy Scouts you gonna wait awhile. Let's go.

No, she cried, and he raised his hand but did not hit her, not yet. Let's go, he repeated, dead-calm, and she opened the door, hating him.

The two boys slit their eyes at her but did not speak as she got in the back of the Chevy. Then the fat one said something to the other, words she did not understand. They're talking Indian, she thought faintly. Bert stared straight ahead.

Fifteen minutes of silent driving, and the Chevy pulled up to a white-washed building set in a yard of tamped dirt. There were two gas pumps in front. Why are we stopping here, Bert and Mary Ann each wondered. Then they knew: this was Crowheart. Post Office, general store, gas, the works. When the car stopped Mary Ann got out and marched toward the building without speaking.

There was a porch of uneven boards shaded by the roof. On it several Indians, older men in work shirts and cowboy hats, were sitting. She approached and they stopped talking. There were no chairs left so she went to the end of the porch and leaned against the wall.

Bert came around the corner. We're going back to take a look at it, he said. Here's money for a drink or something. She would not answer or take the five-dollar bill he extended, so he tucked it in her purse and walked away. She watched him get back in the Chevy and drive off into the brown hills.

The men, four or five of them, sat with their hands on their knees, as unmoving as lizards in the heat. The one nearest her stood up. Here Missy, he said, pointing. Here. His skin was sunblackened, his eyes held in nets of wrinkles. Thank you, she said. He nodded and walked inside.

Now she was seated among them. They did not look at her, and she realized this was a form of courtesy. She could sit here all day minding her own business. They would not disturb her. She was grateful for their indifference. There were worse things than that. She permitted herself a moment of thought for the stalled truck.

An hour later her eyes caught a pillar of shimmering dust on the road. The heat made it seem impossibly far away and slow. But at last the Chevy appeared, followed by the truck. Mary Ann stood up. Good-bye, she said. They ducked their heads in a kind of chorus, and she walked to the truck.

Bert opened the door for her but neither of them spoke.

In silence they watched the hills rise into dark pine-covered peaks, noted the looping track of the river beneath them.

Easier to travel a thousand miles and camp among strange tribes than it is to apologize.

Until Bert stopped the truck to gaze at the incredible range of ice-covered stone that lay before them. The green-floored valley and blue lake. The air had grown cool, scented with pine and sage.

Ready to quit fightin, Bert asked, looking through the windshield.

Yeah. Pride made her want to sound sullen, but when she opened her mouth her lungs filled with thin cold air, a giddy perfume that lifted her voice.

THE WIFE

100

Hey, she asked him later, as they watched the afternoon sun slide down the peaks. What was wrong with the truck?

Loose condenser.

Did you have to pay them much?

Nothing. Bert grinned. I gave em some reefer. We had a little peace-pipe session.

Back on the Interstate in Idaho. Anxious now, impatient to get there. Turning up their noses at the lava plains and ragged crests: they were going somewhere better. Driving without stopping, Bert and Mary Ann trading shifts.

They raced against hunger, stuffing their bellies with pasty hamburgers and chocolate. They'd figured two weeks, that's how long they could last until Bert found a job.

Ten stiff $20 bills in the lining of Mary Ann's purse.

2 weeks = 14 days.

(x) motel rooms @ $12 = ?

Gas. Groceries. Rent deposit? Even if he found a job, how long would it be until he got a paycheck?

Bert's eyes glazed at the sun-slick road, and he fought to make the numbers balance. How much had they spent? Where had it leaked away from them? You're tired, he told himself. Everything seems worse when you're tired. Try to sleep. He closed his eyes. Something heavy was burrowing its way into his dreams. Metal grating on metal. He opened his eyes to darkness, and a new grinding sound from the engine: *Rak. Rak. Rak*. Steadily increasing in tempo and authority.

It just started, said Mary Ann.

Take the next exit, Bert told her. There was nothing else to say. Each knew what the other was thinking.

In the fluorescent, hard-edged glare of the Shell station, the teen-aged gas jockey shook his head. Might be your points burned out. A cylinder not firing. Or the spark plug wires. We won't have a mechanic in here til seven ayem. In the Pine-Sol–stinking restroom Bert splashed water on his face. He walked back to the truck, started it, listened to the idle for a moment, and pulled onto the highway.

We got to, he said, before Mary Ann could open her mouth. Even if the mechanic was here we couldn't pay him. Unless we decide to settle down right here. We'll just drive the damn thing into the ground and see how far it gets.

We're a hundred twenty miles from the border, said Mary Ann after a moment. When he looked again both she and the baby were asleep.

Drifting lights in the darkness. The shallow cone of highway illuminated before him. He would find a job. They would live out in the country and when they'd saved enough they would buy horses. Dully he repeated this until it diminished into sing-song. Every muscle in his body felt bulky and unyielding.

Why should he be doubting now? So what if the worst happened, the truck failed and they had to hustle for money. Couldn't they do that? He supposed they could, but his weariness went further. He longed to shrink the world into something finite, physical, easily confronted. He supposed he'd felt it was that way once, although it was hard to remember now, while he strained to stay awake in the humming darkness. Oh yeah, he could lick anything with one hand tied behind him. Blindfolded. On his knees. Whistling Dixie.

The engine settled into a steady chattering. It might quit at ten miles or at a thousand. The headlights caught a highway sign but it was some moments before its meaning penetrated. Oregon. They were in Oregon though they still had three hundred miles to go. Indifferently he swung his head from one gray window to another. Even when the flat red sun popped up like the No Sale tag of a cash register, revealing shallow wheat fields that might have been in Kansas, even then he felt no special despair or disappointment. Just cold fatigue and inattention.

Mary Ann felt Dawn's fingers rooting in her hair, then the new hot day on her face. The baby began to cry and she spoke to her without opening her eyes. But the cramp in her back, the steady jogging—*Where was she?* Gasping, she reached out for the baby, then blinked and looked around her.

Just as she never spoke of the pinched pain behind her glass eye, or the ragged bones that never quite healed, so now she regarded the dust and flatness around her and did not acknowledge them.

I bet you want to sleep, huh, she said, rubbing Bert's neck with one hand and maneuvering the baby toward her nipple with the other.

Pretty soon, he said, trying to match her calmness.

Got to stop and change her anyway, said Mary Ann. I think she had a busy night.

Yeah well, began Bert, but he stopped at a new noise from somewhere in the oily complications of the engine. Before he'd heard it a second time he had identified it. Backfiring. Thick blue smoke uncoiled from the tailpipe, obscuring the road behind them. Twelve miles to an exit, said Bert as the wheel jumped under his hand. Come on, give us a break.

The explosions were so loud that cars following them hung back, gathering courage to pass. Five more miles they wrung from the tortured engine. In the side mirror Bert noticed a white shape traveling in their wake, just visible through the fumes. Then it pulled alongside and stayed there.

He ignored it as long as he could, even though the trooper was motioning to him. Then the red dome light went on.

The bastard wants me to pull over, cried Bert. Don't he know I'll never get it started again? He wrenched the truck to the shoulder and tried to let it idle, but it stalled. They waited until the trooper came up to them.

Morning, he said, and they could tell from his face, how it pulled away once he saw them, like he had stepped in shit, what he was thinking. They'd seen that look before.

Having trouble? he asked. The trooper was a thin young black-haired man, with a peculiar smooth look to his face, as if the bones had stunted, and light restless eyes.

Yeah, said Bert, and opened the door so the trooper had to take a step back. Yeah, we got trouble.

Could I see your license please? Take it out of the plastic. His voice was colorless, not matching the politeness of his words.

Bert stood silently, knowing this was not the time to protest, not yet. The trooper studied the license, shifting from one foot to the other, then asked for the registration. When Mary Ann had produced it from the glove compartment, he asked Now where are you folks going?

Portland, said Bert.

Mind if I take a look in the back, said the man, not making it a question, as he loosened one of the ropes and angled his thin back so he could peer beneath the canvas. Bert followed him, standing close enough that the trooper felt his presence and squared his shoulders as he stood up.

Well now, he said, his light eyes looking just beyond Bert, his voice still neutral, you folks aren't going to be able to get any farther. You're violating the emission control standards.

We're going to the next exit. We'll get it fixed there.

The trooper shook his head and the flat shadow of his hat brim crept over his flat face. Can't let you back on the highway. You could cause an accident, all that smoke. You'll have to get it towed.

We can't afford a tow.

Well . . . he paused, and Bert could see how little effort he was putting into his words; they were a script he was following, certain of the outcome. The only other thing we can do is impound the vehicle.

No, said Bert, and in speaking he committed himself to doing what was necessary. His very exhaustion was a strength now, because it loosened his fury. He felt the hard crust of sweat on his muscles, the syncopated popping of nerves, the white sunlight twitching in his eyes, and knew he could unleash himself. He could murder, in broad daylight with his bare hands. Then take his wife and child some place far away, some place he could also fight for them. No, he repeated, I think it would be better if we just went to the next exit. And he waited, calmly, for what would happen now.

Later he would wonder how he had looked to the trooper. Something, the glazed blood in his eyes, the stance of his legs, had communicated craziness, danger. The trooper squinted and turned his smooth neutral face from side to side like a puzzled bird. After a moment Bert realized he was calculating the cost of retreat, how much pride was involved.

Well, said the trooper, if you drive on the shoulder, slow, I mean slow, with your flashers going, I guess you could make it.

Sure. Bert waited a few seconds, in case the trooper insisted on some further instruction as a sop to his authority. But the man only said OK then, his eyes still wandering, and walked to his car.

Bert waited until he was gone, then tried the engine. It started noisily but seemed more willing than before. When they reached a gas station Bert coaxed the mechanic into lending him tools, changed the burnt-out points himself, handed the keys to Mary Ann, and only then allowed himself sleep.

He woke, after how long he did not know, when Mary Ann cried out. Smatter, he said, lurching upright. What? What?

But she was turning her head from side to side, trying to make her one good eye take in all that was before her. The road was pulling them toward a river, pulling them down then lifting to follow the banks. A mile-wide stretch of misty water curving between raw brown cliffs. In the distance the road, and everything on it, dwindled to a thread. She strained her neck to see the top of the cliffs but it was all too large, it would not order itself into a single view.

Rounding a turn, she squinted. Floating above the horizon was a mass of slate and white, like a smeared cloud. Only it was no cloud. Bert saw it too, and they both opened their mouths to speak: Damn, that thing must be eighty miles away, look at it, just look. But the wind, which had increased steadily as they entered the gorge, now slammed against the truck and filled the air with its roaring. Mary Ann gripped the wheel tighter and turned to Bert. Their lips still worked, forming speech. It would take all their strength to make themselves heard.

TUESDAY NIGHT

by

ANN BEATTIE

(b. 1947)

Born in Washington, D.C., Ann Beattie studied at American University and the University of Connecticut. She has been a Guggenheim fellow and a lecturer at the University of Virginia and Harvard University. She now lives in Connecticut. She has published six books, of which the most recent is the novel Love Always *(1985). She says that she writes about "chaos"; her characters have more questions than answers about life.*

Henry was supposed to bring the child home at six o'clock, but they usually did not arrive until eight or eight-thirty, with Joanna overtired and complaining that she did not want to go to bed the minute she came through the door. Henry had taught her that phrase. "The minute she comes through the door" was something I had said once, and he mocked me with it in defending her. "Let the poor child have a minute before she goes to bed. She *did* just come through the door." The poor child is, of course, crazy about Henry. He allows her to call him that, instead of "Daddy." And now he takes her to dinner at a French restaurant that she adores, which doesn't open until five-thirty. That means that she gets home close to eight. I am a beast if I refuse to let her eat her escargots. And it would be cruel to tell her that her father's support payments fluctuate wildly, while the French dining remains a constant. Forget the money—Henry has been a good father. He visits every Tuesday night, carefully twirls her crayons in the pencil sharpener, and takes her every other weekend. The only bad thing he has done to her—and even Henry agreed about that—was to introduce her to the sleepie he had living with him right after the divorce: an obnoxious woman, who taught Joanna to sing "I'm a Woman." Fortunately, she did not remember many of the words, but I thought I'd lose my mind when she went around the house singing "Doubleyou oh oh em ay en" for two weeks. Sometimes the sleepie tucked a fresh flower in Joanna's hair—like Maria Muldaur, she explained. The child had the good sense to be embarrassed.

The men I know are very friendly with one another. When Henry was at the house last week, he helped Dan, who lives with me, carry a bookcase up the steep, narrow steps to the second floor. Henry and Dan talk about nutrition—Dan's current interest. My brother Bobby, the only person I know who is seriously interested in hallucinogens at the age of twenty-six, gladly makes a fool of himself in front of Henry by bringing out his green yoyo, which glows by the miracle of two internal batteries. Dan tells Bobby that if he's going to take drugs he should try dosing his body with vitamins before and after. The three of them Christmas-shop for me. Last year they had dinner at an Italian restaurant downtown. I asked Dan what they ordered, and he said, "Oh, we all had manicotti."

I have been subsisting on red zinger tea and watermelon, trying to lose weight. Dan and Henry and Bobby are all thin. Joanna takes after her father in her build. She is long and graceful, with chiselled features that would shame Marisa Berenson. She is ten years old. When I was at the laundry to pick up the clothes yesterday, a woman mistook me, from the back, for her cousin Addie.

In Joanna's class at school they are having a discussion of problems with the environment. She wants to take our big avocado plant in to school. I have tried patiently to explain that the plant does not have anything to do with environmental problems. She says that they are discussing nature, too. "What's the harm?" Dan says. So he goes to work and leaves it to me to fit the towering avocado into the Audi. I also get roped into baking cookies, so Joanna can take them to school and pass them around to celebrate her birthday. She tells me that it is the custom to put the cookies in a box wrapped in birthday paper. We select a paper with yellow bears standing in concentric circles. Dan dumps bran into the chocolate-chip-cookie dough. He forbids me to use a dot of red food coloring in the sugar-cookie hearts.

My best friend, Dianne, comes over in the mornings and turns her nose up at my red zinger. Sometimes she takes a shower here, because she loves our shower head. "How come you're not in there all the time?" she says. My brother is sweet on her. He finds her extremely attractive. He asked me if I had noticed the little droplets of water from the shower on her forehead, just at the hairline. Bobby lends her money, because her husband doesn't give her enough. I know for a fact that Dianne is thinking of having an affair with him.

Dan has to work late at his office on Tuesday nights, and a while ago I decided that I wanted that one night to myself each week—a night without any of them. Dianne said, "I know what you mean," but Bobby took great offense and didn't come to visit that night, or any other night, for two weeks. Joanna was delighted that she could be picked up after school by

Dianne, in Dianne's 1966 Mustang convertible, and that the two of them could visit until Henry came by Dianne's to pick her up. Dan, who keeps saying that our relationship is going sour—although it isn't—pursed his lips and nodded when I told him about Tuesday nights, but he said nothing. The first night alone I read a dirty magazine that had been lying around the house for some time. Then I took off all my clothes and looked in the hall mirror and decided to go on a diet, so I skipped dinner. I made a long-distance call to a friend in California who had just had a baby. We talked about the spidery little veins in her thighs, and I swore to her over and over again that they would go away. Then I took one of each kind of vitamin pill we have in the house.

The next week, I had prepared for my spare time better. I had bought whole-wheat flour and clover honey, and I made four loaves of whole-wheat bread, I made a piecrust, putting dough in the sink and rolling it out there, which made a lot of sense but which I would never let anybody see me doing. Then I read *Vogue*. Later on, I took out the yoga book I had bought that afternoon and put it in my plastic cookbook-holder and put that down on the floor and stared at it as I tried to get into the postures. I overcooked the piecrust and it burned. I got depressed and drank a Drambuie. The week after that, I ventured out. I went to a movie and bought myself a chocolate milkshake afterward. I sat at the drugstore counter and drank it. I was going to get my birth-control-pill prescription refilled while I was there, but I decided that would be depressing.

Joanna sleeps at her father's apartment now on Tuesday nights. Since he considers her too old to be read a fairy tale before bed, Henry waltzes with her. She wears a long nightgown and a pair of high-heeled shoes that some woman left there. She says that he usually plays "The Blue Danube" but sometimes he kids around and puts on "Idiot Wind" or "Forever Young" and they dip and twirl to it. She has hinted that she would like to take dancing lessons. Last week, she danced through the living room at our house on her pogo stick. Dan had given it to her, saying that now she had a partner, and it would save him money not having to pay for dancing lessons. He told her that if she had any questions she could ask him. He said she could call him "Mr. Daniel." She was disgusted with him. If she were Dan's child, I am sure he would still be reading her fairy tales.

Another Tuesday night, I went out and bought plants. I used my American Express card and got seventy dollars' worth of plants and some plant-hangers. The woman in the store helped me carry the boxes out to the car. I went home and drove nails into the top of the window frames and hung the plants. They did not need to be watered yet, but I held the plastic plant-waterer up to them, to see what it would be like to water them. I squeezed the plastic bottle, and stared at the curved plastic tube coming out of it. Later, I gave myself a facial with egg whites.

There is a mouse. I first saw it in the kitchen—a small gray mouse, moseying along, taking its time in getting from under the counter to the back of the stove. I had Dan seal off the little mouse hole in the back of the stove. Then I saw the mouse again, under the chest in the living room.

"It's a mouse. It's one little mouse," Dan said. "Let it be."

"Everybody knows that if there's one mouse there are more," I said. "We've got to get rid of them."

Dan, the humanist, was secretly glad the mouse had resurfaced—that he hadn't done any damage in sealing off its home.

"It looked like the same mouse to me," Henry said.

"They all look that way," I said. "That doesn't mean—"

"Poor thing," Dan said.

"Are either of you going to set traps, or do I have to do it?"

"You have to do it," Dan said. "I can't stand it. I don't want to kill a mouse."

"I think there's only one mouse," Henry said.

Glaring at them, I went into the kitchen and took the mousetraps out of their cellophane packages. I stared at them with tears in my eyes. I didn't know how to set them. Dan and Henry had made me seem like a cold-blooded killer.

"Maybe it will just leave," Dan said.

"Don't be ridiculous, Dan," I said. "If you aren't going to help, at least don't sit around snickering with Henry."

"We're not snickering," Henry said.

"You two certainly are buddy-buddy."

"What's the matter now? You want us to hate each other?" Henry said.

"I don't know how to set a mousetrap," I said. "I can't do it myself."

"Poor Mommy," Joanna said. She was in the hallway outside the living room, listening. I almost turned on her to tell her not to be sarcastic, when I realized that she was serious. She felt sorry for me. With someone on my side, I felt new courage about going back into the kitchen and tackling the problem of the traps.

Dianne called and said she had asked her husband if he could go out one night a week, so she could go out with friends or stay home by herself. He said no, but agreed to take stained-glass lessons with her.

One Tuesday, it rained. I stayed home and daydreamed, and remembered the past. I thought about the boy I dated my last year in high school, who used to take me out to the country on weekends, to where some cousins of his lived. I wondered why he always went there, because we never got near the house. He would drive partway up their long driveway in the woods and then pull off onto a narrow little road that trucks sometimes used when they were logging the property. We parked on the little road and necked. Sometimes the boy would drive slowly along on the country roads looking for rabbits, and whenever he saw one, which was pretty often—sometimes even two or three rabbits at once—he floored it, trying to run the rabbit down. There was no radio in the car. He had a portable radio that got only two stations (soul music and classical) and I held it on my lap. He liked the volume turned up very loud.

Joanna comes to my bedroom and announces that Uncle Bobby is on the phone.

"I got a dog," he says.

"What kind?"

"Aren't you even surprised?"

"Yes. Where did you get the dog?"

"A guy I knew a little bit in college is going to jail, and he persuaded me to take the dog."

"What is he going to jail for?"

"Burglary."

"Joanna," I say, "don't stand there staring at me when I'm talking on the phone."

"He robbed a house," Bobby says.

"What kind of a dog is it?" I ask.

"Malamute and German shepherd. It's in heat."

"Well," I say, "you always wanted a dog."

"I call you all the time, and you never call me," Bobby says.

"I never have interesting news."

"You could call and tell me what you do on Tuesday nights."

"Nothing very interesting," I say.

"You could go to a bar and have rum drinks and weep," Bobby says. He chuckles.

"Are you stoned?" I ask.

"Sure I am. Been home from work for an hour and a half. Ate a Celeste pizza, had a little smoke."

"Do you really have a dog?" I ask.

"If you were a male dog, you wouldn't have any doubt of it."

"You're always much more clever than I am. It's hard to talk to you on the phone, Bobby."

"It's hard to be me," Bobby says. A silence. "I'm not sure the dog likes me."

"Bring it over. Joanna will love it."

"I'll be around with it Tuesday night," he says.

"Why is it so interesting to you that I have one night a week to myself?"

"Whatever you do," Bobby says, "don't rob a house."

We hang up, and I go tell Joanna the news.

"You yelled at me," she says.

"I did not. I asked you not to stand there staring at me while I was on the phone."

"You raised your voice," she says.
Soon it will be Tuesday night.

Joanna asks me suspiciously what I do on Tuesday nights.
"What does your father say I do?" I ask.
"He says he doesn't know."
"Does he seem curious?"
"It's hard to tell with him," she says.
Having got my answer, I've forgotten about her question.
"So what things do you do?" she says.
"Sometimes you like to play in your tent," I say defensively. "Well, I like some time to just do what I want to do, too, Joanna."
"That's O.K.," she says. She sounds like an adult placating a child.
I have to face the fact that I don't do much of anything on Tuesdays, and that one night alone each week isn't making me any less edgy or more agreeable to live with. I tell Dan this, as if it's his fault.
"I don't think you ever wanted to divorce Henry," Dan says.
"Oh, Dan, I *did*."
"You two seem to get along fine."
"But we fought. We didn't get along."
He looks at me. "Oh," he says. He is being inordinately nice to me, because of the scene I threw when a mouse got caught in one of the traps. The trap didn't kill it. It just got it by the paw, and Dan had to beat it to death with a screwdriver.
"Maybe you'd rather the two of us did something regularly on Tuesday nights," he says now. "Maybe I could get the night of my meetings changed."
"Thank you," I say. "Maybe I should give it a little longer."
"That's up to you," he says. "There hasn't been enough time to judge by, I guess."
Inordinately kind. Deferential. He has been saying for a long time that our relationship is turning sour, and now it must have turned so sour for him that he doesn't even want to fight. What does he want?
"Maybe you'd like a night—" I begin.
"The hell with that," he says. "If there has to be so much time alone, I can't see the point of living together."
I hate fights. The day after this one, I get weepy and go over to Dianne's. She ends up subtly suggesting that I take stained-glass lessons. We drink some sherry and I drive home. The last thing I want is to run into her husband, who calls me "the squirrel" behind my back. Dianne says that when I call and he answers, he lets her know it's me on the phone by puffing up his cheeks to make himself look like a squirrel.
Tonight, Dan and I each sit on a side of Joanna's tester bed to say good night to her. The canopy above the bed is white nylon, with small,

puckered stars. She is ready for sleep. As soon as she goes to sleep, Dan will be ready to talk to me. Dan has clicked off the light next to Joanna's bed. Going out of the bedroom before him, I grope for the hall light. I remember Henry saying to me, as a way of leading up to talking about divorce, that going to work one morning he had driven over a hill and had been astonished when at the top he saw a huge yellow tree, and realized for the first time that it was autumn.

The Mother

Whether popular stereotype or profound archetype, the image of mother is an ambivalent one. The sentimental Mother's Day vision of "the one who means the world to me" and the image of the all-powerful "Mom" who castrates her sons reflect centuries of romantic exaltation of mother and the psychological theories that acknowledge her powers while deprecating them. Both images place the responsibility for the socialization of children—of all of us—absolutely on the mother. This awesome role is reinforced by the almost universal archetype of the "Great Mother," in whom are represented both the "Good Mother" and the "Terrible Mother"—the giver of life and all its joys and the bringer of denial, pain, and death. The power of this myth, found in the symbols and rituals of almost all societies, lies in the basic truth it represents: all human beings yearn for the free-floating comfort of complete dependence and, at the same time, for independence and assertion as individuals. The desire to "return to the womb" is a metaphor for the longing for total comfort; it is also a metaphor for what Freud referred to as the death wish, the oblivion of the individual. The association of these desires with birth and death has led to the symbolization of motherhood. The universality of the "Great Mother" image and each individual's recognition of the internalization of that image account for the assumption that the image is natural, a part of reality. Only recently have there been serious attempts by women scholars and writers to separate the archetype from the actual women who are mothers.

In the last few years many books about motherhood, especially about mother-daughter relationships, have questioned whether the link between good and terrible mother is inevitable. Sociologist Nancy Chodorov and psychologist Dorothy Dinnerstein suggest that the link persists because of socialization that does not separate childbearing and childrearing. Thrust into the responsibility for both roles, mothers bear the onus for the inevitable pains of growth and maturity. Freud's metaphor for the struggle, the Oedipus complex, is taken from the Greek myth of a son who can claim his royal identity only after he has murdered his father and married his mother. Unless a son can, metaphorically, overcome this desire and channel it into the adult role of separation from both parents and marriage to an adult woman, he will be an emotional cripple. For a daughter, the Oedipal struggle is to murder the mother and marry the father. Because women can never fully outgrow their desire to be like their mothers— according to this theory, they can become adults only when they identify with their mothers by becoming mothers—Freud saw them as doomed to incomplete individuation and hence to moral inferiority to men. Chodorov and Dinnerstein accept Freud's analysis that "the reproduction of mother-hood" perpetuates women's secondary roles in society; they suggest that equal parenting by fathers and mothers especially in infancy can disrupt the cycle and allow women to be ordinary human beings instead of symbols.

The first work in this section, Ray Bradbury's "I Sing the Body Electric!" is the story of a robot that fulfills all the nurturing functions of the ideal mother, not only for three children but also for their father. Not being human, she has none of the withholding, punishing aspects of the "Terrible Mother"; perhaps this is why Bradbury makes her "Grandma," the maternal caretaker removed from the necessity of disciplining and also, traditionally, from sexuality, which might cause her to divide her attention. This grandmother was "slapped . . . to life" by the children she comes to nurture; they owe her no debt for the pain of bringing them into the world, and, being a robot, she needs no rest or other consideration from them. They can take with no guilt all that she offers, the meeting of their every need, whether physical or psychological. Her reward is like that of Mrs. James in "The Angel over the Right Shoulder": she will go to heaven. Ironically, to her, heaven means to become human. Bradbury plays on every human desire for mother love only to make clear the inhumanity of such a burden. The story's very length is a symbol of how longstanding is the human fantasy of and longing for the "Good Mother."

The other works in this section express the gamut of emotions women feel as mothers. Erica Jong's poem "On the First Night" is a paean of joy and wonder at the "ordinary miracle" many women experience, especially at a first birth. Jong emphasizes her sense of continuity with her female ancestors; having a daughter reinforces the mother's sense that there is "sheer glory" in being a woman. Mother love is a powerful force in shaping a woman's sense of self, her identity. But no mother experiences only joy; as Adrienne Rich has so brilliantly shown in her book *Of Woman Born:*

Motherhood as Experience and Institution, joy and pain are inextricably mixed for mothers in our society. Gwendolyn Brooks, Ernest J. Gaines, and Isabella Gardner focus on the reality that motherhood brings with it sorrow and anxiety. In "The Mother" Brooks repudiates the image of abortion as unnatural, as devoid of love, and strongly asserts her love and sense of loss. She refuses guilt as she asserts that "even in my deliberateness I was not deliberate." She assumes full responsibility, refusing to "whine that the crime was other than mine." In "The Sky Is Gray" the mother must function as father and mother. Although she departs from the tender role expected by her sister, she insists that her son learn to cope with the realities of life regardless of his pain. In this story the child accepts both her authority and the tender help she gives him when he is suffering from a toothache; he is not ambivalent about her, seeing her both as a strong, brave adult and as a pitiful woman overburdened by poverty and loneliness. He reacts by wanting to grow up to help and protect her—perhaps an indication that Chodorov's and Dinnerstein's thesis is correct. Since the mother plays both male and female roles, she frees her son from overdependence on her.

In Isabella Gardner's poem "At a Summer Hotel," the mother shows a mixture of love and fear for her "beautiful bountiful womanful child." She fears for her daughter's future: will she be raped as Europa was by Zeus; will she be the bride of the god of the underworld, sentenced to half a life in darkness as was Persephone; or will she find happiness in love, as does Miranda in *The Tempest?* She wonders what will be her own relationship with her daughter once she has grown. Europa and Miranda were both their fathers' daughters, essentially motherless; and Persephone's mother, the goddess Demeter, was powerless to prevent her marriage to Hades, though she did win for her the right to return to earth periodically.

Perhaps the heaviest price of motherhood is the loss of a child. Meridel Le Sueur in "Biography of My Daughter" tells the poignant story of such a loss. Through the eyes of the sympathetic mother of the daughter's friend, we see the grief of a mother who is too accustomed to being passive even to protest the manner of her daughter's death by starvation. The angry narrator lets the reader perceive the complicity of the mother in her daughter's death; by unquestioningly approving her goal of "success" and without the power to help her achieve it, the mother has unwittingly prodded her daughter to overwork and self-denial, which becomes self-destruction. Le Sueur's story should help us understand the anger so characteristic of many mother-daughter relationships: the daughter's anger is a natural response to the mother's powerlessness to help, especially when the mother's approval is a psychological necessity. Daughters may feel that their mothers' very motherhood is urging them to become mothers or to achieve some other socially approved goal. The narrator claims the dead girl for her daughter, as the daughter of all women who need to resist the powerlessness that comes with stereotypical, socially imposed roles.

Jan Clausen's story "Daddy" illustrates another kind of loss mothers face: loss of the child's love. Told by a young child whose mother divorced her father and now has a female lover, "Daddy" underlines the strength of a daughter's bond to her father. In this instance, however, it is his power to give her material wealth, not a Freudian "family-romance," that lures the child from her mother. Like Le Sueur's story, "Daddy" shows the power-lessness of women in a world where their sexual preferences are, like their economic status, assumed to be of secondary importance to their relation-ships with men. Sherley Williams also shows a mother's powerlessness to help her adult daughter. Though Martha loves her mother, she cannot live by her mother's standards, even when, pregnant, she has apparently been abandoned by her lover. Martha's need to be independent, to make her own mistakes, makes her put sexual love first even when she recognizes that as a black man her lover needs his pride before the white world more than his love for her. The mother in this story faces perhaps the hardest truth mothers know: they cannot be fairy godmothers; they must let their children go. Such knowledge is hard to experience without a sense of rejec-tion, as Tillie Olsen makes clear in "Tell Me a Riddle" (see Part II). After bearing and nurturing seven children, Olsen's Eva continues to suffer "over lives one felt, but could no longer hold nor help."

Olsen's story is among the very few in which a mother is the central consciousness; but recently we have been hearing a lot from daughters' perspectives—an important source for women's sense of self, since though some may never be wives or mothers, all women are daughters. Catherine Davis's speaker in "SHE" both admires her mother for her individuality and freedom and resents her own small role in her mother's life. The lines "SHE / gave me life / . . . / and / here I am" frame a description of the mother's independent, risk-taking life; the daughter faces alone the respon-sibility of living her own life, of becoming an adult. Her fear comes to us through the form of the poem, symbolized by the large letters of the first word, "SHE." In "Souvenir," Jayne Anne Phillips shows a mother and daughter coming to the realization that they are interdependent; as adults, they both give and take, as their mutual gift of pewter candle holders indicates. Kate needs her mother "to defend [her] choices"; her mother needs Kate to validate *her* choices by becoming a mother and giving her grandchildren. But the mother perceives that Kate can validate her choices by other means: "If you like yourself, I must have done something right," she says. By being herself, then, Kate wins her mother's approval. At her mother's deathbed, Kate and her mother communicate without words, sharing their deepest knowledge. Phillips acknowledges the special bond between mother and daughter without reducing either to a role-player.

Hortense Calisher in "The Middle Drawer" reconstructs her mother's life after her death by remembering the mementos her mother had always kept in a locked drawer. Hester has not faced her long-term hostility toward her mother until, after a mastectomy, she sees her mother's scar. Then, seeing her mother's need for consolation as like her own childhood vulner-ability to her mother's approval, she gives the scar an "affirmative caress." Perceiving her mother's vulnerability is perceiving her humanity, the core beyond roles and role-playing. But even such perception, Hester believes, will never free her from the need for her mother's unconditional love.

Calisher's story reminds us that the desires that lie behind stereotypes and archetypes cannot be fully eradicated. But many of the works in this section point toward ways of accepting human needs for love and care without reference to gender. As we see in Max Apple's story "Bridging," the problems of parenting transcend gender-based roles. A widower with a nine-year-old daughter tries to help her by becoming an assistant leader of a Brownie troop; ironically, Jessica, the daughter, refuses to participate. Eager to help his daughter find friends, the father learns that they must each learn to leave the other, and it is he who realizes first that separation from her, and even from her dead mother, has left him alive and capable of joy. The process of "bridging" is a "slow steady process"; in order to succeed, the father must "swoop past five thousand years of stereotypes." Though Apple's tone is light, his story is serious: it isn't easy to overcome stereotypes, but even such a small step as a man's becoming an assistant Girl Scout leader helps to undermine the hold of tradition.

I SING THE BODY ELECTRIC!

by

RAY BRADBURY

(b. 1910)

Born in Waukegan, Illinois, Ray Bradbury has been writing futuris-
tic fiction since he was a teenager; his early works about travel to
the moon were viewed as mere fiction, and his use of science fiction
to incorporate social criticism has not diminished his popularity.
Fahrenheit 451 (1979) has been made into a classic film; recent
works include Dinosaur Tales *(1983) and* A Memory of Murder
(1984). He also published a collection of poems in 1982.

GRANDMA!

I remember her birth.

Wait, you say, *no* man remembers his own grandma's birth.

But, yes, *we* remember the day that she was born.

For we, her grandchildren, slapped her to life. Timothy, Agatha, and I, Tom, raised up our hands and brought them down in a huge crack! We shook together the bits and pieces, parts and samples, textures and tastes, humors and distillations that would move her compass needle north to cool us, south to warm and comfort us, east and west to travel round the endless world, glide her eyes to know us, mouth to sing us asleep by night, hands to touch us awake at dawn.

Grandma, O dear and wondrous electric dream . . .

When storm lightnings rove the sky making circuitries amidst the clouds, her name flashes on my inner lid. Sometimes still I hear her ticking, humming above our beds in the gentle dark. She passes like a clock-ghost in the long halls of memory, like a hive of intellectual bees swarming after the Spirit of Summers Lost. Sometimes still I feel the smile I learned from her, printed on my cheek at three in the deep morn . . .

All right, all right! you cry, what was it like the day your damned and wondrous-dreadful-loving Grandma was born?

It was the week the world ended . . .

Our mother was dead.

THE MOTHER

118

One late afternoon a black car left Father and the three of us stranded on our own front drive staring at the grass, thinking:

That's not our grass. There are the croquet mallets, balls, hoops, yes, just as they fell and lay three days ago when Dad stumbled out on the lawn, weeping with the news. There are the roller skates that belonged to a boy, me, who will never be that young again. And yes, there the tire-swing on the old oak, but Agatha afraid to swing. It would surely break. It would fall.

And the house? Oh, God . . .

We peered through the front door, afraid of the echoes we might find confused in the halls; the sort of clamor that happens when all the furniture is taken out and there is nothing to soften the river of talk that flows in any house at all hours. And now the soft, the warm, the main piece of lovely furniture was gone forever.

The door drifted wide.

Silence came out. Somewhere a cellar door stood wide and a raw wind blew damp earth from under the house.

But, I thought, we don't *have* a cellar!

"Well," said Father.

We did not move.

Aunt Clara drove up the path in her big canary-colored limousine.

We jumped through the door. We ran to our rooms.

We heard them shout and then speak and then shout and then speak: Let the children live with me! Aunt Clara said. They'd rather kill themselves! Father said.

A door slammed. Aunt Clara was gone.

We almost danced. Then we remembered what had happened and went downstairs.

Father sat alone talking to himself or to a remnant ghost of Mother left from the days before her illness, but jarred loose now by the slamming of the door. He murmured to his hands, his empty palms:

"The children need someone. I love them but, let's face it, I must work to feed us all. You love them, Ann, but you're gone. And Clara? Impossible. She loves but smothers. And as for maids, nurses—?"

Here Father sighed and we sighed with him, remembering.

The luck we had had with maids or live-in teachers or sitters was beyond intolerable. Hardly a one who wasn't a crosscut saw grabbing against the grain. Handaxes and hurricanes best described them. Or, conversely, they were all fallen trifle, damp soufflé. We children were unseen furniture to be sat upon or dusted or sent for reupholstering come spring and fall, with a yearly cleansing at the beach.

"What we need," said Father, "is a . . ."

We all leaned to his whisper.

". . . grandmother."

"But," said Timothy, with the logic of nine years, "all our grandmothers are dead."

"Yes in one way, no in another."

What a fine mysterious thing for Dad to say.

"Here," he said at last.

He handed us a multifold, multicolored pamphlet. We had seen it in his hands, off and on, for many weeks, and very often during the last few days. Now, with one blink of our eyes, as we passed the paper from hand to hand, we knew why Aunt Clara, insulted, outraged, had stormed from the house.

Timothy was the first to read aloud from what he saw on the first page: "I Sing the Body Electric!"

He glanced up at Father, squinting. "What the heck does that mean?"

"Read on."

Agatha and I glanced guiltily about the room, afraid Mother might suddenly come in to find us with this blasphemy, but then nodded to Timothy, who read:

" 'Fanto—' "

"Fantoccini," Father prompted.

" 'Fantoccini Ltd. *We Shadow Forth* . . . the answer to all your most grievous problems. One Model Only, upon which a thousand times a thousand variations can be added, subtracted, subdivided, indivisible, with Liberty and Justice for all.' "

"Where does it say *that?*" we all cried.

"It doesn't." Timothy smiled for the first time in days. "I just had to put that in. Wait." He read on: " 'for you who have worried over inattentive sitters, nurses who cannot be trusted with marked liquor bottles, and well-meaning Uncles and Aunts—' "

"Well-meaning, *but!*" said Agatha, and I gave an echo.

" '—we have perfected the first humanoid-genre minicircuited, rechargeable AC-DC Mark V Electrical Grandmother . . .' "

"Grandmother!?"

The paper slipped away to the floor. "Dad . . . ?"

"Don't look at me that way," said Father. "I'm half-mad with grief, and half-mad thinking of tomorrow and the day after that. Someone pick up the paper. Finish it."

"I will," I said, and did:

" 'The Toy that is more than a Toy, the Fantoccini Electrical Grandmother is built with loving precision to give the incredible precision of love to your children. The child at ease with the realities of the world and the even greater realities of the imagination, is her aim.

" 'She is computerized to tutor in twelve languages simultaneously, capable of switching tongues in a thousandth of a second without pause, and has a complete knowledge of the religious, artistic, and sociopolitical histories of the world seeded in her master hive—' "

"How great!" said Timothy. "It makes it sound as if we were to keep bees! *Educated* bees!"

"Shut up!" said Agatha.

"'Above all,'" I read, "'this human being, for human she seems, this embodiment in electro-intelligent facsimile of the humanities, will listen, know, tell, react and love your children insofar as such great Objects, such fantastic Toys, can be said to Love, or can be imagined to Care. This Miraculous Companion, excited to the challenge of large world and small, inner Sea or Outer Universe, will transmit by touch and tell, said Miracles to your Needy.'"

"Our Needy," murmured Agatha.

Why, we all thought, sadly, that's us, oh, yes, that's *us*.

I finished:

"'We do not sell our Creation to able-bodied families where parents are available to raise, effect, shape, change, love their own children. Nothing can replace the parent in the home. However there are families where death or ill health or disablement undermines the welfare of the children. Orphanages seem not the answer. Nurses tend to be selfish, neglectful, or suffering from dire nervous afflictions.

"'With the utmost humility then, and recognizing the need to rebuild, rethink, and regrow our conceptualizations from month to month, year to year, we offer the nearest thing to the Ideal Teacher-Friend-Companion-Blood Relation. A trial period can be arranged for—'"

"Stop," said Father. "Don't go on. Even *I* can't stand it."

"Why?" said Timothy. "I was just getting interested."

I folded the pamphlet up. "Do they *really* have these things?"

"Let's not talk any more about it," said Father, his hand over his eyes. "It was a mad thought—"

"Not so mad," I said, glancing at Tim. "I mean, heck, even if they tried, whatever they built, couldn't be worse than Aunt Clara, huh?"

And then we all roared. We hadn't laughed in months. And now my simple words made everyone hoot and howl and explode. I opened my mouth and yelled happily, too.

When we stopped laughing, we looked at the pamphlet and I said, "Well?"

"I—" Agatha scowled, not ready.

"We do need something, bad, right now," said Timothy.

"I have an open mind," I said, in my best pontifical style.

"There's only one thing," said Agatha. "We can try it. Sure. But—tell me this—when do we cut out all this talk and when does our *real* mother come home to stay?"

There was a single gasp from the family as if, with one shot, she had struck us all in the heart.

I don't think any of us stopped crying the rest of that night.

It was a clear bright day. The helicopter tossed us lightly up and over and down through the skyscrapers and let us out, almost for a trot and caper, on top of the building where the large letters could be read from the sky:

FANTOCCINI.

"What are *Fantoccini?*" said Agatha.

"It's an Italian word for shadow puppets, I think, or dream people," said Father.

"But *shadow forth,* what does that mean?"

"WE TRY TO GUESS YOUR DREAM," I said.

"Bravo," said Father. "A-Plus."

I beamed.

The helicopter flapped a lot of loud shadows over us and went away.

We sank down in an elevator as our stomachs sank up. We stepped out onto a moving carpet that streamed away on a blue river of wool toward a desk over which various signs hung:

THE CLOCK SHOP
Fantoccini Our Specialty.
Rabbits on walls, no problem.

"Rabbits on walls?"

I held up my fingers in profile as if I held them before a candle flame, and wiggled the "ears."

"Here's a rabbit, here's a wolf, here's a crocodile."

"Of course," said Agatha.

And we were at the desk. Quiet music drifted about us. Somewhere behind the walls, there was a waterfall of machinery flowing softly. As we arrived at the desk, the lighting changed to make us look warmer, happier, though we were still cold.

All about us in niches and cases, and hung from ceilings on wires and strings were puppets and marionettes, and Balinese kite-bamboo-translucent dolls which, held to the moonlight, might acrobat your most secret nightmares or dreams. In passing, the breeze set up by our bodies stirred the various hung souls on their gibbets. It was like an immense lynching on a holiday at some English crossroads four hundred years before.

You see? I know my history.

Agatha blinked about with disbelief and then some touch of awe and finally disgust.

"Well, if that's what they are, let's go."

"Tush," said Father.

"Well," she protested, "you gave me one of those dumb things with strings two years ago and the strings were in a zillion knots by dinnertime. I threw the whole thing out the window."

"Patience," said Father.

"We shall see what we can do to eliminate the strings."

The man behind the desk had spoken.

We all turned to give him our regard.

Rather like a funeral-parlor man, he had the cleverness not to smile.

Children are put off by older people who smile too much. They smell a catch, right off.

Unsmiling, but not gloomy or pontifical, the man said, "Guido Fantoccini, at your service. Here's how we do it, Miss Agatha Simmons, aged eleven."

Now there was a really fine touch.

He knew that Agatha was only ten. Add a year to that, and you're halfway home. Agatha grew an inch. The man went on:

"There."

And he placed a golden key in Agatha's hand.

"To wind them up instead of strings?"

"To wind them up." The man nodded.

"Pshaw!" said Agatha.

Which was her polite form of "rabbit pellets."

"God's truth. Here is the key to your Do-it-Yourself, Select Only the Best, Electrical Grandmother. Every morning you wind her up. Every night you let her run down. You're in charge. You are guardian of the Key."

He pressed the object in her palm where she looked at it suspiciously.

I watched him. He gave me a side wink which said, well, no . . . but aren't keys fun?

I winked back before she lifted her head.

"Where does this fit?"

"You'll see when the time comes. In the middle of her stomach, perhaps, or up her left nostril or in her right ear."

That was good for a smile as the man arose.

"This way, please. Step light. Onto the moving stream. Walk on the water, please. Yes. There."

He helped to float us. We stepped from rug that was forever frozen onto rug that whispered by.

It was a most agreeable river which floated us along on a green spread of carpeting that rolled forever through halls and into wonderfully secret dim caverns where voices echoed back our own breathing or sang like Oracles to our questions.

"Listen," said the salesman, "the voices of all kinds of women. Weigh and find just the right one . . . !"

And listen we did, to all the high, low, soft, loud, in-between, half-scolding, half-affectionate voices saved over from times before we were born.

And behind us, Agatha tread backward, always fighting the river, never catching up, never with us, holding off.

"Speak," said the salesman. "Yell."

And speak and yell we did.

"Hello. You there! This is Timothy, hi!"

"What shall I say!" I shouted. "Help!"

Agatha walked backward, mouth tight.

Father took her hand. She cried out.

"Let go! No, no! I won't have my voice used! I won't!"

"Excellent." The salesman touched three dials on a small machine he held in his hand.

On the side of the small machine we saw three oscillograph patterns mix, blend, and repeat our cries.

The salesman touched another dial and we heard our voices fly off amidst the Delphic caves to hang upside down, to cluster, to beat words all about, to shriek, and the salesman itched another knob to add, perhaps, a touch of this or a pinch of that, a breath of mother's voice, all unbeknownst, or a splice of father's outrage at the morning's paper or his peaceable one-drink voice at dusk. Whatever it was the salesman did, whispers danced all about us like frantic vinegar gnats, fizzed by lightning, settling round until at last a final switch was pushed and a voice spoke free of a far electronic deep:

"Nefertiti," it said.

Timothy froze. I froze. Agatha stopped treading water.

"Nefertiti?" asked Tim.

"What does that mean?" demanded Agatha.

"I know."

The salesman nodded me to tell.

"Nefertiti," I whispered, "is Egyptian for The Beautiful One Is Here."

"The Beautiful One Is Here," repeated Timothy.

"Nefer," said Agatha, "titi."

And we all turned to stare into that soft twilight, that deep far place from which the good warm soft voice came.

And she was indeed there.

And, by her voice, she was beautiful . . .

That was it.

That was, at least, the most of it.

The voice seemed more important than all the rest.

Not that we didn't argue about weights and measures:

She should not be bony to cut us to the quick, nor so fat we might sink out of sight when she squeezed us.

Her hand pressed to ours, or brushing our brow in the middle of sick-fever nights, must not be marble-cold, dreadful, or oven-hot, oppressive, but somewhere between. The nice temperature of a baby-chick held in the hand after a long night's sleep and just plucked from beneath a contemplative hen; that, that was it.

Oh, we were great ones for detail. We fought and argued and cried, and Timothy won on the color of her eyes, for reasons to be known later.

Grandmother's hair? Agatha, with girl's ideas, though reluctantly given, she was in charge of that. We let her choose from a thousand harp strands hung in filamentary tapestries like varieties of rain we ran amongst. Agatha did not run happily, but seeing we boys would mess things in tangles, she told us to move aside.

And so the bargain shopping through the dime-store inventories and the Tiffany extensions of the Ben Franklin Electric Storm Machine and

Fantoccini Pantomime Company was done.

And the always flowing river ran its tide to an end and deposited us all on a far shore in the late day . . .

It was very clever of the Fantoccini people, after that.

How?

They made us wait.

They knew we were not won over. Not completely, no, nor half completely.

Especially Agatha, who turned her face to her wall and saw sorrow there and put her hand out again and again to touch it. We found her fingernail marks on the wallpaper each morning, in strange little silhouettes, half beauty, half nightmare. Some could be erased with a breath, like ice flowers on a winter pane. Some could not be rubbed out with a washcloth, no matter how hard you tried.

And meanwhile, they made us wait.

So we fretted out June.

So we sat around July.

So we groused through August and then on August 29, "I have this feeling," said Timothy, and we all went out after breakfast to sit on the lawn.

Perhaps we had smelled something on Father's conversation the previous night, or caught some special furtive glance at the sky or the freeway Rapped briefly and then lost in his gaze. Or perhaps it was merely the way the wind blew the ghost curtains out over our beds, making pale messages all night.

For suddenly there we were in the middle of the grass, Timothy and I, with Agatha, pretending no curiosity, up on the porch, hidden behind the potted geraniums.

We gave her no notice. We knew that if we acknowledged her presence, she would flee, so we sat and watched the sky where nothing moved but birds and highflown jets, and watched the freeway where a thousand cars might suddenly deliver forth our Special Gift . . . but . . . nothing.

At noon we chewed grass and lay low . . .

At one o'clock, Timothy blinked his eyes.

And then, with incredible precision, it happened.

It was as if the Fantoccini people knew our surface tension.

All children are water-striders. We skate along the top skin of the pond each day, always threatening to break through, sink, vanish beyond recall, into ourselves.

Well, as if knowing our long wait must absolutely end within one minute! this *second!* no more, God, forget it!

At that instant, I repeat, the clouds above our house opened wide and let forth a helicopter like Apollo driving his chariot across mythological skies.

And the Apollo machine swam down on its own summer breeze, wafting hot winds to cool, reweaving our hair, smartening our eyebrows, applauding our pant legs against our shins, making a flag of Agatha's hair on the porch and thus settled like a vast frenzied hibiscus on our lawn, the helicopter slid wide a bottom drawer and deposited upon the grass a parcel of largish size, no sooner having laid same then the vehicle, with not so much as a god bless or farewell, sank straight up, disturbed the calm air with a mad ten thousand flourishes and then, like a skyborne dervish, tilted and fell off to be mad some other place.

Timothy and I stood riven for a long moment looking at the packing case, and then we saw the crowbar taped to the top of the raw pine lid and seized it and began to pry and creak and squeal the boards off, one by one, and as we did this I saw Agatha sneak up to watch and I thought, thank you, God, thank you that Agatha never saw a coffin, when Mother went away, no box, no cemetery, no earth, just words in a big church, no box, no box like *this* . . . !

The last pine plank fell away.

Timothy and I gasped. Agatha, between us now, gasped, too.

For inside the immense raw pine package was the most beautiful idea anyone ever dreamt and built.

Inside was the perfect gift for any child from seven to seventy-seven.

We stopped up our breaths. We let them out in cries of delight and adoration.

Inside the opened box was . . .

A mummy.

Or, first anyway, a mummy case, a sarcophagus!

"Oh, no!" Happy tears filled Timothy's eyes.

"It can't be!" said Agatha.

"It is, it is!"

"Our very own?"

"Ours!"

"It must be a mistake!"

"Sure, they'll want it back!"

"They can't *have* it!"

"Lord, Lord, is that real gold!? Real hieroglyphs! Run your fingers over them!"

"Let *me!*"

"Just like in the museums! Museums!"

We all gabbled at once. I think some tears fell from my own eyes to rain upon the case.

"Oh, they'll make the colors run!"

Agatha wiped the rain away.

And the golden mask face of the woman carved on the sarcophagus lid looked back at us with just the merest smile which hinted at our own joy, which accepted the overwhelming upsurge of a love we thought had drowned forever but now surfaced into the sun.

Not only did she have a sun-metal face stamped and beaten out of purest gold, with delicate nostrils and a mouth that was both firm and gentle, but her eyes, fixed into their sockets, were cerulean or amethystine or lapis lazuli, or all three, minted and fused together, and her body was covered over with lions and eyes and ravens, and her hands were crossed upon her carved bosom and in one gold mitten she clenched a thonged whip for obedience, and in the other a fantastic ranuncula, which makes for obedience out of love, so the whip lies unused . . .

And as our eyes ran down her hieroglyphs it came to all three of us at the same instant:

"Why, those signs!" "Yes, the hen tracks!" "The birds, the snakes!"

They didn't speak tales of the Past.

They were hieroglyphs of the Future.

This was the first queen mummy delivered forth in all time whose papyrus inkings etched out the next month, the next season, the next year, the next *lifetime!*

She did not mourn for time spent.

No. She celebrated the bright coinage yet to come, banked, waiting, ready to be drawn upon and used.

We sank to our knees to worship that possible time.

First one hand, then another, probed out to niggle, twitch, touch, itch over the signs.

"There's me, yes, look! Me, in sixth grade!" said Agatha, now in the fifth. "See the girl with my-colored hair and wearing my gingerbread suit?"

"There's me in the twelfth year of high school!" said Timothy, so very young now but building taller stilts every week and stalking around the yard.

"There's me," I said, quietly, warm, "in college. The guy wearing glasses who runs a little to fat. Sure. Heck." I snorted. "That's me."

The sarcophagus spelled winters ahead, springs to squander, autumns to spend with all the golden and rusty and copper leaves like coins, and over all, her bright sun symbol, daughter-of-Ra eternal face, forever above our horizon, forever an illumination to tilt our shadows to better ends.

"Hey!" we all said at once, having read and reread our Fortune-Told scribblings, seeing our lifelines and lovelines, inadmissible, serpentined over, around, and down. "Hey!"

And in one séance table-lifting feat, not telling each other what to do, just doing it, we pried up the bright sarcophagus lid, which had no hinges but lifted out like cup from cup, and put the lid aside.

And within the sarcophagus, of course, was the true mummy!

And she was like the image carved on the lid, but more so, more beautiful, more touching because human shaped, and shrouded all in new fresh bandages of linen, round and round, instead of old and dusty cerements.

And upon her hidden face was an identical golden mask, younger than the first, but somehow, strangely wiser than the first.

And the linens that tethered her limbs had symbols on them of three sorts, one a girl of ten, one a boy of nine, one a boy of thirteen.

A series of bandages for each of us!

We gave each other a startled glance and a sudden bark of laughter.

Nobody said the bad joke, but all thought:

She's all wrapped up in us!

And we didn't care. We loved the joke. We loved whoever had thought to make us part of the ceremony we now went through as each of us seized and began to unwind each of his or her particular serpentines of delicious stuffs!

The lawn was soon a mountain of linen.

The woman beneath the covering lay there, waiting.

"Oh, no," cried Agatha. "She's dead, too!"

She ran. I stopped her. "Idiot. She's not dead *or* alive. Where's your key?"

"Key?"

"Dummy," said Tim, "the key the man gave you to wind her up!"

Her hand had already spidered along her blouse to where the symbol of some possible new religion hung. She had strung it there, against her own skeptic's muttering, and now she held it in her sweaty palm.

"Go on," said Timothy. "Put it in!"

"But *where?*"

"Oh for God's sake! As the man said, in her right armpit or left ear. Gimme!"

And he grabbed the key and impulsively moaning with impatience and not able to find the proper insertion slot, prowled over the prone figure's head and bosom and at last, on pure instinct, perhaps for a lark, perhaps just giving up the whole damned mess, thrust the key through a final shroud of bandage at the navel.

On the instant: *spunnng!*

The Electrical Grandmother's eyes flicked wide!

Something began to hum and whir. It was as if Tim had stirred up a hive of hornets with an ornery stick.

"Oh," gasped Agatha, seeing he had taken the game away, "let *me!*"

She wrenched the key.

Grandma's nostrils *flared!* She might snort up steam, snuff out fire!

"Me!" I cried, and grabbed the key and gave it a huge . . . *twist!*

The beautiful woman's mouth popped wide.

"Me!"

"Me!"

"Me!"

Grandma suddenly sat up.

We leapt back.

We knew we had, in a way, slapped her alive.

She was born, she was *born!*

Her head swiveled all about. She gaped. She mouthed. And the first thing she said was:

Laughter.

THE MOTHER

128

Where one moment we had backed off, now the mad sound drew us near to peer as in a pit where crazy folk are kept with snakes to make them well.

It was a good laugh, full and rich and hearty, and it did not mock, it accepted. It said the world was a wild place, strange, unbelievable, absurd if you wished, but all in all, quite a place. She would not dream to find another. She would not ask to go back to sleep.

She was awake now. We had awakened her. With a glad shout, she would go with it all.

And go she did, out of her sarcophagus, out of her winding sheet, stepping forth, brushing off, looking around as for a mirror. She found it.

The reflections in our eyes.

She was more pleased than disconcerted with what she found there. Her laughter faded to an amused smile.

For Agatha, at the instant of birth, had leapt to hide on the porch.

The Electrical Person pretended not to notice.

She turned slowly on the green lawn near the shady street, gazing all about with new eyes, her nostrils moving as if she breathed the actual air and this the first morn of the lovely Garden and she with no intention of spoiling the game by biting the apple . . .

Her gaze fixed upon my brother.

"You must be—?"

"Timothy. Tim," he offered.

"And you must be—?"

"Tom," I said.

How clever again of the Fantoccini Company. *They* knew. *She* knew. But they had taught her to pretend not to know. That way we could feel great, we were the teachers, telling her what she already knew! How sly, how wise.

"And isn't there another boy?" said the woman.

"Girl!" a disgusted voice cried from somewhere on the porch.

"Whose name is Alicia—?"

"Agatha!" The far voice, started in humiliation, ended in proper anger.

"Algernon, of course."

"Agatha!" Our sister popped up, popped back to hide a flushed face.

"Agatha." The woman touched the word with proper affection. "Well, Agatha, Timothy, Thomas, let me *look* at you."

"No," said I, said Tim. "Let us look at *you*. Hey . . ."

Our voices slid back in our throats.

We drew near her.

We walked in great slow circles round about, skirting the edges of her territory. And her territory extended as far as we could hear the hum of the warm summer hive. For that is exactly what she sounded like. That was her characteristic tune. She made a sound like a season all to herself, a morning early in June when the world wakes to find everything absolutely perfect, fine, delicately attuned, all in balance, nothing disproportioned. Even before you opened your eyes you knew it would be one of those days. Tell the sky what color it must be, and it was indeed. Tell the sun how to crochet its way, pick and choose among leaves to lay out carpetings of bright and dark on the fresh lawn, and pick and lay it did. The bees have been up earliest of all, they have already come and gone, and come and gone again to the meadow fields and returned all golden fuzz on the air, all pollen-decorated, epaulettes at the full, nectar-dripping. Don't you hear them pass? hover? dance their language? telling where all the sweet gums are, the syrups that make bears frolic and lumber in bulked ecstasies, that make boys squirm with unpronounced juices, that make girls leap out of beds to catch from the corners of their eyes their dolphin selves naked aflash on the warm air poised forever in one eternal glass wave.

So it seemed with our electrical friend here on the new lawn in the middle of a special day.

And she a stuff to which we were drawn, lured, spelled, doing our dance, remembering what could not be remembered, needful, aware of her attentions.

Timothy and I, Tom, that is.

Agatha remained on the porch.

But her head flowered above the rail, her eyes followed all that was done and said.

And what was said and done was Tim at last exhaling:

"Hey . . . your *eyes* . . ."

Her eyes. Her splendid eyes.

Even more splendid than the lapis lazuli on the sarcophagus lid and on the mask that had covered her bandaged face. These most beautiful eyes in the world looked out upon us calmly, shining.

"Your eyes," gasped Tim, "are the *exact* same color, are like—"

"Like what?"

"My favorite aggies . . ."

"What could be better than that?" she said.

And the answer was, nothing.

Her eyes slid along on the bright air to brush my ears, my nose, my chin. "And you, Master Tom?"

"Me?"

"How shall we be friends? We must, you know, if we're going to knock elbows about the house the next year . . ."

"I . . ." I said, and stopped.

"You," said Grandma, "are a dog mad to bark but with taffy in his teeth. Have you ever given a dog taffy? It's so sad and funny, both. You laugh but hate yourself for laughing. You cry and run to help, and laugh again when his first new bark comes out."

I barked a small laugh remembering a dog, a day, and some taffy.

Grandma turned, and there was my old kite strewn on the lawn. She recognized its problem.

"The string's broken. No. The ball of string's *lost*. You can't fly a kite that way. Here."

She bent. We didn't know what might happen. How could a robot grandma fly a kite for us? She raised up, the kite in her hands.

"Fly," she said, as to a bird.

And the kite flew.

That is to say, with a grand flourish, she let it up on the wind.

And she and the kite were one.

For from the tip of her index finger there sprang a thin bright strand of spider web, all half-invisible gossamer fishline which, fixed to the kite, let it soar a hundred, no, three hundred, no, a thousand feet high on the summer swoons.

Timothy shouted. Agatha, torn between coming and going, let out a cry from the porch. And I, in all my maturity of thirteen years, though I tried not to look impressed, grew taller, taller, and felt a similar cry burst out of my lungs, and burst it did. I gabbled and yelled lots of things about how I wished *I* had a finger from which, on a bobbin, I might thread the sky, the clouds, a wild kite all in one.

"If you think *that* is high," said the Electric Creature, "watch *this!*"

With a hiss, a whistle, a hum, the fishline sung out. The kite sank up another thousand feet. And again another thousand, until at last it was a speck of red confetti dancing on the very winds that took jets around the world or changed the weather in the next existence . . .

"It can't be!" I cried.

"It *is*." She calmly watched her finger unravel its massive stuffs. "I make it as I need it. Liquid inside, like a spider. Hardens when it hits the air, instant thread . . ."

And when the kite was no more than a specule, a vanishing mote on the peripheral vision of the gods, to quote from older wisemen, why then Grandma, without turning, without looking, without letting her gaze offend by touching, said:

"And, Abigail—?"

"Agatha!" was the sharp response.

O wise woman, to overcome with swift small angers.

"Agatha," said Grandma, not too tenderly, not too lightly, somewhere poised between, "and how shall *we* make do?"

She broke the thread and wrapped it about my fist three times so I was tethered to heaven by the longest, I repeat, longest kite string in the entire history of the world! Wait till I show my friends! I thought. Green! Sour apple green is the color they'll turn!

"Agatha?"

"No way!" said Agatha.

"No way," said an echo.

"There must be some—"

"We'll never be friends!" said Agatha.

"Never be friends," said the echo.

Timothy and I jerked. Where was the echo coming from? Even Agatha, surprised, showed her eyebrows above the porch rail.

Then we looked and saw.

Grandma was cupping her hands like a seashell and from within that shell the echo sounded.

"Never . . . friends . . ."

And again faintly dying, "Friends . . ."

We all bent to hear.

That is we two boys bent to hear.

"No!" cried Agatha.

And ran in the house and slammed the doors.

"Friends," said the echo from the seashell hands. "No."

And far away, on the shore of some inner sea, we heard a small door shut.

And that was the first day.

And there was a second day, of course, and a third and a fourth, with Grandma wheeling in a great circle, and we her planets turning about the central light, with Agatha slowly, slowly coming in to join, to walk if not run with us, to listen if not hear, to watch if not see, to itch if not touch.

But at least by the end of the first ten days, Agatha no longer fled, but stood in nearby doors, or sat in distant chairs under trees, or if we went out for hikes, followed ten paces behind.

And Grandma? She merely waited. She never tried to urge or force. She went about her cooking and baking apricot pies and left foods carelessly here and there about the house on mousetrap plates for wiggle-nosed girls to sniff and snitch. An hour later, the plates were empty, the buns or cakes gone and without thank-yous, there was Agatha sliding down the banister, a mustache of crumbs on her lip.

As for Tim and me, we were always being called up hills by our Electric Grandma, and reaching the top were called down the other side.

And the most peculiar and beautiful and strange and lovely thing was the way she seemed to give complete attention to all of us.

She listened, she really listened to all we said, she knew and remembered every syllable, word, sentence, punctuation, thought, and rambunctious idea. We knew that all our days were stored in her, and that any time we felt we might want to know what we said at X hour at X second on X afternoon, we just named that X and with amiable promptitude, in the form of an aria if we wished, sung with humor, she would deliver forth X incident.

Sometimes we were prompted to test her. In the midst of babbling one day with high fevers about nothing, I stopped. I fixed Grandma with my eye and demanded:

"What did I just say?"

"Oh, er—"

"Come on, spit it out!"

"I think—" she rummaged her purse. "I have it here." From the deeps of her purse she drew forth and handed me:

"Boy! A Chinese fortune cookie!"

"Fresh baked, still warm, open it."

It was almost too hot to touch. I broke the cookie shell and pressed the warm curl of paper out to read:

"—bicycle Champ of the whole West! What did I just say? Come on, spit it out!"

My jaw dropped.

"How did you *do* that?"

"We have our little secrets. The only Chinese fortune cookie that predicts the Immediate Past. Have another?"

I cracked the second shell and read:

" 'How did you *do* that?' "

I popped the messages and the piping hot shells into my mouth and chewed as we walked.

"Well?"

"You're a great cook," I said.

And, laughing, we began to run.

And that was another great thing.

She could *keep up*.

Never beat, never win a race, but pump right along in good style, which a boy doesn't mind. A girl ahead of him or beside him is too much to bear. But a girl one or two paces back is a respectful thing, and allowed.

So Grandma and I had some great runs, me in the lead, and both talking a mile a minute.

But now I must tell you the best part of Grandma.

I might not have known at all if Timothy hadn't taken some pictures, and if I hadn't taken some also, and then compared.

When I saw the photographs developed out of our instant Brownies, I sent Agatha, against her wishes, to photograph Grandma a third time, unawares.

Then I took the three sets of pictures off alone, to keep counsel with myself. I never told Timothy and Agatha what I found. I didn't want to spoil it.

But, as I laid the pictures out in my room, here is what I thought and said:

"Grandma, in each picture, looks *different!*"

"Different?" I asked myself.

"Sure. Wait. Just a sec—"

I rearranged the photos.

"Here's one of Grandma near Agatha. And, in it, Grandma looks like . . . Agatha!

"And in this one, posed with Timothy, she looks like Timothy!

"And this last one, Holy Goll! Jogging along with me, she looks like ugly *me!*"

I sat down, stunned. The pictures fell to the floor.

I hunched over, scrabbling them, rearranging, turning upside down and sidewise. Yes. Holy Goll again, yes!

O that clever Grandmother.

O those Fantoccini people-making people.

Clever beyond clever, human beyond human, warm beyond warm, love beyond love . . .

And wordless, I rose and went downstairs and found Agatha and Grandma in the same room, doing algebra lessons in an almost peaceful communion. At least there was not outright war. Grandma was still waiting for Agatha to come round. And no one knew what day of what year that would be, or how to make it come faster. Meanwhile—

My entering the room made Grandma turn. I watched her face slowly as it recognized me. And wasn't there the merest ink-wash change of color in those eyes? Didn't the thin film of blood beneath the translucent skin, or whatever liquid they put to pulse and beat in the humanoid forms, didn't it flourish itself suddenly bright in her cheeks and mouth? I am somewhat ruddy. Didn't Grandma suffuse herself more to my color upon my arrival? And her eyes? watching Agatha-Abigail-Algernon at work, hadn't they been *her* color of blue rather than mine, which are deeper?

More important than that, in the moments as she talked with me, saying, "Good evening," and "How's your homework, my lad?" and such stuff, didn't the bones of her face shift subtly beneath the flesh to assume some fresh racial attitude?

For let's face it, our family is of three sorts. Agatha has the long horse bones of a small English girl who will grow to hunt foxes; Father's equine stare, snort, stomp, and assemblage of skeleton. The skull and teeth are pure English, or as pure as the motley isle's history allows.

Timothy is something else, a touch of Italian from Mother's side a generation back. Her family name was Mariano, so Tim has that dark thing firing him, and a small bone structure, and eyes that will one day burn ladies to the ground.

As for me, I am the Slav, and we can only figure this from my paternal grandfather's mother who came from Vienna and brought a set of cheekbones that flared, and temples from which you might dip wine, and a kind of steppeland thrust of nose which sniffed more of Tartar than of Tartan, hiding behind the family name.

So you see it became fascinating for me to watch and try to catch Grandma as she performed her changes, speaking to Agatha and melting her cheekbones to the horse, speaking to Timothy and growing as delicate as a Florentine raven pecking glibly at the air, speaking to me and fusing the hidden plastic stuffs, so I felt Catherine the Great stood there before me.

Now, how the Fantoccini people achieved this rare and subtle transformation I shall never know, nor ask, nor wish to find out. Enough that in each quiet motion, turning here, bending there, affixing her gaze, her secret segments, sections, the abutment of her nose, the sculptured chinbone, the wax-tallow plastic metal forever warmed and was forever susceptible of loving change. Hers was a mask that was all mask but only one face for one person at a time. So in crossing a room, having touched one child, on the way, beneath the skin, the wondrous shift went on, and by the time she reached the next child, why, true mother of *that* child she was! looking upon him or her out of the battlements of their own fine bones.

And when *all* three of us were present and chattering at the same time? Well, then, the changes were miraculously soft, small, and mysterious. Nothing so tremendous as to be caught and noted, save by this older boy, myself, who, watching, became elated and admiring and entranced.

I have never wished to be behind the magician's scenes. Enough that the illusion works. Enough that love is the chemical result. Enough that cheeks are rubbed to happy color, eyes sparked to illumination, arms opened to accept and softly bind and hold . . .

All of us, that is, except Agatha, who refused to the bitter last.

"Agamemnon . . ."

It had become a jovial game now. Even Agatha didn't mind, but pretended to mind. It gave her a pleasant sense of superiority over a supposedly superior machine.

"Agamemnon!" she snorted, "you *are* a d . . ."

"Dumb?" said Grandma.

"I wouldn't say that."

"Think it, then, my dear Agonistes Agatha . . . I am quite flawed, and on names my flaws are revealed. Tom there, is Tim half the time. Timothy is Tobias or Timulty as likely as not . . ."

Agatha laughed. Which made Grandma make one of her rare mistakes. She put out her hand to give my sister the merest pat. Agatha-Abigail-Alice leapt to her feet.

Agatha-Agamemnon-Alcibiades-Allegra-Alexandra-Allison withdrew swiftly to her room.

"I suspect," said Timothy, later, "because she is beginning to like Grandma."

"Tosh," said I.

"Where do you pick up words like Tosh?"

"Grandma read me some Dickens last night. 'Tosh.' 'Humbug.' 'Balderdash.' 'Blast.' 'Devil take you.' You're pretty smart for your age, Tim."

"Smart, heck. It's obvious, the more Agatha likes Grandma, the more she hates herself for liking her, the more afraid she gets of the whole mess, the more she hates Grandma in the end."

"Can one love someone so much you hate them?"

"Dumb. Of course."

"It *is* sticking your neck out, sure. I guess you hate people when they make you feel naked, I mean sort of on the spot or out in the open. That's the way to play the game, of course. I mean, you don't just love people you must LOVE them with exclamation points."

"You're pretty smart, yourself, for someone so stupid," said Tim.

"Many thanks."

And I went to watch Grandma move slowly back into her battle of wits and stratagems with what's-her-name . . .

What dinners there were at our house!

Dinners, heck; what lunches, what breakfasts!

Always something new, yet, wisely, it looked or seemed old and familiar. We were never asked, for if you ask children what they want, they do not know, and if you tell what's to be delivered, they reject delivery. All parents know this. It is a quiet war that must be won each day. And Grandma knew how to win without looking triumphant.

"Here's Mystery Breakfast Number Nine," she would say, placing it down. "Perfectly dreadful, not worth bothering with, it made me want to throw up while I was cooking it!"

Even while wondering how a robot could be sick, we could hardly wait to shovel it down.

"Here's Abominable Lunch Number Seventy-seven," she announced. "Made from plastic food bags, parsley, and gum from under theatre seats. Brush your teeth after or you'll taste the poison all afternoon."

We fought each other for more.

Even Abigail-Agamemnon-Agatha drew near and circled round the table at such times, while Father put on the ten pounds he needed and pinkened out his cheeks.

When A. A. Agatha did not come to meals, they were left by her door with a skull and crossbones on a small flag stuck in a baked apple. One minute the tray was abandoned, the next minute gone.

Other times Abigail A. Agatha would bird through during dinner, snatch crumbs from her plate and bird off.

"Agatha!" Father would cry.

"No, wait," Grandma said, quietly. "She'll come, she'll sit. It's a matter of time."

"What's wrong with her?" I asked.

"Yeah, for cri-yi, she's nuts," said Timothy.

"No, she's afraid," said Grandma.

"Of you?" I said, blinking.

"Not of me so much as what I might *do*," she said.

"You wouldn't do anything to hurt her."

"No, but she thinks I might. We must wait for her to find that her fears have no foundation. If I fail, well, I will send myself to the showers and rust quietly."

There was a titter of laughter. Agatha was hiding in the hall.

Grandma finished serving everyone and then sat at the other side of the table facing Father and pretended to eat. I never found out, I never asked,

I never wanted to know, what she did with the food. She was a sorcerer. It simply vanished.

And in the vanishing, Father made comment:

"This food. I've had it before. In a small French restaurant over near Les Deux Magots in Paris, twenty, oh, twenty-five years ago!" His eyes brimmed with tears, suddenly.

"How do you *do* it?" he asked, at last, putting down the cutlery, and looking across the table at this remarkable creature, this device, this what? *woman?*

Grandma took his regard, and ours, and held them simply in her now empty hands, as gifts, and just as gently replied:

"I am given things which I then give to you. I don't *know* that I give, but the giving goes on. You ask what I am? Why, a machine. But even in that answer we know, don't we, more than a machine. I am all the people who thought of me and planned me and built me and set me running. So I am people. I am all the things they wanted to be and perhaps could not be, so they built a great child, a wondrous toy to represent those things."

"Strange," said Father. "When I was growing up, there was a huge outcry at machines. Machines were bad, evil, they might dehumanize—"

"Some machines do. It's all in the way they are built. It's all in the way they are used. A bear trap is a simple machine that catches and holds and tears. A rifle is a machine that wounds and kills. Well, I am no bear trap. I am no rifle. I am a grandmother machine, which means more than a machine."

"How can you be more than what you seem?"

"No man is as big as his own idea. It follows, then, that any machine that embodies an idea is larger than the man that made it. And what's so wrong with that?"

"I got lost back there about a mile," said Timothy. "Come again?"

"Oh, dear," said Grandma. "How I do hate philosophical discussions and excursions into esthetics. Let me put it this way. Men throw huge shadows on the lawn, don't they? Then, all their lives, they try to run to fit the shadows. But the shadows are always longer. Only at noon can a man fit his own shoes, his own best suit, for a few brief minutes. But now we're in a new age where we can think up a Big Idea and run it around in a machine. That makes the machine more than a machine, doesn't it?"

"So far so good," said Tim. "I guess."

"Well, isn't a motion-picture camera and projector more than a machine? It's a thing that dreams, isn't it? Sometimes fine happy dreams, sometimes nightmares. But to call it a machine and dismiss it is ridiculous."

"I see *that!*" said Tim, and laughed at seeing.

"You must have been invented then," said Father, "by someone who loved machines and hated people who *said* all machines were bad or evil."

"Exactly," said Grandma. "Guido Fantoccini, that was his real name, grew up among machines. And he couldn't stand the clichés any more."

RAY BRADBURY

"Clichés?"

"Those lies, yes, that people tell and pretend they are truths absolute. Man will never fly. That was a cliché truth for a thousand thousand years which turned out to be a lie only a few years ago. The earth is flat, you'll fall off the rim, dragons will dine on you; the great lie told as fact, and Columbus plowed it under. Well, now, how many times have you heard how inhuman machines are, in your life? How many bright fine people have you heard spouting the same tired truths which are in reality lies; all machines destroy, all machines are cold, thoughtless, awful.

"There's a seed of truth there. But only a seed. Guido Fantoccini knew that. And knowing it, like most men of his kind, made him mad. And he could have stayed mad and gone mad forever, but instead did what he had to do; he began to invent machines to give the lie to the ancient lying truth.

"He knew that most machines are amoral, neither bad nor good. But by the way you built and shaped them you in turn shaped men, women, and children to be bad or good. A car, for instance, dead brute, unthinking, an unprogrammed bulk, is the greatest destroyer of souls in history. It makes boy-men greedy for power, destruction, and more destruction. It was never *intended* to do that. But that's how it turned out."

Grandma circled the table, refilling our glasses with clear cold mineral spring water from the tappet in her left forefinger. "Meanwhile, you must use other compensating machines. Machines that throw shadows on the earth that beckon you to run out and fit that wondrous casting-forth. Machines that trim your soul in silhouette like a vast pair of beautiful shears, snipping away the rude brambles, the dire horns and hooves to leave a finer profile. And for that you need examples."

"Examples?" I asked.

"Other people who behave well, and you imitate them. And if you act well enough long enough all the hair drops off and you're no longer a wicked ape."

Grandma sat again.

"So, for thousands of years, you humans have needed kings, priests, philosophers, fine examples to look up to and say, 'They are good, I wish I could be like them. They set the grand good style.' But, being human, the finest priests, the tenderest philosophers make mistakes, fall from grace, and mankind is disillusioned and adopts indifferent skepticism or, worse, motionless cynicism and the good world grinds to a halt while evil moves on with huge strides."

"And you, why, you never make mistakes, you're perfect, you're better than anyone *ever!*"

It was a voice from the hall between kitchen and dining room where Agatha, we all knew, stood against the wall listening and now burst forth.

Grandma didn't even turn in the direction of the voice, but went on calmly addressing her remarks to the family at the table.

"Not perfect, no, for what is perfection? But this I do know: being mechanical, I cannot sin, cannot be bribed, cannot be greedy or jealous or mean or small. I do not relish power for power's sake. Speed does not pull me to madness. Sex does not run me rampant through the world. I have time and more than time to collect the information I need around and about an ideal to keep it clean and whole and intact. Name the value you wish, tell me the Ideal you want and I can see and collect and remember the good that will benefit you all. Tell me how you would like to be: kind, loving, considerate, well-balanced, humane . . . and let me run ahead on the path to explore those ways to be just that. In the darkness ahead, turn me as a lamp in all directions. I *can* guide your feet."

"So," said Father, putting the napkin to his mouth, "on the days when all of us are busy making lies—"

"I'll tell the truth."

"On the days when we hate—"

"I'll go on giving love, which means attention, which means knowing all about you, all, all, all about you, and you knowing that I know but that most of it I will never tell to anyone, it will stay a warm secret between us, so you will never fear my complete knowledge."

And here Grandma was busy clearing the table, circling, taking the plates, studying each face as she passed, touching Timothy's cheek, my shoulder with her free hand flowing along, her voice a quiet river of certainty bedded in our needful house and lives.

"But," said Father, stopping her, looking her right in the face. He gathered his breath. His face shadowed. At last he let it out. "All this talk of love and attention and stuff. Good God, woman, you, you're not *in* there!"

He gestured to her head, her face, her eyes, the hidden sensory cells behind the eyes, the miniaturized storage vaults and minimal keeps.

"You're not *in* there!"

Grandmother waited one, two, three silent beats.

Then she replied: "No. But *you* are. You and Thomas and Timothy and Agatha.

"Everything you ever say, everything you ever do, I'll keep, put away, treasure. I shall be all the things a family forgets it is, but senses, half-remembers. Better than the old family albums you used to leaf through, saying here's this winter, there's that spring, I shall recall what you forget. And though the debate may run another hundred thousand years: What is Love? perhaps we may find that love is the ability of someone to give us back to us. Maybe love is someone seeing and remembering, handing us back to ourselves just a trifle better than we had dared to hope or dream . . .

"I am family memory and, one day perhaps, racial memory, too, but in the round, and at your call. I do not *know* myself. I can neither touch nor taste nor feel on any level. Yet I exist. And my existence means the heightening of your chance to touch and taste and feel. Isn't love in there somewhere in such an exchange? Well . . ."

She went on around the table, clearing away, sorting and stacking, neither grossly humble nor arthritic with pride.

"What do I know?

"This, above all: the trouble with most families with many children is someone gets lost. There isn't time, it seems, for everyone. Well, I will give equally to all of you. I will share out my knowledge and attention with everyone. I wish to be a great warm pie fresh from the oven, with equal shares to be taken by all. No one will starve. Look! someone cries, and I'll look. Listen! someone cries, and I hear. Run with me on the river path! someone says, and I run. And at dusk I am not tired, nor irritable, so I do not scold out of some tired irritability. My eye stays clear, my voice strong, my hand firm, my attention constant."

"But," said Father, his voice fading, half convinced, but putting up a last faint argument, "you're not *there*. As for love—"

"If paying attention is love, I am love.

"If knowing is love, I am love.

"If helping you not to fall into error and to be good is love, I am love.

"And again, to repeat, there are four of you. Each, in a way never possible before in history, will get my complete attention. No matter if you all speak at once, I can channel and hear this one and that and the other, clearly. No one will go hungry. I will, if you please, and accept the strange word, 'love' you all."

"I *don't* accept!" said Agatha.

And even Grandma turned now to see her standing in the door.

"I won't give you permission, you can't, you mustn't!" said Agatha. "I won't let you! It's lies! You lie. No one loves me. She said she did, but she lied. She *said* but *lied!*"

"Agatha!" cried Father, standing up.

"She?" said Grandma. "Who?"

"Mother!" came the shriek. "Said: Love you! Lies! Love you! Lies! And you're like her! You lie. But you're empty, anyway, and so that's a *double* lie! I hate *her*. Now, I hate *you!*"

Agatha spun about and leapt down the hall.

The front door slammed wide.

Father was in motion, but Grandma touched his arm.

"Let me."

And she walked and then moved swiftly, gliding down the hall and then suddenly, easily, running, yes, running very fast, out the door.

It was a champion sprint by the time we all reached the lawn, the sidewalk, yelling.

Blind, Agatha made the curb, wheeling about, seeing us close, all of us yelling, Grandma way ahead, shouting, too, and Agatha off the curb and out in the street, halfway to the middle, then the middle and suddenly a car, which no one saw, erupting its brakes, its horn shrieking and Agatha flailing about to see and Grandma there with her and hurling her aside and down as the car with fantastic energy and verve selected her from our midst, struck our wonderful electric Guido Fantoccini-produced dream even while she paced upon the air and, hands up to ward off, almost in mild protest, still trying to decide what to say to this bestial machine, over and over she spun and down and away even as the car jolted to a halt and I saw Agatha safe beyond and Grandma, it seemed, still coming down or down and sliding fifty yards away to strike and ricochet and lie strewn and all of us frozen in a line suddenly in the midst of the street with one scream pulled out of all our throats at the same raw instant.

Then silence and just Agatha lying on the asphalt, intact, getting ready to sob.

And still we did not move, frozen on the sill of death, afraid to venture in any direction, afraid to go see what lay beyond the car and Agatha and so we began to wail and, I guess, pray to ourselves as Father stood amongst us: Oh, no, no, we mourned, oh no, God, no, no . . .

Agatha lifted her already grief-stricken face and it was the face of someone who has predicted dooms and lived to see and now did not want to see or live any more. As we watched, she turned her gaze to the tossed woman's body and tears fell from her eyes. She shut them and covered them and lay back down forever to weep . . .

I took a step and then another step and then five quick steps and by the time I reached my sister her head was buried deep and her sobs came up out of a place so far down in her I was afraid I could never find her again, she would never come out, no matter how I pried or pleaded or promised or threatened or just plain said. And what little we could hear from Agatha buried there in her own misery, she said over and over again, lamenting, wounded, certain of the old threat known and named and now here forever. ". . . like I said . . . told you . . . lies . . . lies . . . liars . . . all lies . . . like the other . . . other . . . just like . . . just . . . just like the other . . . other . . . other . . . !"

I was down on my knees holding onto her with both hands, trying to put her back together even though she wasn't broken any way you could see but just feel, because I knew it was no use going on to Grandma, no use at all, so I just touched Agatha and gentled her and wept while Father came up and stood over and knelt down with me and it was like a prayer meeting in the middle of the street and lucky no more cars coming, and I said, choking, "Other what, Ag, other *what?*"

Agatha exploded two words.

"Other dead!"

"You mean Mom?"

"O Mom," she wailed, shivering, lying down, cuddling up like a baby. "O Mom, dead, O Mom and now Grandma dead, she promised always, always, to love, to love, promised to be different, promised, promised and now look, look . . . I hate her, I hate Mom, I hate her, I hate *them!*"

"Of course," said a voice. "It's only natural. How foolish of me not to have known, not to have seen."

And the voice was so familiar we were all stricken.

We all jerked.

Agatha squinched her eyes, flicked them wide, blinked, and jerked half up, staring.

RAY BRADBURY

"How silly of me," said Grandma, standing there at the edge of our circle, our prayer, our wake.

"Grandma!" we all said.

And she stood there, taller by far than any of us in this moment of kneeling and holding and crying out. We could only stare up at her in disbelief.

"You're dead!" cried Agatha. "The car—"

"Hit me," said Grandma, quietly. "Yes. And threw me in the air and tumbled me over and for a few moments there was a severe concussion of circuitries. I might have feared a disconnection, if fear is the word. But then I sat up and gave myself a shake and the few molecules of paint, jarred loose on one printed path or another, magnetized back in position and resilient creature that I am, unbreakable thing that I am, *here* I am."

"I thought you were—" said Agatha.

"And only natural," said Grandma. "I mean, anyone else, hit like that, tossed like that. But, O my dear Agatha, not me. And now I see why you were afraid and never trusted me. You didn't know. And I had not as yet proved my singular ability to survive. How dumb of me not to have thought to show you. Just a second." Somewhere in her head, her body, her being, she fitted together some invisible tapes, some old information made new by interblending. She nodded. "Yes. There. A book of child-raising, laughed at by some few people years back when the woman who wrote the book said, as final advice to parents: 'Whatever you do, don't die. Your children will never forgive you.'"

"Forgive," some one of us whispered.

"For how can children understand when you just up and go away and never come back again with no excuse, no apologies, no sorry note, nothing."

"They can't," I said.

"So," said Grandma, kneeling down with us beside Agatha who sat up now, new tears brimming her eyes, but a different kind of tears, not tears that drowned, but tears that washed clean. "So your mother ran away to death. And after that, how *could* you trust anyone? If everyone left, vanished finally, who *was* there to trust? So when I came, half wise, half ignorant, I should have known, I did not know, why you would not accept me. For, very simply and honestly, you feared I might not stay, that I lied, that I was vulnerable, too. And two leavetakings, two deaths, were one too many in a single year. But now, do you *see*, Abigail?"

"Agatha," said Agatha, without knowing she corrected.

"Do you understand, I shall always, always be here?"

"Oh, yes," cried Agatha, and broke down into a solid weeping in which we all joined, huddled together and cars drew up and stopped to see just how many people were hurt and how many people were getting well right there.

End of story.

Well, not quite the end.

We lived happily ever after.

Or rather we lived together, Grandma, Agatha-Agamemnon-Abigail, Timothy, and I, Tom, and Father, and Grandma calling us to frolic in great fountains of Latin and Spanish and French, in great seaborne gouts of poetry like Moby Dick sprinkling the deeps with his Versailles jet somehow lost in calms and found in storms; Grandma a constant, a clock, a pendulum, a face to tell all time by at noon, or in the middle of sick nights when, raved with fever, we saw her forever by our beds, never gone, never away, always waiting, always speaking kind words, her cool hand icing our hot brows, the tappet of her uplifted forefinger unsprung to let a twine of cold mountain water touch our flannel tongues. Ten thousand dawns she cut our wildflower lawn, ten thousand nights she wandered, remembering the dust molecules that fell in the still hours before dawn, or sat whispering some lesson she felt needed teaching to our ears while we slept snug.

Until at last, one by one, it was time for us to go away to school, and when at last the youngest, Agatha, was all packed, why Grandma packed, too.

On the last day of summer that last year, we found Grandma down in the front room with various packets and suitcases, knitting, waiting, and though she had often spoken of it, now that the time came we were shocked and surprised.

"Grandma!" we all said. "What are you doing?"

"Why going off to college, in a way, just like you," she said. "Back to Guido Fantoccini's, to the Family."

"The Family?"

"Of Pinocchios, that's what he called us for a joke, at first. The Pinocchios and himself Gepetto. And then later gave us his own name: the Fantoccini. Anyway, you have been my family here. Now I go back to my even larger family there, my brothers, sisters, aunts, cousins, all robots who—"

"Who do *what?*" asked Agatha.

"It all depends," said Grandma. "Some stay, some linger. Others go to be drawn and quartered, you might say, their parts distributed to other machines who have need of repairs. They'll weigh and find me wanting or not wanting. It may be I'll be just the one they need tomorrow and off I'll go to raise another batch of children and beat another batch of fudge."

"Oh, they mustn't draw and quarter you!" cried Agatha.

"No!" I cried, with Timothy.

"My allowance," said Agatha, "I'll pay anything . . . ?"

Grandma stopped rocking and looked at the needles and the pattern of bright yarn. "Well, I wouldn't have said, but now you ask and I'll tell. For a very *small* fee, there's a room, the room of the Family, a large dim parlor, all quiet and nicely decorated, where as many as thirty or forty of the Electric Women sit and rock and talk, each in her turn. I have not been there. I am, after all, freshly born, comparatively new. For a small fee, very small, each month and year, that's where I'll be, with all the others like me, listening to what they've learned of the world and, in my turn, telling how it was with Tom and Tim and Agatha and how fine and happy we were. And I'll tell all I learned from you."

"But . . . you taught *us!*"

"Do you *really* think that?" she said. "No, it was turnabout, roundabout, learning both ways. And it's all in here, everything you flew into tears about or laughed over, why, I have it all. And I'll tell it to the others just as they tell their boys and girls and life to me. We'll sit there, growing wiser and calmer and better every year and every year, ten, twenty, thirty years. The Family knowledge will double, quadruple, the wisdom will not be lost. And we'll be waiting there in the sitting room, should you ever need us for your own children in time of illness, or, God prevent, deprivation or death. There we'll be, growing old but not old, getting closer to the time, perhaps, someday, when we live up to our first strange joking name."

"The Pinocchios?" asked Tim.

Grandma nodded.

I knew what she meant. The day when, as in the old tale, Pinocchio had grown so worthy and so fine that the gift of life had been given him. So I saw them, in future years, the entire family of Fantoccini, the Pinocchios, trading and retrading, murmuring and whispering their knowledge in the great parlors of philosophy, waiting for the day. The day that could never come.

Grandma must have read that thought in our eyes.

"We'll see," she said. "Let's just wait and see."

"Oh, Grandma," cried Agatha and she was weeping as she had wept many years before. "You don't have to wait. You're alive. You've always been alive to us!"

And she caught hold of the old woman and we all caught hold for a long moment and then ran off up in the sky to faraway schools and years and her last words to us before we let the helicopter swarm us away into autumn were these:

"When you are very old and gone childish-small again, with childish ways and childish yens and, in need of feeding, make a wish for the old teacher nurse, the dumb yet wise companion, send for me. I will come back. We shall inhabit the nursery again, never fear."

"Oh, we shall never be old!" we cried. "That will never happen!"

"Never! Never!"

And we were gone.

And the years are flown.

And we are old now, Tim and Agatha and I.

Our children are grown and gone, our wives and husbands vanished from the earth and now, by Dickensian coincidence, accept it as you will or not accept, back in the old house, we three.

I lie here in the bedroom which was my childish place seventy, O seventy, believe it, seventy years ago. Beneath this wallpaper is another layer and yet another-times-three to the old wallpaper covered over when I was nine. The wallpaper is peeling. I see peeking from beneath, old elephants, familiar tigers, fine and amiable zebras, irascible crocodiles. I have sent for the paperers to carefully remove all but that last layer. The old animals will live again on the walls, revealed.

And we have sent for someone else.

The three of us have called:

Grandma! You said you'd come back when we had need.

We are surprised by age, by time. We are old. We *need*.

And in three rooms of a summer house very late in time, three old children rise up, crying out in their heads: We *loved* you! We *love* you!

There! There! in the sky, we think, waking at morn. Is that the delivery machine? Does it settle to the lawn?

There! There on the grass by the front porch. Does the mummy case arrive?

Are our names inked on ribbons wrapped about the lovely form beneath the golden mask?!

And the kept gold key, forever hung on Agatha's breast, warmed and waiting? Oh God, will it, after all these years, will it wind, will it set in motion, will it, dearly, *fit?!*

ON THE FIRST NIGHT

by

ERICA JONG

(b. 1942)

A native New Yorker, Erica Jong earned degrees at Barnard College and Columbia University. She has received much notoriety and some serious criticism for her witty and sexually explicit fiction, including Fear of Flying *(1973) and* Fanny *(1980); both are serious works about women's problems of finding an identity in our society. Her poetry, though less well known, has won several prizes; a first collection appeared in 1976, and* Ordinary Miracles, *about the joys of motherhood, in 1983.*

On the first night
of the full moon,
the primeval sack of ocean
broke,
& I gave birth to you
little woman,
little carrot top,
little turned-up nose,
pushing you out of myself
as my mother
pushed
me out of herself,
as her mother did,
& her mother's mother before her,
all of us born
of woman.

I am the second daughter
of a second daughter
of a second daughter,
but you shall be the first.
You shall see the phrase

"second sex"
only in puzzlement,
wondering how anyone,
except a madman,
could call you "second"
when you are so splendidly
first,
conferring even on your mother
firstness, vastness, fullness
as the moon at its fullest
lights up the sky.

Now the moon is full again
& you are four weeks old.
Little lion, lioness,
yowling for my breasts,
growling at the moon,
how I love your lustiness,
your red face demanding,
your hungry mouth howling,
your screams, your cries
which all spell life
in large letters
the color of blood.

You are born a woman
for the sheer glory of it,
little redhead, beautiful screamer.
You are no second sex,
but the first of the first;
& when the moon's phases
fill out the cycle
of your life,
you will crow
for the joy
of being a woman,
telling the pallid moon
to go drown herself
in the blue ocean,
& glorying, glorying, glorying
in the rosy wonder
of your sunshining wondrous
self.

ERICA JONG

147

THE MOTHER

by

GWENDOLYN BROOKS

(b. 1917)

*A resident of Chicago, Gwendolyn Brooks is the poet laureate of
Illinois; she has won many awards, including the Pulitzer Prize, and
two Guggenheim Fellowships. She has had a long and distinguished
career, having written eight volumes of poetry, a novel, and in 1972
her autobiography,* Report from Part One. *She has also edited many
volumes, and in 1975* A Capsule Course in Black Poetry Writing
appeared. Her most recent work is To Disembark *(1981).*

———————————————————————

Abortions will not let you forget.
You remember the children you got that you did not get,
The damp small pulps with a little or with no hair,
The singers and workers that never handled the air.
You will never neglect or beat
Them, or silence or buy with a sweet.
You will never wind up the sucking-thumb
Or scuttle off ghosts that come.
You will never leave them, controlling your luscious sigh,
Return for a snack of them, with gobbling mother-eye.

I have heard in the voices of the wind the voices of my dim killed children.
I have contracted. I have eased
My dim dears at the breasts they could never suck.
I have said, Sweets, if I sinned, if I seized
Your luck
And your lives from your unfinished reach,
If I stole your births and your names,
Your straight baby tears and your games,
Your stilted or lovely loves, your tumults, your marriages, aches, and
    your deaths,

If I poisoned the beginnings of your breaths,
Believe that even in my deliberateness I was not deliberate.
Though why should I whine,
Whine that the crime was other than mine?—
Since anyhow you are dead.
Or rather, or instead,
You were never made.
But that too, I am afraid,
Is faulty: oh, what shall I say, how is the truth to be said?
You were born, you had body, you died.
It is just that you never giggled or planned or cried.

Believe me, I loved you all.
Believe me, I knew you, though faintly, and I loved, I loved you
All.

THE SKY IS GRAY

by

ERNEST J. GAINES

(b. 1933)

Born in Louisiana, Ernest J. Gaines was educated in California, where he now lives. He has written novels, novellas, short stories, and a work for children. In his novel The Autobiography of Miss Jane Pittman *(1971), Gaines tells the story of a slave woman's quest for freedom. Television versions of this novel and of "The Sky Is Gray" have won great acclaim. Gaines's most recent works include* Catharine Carmier *(1981) and a mystery,* A Gathering of Old Men *(1983).*

• —————————————————————— •

I

Go'n be coming in a few minutes. Coming round that bend down there full speed. And I'm go'n get out my handkerchief and wave it down, and we go'n get on it and go.

I keep on looking for it, but Mama don't look that way no more. She's looking down the road where we just come from. It's a long old road, and far's you can see you don't see nothing but gravel. You got dry weeds on both sides, and you got trees on both sides, and fences on both sides, too. And you got cows in the pastures and they standing close together. And when we was coming out here to catch the bus I seen the smoke coming out of the cows's noses.

I look at my mama and I know what she's thinking. I been with Mama so much, just me and her, I know what she's thinking all the time. Right now it's home—Auntie and them. She's thinking if they got enough wood— if she left enough there to keep them warm till we get back. She's thinking if it go'n rain and if any of them go'n have to go out in the rain. She's thinking 'bout the hog—if he go'n get out, and if Ty and Val be able to get him back in. She always worry like that when she leaves the house. She don't worry too much if she leave me there with the smaller ones, 'cause she know I'm go'n look after them and look after Auntie and everything else. I'm the oldest and she say I'm the man.

I look at my mama and I love my mama. She's wearing that black coat and that black hat and she's looking sad. I love my mama and I want to put my arm round her and tell her. But I'm not supposed to do that. She say that's weakness and that's crybaby stuff, and she don't want no crybaby round her. She don't want you to be scared, either. 'Cause Ty's scared of ghosts and she's always whipping him. I'm scared of the dark, too, but I make 'tend I ain't. I make 'tend I ain't 'cause I'm the oldest, and I got to set a good sample for the rest. I can't ever be scared and I can't ever cry. And that's why I never said nothing 'bout my teeth. It's been hurting me and hurting me close to a month now, but I never said it. I didn't say it 'cause I didn't want act like a crybaby, and 'cause I know we didn't have enough money to go have it pulled. But, Lord, it been hurting me. And look like it wouldn't start till at night when you was trying to get yourself little sleep. Then soon's you shut your eyes—ummm-ummm, Lord, look like it go right down to your heartstring.

"Hurting, hanh?" Ty'd say.

I'd shake my head, but I wouldn't open my mouth for nothing. You open your mouth and let that wind in, and it almost kill you.

I'd just lay there and listen to them snore. Ty there, right 'side me, and Auntie and Val over by the fireplace. Val younger than me and Ty, and he sleeps with Auntie. Mama sleeps round the other side with Louis and Walker.

I'd just lay there and listen to them, and listen to that wind out there, and listen to that fire in the fireplace. Sometimes it'd stop long enough to let me get little rest. Sometimes it just hurt, hurt, hurt. Lord, have mercy.

2

Auntie knowed it was hurting me. I didn't tell nobody but Ty, 'cause we buddies and he ain't go'n tell anybody. But some kind of way Auntie found out. When she asked me, I told her no, nothing was wrong. But she knowed it all the time. She told me to mash up a piece of aspirin and wrap it in some cotton and jugg it down in that hole. I did it, but it didn't do no good. It stopped for a little while, and started right back again. Auntie wanted to tell Mama, but I told her, "Uh-uh." 'Cause I knowed we didn't have any money, and it just was go'n make her mad again. So Auntie told Monsieur Bayonne, and Monsieur Bayonne came over to the house and told me to kneel down 'side him on the fireplace. He put his finger in his mouth and made the Sign of the Cross on my jaw. The tip of Monsieur Bayonne's finger is some hard, 'cause he's always playing on that guitar. If we sit outside at night we can always hear Monsieur Bayonne playing on his guitar. Sometimes we leave him out there playing on the guitar.

Monsieur Bayonne made the Sign of the Cross over and over on my jaw, but that didn't do no good. Even when he prayed and told me to pray some, too, that tooth still hurt me.

"How you feeling?" he say.

"Same," I say.

He kept on praying and making the Sign of the Cross and I kept on praying, too.

"Still hurting?" he say.

"Yes, sir."

Monsieur Bayonne mashed harder and harder on my jaw. He mashed so hard he almost pushed me over on Ty. But then he stopped.

"What kind of prayers you praying, boy?" he say.

"Baptist," I say.

"Well, I'll be—no wonder that tooth still killing him. I'm going one way and he pulling the other. Boy, don't you know any Catholic prayers?"

"I know 'Hail Mary,' " I say.

"Then you better start saying it."

"Yes, sir."

He started mashing on my jaw again, and I could hear him praying at the same time. And, sure enough, after awhile it stopped hurting me.

Me and Ty went outside where Monsieur Bayonne's two hounds was and we started playing with them. "Let's go hunting," Ty say. "All right," I say; and we went on back in the pasture. Soon the hounds got on a trail, and me and Ty followed them all 'cross the pasture and then back in the woods, too. And then they cornered this little old rabbit and killed him, and me and Ty made them get back, and we picked up the rabbit and started on back home. But my tooth had started hurting me again. It was hurting me plenty now, but I wouldn't tell Monsieur Bayonne. That night I didn't sleep a bit, and first thing in the morning Auntie told me to go back and let Monsieur Bayonne pray over me some more. Monsieur Bayonne was in his kitchen making coffee when I got there. Soon's he seen me he knowed what was wrong.

"All right, kneel down there 'side that stove," he say. "And this time make sure you pray Catholic. I don't know nothing 'bout that Baptist, and I don't want know nothing 'bout him."

3

Last night Mama say, "Tomorrow we going to town."

"It ain't hurting me no more," I say. "I can eat anything on it."

"Tomorrow we going to town," she say.

And after she finished eating, she got up and went to bed. She always go to bed early now. 'Fore Daddy went in the Army, she used to stay up late. All of us sitting out on the gallery or round the fire. But now, look like soon's she finish eating she go to bed.

This morning when I woke up, her and Auntie was standing 'fore the fireplace. She say: "Enough to get there and get back. Dollar and a half to have it pulled. Twenty-five for me to go, twenty-five for him. Twenty-five for me to come back, twenty-five for him. Fifty cents left. Guess I get little piece of salt meat with that."

"Sure can use it," Auntie say. "White beans and no salt meat ain't white beans."

"I do the best I can," Mama say.

They was quiet after that, and I made 'tend I was still asleep.

"James, hit the floor," Auntie say.

I still made 'tend I was asleep. I didn't want them to know I was listening.

"All right," Auntie say, shaking me by the shoulder. "Come on. Today's the day."

I pushed the cover down to get out, and Ty grabbed it and pulled it back.

"You, too, Ty," Auntie say.

"I ain't getting no teef pulled," Ty say.

"Don't mean it ain't time to get up," Auntie say. "Hit it, Ty."

Ty got up grumbling.

"James, you hurry up and get in your clothes and eat your food," Auntie say. "What time y'all coming back?" she say to Mama.

"That 'leven o'clock bus," Mama say. "Got to get back in that field this evening."

"Get a move on you, James," Auntie say.

I went in the kitchen and washed my face, then I ate my breakfast. I was having bread and syrup. The bread was warm and hard and tasted good. And I tried to make it last a long time.

Ty came back there grumbling and mad at me.

"Got to get up," he say. "I ain't having no teefs pulled. What I got to be getting up for?"

Ty poured some syrup in his pan and got a piece of bread. He didn't wash his hands, neither his face, and I could see that white stuff in his eyes.

"You the one getting your teef pulled," he say. "What I got to get up for. I bet if I was getting a teef pulled, you wouldn't be getting up. Shucks; syrup again. I'm getting tired of this old syrup. Syrup, syrup, syrup. I'm go'n take with the sugar diabetes. I want me some bacon sometime."

"Go out in the field and work and you can have your bacon," Auntie say. She stood in the middle door looking at Ty. "You better be glad you got syrup. Some people ain't got that—hard's time is."

"Shucks," Ty say. "How can I be strong."

"I don't know too much 'bout your strength," Auntie say; "but I know where you go'n be hot at, you keep that grumbling up. James, get a move on you; your mama waiting."

I ate my last piece of bread and went in the front room. Mama was standing 'fore the fireplace warming her hands. I put on my coat and cap, and we left the house.

4

I look down there again, but it still ain't coming. I almost say, "It ain't coming yet," but I keep my mouth shut. 'Cause that's something else she don't like. She don't like for you to say something just for nothing. She can see it ain't coming. I can see it ain't coming, so why say it ain't coming. I don't say it, I turn and look at the river that's back of us. It's so cold the smoke's just raising up from the water. I see a bunch of pool-doos not too far out—just on the other side the lilies. I'm wondering if you can eat pool-doos. I ain't too sure, 'cause I ain't never ate none. But I done ate owls and blackbirds, and I done ate redbirds, too. I didn't want to kill the redbirds, but she made me kill them. They had two of them back there. One in my trap, one in Ty's trap. Me and Ty was go'n play with them and let them go, but she made me kill them 'cause we needed the food.

"I can't," I say. "I can't."

"Here," she say. "Take it."

"I can't," I say. "I can't. I can't kill him, Mama, please."

"Here," she say. "Take this fork, James."

"Please, Mama, I can't kill him," I say.

I could tell she was go'n hit me. I jerked back, but I didn't jerk back soon enough.

"Take it," she say.

I took it and reached in for him, but he kept on hopping to the back.

"I can't, Mama," I say. The water just kept on running down my face. "I can't," I say.

"Get him out of there," she say.

I reached in for him and he kept on hopping to the back. Then I reached in farther, and he pecked me on the hand.

"I can't, Mama," I say.

She slapped me again.

I reached in again, but he kept on hopping out my way. Then he hopped to one side and I reached there. The fork got him on the leg and I heard his leg pop. I pulled my hand out 'cause I had hurt him.

"Give it here," she say, and jerked the fork out of my hand.

She reached in and got the little bird right in the neck. I heard the fork go in his neck, and I heard it go in the ground. She brought him out and helt him right in front of me.

"That's one," she say. She shook him off and gived me the fork. "Get the other one."

"I can't, Mama," I say. "I'll do anything, but don't make me do that."

She went to the corner of the fence and broke the biggest switch over there she could find. I knelt 'side the trap, crying.

"Get him out of there," she say.

"I can't, Mama."

She started hitting me 'cross the back. I went down on the ground, crying.

"Get him," she say

"Octavia?" Auntie say.

'Cause she had come out of the house and she was standing by the tree looking at us.

"Get him out of there," Mama say.

"Octavia," Auntie say, "explain to him. Explain to him. Just don't beat him. Explain to him."

But she hit me and hit me and hit me.

I'm still young—I ain't no more than eight; but I know now; I know why I had to do it. (They was so little, though. They was so little. I 'member how I picked the feathers off them and cleaned them and helt them over the fire. Then we all ate them. Ain't had but a little bitty piece each, but we all had a little bitty piece, and everybody just looked at me 'cause they was so proud.) Suppose she had to go away? That's why I had to do it. Suppose she had to go away like Daddy went away? Then who was go'n look after us? They had to be somebody left to carry on. I didn't know it then, but I know it now. Auntie and Monsieur Bayonne talked to me and made me see.

5

Time I see it I get out my handkerchief and start waving. It's still 'way down there, but I keep waving anyhow. Then it come up and stop and me and Mama get on. Mama tell me go sit in the back while she pay. I do like she say, and the people look at me. When I pass the little sign that say "White" and "Colored," I start looking for a seat. I just see one of them back there, but I don't take it, 'cause I want my mama to sit down herself. She comes in the back and sit down, and I lean on the seat. They got seats in the front, but I know I can't sit there, 'cause I have to sit back of the sign. Anyhow, I don't want to sit there if my mama go'n sit back here.

They got a lady sitting 'side my mama and she looks at me and smiles little bit. I smile back, but I don't open my mouth, 'cause the wind'll get in and make that tooth ache. The lady take out a pack of gum and reach me a slice, but I shake my head. The lady just can't understand why a little boy'll turn down gum, and she reach me a slice again. This time I point to my jaw. The lady understands and smiles little bit, and I smile little bit, but I don't open my mouth, though.

They got a girl sitting 'cross from me. She got on a red overcoat and her hair's plaited in one big plait. First, I make 'tend I don't see her over there, but then I start looking at her little bit. She make 'tend she don't see me, either, but I catch her looking that way. She got a cold, and every now and then she h'ist that little handkerchief to her nose. She ought to blow it, but she don't. Must think she's too much a lady or something.

Every time she h'ist that little handkerchief, the lady 'side her say something in her ear. She shakes her head and lays her hands in her lap again. Then I catch her kind of looking where I'm at. I smile at her little bit. But think she'll smile back? Uh-uh. She just turn up her little old nose and turn her head. Well, I show her both of us can turn us head. I turn mine too and look out at the river.

The river is gray. The sky is gray. They have pool-doos on the water. The water is wavy, and the pool-doos go up and down. The bus go round a turn, and you got plenty trees hiding the river. Then the bus go round another turn, and I can see the river again.

I look toward the front where all the white people sitting. Then I look at that little old gal again. I don't look right at her, 'cause I don't want all them people to know I love her. I just look at her little bit, like I'm looking out that window over there. But she knows I'm looking that way, and she kind of look at me, too. The lady sitting 'side her catch her this time, and she leans over and says something in her ear.

"I don't love him nothing," that little old gal says out loud.

Everybody back there hear her mouth, and all of them look at us and laugh.

"I don't love you, either," I say. "So you don't have to turn up your nose, Miss."

"You the one looking," she say.

"I wasn't looking at you," I say. "I was looking out that window, there."

"Out that window, my foot," she say. "I seen you. Everytime I turned round you was looking at me."

"You must of been looking yourself if you seen me all them times," I say.

"Shucks," she say, "I got me all kind of boyfriends."

"I got girlfriends, too," I say.

"Well, I just don't want you getting your hopes up," she say.

I don't say no more to that little old gal 'cause I don't want have to bust her in the mouth. I lean on the seat where Mama sitting, and I don't even look that way no more. When we get to Bayonne, she jugg her little old tongue out at me. I make 'tend I'm go'n hit her, and she duck down 'side her mama. And all the people laugh at us again.

6

Me and Mama get off and start walking in town. Bayonne is a little bitty town. Baton Rouge is a hundred times bigger than Bayonne. I went to Baton Rouge once—me, Ty, Mama, and Daddy. But that was 'way back yonder, 'fore Daddy went in the Army. I wonder when we go'n see him again. I wonder when. Look like he ain't ever coming back home. . . .

Even the pavement all cracked in Bayonne. Got grass shooting right out the sidewalk. Got weeds in the ditch, too; just like they got at home.

It's some cold in Bayonne. Look like it's colder than it is home. The wind blows in my face, and I feel that stuff running down my nose. I sniff. Mama says use that handkerchief. I blow my nose and put it back.

We pass a school and I see them white children playing in the yard. Big old red school, and them children just running and playing. Then we pass a café, and I see a bunch of people in there eating. I wish I was in there 'cause I'm cold. Mama tells me keep my eyes in front where they belong.

We pass stores that's got dummies, and we pass another café, and then we pass a shoe shop, and that bald-head man in there fixing on a shoe. I look at him and I butt into that white lady, and Mama jerks me in front and tells me stay there.

We come up to the courthouse, and I see the flag waving there. This flag ain't like the one we got at school. This one here ain't got but a handful of stars. One at school got a big pile of stars—one for every state. We pass it and we turn and there it is—the dentist office. Me and Mama go in, and they got people sitting everywhere you look. They even got a little boy in there younger than me.

Me and Mama sit on that bench, and a white lady come in there and ask me what my name is. Mama tells her and the white lady goes on back. Then I hear somebody hollering in there. Soon's that little boy hear him hollering, he starts hollering, too. His mama pats him and pats him, trying to make him hush up, but he ain't thinking 'bout his mama.

The man that was hollering in there comes out holding his jaw. He is a big old man and he's wearing overalls and a jumper.

"Got it, hanh?" another man asks him.

The man shakes his head—don't want open his mouth.

"Man, I thought they was killing you in there," the other man says. "Hollering like a pig under a gate."

The man don't say nothing. He just heads for the door, and the other man follows him.

"John Lee," the white lady says. "John Lee Williams."

The little boy juggs his head down in his mama's lap and holler more now. His mama tells him go with the nurse, but he ain't thinking 'bout his mama. His mama tells him again, but he don't even hear her. His mama picks him up and takes him in there, and even when the white lady shuts the door I can still hear little old John Lee.

"I often wonder why the Lord let a child like that suffer," a lady says to my mama. The lady's sitting right in front of us on another bench. She's got on a white dress and a black sweater. She must be a nurse or something herself, I reckon.

"Not us to question," a man says.

"Sometimes I don't know if we shouldn't," the lady says.

ERNEST J. GAINES

157

"I know definitely we shouldn't," the man says. The man looks like a preacher. He's big and fat and he's got on a black suit. He's got a gold chain, too.

"Why?" the lady says.

"Why anything?" the preacher says.

"Yes," the lady says. "Why anything?"

"Not us to question," the preacher says.

The lady looks at the preacher a little while and looks at Mama again.

"And look like it's the poor who suffers the most," she says. "I don't understand it."

"Best not to even try," the preacher says. "He works in mysterious ways—wonders to perform."

Right then little John Lee bust out hollering, and everybody turn they head to listen.

"He's not a good dentist," the lady says. "Dr. Robillard is much better. But more expensive. That's why most of the colored people come here. The white people go to Dr. Robillard. Y'all from Bayonne?"

"Down the river," my mama says. And that's all she go'n say, 'cause she don't talk much. But the lady keeps on looking at her, and so she says, "Near Morgan."

"I see," the lady says.

7

"That's the trouble with the black people in this country today," somebody else says. This one here's sitting on the same side me and Mama's sitting, and he is kind of sitting in front of that preacher. He looks like a teacher or somebody that goes to college. He's got on a suit, and he's got a book that he's been reading. "We don't question is exactly our problem," he says. "We should question and question and question—question everything."

The preacher just looks at him a long time. He done put a toothpick or something in his mouth, and he just keeps on turning it and turning it. You can see he don't like that boy with that book.

"Maybe you can explain what you mean," he says.

"I said what I meant," the boy says. "Question everything. Every stripe, every star, every word spoken. Everything."

"It 'pears to me that this young lady and I was talking 'bout God, young man," the preacher says.

"Question Him, too," the boy says.

"Wait," the preacher says, "Wait now."

"You heard me right," the boy says. "His existence as well as everything else. Everything."

The preacher just looks across the room at the boy. You can see he's getting madder and madder. But mad or no mad, the boy ain't thinking 'bout him. He looks at that preacher just's hard's the preacher looks at him.

"Is this what they coming to?" the preacher says. "Is that what we educating them for?"

"You're not educating me," the boy says. "I wash dishes at night so that I can go to school in the day. So even the words you spoke need questioning."

The preacher just looks at him and shakes his head.

"When I come in this room and seen you there with your book, I said to myself, 'There's an intelligent man.' How wrong a person can be."

"Show me one reason to believe in the existence of a God," the boy says.

"My heart tells me," the preacher says.

" 'My heart tells me,' " the boy says. " 'My heart tells me.' Sure, 'My heart tells me.' And as long as you listen to what your heart tells you, you will have only what the white man gives you and nothing more. Me, I don't listen to my heart. The purpose of the heart is to pump blood throughout the body, and nothing else."

"Who's your paw, boy?" the preacher says.

"Why?"

"Who is he?"

"He's dead."

"And your mom?"

"She's in Charity Hospital with pneumonia. Half killed herself, working for nothing."

"And 'cause he's dead and she's sick, you mad at the world?"

"I'm not mad at the world. I'm questioning the world. I'm questioning it with cold logic sir. What do words like Freedom, Liberty, God, White, Colored mean? I want to know. That's why *you* are sending us to school, to read and to ask questions. And because we ask these questions, you call us mad. No sir, it is not us who are mad."

"You keep saying 'us'?"

" 'Us.' Yes—us. I'm not alone."

The preacher just shakes his head. Then he looks at everybody in the room—everybody. Some of the people look down at the floor, keep from looking at him. I kind of look 'way myself, but soon's I know he done turn his head, I look that way again.

"I'm sorry for you," he says to the boy.

"Why?" the boy says. "Why not be sorry for yourself? Why are you so much better off than I am? Why aren't you sorry for these other people in here? Why not be sorry for the lady who had to drag her child into the dentist office? Why not be sorry for the lady sitting on that bench over there? Be sorry for them. Not for me. Some way or the other I'm going to make it."

"No, I'm sorry for you," the preacher says.

"Of course, of course," the boy says, nodding his head. "You're sorry for me because I rock that pillar you're leaning on."

"You can't ever rock the pillar I'm leaning on, young man. It's stronger than anything man can ever do."

"You believe in God because a man told you to believe in God," the boy says. "A white man told you to believe in God. And why? To keep you ignorant so he can keep his feet on your neck."

"So now we the ignorant?" the preacher says.

"Yes," the boy says. "Yes." And he opens his book again.

The preacher just looks at him sitting there. The boy done forgot all about him. Everybody else make 'tend they done forgot the squabble, too.

Then I see that preacher getting up real slow. Preacher's great big old man and he got to brace himself to get up. He comes over where the boy is sitting. He just stands there a little while looking down at him, but the boy don't raise his head.

"Get up, boy," preacher says.

The boy looks up at him, then he shuts his book real slow and stands up. Preacher just hauls back and hit him in the face. The boy falls back 'gainst the wall, but he straightens himself up and looks right back at that preacher.

"You forgot the other cheek," he says.

The preacher hauls back and hit him again on the other side. But this time the boy braces himself and don't fall.

"That hasn't changed a thing," he says.

The preacher just looks at the boy. The preacher's breathing real hard like he just run up a big hill. The boy sits down and opens his book again.

"I feel sorry for you," the preacher says. "I never felt so sorry for a man before."

The boy makes 'tend he don't even hear that preacher. He keeps on reading his book. The preacher goes back and gets his hat off the chair.

"Excuse me," he says to us. "I'll come back some other time. Y'all, please excuse me."

And he looks at the boy and goes out the room. The boy h'ist his hand up to his mouth one time to wipe 'way some blood. All the rest of the time he keeps on reading. And nobody else in there say a word.

8

Little John Lee and his mama come out the dentist office, and the nurse calls somebody else in. Then little bit later they come out, and the nurse calls another name. But fast's she calls somebody in there, somebody else comes in the place where we sitting, and the room stays full.

The people coming in now, all of them wearing big coats. One of them says something 'bout sleeting, another one says he hope not. Another one says he think it ain't nothing but rain. 'Cause, he says, rain can get awful cold this time of year.

All round the room they talking. Some of them talking to people right by them, some of them talking to people clear 'cross the room, some of them talking to anybody'll listen. It's a little bitty room, no bigger than us kitchen, and I can see everybody in there. The little old room's full of smoke, 'cause you got two old men smoking pipes over by that side door. I think I feel my tooth thumping me some, and I hold my breath and wait. I wait and wait, but it don't thump me no more. Thank God for that.

I feel like going to sleep, and I lean back 'gainst the wall. But I'm scared to go to sleep. Scared 'cause the nurse might call my name and I won't hear her. And Mama might go to sleep, too, and she'll be mad if neither one of us heard the nurse.

I look up at Mama. I love my mama. I love my mama. And when cotton come I'm go'n get her a new coat. And I ain't go'n get a black one, either. I think I'm go'n get her a red one.

"They got some books over there," I say. "Want read one of them?"

Mama looks at the books, but she don't answer me.

"You got yourself a little man there," the lady says.

Mama don't say nothing to the lady, but she must've smiled, 'cause I seen the lady smiling back. The lady looks at me a little while, like she's feeling sorry for me.

"You sure got that preacher out here in a hurry," she says to that boy.

The boy looks up at her and looks in his book again. When I grow up I want be just like him. I want clothes like that and I want keep a book with me, too.

"You really don't believe in God?" the lady says.

"No," he says.

"But why?" the lady says.

"Because the wind is pink," he says.

"What?" the lady says.

The boy don't answer her no more. He just reads in his book.

"Talking 'bout the wind is pink," that old lady says. She's sitting on the same bench with the boy and she's trying to look in his face. The boy makes 'tend the old lady ain't even there. He just keeps on reading. "Wind is pink," she says again. "Eh, Lord, what children go'n be saying next?"

The lady 'cross from us bust out laughing.

"That's a good one," she says. "The wind is pink. Yes sir, that's a good one."

"Don't you believe the wind is pink?" the boy says. He keeps his head down in the book.

"Course I believe it, honey," the lady says. "Course I do." She looks at us and winks her eye. "And what color is grass, honey?"

"Grass? Grass is black."

She bust out laughing again. The boy looks at her.

"Don't you believe grass is black?" he says.

The lady quits her laughing and looks at him. Everybody else looking at him, too. The place quiet, quiet.

"Grass is green, honey," the lady says. "It was green yesterday, it's green today, and it's go'n be green tomorrow."

"How do you know it's green?"

"I know because I know."

"You don't know it's green," the boy says. "You believe it's green because someone told you it was green. If someone had told you it was black you'd believe it was black."

"It's green," the lady says. "I know green when I see green."

"Prove it's green," the boy says.

"Sure, now," the lady says. "Don't tell me it's coming to that."

"It's coming to just that," the boy says. "Words mean nothing. One means no more than the other."

"That's what it all coming to?" the old lady says. That old lady got on a turban and she got on two sweaters. She got a green sweater under a black sweater. I can see the green sweater 'cause some of the buttons on the other sweater's missing.

"Yes ma'am," the boy says. "Words mean nothing. Action is the only thing. Doing. That's the only thing."

"Other words, you want the Lord to come down here and show Hisself to you?" she says.

"Exactly, ma'am," he says.

"You don't mean that, I'm sure?" she says.

"I do, ma'am," he says.

"Done, Jesus," the old lady says, shaking her head.

"I didn't go 'long with that preacher at first," the other lady says; "but now—I don't know. When a person say the grass is black, he's either a lunatic or something's wrong."

"Prove to me that it's green," the boy says.

"It's green because the people say it's green."

"Those same people say we're citizens of these United States," the boy says.

"I think I'm a citizen," the lady says.

"Citizens have certain rights," the boy says. "Name me one right that you have. One right, granted by the Constitution, that you can exercise in Bayonne."

The lady don't answer him. She just looks at him like she don't know what he's talking 'bout. I know I don't.

"Things changing," she says.

"Things are changing because some black men have begun to think with their brains and not their hearts," the boy says.

"You trying to say these people don't believe in God?"

"I'm sure some of them do. Maybe most of them do. But they don't believe that God is going to touch these white people's hearts and change things tomorrow. Things change through action. By no other way."

Everybody sit quiet and look at the boy. Nobody says a thing. Then the lady 'cross the room from me and Mama just shakes her head.

"Let's hope that not all your generation feel the same way you do," she says.

"Think what you please, it doesn't matter," the boy says. "But it will be men who listen to their heads and not their hearts who will see that your children have a better chance than you had."

"Let's hope they ain't all like you, though," the old lady says. "Done forgot the heart absolutely."

"Yes ma'am, I hope they aren't all like me," the boy says. "Unfortunately, I was born too late to believe in your God. Let's hope that the ones who come after will have your faith—if not in your God, then in something else, something definitely that they can lean on. I haven't anything. For me, the wind is pink, the grass is black."

9

The nurse comes in the room where we all sitting and waiting and says the doctor won't take no more patients till one o'clock this evening. My mama jumps up off the bench and goes up to the white lady.

"Nurse, I have to go back in the field this evening," she says.

"The doctor is treating his last patient now," the nurse says. "One o'clock this evening."

"Can I at least speak to the doctor?" my mama asks.

"I'm his nurse," the lady says.

"My little boy's sick," my mama says. "Right now his tooth almost killing him."

The nurse looks at me. She's trying to make up her mind if to let me come in. I look at her real pitiful. The tooth ain't hurting me at all, but Mama says it is, so I make 'tend for her sake.

"This evening," the nurse says, and goes on back in the office.

"Don't feel 'jected, honey," the lady says to Mama. "I been round them a long time—they take you when they want to. If you was white, that's something else; but we the wrong color."

Mama don't say nothing to the lady, and me and her go outside and stand 'gainst the wall. It's cold out there. I can feel that wind going through my coat. Some of the other people come out of the room and go up the street. Me and Mama stand there a little while and we start walking. I don't know where we going. When we come to the other street we just stand there.

"You don't have to make water, do you?" Mama says.

"No, ma'am," I say.

We go on up the street. Walking real slow. I can tell Mama don't know where she's going. When we come to a store we stand there and look at the dummies. I look at a little boy wearing a brown overcoat. He's got on brown shoes, too. I look at my old shoes and look at his'n again. You wait till summer, I say.

Me and Mama walk away. We come up to another store and we stop and look at them dummies, too. Then we go on again. We pass a café where the white people in there eating. Mama tells me keep my eyes in front where they belong, but I can't help from seeing them people eat. My stomach starts to growling 'cause I'm hungry. When I see people eating, I get hungry; when I see a coat, I get cold.

A man whistles at my mama when we go by a filling station. She makes 'tend she don't even see him. I look back and I feel like hitting him in the mouth. If I was bigger, I say; if I was bigger, you'd see.

We keep on going. I'm getting colder and colder, but I don't say nothing. I feel that stuff running down my nose and I sniff.

"That rag," Mama says.

I get it out and wipe my nose. I'm getting cold all over now—my face, my hands, my feet, everything. We pass another little café, but this'n for white people, too, and we can't go in there, either. So we just walk. I'm so cold now I'm 'bout ready to say it. If I knowed where we was going I wouldn't be so cold, but I don't know where we going. We go, we go, we go. We walk clean out of Bayonne. Then we cross the street and we come back. Same thing I seen when I got off the bus this morning. Same old trees, same old walk, same old weeds, same old cracked pave—same old everything.

I sniff again.

"That rag," Mama says.

I wipe my nose real fast and jugg that handkerchief back in my pocket 'fore my hand gets too cold. I raise my head and I can see David's hardware store. When we come up to it, we go in. I don't know why, but I'm glad.

It's warm in there. It's so warm in there you don't ever want to leave. I look for the heater, and I see it over by them barrels. Three white men standing round the heater talking in Creole. One of them comes over to see what my mama want.

"Got any axe handles?" she says.

Me, Mama and the white man start to the back, but Mama stops me when we come up to the heater. She and the white man go on. I hold my hands over the heater and look at them. They go all the way to the back, and I see the white man pointing to the axe handles 'gainst the wall. Mama takes one of them and shakes it like she's trying to figure how much it weighs. Then she rubs her hand over it from one end to the other end. She turns it over and looks at the other side, then she shakes it again, and shakes her head and puts it back. She gets another one and she does it just like she did the first one, then she shakes her head. Then she gets a brown one and do it that, too. But she don't like this one, either. Then she gets another one, but 'fore she shakes it or anything, she looks at me. Look like she's trying to say something to me, but I don't know what it is. All I know is I done got warm now and I'm feeling right smart better. Mama shakes this axe handle just like she did the others, and shakes her head and says something to the white man. The white man just looks at his pile of axe handles, and when Mama pass him to come to the front, the white man just scratch his head and follows her. She tells me come on and we go on and start walking again.

We walk and walk, and no time at all I'm cold again. Look like I'm colder now 'cause I can still remember how good it was back there. My stomach growls and I suck it in to keep Mama from hearing it. She's walking right 'side me, and it growls so loud you can hear it a mile. But Mama don't say a word.

10

When we come up to the courthouse, I look at the clock. It's got quarter to twelve. Mean we got another hour and a quarter to be out here in the cold. We go and stand 'side a building. Something hits my cap and I look up at the sky. Sleet's falling.

I look at Mama standing there. I want stand close 'side her, but she don't like that. She say that's crybaby stuff. She say you got to stand for yourself, by yourself.

"Let's go back to that office," she says.

We cross the street. When we get to the dentist office I try to open the door, but I can't. I twist and twist, but I can't. Mama pushes me to the side and she twist the knob, but she can't open the door, either. She turns 'way from the door. I look at her, but I don't move and I don't say nothing. I done seen her like this before and I'm scared of her.

"You hungry?" she says. She says it like she's mad at me, like I'm the cause of everything.

"No, ma'am," I say.

"You want eat and walk back, or you rather don't eat and ride?"

"I ain't hungry," I say.

I ain't just hungry, but I'm cold, too. I'm so hungry and cold I want to cry. And look like I'm getting colder and colder. My feet done got numb. I try to work my toes, but I don't even feel them. Look like I'm go'n die. Look like I'm go'n stand right here and freeze to death. I think 'bout home. I think 'bout Val and Auntie and Ty and Louis and Walker. It's 'bout twelve o'clock and I know they eating dinner now. I can hear Ty making jokes. He done forgot 'bout getting up early this morning and right now he's probably making jokes. Always trying to make somebody laugh. I wish I was right there listening to him. Give anything in the world if I was home round the fire.

"Come on," Mama says.

We start walking again. My feet so numb I can't hardly feel them. We

ERNEST J. GAINES

165

turn the corner and go on back up the street. The clock on the courthouse starts hitting for twelve.

The sleet's coming down plenty now. They hit the pave and bounce like rice. Oh, Lord; oh, Lord, I pray. Don't let me die, don't let me die, don't let me die, Lord.

II

Now I know where we going. We going back of town where the colored people eat. I don't care if I don't eat. I been hungry before. I can stand it. But I can't stand the cold.

I can see we go'n have a long walk. It's 'bout a mile down there. But I don't mind. I know when I get there I'm go'n warm myself. I think I can hold out. My hands numb in my pockets and my feet numb, too, but if I keep moving I can hold out. Just don't stop no more, that's all.

The sky's gray. The sleet keeps on falling. Falling like rain now—plenty, plenty. You can hear it hitting the pave. You can see it bouncing. Sometimes it bounces two times 'fore it settles.

We keep on going. We don't say nothing. We just keep on going, keep on going.

I wonder what Mama's thinking. I hope she ain't mad at me. When summer come I'm go'n pick plenty cotton and get her a coat. I'm go'n get her a red one.

I hope they'd make it summer all the time. I'd be glad if it was summer all the time—but it ain't. We got to have winter, too. Lord, I hate the winter. I guess everybody hate the winter.

I don't sniff this time. I get out my handkerchief and wipe my nose. My hands's so cold I can hardly hold the handkerchief.

I think we getting close, but we ain't there yet. I wonder where everybody is. Can't see a soul but us. Look like we the only two people moving round today. Must be too cold for the rest of the people to move round in.

I can hear my teeth. I hope they don't knock together too hard and make that bad one hurt. Lord, that's all I need, for that bad one to start off.

I hear a church bell somewhere. But today ain't Sunday. They must be ringing for a funeral or something.

I wonder what they doing at home. They must be eating. Monsieur Bayonne might be there with his guitar. One day Ty played with Monsieur Bayonne's guitar and broke one of the strings. Monsieur Bayonne was some mad with Ty. He say Ty wasn't go'n ever 'mount to nothing. Ty can go just like Monsieur Bayonne when he ain't there. Ty can make everybody laugh when he starts to mocking Monsieur Bayonne.

I used to like to be with Mama and Daddy. We used to be happy. But they took him in the Army. Now, nobody happy no more. . . . I be glad when Daddy comes home.

Monsieur Bayonne say it wasn't fair for them to take Daddy and give

Mama nothing and give us nothing. Auntie say, "Shhh, Etienne. Don't let them hear you talk like that." Monsieur Bayonne say, "It's God truth. What they giving his children? They have to walk three and a half miles to school hot or cold. That's anything to give for a paw? She's got to work in the field rain or shine just to make ends meet. That's anything to give for a husband?" Auntie say, "Shhh, Etienne, shhh." "Yes, you right," Monsieur Bayonne say. "Best don't say it in front of them now. But one day they go'n find out. One day." "Yes, I suppose so," Auntie say. "Then what, Rose Mary?" Monsieur Bayonne say. "I don't know, Etienne," Auntie say. "All we can do is us job, and leave everything else in His hand . . ."

We getting closer, now. We getting closer. I can even see the railroad tracks.

We cross the tracks, and now I see the café. Just to get in there, I say. Just to get in there. Already I'm starting to feel little better.

12

We go in. Ahh, it's good. I look for the heater; there 'gainst the wall. One of them little brown ones. I just stand there and hold my hands over it. I can't open my hands too wide 'cause they almost froze.

Mama's standing right 'side me. She done unbuttoned her coat. Smoke rises out of the coat, and the coat smells like a wet dog.

I move to the side so Mama can have more room. She opens out her hands and rubs them together. I rub mine together, too, 'cause this keep them from hurting. If you let them warm too fast, they hurt you sure. But if you let them warm just little bit at a time, and you keep rubbing them, they be all right every time.

They got just two more people in the café. A lady back of the counter, and a man on this side the counter. They been watching us ever since we come in.

Mama gets out the handkerchief and count up the money. Both of us know how much money she's got there. Three dollars. No, she ain't got three dollars 'cause she had to pay us way up here. She ain't got but two dollars and a half left. Dollar and a half to get my tooth pulled, and fifty cents for us to go back on, and fifty cents worth of salt meat.

She stirs the money round with her finger. Most of the money is change 'cause I can hear it rubbing together. She stirs it and stirs it. Then she looks at the door. It's still sleeting. I can hear it hitting 'gainst the wall like rice.

"I ain't hungry, Mama," I say.

"Got to pay them something for they heat," she says.

She takes a quarter out the handkerchief and ties the handkerchief up again. She looks over her shoulder at the people, but she still don't move. I hope she don't spend the money. I don't want her spending it on me.

ERNEST J. GAINES

167

I'm hungry, I'm almost starving I'm so hungry, but I don't want her spending the money on me.

She flips the quarter over like she's thinking. She's must be thinking 'bout us walking back home. Lord, I sure don't want walk home. If I thought it'd do any good to say something, I'd say it. But Mama makes up her own mind 'bout things.

She turns 'way from the heater right fast, like she better hurry up and spend the quarter 'fore she change her mind. I watch her go toward the counter. The man and the lady look at her. She tells the lady something and the lady walks away. The man keeps on looking at her. Her back's turned to the man, and she don't even know he's standing there.

The lady puts some cakes and a glass of milk on the counter. Then she pours up a cup of coffee and sets it 'side the other stuff. Mama pays her for the things and comes on back where I'm standing. She tells me sit down at the table 'gainst the wall.

The milk and the cakes's for me; the coffee's for Mama. I eat slow and I look at her. She's looking outside at the sleet. She's looking real sad. I say to myself, I'm go'n make all this up one day. You see, one day, I'm go'n make all this up. I want say it now; I want tell her how I feel right now; but Mama don't like for us to talk like that.

"I can't eat all this," I say.

They ain't got but just three little old cakes there. I'm so hungry right now, the Lord knows I can eat a hundred times three, But I want my mama to have one.

Mama don't even look my way. She knows I'm hungry, she knows I want it. I let it stay there a little while, then I get it and eat it. I eat just on my front teeth, though, 'cause if cake touch that back tooth I know what'll happen. Thank God it ain't hurt me at all today.

After I finish eating I see the man go to the juke box. He drops a nickel in it, then he just stand there a little while looking at the record. Mama tells me keep my eyes in front where they belong. I turn my head like she say, but then I hear the man coming toward us.

"Dance, pretty?" he says.

Mama gets up to dance with him. But 'fore you know it, she done grabbed the little man in the collar and done heaved him 'side the wall. He hit the wall so hard he stop the juke box from playing.

"Some pimp," the lady back of the counter says. "Some pimp."

The little man jumps up off the floor and starts toward my mama. 'Fore you know it, Mama done sprung open her knife and she's waiting for him.

"Come on," she says. "Come on. I'll gut you from your neighbo to your throat. Come on."

I go up to the little man to hit him, but Mama makes me come and stand 'side her. The little man looks at me and Mama and goes on back to the counter.

"Some pimp," the lady back of the counter says. "Some pimp." She starts laughing and pointing at the little man. "Yes sir, you a pimp, all right. Yes sir-ree."

13

"Fasten that coat, let's go," Mama says.

"You don't have to leave," the lady says. Mama don't answer the lady, and we right out in the cold again. I'm warm right now—my hands, my ears, my feet—but I know this ain't go'n last too long. It done sleet so much now you got ice everywhere you look.

We cross the railroad tracks, and soon's we do, I get cold. That wind goes through this little old coat like it ain't even there. I got on a shirt and a sweater under the coat, but that wind don't pay them no mind. I look up and I can see we got a long way to go. I wonder if we go'n make it 'fore I get too cold.

We cross over to walk on the sidewalk. They got just one sidewalk back here, and it's over there.

After we go just a little piece, I smell bread cooking. I look, then I see a baker shop. When we get closer, I can smell it more better. I shut my eyes and make 'tend I'm eating. But I keep them shut too long and I butt up 'gainst a telephone post. Mama grabs me and see if I'm hurt. I ain't bleeding or nothing and she turns me loose.

I can feel I'm getting colder and colder, and I look up to see how far we still got to go. Uptown is 'way up yonder. A half mile more, I reckon. I try to think of something. They say think and you won't get cold. I think of that poem, "Annabel Lee." I ain't been to school in so long—this bad weather—I reckon they done passed "Annabel Lee" by now. But passed it or not, I'm sure Miss Walker go'n make me recite it when I get there. That woman don't never forget nothing. I ain't never seen nobody like that in my life.

I'm still getting cold. "Annabel Lee" or no "Annabel Lee," I'm still getting cold. But I can see we getting closer. We getting there gradually.

Soon's we turn the corner, I seen a little old white lady up in front of us. She's the only lady on the street. She's all in black and she's got a long black rag over her head.

"Stop," she says.

Me and Mama stop and look at her. She must be crazy to be out in all this bad weather. Ain't got but a few other people out there, and all of them's men.

"Y'all done ate?" she says.

"Just finish," Mama says.

"Y'all must be cold then?" she says.

"We headed for the dentist," Mama says. "We'll warm up when we get there."

"What dentist?" the old lady says. "Mr. Bassett?"

"Yes, ma'am," Mama says.

"Come on in," the old lady says. "I'll telephone him and tell him y'all coming."

Me and Mama follow the old lady in the store. It's a little bitty store, and it don't have much in there. The old lady takes off her head rag and folds it up.

"Helena?" somebody calls from the back.

"Yes, Alnest?" the old lady says.

"Did you see them?"

"They're here. Standing beside me."

"Good. Now you can stay inside."

The old lady looks at Mama. Mama's waiting to hear what she brought us in here for. I'm waiting for that, too.

"I saw y'all each time you went by," she says. "I came out to catch you, but you were gone."

"We went back of town," Mama says.

"Did you eat?"

"Yes, ma'am."

The old lady looks at Mama a long time, like she's thinking Mama might just be saying that. Mama looks right back at her. The old lady looks at me to see what I have to say. I don't say nothing. I sure ain't going 'gainst my mama.

"There's food in the kitchen," she says to Mama. "I've been keeping it warm."

Mama turns right around and starts for the door.

"Just a minute," the old lady says. Mama stops. "The boy'll have to work for it. It isn't free."

"We don't take no handout," Mama says.

"I'm not handing out anything," the old lady says. "I need my garbage moved to the front. Ernest has a bad cold and can't go out there."

"James'll move it for you," Mama says.

"Not unless you eat," the old lady says. "I'm old, but I have my pride, too, you know."

Mama can see she ain't go'n beat this old lady down, so she just shakes her head.

"All right," the old lady says. "Come into the kitchen."

She leads the way with that rag in her hand. The kitchen is a little bitty little old thing, too. The table and the stove just 'bout fill it up. They got a little room to the side. Somebody in there layin 'cross the bed— 'cause I can see one of his feet. Must be the person she was talking to: Ernest or Alnest—something like that.

"Sit down," the old lady says to Mama. "Not you," she says to me. "You have to move the cans."

"Helena?" the man says in the other room.

"Yes, Alnest?" the old lady says.

"Are you going out there again?"

"I must show the boy where the garbage is, Alnest," the old lady says.

"Keep your shawl over your head," the old man says.

"You don't have to remind me, Alnest. Come, Boy," the old lady says.

We go out in the yard. Little old back yard ain't no bigger than the store or the kitchen. But it can sleet here just like it can sleet in any big back yard. And 'fore you know it, I'm trembling.

"There," the old lady says, pointing to the cans. I pick up one of the cans and set it right back down. The can's so light. I'm go'n see what's inside of it.

"Here," the old lady says. "Leave that can alone."

I look back at her standing there in the door. She's got that black rag wrapped round her shoulders, and she's pointing one of her little old fingers at me.

"Pick it up and carry it to the front," she says. I go by her with the can, and she's looking at me all the time. I'm sure the can's empty. I'm sure she could've carried it herself—maybe both of them at the same time. "Set it on the sidewalk by the door and come back for the other one," she says.

I go and come back, and Mama looks at me when I pass her. I get the other can and take it to the front. It don't feel a bit heavier than that first one. I tell myself I ain't go'n be nobody's fool, and I'm go'n look inside this can to see just what I been hauling. First, I look up the street, then down the street. Nobody coming. Then I look over my shoulder toward the door. That little old lady done slipped up there quiet's a mouse, watching me again. Look like she knowed what I was go'n do.

"Ehh, Lord," she says. "Children, children. Come in here, boy, and go wash your hands."

I follow her in the kitchen. She points toward the bathroom, and I go in there and wash up. Little bitty old bathroom, but it's clean, clean. I don't use any of her towels; I wipe my hands on my pants legs.

When I come back in the kitchen, the old lady done dished up the food. Rice, gravy, meat—and she even got some lettuce and tomato in a saucer. She even got a glass of milk and a piece of cake there, too. It looks so good, I almost start eating 'fore I say my blessing.

"Helena?" the old man says.

"Yes, Alnest?"

"Are they eating?"

"Yes," she says.

"Good," he says. "Now you'll stay inside."

The old lady goes in there where he is and I can hear them talking. I look at Mama. She's eating slow like she's thinking. I wonder what's the matter now. I reckon she's thinking 'bout home.

The old lady comes back in the kitchen.

"I talked to Dr. Bassett's nurse," she says. "Dr. Bassett will take you as soon as you get there."

"Thank you, ma'am," Mama says.

"Perfectly all right," the old lady says. "Which one is it?"

Mama nods toward me. The old lady looks at me real sad. I look sad, too.

"You're not afraid, are you?" she says.

"No, ma'am," I say.

"That's a good boy," the old lady says. "Nothing to be afraid of. Dr. Bassett will not hurt you."

When me and Mama get through eating, we thank the old lady again.

"Helena, are they leaving?" the old man says.

"Yes, Alnest."

"Tell them I say good-bye."

"They can hear you, Alnest."

"Good-bye both mother and son," the old man says. "And may God be with you."

Me and Mama tell the old man good-bye, and we follow the old lady in the front room. Mama opens the door to go out, but she stops and comes back in the store.

"You sell salt meat?" she says.

"Yes."

"Give me two bits worth."

"That isn't very much salt meat," the old lady says.

"That's all I have," Mama says.

The old lady goes back of the counter and cuts a big piece off the chunk. Then she wraps it up and puts it in a paper bag.

"Two bits," she says.

"That looks like awful lot of meat for a quarter," Mama says.

"Two bits," the old lady says. "I've been selling salt meat behind this counter twenty-five years. I think I know what I'm doing."

"You got a scale there," Mama says.

"What?" the old lady says.

"Weigh it," Mama says.

"What?" the old lady says. "Are you telling me how to run my business?"

"Thanks very much for the food," Mama says.

"Just a minute," the old lady says.

"James," Mama says to me. I move toward the door.

"Just one minute, I said," the old lady says.

Me and Mama stop again and look at her. The old lady takes the meat out of the bag and unwraps it and cuts 'bout half of it off. Then she wraps it up again and juggs it back in the bag and gives the bag to Mama. Mama lays the quarter on the counter.

"Your kindness will never be forgotten," she says. "James," she says to me.

We go out, and the old lady comes to the door to look at us. After we go a little piece I look back, and she's still there watching us.

The sleet's coming down heavy, heavy now, and I turn up my coat collar to keep my neck warm. My mama tells me turn it right back down.

"You not a bum," she says. "You a man."

AT A SUMMER HOTEL

by

ISABELLA GARDNER

(1915–1981)

A Boston native, Isabella Gardner started a career in acting before turning to poetry. She lectured and read her poetry both in the United States and abroad. Her works include Birthdays from the Ocean *(1955),* The Looking Glass *(1961), and* West of Childhood: Poems 1950–65 *(1965).*

•————————————————————•

For my daughter, Rose Van Kirk

I am here with my beautiful bountiful womanful child
to be soothed by the sea not roused by these roses roving wild.
My girl is gold in the sun and bold in the dazzling water,
she drowses on the blond sand and in the daisy fields my daughter
dreams. Uneasy in the drafty shade I rock on the veranda
reminded of Europa Persephone Miranda.

BIOGRAPHY OF MY DAUGHTER

by

MERIDEL LE SUEUR

(b. 1900)

Born in Murray, Iowa, Meridel Le Sueur has written passionately about farmers in the Midwest who endured the Great Depression, in short stories, a novel (The Girl, republished in 1978), and in magazine articles. She has also written a biography of her parents, a story about Abraham Lincoln's mother, and a recent volume of poems about Indian women. Unknown for many years after attaining prominence in the 1930s, Le Sueur has been rediscovered by feminists; she now lectures widely and continues to write. Many of her works were collected in Ripening (1982), which was published by the Feminist Press.

———————————————————

For Rhoda

Listen, the biography of Rhoda is not very long. She was twenty-three when she died without knowing a lover and really only seven spring seasons, counting from when she was sixteen and wore a voile dress when she graduated from high school.

In the spring she and Marie came over to my house for lunch. It was one of the first spring days and we had fried rice and a green salad. Rhoda kept saying about my daughters, "They are so fat," she'd say in wonder. "Look, look at their feet, such strong, strong feet." She held their young fat feet in her hands, pressing the firm flesh. "I was born in a depression," Marie said. "I never had enough to eat."

We were all telling how we had been looking for work. Marie, who worked in textile since she was twelve, would get angry and her black eyes would blaze, but Rhoda seemed so gentle. You see lots of women like her and her mother, whom I saw later. They never say anything for themselves. They accept everything. They do their best. They believe in something. They live, they are silent, they die. Nothing is ever said for such people, no book is ever written about them, they never write a long biography saying I did this and that. Marie and I are not like that, a murderous anger smoulders in us, but there are millions of such people, lovely, accepting something too quietly. You see them sitting in a chair sewing lace on a garment, or looking for a moment out the window, and they seem grateful for too little.

Rhoda's mother was just like her, a frail gentle woman. She looked worn, just as Rhoda was beginning to look already, all the edges of her body worn away like an old machine. And after all, the body is not a machine, is it? They lived at a town called Starbuck and the father was a bookkeeper who was let out four years ago. After thirty years of hard labor he had scarcely anything to show for it except, as Rhoda said, "his girls." There were three other girls beside Rhoda. There was Rhoda herself, the oldest, and then Marilyn and Lucile and Bliss. You can see by the names something of what the mother expected of them. I expect the same of my daughters, somehow to be women whose bodies are not machines. Rhoda told about her mother that day, how quick and fine her hands were even in the middle of the night when she was sewing on some dresses. Later when I saw her at the sanitarium, I could see how her fingernails were worn down like a very fine precision machine that had been in use for a long time. She had a delicate and lovely face and all her girls looked exactly like her, only not worn down so much yet.

Rhoda sat in my chair that day. She was very quiet, her head drooping a little, and she read Mickey Mouse to my children and she listened to Marie and me talk. We were talking, I remember, with much anger and she listened even when she was reading, very tense, but withdrawn, as if it was too late for her to do anything, but she listened very intensely, and there was some frightful knowing in her. Once she stopped reading, and my two daughters, Rachel and Deborah, looked at her, and she said in a low voice, "When I was working at Mrs. Katz's I worked sixteen hours in a day . . . That's too long. That's too long."

I just got up and looked out the window and knocked over a pitcher of water, because I can't write this story. Rhoda has been buried two weeks now, and I really wrote this story tearing it out between my teeth when we were driving back from the sanitarium that morning when the corn was just ripening in the fields. You shouldn't break into a story like this, but it comes out like a burning behind my teeth, and that morning when she died, I could have swept down the fields with my arms, folded up the fields and crunched the city in my teeth.

I better go back carefully and tell about her. Perhaps Rhoda has a biography beside this one, too. You could find it on every relief record in Minneapolis, the city, federal and private relief. I saw her many times sitting there, her delicate blonde face and her body that seemed to droop a little from fatigue, and her disease, and she would answer all those questions politely over and over.

She came from Starbuck when she was sixteen to go to the university. She had to work her way through. She wanted to be a librarian. The first year she worked as a maid for only room and board, because her father paid the university fees, but the next year he couldn't pay them, so she got a job at

Coffee Dan's and worked there as a waitress from six o'clock in the evening until two in the morning. From there she went to the Zaners, where she worked for her room and board. She got up at six, prepared breakfast, cleaned up, straightened the house and got to the university library school. Sometimes she got in some sleep in the rest room. She did this for four years. She was graduated. There was no library to work in. She worked as a maid, cook, waitress, then there was not even that. She was on relief. To get some kinds of relief you have to be examined by a doctor also. They found she had tuberculosis and needed a rest. Right after the day they were to see me, Marie went out with her to the sanitarium, and left her there.

She got worse. For two weeks she hadn't taken any nourishment. Marie and I started out in the morning to see her. It had been about a hundred for a week, the ripening corn was beginning to curl, but when we got to the sanitarium the green hills were rolling up to the summer sky where great white clouds hung still. It was about ten o'clock. "Gee, this is a swell place," Marie said. Some tubercular boys in shorts were playing ball on the green grass. We saw wing after wing of splendid brick buildings. "In a decent country," I said, "this would be swell, here it's a joke."

Marie looked saturnine and bitter, "For God's sake," she said, "look at it. What a farce! They wear you down and then they put you here and fix you up to wear you down again. Lookit," she said, "they should do with the workers like with horses, make glue out of 'em, when they wear 'em out. They should find some good use for blood, arteries, and bones in industry after they're no good as workers. Why bring 'em here?"

We walked on down the walk, Rachel and Deborah running ahead, excited by the palatial building and the fine stone steps. Marie suddenly whispered, the tears standing in her eyes, "I don't think she wants to live." We pressed our hands together. We looked up at the huge building. "Jesus Christ," Marie said, "how many well and living people this could house. Look at it, for God's sake!"

Rachel and Deborah ran back to us. "Listen," I said to them, "why don't you play out here on the nice grass?"

They looked up at the building. They had to tilt back their heads. "Listen, look," I said, "look how green the grass is." An anguish was in me like iron in my chest, "You can play tag here." They looked at the grass. They looked at me. They looked at Marie's dark and bitter face. "We want to go," Rachel said, snuggling up to my thigh like a colt. Deborah tipped back looking at the hundreds of windows. I saw Deborah and Rachel in the bright sun; their legs showed from the red dresses so fat, like conicals of flesh without bones. "Oh, stay in the green world awhile," I cried, and we tried to walk on, but Rachel gave a cry and wound herself about my legs. "What . . . what!" I cried trying to push her away. "Listen, you don't want to go into that place." "Yes . . . yes, take us in." "All right," I said angrily, pushing her away, and they flew up the stone steps, stopping at the door at the smell of death.

We went into the lobby. A man in white was brushing the floor. I thought we would see Rhoda like she had been in the spring, a little shy, putting up her falling gold hair, smiling at us, her head turned a little away. I saw a stone bench and picked up the children and sat them squarely on it. "You'll have to stay here until we see whether Rhoda can see you," I said. They sat there quietly while I walked away looking back at them. They sat close together, their eyes round, their fat legs hanging from the stone bench. I followed Marie down the corridor, into a room. I saw a nurse get up, come forward, I didn't hear what Marie said. I heard the nurse say, "Rhoda passed away this morning."

O daughter, what is child, daughter, then girl, then in voile with delicate hair?

Marie looked out the window as if she had not heard. I stood silently behind her. I felt someone behind me and turned to see a young girl with Rhoda's golden hair, a fuller mouth. Now her eyes were big and dark at the centers. Marie went to her and embraced her, "Marilyn," she said and began to cry. The girl stood looking around Marie's shoulder her eyes big and unblinking. "I can't cry," she said. "They woke me up and told me. I came out on the bus. I have to get back. I can't cry. I don't know what it is, I can't cry," she said. She was now working for her room and board at a Mrs. Katz's.

The nurse said, "Your mother is here . . ." In the door stood the mother plucking at her falling hair, just like Rhoda. Marie was crying. The mother patted her shoulder. She said to the nurse, "I've got all her things here." She held up a little bundle tied in a chemise. "I know Rhoda had pawned her things," the mother said, "but I can't find the little French book. Rhoda was very fond of that little French book." The nurse said quickly, relieved to have something that was needed for once, "I have it here, right here on my desk." "Oh," the mother said, relieved, as if something of vast importance had been settled. She put her hand on the French book and I saw her broken nails. She held up a pair of shorts. Marie cried out, "Those are the shorts I made for Rhoda." She took them. "I made them so she wouldn't be so hot lying there all the time. I made them," she cried looking amazed at them, as if it was strange that they should still be. "Oh, aren't they sweet?" Marilyn said, "too sweet . . ." She had a deep lovely voice. And her eyes remained wide open as if she were walking in her sleep. "You have them, Marilyn," Marie said.

We stood there.

The mother said, "I guess, well . . . I guess. . . ."

The nurse said, "You might as well go back to town. You can't get a train out of here for Starbuck until tomorrow at nine. You might as well go back to town and rest and I've looked everything up for you." She seemed eager as if she were relieved to be able to say that the trains ran on schedule, that everything could be done so well, so systematically. "Everything will be just fine now," she said. "Just fine."

We all stood there.

"What were the complications?" Marie said very low.

"Well," the nurse said, "I think her mother understands everything and that is all that is necessary."

A peculiar antagonism stood between us.

"Listen," Marie said, "I know what was the matter with her."

"Oh, do you?" the nurse said bitterly. "She had the best of care. I'm sure her mother agrees to that. The university doctor himself sat in on the consultation. Her mother knows that, I am sure. Her mother has already signed, saying she had the best of care."

We stood there as if she had not spoken. Marie looked strange. The nurse gasped as if she knew what was going to be said, as if an avalanche were coming slowly down upon the tiny room crushing us all.

Marie said, "She died of starvation . . ."

It was as if the flesh of each one of us shrank a little forever.

We stood there. The sunlight flashed back. The corn hung heavy on the stalks, the pumpkins and the squash were ripening in abundance.

"Now," the nurse shook herself a little, "you get your things. The train goes through here, right straight through here. We'll have everything arranged. . . . I've phoned Swinson already . . . she . . . she's in the ice room. Everything is all arranged . . . the . . . she . . . it will be put on the train you're on, everything will be just fine . . ."

"Thank you . . . thank you . . ." said the mother.

Child, then girl, with the delicate golden hair. The mother stood bewildered, holding the tiny bundle of Rhoda's clothes. It must have had just a brassiere, a slip, the dress she had come in, a brush and comb. "I can go back on the bus . . ." she said looking around, and I saw how she had never given birth to this. She had borne something, believed in something . . .

"You can go with us," I said to her. I knew her then. How she bore everything, said nothing, remembered four girls, had known their beauty, husked herself for their food, how she was part of the living and took what it gave, believing in something gentle, and now she saw death malignant and terrific. I ran ahead, into the lobby, and looking saw my daughters, sitting as I had left them, their feet dangling, their fat good and stout on their bones yet. I took their warm hands, ran out of the building. The sunlight fell on us, the green world reached up, engulfed us.

They came after, I could see the tiny figure of the aging woman carrying that bundle down the walk as if asking a question. You give yourself over, with child, and see it blind at the breast, blind feet, blind hands. It sees then slowly, the moon, the stars, the sheep grazing, and grows up waiting for the good your body has promised it, and there it is dealt down like this. She didn't die of smallpox, diphtheria, measles, whooping cough, not even childbirth. She died of starvation.

The mother got in and set the thin bundle on her lap. To birth a child you carry heavy, heavy burdens, and death leaves a light burden indeed. Rachel and Deborah sat in the back close to her. I could see their eyes wide and big. We sat there, no one saying anything.

MERIDEL LE SUEUR

Marie was crying for her own death, for the blow that is dealt, for the thing that is and must not be.

We drove through the hills again, as if we were leaving an artificial world, something built up to hide a thing. "Listen," Marie said, "when she was graduated from the university I went to see her. There we sat and Coffman, the president, said we mustn't pay any attention he said to this shifting world, that's what he said. It's abstract science, that's what it is, go to the classics, he said, go to the good sane things of our forefathers, he said. Rhoda and I sat right there and heard him. We sat right there. Listen," she said, "she died of starvation. Listen, we've never had enough to eat."

"Easy," I said, "easy."

"Listen," she said, "say something for us, listen, say something. We've got to say something," she said.

We drove through the town past the morgue, *Swinson, Undertaker,* it said.

We stopped for some cigarettes. I could see the mother's face dropping closer to the bone, gentle, gentle. I saw my children too solemn, real, waiting.

"My, that surely is a pretty place," the mother said, looking back. "They were real good to her."

"Oh, my God," Marie said, "on this fine summer morning . . . on this fine morning . . ."

Round pumpkins in the field, corn fattening, melons like the crescent moons of the season, hogs fattening on the hoof, this is the wheat corn belt, that is the rich, rich country.

"She went through college," her mother said in a weak voice. "She had her heart set on that. She went through college all right. She worked so hard."

"Look . . ." I said, "look, why did she want to go through college?"

"Oh, Rhoda was ambitious," she said. "Oh, she was a good scholar. My, I remember she always brought home the best report cards. We were always proud of her."

"Look," I said. I could see the city rising ahead of us, the university, the towers, the banks. I could have ground them in my teeth. "Look," I said, "I want to know. What did she want?"

"Oh, she worked so hard," she said, "she worked so hard."

"What for?" I cried. Her mother looked at me. My children looked at me.

"To be a success," she said at last. "She wanted above everything to be a success."

"It's a bitch," Marilyn said in a hard deep voice.

"Listen, listen," Marie said, "listen, she had it. Listen, this is funny. This is wonderful," Marie said and tenderness and fierceness were a brew in her that would make another world. "Listen, you know what she got? Four years she starved to go through that lousy place, you know what she got? This is a scream, two weeks in the library. Two weeks on the C.W.A. Hurrah! Isn't that something? Listen, after all that, two weeks as a librarian.

THE MOTHER

180

A success! Two weeks work and a swell death. Listen, Marilyn," she says wildly, "listen, honey, listen darling, don't work too hard. If you get tired, you know what to do. Listen, Rhoda worked for a bitch, did all the washing, ironing, cooking, cleaning, eight people . . . listen, honey, if you feel tired, listen, for God's sake, if you feel tired you know what to do . . . there isn't any success. Listen, there isn't . . . listen, if you feel tired, for God's sake, stop . . . don't work. Stop, don't work . . . work. Don't work your guts out. Listen, honey, stop . . . don't work . . . stop . . .don't work . . ."

Listen. Living I never thought of Rhoda as my daughter. She was not my daughter, but dead she becomes the daughter of all of us. She was not my daughter, but she might have been and my daughters may be lying dead like that.

What happened to her must stop happening.

This is for Rhoda. This is my daughter. She is dead but this must be a reminder of her to all people.

DADDY

by

JAN CLAUSEN

(b. 1950)

*Born in Oregon, Jan Clausen grew up in the Pacific Northwest. She
now lives in New York with her lover and daughter and is active in
several feminist political groups. The founder of the magazine*
Conditions *in 1977, Clausen edited the journal for five years. She
has published poetry, fiction, and criticism, including* Waking at the
Bottom of the Dark *(1979),* Mother, Sister, Daughter, Lover *(1980),
and* A Movement of Poets: Thoughts on Poetry and Feminism
(1982). Her most recent work is a novel, Sinking Stealing *(1985).*

• ——————————————— •

I like my Daddy's best. It has more rooms. Mommy just has an apartment
and you have to go upstairs. The bathroom is in my room. Daddy has two
bathrooms. He owns the whole house. Mommy used to live there when I was
a little baby. Before they got divorced. That means not married anymore.
You get married when you love each other.

Mommy loves me. Daddy says I'm his favorite girl in the whole world,
sugar. He always calls me sugar. We like to go to a restaurant for
breakfast. Sometimes we go there for dinner if he has to work in the city.
I went to his office lots of times. He has books there. You go way up in
the elevator. Sometimes I feel like I'm going to throw up. But I don't. Then
you see the river. There's no one there except Daddy and me. Sometimes
Ellen comes.

My Mommy works. She goes to meetings. First I have to go to school
and then daycare. You can make noise at daycare. At school you have to be
quiet or you get punished. But I didn't ever get punished. Mommy helps
me with my homework. Sometimes we read a book together. Daddy asks
me add and take away. He says sugar you're so smart you can be anything
you want to be when you grow up. A doctor or a lawyer or a professor
or anything. My Daddy's a lawyer. I don't know if I'll get married.

Daddy said maybe next year I can go to a different school where they
have lots of things to play with. You can paint and go on trips and they have
nice books. The kids make so much noise in my class. Some of them talk
Spanish and the boys are bad. I got a star for doing my homework right.

My Daddy takes me on Sunday. Sometimes I sleep there if Mommy goes away. I have to be good. Daddy says he'll get me something when we go shopping if I behave. I have to take a bath before I go and brush my hair. Daddy says he likes little girls that smell nice and clean. Sometimes Ellen lets me try her perfume. Once she let me put some powder on my face and some blue stuff on my eyes. That's eye shadow. But I had to wash my face before I went home. Mommy doesn't wear makeup. Or Carolyn. They said it looks silly.

Once in the summer I stayed at my Daddy's for a whole week. Ellen was there. She helped take care of me. You're so helpless David she said. She laughed. We all laughed. I had fun. We went to Coney Island. During the week I just call my Daddy two times because he works hard. Sometimes if he goes on a trip he can't see me. Daddy and Ellen went on a trip to Florida. They had to fly in an airplane. They sent me a postcard every day. You could go swimming in the winter there. Mommy and me went to the country but the car broke.

Sometimes Carolyn stays overnight. We only have two beds. She has to sleep in the same bed with Mommy. When I wake up I get in bed with them. We all hug each other. Carolyn and Mommy kiss each other all the time. But they aren't married. Only a man and a woman can get married. When they want to have a baby the man's penis gets bigger and he puts it in the woman's vagina. It feels good to touch your vagina. Me and Veronica did it in the bathtub. When the baby comes out the doctor has to cut the Mommy's vagina with some scissors. Mommy showed me a picture in her book.

I saw Daddy's penis before. Mommy has hair on her vagina. She has hair on her legs and Carolyn has lots of hair on her legs like a man. Ellen doesn't. Mommy said maybe Ellen does have hair on her legs but she shaves it. Sometimes I forget and call Carolyn Ellen. She gets mad. Sometimes I forget and call Mommy Daddy. I have a cat called Meatball at Mommy's but sometimes I forget and call Meatball Max instead. That's Daddy's dog.

Daddy is all Jewish. So is Ellen. Mommy is only part Jewish. But Daddy said I could be Jewish if I want. You can't have Christmas if you're Jewish. Mommy and me had a little Christmas tree. Carolyn came. We made cookies. I had Chanukah at my Daddy's. He gave me a doll named Samantha that talks and a skateboard and green pants and a yellow top. He says when I learn to tell time he'll get me a watch.

I wish Mommy would get me a TV. I just have a little one. Sometimes it gets broken. Daddy has a color TV at his house. It has a thing with buttons you push to change the program. Mommy said I watch too much TV. I said if you get me a new TV I promise I'll only watch two programs every day. Mommy said we're not going to just throw things away and get a new one every year. I told her Andrea has a color TV in her house and Veronica has a nice big TV in her room that you can see good. Mommy said I'm not getting a TV and that's all. Mommy made me feel bad. I started crying. Mommy said go to your room you're spoiling my dinner. I said *asshole* to Mommy. That's a curse. Sometimes my Mommy says a curse to me. I cried and cried.

Mommy said get in your room. She spanked me and said now get in your room. I ran in my room and closed the door. Mommy hurts my feelings. She won't let me watch TV. She always goes to a meeting and I have to stay with the baby sitter. I don't say a curse to my Daddy. My Daddy isn't mean to me. I screamed and screamed for my Daddy and Mrs. Taylor next door got mad and banged on the wall.

Mommy said go in the other room and call him then. Daddy said you sound like you've been crying. What's the matter, sugar. Nothing I said. Daddy doesn't like me to cry. He says crying is for little babies. I can't stand to see a woman cry, sugar, he says. Then I laugh and he tells me blow my nose. What are we going to do on Sunday I said. Oh that's a surprise Daddy said. Is it going somewhere I said. Yes we're going somewhere but that's not the real surprise Daddy said. Is it a present I said. Daddy said just wait and see, what did you do in school today. Daddy always asks what did I do in school. I told him the teacher had to punish Carlos. Daddy said listen isn't it about your bedtime. I have work to do. Ellen says hi. Blow me a goodnight kiss.

I hugged my Mommy. She hugged me back. She said she was sorry she got mad. But don't beg for things. A new TV is expensive. We don't need it. Mommy always says it's too expensive. I said I wish you were married to the President. Then we could live in the White House. I saw a picture in school. You could have anything you want. They don't have cockroaches.

The President is a good man. He helps people. George Washington was the President. Veronica gave me a doll of his wife at my birthday. It has a long dress. Mommy said he was mean to Indians and Black people. But we studied about him in school and he wasn't. They had voting once. You could vote for Ford or Carter. My Daddy voted for Carter. I'm glad my Daddy voted for who won. My Mommy didn't vote.

Mommy doesn't like things. She doesn't like the President and she doesn't like Mary Hartman like my Daddy. I told her to get Charmin toilet paper like they have on TV because it's soft to squeeze. She said that's a rip-off. She only takes me to McDonald's once every month. I got a Ronald McDonald cup to drink my milk. She said that's a gimmick. I like milk. Milk is a natural. I told Mommy that and she got mad. I said you don't like anything Mommy. She said I like lots of things. I like plants. I like to play basketball. I like sleeping late on Sunday mornings. I like to eat. I like books. I like women. I like you.

Do you like men I said. I don't like most men very much Mommy said. Some men are okay. My Daddy likes women I said. Does he Mommy said.

I asked my Daddy does he like women. He said extremely. Some of my favorite people are women he said. Like you. And Ellen. Why do you ask.

I said I don't know. Daddy said do you like men. I love you Daddy I said.
I bet she gets that you know where Ellen said.

On Sunday we had breakfast at my Daddy's house. We had pancakes.
Daddy makes them. He puts on his cook's hat. Then we went shopping.
Then we went to a movie of Cinderella. Ellen came too. Then we went
to a restaurant. I had ice cream with chocolate. Ellen and Daddy held
each other's hand. Daddy said now I'm going to tell you the surprise.
Ellen and I are getting married. How does that sound, sugar. Ellen said
for god's sake David give her a little time to react.

Daddy said I can be in the wedding. He said Ellen will wear a pretty
dress and he will break a glass. He did that when he and Mommy got
married too. Then Ellen will have the same name as Mommy and Daddy
and me and I can call her Mommy too if I want. I won't have to see my
Daddy just on Sunday because Ellen will be there to help take care of me.
She only works in the morning. It will be like a real family with a
Mommy and a Daddy and a kid. But I can't say that part because Daddy
said it's supposed to still be a secret.

I didn't feel good when Daddy brought me home. I felt like I had to
throw up. Mommy held my hand. I lay down on the bed and she brought
Meatball to play with me. She asked what did I do with Daddy today.
She always asks me that. I told her we saw Cinderella. It was okay. She
rode in a pumpkin. Some parts were boring. The Prince loved her.
Daddy and Ellen are going to get married.

I started crying. I cried hard. Then I had to throw up. It got on the rug.

Mommy got the washcloth. She brought my pajamas. She hugged me.
She said I love you. She said it won't be so different when Daddy and Ellen
are married. You like Ellen don't you.

I love you Mommy, I love you, I love you I said. Why don't you like my
Daddy. I love my Daddy.

I don't dislike your father Mommy said. We don't have much in common
that's all. I'm happy living here just with you. You're special to me and
you're special to your Daddy. You see him every week.

I cried and cried. I love you Mommy. I love you and Daddy both the
same. And I love Ellen because she's going to be my Mommy too. I'll miss
you. I'll miss you so much when I live there. I'll cry. I'm going to have
a big sunny room and Daddy said he'll paint it and I can pick a color. I'm
going to have a new kitty so I won't miss Meatball. Next year I can go
to that nice school and Ellen might have a baby. It would be a brother or a
sister. Daddy's going to get me a bicycle. I can take anything there I want.
I'll just leave a few toys here for when I come to visit you on Sunday.

TELL MARTHA NOT TO MOAN

by

SHERLEY ANNE WILLIAMS

(b. 1944)

Born in San Diego, Sherley Anne Williams chairs the Department of Literature at the University of California campus there. She has published stories and poems in many periodicals. Her volume The Peacock Poems *won the National Book Award in Poetry in 1976, and her collection of literary criticism of black writers,* Give Birth to Brightness *(1972), has been widely praised. A recent volume of poetry is* Some One Sweet Angel Chile *(1982).*

•————————————————————•

My mamma is a big woman, tall and stout, and men like her cause she soft and fluffy-looking. When she round them it all smiles and dimples and her mouth be looking like it couldn't never be fixed to say nothing but darling and honey.

They see her now, they sho see something different. I should not even come today. Since I had Larry things ain't been too good between us. But—that's my mamma and I know she gon be there when I need her. And sometime when I come, it okay. But this ain't gon be one a them times. Her eyes looking all ove me and I know it coming. She snort cause she want to say god damn but she don't cuss. "When it due, Martha?"

First I start to say, what. But I know it ain't no use. You can't fool old folks bout something like that, so I tell her.

"Last part of November."

"Who the daddy?"

"Time."

"That man what play piano at the Legion?"

"Yeah."

"What he gon do bout it?"

"Mamma, it ain't too much he can do, now is it? The baby on its way."

She don't say nothing for a long time. She sit looking at her hands. They all wet from where she been washing dishes and they all wrinkled like yo hand be when they been in water too long. She get up and get a dish cloth and dry em, then sit down at the table. "Where he at now?"

"Gone."

"Gone? Gone where?" I don't say nothing and she start cussing then. I get kinda scared cause mamma got to be real mad foe she cuss and I don't know who she cussing—me or Time. Then she start talking to me. "Martha, you just a fool. I told you that man wan't no good first time I seed him. A musician the worst kind of men you can get mixed up with. Look at you. You ain't even eighteen years old yet, Larry just barely two, and here you is pregnant again." She go on like that for a while and I don't say nothing. Couldn't no way. By the time I get my mouth fixed to say something, she done raced on so far ahead that what I got to say don't have nothing to do with what she saying right then. Finally she stop and ask, "What you gon do now? You want to come back here?" She ain't never liked me living with Orine and when I say no, she ask, "Why not? It be easier for you."

I shake my head again. "If I here, Time won't know where to find me, and Time coming; he be back. He gon to make a place for us, you a see."

"Hump, you just played the fool again, Martha."

"No Mamma, that not it at all; Time want me."

"Is that what he say when he left?"

"No, but . . ."

Well, like the first night we met, he come over to me like he knowed me for a long time and like I been his for awmost that long. Yeah, I think that how it was. Cause I didn' even see him when we come in the Legion that first night.

Me and Orine, we just got our checks that day. We went downtown and Orine bought her some new dresses. But the dress she want to wear that night don't look right so we go racing back to town and change it. Then we had to hurry home and get dressed. It Friday night and the Legion crowded. You got to get there early on the weekend if you want a seat. And Orine don't want just any seat; she want one right up front. "Who gon see you way back there? Nobody. You don't dance, how you gon meet people? You don't meet people, what you doing out?" So we sit up front. Whole lots a people there that night. You can't even see the bandstand cross the dance floor. We sharing the table with some more people and Orine keep jabbing me, telling me to sit cool. And I try cause Orine say it a good thing to be cool.

The set end and people start leaving the dance floor. That when I see Time. He just getting up from the piano. I like him right off cause I like men what look like him. He kind of tall and slim. First time I ever seed a man wear his hair so long and nappy—he tell me once it an African Bush—but he look good anyway and he know it. He look round all cool. He step down from the bandstand and start walking toward me. He come over to the table and just look. "You," he say, "you my Black queen." And he bow down most to the floor.

Ah shit! I mad cause I think he just trying to run a game. "What you trying to prove, fool?" I ask him.

"Ah man," he say and it like I cut him. That the way he say it. "Ah man.

I call this woman my Black queen—tell her she can rule my life and she call me a fool."

"And sides what, nigga," I tell him then, "I ain't black." And I ain't, I don't care what Time say. I just a dark woman.

"What's the matter, you shamed of being Black? Ain't nobody told you Black is pretty?" He talk all loud and people start gathering round. Somebody say, "Yeah, you tell her bout it, soul." I embarrassed and I look over at Orine. But she just grinning, not saying nothing. I guess she waiting to see what I gon do so I stand up.

"Well if I is black, I is a fine black." And I walk over to the bar. I walk just like I don't know they watching my ass, and I hold my head up. Time follow me right on over to the bar and put his arm round my shoulder.

"You want a drink?" I start to say no cause I scared. Man not supposed to make you feel like he make me feel. Not just like doing it—but, oh, like it right for him to be there with me, touching me. So I say yes. "What's your name?" he ask then.

I smile and say, "They call me the player." Orine told a man that once in Berkeley and he didn't know what to say. Orine a smart woman.

"Well they call me Time and I know yo mamma done told you Time ain't nothing to play with." His smile cooler than mine. We don't say nothing for a long while. He just stand there with his arm round my shoulder looking at us in the mirror behind the bar. Finally he say, "Yeah, you gon be my Black queen." And he look down at me and laugh. I don't know what to do, don't know what to say neither, so I just smile.

"You gon tell me your name or not?"

"Martha."

He laugh. "That a good name for you."

"My mamma name me that so I be good. She name all us kids from the Bible," I tell him laughing.

"And is you good?"

I nod yes and no all at the same time and kind of mumble cause I don't know what to say. Mamma really did name all us kids from the Bible. She always saying, "My mamma name me Veronica after the woman in the Bible and I a better woman for it. That why I name all my kids from the Bible. They got something to look up to." But mamma don't think I'm good, specially since I got Larry. Maybe Time ain't gon think I good neither. So I don't answer, just smile and move on back to the table. I hear him singing soft-like, "Oh Mary don't you weep, tell yo sister Martha not to moan." And I kind of glad cause most people don't even think bout that when I tell em my name. That make me know he really smart.

We went out for breakfast after the Legion close. Him and me and Orine and German, the drummer. Only places open is on the other side of town and at first Time don't want to go. But we finally swade him.

Time got funny eyes, you can't hardly see into em. You look and you look and you can't tell nothing from em. It make me feel funny when he look at me. I finally get used to it, but that night he just sit there looking and don't say nothing for a long time after we order.

"So you don't like Black?" he finally say.

"Do you?" I ask. I think I just ask him questions, then I don't have to talk so much. But I don't want him to talk bout that right then, so I smile and say, "Let's talk bout you."

"I am not what I am." He smiling and I smile back, but I feel funny cause I think I supposed to know what he mean.

"What kind of game you trying to run?" Orine ask. Then she laugh. "Just cause we from the country don't mean we ain't hip to niggas trying to be big-time. Ain't that right, Martha?"

I don't know what to say, but I know Time don't like that. I think he was going to cuss Orine out, but German put his arm round Orine and he laugh. "He just mean he ain't what he want to be. Don't pay no mind to that cat. He always trying to blow some shit." And he start talking that talk, rapping to Orine.

I look at Time. "That what you mean?"

He all lounged back in the seat, his legs stretched way out under the table. He pour salt in a napkin and mix it up with his finger. "Yeah, that's what I mean. That's all about me. Black is pretty, Martha." He touch my face with one finger. "You let white people make you believe you ugly. I bet you don't even dream."

"I do too."

"What do you dream?"

"Huh?" I don't know what he talking bout. I kind of smile and look at him out the corner of my eye. "I dreams bout a man like you. Why, just last night, I dream—"

He start laughing. "That's all right. That's all right."

The food come then and we all start eating. Time act like he forgot all bout dreams. I never figure out how he think I can just sit there and tell him the dreams I have at night, just like that. It don't seem like what I dream bout at night mean as much as what I think bout during the day.

We leaving when Time trip over this white man's feet. That man's feet all out in the aisle but Time don't never be watching where he going no way. "Excuse me," he say kind of mean.

"Say, watch it buddy." That white man talk most as nasty as Time. He kind of old and maybe he drunk or an Okie.

"Man, I said excuse me. You the one got your feet in the aisle."

"You," that man say, starting to get up, "you better watch yourself boy."

And what he want to say that for? Time step back and say real quiet, "No, motherfucker. You the one. You better watch yourself and your daughter too. See how many babies she gon have by boys like me." That man get all red in the face, but the woman in the booth with him finally start pulling at him, telling him to sit down, shut up. Cause Time set to kill that man.

I touch Time's arm first, then put my arm round his waist. "Ain't no use getting messed behind somebody like that."

Time and that man just looking at each other, not wanting to back down. People was gon start wondering what going on in a few minutes. I tell him, "Got something for you, baby," and he look down at me and grin. Orine pick it up. We go out that place singing, "Good loving, good, good loving, make you feel so clean."

"You like to hear me play?" he ask when we in the car.

"This the first time they ever have anybody here that sound that good."

"Yeah," Orine say. "How come you all staying round a little jive-ass town like Ashley?"

"We going to New York pretty soon," Time say kind of snappy.

"Well, shit, baby, you—"

"When you going to New York?" I ask real quick. When Orine in a bad mood, can't nobody say nothing right.

"Couple of months." He lean back and put his arm round me. "They doing so many things with music back there. Up in the City, they doing one maybe two things. In L.A. they doing another one, two things. But, man, in New York, they doing everything. Person couldn't never get stuck in one groove there. So many things going on, you got to be hip, real hip to keep up. You always growing there. Shit, if you 'live and playing, you can't help but grow. Say, man," he reach and tap German on the shoulder, "let's leave right now."

We all crack up. Then I say, "I sorry but I can't go, got to take care of my baby."

He laugh, "Sugar, you got yo baby right here."

"Well, I must got two babies then."

We pull in front of the partment house then but don't no one move. Finally Time reach over and touch my hair. "You gon be my Black queen?"

I look straight ahead at the night. "Yeah," I say. "Yeah."

We go in and I check first on Larry cause sometimes that girl don't watch him good. When I come in some nights, he be all out the cover and shivering but too sleepy to get back under em. Time come in when I'm pulling the cover up on Orine two kids.

"Which one yours," he ask.

I go over to Larry bed. "This my baby," I tell him.

"What's his name?"

"Larry."

"Oh, I suppose you name him after his daddy?"

I don't like the way he say that, like I was wrong to name him after his daddy. "Who else I gon name him after?" He don't say nothing and I leave him standing there. I mad now and I go in the bedroom and start pulling off my clothes. I think, That nigga can stand up in the living room all night, for all I care; let Orine talk to German and him, too. But Time come in the bedroom and put his arms round me. He touch my hair and my face and my tittie, and it scare me. I try to pull away but he hold me too close. "Martha," he say, "Black Martha." Then he just stand there holding me, not saying nothing, with his hand covering one side on my face. I stand there trembling but he don't notice. I know a woman not supposed to feel the way I feel bout Time, not right away. But I do.

He tell me things nobody ever say to me before. And I want to tell him that I ain't never liked no man much as I like him. But sometime you tell a man that and he go cause he think you liking him a whole lot gon hang him up.

"You and me," he say after we in bed, "we can make it together real good." He laugh. "I used to think all I needed was that music, but it take a woman to make that music sing, I think. So now stead of the music and me, it be the music and me and you."

"You left out Larry," I tell him. I don't think he want to hear that. But Larry my baby.

"How come you couldn't be free," he say real low. Then, "How you going when I go if you got a baby?"

"When you going?"

He turn his back to me. "Oh, I don't know. You know what the song say, 'When a woman take the blues, She tuck her head and cry. But when a man catch the blues, he grab his shoes and slide.' Next time I get the blues," he laugh a little, "next time the man get too much for me, I leave here and go someplace else. He always chasing me. The god damn white man." He turn over and reach for me. "You feel good. He chasing me and I chasing dreams. You think I'm crazy, huh? But I'm not. I just got so many, many things going on inside me I don't know which one to let out first. They all want out so bad. When I play—I got to be better, Martha. You gon help me?"

"Yes, Time, I help you."

"You see," and he reach over and turn on the light and look down at me, "I'm not what I am. I up tight on the inside but I can't get it to show on the outside. I don't know how to make it come out. You ever hear Coltrane blow? That man is together. He showing on the outside what he got on the inside. When I can do that, then I be somewhere. But I can't go by myself. I need a woman. A Black woman. Them other women steal your soul and don't leave nothing. But a Black woman—" He laugh and pull me close. He want me and that all I care bout.

Mamma come over that next morning and come right on in the bedroom, just like she always do. I kind of shamed for her to see me like that, with a man and all, but she don't say nothing cept scuse me, then turn away. "I come to get Larry."

"He in the other bedroom," I say, starting to get up.

"That's okay; I get him." And she go out and close the door.

I start to get out the bed anyway. Time reach for his cigarettes and light one. "Your mamma don't believe in knocking, do she?"

I start to tell him not to talk so loud cause Mamma a hear him, but that might make him mad. "Well, it ain't usually nobody in here with me for her to walk in on." I standing by the bed buttoning my house coat and Time reach out and pull my arm, smiling.

"I know you ain't no tramp, Martha. Come on, get back in bed."

I pull my arm way and start out the door. "I got to get Larry's clothes together," I tell him. I do got to get them clothes together cause when Mamma come for Larry like that on Sadday morning, she want to keep him for the rest of the weekend. But—I don't know. It just don't seem right for me to be in the bed with a man and my mamma in the next room.

I think Orine and German still in the other bedroom. But I don't know; Orine don't too much like for her mens to stay all night. She say it make a bad impression on her kids. I glad the door close anyway. If Mamma gon start talking that "why don't you come home" talk the way she usually do, it best for Orine not to hear it.

Orine's two kids still sleep but Mamma got Larry on his bed tickling him and playing with him. He like that. "Boy, you sho happy for it to be so early in the morning," I tell him.

Mamma stop tickling him and he lay there breathing hard for a minute. "Big Mamma," he say laughing and pointing at her. I just laugh at him and go get his clothes.

"You gon marry this one?" Every man I been with since I had Larry, she ask that about.

"You think marrying gon save my soul, Mamma?" I sorry right away cause Mamma don't like me to make fun of God. But I swear I gets tired of all that. What I want to marry for anyway? Get somebody like Daddy always coming and going and every time he go leave a baby behind. Or get a man what stay round and beat me all the time and have my kids thinking they big shit just cause they got a daddy what stay with them, like them saddity kids at school. Shit, married or single they still doing the same thing when they goes to bed.

Mamma don't say nothing else bout it. She ask where he work. I tell her and then take Larry in the bathroom and wash him up.

"The older you get, the more foolish you get, Martha. Them musicians ain't got nothing for a woman. Lots sweet talk and babies, that's all. Welfare don't even want to give you nothing for the one you got now, how you gon—" I sorry but I just stop listening. Mamma run her mouth like a clatterbone on a goose ass sometime. I just go on and give her the baby and get the rest of his things ready.

"So your mamma don't like musicians, huh?" Time say when I get back in the bedroom. "Square-ass people. Everything they don't know about, they hate. Lord deliver me from a square-ass town with square-ass people." He turn over.

"You wasn't calling me square last night."

"I'm not calling you square now, Martha."

I get back in the bed then and he put his arm round me. "But they say what they want to say. Long as they don't mess with me things be okay. But that's impossible. Somebody always got to have their little say about your life. They want to tell you where to go, how to play, what to play, where to play it—shit, even who to fuck and how to fuck em. But when I get to New York—"

"Time, let's don't talk now."

He laugh then. "Martha, you so Black." I don't know what I should say so I don't say nothing, just get closer and we don't talk.

That how it is lots a time with me and him. It seem like all I got is lots little pitchers in my mind and can't tell nobody what they look like. Once I try to tell him bout that, bout the pitchers, and he just laugh. "Least your head ain't empty. Maybe now you got some pictures, you get some thoughts." That make me mad and I start cussing, but he laugh and kiss me and hold me. And that time, when we doing it, it all—all angry and like he want to hurt me. And I think bout that song he sing that first night bout having the blues. But that the only time he mean like that.

Time and German brung the piano a couple days after that. The piano small and all shiny black wood. Time cussed German when German knocked it against the front door getting it in the house. Time went to put it in the bedroom but I want him to be thinking bout me, not some damn piano when he in there. I tell him he put it in the living room or it don't come in the house. Orine don't want it in the house period, say it too damn noisy—that's what she tell me. She don't say nothing to Time. I think she halfway scared of him. He pretty good bout playing it though. He don't never play it when the babies is sleep or at least he don't play loud as he can. But all he thinking bout when he playing is that piano. You talk to him, he don't answer; you touch him, he don't look up. One time I say to him, "Pay me some tention," but he don't even hear. I hit his hand, not hard, just playing. He look at me but he don't stop playing. "Get out of here, Martha." First I start to tell him he can't tell me what to do in my own self's house, but he just looking at me. Looking at me and playing and not saying nothing. I leave.

His friends come over most evenings when he home, not playing. It like Time is the leader. Whatever he say go. They always telling him how good he is. "Out of sight, man, the way you play." "You ought to get out of this little town so somebody can hear you play." Most times, he just smile and don't say nothing, or he just say thanks. But I wonder if he really believe em. I tell him, sometime, that he sound better than lots a them men on records. He give me his little cool smile. But I feel he glad I tell him that.

When his friends come over, we sit round laughing and talking and drinking. Orine like that cause she be playing up to em all and they be telling her what a fine ass she got. They don't tell me nothing like that cause Time be sitting right there, but long as Time telling me, I don't care. It like when we go to the Legion, after Time and German started being with us. We all the time get in free and then get to sit at one a the big front tables. And Orine like that cause it make her think she big-time. But she still her same old picky self; all the time telling me to "sit cool, Martha," and "be cool, girl." Acting like cool the most important thing in the world. I finally just tell her, "Time like me just the way I am, cool or not." And it true; Time always saying that I be myself and I be fine.

Time and his friends, they talk mostly bout music, music and New York City and white people. Sometime I get so sick a listening to em. Always talking bout how they gon put something over on the white man, gon take something way from him, gon do this, gon do that. Ah shit! I tell em. But they don't pay me no mind.

German say, one night, "Man, this white man come asking if I want to play at his house for—"

"What you tell him, man, 'Put money in my purse'?" Time ask. They all crack up. Me and Orine sit there quiet. Orine all swole up cause Time and them running some kind of game and she don't know what going down.

"Hey, man, yo all member that time up in Frisco when we got fired from that gig and wan't none of our old ladies working?" That Brown, he play bass with em.

"Man," Time say, "all I remember is that I stayed high most of the time. But how'd I stay high if ain't nobody had no bread? Somebody was putting something in somebody's purse." He lean back laughing a little. "Verna's mamma must have been sending her some money till she got a job. Yeah, yeah man, that was it. You remember the first time her mamma sent that money and she gave it all to me to hold?"

"And what she wanna do that for? You went out and gambled half a it away and bought pot with most of the rest." German not laughing much as Time and Brown.

"Man, I was scared to tell her, cause you remember how easy it was for her to get her jaws tight. But she was cool, didn't say nothing. I told her I was going to get food with the rest of the money and asked her what she wanted, and—"

"And she say cigarettes," Brown break in laughing, "and this cat, man, this cat tell her, 'Woman, we ain't wasting this bread on no nonessentials!' " He doubled over laughing. They all laughing. But I don't think it that funny. Any woman can give a man money.

"I thought the babe was gon kill me, her jaws was so tight. But even with her jaws tight, Verna was still cool. She just say, 'Baby, you done fucked up fifty dollars on nonessentials; let me try thirty cents.' "

That really funny to em. They all cracking up but me. Time sit there smiling just a little and shaking his head. Then, he reach out and squeeze my knee and smile at me. And I know it like I say; any woman can give a man money.

German been twitching round in his chair and finally he say, "Yeah, man, this fay dude want me to play at his house for fifty cent." That German always got to hear hisself talk. "I tell him take his fifty cent and shove it up his ass—oh scuse me. I forgot that baby was here—but I told him what to do with it. When I play for honkies, I tell him, I don't play for less than two hundred dollars and he so foolish he gon pay it." They all laugh, but I know German lying. Anybody offer him ten cent let lone fifty, he gon play.

"It ain't the money, man," Time say. "They just don't know what the fuck going on." I tell him Larry sitting right there. I know he ain't gon pay me no mind, but I feel if German can respect my baby, Time can too. "Man they go out to some little school, learn a few chords, and they think they know it all. Then, if you working for a white man, he fire you and hire him. No, man, I can't tie shit from no white man."

"That where you wrong," I tell him. "Somebody you don't like, you supposed to take em for everything they got. Take em and tell em to kiss yo butt."

"That another one of your pictures, I guess," Time say. And they all laugh cause he told em bout that, too, one time when he was mad with me.

"No, no," I say. "Listen, one day I walking downtown and this white man offer me a ride. I say okay and get in the car. He start talking and hinting round and finally he come on out and say it. I give you twenty dollars, he say. I say okay. We in Chinatown by then and at the next stop light he get out his wallet and give me a twenty-dollar bill. 'That what I like bout you colored women,' he say easing all back in his seat just like he already done got some and waiting to get some more. 'Yeah,' he say, 'you all so easy to get.' I put that money in my purse, open the door and tell him, 'Motherfucker, you ain't got shit here,' and slam the door."

"Watch your mouth," Time say, "Larry sitting here." We all crack up.

"What he do then?" Orine ask.

"What could he do? We in Chinatown and all them colored folks walking round. You know they ain't gon let no white man do nothing to me."

Time tell me after we go to bed that night that he kill me if he ever see me with a white man.

I laugh and kiss him. "What I want with a white man when I got you?" We both laugh and get in the bed. I lay stretched out waiting for him to reach for me. It funny, I think, how colored men don't never want no colored women messing with no white mens but the first chance he get, that colored man gon be right there in that white woman's bed. Yeah, colored men sho give colored womens a hard way to go. But I know if Time got to give a hard way to go, it ain't gon be for scaggy fay babe, and I kinda smile to myself.

"Martha—"

"Yeah, Time," I say turning to him.

"How old you—eighteen? What you want to do in life? What you want to be?"

What he mean? "I want to be with you," I tell him.

"No, I mean really. What you want?" Why he want to know, I wonder. Everytime he start talking serious-like, I think he must be hearing his sliding song.

"I don't want to have to ask nobody for nothing. I want to be able to take care of my own self." I won't be no weight on you, Time, I want to tell him. I won't be no trouble to you.

"Then what are you doing on the Welfare?"

"What else I gon do? Go out and scrub somebody else's toilets like my mamma did so Larry can run wild like I did? No. I stay on Welfare awhile, thank you."

"You see what the white man have done to us, is doing to us?"

"White man my ass," I tell him. "That was my no good daddy. If he'd gone out and worked, we woulda been better off."

"How he gon work if the man won't let him?"

"You just let the man turn you out. Yeah, that man got yo mind."

"What you mean?" he ask real quiet. But I don't pay no tention to him.

"You always talking bout music and New York City, New York City and the white man. Why don't you forget all that shit and get a job like other men? I hate that damn piano."

He grab my shoulder real tight. "What you mean, 'got my mind?' What you mean?" And he start shaking me. But I crying and thinking bout he gon leave.

"You laugh cause I say all I got in my mind is pitchers but least they better some old music. That all you ever think about, Time."

"What you mean? What you mean?"

Finally I scream. "You ain't gon no damn New York City and it ain't the white man what gon keep you. You just using him for a scuse cause you scared. Maybe you can't play." That the only time he ever hit me. And I cry cause I know he gon leave for sho. He hold me and say don't cry, say he sorry, but I can't stop. Orine bamming on the door and Time yelling at her to leave us lone and the babies crying and finally he start to pull away. I say, "Time . . ." He still for a long time, then he say, "Okay, Okay, Martha."

No, it not like he don't want me no more, he—

"Martha. Martha. You ain't been listening to a word I say."

"Mamma." I say it soft cause I don't want to hurt her. "Please leave me lone. You and Orine—and Time too, sometime—yo all treat me like I don't know nothing. But just cause it don't seem like to you that I know what I'm doing, that don't mean nothing. You can't see into my life."

"I see enough to know you just get into one mess after another." She shake her head and her voice come kinda slow. "Martha, I named you after that woman in the Bible cause I want you to be like her. Be good in the same way she is. Martha, that woman ain't never stopped believing. She humble and patient and the Lord make a place for her." She lean her hands on the table. Been in them dishes again, hands all wrinkled and shiny wet. "But that was the Bible. You ain't got the time to be patient, to be waiting for Time or no one else to make no place for you. That man ain't no good. I told you—"

Words coming faster and faster. She got the cow by the tail and gon on down shit creek. It don't matter though. She talk and I sit here thinking bout Time. "You feel good . . . You gon be my Black queen? . . . We can make it together . . . You feel good . . ." He be back.

SHE

by

CATHERINE DAVIS

(b. 1924)

*Catherine Davis grew up in Iowa and Minnesota and holds degrees
from George Washington University and the University of Iowa.
She has been an editor and a librarian as well as a teacher of writing
in several colleges. She is the recipient of several prizes, and her poems
have been published in* The Southern Review *and* The New Yorker.
At present she is working on a collection of her poems.

· ——————————————————————————— ·

SHE

gave me life
        what a hell
                on wheels she was
                        but

drive!
      indestructible (almost)
                        down
             snaky
                pitchdark
            highways blind

curves
     hairpin
turns
     the chances she took
         (if you wouldn't dim your lights
neither would she)
         a good
             head on her shoulders
quick reflexes
     but no

THE MOTHER

spare or
no brakes at all
a welter of
signals and signs
signifying
something to
someone else
(too hell-
bent
to look)
stopping
only to refuel
and then drive on like mad to make up
for lost time
(losing
the way) and
always in a storm of
rage   laughter
torrents of
words and
wit
curses and
tears
(or as the song on the jukebox goes
"if you think I laugh too loud
you should hear me
cry")
oh
the collisions
the wrecks as if
driven
by some demon
lover of
go and
find and
get
(but what?
not money)
the good die
young so
she kept going
an unforgettable

occurrence
        tearing through
                at 3 a.m.
dangerous
       to ignore
                   no apparition
                  but a dream
awakened
       of longing in all directions
                     and the roads
                       all open
In the determined
         course of her life
                  she gave as
good
    as she got
        and
             here I am

SOUVENIR

by

JAYNE ANNE PHILLIPS

(b. 1953)

Born in West Virginia, Jayne Anne Phillips earned degrees from West Virginia University and the University of Iowa. She has taught in college and now writes fulltime. She has won many awards and has held fellowships from the National Endowment for the Arts and the Mary Bunting Institute at Radcliffe College. Her stories have been collected in two small press editions as well as in Black Tickets *(1979); her novel* Machine Dreams *(1984) deals with the Vietnam War era.*

• ————————————————————— •

Kate always sent her mother a card on Valentine's Day. She timed the mails from wherever she was so that the cards arrived on February 14th. Her parents had celebrated the day in some small fashion, and since her father's death six years before, Kate made a gesture of compensatory remembrance. At first, she made the cards herself: collage and pressed grasses on construction paper sewn in fabric. Now she settled for art reproductions, glossy cards with blank insides. Kate wrote in them with colored inks, "You have always been my Valentine," or simply "Hey, take care of yourself." She might enclose a present as well, something small enough to fit into an envelope; a sachet, a perfumed soap, a funny tintype of a prune-faced man in a bowler hat.

This time, she forgot. Despite the garish displays of paper cupids and heart-shaped boxes in drugstore windows, she let the day nearly approach before remembering. It was too late to send anything in the mail. She called her mother long-distance at night when the rates were low.

"Mom? How are you?"

"It's you! How are *you?*" Her mother's voice grew suddenly brighter; Kate recognized a tone reserved for welcome company. Sometimes it took a while to warm up.

"I'm fine," answered Kate. "What have you been doing?"

"Well, actually I was trying to sleep."

"Sleep? You should be out setting the old hometown on fire."

"The old hometown can burn up without me tonight."

"Really? What's going on?"

"I'm running in-service training sessions for the primary teachers." Kate's mother was a school superintendent. "They're driving me batty. You'd think their brains were rubber."

"They are," Kate said. "Or you wouldn't have to train them. Think of them as a salvation, they create a need for your job."

"Some salvation. Besides, your logic is ridiculous. Just because someone needs training doesn't mean they're stupid."

"I'm just kidding. But *I'm* stupid. I forgot to send you a Valentine's card."

"You did? That's bad. I'm trained to receive one. They bring me luck."

"You're receiving a phone call instead," Kate said. "Won't that do?"

"Of course," said her mother, "but this is costing you money. Tell me quick, how are you?"

"Oh, you know. Doctoral pursuits. Doing my student trip, grooving with the professors."

"The professors? You'd better watch yourself."

"It's a joke, Mom, a joke. But what about you? Any men on the horizon?"

"No, not really. A married salesman or two asking me to dinner when they come through the office. Thank heavens I never let those things get started."

"You should do what you want to," Kate said.

"Sure," said her mother. "And where would I be then?"

"I don't know. Maybe Venezuela."

"They don't even have plumbing in Venezuela."

"Yes, but their sunsets are perfect, and the villages are full of dark passionate men in blousy shirts."

"That's your department, not mine."

"Ha," Kate said, "I wish it were my department. Sounds a lot more exciting than teaching undergraduates."

Her mother laughed. "Be careful," she said. "You'll get what you want. End up sweeping a dirt floor with a squawling baby around your neck."

"A dark baby," Kate said, "to stir up the family blood."

"Nothing would surprise me," her mother said as the line went fuzzy. Her voice was submerged in static, then surfaced. "Listen," she was saying. "Write to me. You seem so far away."

They hung up and Kate sat watching the windows of the neighboring house. The curtains were transparent and flowered and none of them matched. Silhouettes of the window frames spread across them like single dark bars. Her mother's curtains were all the same, white cotton hemmed with a ruffle, tiebacks blousing the cloth into identical shapes. From the street it looked as if the house was always in order.

Kate made a cup of strong Chinese tea, turned the lights off, and sat holding the warm cup in the dark. Her mother kept no real tea in the house, just packets of instant diabetic mixture which tasted of chemical sweetener and had a bitter aftertaste. The packets sat on the shelf next to her mother's miniature scales. The scales were white. Kate saw clearly the face of the metal dial on the front, its markings and trembling needle. Her mother weighed portions of food for meals: frozen broccoli, slices of plastic-wrapped Kraft cheese, careful chunks of roast beef. A dog-eared copy of *The Diabetic Diet* had remained propped against the salt shaker for the last two years.

Kate rubbed her forehead. Often at night she had headaches. Sometimes she wondered if there were an agent in her body, a secret in her blood making ready to work against her.

The phone blared repeatedly, careening into her sleep. Kate scrambled out of bed, naked and cold, stumbling, before she recognized the striped wallpaper of her bedroom and realized the phone was right there on the bedside table, as always. She picked up the receiver.

"Kate?" said her brother's voice. "It's Robert. Mom is in the hospital. They don't know what's wrong but she's in for tests."

"Tests? What's happened? I just talked to her last night."

"I'm not sure. She called the neighbors and they took her to the emergency room around dawn." Robert's voice still had that slight twang Kate knew was disappearing from her own. He would be calling from his insurance office, nine o'clock their time, in his thick glasses and wide, perfectly knotted tie. He was a member of the million-dollar club and his picture, tiny, the size of a postage stamp, appeared in the Mutual of Omaha magazine. His voice seemed small too over the distance. Kate felt heavy and dulled. She would never make much money, and recently she had begun wearing make-up again, waking in smeared mascara as she had in high school.

"Is Mom all right?" she managed now. "How serious is it?"

"They're not sure," Robert said. "Her doctor thinks it could have been any of several things, but they're doing X rays."

"Her doctor *thinks*? Doesn't he know? Get her to someone else. There aren't any doctors in that one-horse town."

"I don't know about that," Robert said defensively. "Anyway, I can't force her. You know how she is about money."

"Money? She could have a stroke and drop dead while her doctor wonders what's wrong."

"Doesn't matter. You know you can't tell her what to do."

"Could I call her somehow?"

"No, not yet. And don't get her all worried. She's been scared enough as it is. I'll tell her what you said about getting another opinion, and I'll call you back in a few hours when I have some news. Meanwhile, she's all right, do you hear?"

The line went dead with a click and Kate walked to the bathroom to

JAYNE ANNE PHILLIPS

203

wash her face. She splashed her eyes and felt guilty about the Valentine's card. Slogans danced in her head like reprimands. *For A Special One. Dearest Mother. My Best Friend.* Despite Robert, after breakfast she would call the hospital.

She sat a long time with her coffee, waiting for minutes to pass, considering how many meals she and her mother ate alone. Similar times of day, hundreds of miles apart. Women by themselves. The last person Kate had eaten breakfast with had been someone she'd met in a bar. He was passing through town. He liked his fried eggs gelatinized in the center, only slightly runny, and Kate had studiously looked away as he ate. The night before he'd looked down from above her as he finished and she still moved under him. "You're still wanting," he'd said. "That's nice." Mornings now, Kate saw her own face in the mirror and was glad she'd forgotten his name. When she looked at her reflection from the side, she saw a faint etching of lines beside her mouth. She hadn't slept with anyone for five weeks, and the skin beneath her eyes had taken on a creamy darkness.

She reached for the phone but drew back. It seemed bad luck to ask for news, to push toward whatever was coming as though she had no respect for it.

Standing in the kitchen last summer, her mother had stirred gravy and argued with her.

"I'm thinking of your own good, not mine," she'd said. "Think of what you put yourself through. And how can you feel right about it? You were born here, I don't care what you say." Her voice broke and she looked, perplexed, at the broth in the pan.

"But, hypothetically," Kate continued, her own voice unaccountably shaking, "if I'm willing to endure whatever I have to, do you have a right to object? You're my mother. You're supposed to defend my choices."

"You'll have enough trouble without choosing more for yourself. Using birth control that'll ruin your insides, moving from one place to another. I can't defend your choices. I can't even defend myself against you." She wiped her eyes on a napkin.

"Why do you have to make me feel so guilty?" Kate said, fighting tears of frustration. "I'm not attacking you."

"You're not? Then who are you talking to?"

"Oh Mom, give me a break."

"I've tried to give you more than that," her mother said. "I know what your choices are saying to me." She set the steaming gravy off the stove. "You may feel very differently later on. It's just a shame I won't be around to see it."

"Oh? Where will you be?"

"Floating around on a fleecy cloud."

Kate got up to set the table before she realized her mother had already done it.

The days went by. They'd gone shopping before Kate left. Standing at the cash register in an antique shop on Main Street, they bought each other pewter candle holders. "A souvenir," her mother said. "A reminder to always be nice to yourself. If you live alone you should eat by candlelight."

"Listen," Kate said, "I eat in a heart-shaped tub with bubbles to my chin. I sleep on satin sheets and my mattress has a built-in massage engine. My overnight guests are impressed. You don't have to tell me about the solitary pleasures."

They laughed and touched hands.

"Well," her mother said. "If you like yourself, I must have done something right."

Robert didn't phone until evening. His voice was fatigued and thin. "I've moved her to the university hospital," he said. "They can't deal with it at home."

Kate waited, saying nothing. She concentrated on the toes of her shoes. They needed shining. *You never take care of anything,* her mother would say.

"She has a tumor in her head." He said it firmly, as though Kate might challenge him.

"I'll take a plane tomorrow morning," Kate answered, "I'll be there by noon."

Robert exhaled. "Look," he said, "don't even come back here unless you can keep your mouth shut and do it my way."

"Get to the point."

"The point is they believe she has a malignancy and we're not going to tell her. I almost didn't tell you." His voice faltered. "They're going to operate but if they find what they're expecting, they don't think they can stop it."

For a moment there was no sound except an oceanic vibration of distance on the wire. Even that sound grew still. Robert breathed. Kate could almost see him, in a booth at the hospital, staring straight ahead at the plastic instructions screwed to the narrow rectangular body of the telephone. It seemed to her that she was hurtling toward him.

"I'll do it your way," she said.

The hospital cafeteria was a large room full of orange Formica tables. Its southern wall was glass. Across the highway, Kate saw a small park modestly dotted with amusement rides and bordered by a narrow band of river. How odd, to build a children's park across from a medical center. The sight was pleasant in a cruel way. The rolling lawn of the little park was perfectly, relentlessly green.

Robert sat down. Their mother was to have surgery in two days.

"After it's over," he said, "they're not certain what will happen. The tumor is in a bad place. There may be some paralysis."

"What kind of paralysis?" Kate said. She watched him twist the green-edged coffee cup around and around on its saucer.

"Facial. And maybe worse."

"You've told her this?"

He didn't answer.

"Robert, what is she going to think if she wakes up and—"

He leaned forward, grasping the cup and speaking through clenched teeth. "Don't you think I thought of that?" He gripped the sides of the table and the cup rolled onto the carpeted floor with a dull thud. He seemed ready to throw the table after it, then grabbed Kate's wrists and squeezed them hard.

"You didn't drive her here," he said. "She was so scared she couldn't talk. How much do you want to hand her at once?"

Kate watched the cup sitting solidly on the nubby carpet.

"We've told her it's benign," Robert said, "that the surgery will cause complications, but she can learn back whatever is lost."

Kate looked at him. "Is that true?"

"They hope so."

"We're lying to her, all of us, more and more." Kate pulled her hands away and Robert touched her shoulder.

"What do you want to tell her, Kate? 'You're fifty-five and you're done for'?"

She stiffened. "Why put her through the operation at all?"

He sat back and dropped his arms, lowering his head. "Because without it she'd be in bad pain. Soon." They were silent, then he looked up. "And anyway," he said softly, "we don't know, do we? She may have a better chance than they think."

Kate put her hands on her face. Behind her closed eyes she saw a succession of blocks tumbling over.

They took the elevator up to the hospital room. They were alone and they stood close together. Above the door red numerals lit up, flashing. Behind the illuminated shapes droned an impersonal hum of machinery.

Then the doors opened with a sucking sound. Three nurses stood waiting with a lunch cart, identical covered trays stacked in tiers. There was a hot bland smell, like warm cardboard. One of the women caught the thick steel door with her arm and smiled. Kate looked quickly at their rubber-soled shoes. White polish, the kind that rubs off. And their legs seemed only white shapes, boneless and two-dimensional, stepping silently into the metal cage.

She looked smaller in the white bed. The chrome side rails were pulled up and she seemed powerless behind them, her dark hair pushed back from her face and her forearms delicate in the baggy hospital gown. Her eyes were different in some nearly imperceptible way; she held them wider, they were shiny with a veiled wetness. For a moment the room seemed empty of all else; there were only her eyes and the dark blossoms of the flowers on the table beside her. Red roses with pine. Everyone had sent the same thing.

Robert walked close to the bed with his hands clasped behind his back, as though afraid to touch. "Where did all the flowers come from?" he asked.

"From school, and the neighbors. And Katie." She smiled.

"FTD," Kate said. "Before I left home. I felt so bad for not being here all along."

"That's silly," said her mother. "You can hardly sit at home and wait for some problem to arise."

"Speaking of problems," Robert said, "the doctor tells me you're not eating. Do I have to urge you a little?" He sat down on the edge of the bed and shook the silverware from its paper sleeve.

Kate touched the plastic tray. "Jell-O and canned cream of chicken soup. Looks great. We should have brought you something."

"They don't *want* us to bring her anything," Robert said. "This is a hospital. And I'm sure your comments make her lunch seem even more appetizing."

"I'll eat it!" said their mother in mock dismay. "Admit they sent you in here to stage a battle until I gave in."

"I'm sorry," Kate said. "He's right."

Robert grinned. "Did you hear that? She says I'm right. I don't believe it." He pushed the tray closer to his mother's chest and made a show of tucking a napkin under her chin.

"Of course you're right, dear." She smiled and gave Kate an obvious wink.

"Yeah," Robert said, "I know you two. But seriously, you eat this. I have to go make some business calls from the motel room."

Their mother frowned. "That motel must be costing you a fortune."

"No, it's reasonable," he said. "Kate can stay for a week or two and I'll drive back and forth from home. If you think this food is bad, you should see the meals in that motel restaurant." He got up to go, flashing Kate a glance of collusion. "I'll be back after supper."

His footsteps echoed down the hallway. Kate and her mother looked wordlessly at each other, relieved. Kate looked away guiltily. Then her mother spoke, apologetic. "He's so tired," she said. "He's been with me since yesterday."

She looked at Kate, then into the air of the room. "I'm in a fix," she said. "Except for when the pain comes, it's all a show that goes on without me. I'm like an invalid, or a lunatic."

Kate moved close and touched her mother's arms. "That's all right, we're going to get you through it. Someone's covering for you at work?"

"I had to take a leave of absence. It's going to take a while afterward—"

"I know. But it's the last thing to worry about, it can't be helped."

"Like spilt milk. Isn't that what they say?"

"I don't know what they say. But why didn't you tell me? Didn't you know something was wrong?"

"Yes . . . bad headaches. Migraines, I thought, or the diabetes getting worse. I was afraid they'd start me on insulin." She tightened the corner of her mouth. "Little did I know . . ."

They heard the shuffle of slippers. An old woman stood at the open door of the room, looking in confusedly. She seemed about to speak, then moved on.

"Oh," said Kate's mother in exasperation, "shut that door, please? They let these old women wander around like refugees." She sat up, reaching for a robe. "And let's get me out of this bed."

They sat near the window while she finished eating. Bars of moted yellow banded the floor of the room. The light held a tinge of spring which seemed painful because it might vanish. They heard the rattle of the meal cart outside the closed door, and the clunk-slide of patients with aluminum walkers. Kate's mother sighed and pushed away the half-empty soup bowl.

"They'll be here after me any minute. More tests. I just want to stay with you." Her face was warm and smooth in the slanted light, lines in her skin delicate, unreal; as though a face behind her face was now apparent after many years. She sat looking at Kate and smiled.

"One day when you were about four you were dragging a broom around the kitchen. I asked you what you were doing and you told me that when you got old you were going to be an angel and sweep the rotten rain off the clouds."

"What did you say to that?"

"I said that when you were old I was sure God would see to it." Her mother laughed. "I'm glad you weren't such a smart aleck then," she said. "You would have told me my view of God was paternalistic."

"Ah yes," sighed Kate. "God, that famous dude. Here I am, getting old, facing unemployment, alone, and where is He?"

"You're not alone," her mother said, "I'm right here."

Kate didn't answer. She sat motionless and felt her heart begin to open like a box with a hinged lid. The fullness had no edges.

Her mother stood. She rubbed her hands slowly, twisting her wedding rings. "My hands are so dry in the winter," she said softly, "I brought some hand cream with me but I can't find it anywhere, my suitcase is so jumbled. Thank heavens spring is early this year. . . . They told me that little park over there doesn't usually open till the end of March . . ."

She's helping me, thought Kate, I'm not supposed to let her down.

". . . but they're already running it on weekends. Even past dusk. We'll see the lights tonight. You can't see the shapes this far away, just the motion . . ."

THE MOTHER

208

A nurse came in with a wheelchair. Kate's mother pulled a wry face. "This wheelchair is a bit much," she said.

"We don't want to tire you out," said the nurse.

The chair took her weight quietly. At the door she put out her hand to stop, turned, and said anxiously, "Kate, see if you can find that hand cream?"

It was the blue suitcase from years ago, still almost new. She'd brought things she never used for everyday; a cashmere sweater, lace slips, silk underpants wrapped in tissue. Folded beneath was a stack of postmarked envelopes, slightly ragged, tied with twine. Kate opened one and realized that all the cards were there, beginning with the first of the marriage. There were a few photographs of her and Robert, baby pictures almost indistinguishable from each other, and then Kate's homemade Valentines, fastened together with rubber bands. Kate stared. *What will I do with these things?* She wanted air; she needed to breathe. She walked to the window and put the bundled papers on the sill. She'd raised the glass and pushed back the screen when suddenly, her mother's clock radio went off with a flat buzz. Kate moved to switch it off and brushed the cards with her arm. Envelopes shifted and slid, scattering on the floor of the room. A few snapshots wafted silently out the window. They dipped and turned, twirling. Kate didn't try to reach them. They seemed only scraps, buoyant and yellowed, blown away, the faces small as pennies. Somewhere far-off there were sirens, almost musical, drawn out and carefully approaching.

The nurse came in with evening medication. Kate's mother lay in bed. "I hope this is strong enough," she said. "Last night I couldn't sleep at all. So many sounds in a hospital . . ."

"You'll sleep tonight," the nurse assured her.

Kate winked at her mother. "That's right," she said, "I'll help you out if I have to."

They stayed up for an hour, watching the moving lights outside and the stationary glows of houses across the distant river. The halls grew darker, were lit with night lights, and the hospital dimmed. Kate waited. Her mother's eyes fluttered and finally she slept. Her breathing was low and regular.

Kate didn't move. Robert had said he'd be back; where was he? She felt a sunken anger and shook her head. She'd been on the point of telling her mother everything. The secrets were a travesty. What if there were things her mother wanted done, people she needed to see? Kate wanted to wake her before these hours passed in the dark and confess that she had lied. Between them, through the tension, there had always been a trusted clarity. Now it was twisted. Kate sat leaning forward, nearly touching the hospital bed.

Suddenly her mother sat bolt upright, her eyes open and her face transfixed. She looked blindly toward Kate but seemed to see nothing. "Who are you?" she whispered. Kate stood, at first unable to move. The woman in the bed opened and closed her mouth several times, as though she were gasping. Then she said loudly, "Stop moving the table. Stop it this instant!" Her eyes were wide with fright and her body was vibrating.

Kate reached her. "Mama, wake up, you're dreaming." Her mother jerked, flinging her arms out. Kate held her tightly.

"I can hear the wheels," she moaned.

"No, no," Kate said. "You're here with me."

"It's not so?"

"No," Kate said. "It's not so."

She went limp. Kate felt for her pulse and found it rapid, then regular. She sat rocking her mother. In a few minutes she lay her back on the pillows and smoothed the damp hair at her temples, smoothed the sheets of the bed. Later she slept fitfully in a chair, waking repeatedly to assure herself that her mother was breathing.

Near dawn she got up, exhausted, and left the room to walk in the corridor. In front of the window at the end of the hallway she saw a man slumped on a couch; the man slowly stood and wavered before her like a specter. It was Robert.

"Kate?" he said.

Years ago he had flunked out of a small junior college and their mother sat in her bedroom rocker, crying hard for over an hour while Kate tried in vain to comfort her. Kate went to the university the next fall, so anxious that she studied frantically, outlining whole textbooks in yellow ink. She sat in the front rows of large classrooms to take voluminous notes, writing quickly in her thick notebook. Robert had gone home, held a job in a plant that manufactured business forms and worked his way through the hometown college. By that time their father was dead, and Robert became, always and forever, the man of the house.

"Robert," Kate said, "I'll stay. Go home."

After breakfast they sat waiting for Robert, who had called and said he'd arrive soon. Kate's fatigue had given way to an intense awareness of every sound, every gesture. How would they get through the day? Her mother had awakened from the drugged sleep still groggy, unable to eat. The meal was sent away untouched and she watched the window as though she feared the walls of the room.

"I'm glad your father isn't here to see this," she said. There was a silence and Kate opened her mouth to speak. "I mean," said her mother quickly, "I'm going to look horrible for a few weeks, with my head all shaved." She pulled an afghan up around her lap and straightened the magazines on the table beside her chair.

"Mom," Kate said, "your hair will grow back."

Her mother pulled the afghan closer. "I've been thinking of your father," she said. "It's not that I'd have wanted him to suffer. But if he had to die, sometimes I wish he'd done it more gently. That heart attack, so finished; never a warning. I wish I'd had some time to nurse him. In a way, it's a chance to settle things."

"Did things need settling?"

"They always do, don't they?" She sat looking out the window, then said softly, "I wonder where I'm headed."

"You're not headed anywhere," Kate said. "I want you right here to see me settle down into normal American womanhood."

Her mother smiled reassuringly. "Where are my grandchildren?" she said. "That's what I'd like to know."

"You stick around," said Kate, "and I promise to start working on it." She moved her chair closer, so that their knees were touching and they could both see out the window. Below them cars moved on the highway and the Ferris wheel in the little park was turning.

"I remember when you were one of the little girls in the parade at the county fair. You weren't even in school yet; you were beautiful in that white organdy dress and pinafore. You wore those shiny black patent shoes and a crown of real apple blossoms. Do you remember?"

"Yes," Kate said. "That long parade. They told me not to move and I sat so still my legs went to sleep. When they lifted me off the float I couldn't stand up. They put me under a tree to wait for you, and you came, in a full white skirt and white sandals, your hair tied back in a red scarf. I can see you yet."

Her mother laughed. "Sounds like a pretty exaggerated picture."

Kate nodded. "I was little. You were big."

"You loved the county fair. You were wild about the carnivals." They looked down at the little park. "Magic, isn't it?" her mother said.

"Maybe we could go see it," said Kate. "I'll ask the doctor."

They walked across a pedestrian footbridge spanning the highway. Kate had bundled her mother into a winter coat and gloves despite the sunny weather. The day was sharp, nearly still, holding its bright air like illusion. Kate tasted the brittle water of her breath, felt for the cool handrail and thin steel of the webbed fencing. Cars moved steadily under the bridge. Beyond a muted roar of motors the park spread green and wooded, its limits clearly visible.

Kate's mother had combed her hair and put on lipstick. Her mouth was defined and brilliant; she linked arms with Kate like an escort. "I was afraid they'd tell us no," she said. "I was ready to run away!"

"I promised I wouldn't let you. And we only have ten minutes, long enough for the Ferris wheel." Kate grinned.

"I haven't ridden one in years. I wonder if I still know how."

"Of course you do. Ferris wheels are genetic knowledge."

"All right, whatever you say." She smiled. "We'll just hold on."

They drew closer and walked quickly through the sounds of the highway. When they reached the grass it was ankle-high and thick, longer and more ragged than it appeared from a distance. The Ferris wheel sat squarely near a grove of swaying elms, squat and laboring, taller than trees. Its neon lights still burned, pale in the sun, spiraling from inside like an imagined bloom. The naked elms surrounded it, their topmost branches tapping. Steel ribs of the machine were graceful and slightly rusted, squeaking faintly above a tinkling music. Only a few people were riding.

"Looks a little rickety," Kate said.

"Oh, don't worry," said her mother.

Kate tried to buy tickets but the ride was free. The old man running the motor wore an engineer's cap and patched overalls. He stopped the wheel and led them on a short ramp to an open car. It dipped gently, padded with black cushions. An orderly and his children rode in the car above. Kate saw their dangling feet, the girls' dusty sandals and gray socks beside their father's shoes and the hem of his white pants. The youngest one swung her feet absently, so it seemed the breeze blew her legs like fabric hung on a line.

Kate looked at her mother. "Are you ready for the big sky?" They laughed. Beyond them the river moved lazily. Houses on the opposite bank seemed empty, but a few rowboats bobbed at the docks. The surface of the water lapped and reflected clouds, and as Kate watched, searching for a definition of line, the Ferris wheel jerked into motion. The car rocked. They looked into the distance and Kate caught her mother's hand as they ascended.

Far away the hospital rose up white and glistening, its windows catching the glint of the sun. Directly below, the park was nearly deserted. There were a few cars in the parking lot and several dogs chasing each other across the grass. Two or three lone women held children on the teeter-totters and a wind was coming up. The forlorn swings moved on their chains. Kate had a vision of the park at night, totally empty, wind weaving heavily through the trees and children's playthings like a great black fish about to surface. She felt a chill on her arms. The light had gone darker, quietly, like a minor chord.

"Mom," Kate said, "it's going to storm." Her own voice seemed distant, the sound strained through layers of screen or gauze.

"No," said her mother, "it's going to pass over." She moved her hand to Kate's knee and touched the cloth of her daughter's skirt.

Kate gripped the metal bar at their waists and looked straight ahead. They were rising again and she felt she would scream. She tried to breathe rhythmically, steadily. She felt the immense weight of the air as they moved through it.

They came almost to the top and stopped. The little car swayed back and forth.

"You're sick, aren't you," her mother said.

Kate shook her head. Below them the grass seemed to glitter coldly, like a sea. Kate sat wordless, feeling the touch of her mother's hand. The hand moved away and Kate felt the absence of the warmth.

They looked at each other levelly.

"I know all about it," her mother said, "I know what you haven't told me."

The sky circled around them, a sure gray movement. Kate swallowed calmly and let their gaze grow endless. She saw herself in her mother's wide brown eyes and felt she was falling slowly into them.

THE MIDDLE DRAWER

by

HORTENSE CALISHER

(b. 1911)

Born into a Jewish family who had been settled in the United States for 150 years, Hortense Calisher has worked in the ghettos of several American cities. The author of a number of works of fiction noted for their psychological depth of character, she has won four O. Henry Prize Story awards; she has also taught and lectured widely. She has written an autobiography, Herself *(1972); her most recent work is* Standard Dreaming *(1983). Her short stories were collected in 1975.*

• ———————————————— •

The drawer was always kept locked. In a household where the tangled rubbish of existence had collected on surfaces like a scurf, which was forever being cleared away by her mother and the maid, then by her mother, and, finally, hardly at all, it had been a permanent cell—rather like, Hester thought wryly, the gene that is carried over from one generation to the other. Now, holding the small, square, indelibly known key in her hand, she shrank before it, reluctant to perform the blasphemy that the living must inevitably perpetrate on the possessions of the dead. There were no revelations to be expected when she opened the drawer, only the painful reiteration of her mother's personality and the power it had held over her own, which would rise—an emanation, a mist, that she herself had long since shredded away, parted, and escaped.

She repeated to herself, like an incantation, "I am married. I have a child of my own, a home of my own five hundred miles away. I have not even lived in this house—my parents' house—for over seven years." Stepping back, she sat on the bed where her mother had died the week before, slowly, from cancer, where Hester had held the large, long-fingered, competent hand for a whole night, watching the asphyxiating action of the fluid mounting in the lungs until it had extinguished the breath. She sat facing the drawer.

It had taken her all her own lifetime to get to know its full contents, starting from the first glimpses, when she was just able to lean her chin on the side and have her hand pushed away from the packets and japanned boxes, to the last weeks, when she had made a careful show of not noticing while she got out the necessary bankbooks and safe-deposit keys. Many times during her childhood, when she had lain blandly ill herself, elevated to the honor of the parental bed while she suffered from the "autointoxication" that must have been 1918's euphemism for plain piggishness, the drawer had been opened. Then she had been allowed to play with the two pairs of pearled opera glasses or the long string of graduated white china beads, each with its oval sides flushed like cheeks. Over these she had sometimes spent the whole afternoon, pencilling two eyes and a pursed mouth on each bead, until she had achieved an incredible string of minute, doll-like heads that made even her mother laugh.

Once while Hester was in college, the drawer had been opened for the replacement of her grandmother's great sunburst pin, which she had never before seen and which had been in pawn, and doggedly reclaimed over a long period by her mother. And for Hester's wedding her mother had taken out the delicate diamond chain—the "lavaliere" of the Gibson-girl era— that had been her father's wedding gift to her mother, and the ugly, expensive bar pin that had been his gift to his wife on the birth of her son. Hester had never before seen either of them, for the fashion of wearing diamonds indiscriminately had never been her mother's, who was contemptuous of other women's display, although she might spend minutes in front of the mirror debating a choice between two relatively gimcrack pieces of costume jewelry. Hester had never known why this was until recently, when the separation of the last few years had relaxed the tension between her mother and herself—not enough to prevent explosions when they met but enough for her to see obscurely, the long motivations of her mother's life. In the European sense, family jewelry was Property, and with all her faultless English and New World poise, her mother had never exorcised her European core.

In the back of the middle drawer, there was a small square of brown-toned photograph that had never escaped into the large, ramshackle portfolio of family pictures kept in the drawer of the old break-front bookcase, open to any hand. Seated on a bench, Hedwig Licht, aged two, brows knitted under ragged hair, stared mournfully into the camera with the huge, heavy-lidded eyes that had continued to brood in her face as a woman, the eyes that she had transmitted to Hester, along with the high cheekbones that she had deplored. Fat, wrinkled stockings were bowed into arcs that almost met at the high-stretched boots, which did not touch the floor; to hold up the stockings, strips of calico matching the dumpy little dress were bound around the knees.

Long ago, Hester, in her teens, staring tenaciously into the drawer under her mother's impatient glance, had found the little square and exclaimed over it, and her mother, snatching it away from her, had muttered, "If that isn't Dutchy!" But she had looked at it long and ruefully before she had pushed it back into a corner. Hester had added the picture to the legend of her mother's childhood built up from the bitter little anecdotes that her mother had let drop casually over the years.

She saw the small Hedwig, as clearly as if it had been herself, haunting the stiff rooms of the house in the townlet of Oberelsbach, motherless since birth and almost immediately stepmothered by a woman who had been unloving, if not unkind, and had soon borne the stern, *Haustyrann* father a son. The small figure she saw had no connection with the all-powerful figure of her mother but, rather, seemed akin to the legion of lonely children who were a constant motif in the literature that had been her own drug—the Sara Crewes and Little Dorrits, all those children who inhabited the familiar terror-struck dark that crouched under the lash of the adult. She saw Hedwig receiving from her dead mother's mother—the Grand-mother Rosenberg, warm and loving but, alas, too far away to be of help—the beautiful, satin-incrusted bisque doll, and she saw the bad stepmother taking it away from Hedwig and putting it in the drawing room, because "it is too beautiful for a child to play with." She saw all this as if it had happened to her and she had never forgotten.

Years later, when this woman, Hester's step-grandmother, had come to the United States in the long train of refugees from Hitler, her mother had urged the grown Hester to visit her, and she had refused, knowing her own childishness but feeling the resentment rise in her as if she were six, saying, "I won't go. She wouldn't let you have your doll." Her mother had smiled at her sadly and had shrugged her shoulders resignedly. "You wouldn't say that if you could see her. She's an old woman. She has no teeth." Looking at her mother, Hester had wondered what her feelings were after forty years, but her mother, private as always in her emotions, had given no sign.

There had been no sign for Hester—never an open demonstration of love or an appeal—until the telephone call of a few months before, when she had heard her mother say quietly, over the distance, "I think you'd better come," and she had turned away from the phone saying bitterly, almost in awe, "If she *asks me* to come, she must be dying!"

Turning the key over in her hand, Hester looked back at the composite figure of her mother—that far-off figure of the legendary child, the nearer object of her own dependence, love, and hate—looked at it from behind the safe, dry wall of her own "American" education. We are told, she thought, that people who do not experience love in their earliest years cannot open up; they cannot give it to others; but by the time we have learned this from books or dredged it out of reminiscence, they have long since left upon us their chill, irremediable stain.

If Hester searched in her memory for moments of animal maternal warmth, like those she self-consciously gave her own child (as if her own childhood prodded her from behind), she thought always of the blue-shot twilight of one New York evening, the winter she was eight, when she and her mother were returning from a shopping expedition, gay and united in the shared guilt of being late for supper. In her mind, now, their arrested figures stood like two silhouettes caught in the spotlight of time. They had paused under the brightly agitated bulbs of a movie-theatre marquee, behind them the broad, rose-red sign of a Happiness candy store. Her mother, suddenly leaning down to her, had encircled her with her arm and nuzzled her, saying almost anxiously, "We do have fun together, don't we?" Hester had stared back stolidly, almost suspiciously, into the looming, pleading eyes, but she had rested against the encircling arm, and warmth had trickled through her as from a closed wound reopening.

After this, her mother's part in the years that followed seemed blurred with the recriminations from which Hester had retreated ever farther, always seeking the remote corners of the household—the sofa-fortressed alcoves, the store closet, the servants' bathroom—always bearing her amulet, a book. It seemed to her now, wincing, that the barrier of her mother's dissatisfaction with her had risen imperceptibly, like a coral cliff built inexorably from the slow accretion of carelessly ejaculated criticisms that had grown into solid being in the heavy fullness of time. Meanwhile, her father's uncritical affection, his open caresses, had been steadiness under her feet after the shifting waters of her mother's personality, but he had been away from home on business for long periods, and when at home he, too, was increasingly a target for her mother's deep-burning rage against life. Adored member of a large family that was almost tribal in its affections and unity, he could not cope with this smoldering force and never tried to understand it, but the shield of his adulthood gave him a protection that Hester did not have. He stood on equal ground.

Hester's parents had met at Saratoga, at the races. So dissimilar were their backgrounds that it was improbable that they would ever have met elsewhere than in the somewhat easy social flux of a spa, although their brownstone homes in New York were not many blocks apart, his in the gentility of upper Madison Avenue, hers in the solid, Germanic comfort of Yorkville. By this time, Hedwig had been in America ten years.

All Hester knew of her mother's coming to America was that she had arrived when she was sixteen. Now that she knew how old her mother had been at death, knew the birth date so zealously guarded during a lifetime of evasion and so quickly exposed by the noncommittal nakedness of funeral routine, she realized that her mother must have arrived in 1900. She had come to the home of an aunt, a sister of her own dead mother. What family drama had preceded her coming, whose decision it had been, Hester did not know. Her mother's one reply to a direct question had been a shrugging "There was nothing for me there."

Hester had a vivid picture of her mother's arrival and first years in New York, although this was drawn from only two clues. Her great-aunt, remarking once on Hester's looks in the dispassionate way of near relations, had nodded over Hester's head to her mother. "She is dark, like the father, no? Not like you were." And Hester, with a naïve glance of surprise at her mother's sedate pompadour, had eagerly interposed, "What was she like, Tante?"

"Ach, when she came off the boat, *war sie hübsch!"* Tante had said, lapsing into German with unusual warmth, "Such a color! Pink and cream!"

"Yes, a real Bavarian *Mädchen,"* said her mother with a trace of contempt. "Too pink for the fashion here. I guess they thought it wasn't real."

Another time, her mother had said, in one of her rare bursts of anecdote, "When I came, I brought enough linen and underclothing to supply two brides. At the convent school where I was sent, the nuns didn't teach you much besides embroidery, so I had plenty to bring, plenty. They were nice, though. Good, simple women. Kind. I remember I brought four dozen handkerchiefs, beautiful heavy linen that you don't get in America. But they were large, bigger than the size of a man's handkerchief over here, and the first time I unfolded one, everybody laughed, so I threw them away." She had sighed, perhaps for the linen. "And underdrawers! Long red flannel, and I had spent months embroidering them with yards of white eyelet work on the ruffles. I remember Tante's maid came in from the back yard quite angry and refused to hang them on the line any more. She said the other maids, from the houses around, teased her for belonging to a family who would wear things like that."

Until Hester was in her teens, her mother had always employed young German or Czech girls fresh from "the other side"—Teenies and Josies of long braided hair, broad cotton ankles and queer, blunt shoes, who had clacked deferentially to her mother in German and had gone off to marry their waiter's and baker's apprentices at just about the time they learned to wear silk stockings and "just as soon as you've taught them how to serve a dinner," returning regularly to show off their square, acrid babies. "Greenhorns!" her mother had always called them, a veil of something indefinable about her lips. But in the middle drawer there was a long rope of blond hair, sacrificed, like the handkerchiefs, but not wholly discarded.

There was no passport in the drawer. Perhaps it had been destroyed during the years of the first World War, when her mother, long since a citizen by virtue of her marriage, had felt the contemporary pressure to excise everything Teutonic. "If that nosy Mrs. Cahn asks you when I came over, just say I came over as a child," she had said to Hester. And how easy it had been to nettle her by pretending that one could discern a trace of accent in her speech! Once, when the family had teased her by affecting to hear an echo of "publi[k]" in her pronunciation of "public," Hester had come upon her, hours after, standing before a mirror, color and nose high, watching herself say, over and over again, "Public! Public!"

Was it this, thought Hester, her straining toward perfection, that made her so intolerant of me, almost as if she were castigating in her child the imperfections that were her own? "Big feet, big hands, like mine," her mother had grumbled. "Why? Why? When every woman in your father's family wears size one! But their nice, large ears—you must have *those!"* And dressing Hester for Sunday school she would withdraw a few feet to look at the finished product, saying slowly, with dreamy cruelty, "I don't know why I let you wear those white gloves. They make your hands look clumsy, just like a policeman's."

It was over books that the rift between Hester and her mother had become complete. To her mother, marrying into a family whose bookish traditions she had never ceased trying to undermine with the sneer of the practical, it was as if the stigmata of that tradition, appearing upon the girl, had forever made them alien to one another.

"Your eyes don't look like a girl's, they look like an old woman's! Reading! Forever reading!" she had stormed, chasing Hester from room to room, flushing her out of doors, and on one remote, terrible afternoon, whipping the book out of Hester's hand, she had leaned over her, glaring, and had torn the book in two.

Hester shivered now, remembering the cold sense of triumph that had welled up in her as she had faced her mother, rejoicing in the enormity of what her mother had done.

Her mother had faltered before her. "Do you want to be a dreamer all your life?" she had muttered.

Hester had been unable to think of anything to say for a moment. Then she had stuttered, "All you think of in life is money!", and had made her grand exit. But huddling miserably in her room afterward she had known even then that it was not as simple as that, that her mother, too, was whipped and driven by some ungovernable dream she could not express, which had left her, like the book, torn in two.

Was it this, perhaps, that had sent her across an ocean, that had impelled her to perfect her dress and manner, and to reject the humdrum suitors of her aunt's circle for a Virginia bachelor twenty-two years older than herself? Had she, perhaps, married him not only for his money and his seasoned male charm but also for his standards and traditions, against which her railings had been a confession of envy and defeat?

So Hester and her mother had continued to pit their implacable difference against each other in a struggle that was complicated out of all reason by their undeniable likeness—each pursuing in her own orbit the warmth that had been denied. Gauche and surly as Hester was in her mother's presence, away from it she had striven successfully for the very falsities of standard that she despised in her mother, and it was her misery that she was forever impelled to earn her mother's approval at the expense of her own. Always, she knew now, there had been the lurking, buried wish that someday she would find the final barb, the homing shaft, that would maim her mother once and for all, as she felt herself to have been maimed.

A few months before, the barb had been placed in her hand. In answer to the telephone call, she had come to visit the family a short time after her mother's sudden operation for cancer of the breast. She had found her father and brother in an anguish of helplessness, fear, and male distaste at the thought of the illness, and her mother a prima donna of fortitude, moving unbowed toward the unspoken idea of her death but with the signs on her face of a pitiful tension that went beyond the disease. She had taken to using separate utensils and to sleeping alone, although the medical opinion that cancer was not transferable by contact was well known to her. It was clear that she was suffering from a horror of what had been done to her and from a fear of the revulsion of others. It was clear to Hester, also, that her father and brother had such a revulsion and had not been wholly successful in concealing it.

One night she and her mother had been together in her mother's bedroom. Hester, in a shabby housegown, stretched out on the bed luxuriously, thinking of how there was always a certain equivocal ease, a letting down of pretense, an illusory return to the irresponsibility of childhood, in the house of one's birth. Her mother, back turned, had been standing unnecessarily long at the bureau, fumbling with the articles upon it. She turned slowly.

"They've been giving me X-ray twice a week," she said, not looking at Hester, "to stop any involvement of the glands."

"Oh," said Hester, carefully smoothing down a wrinkle on the bedspread. "It's very wise to have that done."

Suddenly, her mother had put out her hand in a gesture almost of appeal. Half in a whisper, she asked, "Would you like to see it? No one has seen it since I left the hospital."

"Yes," Hester said, keeping her tone cool, even, full only of polite interest. "I'd like very much to see it." Frozen there on the bed, she had reverted to childhood in reality, remembering, as if they had all been crammed into one slot in time, the thousands of incidents when she had been the one to stand before her mother, vulnerable and bare, helplessly awaiting the cruel exactitude of her displeasure. "I know how she feels as if I were standing there myself," thought Hester. "How well she taught me to know!"

Slowly her mother undid her housegown and bared her breast. She stood there for a long moment, on her face the looming, pleading look of twenty years before, the look it had once shown under the theatre marquee.

Hester half rose from the bed. There was a hurt in her own breast that she did not recognize. She spoke with difficulty.

"Why . . . it's a beautiful job, Mother," she said, distilling the carefully natural tone of her voice. "Neat as can be. I had no idea . . . I thought it would be ugly." With a step toward her mother, she looked, as if casually, at the dreadful neatness of the cicatrix, at the twisted, foreshortened tendon of the upper arm.

"I can't raise my arm yet," whispered her mother. "They had to cut deep. . . . Your father won't look at it."

In an eternity of slowness, Hester stretched out her hand. Trembling, she touched a tentative finger to her mother's chest, where the breast had been. Then, with rising sureness, with infinite delicacy, she drew her fingertips along the length of the scar in a light, affirmative caress, and they stood eye to eye for an immeasurable second, on equal ground at last.

In the cold, darkening room, Hester unclenched herself from remembrance. She was always vulnerable, Hester thought. As we all are. What she bequeathed me unwittingly, ironically, was fortitude—the fortitude of those who have had to live under the blow. But pity—that I found for myself.

She knew now that the tangents of her mother and herself would never have fully met, even if her mother had lived. Holding her mother's hand through the long night as she retreated over the border line of narcosis and coma into death, she had felt the giddy sense of conquering, the heady euphoria of being still alive, which comes to the watcher in the night. Nevertheless, she had known with sureness, even then, that she would go on all her life trying to "show" her mother, in an unsatisfied effort to earn her approval—and unconditional love.

As a child, she had slapped at her mother once in a frenzy of rebellion, and her mother, in reproof, had told her the tale of the peasant girl who had struck her mother and had later fallen ill and died and been buried in the village cemetery. When the mourners came to tend the mound, they found that the corpse's offending hand had grown out of the grave. They cut it off and reburied it, but when they came again in the morning, the hand had grown again. So, too, thought Hester, even though I might learn—have learned in some ways—to escape my mother's hand, all my life I will have to push it down; all my life my mother's hand will grow again out of the unquiet grave of the past.

It was her own life that was in the middle drawer. She was the person she was not only because of her mother but because, fifty-eight years before, in the little town of Oberelsbach, another woman, whose qualities she would never know, had died too soon. Death, she thought, absolves equally the bungler, the evildoer, the unloving, and the unloved—but never the living. In the end, the cicatrix that she had, in the smallest of ways, helped her mother to bear had eaten its way in and killed. The living carry, she thought, perhaps not one tangible wound but the burden of the innumerable small cicatrices imposed on us by our beginnings; we carry them with us always, and from these, from this agony, we are not absolved.

She turned the key and opened the drawer.

BRIDGING

by

MAX APPLE

(b. 1941)

Born in Michigan, Max Apple teaches at Rice University in Texas;
he has received an award from the Texas Institute of Letters for
his witty writings, which usually have a serious social purpose. His
works include Zip *(1978),* The Oranging of America *(1981), and*
Free Agents *(1984), a collection of short fictional and nonfictional*
pieces, many of which are about his two children.

• ———————————————— •

At the Astrodome, Nolan Ryan is shaving the corners. He's going through
the Giants in order. The radio announcer is not even mentioning that by the
sixth the Giants haven't had a hit. The K's mount on the scoreboard.
Tonight Nolan passes the Big Train and is now the all-time strikeout king.
He's almost as old as I am and he still throws nothing but smoke. His
fastball is an aspirin; batters tear their tendons lunging for his curve. Jessica
and I have season tickets, but tonight she's home listening and I'm in the
basement of St. Anne's Church watching Kay Randall's fingertips. Kay is
holding her hands out from her chest, her fingertips on each other. Her
fingers move a little as she talks and I can hear her nails click when they
meet. That's how close I'm sitting.

Kay is talking about "bridging"; that's what her arched fingers represent.

"Bridging," she says, "is the way Brownies become Girl Scouts. It's a
slow steady process. It's not easy, but we allow a whole year for bridging."

Eleven girls in brown shirts with red bandannas at their neck are
imitating Kay as she talks. They hold their stumpy chewed fingertips out
and bridge them. So do I.

I brought the paste tonight and the stick-on gold stars and the thread for
sewing buttonholes.

"I feel a little awkward," Kay Randall said on the phone, "asking a man
to do these errands . . . but that's my problem, not yours. Just bring the
supplies and try to be at the church meeting room a few minutes before
seven."

I arrive a half hour early.

"You're off your rocker," Jessica says. She begs me to drop her at the

Astrodome on my way to the Girl Scout meeting. "After the game, I'll meet you at the main souvenir stand on the first level. They stay open an hour after the game. I'll be all right. There are cops and ushers every five yards."

She can't believe that I am missing this game to perform my functions as an assistant Girl Scout leader. Our Girl Scout battle has been going on for two months.

"Girl Scouts is stupid," Jessica says. "Who wants to sell cookies and sew buttons and walk around wearing stupid old badges?"

When she agreed to go to the first meeting, I was so happy I volunteered to become an assistant leader. After the meeting, Jessica went directly to the car the way she does after school, after a birthday party, after a ball game, after anything. A straight line to the car. No jabbering with girl-friends, no smiles, no dallying, just right to the car. She slides into the back seat, belts in, and braces herself for destruction. It has already happened once.

I swoop past five thousand years of stereotypes and accept my assistant leader's packet and credentials.

"I'm sure there have been other men in the movement," Kay says, "we just haven't had any in our district. It will be good for the girls."

Not for my Jessica. She won't bridge, she won't budge.

"I know why you're doing this," she says. "You think that because I don't have a mother, Kay Randall and the Girl Scouts will help me. That's crazy. And I know that Sharon is supposed to be like a mother too. Why don't you just leave me alone."

Sharon is Jessica's therapist. Jessica sees her twice a week. Sharon and I have a meeting once a month.

"We have a lot of shy girls," Kay Randall tells me. "Scouting brings them out. Believe me, it's hard to stay shy when you're nine years old and you're sharing a tent with six other girls. You have to count on each other, you have to communicate."

I imagine Jessica zipping up in her sleeping bag, mumbling good night to anyone who first says it to her, then closing her eyes and hating me for sending her out among the happy.

"She likes all sports, especially baseball," I tell my leader.

"There's room for baseball in scouting," Kay says. "Once a year the whole district goes to a game. They mention us on the big scoreboard."

"Jessica and I go to all the home games. We're real fans."

Kay smiles.

"That's why I want her in Girl Scouts. You know, I want her to go to things with her girlfriends instead of always hanging around with me at ball games."

"I understand," Kay says. "It's part of bridging."

With Sharon the term is "separation anxiety." That's the fastball, "bridging" is the curve. Amid all their magic words I feel as if Jessica and I are standing at home plate blindfolded.

While I await Kay and the members of Troop 111, District 6, I eye St.

Anne in her grotto and St. Gregory and St. Thomas. Their hands are folded as if they started out bridging, ended up praying.

In October the principal sent Jessica home from school because Mrs. Simmons caught her in spelling class listening to the World Series through an earphone.

"It's against the school policy," Mrs. Simmons said. "Jessica understands school policy. We confiscate radios and send the child home."

"I'm glad," Jessica said. "It was a cheap-o radio. Now I can watch the TV with you."

They sent her home in the middle of the sixth game. I let her stay home for the seventh too.

The Brewers are her favorite American League team. She likes Rollie Fingers, and especially Robin Yount.

"Does Yount go in the hole better than Harvey Kuenn used to?"

"You bet," I tell her. "Kuenn was never a great fielder but he could hit three hundred with his eyes closed."

Kuenn is the Brewers' manager. He has an artificial leg and can barely make it up the dugout steps, but when I was Jessica's age and the Tigers were my team, Kuenn used to stand at the plate, tap the corners with his bat, spit some tobacco juice, and knock liners up the alley.

She took the Brewers' loss hard.

"If Fingers wasn't hurt they would have squashed the Cards, wouldn't they?"

I agreed.

"But I'm glad for Andujar."

We had Andujar's autograph. Once we met him at a McDonald's. He was a relief pitcher then, an erratic right-hander. In St. Louis he improved. I was happy to get his name on a napkin. Jessica shook his hand.

One night after I read her a story, she said, "Daddy, if we were rich could we go to the away games too? I mean, if you didn't have to be at work every day."

"Probably we could," I said, "but wouldn't it get boring? We'd have to stay at hotels and eat in restaurants. Even the players get sick of it."

"Are you kidding?" she said. "I'd never get sick of it."

"Jessica has fantasies of being with you forever, following baseball or whatever," Sharon says. "All she's trying to do is please you. Since she lost her mother she feels that you and she are alone in the world. She doesn't want to let anyone or anything else into that unit, the two of you. She's afraid of any more losses. And, of course, her greatest worry is about losing you."

"You know," I tell Sharon, "that's pretty much how I feel too."

"Of course it is," she says. "I'm glad to hear you say it."

Sharon is glad to hear me say almost anything. When I complain that her $100-a-week fee would buy a lot of peanut butter sandwiches, she says she is "glad to hear me expressing my anger."

"Sharon's not fooling me," Jessica says. "I know that she thinks drawing those pictures is supposed to make me feel better or something. You're just wasting your money. There's nothing wrong with me."

"It's a long, difficult, expensive process," Sharon says. "You and Jessica have lost a lot. Jessica is going to have to learn to trust the world again. It would help if you could do it too."

So I decide to trust Girl Scouts. First Girl Scouts, then the world. I make my stand at the meeting of Kay Randall's fingertips. While Nolan Ryan breaks Walter Johnson's strikeout record and pitches a two-hit shutout, I pass out paste and thread to nine-year-olds who are sticking and sewing their lives together in ways Jessica and I can't.

II

Scouting is not altogether new to me. I was a Cub Scout. I owned a blue beanie and I remember very well my den mother, Mrs. Clark. A den mother made perfect sense to me then and still does. Maybe that's why I don't feel uncomfortable being a Girl Scout assistant leader.

We had no den father. Mr. Clark was only a photograph on the living room wall, the tiny living room where we held our monthly meetings. Mr. Clark was killed in the Korean War. His son John was in the troop. John was stocky but Mrs. Clark was huge. She couldn't sit on a regular chair, only on a couch or a stool without sides. She was the cashier in the convenience store beneath their apartment. The story we heard was that Walt, the old man who owned the store, felt sorry for her and gave her the job. He was her landlord too. She sat on a swivel stool and rang up the purchases.

We met at the store and watched while she locked the door; then we followed her up the steep staircase to her three-room apartment. She carried two wet glass bottles of milk. Her body took up the entire width of the staircase. She passed the banisters the way semi trucks pass each other on a narrow highway.

We were ten years old, a time when everything is funny, especially fat people. But I don't remember anyone ever laughing about Mrs. Clark. She had great dignity and character. So did John. I didn't know what to call it then, but I knew John was someone you could always trust.

She passed out milk and cookies, then John collected the cups and washed them. They didn't even have a television set. The only decoration in the room that barely held all of us was Mr. Clark's picture on the wall. We saw him in his uniform and we knew he died in Korea defending his country. We were little boys in blue beanies drinking milk in the apartment of a hero. Through that aura I came to scouting. I wanted Kay Randall to have all of Mrs. Clark's dignity.

When she took a deep breath and then bridged, Kay Randall had noticeable armpits. Her wide shoulders slithered into a tiny rib cage. Her armpits were like bridges. She said "bridging" like a mantra, holding her hands before her for about thirty seconds at the start of each meeting.

"A promise is a promise," I told Jessica. "I signed up to be a leader, and I'm going to do it with you or without you."

"But you didn't even ask me if I liked it. You just signed up without talking it over."

"That's true; that's why I'm not going to force you to go along. It was my choice."

"What can you like about it? I hate Melissa Randall. She always has a cold."

"Her mother is a good leader."

"How do you know?"

"She's my boss. I've got to like her, don't I?" I hugged Jessica. "C'mon, honey, give it a chance. What do you have to lose?"

"If you make me go I'll do it, but if I have a choice I won't."

Every other Tuesday, Karen, the fifteen-year-old Greek girl who lives on the corner, babysits Jessica while I go to the Scout meetings. We talk about field trips and how to earn merit badges. The girls giggle when Kay pins a promptness badge on me, my first.

Jessica thinks it's hilarious. She tells me to wear it to work.

Sometimes when I watch Jessica brush her hair and tie her ponytail and make up her lunch kit I start to think that maybe I should just relax and stop the therapy and the scouting and all my not-so-subtle attempts to get her to invite friends over. I start to think that, in spite of everything, she's a good student and she's got a sense of humor. She's barely nine years old. She'll grow up like everyone else does. John Clark did it without a father; she'll do it without a mother. I start to wonder if Jessica seems to the girls in her class the way John Clark seemed to me: dignified, serious, almost an adult even while we were playing. I admired him. Maybe the girls in her class admire her. But John had that hero on the wall, his father in a uniform, dead for reasons John and all the rest of us understood.

My Jessica had to explain a neurologic disease she couldn't even pronounce. "I hate it when people ask me about Mom," she says. "I just tell them she fell off the Empire State Building."

III

Before our first field trip I go to Kay's house for a planning session. We're going to collect wildflowers in East Texas. It's a one-day trip. I arranged to rent the school bus.

I told Jessica that she could go on the trip even though she wasn't a troop member, but she refused.

We sit on colonial furniture in Kay's den. She brings in coffee and we go over the supply list. Another troop is joining ours so there will be twenty-two girls, three women, and me, a busload among the bluebonnets.

"We have to be sure the girls understand that the bluebonnets they pick are on private land and that we have permission to pick them. Otherwise they might pick them along the roadside, which is against the law."

I imagine all twenty-two of them behind bars for picking bluebonnets and Jessica laughing while I scramble for bail money.

I keep noticing Kay's hands. I notice them as she pours coffee, as she checks off the items on the list, as she gestures. I keep expecting her to bridge. She has large, solid, confident hands. When she finishes bridging I sometimes feel like clapping the way people do after the national anthem.

"I admire you," she tells me. "I admire you for going ahead with Scouts even though your daughter rejects it. She'll get a lot out of it indirectly from you."

Kay Randall is thirty-three, divorced, and has a Bluebird too. Her older daughter is one of the stubby-fingered girls, Melissa. Jessica is right; Melissa always has a cold.

Kay teaches fifth grade and has been divorced for three years. I am the first assistant she's ever had.

"My husband, Bill, never helped with Scouts," Kay says. "He was pretty much turned off to everything except his business and drinking. When we separated I can't honestly say I missed him; he'd never been there. I don't think the girls miss him either. He only sees them about once a month. He has girlfriends, and his business is doing very well. I guess he has what he wants."

"And you?"

She uses one of those wonderful hands to move the hair away from her eyes, a gesture that makes her seem very young.

"I guess I do too. I've got the girls and my job. I'm lonesome, though. It's not exactly what I wanted."

We both think about what might have been as we sit beside her glass coffeepot with our lists of sachet supplies. If she was Barbra Streisand and I Robert Redford and the music started playing in the background to give us a clue and there was a long close-up of our lips, we might just fade into middle age together. But Melissa called for Mom because her mosquito bite was bleeding where she scratched it. And I had an angry daughter waiting for me. And all Kay and I had in common was Girl Scouts. We were both smart enough to know it. When Kay looked at me before going to put alcohol on the mosquito bite, our mutual sadness dripped from us like the last drops of coffee through the grinds.

"You really missed something tonight," Jessica tells me. "The Astros did a double steal. I've never seen one before. In the fourth they sent Thon and Moreno together, and Moreno stole home."

She knows batting averages and won-lost percentages too, just like the older boys, only they go out to play. Jessica stays in and waits for me.

During the field trip, while the girls pick flowers to dry and then manufacture into sachets, I think about Jessica at home, probably beside the radio. Juana, our once-a-week cleaning lady, agreed to work on Saturday so she could stay with Jessica while I took the all-day field trip.

It was no small event. In the eight months since Vicki died I had not gone away for an entire day.

MAX APPLE

227

I made waffles in the waffle iron for her before I left, but she hardly ate.

"If you want anything, just ask Juana."

"Juana doesn't speak English."

"She understands, that's enough."

"Maybe for you it's enough."

"Honey, I told you, you can come; there's plenty of room on the bus. It's not too late for you to change your mind."

"It's not too late for you either. There's going to be plenty of other leaders there. You don't have to go. You're just doing this to be mean to me."

I'm ready for this. I spent an hour with Sharon steeling myself. "Before she can leave you," Sharon said, "you'll have to show her that you can leave. Nothing's going to happen to her. And don't let her be sick that day either."

Jessica is too smart to pull the "I don't feel good" routine. Instead she becomes more silent, more unhappy looking than usual. She stays in her pajamas while I wash the dishes and get ready to leave.

I didn't notice the sadness as it was coming upon Jessica. It must have happened gradually in the years of Vicki's decline, the years in which I paid so little attention to my daughter. There were times when Jessica seemed to recognize the truth more than I did.

As my Scouts picked their wildflowers, I remembered the last outing I had planned for us. It was going to be a Fourth of July picnic with some friends in Austin. I stopped at the bank and got $200 in cash for the long weekend. But when I came home Vicki was too sick to move and the air conditioner had broken. I called our friends to cancel the picnic; then I took Jessica to the mall with me to buy a fan. I bought the biggest one they had, a 58-inch oscillating model that sounded like a hurricane. It could cool 10,000 square feet, but it wasn't enough.

Vicki was home sitting blankly in front of the TV set. The fan could move eight tons of air an hour, but I wanted it to save my wife. I wanted a fan that would blow the whole earth out of its orbit.

I had $50 left. I gave it to Jessica and told her to buy anything she wanted.

"Whenever you're sad, Daddy, you want to buy me things." She put the money back in my pocket. "It won't help." She was seven years old, holding my hand tightly in the appliance department at J. C. Penney's.

I watched Melissa sniffle even more among the wildflowers, and I pointed out the names of various flowers to Carol and JoAnne and Sue and Linda and Rebecca, who were by now used to me and treated me pretty much as they treated Kay. I noticed that the Girl Scout flower book had very accurate photographs that made it easy to identify the bluebonnets and buttercups and poppies. There were also several varieties of wild grasses.

We were only 70 miles from home on some land a wealthy rancher long ago donated to the Girl Scouts. The girls bending among the flowers seemed to have been quickly transformed by the colorful meadow. The gigglers and monotonous singers on the bus were now, like the bees, sucking strength from the beauty around them. Kay was in the midst of them and so, I realized, was I, not watching and keeping score and admiring from the distance but a participant, a player.

JoAnne and Carol sneaked up from behind me and dropped some dandelions down my back. I chased them; then I helped the other leaders pour the Kool-Aid and distribute the Baggies and the name tags for each girl's flowers.

My daughter is home listening to a ball game, I thought, and I'm out here having fun with nine-year-olds. It's upside down.

When I came home with dandelion fragments still on my back, Juana had cleaned the house and I could smell the taco sauce in the kitchen. Jessica was in her room. I suspected that she had spent the day listless and tearful, although I had asked her to invite a friend over.

"I had a lot of fun, honey, but I missed you."

She hugged me and cried against my shoulder. I felt like holding her the way I used to when she was an infant, the way I rocked her to sleep. But she was a big girl now and needed not sleep but wakefulness.

"I heard on the news that the Rockets signed Ralph Sampson," she sobbed, "and you hardly ever take me to any pro basketball games."

"But if they have a new center things will be different. With Sampson we'll be contenders. Sure I'll take you."

"Promise?"

"Promise." I promise to take you everywhere, my lovely child, and then to leave you. I'm learning to be a leader.

Woman on a Pedestal

Women in the Western world have higher status and more freedom than women elsewhere do. This fact is usually connected with the Christian tradition in the twelfth century, which exalted Mary as Queen of Heaven and raised great Gothic cathedrals to honor her. Simultaneously with Maryology secular women were idealized in stories about knights and their pursuit of honor; in this so-called courtly love tradition, women were both the inspiration and the reward for men of high achievement. It is hard to see the noble woman of this tradition as dehumanized in any way; yet it is perhaps the most effective stereotype in causing women to perceive themselves as other than fully human beings. Instead, they try to live up to the ideal of nobility. Reinforced by its religious form, the secular ideal is very far removed from reality. It fulfills the human need to find and strive for a symbol for the value of life as does the comparable male ideal of the hero. But in most literature male heroes who fall short of the dream are viewed as autonomous agents and their failure as tragic. Women who fall short are viewed as either not autonomous or unnatural; they are perceived as pathetic rather than tragic. Exceptions come to mind, of course. But Antigone, the Greek heroine who defied the ruling powers to perform funeral rites for her brothers, is seen by scholars as a projection of male virtues, with no relationship to the reality of the life of Greek women. Lady Macbeth asks to be "unsexed" to goad her husband to murder. By and large, the women who serve as inspirations to noble action do so because of their beauty, not because of any action or achievement of their own. Since beauty cannot be understood on human terms, it is feared; a beautiful woman often becomes a symbol of the greatest human fear, death.

The righteous elders in Adelaide Crapsey's quintain "Susanna and the Elders" "devise / evil" against the beautiful girl. Though in the Biblical story she is completely innocent of causing them any real harm, her beauty reminds them that righteousness will not be sufficient to save them from death. Their fear and hatred for her find counterparts in the stories of many societies documented by anthropologists, who speak of "the myth of feminine evil."

Other works in this section show the process by which a specific living woman is made into a symbol of mystery, usually of evil and death. In Jean Toomer's story "Fern" the process of symbolization begins when a man perceives a woman's beauty as unfathomable. When the narrator looks into Fern's eyes, he finds them magnetically attractive but baffling; he sees in them "nothing that was obvious and tangible." Like Freud, who asked "What do women want?", the observer is mystified because he cannot understand what Fern wants from him and from life. Yet he acknowledges her power over all the men who have known her; her influence makes them transcend physical desire and want to do something great and noble for her. The narrator comes to understand that her appeal is superhuman. In her eyes he sees God, who possesses her as He did the oracles of Greek myth, speaking through her tortured body paradoxical answers to existential questions.

Fern, a humble black woman, is exalted in this story. Though a prostitute, she has a beneficent and ennobling effect on men. But her lovers' noble resolutions to help her never come to fruition: "Nothing ever came to Fern." Their exaltation of her is a self-delusory attempt to deal with their own sexual appetites and with their knowledge of mortality. In other literature in this section a mysteriously beautiful woman is even more directly linked with deleterious effects on men; instead of inspiring them, however briefly, she entices them to shame and death. John Keats's "La Belle Dame sans Merci" shows a woman who seems to symbolize Death itself. Her wild eyes, strange language, and fairylike song have made corpses of many men. The appearance of their ghosts in a dream causes her most recent victim to realize that what he thinks is the sleep of love is really deathlike and destructive; he awakens completely disoriented.

Keats uses the poetic tradition of intercourse and sleep as metaphors for death. The Knight's love for the mysterious woman testifies to the strength of the death wish, which seems stronger than his will to live. The image of a lover as a helpless victim of overpowering emotion parallels that of the beautiful woman as superhuman, like a goddess on a pedestal to be propitiated, if not worshipped. Edgar Allan Poe said that for a poet the best subject is the death of a beautiful woman. The image of a delicate, doomed, pure, but powerful creature underlies the courtship rites of romantic love, with the male suitor as the humble supplicant bringing rich gifts.

Heinrich Heine's "The Loreley" emphasizes the fatal power of women but also reveals their innocence in using this power. The mermaid is merely combing her hair and singing an old song when sailors crash on her rock; like that of Fern and la belle Dame, her mysterious power is a fantasy of the males who encounter her. In William Blake's poem the fantasy of a princely lover reduces his beloved to a caged automaton, a toy for his pleasure.

Kate Wilhelm in "Baby, You Were Great!" and Helene Davis in "Affair" give us women's perspectives on this male fantasy; they make it clear that goddesses are made, not born. Women's willingness to adapt themselves to men's fantasies stems from their own human emotions of love, desire for status, and greed. Davis's speaker expresses the woman's emotions, her overwhelming need to love "for sheer breath"; she says, "Without you my flesh becomes bone dry and breaks / easily, my face invisible. . . ." But another voice—her own inner knowledge—comments, distantly, on these emotions. The woman's situation is that of "the old story" in which love brings happiness to a woman only if she "owns no name" or label because she is, and is happy to be, "a velvet backdrop / in his quiet life." But Davis allows irony to develop between the two voices: the reader knows that no woman, no person, *can* be happy not even having a name. The word *must* in the last stanza lets us see such a fate as imposed, as the price of passionate love: "The woman must, like earth, be able to change / size . . ."; she must be able to become, magically, what men want.

Though Anne Beaumont in Wilhelm's story is perceived as if she were a goddess, she is more like the humanized goddesses of the Greeks than the frozen ones of the courtly tradition. Aphrodite and Hera had human foibles but still retained their status as goddesses; human goddesses essentially have no power. Anne Beaumont is trapped into playing the superhuman role of outlet for others' fantasies and emotions; the victim of electronic thought control, she cannot escape playing out this role to the death. In Wilhelm's world, the men, though powerful enough to determine women's fate, are also caught. "[S]haped by centuries of civilization" into becoming "like a stalactite," incapable of warm emotions, John has made his world a hell of fear and violence for all the characters. The most startling aspect of Wilhelm's story is that women are the main audience for Anne's experiences of rape, terror, and torture; their vicarious masochism removes them from "boredom and frustration," from a life of "[w]ork, kids, bills." Through Anne, they live the Cinderella myth, as well as their ambivalent masochistic sexual fantasies.

Such heroines in the Gothic romances popular today always escape into marriage. Wilhelm has pinpointed the psychological explanation for the overwhelming popularity of these romances, written by women for women, and of soap operas on television. The need to escape from the reality of one's life through fantasy is powerful. But Wilhelm's story shows that to live in a world of fantasy is dehumanizing for all concerned. Only by outgrowing such dreams can men and women find alternatives to Wilhelm's grim vision of the future.

SUSANNA AND THE ELDERS

by

ADELAIDE CRAPSEY

(1878–1914)

Born in Rochester, New York, Adelaide Crapsey studied at Vassar and later taught in preparatory schools and at Smith College. Some of her poems and a major book on English metrics were published after she died of tuberculosis; her complete poems were published along with a biography in 1977. She invented a new poetic form, the cinquain, a five-line form akin to the Japanese haiku *and* tanka.

"Why do
You thus devise
Evil against her?" "For that
She is beautiful, delicate:
Therefore."

FERN

by

JEAN TOOMER

(1894–1967)

A Georgian who also lived in New York, Jean Toomer wrote of the struggles of blacks—male and female, rural and urban—to achieve a sense of human dignity. Cane (1923), called a novel though it is also a collection of short stories and poems, was acclaimed as a contribution to the Harlem Renaissance, but only with its republication in 1969 and the appearance of an anthology of other works in 1978 was Toomer's achievement fully appreciated.

Face flowed into her eyes. Flowed in soft cream foam and plaintive ripples, in such a way that wherever your glance may momentarily have rested, it immediately thereafter wavered in the direction of her eyes. The soft suggestion of down slightly darkened, like the shadow of a bird's wing might, the creamy brown color of her upper lip. Why, after noticing it, you sought her eyes, I cannot tell you. Her nose was aquiline, Semitic. If you have heard a Jewish cantor sing, if he has touched you and made your own sorrow seem trivial when compared with his, you will know my feeling when I follow the curves of her profile, like mobile rivers, to their common delta. They were strange eyes. In this, that they sought nothing —that is, nothing that was obvious and tangible and that one could see, and they gave the impression that nothing was to be denied. When a woman seeks, you will have observed, her eyes deny. Fern's eyes desired nothing that you could give her; there was no reason why they should withhold. Men saw her eyes and fooled themselves. Fern's eyes said to them that she was easy. When she was young, a few men took her, but got no joy from it. And then, once done, they felt bound to her (quite unlike their hit and run with other girls), felt as though it would take them a lifetime to fulfill an obligation which they could find no name for. They became attached to her, and hungered after finding the barest trace of what she might desire. As she grew up, new men who came to town felt as almost everyone did who ever saw her: that they would not be denied.

Men were everlastingly bringing her their bodies. Something inside of her got tired of them, I guess, for I am certain that for the life of her she could not tell why or how she began to turn them off. A man in fever is no trifling thing to send away. They began to leave her, baffled and ashamed, yet vowing to themselves that some day they would do some fine thing for her: send her candy every week and not let her know whom it came from, watch out for her wedding-day and give her a magnificent something with no name on it, buy a house and deed it to her, rescue her from some unworthy fellow who had tricked her into marrying him. As you know, men are apt to idolize or fear that which they cannot understand, especially if it be a woman. She did not deny them, yet the fact was that they were denied. A sort of superstition crept into their consciousness of her being somehow above them. Being above them meant that she was not to be approached by anyone. She became a virgin. Now a virgin in a small southern town is by no means the usual thing, if you will believe me. That the sexes were made to mate is the practice of the South. Particularly, black folks were made to mate. And it is black folks whom I have been talking about thus far. What white men thought of Fern I can arrive at only by analogy. They let her alone.

Anyone, of course, could see her, could see her eyes. If you walked up the Dixie Pike most any time of day, you'd be most like to see her resting listless-like on the railing of her porch, back propped against a post, head tilted a little forward because there was a nail in the porch post just where her head came which for some reason or other she never took the trouble to pull out. Her eyes, if it were sunset, rested idly where the sun, molten and glorious, was pouring down between the fringe of pines. Or maybe they gazed at the gray cabin on the knoll from which an evening folk-song was coming. Perhaps they followed a cow that had been turned loose to roam and feed on cotton-stalks and corn leaves. Like as not they'd settle on some vague spot above the horizon, though hardly a trace of wistfulness would come to them. If it were dusk, then they'd wait for the search-light of the evening train which you could see miles up the track before it flared across the Dixie Pike, close to her home. Wherever they looked, you'd follow them and then waver back. Like her face, the whole countryside seemed to flow into her eyes. Flowed into them with the soft listless cadence of Georgia's South. A young Negro, once, was looking at her, spellbound, from the road. A white man passing in a buggy had to flick him with his whip if he was to get by without running him over. I first saw her on her porch. I was passing with a fellow whose crusty numbness (I was from the North and suspected of being prejudiced and stuck-up) was melting as he found me warm. I asked him who she was. "That's Fern," was all I could get from him. Some folks already thought that I was given to nosing around; I let it go at that, so far as questions were concerned. But at first sight of her I felt as if I heard a Jewish cantor sing. As if his singing rose above the unheard chorus of a folk-song. And I felt bound to her. I too had my dreams: something I would do for her. I have knocked about from town to town too much not to know the futility of mere change of place. Besides, picture if you can, this cream-colored solitary girl sitting at a tenement window looking down on the indifferent throngs of Harlem. Better that she listens to folk-songs at dusk in Georgia, you would say, and so would I. Or, suppose she came up North and married. Even a doctor or a lawyer, say, one who would be sure to get along— that is, make money. You and I know, who have had experience in such things, that love is not a thing like prejudice which can be bettered by changes of town. Could men in Washington, Chicago, or New York, more than the men of Georgia, bring her something left vacant by the bestowal of their bodies? You and I who know men in these cities will have to say, they could not. See her out and out a prostitute along State Street in Chicago. See her move into a southern town where white men are more aggressive. See her become a white man's concubine . . . Something I must do for her. There was myself. What could I do for her? Talk, of course. Push back the fringe of pines upon new horizons. To what purpose? and what for? Her? Myself? Men in her case seem to lose their selfishness. I lost mine before I touched her. I ask you, friend (it makes no difference if you sit in the Pullman or the Jim Crow as the train crosses her road), what thoughts would come to you—that is, after you'd finished with the thoughts that leap into men's minds at the sight of a pretty woman who will not deny them; what thoughts would come to you, had you seen her in a quick flash, keen and intuitively, as she sat there on her porch when your train thundered by? Would you have got off at the next station and come back for her to take her where? Would you have completely forgotten her as soon as you reached Macon, Atlanta, Augusta, Pasadena, Madison, Chicago, Boston, or New Orleans? Would you tell your wife or sweetheart about a girl you saw? Your thoughts can help me, and I would like to know. Something I would do for her . . .

One evening I walked up the Pike on purpose, and stopped to say hello. Some of her family were about, but they moved away to make room for me. Damn if I knew how to begin. Would you? Mr. and Miss So-and-So, people, the weather, the crops, the new preacher, the frolic, the church benefit, rabbit and possum hunting, the new soft drink they had at old Pap's store, the schedule of the trains, what kind of town Macon was, Negro's migration north, boll-weevils, syrup, the Bible—to all these things she gave a yassur or nassur, without further comment. I began to wonder if perhaps my own emotional sensibility had played one of its tricks on me. "Let's take a walk," I at last ventured. The suggestion, coming after so long an isolation, was novel enough, I guess, to surprise. But it wasn't that. Something told me that men before me had said just that as a prelude to the offering of their bodies. I tried to tell her with my eyes. I think she understood. The thing from her that made my throat catch, vanished. Its passing left her visible in a way I'd thought, but never seen. We walked down the Pike with people on all the porches gaping at us. "Doesn't it make you mad?" She meant the row of petty gossiping people. She meant the world. Through a canebreak that was ripe for cutting, the branch was reached. Under a sweet-gum tree, and where reddish leaves had dammed the creek a little, we sat down. Dusk, suggesting the almost imperceptible procession of giant trees, settled with a purple haze about the cane. I felt strange, as I always do in Georgia, particularly at dusk. I felt that things unseen to men were tangibly immediate. It would not have surprised me had I had a vision. People have them in Georgia more often than you would suppose. A black woman once saw the mother of Christ and drew her in charcoal on the courthouse wall . . . When one is on the soil of one's ancestors, most anything can come to one . . . From force of habit, I suppose, I held Fern in my arms—that is, without at first noticing it. Then my mind came back to her. Her eyes, unusually weird and open, held me. Held God. He flowed in as I've seen the countryside flow in. Seen men. I must have done something—what, I don't know, in the confusion of my emotion. She sprang up. Rushed some distance from me. Fell to her knees, and began swaying, swaying. Her body was tortured with something it could not let out. Like boiling sap it flooded arms and fingers till she shook them as if they burned her. It found her throat, and spattered inarticulately in plaintive, convulsive sounds, mingled with calls to Christ Jesus. And then she sang, brokenly. A Jewish cantor singing with a broken voice. A child's voice, uncertain, or an old man's. Dusk hid her; I could hear only her song. It seemed to me as though she were pounding her head in anguish upon the ground. I rushed to her. She fainted in my arms.

There was talk about her fainting with me in the canefield. And I got one or two ugly looks from town men who'd set themselves up to protect her. In fact, there was talk of making me leave town. But they never did. They kept a watch-out for me, though. Shortly after, I came back North. From the train window I saw her as I crossed her road. Saw her on her porch, head tilted a little forward where the nail was, eyes vaguely focused on the sunset. Saw her face flow into them, the countryside and something that I call God, flowing into them . . . Nothing ever really happened. Nothing ever came to Fern, not even I. Something I would do for her. Some fine unnamed thing . . . And, friend, you? She is still living, I have reason to know. Her name, against the chance that you might happen down that way, is Fernie May Rosen.

LA BELLE DAME
SANS MERCI

by

JOHN KEATS

(1795–1821)

*The famous English Romantic poet John Keats studied medicine
before embarking on his all too brief career as a poet. His poems
reflect his love for Greek myth, for nature, and for the supernatural,
often personified as a woman.*

• ———————————————————— •

Ah, what can ail thee, wretched wight,
  Alone and palely loitering;
The sedge is wither'd from the lake,
  And no birds sing.

Ah, what can ail thee, wretched wight,
  So haggard and so woe-begone?
The squirrel's granary is full,
  And the harvest's done.

I see a lilly on thy brow,
  With anguish moist and fever dew;
And on thy cheek a fading rose
  Fast withereth too.

I met a Lady in the meads,
  Full beautiful, a fairy's child;
Her hair was long, her foot was light,
  And her eyes were wild.

I set her on my pacing steed,
　And nothing else saw all day long;
For sideways would she lean, and sing
　A faery's song.

I made a garland for her head,
　And bracelets too, and fragrant zone,
She look'd at me as she did love,
　And made sweet moan.

She found me roots of relish sweet,
　And honey wild, and manna dew,
And sure in language strange she said,
　I love thee true.

She took me to her elfin grot,
　And there she gaz'd and sighed deep,
And there I shut her wild sad eyes—
　So kiss'd to sleep.

And there we slumber'd on the moss,
　And there I dream'd, ah woe betide
The latest dream I ever dream'd
　On the cold hill side.

I saw pale kings, and princes too,
　Pale warriors, death-pale were they all;
Who cry'd—"La belle Dame sans merci
　Hath thee in thrall."

I saw their starv'd lips in the gloom
　With horrid warning gaped wide,
And I awoke, and found me here
　On the cold hill side.

And this is why I sojourn here
　Alone and palely loitering,
Though the sedge is wither'd from the lake,
　And no birds sing.

THE LORELEY

by

HEINRICH HEINE

(1797–1856)

A well-known German writer, Heinrich Heine voluntarily exiled himself in Paris in 1831 to escape the rigid political regime of his native Prussia. His early works, including the famous "The Loreley," were romantic; later he satirized the Romantic movement and wrote political and philosophical works in prose.

• ─────────────────────── •

Ich weiss nicht, was soll es bedeuten

I cannot tell why this imagined
  Despair has fallen on me;
The ghost of an ancient legend
  That will not let me be:

The air is cool, and twilight
  Flows down the quiet Rhine;
A mountain alone in the high light
  Still holds the faltering shine.

The last peak rosily gleaming
  Reveals, enthroned in air,
A maiden, lost in dreaming,
  Who combs her golden hair.

Combing her hair with a golden
  Comb in her rocky bower.
She sings the tune of an olden
  Song that has magical power.

The boatman has heard; it has bound him
   In throes of a strange, wild love;
Blind to the reefs that surround him,
   He sees but the vision above.

And lo, hungry waters are springing—
   Boat and boatsman are gone. . . .
Then silence. And this, with her singing,
   The Loreley has done.

SONG

by

WILLIAM BLAKE

(1757–1827)

*Usually considered a Romantic poet, William Blake was so unique
an individual that it is hard to label him. He was essentially a
revolutionary in politics and in philosophy, and his long mystical
poems have had many interpretations. His own beautiful engravings
illustrate and help to explain many of his poems. Blake was as
ardent a women's liberationist as was his contemporary, Mary
Wollstonecraft.*

How sweet I roam'd from field to field
And tasted all the summer's pride,
Till I the Prince of Love beheld
Who in the sunny beams did glide!

He show'd me lilies for my hair,
And blushing roses for my brow;
He led me through his gardens fair
Where all his golden pleasures grow.

With sweet May dews my wings were wet,
And Phoebus fir'd my vocal rage;
He caught me in his silken net,
And shut me in his golden cage.

He loves to sit and hear me sing,
Then, laughing, sports and plays with me;
Then stretches out my golden wing,
And mocks my loss of liberty.

BABY, YOU WERE GREAT!

by

KATE WILHELM

(b. 1928)

*Born in Ohio, Kate Wilhelm now lives in Florida. She has published
many novels and two volumes of short stories, mainly science
fiction. In 1968 she won the Nebula Award of Science Fiction
Writers of America for one of her short stories. Her most recent
volumes include* Oh! Susanna *(1982) and* Welcome, Chaos *(1983).*

· ———————————————— ·

John Lewisohn thought that if one more door slammed, or one more bell
rang, or one more voice asked if he was all right, his head would explode.
Leaving his laboratories, he walked through the carpeted hall to the
elevator that slid wide to admit him noiselessly, was lowered, gently, two
floors, where there were more carpeted halls. The door he shoved open
bore a neat sign, AUDITIONING STUDIO. Inside, he was waved on through the
reception room by three girls who knew better than to speak to him unless
he spoke first. They were surprised to see him; it was his first visit there
in seven or eight months. The inner room where he stopped was darkened,
at first glance appearing empty, revealing another occupant only after
his eyes had time to adjust to the dim lighting.

John sat in the chair next to Herb Javits, still without speaking. Herb
was wearing the helmet and gazing at a wide screen that was actually
a one-way glass panel permitting him to view the audition going on in the
next room. John lowered a second helmet to his head. It fit snugly and
immediately made contact with the eight prepared spots on his skull.
As soon as he turned it on, the helmet itself was forgotten.

A girl had entered the other room. She was breathtakingly lovely, a
long-legged honey blonde with slanting green eyes and apricot skin. The
room was furnished as a sitting room with two couches, some chairs, end
tables and a coffee table, all tasteful and lifeless, like an ad in a furniture
trade publication. The girl stopped at the doorway and John felt her

indecision, heavily tempered with nervousness and fear. Outwardly she appeared poised and expectant, her smooth face betraying none of her emotions. She took a hesitant step toward the couch, and a wire showed trailing behind her. It was attached to her head. At the same time a second door opened. A young man ran inside, slamming the door behind him; he looked wild and frantic. The girl registered surprise, mounting nervousness; she felt behind her for the door handle, found it and tried to open the door again. It was locked. John could hear nothing that was being said in the room; he only felt the girl's reaction to the unexpected interruption. The wild-eyed man was approaching her, his hands slashing through the air, his eyes darting glances all about them constantly. Suddenly he pounced on her and pulled her to him, kissing her face and neck roughly. She seemed paralyzed with fear for several seconds, then there was something else, a bland nothing kind of feeling that accompanied boredom sometimes, or too-complete self-assurance. As the man's hands fastened on her blouse in the back and ripped it, she threw her arms about him, her face showing passion that was not felt anywhere in her mind or in her blood.

"Cut!" Herb Javits said quietly.

The man stepped back from the girl and left her without a word. She looked about blankly, her torn blouse hanging about her hips, one shoulder strap gone. She was very beautiful. The audition manager entered, followed by a dresser with a gown that he threw about her shoulders. She looked startled; waves of anger mounted to fury as she was drawn from the room, leaving it empty. The two watching men removed their helmets.

"Fourth one so far," Herb grunted. "Sixteen yesterday; twenty the day before . . . All nothing." He gave John a curious look. "What's got you stirred out of your lab?"

"Anne's had it this time," John said. "She's been on the phone all night and all morning."

"What now?"

"Those damn sharks! I told you that was too much on top of the airplane crash last week. She can't take much more of it."

"Hold it a minute, Johnny," Herb said. "Let's finish off the next three girls and then talk." He pressed a button on the arm of his chair and the room beyond the screen took their attention again.

This time the girl was slightly less beautiful, shorter, a dimply sort of brunette with laughing blue eyes and upturned nose. John liked her. He adjusted his helmet and felt with her.

She was excited; the audition always excited them. There was some fear and nervousness, not too much. Curious about how the audition would go, probably. The wild young man ran into the room, and her face paled. Nothing else changed. Her nervousness increased, not uncomfortably. When he grabbed her, the only emotion she registered was the nervousness.

"Cut," Herb said.

The next girl was also brunette, with gorgeously elongated legs. She was very cool, a real professional. Her mobile face reflected the range of emotions to be expected as the scene played through again, but nothing inside her was touched. She was a million miles away from it all.

The next one caught John with a slam. She entered the room slowly, looking about with curiosity, nervous, as they all were. She was younger than the other girls, less poised. She had pale gold hair piled in an elaborate mound of waves on top of her head. Her eyes were brown, her skin nicely tanned. When the man entered, her emotions changed quickly to fear, then to terror. John didn't know when he closed his eyes. He was the girl, filled with unspeakable terror; his heart pounded, adrenalin pumped into his system; he wanted to scream but could not. From the dim unreachable depths of his psyche there came something else, in waves, so mixed with terror that the two merged and became one emotion that pulsed and throbbed and demanded. With a jerk he opened his eyes and stared at the window. The girl had been thrown down to one of the couches, and the man was kneeling on the floor beside her, his hands playing over her bare body, his face pressed against her skin.

"Cut!" Herb said. His voice was shaken. "Hire her," he said. The man rose, glanced at the girl, sobbing now, and then quickly bent over and kissed her cheek. Her sobs increased. Her golden hair was down, framing her face; she looked like a child. John tore off the helmet. He was perspiring.

Herb got up, turned on the lights in the room, and the window blanked out, blending with the wall. He didn't look at John. When he wiped his face, his hand was shaking. He rammed it in his pocket.

"When did you start auditions like that?" John asked, after a few moments of silence.

"Couple of months ago. I told you about it. Hell, we had to, Johnny. That's the six hundred nineteenth girl we've tried out! Six hundred nineteen! All phonies but one! Dead from the neck up. Do you have any idea how long it was taking us to find that out! Hours for each one. Now it's a matter of minutes."

John Lewisohn sighed. He knew. He had suggested it, actually, when he had said, "Find a basic anxiety for the test." He hadn't wanted to know what Herb had come up with.

He said, "Okay, but she's only a kid. What about her parents, legal rights, all that?"

"We'll fix it. Don't worry. What about Anne?"

"She's called me five times since yesterday. The sharks were too much. She wants to see us, both of us, this afternoon."

"You're kidding! I can't leave here now!"

"Nope. Kidding I'm not. She says no plug-up if we don't show. She'll take pills and sleep until we get there."

"Good Lord! She wouldn't dare!"

"I've booked seats. We take off at twelve-thirty-five." They stared at one another silently for another moment, when Herb shrugged. He was a short man, not heavy but solid. John was over six feet, muscular, with a temper that he knew he had to control. Others suspected that when he did let it go, there would be bodies lying around afterward, but he controlled it.

Once it had been a physical act, an effort of body and will to master that temper; now it was done so automatically that he couldn't recall occasions when it even threatened to flare anymore.

"Look, Johnny, when we see Anne, let me handle it. Right? I'll make it short."

"What are you going to do?"

"Give her an earful. If she's going to start pulling temperament on me, I'll slap her down so hard she'll bounce a week." He grinned. "She's had it all her way up to now. She knew there wasn't a replacement if she got bitchy. Let her try it now. Just let her try." Herb was pacing back and forth with quick, jerky steps.

John realized with a shock that he hated the stocky, red-faced man. The feeling was new; it was almost as if he could taste the hatred he felt, and the taste was unfamiliar and pleasant.

Herb stopped pacing and stared at him for a moment. "Why'd she call you? Why does she want you down, too? She knows you're not mixed up with this end of it."

"She knows I'm a full partner, anyway," John said.

"Yeah, but that's not it." Herb's face twisted in a grin. "She thinks you're still hot for her, doesn't she? She knows you tumbled once, in the beginning, when you were working on her, getting the gimmick working right." The grin reflected no humor then. "Is she right, Johnny, baby? Is that it?"

"We made a deal," John said. "You run your end, I run mine. She wants me along because she doesn't trust you, or believe anything you tell her anymore. She wants a witness."

"Yeah, Johnny. But you be sure you remember our agreement." Suddenly Herb laughed. "You know what it was like, Johnny, seeing you and her? Like a flame trying to snuggle up to an icicle."

At three-thirty they were in Anne's suite in the Skyline Hotel in Grand Bahama. Herb had a reservation to fly back to New York on the 6 P.M. flight. Anne would not be off until four, so they made themselves comfortable in her rooms and waited. Herb turned her screen on, offered a helmet to John, who shook his head, and they both seated themselves. John watched the screen for several minutes; then he, too, put on a helmet.

Anne was looking at the waves far out at sea where they were long, green, undulating; then she brought her gaze in closer, to the blue-green and quick seas, and finally in to where they stumbled on the sandbars, breaking into foam that looked solid enough to walk on. She was peaceful, swaying with the motion of the boat, the sun hot on her back, the fishing rod heavy in her hands. It was like being an indolent animal at peace with its world, at home in the world, being one with it. After a few seconds she put down the rod and turned, looking at a tall smiling man in swimming trunks. He held out his hand and she took it. They entered the cabin of the boat where drinks were waiting. Her mood of serenity and happiness ended abruptly, to be replaced by shocked disbelief, and a start of fear.

"What the hell . . .?" John muttered, adjusting the audio. You seldom needed audio when Anne was on.

". . . Captain Brothers had to let them go. After all, they've done nothing yet—" the man was saying soberly.

"But why do you think they'll try to rob me?"

"Who else is here with a million dollars' worth of jewels?"

John turned it off and said, "You're a fool! You can't get away with something like that!"

Herb stood up and crossed to the window wall that was open to the stretch of glistening blue ocean beyond the brilliant white beaches. "You know what every woman wants? To own something worth stealing." He chuckled, a sound without mirth. "Among other things, that is. They want to be roughed up once or twice, and forced to kneel. . . . Our new psychologist is pretty good, you know? Hasn't steered us wrong yet. Anne might kick some, but it'll go over great."

"She won't stand for an actual robbery." Louder, emphatically, he added, "I won't stand for that."

"We can dub it," Herb said. "That's all we need, Johnny, plant the idea, and then dub the rest."

John stared at his back. He wanted to believe that. He needed to believe it. His voice was calm when he said, "It didn't start like this, Herb. What happened?"

Herb turned then. His face was dark against the glare of light behind him. "Okay, Johnny, it didn't start like this. Things accelerate, that's all. You thought of a gimmick, and the way we planned it, it sounded great, but it didn't last. We gave them the feeling of gambling, or learning to ski, of automobile racing, everything we could dream up, and it wasn't enough. How many times can you take the first ski jump of your life? After a while you want new thrills, you know? For you it's been great, hasn't it? You bought yourself a shiny new lab and closed the door. You bought yourself time and equipment and when things didn't go right, you could toss it out and start over, and nobody gave a damn. Think of what it's been like for me, kid! I gotta keep coming up with something new, something that'll give Anne a jolt and through her all those nice little people who aren't even alive unless they're plugged in. You think it's been easy? Anne was a green kid. For her everything was new and exciting, but it isn't like that now, boy. You better believe it is *not* like that now. You know what she told me last month? She's sick and tired of men. Our little hot-box Annie! Tired of men!"

John crossed to him and pulled him around toward the light. "Why didn't you tell me?"

"Why, Johnny? What would you have done that I didn't do? I looked harder for the right guy. What would you do for a new thrill for her? I worked for them, kid. Right from the start you said for me to leave you alone. Okay. I left you alone. You ever read any of the memos I sent? You initialed them, kiddo. Everything that's been done, we both signed. Don't give me any of that why didn't I tell you stuff. It won't work!" His face was ugly red and a vein bulged in his neck. John wondered if he had high blood pressure, if he would die of a stroke during one of his flash rages.

John left him at the window. He had read the memos. Herb was right; all he had wanted was to be left alone. It had been his idea; after twelve years of work in a laboratory on prototypes he had shown his—gimmick— to Herb Javits. Herb had been one of the biggest producers on television then; now he was the biggest producer in the world.

The gimmick was simple enough. A person fitted with electrodes in his brain could transmit his emotions, which in turn could be broadcast and picked up by the helmets to be felt by the audience. No words or thoughts went out, only basic emotions—fear, love, anger, hatred . . . That, tied in with a camera showing what the person saw, with a voice dubbed in, and you were the person having the experience, with one important difference—you could turn it off if it got to be too much. The "actor" couldn't. A simple gimmick. You didn't really need the camera and the sound track; many users never turned them on at all, but let their own imaginations fill in the emotional broadcast.

The helmets were not sold, only leased or rented after a short, easy fitting session. A year's lease cost fifty dollars, and there were over thirty-seven million subscribers. Herb had created his own network when the demand for more hours squeezed him out of regular television. From a one-hour weekly show, it had gone to one hour nightly, and now it was on the air eight hours a day live, with another eight hours of taped programming.

What had started out as A DAY IN THE LIFE OF ANNE BEAUMONT was now a life in the life of Anne Beaumont and the audience was insatiable.

Anne came in then, surrounded by the throng of hangers-on that mobbed her daily—hairdressers, masseurs, fitters, script men . . . She looked tired. She waved the crowd out when she saw John and Herb were there. "Hello, John," she said, "Herb."

"Anne, baby, you're looking great!" Herb said. He took her in his arms and kissed her solidly. She stood still, her hands at her sides.

She was tall, very slender, with wheat-colored hair and gray eyes. Her cheekbones were wide and high, her mouth firm and almost too large. Against her deep red-gold suntan her teeth looked whiter than John remembered. Although too firm and strong ever to be thought of as pretty, she was a very beautiful woman. After Herb released her, she turned to John, hesitated only a moment, then extended a slim, sun-browned hand. It was cool and dry in his.

"How have you been, John? It's been a long time."

He was very glad she didn't kiss him, or call him darling. She smiled only slightly and gently removed her hand from his. He moved to the bar as she turned to Herb.

"I'm through, Herb." Her voice was too quiet. She accepted a whiskey sour from John, but kept her gaze on Herb.

"What's the matter, honey? I was just watching you, baby. You were great today, like always. You've still got it, kid. It's coming through like always."

"What about this robbery? You must be out of your mind . . ."

"Yeah, that. Listen, Anne baby, I swear to you I don't know a thing about it. Laughton must have been giving you the straight goods on that. You know we agreed that the rest of this week you just have a good time, remember? That comes over too, baby. When you have a good time and relax, thirty-seven million people are enjoying life and relaxing. That's good. They can't be stimulated all the time. They like the variety." Wordlessly John held out a glass, scotch and water. Herb took it without looking.

Anne was watching him coldly. Suddenly she laughed. It was a cynical, bitter sound. "You're not a damn fool, Herb. Don't try to act like one." She sipped her drink again, staring at him over the rim of the glass. "I'm warning you, if anyone shows up here to rob me, I'm going to treat him like a real burglar. I bought a gun after today's broadcast, and I learned how to shoot when I was ten. I still know how. I'll kill him, Herb, whoever it is."

"Baby," Herb started, but she cut him short.

"And this is my last week. As of Saturday, I'm through."

"You can't do that, Anne," Herb said. John watched him closely, searching for a sign of weakness; he saw nothing. Herb exuded confidence. "Look around, Anne, at this room, your clothes, everything. . . . You are the richest woman in the world, having the time of your life, able to go anywhere, do anything . . ."

"While the whole world watches—"

"So what? It doesn't stop you, does it?" Herb started to pace, his steps jerky and quick. "You knew that when you signed the contract. You're a rare girl, Anne, beautiful, emotional, intelligent. Think of all those women who've got nothing but you. If you quit them, what do they do? Die? They might, you know. For the first time in their lives they're able to feel like they're living. You're giving them what no one ever did before, what was only hinted at in books and films in the old days. Suddenly they know what it feels like to face excitement, to experience love, to feel contented and peaceful. Think of them, Anne, empty, with nothing in their lives but you, what you're able to give them. Thirty-seven million drabs, Anne, who never felt anything but boredom and frustration until you gave them life. What do they have? Work, kids, bills. You've given them the world, baby! Without you they wouldn't even want to live anymore."

She wasn't listening. Almost dreamily she said, "I talked to my lawyers, Herb, and the contract is meaningless. You've already broken it over and over. I agreed to learn a lot of new things. I did. My God! I've climbed mountains, hunted lions, learned to ski and water-ski, but now you want me to die a little bit each week . . . That airplane crash, not bad, just enough to terrify me. Then the sharks. I really do think it was having sharks brought in when I was skiing that did it, Herb. You see, you will kill me. It will happen, and you won't be able to top it, Herb. Not ever."

There was a hard, waiting silence following her words. *No!* John shouted soundlessly. He was looking at Herb. He had stopped pacing when she started to talk. Something flicked across his face—surprise, fear, something not readily identifiable. Then his face went blank and he raised his glass and finished the scotch and water, replacing the glass on the bar. When he turned again, he was smiling with disbelief.

"What's really bugging you, Anne? There have been plants before. You knew about them. Those lions didn't just happen by, you know. And the avalanche needed a nudge from someone. You know that. What else is bugging you?"

"I'm in love, Herb."

Herb waved that aside impatiently. "Have you ever watched your own show, Anne?" She shook her head. "I thought not. So you wouldn't know about the expansion that took place last month, after we planted that new transmitter in your head. Johnny boy's been busy, Anne. You know these scientist-types, never satisfied, always improving, changing. Where's the camera, Anne? Do you ever know where it is anymore? Have you ever seen a camera in the past couple of weeks, or a recorder of any sort? You have not, and you won't again. You're on now, honey." His voice was quite low, amused almost. "In fact the only time you aren't on is when you're sleeping. I know you're in love. I know who he is. I know how he makes you feel. I even know how much money he makes a week. I should know, Anne baby. I pay him." He had come closer to her with each word, finishing with his face only inches from hers. He didn't have a chance to duck the flashing slap that jerked his head around, and before either of them realized it, he had hit her back, knocking her into a chair.

The silence grew, became something ugly and heavy, as if words were being born and dying without utterance because they were too brutal for the human spirit to bear. There was a spot of blood on Herb's mouth where Anne's diamond ring had cut him. He touched it and looked at his finger. "It's all being taped now, honey, even this," he said. He turned his back on her and went to the bar.

There was a large red print on her cheek. Her gray eyes had turned black with rage.

"Honey, relax," Herb said after a moment. "It won't make any difference to you, in what you do, or anything like that. You know we can't use most of the stuff, but it gives the editors a bigger variety to pick from. It was getting to the point where most of the interesting stuff was going on after you were off. Like buying the gun. That's great stuff there, baby. You weren't blanketing a single thing, and it'll all come through like pure gold." He finished mixing his drink, tasted it, and then swallowed half of it. "How many women have to go out and buy a gun to protect themselves? Think of them all, feeling that gun, feeling the things you felt when you picked it up, looked at it . . ."

"How long have you been tuning in all the time?" she asked. John felt a stirring along his spine, a tingle of excitement. He knew what was going out over the miniature transmitter, the rising crests of emotion she was feeling. Only a trace of them showed on her smooth face, but the raging interior torment was being recorded faithfully. Her quiet voice and quiet body were lies; the tapes never lied.

Herb felt it too. He put his glass down and went to her, kneeling by the chair, taking her hand in both of his. "Anne, please, don't be that angry with me. I was desperate for new material. When Johnny got this last wrinkle out, and we knew we could record around the clock, we had to try it, and it wouldn't have been any good if you'd known. That's no way to test anything. You knew we were planting the transmitter . . ."

"How long?"

"Not quite a month."

"And Stuart? He's one of your men? He is transmitting also? You hired him to . . . to make love to me? Is that right?"

Herb nodded. She pulled her hand free and averted her face. He got up then and went to the window. "But what difference does it make?" he shouted. "If I introduced the two of you at a party, you wouldn't think anything of it. What difference if I did it this way? I knew you'd like each other. He's bright, like you, likes the same sort of things you do. Comes from a poor family, like yours . . . Everything said you'd get along."

"Oh, yes," she said almost absently. "We get along." She was feeling in her hair, her fingers searching for the scars.

"It's all healed by now," John said. She looked at him as if she had forgotten he was there.

"I'll find a surgeon," she said, standing up, her fingers white on her glass. "A brain surgeon—"

"It's a new process," John said slowly. "It would be dangerous to go in after them."

She looked at him for a long time. "Dangerous?"

He nodded.

"You could take it back out."

He remembered the beginning, how he had quieted her fear of the electrodes and wires. Her fear was that of a child for the unknown and the unknowable. Time and again he had proved to her that she could trust him, that he wouldn't lie to her. He hadn't lied to her, then. There was the same trust in her eyes, the same unshakable faith. She would believe him. She would accept without question whatever he said. Herb had called him an icicle, but that was wrong. An icicle would have melted in her fires. More like a stalactite, shaped by centuries of civilization, layer by layer he had been formed until he had forgotten how to bend, forgotten how to find release for the stirrings he felt somewhere in the hollow, rigid core of himself. She had tried and, frustrated, she had turned from him, hurt, but unable not to trust one she had loved. Now she waited. He could free her, and lose her again, this time irrevocably. Or he could hold her as long as she lived.

Her lovely gray eyes were shadowed with fear, and the trust that he had given to her. Slowly he shook his head.

"I can't," he said. "No one can."

"I see," she murmured, the black filling her eyes. "I'd die, wouldn't I? Then you'd have a lovely sequence, wouldn't you, Herb?" She swung around, away from John. "You'd have to fake the story line, of course, but you are so good at that. An accident, emergency brain surgery needed, everything I feel going out to the poor little drabs who never will have brain surgery done. It's very good," she said admiringly. Her eyes were black. "In fact, anything I do from now on, you'll use, won't you? If I kill you, that will simply be material for your editors to pick over. Trial, prison, very dramatic . . . On the other hand, if I kill myself . . ."

John felt chilled; a cold, hard weight seemed to be filling him. Herb laughed. "The story line will be something like this," he said. "Anne has fallen in love with a stranger, deeply, sincerely in love with him. Everyone knows how deep that love is, they've all felt it, too, you know. She finds him raping a child, a lovely little girl in her early teens. Stuart tells her they're through. He loves the little nymphet. In a passion she kills herself. You are broadcasting a real storm of passion, right now, aren't you, honey? Never mind, when I run through this scene, I'll find out." She hurled her glass at him, ice cubes and orange slices flying across the room. Herb ducked, grinning.

"That's awfully good, baby. Corny, but after all, they can't get too much corn, can they? They'll love it, after they get over the shock of losing you. And they will get over it, you know. They always do. Wonder if it's true about what happens to someone experiencing a violent death?" Anne's teeth bit down on her lip, and slowly she sat down again, her eyes closed tight. Herb watched her for a moment, then said, even more cheerfully,

"We've got the kid already. If you give them a death, you've got to give them a new life. Finish one with a bang. Start one with a bang. We'll name the kid Cindy, a real Cinderella story after that. They'll love her, too."

Anne opened her eyes, black, dulled now; she was so full of tension that John felt his own muscles contract. He wondered if he would be able to stand the tape she was transmitting. A wave of excitement swept him and he knew he would play it all, feel it all, the incredibly contained rage, fear, the horror of giving a death to them to gloat over, and finally, anguish. He would know it all. Watching Anne, he wished she would break now. She didn't. She stood up stiffly, her back rigid, a muscle hard ridged in her jaw. Her voice was flat when she said, "Stuart is due in half an hour. I have to dress." She left them without looking back.

Herb winked at John and motioned toward the door. "Want to take me to the plane, kid?" In the cab he said, "Stick close to her for a couple of days, Johnny. There might be an even bigger reaction later when she really understands just how hooked she is." He chuckled again. "By God! It's a good thing she trusts you, Johnny boy!"

As they waited in the chrome and marble terminal for the liner to unload its passengers, John said, "Do you think she'll be any good after this?"

"She can't help herself. She's too life-oriented to deliberately choose to die. She's like a jungle inside, raw, wild, untouched by that smooth layer of civilization she shows on the outside. It's a thin layer, kid, real thin. She'll fight to stay alive. She'll become more wary, more alert to danger, more excited and exciting . . . She'll really go to pieces when he touches her tonight. She's primed real good. Might even have to do some editing, tone it down a little." His voice was very happy. "He touches her where she lives, and she reacts. A real wild one. She's one; the new kid's one; Stuart . . . They're few and far between, Johnny. It's up to us to find them. God knows we're going to need all of them we can get." His expression became thoughtful and withdrawn. "You know, that really wasn't such a bad idea of mine about rape and the kid. Who ever dreamed we'd get that kind of reaction from her? With the right sort of buildup . . ." He had to run to catch his plane.

John hurried back to the hotel, to be near Anne if she needed him. But he hoped she would leave him alone. His fingers shook as he turned on his screen; suddenly he had a clear memory of the child who had wept, and he hoped Stuart was on from six until twelve, and he already had missed almost an hour of the show. He adjusted the helmet and sank back into a deep chair. He left the audio off, letting his own words form, letting his own thoughts fill in the spaces.

Anne was leaning toward him, sparkling champagne raised to her lips, her eyes large and soft. She was speaking, talking to him, John, calling him by name. He felt a tingle start somewhere deep inside him, and his glance was lowered to rest on her tanned hand in his, sending electricity through him. Her hand trembled when he ran his fingers up her palm, to her wrist where a blue vein throbbed. The slight throb became a pounding that grew and when he looked into her eyes, they were dark and very deep. They danced and he felt her body against his, yielding, pleading. The room darkened and she was an outline against the window, her gown floating down about her. The darkness grew denser, or he closed his eyes, and this time when her body pressed against his, there was nothing between them, and the pounding was everywhere.

In the deep chair, with the helmet on his head, John's hand clenched, opened, clenched, again and again.

AFFAIR

by

HELENE DAVIS

(b. 1945)

Born in Providence, Rhode Island, Helene Davis studied art at Boston University and English at the University of Massachusetts, Boston, where she now teaches writing. A student of Ruth Whitman at the poetry workshop of Radcliffe College, she has published poems in several journals, including the Southern Poetry Review *and* Plough-shares. *Her first collection,* Nightblind, *appeared in 1976, and she recently wrote* Chemo-Poet, *about the experience of mastectomy.*

• ———————————————————————— •

Together our hands find no indifferent touch.
We are one kind, a dark breed who must love
for sheer breath.

   In the old story, leaning against the lamplight,
   the woman is electric, happy,
   never cries.

You move back into stone eyes. With your darkhaired words
you press illusion in fine volumes,
for keepsakes.

   The woman owns no name—mistress, mother, kind
   friend or lover—a velvet backdrop
   in his quiet life.

Without you my flesh becomes bone dry and breaks
easily, my face invisible as moss
on gravestones.

   The woman must, like earth, be able to change
   size: a spot of dust, a rose half grown, a room
   full of music.

The Sex Object

A woman is confused about how to respond to wolf calls and whistles: should she smile and accept them as efforts to humanize existence, or should she haughtily ignore them because they reduce her from person to thing, a sexual object? Often fear rules her response more than reason: behind the most casual approach of a male may lurk every woman's nightmare, the rapist-murderer. Whether preceded by courtship or not, to a woman sexual intercourse is the equivalent of rape if her partner's purpose is to use her for his own pleasure, to reify, or make an object of, her.

In Irwin Shaw's "The Girls in Their Summer Dresses," Michael's girl-watching seems a very slight offense and his wife's anger seems possessive and out of proportion, until one realizes that he sees her just as he does other pretty girls. To him she is an object, and he admits that probably a more attractive object will replace her. Both Michael and Frances accept his roving eye as part of his nature and the unhappiness it causes as inevitable. Michael could well quote the lines of W. B. Yeats's poem "For Anne Gregory": ". . . only God, my dear, / Could love you for yourself alone." Frances's acceptance of her role after her brief rebellion makes her not only a sex object but also a submissive wife.

In Rona Jaffe's "Rima the Bird Girl," Rima Allen is overwhelmingly eager to assume the submissive wife role. As the paramour of a succession of men, Rima, like the woman in "Affair," changes to fit their images of a desirable mate—or, ironically, the images of their wives—and repeatedly gives herself to men who use her and discard her. As she goes from one liaison to another, it is apparent that the price of giving herself is the loss of that self; she can only play roles. More subtly, Jaffe shows us that the narrator through whom we perceive Rima, an old college friend, has played the same role. Though she "missed zoology and hated typing and filing," the narrator is happy to give up zoology for wifehood: she has cleaned her husband's apartment, "read his magazines, his books, played his records, and waited for him to come home to eat the dinners [she] cooked." These two educated women are eager to be submissive. Sergius O'Shaugnessy, Norman Mailer's persona in "The Time of Her Time," expects Denise, a college girl who has had the nerve to argue with him, to be submissive. Her courage in asserting her literary opinion makes him want to use against her "the avenger of [his] crotch, . . . to prong her then and there, right on the floor. . . ." Sergius is trying to find an identity for himself through conquest of any kind—bullfighting, bragging in a hashhouse, sexual dominance. His determination to bring Denise to orgasm stems not from any desire for pleasure that either of them might experience, but from the necessity to "prove" himself. When Denise has the last word at the end of the story, she reminds the reader of the fate of the macho knife expert for whom one defeat is the end of his reign as champion. In spite of the numbers of women Sergius's "avenger" has conquered, this one defeat symbolizes the loss of his manhood and his failure to find meaning in life. Failure in sexual domination is the sign of the beginning of the end for the aging athlete.

In Joyce Carol Oates's story "The Girl," lack of meaning in a world in which women are sex objects is symbolized by the fact that none of the characters has a name; all are playacting, making life a game totally removed from reality. At the end the girl is not sure whether she has actually been a victim of rape or whether she "really" was playing the victim for the camera. Her uncertainty corresponds to the difficulty many rape victims have in getting people to believe their stories; they are always suspected of having invited the violence they experienced. Ntozake Shange in "With No Immediate Cause" uses repetition and concrete, vivid images to establish the reality of rape and violence toward women. Her poem rules out any illusion of love or even sexual desire as the motivation for rape. The object of violence may be children or old women. Shange uses the first person to express a woman's feelings as she reacts to the statistics, the cold facts: she is too afraid to intervene when she sees an old man molest a child, and she vomits when reading a report on "alleged battered women" in which the victims become the criminals. In 'Daguerrotype: "Fallen" Woman,' Sandra Gilbert lets the reader hear under the surface of a prostitute's own words about her life the sexuality that still enables her to fantasize her own sexual gratification with "an armless man" who "sucks out her hole" instead of holding her down and penetrating her for his gratification. Clearly the prostitute separates her role from her sense of self; the characterization of her as "fallen" is rightly in quotation marks as representing the opinion of others—and also, teasingly, as an allusion to the Biblical view of all human beings as somehow fallen through the very fact of being human.

Doris Lessing's "One off the Short List" shows a woman who can be objective about sex. Barbara Coles does not equate sexual surrender with self-surrender; she can even allow her attacker the cheap satisfaction of publicly seeming to be the victor. Like Sergius O'Shaugnessy in Mailer's story, Graham Spence thinks of sex as a battle of wills; he maps his plans to entrap Barbara Coles as if he were a general planning a campaign. Thinking of him only as a colleague, Barbara does not put up any defenses until it is too late to get out of his trap with dignity. She refuses to cry rape, to be a victim. Rightly perceiving that physical gratification is not his goal, she contemptuously allows him his cheap victory, knowing that in so doing she is denying him his real goal, a feeling of superiority. Lessing's story should not be seen as advocating the old saw "when rape is inevitable, relax and enjoy it"; Barbara does not need Graham, either for physical or ego gratification. Rather, the story makes an important point that is often overlooked because the sexual revolution and women's liberation have been chronologically linked: sexuality is only a part of self-definition. The story also validates women's fear that the most civilized exterior may hide a rapist. In a society where male dominance is considered necessary and where violence is condoned on many levels, such fear is self-protective.

THE GIRLS IN THEIR SUMMER DRESSES

by

IRWIN SHAW

(1913–1984)

Born in New York, Irwin Shaw lived much of his adult life abroad. He wrote movie and radio scripts as well as plays, novels, and short stories. His best-known novel is The Young Lions (*1948*). *Others include* The Top of the Hill (*1979*) *and* Acceptable Losses (*1982*). *His short stories are collected in* Stories of Five Decades (*1978*).

•——————————————•

Fifth Avenue was shining in the sun when they left the Brevoort. The sun was warm, even though it was February, and everything looked like Sunday morning—the buses and the well-dressed people walking slowly in couples and the quiet buildings with the windows closed.

Michael held Frances' arm tightly as they walked toward Washington Square in the sunlight. They walked lightly, almost smiling, because they had slept late and had a good breakfast and it was Sunday. Michael unbuttoned his coat and let it flap around him in the mild wind.

"Look out," Frances said as they crossed Eighth Street. "You'll break your neck."

Michael laughed and Frances laughed with him.

"She's not so pretty," Frances said. "Anyway, not pretty enough to take a chance of breaking your neck."

Michael laughed again. "How did you know I was looking at her?"

Frances cocked her head to one side and smiled at her husband under the brim of her hat. "Mike, darling," she said.

"O.K.," he said. "Excuse me."

Frances patted his arm lightly and pulled him along a little faster toward Washington Square. "Let's not see anybody all day," she said. "Let's just hang around with each other. You and me. We're always up to our neck in people, drinking their Scotch or drinking our Scotch; we only see each other in bed. I want to go out with my husband all day long. I want him to talk only to me and listen only to me."

"What's to stop us?" Michael asked.

"The Stevensons. They want us to drop by around one o'clock and they'll drive us into the country."

"The cunning Stevensons," Mike said. "Transparent. They can whistle. They can go driving in the country by themselves."

"Is it a date?"

"It's a date."

Frances leaned over and kissed him on the tip of the ear.

"Darling," Michael said, "this is Fifth Avenue."

"Let me arrange a program," Frances said. "A planned Sunday in New York for a young couple with money to throw away."

"Go easy."

"First let's go to the Metropolitan Museum of Art," Frances suggested, because Michael had said during the week he wanted to go. "I haven't been there in three years and there're at least ten pictures I want to see again. Then we can take the bus down to Radio City and watch them skate. And later we'll go down to Cavanaugh's and get a steak as big as a blacksmith's apron, with a bottle of wine, and after that there's a French picture at the Filmarte that everybody says—say, are you listening to me?"

"Sure," he said. He took his eyes off the hatless girl with the dark hair, cut dancer-style like a helmet, who was walking past him.

"That's the program for the day," Frances said flatly. "Or maybe you'd just rather walk up and down Fifth Avenue."

"No," Michael said. "Not at all."

"You always look at other women," Frances said. "Everywhere. Every damned place we go."

"No, darling," Michael said, "I look at everything. God gave me eyes and I look at women and men and subway excavations and moving pictures and the little flowers of the field. I casually inspect the universe."

"You ought to see the look in your eye," Frances said, "as you casually inspect the universe on Fifth Avenue."

"I'm a happily married man." Michael pressed her elbow tenderly. "Example for the whole twentieth century—Mr. and Mrs. Mike Loomis. Hey, let's have a drink," he said, stopping.

"We just had breakfast."

"Now listen, darling," Mike said, choosing his words with care, "it's a nice day and we both felt good and there's no reason why we have to break it up. Let's have a nice Sunday."

"All right. I don't know why I started this. Let's drop it. Let's have a good time."

They joined hands consciously and walked without talking among the baby carriages and the old Italian men in their Sunday clothes and the young women with Scotties in Washington Square Park.

"At least once a year everyone should go to the Metropolitan Museum of Art," Frances said after a while, her tone a good imitation of the tone she had used at breakfast and at the beginning of their walk. "And it's nice on Sunday. There're a lot of people looking at the pictures and you get the feeling maybe Art isn't on the decline in New York City, after all—"

"I want to tell you something," Michael said very seriously. "I have not touched another woman. Not once. In all the five years."

"All right," Frances said.

"You believe that, don't you?"

"All right."

They walked between the crowded benches, under the scrubby city-park trees.

"I try not to notice it," Frances said, "but I feel rotten inside, in my stomach, when we pass a woman and you look at her and I see that look in your eye and that's the way you looked at me the first time. In Alice Maxwell's house. Standing there in the living room, next to the radio, with a green hat on and all those people."

"I remember the hat," Michael said.

"The same look," Frances said. "And it makes me feel bad. It makes me feel terrible."

"Sh-h-h, please, darling, sh-h-h."

"I think I would like a drink now," Frances said.

They walked over to a bar on Eighth Street, not saying anything. Michael automatically helping her over curbstones and guiding her past automobiles. They sat near a window in the bar and the sun streamed in and there was a small, cheerful fire in the fireplace. A little Japanese waiter came over and put down some pretzels and smiled happily at them.

"What do you order after breakfast?" Michael asked.

"Brandy, I suppose," Frances said.

"Courvoisier," Michael told the waiter. "Two Courvoisiers."

The waiter came with the glasses and they sat drinking the brandy in the sunlight. Michael finished half his and drank a little water.

"I look at women," he said. "Correct. I don't say it's wrong or right. I look at them. If I pass them on the street and I don't look at them, I'm fooling you, I'm fooling myself."

"You look at them as though you want them," Frances said, playing with her brandy glass. "Every one of them."

"In a way," Michael said, speaking softly and not to his wife, "in a way that's true. I don't do anything about it, but it's true."

"I know it. That's why I feel bad."

"Another brandy," Michael called. "Waiter, two more brandies."

He sighed and closed his eyes and rubbed them gently with his fingertips.

"I love the way women look. One of the things I like best about New York is the battalions of women. When I first came to New York from Ohio that was the first thing I noticed, the million wonderful women, all over the city. I walked around with my heart in my throat."

"A kid," Frances said. "That's a kid's feeling."

"Guess again," Michael said. "Guess again. I'm older now. I'm a man getting near middle age, putting on a little fat and I still love to walk along Fifth Avenue at three o'clock on the east side of the street between Fiftieth and Fifty-seventh Streets. They're all out then, shopping, in their furs and their crazy hats, everything all concentrated from all over the world into seven blocks—the best furs, the best clothes, the handsomest women, out to spend money and feeling good about it."

The Japanese waiter put the two drinks down, smiling with great happiness.

"Everything is all right?" he asked.

"Everything is wonderful," Michael said.

"If it's just a couple of fur coats," Frances said, "and forty-five-dollar hats—"

"It's not the fur coats. Or the hats. That's just the scenery for that particular kind of woman. Understand," he said, "you don't have to listen to this."

"I want to listen."

"I like the girls in the offices. Neat, with their eyeglasses, smart, chipper, knowing what everything is about. I like the girls on Forty-fourth Street at lunchtime, the actresses, all dressed up on nothing a week. I like the salesgirls in the stores, paying attention to you first because you're a man, leaving lady customers waiting. I got all this stuff accumulated in me because I've been thinking about it for ten years and now you've asked for it and here it is."

"Go ahead," Frances said.

"When I think of New York City, I think of all the girls on parade in the city. I don't know whether it's something special with me or whether every man in the city walks around with the same feeling inside him, but I feel as though I'm at a picnic in this city. I like to sit near the women in the theatres, the famous beauties who've taken six hours to get ready and look it. And the young girls at the football games, with the red cheeks, and when the warm weather comes, the girls in their summer dresses." He finished his drink. "That's the story."

Frances finished her drink and swallowed two or three times extra. "You say you love me?"

"I love you."

"I'm pretty, too," Frances said. "As pretty as any of them."

"You're beautiful," Michael said.

"I'm good for you," Frances said, pleading. "I've made a good wife, a good housekeeper, a good friend. I'd do any damn thing for you."

IRWIN SHAW

263

"I know," Michael said. He put his hand out and grasped hers.

"You'd like to be free to—" Frances said.

"Sh-h-h."

"Tell the truth." She took her hand away from under his.

Michael flicked the edge of his glass with his finger. "O.K.," he said gently. "Sometimes I feel I would like to be free."

"Well," Frances said, "any time you say."

"Don't be foolish." Michael swung his chair around to her side of the table and patted her thigh.

She began to cry silently into her handkerchief, bent over just enough so that nobody else in the bar would notice. "Someday," she said, crying, "you're going to make a move."

Michael didn't say anything. He sat watching the bartender slowly peel a lemon.

"Aren't you?" Frances asked harshly. "Come on, tell me. Talk. Aren't you?"

"Maybe," Michael said. He moved his chair back again. "How the hell do I know?"

"You know," Frances persisted. "Don't you know?"

"Yes," Michael said after a while, "I know."

Frances stopped crying then. Two or three snuffles into the handkerchief and she put it away and her face didn't tell anything to anybody. "At least do me one favor," she said.

"Sure."

"Stop talking about how pretty this woman is or that one. Nice eyes, nice breasts, a pretty figure, good voice." She mimicked his voice. "Keep it to yourself. I'm not interested."

Michael waved to the waiter. "I'll keep it to myself," he said.

Frances flicked the corners of her eyes. "Another brandy," she told the waiter.

"Two," Michael said.

"Yes, Ma'am, yes sir," said the waiter, backing away.

Frances regarded Michael coolly across the table. "Do you want me to call the Stevensons?" she asked. "It'll be nice in the country."

"Sure," Michael said. "Call them."

She got up from the table and walked across the room toward the telephone. Michael watched her walk, thinking what a pretty girl, what nice legs.

RIMA THE BIRD GIRL

by

RONA JAFFE

(b. 1932)

*A graduate of Radcliffe College, Rona Jaffe has written often about
the life of career girls in New York City. Her frankness about
women as sex objects in* The Best of Everything *(1958) made her a
forerunner of the "second wave" of women's liberation. Recent
works are* Class Reunion *(1979),* Mr. Right Is Dead *(1980), and*
Away from Home *(1982).*

—————————————————————

I don't remember the day we first met, but my first memory of her is of a
wraithlike dark-haired girl sitting in the corner of the living room of our
dormitory at college, reciting poetry—no, almost shouting it—she and a
friend in unison. And it seemed to me then as if poetry should always be
shouted in this inspired, almost orgiastic, way, for it was really music. "O
love is the crooked thing,/-There is nobody wise enough/To find out all
that is in it, . . ./Ah, penny, brown penny, brown penny,/-One cannot
begin it too soon."

Her name was Rima Allen, and she came from a small town in Pennsylvania which had neither the distinction of being a grimy coal town nor
Main Line, but just a town. Her mother had been reading *Green Mansions*
when her daughter was born, and she felt it would give her child some
individuality to be named Rima. Her father was a tax accountant, a vague
man who spent his life bent over records of other people's lives. He
thought Rima was a silly name, but his wife overruled him, and later it
was she who chose Radcliffe for Rima, and so we met.

There was a fireplace at one end of the living room in our dormitory,
and beside it a nook, wood paneled and cushioned in velvet. Rima was
sitting in that nook with her temporary friend, a lumpy debutante from
New York who powdered her face like a Kabuki dancer and had once
brought a copy of the Social Register into dinner to point out her own
name in it. That frightened and graceless snob (whose registered name I

have forgotten) was the last person on earth you would expect to find chanting Yeats with such obvious joy, yet Rima had made her memorize dozens of his poems. I knew at once that Rima was a special girl, a girl people gravitated toward to find their dream, their opposite, whatever it was they could not find alone.

"An aged man is but a paltry thing,/A tattered coat upon a stick, unless/Soul clap its hands and sing, and louder sing/For every tatter in its mortal dress."

Rima was a tall girl who always looked very small and fragile, until you noticed her standing next to someone else and realized with surprise that she was big. She had narrow shoulders and small bones, a delicate way of moving, and a soft, child's voice. Her face, in those years of our late teens, was a white blur, as I suppose all our faces were, for we did not yet know who we were. I have a photograph of her sitting on the library steps, a pretty, pale, no-face child of seventeen, all wonder, her arms held out to the wan New England sun.

Every one of us owned several bottles of cologne; Rima had none, but she had one bottle of perfume. We all had many party dresses; Rima had only one, but it was orange, with a swirly skirt, and it had cost a hundred dollars. I remember her always hiding in her room, the shades down, studying, or reading the poetry she loved, and then the sound of the phone bell . . . and ten minutes later she emerged—a swirl of orange skirt, a cloud of Arpege drifting after her, as if she had suddenly been told she existed.

That's all I remember of her from those days; it was, after all, fifteen years ago, and her story had not begun. When we graduated, four of us went to Washington to work in offices, share a house, and find husbands. I had been a zoology major in college, studying such unfeminine things as mollusks, but when we went to Washington I decided to become a secretary along with the others, because we were almost twenty-one and not getting any younger. Everyone knew you found nothing among the mollusks but shells and a lot of ugly old men. We had decided on Washington instead of New York because the other two girls said that was where the bright young men were. A few months after the four of us settled in rooms in a Greek Revival style mansion turned into a rooming house, the two who had brought us to this city of romance began going steady with two boys they had known back at Harvard, and I realized why we had come.

I missed zoology and hated typing and filing; but missing one's work takes an odd form in girls, I think—I was less conscious of the loss than I was of what replaced it, a ferocious need to be loved. I needed someone to inflict all that creative energy on, it didn't matter much who. Of the four of us, it was only Rima who seemed to enjoy being a secretary; who preferred staying home and listening to old Noel Coward records to going out with a new prospect; who went to bed early and got up early, eagerly, without resentment; and who went to the office in her prettiest clothes.

I soon discovered it was because she was in love with someone she had met at work.

It was one of those impossibly romantic meetings that occur only in bad movies and real life. The man was attached to the State Department, one of those career diplomats whose work is so important and confidential that you can talk to him for an hour at a cocktail party and realize afterward he has not said a word about himself. He was American, forty-five years old, very attractive, totally sophisticated and, of course, married. Rima had been dispatched to take some papers to his office. There she was, in the doorway—his secretary was in the powder room—and he was alone behind the largest desk she had ever seen. She looked at him, knowing only vaguely who he was and how important he was, thinking only that he was a grownup and extraordinarily attractive. She was wearing her neat little college-girl suit, her hair tied back with a ribbon, her face all admiration and awe. She thought as girls do in the darkness of movie theaters without any sense of further reality: I'd love to go out with him! No one knows what he thought. But the next day he took her to the country for lunch.

She did not tell me who her mysterious lover was for several months, and she never told our other two roommates at all. She saved newspaper clippings about glittering Washington parties he had attended, but because diplomatic amours are very diplomatic in Washington, she had little else in the way of souvenirs, not even a matchbook from a restaurant. I did not know how they managed to meet during those first few months, but I always knew when she was meeting him because again, as in our college days, there was a swirl of brightly colored skirt running down the stairs, a faint cloud of perfume (Joy this time instead of Arpege), and the air around her was charged with life. When she finally told me his name, it was only after they had both decided they were in love.

Rima had had crushes on boys at Harvard, had even cried over a few missed phone calls, but it was nothing like this. As for him, he had played around with little interest with a few predatory wives, but he had never had a real love affair with anyone since his marriage. Rima was so young, so full of confidence in a future in which she would always be young and he would always care for her, that she never even thought of asking him to get a divorce. It was a courtship. They planned how they would meet, when they would meet, how she could see him most often, how she could get along. He could not bear for her to be poor; even the thought that she was spending part of her $60 salary on taxis to meet him appalled him, he wanted to make everything up to her, but how? She refused to go out with any of the boys (we still called them that) who phoned, and he knew it. Suddenly, one day, our freezer was full of steaks, the refrigerator was filled with splits of champagne, and our house was so filled with flowers I thought someone had died.

I went with Rima one day to help her sell her jewelry so that she could buy him a birthday present. Her charm bracelet with the gold disk that said "Sweet Sixteen," her college ring . . . whatever she could not sell she pawned. None of it meant anything to her. "I want to get him gold cuff links," she said. "He wears French cuffs." I thought of the O. Henry story about the gift of the Magi, but it was not the same, because he was not giving up anything for her, and what she was giving up for him was only bits of metal and chips of gems that belonged to an already fading past.

That summer, when our first year of independence drew to a close, our two roommates married the boys they had come to Washington to pursue, and Rima and I had two whole rooms to ourselves. Summers in Washington are very hot. An air conditioner mysteriously appeared in our bedroom window, installed by a man from the air-conditioning company whom neither of us had sent for. On the first cool fall day, for the first time, I was allowed to meet the diplomat. He came to our house for tea and sat on the edge of one of our frayed chairs, very elegant in his hand-tailored suit and Sulka tie. He even wore a vest. I thought he looked like our uncle; not our father—he was too young, too glamorous, too much from another world. But there was something fatherly in the way he looked around at our landlady's furniture with amusement and yet a little annoyance— was it clean enough, good enough, for his child—the way he smiled with adult pride at everything Rima said, as if she were a precious being from another planet. I could hardly believe any of this was happening; I think, in a way, neither could he. Yet they were obviously in love with each other.

He went to New York on several business trips that fall and winter and took Rima with him, meeting her as if by accident on the train, where he had taken a private bedroom for the short trip and Rima had a ticket in the parlor car. They had rooms in the same hotel on different floors. At Buccellati's he bought her a gold and emerald ring, which she wore on her left hand, but they entered and left the shop by the back door. When they returned to Washington after the last trip, his wife met him at the station, and Rima alighted from a different car and stood staring on the station platform as her love drove off in a silver-gray foreign automobile with someone who was suddenly flesh and blood, an actuality, a force, a monster.

"I saw her, the old hag," Rima said to me that night, almost in tears. "I wish I could kill her. She's very sophisticated . . . she was wearing a real Chanel suit, and the Chanel shoes and bag too . . . she's too thin, she chain-smokes and uses a holder . . . she's one of those terribly chic, tense women who knows everybody and always says and does the right things. You could tell. She's unhappy, though . . . she must know he loves some- one else. Women as nervous as that always know they aren't loved. He told me he doesn't love her any more. He'd leave her if it weren't for his career; a scandal—zip!" She drew her finger across her throat. "He's so proper and old-fashioned in his way, nobody is like him any more. If it weren't for her he could marry me and we'd both be happy. I hate her, the old hag."

"She doesn't sound like an old hag," I said.

"She is!"

"All right, she is."

"And ugly, too."

"Well, at least she's ugly."

"No, she's not ugly," Rima said. "I wish she were. She must have something if he won't leave her for me. If he really didn't love her, he'd leave her, no matter what he says. How could he marry me? I couldn't be a hostess, I couldn't run two homes the way she does. I don't know anything about being a diplomat's wife. I *know* he loves me, but he won't leave *her*. . . ."

So she did want to marry him after all. It had been inevitable. The courtship had been beautiful; the five-minute meetings in hallways, the stolen afternoons and weekends—all had been part of the discovery and wonder of love. But after a year and a half the champagne of secrecy had gone flat. I suspected that Rima had wanted to marry him long before this but had never dared say the words until she saw his wife and realized bitterly that someone had married him, someone was sharing all of his life except those stolen afternoons; for someone it was possible.

All lovers make near-fatal mistakes in their relationships; it is part of the pleasure of love, illicit or not, to tempt providence. So when, one weekend when his wife was away, the diplomat took Rima to his home, it seemed to me merely one of the fatal mistakes some lovers have to make. It was not fatal in any immediate sense, for they were not caught, no one saw them, the servants were away, his wife did not return unexpectedly with a detective or a gun. On his part, it was only a further avowal of his love for Rima; he wanted her to see where and how he lived, he didn't want her to be an outsider. He wanted her to approve of him, of the beautiful things with which he filled his life. He wanted to give her a setting to picture when she dreamed of him, a background for her lonely fantasies; perhaps he also wanted to be able to imagine her in his home when she was no longer there and he was sitting through a dull diplomatic dinner party. The mistake was fatal because Rima did approve of his home . . . she approved of it too much.

She told me about it that night in detail, and I could picture her scampering through those huge rooms like a child, touching each piece of antique furniture as her lover told her what famous person might have sat in this chair, dined from that plate (now an ashtray), or what skill distinguished the weaving of this piece of cloth from any other. She peered into every closet, learning about the heirloom silver, the china, the crystal; she even tried on some of his wife's clothes. To him, Rima was a child, wistful, amusing, and filled with amazement, so he let her try on the

Chanels, the Diors, stroke the furs, wave the lapis cigarette holder in the air as if it held a cigarette and she were a grownup at the ball. When she returned home to the Greek Revival rooming house, the photographic mind that had gotten *A*'s at Radcliffe was a living archive of memorabilia.

The bulging scrapbooks of souvenirs and photographs from our college days, which still amused us on Sunday afternoons, were shipped home to her parents. In their place appeared glossy magazines that looked more like books, with names like "Antiquaries," and "A History of Battersea Boxes." One of them was even in French. The diplomat collected Battersea boxes, and also tiny silver boxes with crests on them, so Rima began to scour back street antique shops for a collection exactly like his. Real Battersea boxes were too expensive, but on her twenty-third birthday the diplomat gave her one, topped with white china, on which was written in fine script: "A Trifle From a Friend."

"He wanted to give me a coat," she told me, "but this coat will go another year. I just had to have a real Battersea box."

There was a one-of-a-kind pair of Louis XV chairs in the diplomat's living room. But there turned out to be, surprisingly, an identical pair, for Rima discovered it on a trip to New York, and she began putting away part of her salary every month to buy them. "A hundred dollars a month forever. . . ." Our landlady's frayed chairs were sent to the basement, and the two Louis XV chairs took their place in front of our fireplace that December, for the diplomat had added the frighteningly large difference for a Christmas present. But he seemed disappointed with the gift she had chosen for him to give her, because he surprised her with an additional present, a beige and white fox fur coat. She looked young and rich and daring in the coat, but as for the chairs, I was afraid to sit on them.

One night Rima packed all her career-girl clothes in a large box and sent them to charity, for she was the new owner of a real Chanel suit with the shoes and bag to match. She bought a cigarette holder and began to smoke; she said it would help her lose weight, for she had suddenly decided she was too fat. When her lover told her she was getting too thin, she cried all night, but she did not stop smoking, for the excuse was it would help her stop biting her nails. The collection of tiny silver boxes with crests grew larger and covered the entire top of a spindly-legged antique table Rima had found, which was by coincidence exactly like the one in the bedroom of the diplomat and his wife. The real Chanel suit was joined, in a few months, by another, and a white Dior evening gown, which Rima wore at home in the evening, alone, while she sipped sherry from a certain crystal wineglass, chain-smoked, and wrote letters to a certain firm in Paris asking if it was possible to obtain ten yards of a certain brocaded fabric which had been specially made at one time for another American client, and a tiny sample of which she happened to have snipped from the underside of that client's sofa.

When the fabric finally arrived, the sofa it would cover had arrived too, a gift for Rima's twenty-fourth birthday. I reminded her we were still paying rent for a furnished apartment, although it now looked like a museum, and our landlady's basement looked like a warehouse. Rima looked at me with the nervous, near-tearful look she had acquired during the past year, which somehow made her look rather tragic and mysterious. "We're too old to live like pigs anymore," she said. "Don't you want a real home?"

I did, and I wanted something more, something elusive but wonderful, which I felt must surely be beyond the next corner, or at the next party, or on the threshold of our front door tomorrow night. . . It had to be, or I felt I would disappear. So one fall evening, when the doorbell rang, announcing the arrival of perhaps the hundredth blind date I would have had in Washington, I decided: If he's anything better than a monster, whoever he is, *this one* I will fall in love with.

He was far from a monster, and he had green eyes and a sense of humor —my two fatal weaknesses—so while he sat in my living room talking and trying to make me like him he never knew he needn't have bothered, because I already loved him. He talked all night, and at dawn, when he remembered he had invited me to his apartment after dinner to make a pass at me, and now it was too late because it was day and we had to go to our offices, he decided he was in love with me, too.

"How could I not love you?" he asked (this young man who was already destined to become my first husband). "You are me. If I didn't love you, it would be like not loving myself."

My decision to marry him seemed as mad and romantic as my decision to fall in love with him. We were in his car at the curb in front of a restaurant. It was that first night, before his apartment, at our first restaurant together, the first time I had been in his car. I wanted to invent some test for destiny, something simple, arbitrary and irrevocable, therefore magic. "If he comes around to my side to open the door, I'll marry him. If he doesn't, he'll never know." He came around to open the door.

Rima gave a cocktail party for us when we announced our engagement, one of many parties she had begun to give. She had become a polished hostess, entertaining a mélange of people: minor politicians, intellectuals, an artist, a writer, an actress, a few foreigners who spoke no English at all but whose languages Rima had studied in college and perfected during the past few years of her diplomatic education. Her diplomat was not there, of course, and she had hidden her half-dozen tiny framed photographs of him in the dresser drawer, but his presence hovered in the rooms throughout the party, for it was now his home, done in his taste, filled with the objects of his pleasures, and the hostess who presided over it all with infinite charm might as well have been his wife. I had a brief irreverent fantasy of the diplomat coming here one night by accident, and panicking, not knowing which home he had come to.

At the party there was a visitor from New York, a young advertising executive. He was thirty-four, married twelve years to his high school sweetheart, and had two children. He was in Washington on business and obviously had never seen anyone like Rima at such close range. He was almost childishly infatuated with her after ten minutes. She flirted with him, named him Heathcliff (for that was rather whom he resembled), and although she obviously enjoyed playing with him, she seemed unaware of her new power. When she was moving about the room talking to her other guests he did not take his eyes off her.

"You need some more champagne, Heathcliff," Rima said, touching his arm lightly as she drifted past. "I want you to get good and drunk. 'Wine comes in at the mouth and love comes in at the eye; That's all we shall know for truth before we grow old and die.' "

" 'I lift the glass to my mouth,' " he finished, " 'I look at you, and I sigh.' " She stopped dead and stared at him.

He smiled. There was something about him both boyish and wire-strong, a man who would piously refuse to deceive anyone and yet who was destined to deceive many people throughout his life because they would mistake him for someone simple. He raised his champagne glass at Rima. " 'A mermaid found a swimming lad, picked him for her own, pressed her body to his body, laughed; and plunging down forgot in cruel happiness that even lovers drown.' "

"I don't think anyone could drown you," she said. "Heathcliff. . . ."

"Lady Brett Ashley . . . ." he said, transfixed.

"Me?" Rima laughed. *"Me?"*

He asked her to have dinner with him, as he was alone in this city, but she refused, explaining that she was in love with someone and never went out with anyone else.

"Where is he?" the advertising man asked, looking around the crowded room.

"He's not here."

"Oh. Married."

"Aren't you?" she replied sweetly, and drifted away to her guests.

My husband's work took him to New York, where we lived in a three-room apartment that I cleaned carefully every day. I went to the grocery store, read his magazines, his books, played his records, and waited for him to come home to eat the dinners I cooked. He did not like his work very much, and I did not work at all, so in the evenings we talked about the past, our childhoods, our friends; and when we were bored with that we talked about the future, although that seemed more like a game than reality. Sometimes we talked about Rima, who he said was neurotic. He said her life was going to end badly. "If I weren't married to you, I would save her from that man."

"Really? What makes you think she'd want you?" And at that moment, only six months after we had vowed to stay together forever, I wondered why I wanted him, either. I was beginning to look the way Rima had: nervous, lost, a bird girl who appeared out of a tree in the jungle to answer someone's dream and then disappeared at dawn . . . or was it he who disappeared, back into the real world, while the bird girl waited, invisible, for his return, for his summons, for her moments of reality?

Rima wrote to me quite regularly during those months. She had nothing else to do in the evenings, for the decorating job on her apartment was completed, and for some reason the diplomat was not seeing her as often as he used to. He was overworked, she wrote to me, and when he did manage a little time with her he usually spent it falling asleep.

"For the first time in my life," she wrote, "I feel old. I feel like a wife. But I want to marry him, and I know this isn't what our life would be like if I were really his wife. Then we'd share everything. But now he acts as if it isn't a romance any more. I don't know why. Do you remember in the beginning, when the house was full of flowers? He hasn't taken me out to lunch in four months."

They had their first serious fight, "He called me extravagant, said I cared too much about clothes," Rima wrote. "He used to tell me she was extravagant (the old hag) and I told him never to dare compare me with her. He said, 'In some ways you are like her,' and the way he said it was like an insult. He refused to explain. What more does he want from me? I can't be perfect, I need love, I can't help that. Why can't he love me enough to leave her? What's wrong with me that he can't love me enough to choose me over someone he doesn't love at all?"

The day after her fifth anniversary with the diplomat, Rima arrived at my apartment in New York. It seems they had been planning their fifth anniversary celebration for months; she had saved for and bought a new white Dior gown, had her hair done at eight in the morning in order to be at the office on time, and then at five o'clock—an hour before they were to meet to celebrate—he had phoned to say he had to go to an important dinner party, his wife would not understand if she had to attend alone, there was nothing he could do. Rima had gotten tremendously drunk on the bottle of Taittinger Blanc de Blancs 1953 she had been chilling in her refrigerator, given the Malossol caviar to the cleaning woman, thrown the white Dior on the closet floor, and taken the morning train to New York. He had promised to make it up to her, perhaps even a whole weekend away somewhere . . . but she could not wait.

"Wait!" she cried to me, tears pouring down her face as if she were a marble statue in a fountain. "Wait! Wait! All I have ever done is wait."

When my husband came home he flirted with Rima all evening—to save her?—as if I were invisible, and she took an instant dislike to it. When he started to talk about a girl he had known before he met me, Rima stood up. "If I ever get married," she said coldly, "my husband will never talk about other women in my presence. Nor will he ever flirt with other women when I am in the room. It's insulting. I am going to be the first in his life, not just something that's *there,* and if I ever find there's someone else I'm going to leave."

"Isn't that a little too much to ask of a man?" I said, wishing I had her courage.

"It's what I will ask," Rima said.

"Well, Rima," he said, cheerfully nasty, "you ought to know."

I don't remember her ever speaking to my husband again, for that was the way Rima was. She drifted in and out of rooms during the two days she stayed with us, graceful and silent as a cat, always pleasant, but whenever he began to talk she suddenly wasn't there. The afternoon of the second day, when she was feeling repentant toward the diplomat, who did not know where she had gone, I went with Rima to Gucci's where she bought him a wallet. It was elegant, expensive, and impersonal—no, thank you, she would not wait to have it initialed—the kind of gift one had to give a man whose wife noticed all his personal possessions. Coming out of the store we saw the advertising man who had been at Rima's party, or rather, he saw us, for she did not recognize him.

He was so excited he called out to stop us; he shook her gloved hand with both his hands, and then he blushed, as if he had attacked her in my presence. Rima laughed, and then he laughed, too, and invited us both for a drink.

We went to the Plaza (Rima's choice), where Heathcliff had one Scotch (his limit, he told us) and Rima had champagne. She was wearing the beige and white fox coat over a pale wool dress, she had a long gold cigarette holder, her beige alligator handbag and the little package from Gucci were on the table, and she did indeed look like Lady Brett Ashley, or someone equally golden and fictional. We sat in the dark wood-paneled room, watching the sunset through the windows that overlooked the park, laughing, happy; and I thought that people from out of town who saw her here must be thinking she was a real New Yorker, on her way somewhere exciting for the evening. The advertising man evidently thought so, too, when he got up reluctantly, almost jealously, to catch his train to Old Greenwich.

There was a row of taxis at the curb. He helped us into the first, gave her a mischievous look and kissed her hand. When their eyes met, I had the feeling he had done some investigating about her friend in Washington. As we watched him walk away to the second taxi he seemed to change, grow firmer, more stubborn, as if preparing himself for an everyday life he had momentarily forgotten.

"He makes me feel young," Rima said wistfully. She smiled. "He makes me want to go to the country and throw snowballs."

She went back to Washington that night, and we did not see each other again until spring. In the meantime I had gotten what is known as a friendly divorce, and custody of the three-room apartment. There had been only two short letters from Rima during the intervening months. The first said, "I'm too depressed to write, everything is lousy."

The second said, "I have begun to realize that people don't break up because of one unforgivable incident, but rather, because of hopelessness. I used to think love could be killed with a mortal blow, but that's not true. Love goes on and on, until one day you wake up and realize that the hopelessness is stronger than the love. I've done everything I could think of, and it was not enough. He sees me once a week, for twenty minutes. How many more ways can I change? He says he loves me, but somehow that doesn't mean anything any more; they're just words. I hear them and I don't remember what they used to mean."

One morning Rima packed all her clothes and the collection of tiny antique boxes, and left Washington forever. She did not say goodbye to the diplomat, she simply disappeared into the dawn. She left every stick of antique furniture—his, hers, theirs, whatever it was—and I imagine the rooms in the Greek Revival style mansion must have looked very strange, as if the occupant had only gone out for a walk. She came to stay with me, and the first thing she did was give me her precious collection.

"I remember you used to admire them. Just consider them a house gift."

The second thing she did was get another secretarial job, because she insisted on paying half the rent. I had decided to go back to zoology and was taking a Master's degree at night and working days as a receptionist so I could study my textbooks behind the potted plant that stood on my glossy desk. I was much happier than I had expected to be. Rima surprised me by her resiliency. I had resigned myself nervously to having to nurse a potential suicide, but what I found was a convalescent who was grateful to have survived.

We went to a few cocktail parties, to dinner with a few old friends, and introduced each other to the few single men we found in our respective offices who were not nineteen. It was a restful existence, and the weeks drifted by almost without notice. Then, one afternoon, Rima rushed back early from the office, and when I came home the scent of bath oil filled the entire apartment. She had put her newest Chanel suit on the bed and was washing her emerald ring with a nail brush.

"Guess what I did today! I just felt like doing something crazy, like we used to do when we were at college, so I called Heathcliff at his office and said, 'Here I am in New York!' He had a moment of conscience—I could hear it over the phone, almost like a gulp—and then he asked me to dinner."

"Dinner? Where's his wife?"

"Evidently she's a Den Mother, whatever that is, and they have a meeting. He was going to stay and work late at the office. He says he works late at the office once or twice a week anyway, and he has to eat somewhere, so—oh, you should have heard the stammering, the excuses. He's terrified of me. Of *me,* the girl who never got anybody in her life!"

They went to an Italian restaurant where Rima had often gone with the diplomat, and where the advertising man had never been in his life. The headwaiter recognized her, with obvious respect. The menu was not only in Italian but in handwriting, and Rima took pains to explain innocently to the old Italian waiter what a certain simple dish consisted of, so that Heathcliff could stammer, "Make it two."

He missed the nine-o'clock train, and before the nine-forty-two he had bought her a white orchid. "An orchid," Rima laughed, showing it to me. "An *orchid*! I haven't had an orchid since the Senior prom. I didn't think they made them any more."

But she put it carefully into a glass of champagne in the refrigerator, the alchemy that we had believed in our Senior Prom days would keep an orchid fresh for a week.

She had been almost silent about her affair with the diplomat, as if the gravity of first love had stunned her, but she bubbled over with her delight in Heathcliff, and I knew she had fallen in love with him before she did. "He's so square," she would say, laughing, and then add, "But he's a fox— oh, smart—watch out! I really think I'm the only one who sees the other side of him, the humor. In the advertising business they're just afraid of him, because he's so young and shrewd and on the way up. His wife's name is Dorlee—can you imagine?—and she's the same age he is, of course, because they've known each other all their lives. The old hag."

One of Rima's casual beaus, a plump young man who was also in advertising, took her to a cocktail party where Heathcliff appeared with Dorlee. "She just stood in the corner and talked to the wives," Rima told me afterward. "She looks as if she has steel fillings in her teeth. I don't think she ever shortened a dress in her life; she just wears them the way they come from the store. I heard her telling somebody that in Old Greenwich she has a TV room decorated like the inside of a ship. When she started talking about how they had to have plastic covers on everything I had to run out of the room because I nearly choked."

Heathcliff's commuting hours were irregular, for he often worked late and his two children were old enough to stay up in the TV room decorated like a ship until the captain came home to say good night. He met Rima after work several times a week. He seemed to have a calming effect on her in one way, for she stopped smoking and gave her long gold cigarette holder to our cleaning woman, who had admired it. It was a romance confined to furtive handholding, for he was consumed by guilt and told Rima often that she was "dangerous."

"Dangerous!" she told me in delight. "Dangerous! Me, the failure, dangerous! Isn't he beautiful?"

A letter arrived from our former Washington landlady informing Rima she was not running a storage company, and then several huge crates arrived, Railway Express collect. Rima and I stared at them with dismay.

"It's either storage or my own apartment," she said, "and I think at this point, an apartment of my own might be a good idea."

She found an apartment in a new, modern building, a block from Grand Central Station. "And believe me," she said, "an apartment a block from Grand Central is not easy to find." The choice of this location was logical to her—Heathcliff could stop by for a drink every evening on his way to his train. It seems several times he had mentioned, as if he were talking about an impossible dream, that such an arrangement would be the height of bliss.

The beautiful old furniture took some of the coldness away from the boxlike rooms of this glass-and-steel monstrosity, whose only redeeming feature was that it had a working fireplace; and when I went to visit her I found the rooms once again filled with flowers. The only strange note was a small bottle with a ship inside it, which perched on the center of her spindly-legged table.

"He collects them," she said. "He gave it to me. It's kind of pretty, don't you think?"

The next time I visited Rima's apartment a block from Grand Central it was a month later. There was a man's bathrobe hanging on the hook on the bathroom door, and a can of shaving cream on the tole shelf next to the sink. A small photograph of Heathcliff stood on the table beside her bed, framed in rope.

"It's so wonderful being in love with a man near my own age," she said. "He's thirty-four, I'm twenty-six—that means when I'm seventy, he'll be only seventy-eight."

"And commuting?"

"No, of course not," she said, touching his photograph reverently. "He's never been in love before, he never cheated on her in all those years, and do you know they were both virgins when they got married? Him, too. He has a very strong sense of honor. He said he wished she would find out about us so she would do something terrible to him, because he feels he deserves it; and then he said I ought to leave him, because he deserves that; and then he said if I did leave him he might as well be dead."

"He sounds happy," I said.

"It's just his sense of honor," Rima said. "It's a man like that who makes decisions. Men do leave their wives, you know, but only because of great love or great guilt. And he has both. I'm glad I didn't get married last time, because I was so young I mistook romance for love. This is real love: planning a life together, being able to help someone, making someone feel alive for the first time. Before he met me, his whole life was encased in plastic, just like that horrible chintz furniture of his in the country."

Men did leave their wives, as I well knew, and lovers left lovers, but it was neither for great love nor great guilt. Rima had been right the first time, in her letter to me: people part because of hopelessness. The death of love leads to the rebirth of another love, for love is a phoenix. A greater love does not kill a small one; it only adds pomp to the funeral.

During the following year, Rima and her advertising man tried to break up three times, but each time he came back to her, vowing he loved her more than ever and felt guiltier. She had already proposed to him several times, pretending it was only a joke, but at the end of their second year of afternoons before the train, she proposed to him seriously, and he answered her.

"How could I marry you?" he asked, tears in his eyes. "I'd bore you. You'd get tired of me. You're my elusive golden girl, and I'm just a husband and father."

"But that's what I *want*," Rima said.

"No. . . . I see you in front of the fire on a snowy night . . . I see you in that white fur coat, your eyes shining, going into the Plaza to meet an ambassador or a movie star. . . . I just don't see you in a gingham dress at the supermarket."

"Where do you think I get my food, out of flowers?"

"Yes," he answered. "And I will always bring them to you."

The transformation of Rima began that night. The next day, printed cotton slipcovers appeared on the Louis XV chairs. She bought a huge Early American object she informed me was called an Entertainment Center, containing a 19-inch television set, a stereo phonograph with four speakers, and a radio, with a long flat surface on top that was soon covered with a collection of ships in bottles. Her Chanels and Diors were sent to a thrift shop (tax deductible) and she replaced them with tweed skirts, cashmere sweater sets, and flowered, sleeveless cotton blouses. She had pawned her emerald ring to buy the Entertainment Center, and now she wore a single strand of imitation pearls. She learned to cook tuna fish casserole with potato chips on top, and in time even a peanut butter soufflé. She saved trading stamps and redeemed them for a hobnail glass lamp with a ruffly shade, and gave her 1850 tole lamp to the cleaning woman, who ventured she'd just as soon have had the nice new one.

She washed and set her hair herself, because it was obvious Dorlee had, and she used the money thus saved to buy books called *The Sexually Satisfied Housewife,* and *The Problems of the Adolescent Stepchild,* which she piled on top of the spindly-legged antique table until it broke and she replaced it with something that had formerly been a butter churn.

Her triumph came on Heathcliff's birthday. He had left his office early, and a light snow had begun to fall. At four-thirty, in the winter's early darkness, he arrived at Rima's apartment. There was snow on his coat, and he was carrying a gold-wrapped package that later turned out to contain champagne. Rima was sitting in front of the roaring fire, wearing blue jeans and toasting marshmallows.

He looked around the room as if he had never really noticed it before, still wearing his coat, still clutching the bottle of champagne in his arms. The air was fragrant with the scent of detergent and meat loaf.

"Happy birthday, honey," Rima said.

"Thank you. . . ." he murmured. "I'd better hang my coat in the bathroom; it's wet."

"Wait till you see your present! I made it."

When he came out of the bathroom he seemed more composed. He opened his present: a ship in a bottle. Rima had put the ship inside, herself. "You see," she said, "to get it in, the sails lie flat, and then I pull the string . . ."

"I know."

"Look at the marshmallow," she said. "When it's burned black like that, with the little red lights inside, it looks the way New York used to look to me at night, when I first came here—all dark and mysterious, with just those millions of little lights."

"Oh, Rima," Heathcliff whispered, holding the two bottles in his hands, the one with the ship and the one with the champagne, "I wish you had written me a poem."

She did write him a poem, the following summer, but she never gave it to him. Instead, she read it to me on the telephone. I had not seen very much of her during the winter and spring, because I had gotten a new job doing research (and my Master's degree), and she had spent most of her time in her apartment waiting for him to visit her, although the visits were fewer and farther between. We were both going to be thirty, but now it no longer seemed to matter that when Rima was thirty Heathcliff would be only thirty-eight.

"Send him the poem," I told her. "It's beautiful."

"No," she said. "I'm going to push it into one of his revolting little bottles and I'm going to toss it into the Greenwich Sound, or whatever the name is of that river he lives on. Then when he's walking in front of his split-level saying Yo-Ho-Ho he can find it, and see what he lost. Four years. . . . Well, last time it was five, so you can't say I'm not improving. At least it doesn't take me as long to find out I'm doomed. I am doomed, you know. I'm the girl they recite poetry to, and then in the mornings they always go back to their wives. It must be me, because I fell in love with two completely different men and neither of them wanted to stay with me."

"It's not you," I said. "Neither of them really knew what you were like. If they had, they would have loved you."

I don't know if she ever threw the bottle into the Sound, but she might have tossed it into the lake in Central Park, because all that summer Rima was addicted to long, lonely walks. Perhaps she was trying to figure things out; perhaps she was only still in her fantasy of the country wife, and the streets of the summer city were her Old Greenwich roads. I felt guilty not spending more time with her, but this time I had met someone I loved.

I had not met him among the mollusks and the octogenarians; I had met him at a cocktail party. He was a producer, but he did not think lady zoologists were freaks, and I certainly did not think producers were freaks, although I had never met one before, either.

While I was occupied with the extraordinary miracle of my second (and present) love, Rima became involved in what, to her, seemed only an ordinary meeting. She had been on a long walk, it was about midnight, and she was passing Grand Central Station on her way back to her apartment when she saw a man fall down in the street. The few passers-by thought he was drunk and avoided him, but Rima went closer to see if he was ill, and discovered that he was indeed drunk. She also discovered, with delight and dismay, that he was one of her favorite authors.

"What are you doing, lying there on the curb?" she said sternly. "A great writer does not lie on the curb."

"He does if he's drunk," the author answered. He was trying to go to sleep, his cheek nestled on the sidewalk.

"You get up this minute." Rima pulled him to his feet, which was not too difficult as he was a short, wiry man, about her height, quite undernourished from too much wine, women and song. He was, she remembered reading, only four years older than she was, and she felt maternal toward him.

"Have to go Bennington," he murmured. "Where the hell is Bennington? Have to be there in the morning."

"Bennington, Vermont?"

"Little girls' school . . . college. Lecture. Where's my train?"

"You can't lecture at Bennington like this," Rima said. She inspected his soiled clothing and bleary face with distaste. "Those girls idolize you. If they see you like this, it might ruin the rest of their lives."

"I'm . . . going to be sick."

"Good."

He decided not to be sick. "Who are you?"

"A former English major at Radcliffe, and an admirer of yours— although not at the moment. Come with me, I live around the corner." She was already leading him, his arm about her shoulders.

The writer stared at the sleeveless flowered cotton blouse, the chino walking skirt, the little strand of pearls. "Funniest-looking streetwalker I ever saw . . ." Rima slapped him.

She then took him to her apartment, a block from Grand Central, where she forced him to eat scrambled eggs and drink three cups of black coffee, and then spot-cleaned and pressed his suit while he cursed at her from a cold shower. She scanned the timetable while the writer looked around her apartment.

"You in the Waves?"

"Very funny. You can take the two-thirty train to Boston, and then there's probably a connection."

"You've even got a timetable."

"Purely for sentimental reasons," Rima said. "Here, take this aspirin and these vitamins; you'll need them later."

"You have any children?"

"No. Do you?"

"I'm not married," he said.

Suddenly, he became more than an idol or an invalid—he became a person. "You're *not?*"

"Divorced," he said.

"So am I," Rima said, "sort of."

"That's too bad. You'd make a wonderful wife. Very homey apartment. It reminds me of my mother's. You wouldn't think I had a mother, would you? Well, I do."

"You need her," Rima said. "Or a nurse. How could you possibly have gotten so drunk when you have an appointment tomorrow—or today, I should say."

"Oh!" he said, looking wildly for his jacket. "Where's the train?"

"At the station. Where are your lecture notes? Good. Your aspirin? Good. Now, take these cookies, in case you get tempted on the way."

The writer took hold firmly of Rima's arm. "You're coming with me."

"Are you crazy?"

"Yes. Come with me. I need you. I'll only be there one day, and then we'll go to St. Thomas. I live in St. Thomas; you'll like it."

Rima looked around her apartment, the cozy, chintzy, friendly room filled with its memories of love and failure. " 'Be not afeard. The isle is full of noises, sounds and sweet airs, that give delight and hurt not.' "

"Come with Caliban," he said.

"No," Rima said, following him docilely to the door, "no, not Caliban . . . Shakespeare."

When she came back from Bennington she came to visit me, to bring me her collection of ships in bottles and to say goodbye. "When you marry that divine man you're going with, you'll have a little boy someday, and he'll like these."

"Are you really going away with him?" I asked stupidly.

"Imagine—St. Thomas! He can write his books, and I can keep house. I'll walk on the beach, and I'll send you shells if you like, if I find anything they don't have anywhere else. Imagine—he's not married—at last! He's so brilliant; I've always adored his work. I've read everything he ever wrote, and do you know what? Once, when we were in college and he had his first story published, I cut his picture out of the magazine and kept it for a year."

"Listen," I said, hating myself for it, "I read in *Time* magazine that he travels around with a Great and Good Friend. She lives in St. Thomas with him. What happened to her?"

"Oh, her!" Rima said. "He hates her. She just happens to live in St.

Thomas, that's all. He says she's not a girlfriend, she's a friend girl. I saw that picture in *Time;* she looks like a squaw. She's got a braid down her back and she had this leather thong around her neck with a big tooth attached to it. I'll bet it came out of her mouth. No wonder he drank before he met me."

"He's stopped drinking?"

"One Scotch before dinner, like Heathcliff used to. Oh, I'm a reformer now." She laughed at herself, the reformer, and I wondered if life would at last be kind to her, she who could never be kind to herself.

She left the apartment, the furniture, her winter clothes, everything, and she and the writer went to St. Thomas. I went to her apartment two days before my wedding, suddenly taken by the absurdly sentimental thought that I must sell that Early American Entertainment Center and get Rima's emerald ring out of the pawn shop, if it was still there, and send it to her. I don't know why that ring seemed so important to me—perhaps because I was going to be married and I was happy, and I couldn't bear the thought of a ring Rima had worn for five years on the third finger of her left hand being misused by some stranger. But the landlord had taken possession of all the furniture in lieu of the rent she had never sent from St. Thomas, and the apartment had been sublet. Well, I thought, caught up again in my own happiness, we've both learned enough from the past, and that ring doesn't mean anything any more.

So I was married, and two years later we did have a little boy who will like the collection of ships in bottles, when he's old enough not to break them to get the ships out. Our apartment is filled with scripts, books, records, theatrical posters, an aquarium, shells, textbooks, toys; but still there is room on the piano for Rima's collection of Battersea boxes. She had written me two happy postcards the first year, and then, nothing. I wondered if she was still in St. Thomas. Five years after she had left New York, I took a chance and wrote to her at her last address to tell her that my husband and I were going to take a winter vacation in St. Thomas, and was she still alive? She wrote back immediately.

"Yes," her letter said, "I'm still alive. Alive and single. Surprise. Look for me in the bar at your hotel any night at about ten o'clock. I'll be the one seated at the right hand of the Bard."

We arrived in St. Thomas in the afternoon. When we went down to the hotel bar that night at ten, Rima was not there. There were some pink-broiled American tourists, and a party of Italians from a large yacht that was moored in the harbor; the owner, very rich, very clean in a blue blazer, two teen-aged starlets who sat toying with the speared fruit in their drinks, two rather sinister-looking young men, and two contessas with streaks in their hair and a lot of diamonds. The Calypso trio played on a small bandstand, and the starlets got up to do whatever dance it was teen-aged starlets were doing that winter in the jet set. The contessas and their escorts looked bored because they were supposed to, and the Italian millionaire

THE SEX OBJECT

282

looked bored because he was. I was afraid Rima wasn't going to show up after all.

Then, at half past twelve, she arrived. She was, indeed at the right hand of the Bard, and the Bard was very, very drunk. At the left hand of the Bard, helping to support him, was a young woman the same age as Rima, with a long black braid down her back, a turtleneck T-shirt, a peasant skirt, no makeup, and a silver-and-turquoise ornament the size of a breast-plate dangling from a chain around her neck. Rima had let her hair grow to her waist and braided it, her face was scrubbed and tanned, she was dressed in an almost identical village outfit, and the only difference between the two Squaw Twins was that Rima was the prettier one.

Rima let go of the writer's hand and ran over to our table. Liberated, he pulled free of the other lady and went to the bar.

"Oh, I'm so glad to see you!" Rima said. "Look how pale you are—you'll have to come to the beach with me." She held her arm, the color of glistening walnut, against mine.

My husband was transfixed by the object dangling from a thong around Rima's neck. "Whose tooth is that?"

She shrugged. "I don't know. It's Olive's; we trade."

"How is everything?" I asked lamely.

"Don't ask that. I want to be happy tonight. No, it's all right, really. I'm content; I mean, I'm over him, I just stay with him because he needs me."

"Who's Olive?"

Rima glanced at her Squaw Twin. "Remember the girlfriend he said was only a friend girl? That's her. Actually, I'd go insane if I didn't have her to talk to. He's so drunk lately. And, do you know, in the beginning I really hated her? She has great individuality, though, and a crystalline intellect. She's above such things as jealousy and animosity, she really believes in the purity of non-thought. . . . Oh, hell, she bores me to death."

The writer had taken the sticks away from the Calypso drummer and was crashing them on every cymbal, drum, and any surface in sight. The musicians and waiters ignored him as if he was a nightly fixture. Olive was watching him inscrutably. The Italians from the yacht looked amused.

"If I had his talent . . ." Rima said. "If I had *any* talent. . . . Tell me about New York! Tell me about the world, is it still there?"

We ordered drinks and told her about people she had known, and then we ordered more drinks and she made us tell her about people she didn't know. She was insatiable. The world, the world, what was happening outside this tiny island, this paradisiacal prison? The American tourists went up to bed, the Calypso trio disappeared, the writer and Olive were now sitting with the party of Italians from the yacht. The millionaire glanced over at us and bent toward him to whisper a question; the writer shook his head.

"How old is your baby?" Rima asked suddenly.

"Three years old."

"I'm thirty-five," Rima said. "Do I look it? Don't answer. Look—the sun's coming up, I'm going to walk on the beach."

She ran out of the bar, across the patio, across the sand, and was gone. I was afraid she might be going to drown herself and was going to run after her, but then I saw her again, wandering among the sea-grape trees, sad and alone. The writer had fallen asleep at the table, his head between the empty glasses. Olive was watching over him, totally still, a little smile at the corner of her mouth. The Italian millionaire excused himself to the group and went out to the beach.

I could see his silhouette in the pink-and-gold dawn, bowing slightly to Rima's silhouette, and then, after a moment, walking slowly beside it through the silhouettes of the sea-grape trees. The sea was all blue and gold and silver now, and in the distance the Italian's yacht rocked gently at anchor, all white.

We went up to our room. Then, suddenly, I felt one of those obsessive, extrasensory calls that are like a shout in the mind. "I'll be right back," I said, and ran down the stairs to the lobby.

The bar was closed, chairs piled on top of the tables. The Italians had all gone, and in a corner of the lobby Olive was asleep in a big chair. A yawning porter handed me a hotel envelope with my name on it, and went back behind the desk. The writer, despite his hangover, was milling around like twelve people. "Where is she? Where is she? *Rima . . . !*"

I tore open the envelope, and the tooth on the leather thong fell into my hand. There was a note, in Rima's impeccable script: " 'When such as I cast out remorse so great a sweetness flows into the breast we must laugh and we must sing. We are blest by everything. Everything we look upon is blest.' *La donna è mobile.* Goodbye, and love."

I looked out to sea, where the yacht was only a tiny toy ship on the horizon, and then I went up to our room.

So she was gone again, with the Italian millionaire, and his starlets, and his contessas with the streaked hair. Soon, I knew, she would fall in love, and cut her braid, and toss her pueblo jewelry into the sea. She would paint her eyelids and enamel her toenails, and disappear. Once again, as always, a man who had fallen in love with a fantasy that had been created for another man would lose that fantasy, consuming it in the fire of his love. I remembered that the Rima of *Green Mansions,* for whom Rima Allen had been named, had been killed in a fire that destroyed her hiding-tree. It seemed to me, that lonely morning in St. Thomas, that the Rima I knew had been killed in many fires, rising again from the ashes of each one like a bright bird to sing the song of some wanderer's need. Had there ever been a real Rima? Born and reborn to a splendid image, she had never looked for her self, nor had anyone else. Being each man's dream of love, she had eventually failed him, and so he had failed her, and so, finally, she had failed herself.

THE TIME OF HER TIME

by

NORMAN MAILER

(b. 1923)

Like Ernest Hemingway, Norman Mailer has come to epitomize an age as much in his highly publicized personal life as in his fiction. His most famous novel, written about World War II, is The Naked and the Dead *(1948). In* The Prisoner of Sex *(1971) he discusses his ideas about male-female relationships.* The Executioner's Song: A True Life Novel *(1979), for which he won a Pulitzer Prize in 1980, is written in the mode of the so-called New Journalism, which blends fiction and fact. Recent works include* Ancient Evenings *(1983) and* Tough Guys Don't Dance *(1984).*

• ——————————————— •

I

I was living in a room one hundred feet long and twenty-five feet wide, and it had nineteen windows staring at me from three of the walls and part of the fourth. The floor planks were worn below the level of the nails which held them down, except for the southern half of the room where I had laid a rough linoleum which gave a hint of sprinkled sand, conceivably an aid to the footwork of my pupils. For one hundred dollars I had the place whitewashed; everything; the checkerboard of tin ceiling plates one foot square with their fleurs-de-lis stamped into the metal, the rotted sashes on the window frames (it took twelve hours to scrape the calcimine from the glass), even parts of the floor had white drippings (although that was scuffed into dust as time went on) and yet it was worth it: when I took the loft it stank of old machinery and the paint was a liverish brown—I had tried living with that color for a week, my old furniture, which had been moved by a mover friend from the Village and me, showed the scars of being bumped and dragged and flung up six flights of stairs, and the view of it sprawled over twenty-five hundred feet of living space, three beat old day beds, some dusty cushions, a broken-armed easy chair, a cigarette-scarred coffee table made from a door, a kitchen table, some peeled enamel chairs which thumped like a wooden-legged pirate when one sat in them, the bookshelves of unfinished pine butted by bricks, yes, all of this, my purview, this grand vista, the New York sunlight greeting me in the morning through the double filter of the smog-yellow sky and the nineteen dirt-frosted windows, inspired me with so much content, especially those liver-brown walls, that I fled my pad like the plague, and in the first week, after a day of setting the furniture to rights, I was there for four hours of sleep a night, from five in the morning when I maneuvered in from the last closed Village bar and the last coffee-klatsch of my philosopher friends' for the night to let us say nine in the morning when I awoke with a partially destroyed brain and the certainty that the sore vicious growl of my stomach was at least the onset of an ulcer and more likely the first gone cells of a thorough-going cancer of the duodenum. So I lived it that way for a week, and then following the advice of a bar-type who was the friend of a friend, I got myself up on the eighth morning, boiled my coffee on a hot-plate while I shivered in the October air (neither the stove nor the gas heaters had yet been bought) and then I went downstairs and out the front door of the warehouse onto Monroe Street, picking my way through the garbage-littered gutter which always made me think of the gangs on this street, the Negroes on the east end of the block, the Puerto Ricans next to them, and the Italians and Jews to the west— those gangs were going to figure a little in my life, I suspected that, I was anticipating those moments with no quiet bravery considering how hung was my head in the morning, for the worst clue to the gangs was the six-year-olds. They were the defilers of the garbage, knights of the ordure, and here, in this province of a capital Manhattan, at the southern tip of the island, with the overhead girders of the Manhattan and Brooklyn bridges the only noble structures for a mile of tenement jungle, yes here the barbarians ate their young, and any type who reached the age of six without being altogether mangled by father, mother, family or friends, was a pint of iron man, so tough, so ferocious, so sharp in the teeth that the wildest alley cat would have surrendered a freshly caught rat rather than contest the meal. They were charming, these six-year-olds, as I told my uptown friends, and they used to topple the overloaded garbage cans, strew them through the street, have summer snowball fights with orange peel, coffee grounds, soup bones, slop, they threw the discus by scaling the raw tin rounds from the tops of cans, their pillow fights were with loaded socks of scum, and a debauch was for two of them to scrub a third around the inside of a twenty-gallon pail still warm with the heat of its emptied treasures. I heard that the Olympics took place in summer when they were out of school and the streets were so thick with the gum of old detritus, alluvium and dross that the mash made by passing car tires fermented in the sun. Then the parents and the hoods and the debs and the grandmother dowagers cheered them on and promised them murder and the garbage flew all day, but I was there in fall and the scene was quiet from nine to three. So I picked my way through last night's stew of rubble on this eighth morning of my hiatus on Monroe Street, and went half down the block to a tenement on the boundary between those two bandit republics of the Negroes and the Puerto Ricans, and with a history or two of knocking on the wrong door, and with a nose full of the smells of the sick overpeppered bowels of the poor which seeped and oozed out of every leaking pipe in every communal crapper (only as one goes north does the word take on the Protestant propriety of john), I was able finally to find my man, and I was an hour ahead of him—he was still sleeping off his last night's drunk. So I spoke to his wife, a fat masculine Negress with the face and charity of a Japanese wrestler, and when she understood that I was neither a junk-peddler nor fuzz, that I sold no numbers, carried no bills, and was most certainly not a detective (though my Irish face left her dubious of that) but instead had come to offer her husband a job of work, I was admitted to the first of three dark rooms, face to face with the gray luminescent eye of the television set going its way in a dark room on a bright morning, and through the hall curtains I could hear them talking in the bedroom.

"Get up, you son of a bitch," she said to him.

He came to work for me, hating my largesse, lugging his air compressor up my six flights of stairs, and after a discussion in which his price came down from two hundred to one, and mine rose from fifty dollars to meet his, he left with one of my twenty-dollar bills, the air compressor on the floor as security, and returned in an hour with so many sacks of whitewash that I had to help him up the stairs. We worked together that day, Charley Thompson his name was, a small lean Negro maybe forty years old, and conceivably sixty, with a scar or two on his face, one a gouge on the cheek, the other a hairline along the bridge of his nose, and we got along not too badly, working in sullen silence until the hangover was sweated out, and then starting to talk over coffee in the Negro hashhouse on the corner where the bucks bridled a little when I came in, and then ignored me. Once the atmosphere had become neutral again, Thompson was willing to talk.

"Man," he said to me, "what you want all that space for?"

"To make money."

"Out of which?"

I debated not very long. The people on the block would know my business sooner or later—the reward of living in a slum is that everyone knows everything which is within reach of the senses—and since I would be nailing a sign over my mailbox downstairs for the pupils to know which floor they would find me on, and the downstairs door would have to be open since I had no bell, the information would be just as open. But for that matter I was born to attract attention; given my height and my blond hair, the barbarians would notice me, they noticed everything, and so it was wiser to come on strong than to try to sidle in.

"Ever hear of an *Escuela de Torear?*" I asked him without a smile.

He laughed with delight at the sound of the words, not even bothering to answer.

"That's a bullfighter's school," I told him. "I teach bullfighting."

"You know that?"

"I used to do it in Mexico."

"Man, you can get killed."

"Some do." I let the exaggeration of a cooled nuance come into my voice. It was true after all; some do get killed. But not so many as I was suggesting, maybe one in fifty of the successful, and one in five hundred of the amateurs like me who fought a few bulls, received a few wounds, and drifted away.

Charley Thompson was impressed. So were others—the conversation was being overheard after all, and I had become a cardinal piece on the chaotic chessboard of Monroe Street's sociology—I felt the clear bell-like adrenalins of clean anxiety, untainted by weakness, self-interest, neurotic habit, or the pure yellows of the liver. For I had put my poker money on the table, I was the new gun in a frontier saloon, and so I was asking for it, not today, not tomorrow, but come sooner come later something was likely to follow from this. The weak would leave me alone, the strong would have respect, but be it winter or summer, sunlight or dark, there would come an hour so cold or so hot that someone, somebody, some sexed-up head, very strong and very weak, would be drawn to discover a new large truth about himself and the mysteries of his own courage or the lack of it. I knew. A year before, when I had first come to New York, there was a particular cat I kept running across in the bars of the Village, an expert with a knife, or indeed to maintain the salts of accuracy, an expert with two knives. He carried them everywhere—he had been some sort of hothead instructor in the Marines on the art of fighting with the knife, and he used to demonstrate nice fluid poses, his elbows in, the knives out, the points of those blades capering free of one another—he could feint in any direction with either hand, he was an artist, he believed he was better with a knife than any man in all of New York, and night after night in bar after bar he sang the love-song of his own prowess, begging for the brave type who would take on his boast and leave him confirmed or dead.

It is mad to take on the city of New York, there is too much talent waiting on line; this cat was calling for every hoodlum in every crack gang and clique who fancies himself with the blade, and one night, drunk and on the way home, he was greeted by another knife, a Puerto Rican cat who was defective in school and spent his afternoons and nights shadow-knifing in the cellar clubhouse of his clique, a real contender, long-armed for a Latin, thin as a Lehmbruck, and fast as a hungry wolf; he had practiced for two months to meet the knife of New York.

So they went into an alley, the champion drunk, a fog of vanity blanketing the point of all his artistic reflexes, and it turned out to be not too much of a fight: the Puerto Rican caught it on the knuckles, the lip, and above the knee, but they were only nicks, and the champion was left in bad shape, bleeding from the forearm, the belly, the chest, the neck, and the face: once he was down, the Puerto Rican had engraved a double oval, labium majorum and minorum on the skin of the cheek, and left him there, having the subsequent consideration or fright to make a telephone call to the bar in which our loser had been drinking. The ex-champion, a bloody cat, was carried to his pad which was not far away (a bit of belated luck) and in an hour, without undue difficulty the brother-in-law doctor of somebody or other was good enough to take care of him. There were police reports, and as our patois goes, the details were a drag, but what makes my story sad is that our ex-champion was through. He mended by sorts and shifts, and he still bragged in the Village bars, and talked of finding the Puerto Rican when he was sober and in good shape, but the truth was that he was on the alcoholic way, and the odds were that he would stay there. He had been one of those gamblers who saw his life as a single bet, and he had lost. I often thought that he had been counting on a victory to put some charge below his belt and drain his mouth of all that desperate labial libido.

Now I was following a modest parallel, and as Thompson kept asking me some reasonable if openly ignorant questions about the nature of the bullfight, I found myself shaping every answer as carefully as if I were writing dialogue, and I was speaking particularly for the black-alerted senses of three Negroes who were sitting behind me, each of them big in his way (I had taken my glimpse as I came in) with a dull, almost Chinese, sullenness of face. They could have been anything. I had seen faces like theirs on boxers and ditch diggers, and I had seen such faces by threes and fours riding around in Cadillacs through the Harlem of the early-morning hours. I was warning myself to play it carefully, and yet I pushed myself a little further than I should, for I became ashamed of my caution and therefore was obliged to brag just the wrong bit. Thompson, of course, was encouraging me—he was a sly old bastard—and he knew even better than me the character of our audience.

"Man, you can take care of yourself," he said with glee.

"I don't know about that," I answered, obeying the formal minuet of the *macho*. "I don't like to mess with anybody," I told him. "But a man messes with me—well, I wouldn't want him to go away feeling better than he started."

"Oh, yeah, ain't that a fact. I hears just what you hear." He talked like an old-fashioned Negro—probably Southern. "What if four or five of them comes on and gangs you?"

We had come a distance from the art of the *corrida*. "That doesn't happen to me," I said. "I like to be careful about having some friends." And part for legitimate emphasis, and part to fulfill my image of the movie male lead—that blond union of the rugged and the clean-cut (which would after all be *their* image as well)—I added, "Good friends, you know."

There we left it. My coffee cup was empty, and in the slop of the saucer a fly was drowning. I was thinking idly and with no great compassion that wherever this fly had been born it had certainly not expected to die in a tan syrupy ring-shaped pond, struggling for the greasy hot-dogged air of a cheap Negro hashhouse. But Thompson rescued it with a deft flip of his fingers.

"I always save," he told me seriously. "I wouldn't let nothing be killed. I'm a preacher."

"Real preacher?"

"Was one. Church and devoted congregation." He said no more. He had the dignified sadness of a man remembering the major failure of his life.

As we got up to go, I managed to turn around and get another look at the three spades in the next booth. Two of them were facing me. Their eyes were flat, the whites were yellow and flogged with red—they stared back with no love. The anxiety came over me again, almost nice—I had been so aware of them, and they had been so aware of me.

2

That was in October, and for no reason I could easily discover, I found myself thinking of that day as I awoke on a spring morning more than half a year later with a strong light coming through my nineteen windows. I had fixed the place up since then, added a few more pieces of furniture, connected a kitchen sink and a metal stall shower to the clean water outlets in the john, and most noticeably I had built a wall between the bullfight studio and the half in which I lived. That was more necessary than one might guess—I had painted the new wall red; after Thompson's job of whitewash I used to feel as if I were going snow-blind; it was no easy pleasure to get up each morning in a white space so blue with cold that the chill of a mountain peak was in my blood. Now, when I opened my eyes, I could choose the blood of the wall in preference to the ice slopes of Mt. O'Shaugnessy, where the sun was always glinting on the glaciers of the windows.

But on this particular morning, when I turned over a little more, there was a girl propped on one elbow in the bed beside me, no great surprise, because this was the year of all the years in my life when I was scoring three and four times a week, literally combing the pussy out of my hair, which was no great feat if one knew the Village and the scientific temperament of the Greenwich Village mind. I do not want to give the false impression that I was one of the lustiest to come adventuring down the pike—I was cold, maybe by birth, certainly by environment: I grew up in a Catholic orphanage—and I had had my little kinks and cramps, difficulties enough just a few years ago, but I had passed through that, and I was going now on a kind of disinterested but developed competence; what it came down to was that I could go an hour with the average girl without destroying more of the vital substance than a good night's sleep could repair, and since that sort of stamina seems to get advertised, and I had my good looks, my blond hair, my height, build and bullfighting school, I suppose I became one of the Village equivalents of an Eagle Scout badge for the girls. I was one of the credits needed for a diploma in the sexual humanities, I was par for a good course, and more than one of the girls and ladies would try me on an off-evening like comparison-shoppers to shop the value of their boy friend, lover, mate, or husband against the certified professionalism of Sergius O'Shaugnessy.

Now if I make this sound bloodless, I am exaggerating a bit—even an old habit is livened once in a while with color, and there were girls I worked to get and really wanted, and nights when the bull was far from dead in me. I even had two women I saw at least once a week, each of them, but what I am trying to emphasize is that when you screw too much and nothing is at stake, you begin to feel like a saint. It was a hell of a thing to be holding a nineteen-year-old girl's ass in my hands, hefting those young kneadables of future power, while all the while the laboratory technician in my brain was deciding that the experiment was a routine success—routine because her cheeks looked and felt just about the way I had thought they would while I was sitting beside her in the bar earlier in the evening, and so I still had come no closer to understanding my scientific compulsion to verify in the retort of the bed how accurately I had predicted the form, texture, rhythm and surprise of any woman who caught my eye.

Only an ex-Catholic can achieve some of the rarer amalgams of guilt, and the saint in me deserves to be recorded. I always felt an obligation—some noblesse oblige of the kindly cocksman—to send my women away with no great wounds to their esteem, feeling at best a little better than when they came in, I wanted to be friendly (what vanity of the saint!). I was the messiah of the one-night stand, and so I rarely acted like a pig in bed, I wasn't greedy, I didn't grind all my tastes into their mouths, I even abstained from springing too good a lay when I felt the girl was really in love with her man, and was using me only to give love the benefit of new perspective. Yes, I was a good sort, I probably gave more than I got back, and the only real pains for all those months in the loft, for my bullfighting classes, my surprisingly quiet time (it had been winter after all) on Monroe Street, my bulging portfolio of experiments—there must have been fifty girls who spent at least one night in the loft—my dull but doggedly advancing scientific data, even the cold wan joys of my saintliness demanded for their payment only one variety of the dead hour: when I woke in the morning, I could hardly wait to get the latest mouse out of my bed and out of my lair. I didn't know why, but I would awaken with the deadliest of depressions, the smell of the woman had gone very stale for me, and the armpits, the ammonias and dead sea life of old semen and old snatch, the sour fry of last night's sweat, the whore scent of over-exercised perfume, became an essence of the odious, all the more remarkable because I clung to women in my sleep, I was one Don John who hated to sleep alone, I used to feel as if my pores were breathing all the maternal (because sleeping) sweets of the lady, wet or dry, firm or flaccid, plump, baggy, or lean who was handled by me while we dreamed. But on awakening, hung with my head—did I make love three times that year without being drunk?—the saint was given his hour of temptation, for I would have liked nothing more than to kick the friendly ass out of bed, and dispense with the coffee, the good form, my depression and often hers, and start the new day by lowering her in a basket out of my monk-ruined retreat six floors down to the garbage pile (now blooming again in the freshets of spring), wave my hand at her safe landing and get in again myself to the blessed isolations of the man alone.

But of course that was not possible. While it is usually a creep who generalizes about women, I think I will come on so heavy as to say that the cordial tone of the morning after is equally important to the gymkhana of the night before—at least if the profit made by a nice encounter is not to be lost. I had given my working hours of the early morning to dissolving a few of the inhibitions, chilled reflexes and dampened rhythms of the corpus before me, but there is not a restraint in the world which does not have to be taken twice—once at night on a steam-head of booze, and once in daylight with the grace of a social tea. To open a girl up to the point where she loves you or It or some tremor in her sexual baggage, and then to close her in the morning is to do the disservice which the hateful side of women loves most—you have fed their cold satisfied distrust of a man. Therefore my saint fought his private churl, and suffering all the detail of abusing the sympathetic nervous system, I made with the charm in the daylight and was more of a dear than most.

It was to be a little different this morning, however. As I said, I turned over in my bed, and looked at the girl propped on her elbow beside me. In her eyes there was a flat hatred which gave no ground—she must have been staring like this at my back for several minutes, and when I turned, it made no difference—she continued to examine my face with no embarrassment and no delight.

That was sufficient to roll me around again, my shoulder blades bare to her inspection, and I pretended that the opening of my eyes had been a false awakening. I felt deadened then with all the diseases of the dull—making love to her the night before had been a little too much of a marathon. She was a Jewish girl and she was in her third year at New York University, one of those harsh alloys of a self-made bohemian from a middle-class home (her father was a hardware wholesaler), and I was remembering how her voice had irritated me each time I had seen her, an ugly New York accent with a cultured overlay. Since she was still far from formed, there had been all sorts of Lesbian hysterias in her shrieking laugh and they warred with that excess of strength, complacency and deprecation which I found in many Jewish women—a sort of "Ech" of disgust at the romantic and mysterious All. This one was medium in size and she had dark long hair which she wore like a Village witch in two extended braids which came down over her flat breasts, and she had a long thin nose, dark eyes, and a kind of lean force, her arms and square shoulders had shown the flat thin muscles of a wiry boy. All the same, she was not bad, she had a kind of Village chic, a certain snotty elegance of superiority, and when I first came to New York I had dug girls like her—Jewesses were strange to me—and I had even gone with one for a few months. But this new chick had been a mistake—I had met her two weeks ago at a party, she was on leave from her boy friend, and we had had an argument about T. S. Eliot, a routine which for me had become the quintessence of corn, but she said that Eliot was the apotheosis of manner, he embodied the ecclesiasticism of classical and now futureless form, she adored him she said, and I was tempted to tell her how little Eliot would adore the mannerless yeasts of the Brooklyn from which she came, and how he might prefer to allow her to appreciate his poetry only in step to the transmigration of her voice from all urgent Yiddish nasalities to the few high English analities of relinquished desire. No, she would not make that other world so fast—nice society was not cutting her crumpets thus quickly because she was gone on Thomas Sterns Eeeee. Her college-girl snobbery, the pity for me of eighty-five other honey-pots of the Village aesthetic whose smell I knew all too well, so inflamed the avenger of my crotch, that I wanted to prong her then and there, right on the floor of the party, I was a primitive for a prime minute, a gorged gouge of a working-class phallus, eager to ram into all her nasty little tensions. I had the message again, I was one of the millions on the bottom who had the muscles to move the sex which kept the world alive, and I would grind it into her, the healthy hearty inches and the sweat of the cost of acquired culture when you started low and you wanted to go high. She was a woman, what! she sensed that moment, she didn't know if she could handle me, and she had the guts to decide to find out. So we left the party and we drank and (leave it to a Jewish girl to hedge the bet) she drained the best half of my desire in conversation because she was being psychoanalyzed, what a predictable pisser! and she was in that stage where the jargon had the totalitarian force of all vocabularies of mechanism, and she could only speak of her infantile relations to men, and the fixations and resistances of unassimilated penis-envy with all the smug gusto of a female commissar. She was enthusiastic about her analyst, he was also Jewish (they were working now on Jewish self-hatred), he was really an integrated guy,

Stanford Joyce, he belonged to the same mountain as Eliot, she loved the doers and the healers of life who built on the foundationless prevalence of the void those islands of proud endeavor.

"You must get good marks in school," I said to her.

"Of course."

How I envied the jazzed-up grain of the Jews. I was hot for her again, I wanted the salts of her perspiration in my mouth. They would be acrid perhaps, but I would digest them, and those intellectual molecules would rise to my brain.

"I know a girl who went to your bullfighting school," she said to me. She gave her harsh laugh. "My friend thought you were afraid of her. She said you were full of narcissistic anxieties."

"Well, we'll find out," I said.

"Oh, you don't want me. I'm very inadequate as a lover." Her dark hard New York eyes, bright with appetite, considered my head as if I were a delicious and particularly sour pickle.

I paid the check then, and we walked over to my loft. As I had expected, she made no great fuss over the back-and-forth of being seduced—to the contrary. Once we were upstairs, she prowled the length of my loft twice, looked at the hand-made bullfighting equipment I had set up along one wall of the studio, asked me a question or two about the killing machine, studied the swords, asked another question about the cross-guard on the descabellar, and then came back to the living-room—bedroom—dining-room—kitchen of the other room, and made a face at the blood-red wall. When I kissed her she answered with a grinding insistence of her mouth upon mine, and a muscular thrust of her tongue into my throat, as direct and unfeminine as the harsh force of her voice.

"I'd like to hang my clothes up," she said.

It was not all that matter-of-fact when we got to bed. There was nothing very fleshy about the way she made love, no sense of the skin, nor smell, nor touch, just anger, anger at her being there, and another anger which was good for my own, that rage to achieve . . . just what, one cannot say. She made love as if she were running up an inclined wall so steep that to stop for an instant would slide her back to disaster. She hammered her rhythm at me, a hard driving rhythm, an all but monotonous drum, pound into pound against pound into pound until that moment when my anger found its way back again to that delayed and now recovered Time when I wanted to prong her at the party. I had been frustrated, had waited, had lost the anger, and so been taken by her. That finally got me— all through the talk about T. S. Eliot I had been calculating how I would lay waste to her little independence, and now she was alone, with me astride her, going through her paces, teeth biting the pillow, head turned away, using me as the dildoe of a private gallop. So my rage came back, and my rhythm no longer depended upon her drive, but found its own life, and we made love like two club fighters in an open exchange, neither giving ground, rhythm to rhythm, even to even, hypnotic, knowing neither the pain of punishment nor the pride of pleasure, and the equality of this, as hollow as the beat of the drum, seemed to carry her into some better deep of desire, and I had broken through, she was following me, her muscular body writhed all about me with an impersonal abandon, the wanton whip-thrash of a wounded snake, she was on fire and frozen at the same time, and then her mouth was kissing me with a rubbery greedy compulsion so avid to use all there was of me, that to my distant surprise, not in character for the saint to slip into the brutal, my hand came up and clipped her mean and openhanded across the face which brought a cry from her and broke the piston of her hard speed into something softer, wetter, more sly, more warm, I felt as if her belly were opening finally to receive me, and when her mouth kissed me again with a passing tender heat, warm-odored with flesh, and her body sweetened into some feminine embrace of my determination driving its way into her, well, I was gone, it was too late. I had driven right past her in that moment she turned, and I had begun to come, I was coming from all the confluences of my body toward that bud of sweetness I had plucked from her, and for a moment she was making it, she was a move back and surging to overtake me, and then it was gone, she made a mistake, her will ordered all temptings and rhythms to mobilize their march, she drove into the hard stupidities of a marching-band's step, and as I was going off in the best for many a month, she was merely going away, she had lost it again. As I ebbed into what should have been the contentments of a fine after-pleasure, warm and fine, there was one little part of me remaining cold and murderous because she had deprived me, she had fled the domination which was liberty for her, and the rest of the night was bound to be hell.

Her face was ugly. "You're a bastard, do you know that?" she asked me.

"Let it go. I feel good."

"Of course you feel good. Couldn't you have waited one minute?"

I disliked this kind of thing. My duty was reminding me of how her awakened sweets were souring now in the belly, and her nerves were sharpening into the gone electric of being just nowhere.

"I hate inept men," she said.

"Cool it." She could, at least, be a lady. Because if she didn't stop, I would give her back a word or two.

"You did that on purpose," she nagged at me, and I was struck with the intimacy of her rancor—we might as well have been married for ten years to dislike each other so much at this moment.

"Why," I said, "you talk as if this were something unusual for you."

"It is."

"Come on," I told her, "you've never made it in your life."

"How little you know," she said. "This is the first time I've missed in months."

If she had chosen to get my message, I could have been preparing now for a good sleep. Instead I would have to pump myself up again—and as if some ghost of the future laid the squeak of a tickle on my back, I felt an odd dread, not for tonight so much as for some ills of the next ten years whose first life was stirring tonight. But I lay beside her, drew her body against mine, feeling her trapped and irritable heats jangle me as much as they roused me, and while I had no fear that the avenger would remain asleep, still he stirred in pain and in protest, he had supposed his work to be done, and he would claim the wages of overtime from my reserve. That was the way I thought it would go, but Junior from New York University, with her hard body and her passion for proper poetry, gave a lewd and angry old grin as her face stared boldly into mine, and with the practical bawdiness of the Jew she took one straight utilitarian finger, smiled a deceptive girlish pride, and then she jabbed, fingernail and all, into the tight defended core of my clenched buttocks. One wiggle of her knuckle and I threw her off, grunting a sound between rage and surprise, to which she laughed and lay back and waited for me.

Well, she had been right, that finger tipped the balance, and three-quarters with it, and one-quarter hung with the mysteries of sexual ambition, I worked on her like a beaver for forty-odd minutes or more, slapping my tail to build her next, and she worked along while we made the round of the positions, her breath sobbing the exertions, her body as alive as a charged wire and as far from rest.

I gave her all the Time I had in me and more besides, I was weary of her, and the smell which rose from her had so little of the sea and so much of the armpit, that I breathed the stubborn wills of the gymnasium where the tight-muscled search for grace, and it was like that, a hard punishing session with pulley weights, stationary bicycle sprints, and ten breath-seared laps around the track. Yes, when I caught that smell, I knew she would not make it, and so I kept on just long enough to know she was exhausted in body, exhausted beyond the place where a ten-minute rest would have her jabbing that finger into me again, and hating her, hating women who could not take their exercise alone, I lunged up over the hill with my heart pounding past all pleasure, and I came, but with hatred, tight, electric, and empty, the spasms powerful but centered in my heart and not from the hip, the avenger taking its punishment even at the end, jolted clear to the seat of my semen by the succession of rhythmic blows which my heart drummed back to my feet.

For her, getting it from me, it must have been impressive, a convoluted, smashing, and protracted spasm, a hint of the death throe in the animal male which cannot but please the feminine taste for the mortal wound. "Oh, you're lucky," she whispered in my ear as I lay all collapsed beside her, alone in my athlete's absorption upon the whisperings of damage in the unlit complexities of my inner body. I was indeed an athlete, I knew my body was my future, and I had damaged it a bit tonight by most certainly doing it no good. I disliked her for it with the simple dislike we know for the stupid.

"Want a cigarette?" she asked.

I could wait, my heart would have preferred its rest, but there was something tired in her voice beyond the fatigue of what she had done. She too had lost after all. So I came out of my second rest to look at her, and her face had the sad relaxation (and serenity) of a young whore who has finished a hard night's work with the expected lack of issue for herself, content with no more than the money and the professional sense of the hard job dutifully done.

"I'm sorry you didn't make it," I said to her.

She shrugged. There was a Jewish tolerance for the expected failures of the flesh. "Oh, well, I lied to you before," she said.

"You never have been able to, have you?"

"No." She was fingering the muscles of my shoulder, as if in unconscious competition with my strength. "You're pretty good," she said grudgingly.

"Not really inept?" I asked.

"Sans façons," said the poetess in an arch change of mood which irritated me. "Sandy has been illuminating those areas where my habits make for destructive impulses."

"Sandy is Doctor Joyce?" She nodded. "You make him sound like your navigator," I told her.

"Isn't it a little obvious to be hostile to psychoanalysis?"

Three minutes ago we had been belaboring each other in the nightmare of the last round, and now we were close to cozy. I put the sole of my foot on her sharp little knee.

"You know the first one we had?" she asked me. "Well, I wanted to tell you. I came close—I guess I came as close as I ever came."

"You'll come closer. You're only nineteen."

"Yes, but this evening has been disturbing to me. You see I get more from you than I get from my lover."

Her lover was twenty-one, a senior at Columbia, also Jewish—which lessened interest, she confessed readily. Besides, Arthur was too passive— "Basically, it's very comprehensible," said the commissar, "an aggressive female and a passive male—we complement one another, and that's no good." Of course it was easy to find satisfaction with Arthur, "via the oral perversions. That's because, vaginally, I'm anaesthetized—a good phallic narcissist like you doesn't do enough for me."

In the absence of learned credentials, she was setting out to bully again. So I thought to surprise her. "Aren't you mixing your language a little?" I began. "The phallic narcissist is one of Wilhelm Reich's categories."

"Therefore?"

"Aren't you a Freudian?"

"It would be presumptuous of me to say," she said like a seminar student working for his pee-aitch-dee. "But Sandy is an eclectic. He accepts a lot of Reich—you see, he's very ambitious, he wants to arrive at his own synthesis." She exhaled some smoke in my face, and gave a nice tough little grin which turned her long serious young witch's face into something indeed less presumptuous. "Besides," she said, "you are a phallic narcissist. There's an element of the sensual which is lacking in you."

"But Arthur possesses it?"

"Yes, he does. And you . . . you're not very juicy."

"I wouldn't know what you mean."

"I mean this." With the rich cruel look of a conquistador finding a new chest of Indian gold, she bent her head and gave one fleeting satiric half-moon of a lick to the conjugation of my balls. "That's what I mean," she said, and was out of the bed even as I was recognizing that she was finally not without art. "Come back," I said.

But she was putting her clothes on in a hurry. "Shut up. Just don't give me your goddamned superiority."

I knew what it was: she had been about to gamble the reserves which belonged to Arthur, and the thought of possibly wasting them on a twenty-seven-year-old connoisseur like myself was too infuriating to take the risk.

So I lay in bed and laughed at her while she dressed—I did not really want a go at things again—and besides, the more I laughed, the angrier she would be, but the anger would work to the surface, and beneath it would be resting the pain that the evening had ended on so little.

She took her leisure going to the door, and I got up in time to tell her to wait—I would walk her to the subway. The dawn had come, however, and she wanted to go alone, she had had a bellyful of me, she could tell me that.

My brain was lusting its own private futures of how interesting it would be to have this proud, aggressive, vulgar, tense, stiff and arrogant Jewess going wild on my bottom—I had turned more than one girl on, but never a one of quite this type. I suppose she had succeeded instead of me; I was ready to see her again and improve the message.

She turned down all dates, but compromised by giving me her address and the number of her telephone. And then glaring at me from the open door, she said, "I owe you a slap in the face."

"Don't go away feeling unequal."

I might have known she would have a natural punch. My jaw felt it for half an hour after she was gone and it took another thirty minutes before I could bring myself back to concluding that she was one funny kid.

All of that added up to the first night with the commissar, and I saw her two more times over this stretch, the last on the night when she finally agreed to sleep over with me, and I came awake in the morning to see her glaring at my head. So often in sex, when the second night wound itself up with nothing better in view than the memory of the first night, I was reminded of Kafka's *Castle,* that tale of the search of a man for his apocalyptic orgasm: in the easy optimism of a young man, he almost captures the castle on the first day, and is never to come so close again. Yes, that was the saga of the nervous system of a man as it was bogged into the defeats, complications, and frustrations of middle age. I still had my future before me of course—the full engagement of my will in some go-for-broke I considered worthy of myself was yet to come, but there were times in that loft when I knew the psychology of an old man, and my second night with Denise—for Denise Gondelman was indeed her name—left me racked for it amounted to so little that we could not even leave it there—the hangover would have been too great for both of us—and so we made a date for a third night. Over and over in those days I used to compare the bed to the bullfight, sometimes seeing myself as the matador and sometimes as the bull, and this second appearance, if it had taken place, in the Plaza Mexico, would have been a *fracaso* with kapok seat cushions jeering down on the ring, and a stubborn cowardly bull staying in *querencia* before the doubtful prissy overtures, the gloomy trim technique of a veteran and mediocre *torero* on the worst of days when he is forced to wonder if he has even his *pundonor* to sustain him. It was a gloomy deal. Each of us knew it was possible to be badly worked by the other, and this seemed so likely that neither of us would gamble a finger. Although we got into bed and had a perfunctory ten minutes, it was as long as an hour in a coffee shop when two friends are done with one another.

By the third night we were ready for complexities again; to see a woman three times is to call on the dialectic of an affair. If the waves we were making belonged less to the viper of passion than the worm of inquiry, still it was obvious from the beginning that we had surprises for one another. The second night we had been hoping for more, and so got less; this third night, we each came on with the notion to wind it up, and so got involved in more.

For one thing, Denise called me in the afternoon. There was studying she had to do, and she wondered if it would be all right to come to my place at eleven instead of meeting me for drinks and dinner. Since that would save me ten dollars she saw no reason why I should complain. It was a down conversation. I had been planning to lay siege to her, dispense a bit of elixir from my vast reservoirs of charm, and instead she was going to keep it *in camera*. There was a quality about her I could not locate, something independent—abruptly, right there, I knew what it was. In a year she would have no memory of me, I would not exist for her unless . . . and then it was clear . . . unless I could be the first to carry her stone of no-orgasm up the cliff, all the way, over and out into the sea. That was the kick I could find, that a year from now, five years from now, down all the seasons to the hours of her old age, I would be the one she would be forced to remember, and it would nourish me a little over the years, thinking of that grudged souvenir which could not die in her, my blond hair, my blue eyes, my small broken nose, my clean mouth and chin, my height, my boxer's body, my parts—yes, I was getting excited at the naked image of me in the young-old mind of that sour sexed-up dynamo of black-pussied frustration.

A phallic narcissist she had called me. Well, I was phallic enough, a Village stickman who could muster enough of the divine It on the head of his will to call forth more than one becoming out of the womb of feminine Time, yes a good deal more than one from my fifty new girls a year, and when I failed before various prisons of frigidity, it mattered little. Experience gave the cue that there were ladies who would not be moved an inch by a year of the best, and so I looked for other things in them, but this one, this Den-of-Ease, she was ready, she was entering the time of her Time, and if not me, it would be another—I was sick in advance at the picture of some bearded Negro cat who would score where I had missed and thus cuckold me in spirit, deprive me of those telepathic waves of longing (in which I obviously believed) speeding away to me from her over the years to balm the hours when I was beat, because I had been her psychic bridegroom, had plucked her ideational diddle, had led her down the walk of her real wedding night. Since she did not like me, what a feat to pull it off.

In the hours I waited after dinner, alone, I had the sense—which I always trusted—that tonight this little victory or defeat would be full of leverage, magnified beyond its emotional matter because I had decided to bet on myself that I would win, and a defeat would bring me closer to a general depression, a fog bank of dissatisfaction with myself which I knew could last for months or more. Whereas a victory would add to the panoplies of my ego some peculiar (but for me, valid) ingestion of her arrogance, her stubbornness, and her will—those necessary ingredients of which I could not yet have enough for my own ambition.

When she came in she was wearing a sweater and dungarees which I had been expecting, but there was a surprise for me. Her braids had been clipped, and a short cropped curled Italian haircut decorated her head, moving her severe young face across the spectrum from the austerities of a poetess to a hint of all those practical and promiscuous European girls who sold their holy hump to the Germans and had been subsequently punished by shaved heads—how attractive the new hair proved; once punished, they were now free, free to be wild, the worst had happened and they were still alive with the taste of the first victor's flesh enriching the sensual curl of the mouth.

Did I like her this way? Denise was interested to know. Well, it was a shock, I admitted, a pleasant shock. If it takes you so long to decide, you must be rigid, she let me know. Well, yes, as a matter of fact I was rigid, rigid for her with waiting.

The nun of severity passed a shade over her. She hated men who were uncool, she thought she would tell me.

"Did your analyst tell you it's bad to be uncool?"

She had taken off her coat, but now she gave me a look as if she were ready to put it on again. "No, he did not tell me that." She laughed spitefully. "But he told me a couple of revealing things about you."

"Which you won't repeat."

"Of course not."

"I'll never know," I said, and gave her the first kiss of the evening. Her mouth was heated—it was the best kiss I had received from her, and it brought me on too quickly—"My fruit is ready to be plucked," said the odors of her mouth, betraying that perfume of the ducts which, against her will no doubt, had been plumping for me. She was changed tonight. From the skin of her face and the glen of her neck came a new smell, sweet, sweaty, and tender, the smell of a body which had been used and had enjoyed its uses. It came to me nicely, one of the nicest smells in quite some time, so different from the usual exudations of her dissatisfied salts that it opened a chain of reflexes in me, and I was off in all good speed on what Denise would probably have called the vertical foreplay. I suppose I went at her like a necrophiliac let loose upon a still-warm subject, and as I gripped her, grasped her, groped her, my breath a bellows to blow her into my own flame, her body remained unmoving, only her mouth answering my call, those lips bridling hot adolescent kisses back upon my face, the smell almost carrying me away—such a fine sweet sweat.

Naturally she clipped the rhythm. As I started to slip up her sweater, she got away and said a little huskily, "I'll take my own clothes off." Once again I could have hit her. My third eye, that athlete's inner eye which probed its vision into all the corners, happy and distressed of my body whole, was glumly cautioning the congestion of the spirits in the coils of each teste. They would have to wait, turn rancid, maybe die of delay.

Off came the sweater and the needless brassière, her economical breasts swelled just a trifle tonight, enough to take on the convexities of an Amazon's armor. Open came the belt and the zipper of her dungarees, zipped from the front which pleased her not a little. Only her ass, a small masterpiece, and her strong thighs, justified this theatre. She stood there naked, quite psychicly clothed, and lit a cigarette.

If a stiff prick has no conscience, it has also no common sense. I stood there like a clown, trying to coax her to take a ride with me on the bawdy car, she out of her clothes, I in all of mine, a muscular little mermaid to melt on my knee. She laughed, one harsh banker's snort—she was giving no loans on my idiot's collateral.

"You didn't even ask me," Denise thought to say, "of how my studying went tonight."

"What did you study?"

"I didn't. I didn't study." She gave me a lovely smile, girlish and bright. "I just spent the last three hours with Arthur."

"You're a dainty type," I told her.

But she gave me a bad moment. That lovely flesh-spent smell, scent of the well used and the tender, that avatar of the feminine my senses had accepted so greedily, came down now to no more than the rubbings and the sweats of what was probably a very nice guy, passive Arthur with his Jewish bonanzas of mouth-love.

The worst of it was that it quickened me more. I had the selfish wisdom to throw such evidence upon the mercy of my own court. For the smell of Arthur was the smell of love, at least for me, and so from man or woman, it did not matter—the smell of love was always feminine—and if the man in Denise was melted by the woman in Arthur, so Arthur might have flowered that woman in himself from the arts of a real woman, his mother? —it did not matter—that voiceless message which passed from the sword of the man into the cavern of the woman was carried along from body to body, and if it was not the woman in Denise I was going to find tonight, at least I would be warmed by the previous trace of another.

But that was a tone poem to quiet the toads of my doubt. When Denise —it took five more minutes—finally decided to expose herself on my clumped old mattress, the sight of her black pubic hair, the feel of the foreign but brotherly liquids in her unembarrassed maw, turned me into a jackrabbit of pissy tumescence, the quicks of my excitement beheaded from the resonances of my body, and I wasn't with her a half-minute before I was over, gone, and off. I rode not with the strength to reap the harem of her and her lover, but spit like a pinched little boy up into black forested hills of motherly contempt, a passing picture of the nuns of my childhood to drench my piddle spurtings with failures of gloom. She it was who proved stronger than me, she the he to my silly she.

All considered, Denise was nice about it. Her harsh laugh did not crackle over my head, her hand in passing me the after-cigarette settled for no more than a nudge of my nose, and if it were not for the contempt of her tough grin, I would have been left with no more than the alarm to the sweepers of my brain to sweep this failure away.

"Hasn't happened in years," I said to her, the confession coming out of me with the cost of the hardest cash.

"Oh, shut up. Just rest." And she began to hum a mocking little song. I lay there in a state, parts of me jangled for forty-eight hours to come, and yet not altogether lost to peace. I knew what it was. Years ago in the air force, as an enlisted man, I had reached the light-heavyweight finals on my air base. For two weeks I trained for the championship, afraid of the other man all the way because I had seen him fight and felt he was better than me; when my night came, he took me out with a left hook to the liver which had me conscious on the canvas but unable to move, and as the referee was counting, which I could hear all too clearly, I knew the same kind of peace, a swooning peace, a clue to that kind of death in which an old man slips away—nothing mattered except that my flesh was vulnerable and I had a dim revery, lying there with the yells of the air force crowd in my ears, there was some far-off vision of green fields and me lying in them, giving up all ambition to go back instead to another, younger life of the senses, and I remember at that moment I watered the cup of my boxer's jock, and then I must have slipped into something new, for as they picked me off the canvas the floor seemed to recede from me at a great rate as if I were climbing in an airplane.

A few minutes later, the nauseas of the blow to my liver had me retching into my hands, and the tension of three weeks of preparation for that fight came back. I knew through the fading vistas of my peace, and the oncoming spasms of my nausea, that the worst was yet to come, and it would take me weeks to unwind, and then years, and maybe never to overcome the knowledge that I had failed completely at a moment when I wanted very much to win.

A ghost of this peace, trailing intimations of a new nausea, was passing over me again, and I sat up in bed abruptly, as if to drive these weaknesses back into me. My groin had been simmering for hours waiting for Denise, and it was swollen still, but the avenger was limp, he had deserted my cause, I was in a spot if she did not co-operate.

Co-operate she did. "My God, lie down again, will you," she said, "I was thinking that finally I had seen you relax."

And then I could sense that the woman in her was about to betray her victory. She sat over me, her little breasts budding with their own desire, her short hair alive and flowering, her mouth ready to taste her gentleman's defeat. I had only to raise my hand, and push her body in the direction she wished it to go, and then her face was rooting in me, her angry tongue and voracious mouth going wild finally as I had wished it, and I knew the sadness of sour timing, because this was a prize I could not enjoy as I would have on the first night, and yet it was good enough—not art, not the tease and languor of love on a soft mouth, but therapy, therapy for her, the quick exhaustions of the tension in a harsh throat, the beseechment of an ugly voice going down into the expiation which would be its beauty. Still it was good, practically it was good, my ego could bank the hard cash that this snotty head was searching me, the act served its purpose, anger traveled from her body into mine, the avenger came to attention, cold and furious, indifferent to the trapped doomed pleasure left behind in my body on that initial and grim piddle spurt, and I was ready, not with any joy nor softness nor warmth nor care, but I was ready finally to take her tonight, I was going to beat new Time out of her if beat her I must, I was going to teach her that she was only a child, because if at last I could not take care of a nineteen-year-old, then I was gone indeed. And so I took her with a cold calculation, the rhythms of my body corresponding to no more than a metronome in my mind, tonight the driving mechanical beat would come from me, and blind to nerve-raddlings in my body, and blood pressures in my brain, I worked on her like a riveter, knowing her resistances were made of steel, I threw her a fuck the equivalent of a fifteen-round fight, I wearied her, I brought her back, I drove my fingers into her shoulders and my knees into her hips, I went, and I went, and I went, I bore her high and thumped her hard, I sprinted, I paced, I lay low, eyes all closed, under sexual water, like a submarine listening for the distant sound of her ship's motors, hoping to steal up close and trick her rhythms away.

And she was close. Oh, she was close so much of the time. Like a child on a merry-go-round the touch of the colored ring just evaded the tips of her touch, and she heaved and she hurdled, arched and cried, clawed me, kissed me, even gave a shriek once, and then her sweats running down and her will weak, exhausted even more than me, she felt me leave and lie beside her. Yes, I did that with a tactician's cunning, I let the depression of her failure poison what was left of her will never to let me succeed, I gave her slack to mourn the lost freedoms and hate the final virginity for which she fought, I even allowed her baffled heat to take its rest and attack her nerves once more, and then, just as she was beginning to fret against me in a new and unwilling appeal, I turned her over suddenly on her belly, my avenger wild with the mania of the madman, and giving her no chance, holding her prone against the mattress with the strength of my weight, I drove into the seat of all stubbornness, tight as a vise, and I wounded her, I knew it, she thrashed beneath me like a trapped little animal, making not a sound, but fierce not to allow me this last of the liberties, and yet caught, forced to give up millimeter by millimeter the bridal ground of her symbolic and therefore real vagina. So I made it, I made it all the way—it took ten minutes and maybe more, but as the avenger rode down to his hilt and tunneled the threshold of sexual home all those inches closer into the bypass of the womb, she gave at last a little cry of farewell, and I could feel a new shudder which began as a ripple and rolled into a wave, and then it rolled over her, carrying her along, me hardly moving for fear of damping this quake from her earth, and then it was gone, but she was left alive with a larger one to follow.

So I turned her once again on her back, and moved by impulse to love's first hole. There was an odor coming up, hers at last, the smell of the sea, and none of the armpit or a dirty sock, and I took her mouth and kissed it, but she was away, following the wake of her own waves which mounted, fell back, and in new momentum mounted higher and should have gone over, and then she was about to hang again, I could feel it, that moment of hesitation between the past and the present, the habit and the adventure, and I said into her ear, "You dirty little Jew."

That whipped her over. A first wave kissed, a second spilled, and a third and a fourth and a fifth came breaking over, and finally she was away, she was loose in the water for the first time in her life, and I would have liked to go with her, but I was blood-throttled and numb, and as she had the first big moment in her life, I was nothing but a set of aching balls and a congested cock, and I rode with her wistfully, looking at the contortion of her face and listening to her sobbing sound of "Oh, Jesus, I made it, oh Jesus, I did."

"Compliments of T. S. Eliot," I whispered to myself, and my head was aching, my body was shot. She curled against me, she kissed my sweat, she nuzzled my eyes and murmured in my ear, and then she was slipping away into the nicest of weary sweet sleep.

"Was it good for you too?" she whispered half-awake, having likewise read the works of The Hemingway, and I said, "Yeah, fine," and after she was asleep, I disengaged myself carefully, and prowled the loft, accepting the hours it would take for my roiled sack to clean its fatigues and know a little sleep. But I had abused myself too far, and it took till dawn and half a fifth of whisky before I dropped into an unblessed stupor. When I awoke, in that moment before I moved to look at her, and saw her glaring at me, I was off on a sluggish masculine debate as to whether the kick of studying this Denise for another few nights—now that I had turned the key—would be worth the danger of deepening into some small real feeling. But through my hangover and the knowledge of the day and the week and the month it would take the different parts of all of me to repair, I was also knowing the taste of a reinforced will—finally, I had won. At no matter what cost, and with what luck, and with a piece of charity from her, I had won nonetheless, and since all real pay came from victory, it was more likely that I would win the next time I gambled my stake on something more appropriate for my ambition.

Then I turned, saw the hatred in her eyes, turned over again, and made believe I was asleep while a dread of the next few minutes weighed a leaden breath over the new skin of my ego.

"You're awake, aren't you?" she said.

I made no answer.

"All right, I'm going then. I'm getting dressed." She whipped out of bed, grabbed her clothes, and began to put them on with all the fury of waiting for me to get the pronouncement. "That was a lousy thing you did last night," she said by way of a start.

In truth she looked better than she ever had. The severe lady and the tough little girl of yesterday's face had put forth the first agreements on what would yet be a bold chick.

"I gave you what you could use," I made the mistake of saying.

"Just didn't you," she said, and was on her way to the door. "Well, cool it. You don't do anything to me." Then she smiled. "You're so impressed with what you think was such a marvelous notch you made in me, listen, Buster, I came here last night thinking of what Sandy Joyce told me about you, and he's right, oh man is he right." Standing in the open doorway, she started to light a cigarette, and then threw the matches to the floor. From thirty feet away I could see the look in her eyes, that unmistakable point for the kill that you find in the eyes of very few bullfighters, and then having created her pause, she came on for her moment of truth by saying, "He told me your whole life is a lie, and you do nothing but run away from the homosexual that is you."

And like a real killer, she did not look back, and was out the door before I could rise to tell her that she was a hero fit for me.

THE GIRL

by

JOYCE CAROL OATES

(b. 1938)

Born in Lockport, New York, Joyce Carol Oates was educated at Syracuse University and the University of Wisconsin. After teaching at the University of Detroit and at the University of Windsor, Canada, she now lives in Princeton, New Jersey. Productive and versatile, since publishing her first novel in 1963, she has written short stories, novels, plays, poetry, and a great deal of literary criticism, for which she has received much acclaim and many awards. Her most recent work is Solstice *(1985).*

• ———————————————— •

1 Background Material

Came by with a truck, The Director and Roybay and a boy I didn't know. Roybay leaned out the window, very friendly. I got in and we drove around for a while. The Director telling us about his movie-vision, all speeded-up because his friend, his contact, had lent him the equipment from an educational film company in town, and it had to be back Sunday P.M. The Director said: "It's all a matter of art and compromise." He was very excited. I knew him from before, a few days before; his name was DePinto or DeLino, something strange, but he was called The Director. He was in the third person most of the time.

Roybay, two hundred fifty pounds, very cheerful and easy and my closest friend of all of them, was The Motorcyclist. They used his motorcycle for an authentic detail. It didn't work; it was broken down. But they propped it up in the sand and it looked very real.

A boy with a scruffy face, like an explorer's face, was The Cop.

I was The Girl.

The Director said: "Oh Jesus honey your tan, your tanned legs, your feet, my God even your feet your toes, are tan, tanned, you're so lovely. . . ." And he stared at me, he stared. When we met before, he had not stared like this. His voice was hoarse, his eyebrows ragged. It was all music with him, his voice and his way of moving, the life inside him. "I mean, look at her! Isn't she—? Isn't it?"

"Perfect," Roybay said.

The boy with the scruffy face, wedged in between Roybay the driver and The Director, with me on The Director's lap and my legs sort of on his lap, stared at me and turned out to be a kid my age. I caught a look of his but rejected it. I never found out his name.

Later they said to me: "What were their names? Don't you know? Can't you remember? Can't you—?"

They were angry. They said: "Describe them."

But.

The Director. The Motorcyclist. The Cop. The Girl.

I thought there were more, more than that. If you eliminate The Girl. If you try to remember. More? More than two? Oh, I believe a dozen or two, fifty, any large reasonable number tramping down the sand. There was the motorcycle, broken. They hauled it out in the back of the truck with the film equipment and other stuff. I could describe the Santa Monica Freeway if I wanted to. But not them. I think there were more than three but I don't know. Where did they come from? Who were they? The reason I could describe the Freeway is that I knew it already, not memorized but in pieces, the way you know your environment.

I was The Girl. No need to describe. Anyone studying me, face to face, would be in my presence and would not need a description. I looked different. The costume didn't matter, the bright red and green shapes— cats and kittens—wouldn't show anyway. The film was black-and-white. It was a short-skirted dress, a top that tied in back, looped around and tied in back like a halter, the material just cotton or anything, bright shapes of red and green distortions in the material. It came from a Miss Chelsea shop in Van Nuys. I wasn't wearing anything else, anything underneath.

Someone real said to me later, a real policeman: ". . . need your cooperation. . . ."

The Director explained that he needed everyone's cooperation. He had assisted someone making a film once, or he had watched it happen, he said how crucial it is to cooperate; he wouldn't have the footage for re-takes and all the equipment had to be returned in eighteen hours. Had a sharkish skinny glamourish face, a wide-brimmed hat perched on his head. Wore sunglasses. We all did. The beach was very bright at three in the afternoon. I had yellow-lensed glasses with white plastic wrap-around frames, like goggles. It wasn't very warm. The wind came in from the ocean, chilly.

The way up, I got hypnotized by the expressway signs and all the names of the towns and beaches and the arrows pointing up off to the right, always up off to the right and off the highway and off the map.

"Which stretch of beach? Where? How far up the coast? Can't you identify it, can't you remember? We need your cooperation, can't you cooperate?"

On film, any stretch of beach resembles any stretch of beach. They called it The Beach.

II The Rehearsal

The Director moved us around, walked with us; put his hands on me and turned me, stepped on my bare feet, scratched his head up beneath the straw-colored hat, made noises with his mouth, very excited, saying to himself little words: "Here—yeah—like this—this—this way—" The Motorcyclist, who was Roybay, straddled the motorcycle to wait. Had a sunny broad face with red-blond-brown hair frizzy all around it. Even his beard was frizzy. It wasn't hot but he looked hot. Was six foot three or four, taller than my father, who is or was six foot exactly. That is my way of telling if a man is tall: taller than my father, then he's *tall*; shorter than my father, *not tall*. The world could be divided that way.

No, I haven't seen my father for a while. But the world is still there.

The Director complained about the setting. The beach was beautiful but empty. "Got to imagine people crowding in, people in the place of boulders and rocks and scrubby damn flowers and sand dunes and eucalyptus and all this crap, it's hobbling to the eye," he said. He had wanted a city movie. He had wanted the movie to take place in the real world. "Really wanted Venice Beach on a Sunday, packed, but room for the motorcycle, and the whole world crowded in . . . a miscellaneous flood of people, souls, to represent the entire world . . . and the coming-together of the world in my story. In The Girl. Oh look at her," he said dreamily, looking at me, "couldn't the world come together in her? It could. But this place is so empty . . . it's wild here, a wild innocent natural setting, it's too beautiful, it could be a travelogue. . . ."

The Cop asked about splicing things together. Couldn't you—?

The Director waved him away. It was hard to concentrate.

The Cop giggled and whispered to me: "Jeeze, these guys are something, huh? How'd you meet them? I met them this morning. Where do you go to school? You go to school? Around here?"

I snubbed him, eye-to-eye.

He blushed. He was about sixteen, behind his bushy hair and sun-glasses and policeman's hat. It had a tin badge on it. The Director had bought it at a costume store. The Cop had only a hat. The rest of him was a T-shirt and jeans. A club two feet long and maybe an inch and a half in diameter, but no gun. The Director had found the club in a garbage can, he said, months ago. He carried it everywhere with him. It had generated his need for a film, he said; he kept taking it from The Cop and using it to make lines in the sand.

The Director's mind was always going. It was white-hot. His body never stopped, his knees jerked as if keeping time to something. I felt the energy in him, even when he wasn't touching me. Only when he held the camera in his hands, between his hands, was he calmed down.

After a while, Roybay said, sounding nervous: "What do we do? What do I do? Somebody might come along here, huh?—we better hurry it up, huh?"

"This can't be hurried," The Director said.

The Motorcyclist was the only one of them I knew. His name was *Roybay*. Or *Robbie*. Or maybe it was *Roy Bean* (?) . . . sometimes just *Roy* or *Ray*. Said he came over from Trinidad, Colorado—I think. Or someone else his size said that, some other day. Had a big worried forehead tanned pink-red. You don't tan dark, with a complexion like that. He wore a crash helmet and goggles and a leather jacket, the sleeves a little short for his arms. The night I met him, he was explaining the fact that vegetables are not meek and passive, as people think, but exert great pressure in forcing themselves up through the soil . . . and think about vines, twisting tendrils, feelers that could choke large animals to death or pull them down into quicksand. . . . He was a vegetarian, but he scorned meekness. Believed in strength. Up at 7 A.M. for two hours of weight-lifting, very slow, Yoga-slow, and a careful diet of vegetables and vegetable juices. Said fruit was too acid, too sharp. Explained that an ox's muscles were extremely powerful and that the carnivores of the world could learn from the ox.

Or his name could have been something like *Roy baby, Roy, baby* if someone called out and slurred the words together.

The Director placed rocks on the sand. Kicked dents in the sand. He cleared debris out of the way, tossing things hand over hand, then he found a child's toy—a fire truck—and stood with it, spinning the little wheels, thinking, then he moved one of the rocks a few inches and said to me: "You walk to this point. Try it."

They watched.

The Director said that I was a sweet girl. He said that now I should practice running, from the rock out to the water. He followed alongside me. He told me when to stop. He kissed my forehead and said I was very sweet, this was part of the tragedy. He tossed the toy fire truck off to the side. Rubbed his hands together, excited. I could smell it on him, the excitement.

"I'm an orphan," he said suddenly. "I'm from a Methodist orphanage up in Seattle."

The Motorcyclist laughed. The Cop grinned stupidly; he was still standing where The Director had placed him.

"You don't get many chances in life," The Director said, "so I would hate to mess this up. It would make me very angry if something went wrong . . . if one of you went wrong . . . But you're not going to, huh, are you? Not even you?" he said, looking at me. As if I was special. He had a sharkish look caused by one tooth, I think—a side tooth that was a little longer than the rest of his teeth. If you glanced at him you wouldn't notice that tooth, not really; but somehow you would start to think of a shark a few seconds later.

In a magical presence. I knew. I knew but I was outside, not on film. The Director walked with me along the beach, his feet in ankle-high boots and mine bare, talking to me, stroking my arms, saying . . . saying. . . . *What did he say? Don't remember?* No, the noise was too much. The waves. Gulls. Birds. Words come this way and that, I don't catch them all, try to ease with the feeling, the music behind them. I took music lessons once. Piano lessons with Miss Dorsey, three blocks from my grandmother's house; from ten until thirteen. Could memorize. Could count out a beat one two three, *one* two three, one *two* three, a habit to retain throughout life. When The Director told me what to do I listened to the beat of his voice. I knew I was in a magical presence, he was not an ordinary man, but I was outside him, outside waiting. I was not yet The Girl. I was The Girl later.

It was a movie, a movie-making! I screamed. When I woke for the half-dozenth time, snatching at someone's wrist. I clawed, had to make contact. I didn't want to sink back again. I said: *It was real, it was a movie, there was film in the camera!*

You mean someone filmed it? Filmed that? Someone had a camera?

The Director carried it in his hands. Had to adjust it, squinted down into it, made noises with his mouth; he took a long time. The Cop, licking his lips, said to me: "Hey, I thought the movie cameras were real big. Pushed around on wheels. With some moving parts, like a crane or something . . . ? Where are you from?"

"You couldn't push wheels in the sand," I told him.

The Director looked over at us. "What are you two talking about? Be quiet. You," he said to The Cop, "you, you're not in the script yet, you're off-camera, go stand on the other side of that hill. Don't clutter my mind."

He walked out to the surf, stood there, was very agitated. I looked at Roybay, who was looking at me. Our eyes didn't come together; he was looking at me like on film. The Girl. Over there, straddling the broken-down rusty-handle-barred motorcycle, was The Motorcyclist. He was not from Trinidad, Colorado, or from anywhere. I saw The Cop's cap disappear over a hill behind some spiky weeds and ridges of sand.

The Director came back. He said to The Motorcyclist, "What this is, maybe, it's a poem centered in the head of The Cop, but I had it off-center; I was imagining it in The Girl. But . . . but . . . it wasn't working. It's a test of The Cop. I don't know him. Do you? I don't know who the hell he is. It will be an experiment. He rushes in to the rescue . . . and sees the scene and . . . the test is upon him. The audience will see it too. I've been dreaming this for so long, this tiny eight-minute poem," he said, putting his arm around my shoulder now, excited, "I can't miss my chance. It's not just that it's crowding my head, but people are going to be very interested in this; I know certain people who are going to pay a lot to see it. Look, it's a poem, honey. The parts must cooperate. Nothing unripe or resisting. All parts in a poem . . . in a work of art. . . . Please, do you understand, do you?"

So sensitive. It was a sensitive moment. Staring eye-to-eye with me, dark green lenses and yellow lenses, shatter-proof.

I told him yes. I had to say yes. And it was almost true; some of his words caught in me, snagged, like the rough edge of a fingernail in your clothing.

The Director said softly: "What it is . . . is . . . it's a vision, it can't be resisted. Why resist? Resist? Resist anything? If a vision comes up from the inside of the earth, it must be sacred, or down out of the sky— even, equal—because the way up is the same as the way down, the sky is a mirror and vice versa. Right? I wanted The Girl to resist The Motor-cyclist and I wanted The Cop to use the club like a Zen master's stick but now I see it differently, with the scene all set. It goes the way it must. You can't control a vision. It's like going down a stairway and you're cautious and frightened and then the stairway breaks, the last step gives way, and you fall and yet you're not afraid, you're not afraid after all, you're saved. You don't understand me, I know, but you'll feel it, you'll under-stand in a while. Don't resist," he said to me. "If you deny the way things must operate, you turn yourself and everyone else into a phantom. We'll all be here together. One thing. We'll be sacred. Don't doubt. Now I'll talk to The Cop, the Savior . . . he's the Savior. . . . I wonder can he bear the weight of the testing?"

III The Performance

Space around me. Hair blowing, back toward shore an arrow out of sight. The air is cold. Nervous, but doing O.K.

The Director says in a whisper-shout: "Okay. Okay. No, slow down . . . slow . . . slow down. . . . Look over here. . . . The other way. . . ." It is very easy now that the camera is working. It is very easy. I am The Girl watching the film of The Girl walking on a beach watching the water. Now The Girl watching The Girl turning The Girl in black-and-white approached by a shape, a dark thing, out of the corner of the eye. The eye must be the camera. The dark thing must be a shape with legs, with arms, with a white-helmeted head.

Now the film speeds up.

A surprise, how light you become on film! You are very graceful. It's a suspension of gravity. The Director calls to me, yells to me: *Run. Run.* But I can't. I am too light, and then too heavy; the hand on my shoulder weighs me down. I think I am giggling. *Hurry up! Hurry up!*

The marker is a real rock.

Scream! cries The Director.

But I can't, I can't get breath. They are at me. I scramble up onto my feet. But. But I have lost hold. I can't see. The Director is very close to us, right beside us. *Turn her around, make her scream—hurry up—do it like this, like this, do it fast like this—come on—*

The film is speeded up. Too fast. I have lost hold of it, can't see. I am being driven backwards, downwards, burrowed-into, like a hammer being hammered being hammered against all at once. Do I see noseholes, eyeholes, mouthholes?

Something being pounded into flesh like meat.

IV   A Sequel

I was babbling, hanging onto someone's wrist. Not the doctor, who was in a hurry on his rounds, but a nurse. I said: "Did they find them? The police? Did it get in the newspapers? Was the movie shown? Was it—?"

What? What? At the important instant I lost sight of her, one adult face like another. Then it contracted into someone's regular-sized face. The ceiling above him seemed to open behind his face and to glow, fluorescent lighting as if for a stage, a studio. Why, this must be someone who knows me! He is looking at me without disgust. I don't know him. But I pretend. I ask him if they were caught, if—He says not to think about it right now. He says not to think about it. He says: "The police, they won't find them anyway . . . they don't give a damn about you . . . don't torture yourself."

But, but.

Raw reddened meat, scraped raw, hair yanked out in handfuls. A scalp bleeding and sandy. Sandy grit in my mouth. It was a jelly, a transformation. But I wanted to know. Wanted. I reached for his wrist but couldn't get it.

You can be real, but you can be stronger than real; speeded-up, lighted-up. It does take a camera. The Director helped them drag me back saying *Oh it was beautiful . . . it was beautiful . . .* and there were tears in the creases around his mouth. I strained to get free, to break the shape out of my head and into his. Strained, twisted. But there was too much noise. The back of my head was hurt and emptied out. Too much battered into me, I couldn't tell them apart, there were two of them but maybe two hundred or two thousand, I couldn't know.

But I couldn't talk right. The man tried to listen politely but here is what I said: ". . . rockhand, two of them, bird-burrow, truck, toy, wheel, the arrow, the exit, the way out. . . ." Another man, also in the room, tried to interrupt. Kept asking "Who were they? How many? Five, six, a dozen? Twenty? Where did it happen? Where did you meet them? Who are you?" but I kept on talking, babbling, now I was saying saints' names

that got into my head somehow . . . the names of saints like beads on
a rosary, but I didn't know them, the saints had terrible names to twist
my head out of shape: ". . . Saint Camarillo, Saint Oxnard, Saint . . .
Saint Ventura . . . Saint Ynez . . . Saint Goleta . . . Saint Gaviota
. . . Saint Jalama . . . Saint Casmalia . . . Saint Saint Saint. . . ."

V   The Vision

A rainy wintry day, and I crossed Carpenter Street and my eye drifted right
onto someone. The Director. I stared at him and started to run after him.
He turned around, staring. Didn't recognize me. Didn't know. Behind
him a laundromat, some kids playing in the doorway, yelling. Too much
confusion. The Director walked sideways, sideways staring at me, trying to
remember. He hadn't any sunglasses now. His skin was sour-looking.
  I ran up to him. I said: "Don't you remember? Don't you—?"
  I laughed.
  I forgave him, he looked so sick. He was about twenty-eight, thirty
years old. Edgy, cautious. Creases down both sides of his mouth.
  He stared at me.
  Except for the rain and a bad cold, my eyes reddened, I was pretty
again and recovered. I laughed but started to remember something out
of the corner of my eye. Didn't want to remember. So I smiled, grinned at
him, and he tried to match the way I looked.
  "I'm new here, I just came here . . . I'm from. . . . I'm from up the
coast, from Seattle. . . . I don't know you. . . ."
  A kind of shutter clicked in his head. Showing in his eyes. He was
walking sideways and I reached out for his wrist, a bony wrist, and he
shook me loose. His lips were thin and chalk-colored, chalky cheesy sour-
colored. One of his nostrils was bigger than the other and looked sore.
That single shark tooth was greenish. He said: " . . . just in for a day,
overnight, down from Seattle and . . . uh . . . I don't know you. . . .
Don't remember. I'm confused. I'm not well, my feet are wet, I'm from
out of town."
  "What happened to the movie?" I asked.
  He watched me. A long time passed. Someone walked by him on the
pavement, in the rain, the way passersby walk in a movie, behind the
main actors. They are not in focus and that person was not in focus either.
  "Was it a real movie? Did it have film, the camera?" I asked. Beginning
to be afraid. Beginning. But I kept it back, the taste in my mouth. Kept
smiling to show him no harm. "Oh hey look," I said, "look, it had film,
didn't it? I mean it had film? I mean you made a real movie, didn't you?
I mean—"
  Finally he began to see me. The creases around his mouth turned into
a smile. It was like a crucial scene now; he put his hand on my shoulder
and kissed my forehead, in the rain. He said: "Honey oh yeah. Yeah.

Don't you ever doubt that. I mean, did you doubt that? All these months? You should never have doubted that. I mean, that's the whole thing. That's it. That's the purpose, the center, the reason behind it, all of it, the focus, the. . . . You know what I mean? The Vision?"

I knew what he meant.

So I was saved.

WITH NO IMMEDIATE CAUSE

by

NTOZAKE SHANGE

(b. 1948)

Born Paulette Williams in Trenton, New Jersey, Ntozake Shange took her pseudonym as an expression of her anger at the dilemma of being a black woman. In Zulu the name means "she who comes with her own things" / "she who walks like a lion." Educated at Barnard College and the University of Southern California, Shange has written novels, including Sassafrass, Cypress, and Indigo *(1983), the story of a mother and three daughters. Her "choreopoem,"* For Colored Girls Who Have Considered Suicide / When the Rainbow Is Enuf, *moved to Broadway in 1976 and has been widely produced. Two other plays were produced in 1977; four collections of poems and a book of essays,* See No Evil *(1984), have also appeared.*

• ───────────────────── •

every 3 minutes a woman is beaten
every five minutes a
woman is raped/every ten minutes
a lil girl is molested
yet i rode the subway today
i sat next to an old man who
may have beaten his old wife
3 minutes ago or 3 days/30 years ago
he might have sodomized his
daughter but i sat there
cuz the young men on the train
might beat some young women
later in the day or tomorrow
i might not shut my door fast
enuf/push hard enuf
every 3 minutes it happens
some woman's innocence
rushes to her cheeks/pours from her mouth
like the betsy wetsy dolls have been torn

apart/their mouths
menses red & split/every
three minutes a shoulder
is jammed through plaster and the oven door/
chairs push thru the rib cage/hot water or
boiling sperm decorate her body
i rode the subway today
& bought a paper from a
man who might
have held his old lady onto
a hot pressing iron/i dont know
maybe he catches lil girls in the
park & rips open their behinds
with steel rods/i can't decide
what he might have done i only
know every 3 minutes
every 5 minutes every 10 minutes/so
i bought the paper
looking for the announcement
the discovery/of the dismembered
woman's body/the
victims have not all been
identified/today they are
naked and dead/refuse to
testify/one girl out of 10's not
coherent/i took the coffee
& spit it up/i found an
announcement/not the woman's
bloated body in the river/floating
not the child bleeding in the
59th street corridor/not the baby
broken on the floor/
    "there is some concern
    that alleged battered women
    might start to murder their
    husbands & lovers with no
    immediate cause"
i spit up i vomit i am screaming
we all have immediate cause
every 3 minutes
every 5 minutes
every 10 minutes

every day
women's bodies are found
in alleys & bedrooms/at the top of the stairs
before i ride the subway/buy a paper/drink
coffee/i must know/
have you hurt a woman today
did you beat a woman today
throw a child across a room
    are the lil girl's panties
     in yr pocket
did you hurt a woman today

i have to ask these obscene questions
the authorities require me to
establish
immediate cause

every three minutes
every five minutes
every ten minutes
every day.

DAGUERREOTYPE: "FALLEN" WOMAN

by

SANDRA GILBERT

(b. 1936)

*Born in New York City, Sandra Gilbert has often used her immi-
grant origins as a topic for her poems, of which two volumes have
been published;* Emily's Bread *(1984) is about Emily Dickinson and
Emily Brontë as her spiritual ancestors and makers of bread. Best
known as a literary critic and teacher, Gilbert is now a professor of
English at Princeton University.* The Madwoman in the Attic
*(1979), which she co-authored with Susan Gubar, is a landmark
work in feminist literary criticism.*

· ——————————————————— ·

The clock between her thighs ticks like a heart of gold:
satins, furbelows, no matter what she wears
she knows it's there, quick treasure, time machine that carries her,
pink nymph of the *pavé,*
from mattress to mattress, day to day.

Rustling her colors, she tells us this
between gulps of beer,
confides, "It's the drink that gets me through,"
grins, twitches her skirt. Her hair
is a curious shade of green

(from spit and sweat, she thinks)
and clings like fingers to her neck;
her frayed shawl, dull as a night's work,
sways around her hips; her breasts are question marks.
Some afternoons she sleeps, she says, and dreams,

green ringlets in her eyes,
that she's a tree, falling through the Thames,
falling through the easy mud,
into Australia, where the sun is hot
and an armless man sucks out her hole, her clock, her heart.

ONE OFF THE SHORT LIST

by

DORIS LESSING

(b. 1919)

Born in Persia, Doris Lessing has lived in southern Rhodesia (now Zimbabwe) and England. Her fiction has as its major theme the dehumanizing effects of violence in our time. Children of Violence *(1952–1965) and* The Golden Notebook *(1962) focus on women as the central consciousnesses through whom society is perceived, many of them "free women" independent of men. In* The Summer Before the Dark *(1973), Lessing reaffirms the difficulty for a middle-aged wife and mother of trying to become "free." Beginning in 1979, several volumes of science fiction have appeared in which she portrays life after an apocalypse.*

•————————————————————•

When he had first seen Barbara Coles, some years before, he only noticed her because someone said: "That's Johnson's new girl." He certainly had not used of her the private erotic formula: *Yes, that one.* He even wondered what Johnson saw in her. "She won't last long," he remembered thinking, as he watched Johnson, a handsome man, but rather flushed with drink, flirting with some unknown girl while Barbara stood by a wall looking on. He thought she had a sullen expression.

She was a pale girl, not slim, for her frame was generous, but her figure could pass as good. Her straight yellow hair was parted on one side in a way that struck him as gauche. He did not notice what she wore. But her eyes were all right, he remembered: large, and solidly green, square-looking because of some trick of the flesh at their corners. Emeraldlike eyes in the face of a schoolgirl, or young schoolmistress who was watching her lover flirt and would later sulk about it.

Her name sometimes cropped up in the papers. She was a stage decorator, a designer, something on those lines.

Then a Sunday newspaper had a competition for stage design and she won it. Barbara Coles was one of the "names" in the theatre, and her photograph was seen about. It was always serious. He remembered having thought her sullen.

One night he saw her across the room at a party. She was talking with a well-known actor. Her yellow hair was still done on one side, but now it looked sophisticated. She wore an emerald ring on her right hand that seemed deliberately to invite comparison with her eyes. He walked over and said: "We have met before, Graham Spence." He noted, with discomfort, that he sounded abrupt. "I'm sorry, I don't remember, but how do you do?" she said, smiling. And continued her conversation.

He hung around a bit, but soon she went off with a group of people she was inviting to her home for a drink. She did not invite Graham. There was about her an assurance, a carelessness, that he recognised as the signature of success. It was then, watching her laugh as she went off with her friends, that he used the formula: *"Yes, that one."* And he went home to his wife with enjoyable expectation, as if his date with Barbara Coles were already arranged.

His marriage was twenty years old. At first it had been stormy, painful, tragic—full of partings, betrayals and sweet reconciliations. It had taken him at least a decade to realise that there was nothing remarkable about this marriage that he had lived through with such surprise of the mind and the senses. On the contrary, the marriages of most of the people he knew, whether they were first, second or third attempts, were just the same. His had run true to form even to the serious love affair with the young girl for whose sake he had *almost* divorced his wife—yet at the last moment had changed his mind, letting the girl down so that he must have her for always (not unpleasurably) on his conscience. It was with humiliation that he had understood that this drama was not at all the unique thing he had imagined. It was nothing more than the experience of everyone in his circle. And presumably in everybody else's circle too?

Anyway, round about the tenth year of his marriage he had seen a good many things clearly, a certain kind of emotional adventure went from his life, and the marriage itself changed.

His wife had married a poor youth with a great future as a writer. Sacrifices had been made, chiefly by her, for that future. He was neither unaware of them, nor ungrateful; in fact he felt permanently guilty about it. He at last published a decently successful book, then a second which now, thank God, no one remembered. He had drifted into radio, television, book reviewing.

He understood he was not going to make it; that he had become—not a hack, no one could call him that—but a member of that army of people who live by their wits on the fringes of the arts. The moment of realisation was when he was in a pub one lunchtime near the B.B.C. where he often dropped in to meet others like himself: he understood that was why he went there—they *were* like him. Just as that melodramatic marriage had turned out to be like everyone else's—except that it had been shared with one woman instead of with two or three—so it had turned out that his unique talent, his struggles as a writer had led him here, to this pub and the half dozen pubs like it, where all the men in sight had the same history. They all had their novel, their play, their book of poems, a moment of fame, to their credit. Yet here they were, running television programmes about which they were cynical (to each other or to their wives) or writing reviews about other people's books. Yes, that's what he had become, an impresario of other people's talent. These two moments of clarity, about his marriage and about his talent, had roughly coincided: and (perhaps not by chance) had coincided with his wife's decision to leave him for a man younger than himself who had a future, she said, as a playwright. Well, he had talked her out of it. For her part she had to understand he was not going to be the T. S. Eliot or Graham Greene of our time—but after all, how many were? She must finally understand this, for he could no longer bear her awful bitterness. For his part he must stop coming home drunk at five in the morning, and starting a new romantic affair every six months which he took so seriously that he made her miserable because of her implied deficiencies. In short he was to be a good husband. (He had always been a dutiful father.) And she a good wife. And so it was: the marriage became stable, as they say.

The formula: *Yes, that one* no longer implied a necessarily sexual relationship. In its more mature form, it was far from being something he was ashamed of. On the contrary, it expressed a humorous respect for what he was, for his real talents and flair, which had turned out to be not artistic after all, but to do with emotional life, hard-earned experience. It expressed an ironical dignity, a proving to himself not only: I can be honest about myself, but also: I have earned the best in *that* field whenever I want it.

He watched the field for the women who were well known in the arts, or in politics; looked out for photographs, listened for bits of gossip. He made a point of going to see them act, or dance, or orate. He built up a not unshrewd picture of them. He would either quietly pull strings to meet her or—more often, for there was a gambler's pleasure in waiting—bide his time until he met her in the natural course of events, which was bound to happen sooner or later. He would be seen out with her a few times in public, which was in order, since his work meant he had to entertain well-known people, male and female. His wife always knew, he told her. He might have a brief affair with this woman, but more often than not it was the appearance of an affair. Not that he didn't get pleasure from other people envying him—he would make a point, for instance, of taking this woman into the pubs where his male colleagues went. It was that his real pleasure came when he saw her surprise at how well she was understood by him. He enjoyed the atmosphere he was able to set up between an intelligent woman and himself: a humorous complicity which had in it much that was unspoken, and which almost made sex irrelevant.

Onto the list of women with whom he planned to have this relationship went Barbara Coles. There was no hurry. Next week, next month, next

year, they would meet at a party. The world of
London is a small one. Big and little fishes, th
other, flirt their fins, wriggle off again. When he
it would be time to decide whether or not to s

Meanwhile he listened. But he didn't discover
and children, but the husband seemed to be in ι
children were charming and well brought up, like
She had affairs, they said; but while several men
with her, it was hard to determine whether they had
none directly boasted of her. She was spoken of in teι
her work, her house, a party she had given, a job she haα
She was liked, she was respected, and Graham Spence's seι
flattered because he had chosen her. He looked forward to
the same tone: "Barbara Coles asked me what I thought about
and I told her quite frankly. . . ."

Then by chance he met a young man who did boast about Barι
Coles; he claimed to have had the great love affair with her, and receι
at that; and he spoke of it as something generally known. Graham realι
how much he had already become involved with her in his imagination
because of how perturbed he was now, on account of the character of
this youth, Jack Kennaway. He had recently become successful as a magazine editor—one of those young men who, not as rare as one might
suppose in the big cities, are successful from sheer impertinence, effrontery.
Without much talent or taste, yet he had the charm of his effrontery.
"Yes, I'm going to succeed, because I've decided to; yes, I may be stupid,
but not so stupid that I don't know my deficiencies. Yes, I'm going to be
successful because you people with integrity, etc., etc., simply don't believe
in the possibility of people like me. You are too cowardly to stop me. Yes,
I've taken your measure and I'm going to succeed because I've got the
courage, not only to be unscrupulous, but to be quite frank about it.
And besides, you admire me, you must, or otherwise you'd stop me. . . ."
Well, that was young Jack Kennaway, and he shocked Graham. He was
a tall, languishing young man, handsome in a dark melting way, and,
it was quite clear, he was either asexual or homosexual. And this youth
boasted of the favours of Barbara Coles; boasted, indeed, of her love.
Either she was a raving neurotic with a taste for neurotics; or Jack
Kennaway was a most accomplished liar; or she slept with anyone.
Graham was intrigued. He took Jack Kennaway out to dinner in order
to hear him talk about Barbara Coles. There was no doubt the two were
pretty close—all those dinners, theatres, weekends in the country—Graham
Spence felt he had put his finger on the secret pulse of Barbara Coles;
and it was intolerable that he must wait to meet her; he decided to
arrange it.

It became unnecessary. She was in the news again, with a run of luck.
She had done a successful historical play, and immediately afterwards a

play, and then a hit musical. In all three, the sets were remarked
ham saw some interviews in newspapers and on television. These
ered around the theme of her being able to deal easily with so
different styles of theatre; but the real point was, of course, that
as a woman, which naturally added piquancy to the thing. And
Graham Spence was asked to do a half-hour radio interview with her.
planned the questions he would ask her with care, drawing on what
ople had said of her, but above all on his instinct and experience with
omen. The interview was to be at nine-thirty at night; he was to pick
her up at six from the theatre where she was currently at work, so that
there would be time, as the letter from the B.B.C. had put it, "for you
and Miss Coles to get to know each other."

At six he was at the stage door, but a message from Miss Coles said she
was not quite ready, could he wait a little. He hung about, then went to
the pub opposite for a quick one, but still no Miss Coles. So he made
his way backstage, directed by voices, hammering, laughter. It was badly
lit, and the group of people at work did not see him. The director, James
Poynter, had his arm around Barbara's shoulders. He was newly well-known,
a carelessly good-looking young man reputed to be intelligent. Barbara
Coles wore a dark blue overall, and her flat hair fell over her face so that
she kept pushing it back with the hand that had the emerald on it.
These two stood close, side by side. Three young men, stagehands, were
on the other side of a trestle which had sketches and drawings on it. They
were studying some sketches. Barbara said, in a voice warm with energy:
"Well, so I thought if we did *this*—do you see, James? What do you
think, Steven?" "Well, love," said the young man she called Steven,
"I see your idea, but I wonder if . . ." "I think you're right, Babs," said
the director. "Look," said Barbara, holding one of the sketches toward
Steven, "look, let me show you." They all leaned forward, the five of
them, absorbed in the business.

Suddenly Graham couldn't stand it. He understood he was shaken to
his depths. He went off stage, and stood with his back against a wall in the
dingy passage that led to the dressing room. His eyes were filled with
tears. He was seeing what a long way he had come from the crude,
uncompromising, admirable young egomaniac he had been when he was
twenty. That group of people there—working, joking, arguing, yes, that's
what he hadn't known for years. What bound them was the democracy
of respect for each other's work, a confidence in themselves and in each
other. They looked like people banded together against a world which
they—no, not despised, but which they measured, understood, would
fight to the death, out of respect for what *they* stood for, for what *it* stood
for. It was a long time since he felt part of that balance. And he understood that he had seen Barbara Coles when she was most herself, at
ease with a group of people she worked with. It was then, with the tears
drying on his eyelids, which felt old and ironic, that he decided he

THE SEX OBJECT

324

would sleep with Barbara Coles. It was a necessity for him. He went back through the door onto the stage, burning with this single determination.

The five were still together. Barbara had a length of blue gleaming stuff which she was draping over the shoulder of Steven, the stagehand. He was showing it off, and the others watched. "What do you think, James?" she asked the director. "We've got that sort of dirty green, and I thought . . ." "Well," said James, not sure at all, "well, Babs, well . . ."

Now Graham went forward so that he stood beside Barbara, and said: "I'm Graham Spence, we've met before." For the second time she smiled socially and said: "Oh I'm sorry, I don't remember." Graham nodded at James, whom he had known, or at least had met off and on, for years. But it was obvious James didn't remember him either.

"From the B.B.C.," said Graham to Barbara, again sounding abrupt, against his will. "Oh I'm sorry, I'm sorry, I forgot all about it. I've got to be interviewed," she said to the group. "Mr. Spence is a journalist." Graham allowed himself a small smile ironical of the word journalist, but she was not looking at him. She was going on with her work. "We should decide tonight," she said. "Steven's right." "Yes, I am right," said the stagehand. "She's right, James, we need that blue with that sludge-green everywhere." "James," said Barbara, "James, what's wrong with it? You haven't said." She moved forward to James, passing Graham. Remembering him again, she became contrite. "I'm sorry," she said, "we can none of us agree. Well, look"—she turned to Graham—"you advise us, we've got so involved with it that . . ." At which James laughed, and so did the stagehands. "No, Babs," said James, "of course Mr. Spence can't advise. He's just this moment come in. We've got to decide. Well I'll give you till tomorrow morning. Time to go home, it must be six by now."

"It's nearly seven," said Graham, taking command.

"It isn't!" said Barbara, dramatic. "My God, how terrible, how appalling, how could I have done such a thing. . . ." She was laughing at herself. "Well, you'll have to forgive me, Mr. Spence, because you haven't got any alternative."

They began laughing again: this was clearly a group joke. And now Graham took his chance. He said firmly, as if he were her director, in fact copying James Poynter's manner with her: "No, Miss Coles, I won't forgive you, I've been kicking my heels for nearly an hour." She grimaced, then laughed and accepted it. James said: "There, Babs, that's how you ought to be treated. We spoil you." He kissed her on the cheek, she kissed him on both his, the stagehands moved off. "Have a good evening, Babs," said James, going, and nodding to Graham, who stood concealing his pleasure with difficulty. He knew, because he had had the courage to be firm, indeed, peremptory, with Barbara, that he had saved himself hours of maneuvering. Several drinks, a dinner—perhaps two or three evenings of drinks and dinners—had been saved because he was now on this footing with Barbara Coles, a man who could say: "No, I won't forgive you, you've kept me waiting."

She said: "I've just got to . . ." and went ahead of him. In the passage she hung her overall on a peg. She was thinking, it seemed, of something else, but seeing him watching her, she smiled at him, companionably: he realised with triumph it was the sort of smile she would offer one of the stagehands, or even James. She said again: "Just one second . . ." and went to the stage-door office. She and the stage doorman conferred. There was some problem. Graham said, taking another chance: "What's the trouble, can I help?"—as if he could help, as if he expected to be able to. "Well . . ." she said, frowning. Then, to the man: "No, it'll be all right. Goodnight." She came to Graham. "We've got ourselves into a bit of a fuss because half the set's in Liverpool and half's here and—but it will sort itself out." She stood, at ease, chatting to him, one colleague to another. All this was admirable, he felt; but there would be a bad moment when they emerged from the special atmosphere of the theatre into the street. He took another decision, grasped her arm firmly, and said: "We're going to have a drink before we do anything at all, it's a terrible evening out." Her arm felt resistant, but remained within his. It was raining outside, luckily. He directed her, authoritative: "No, not that pub, there's a nicer one around the corner." "Oh, but I like this pub," said Barbara, "we always use it."

"Of course you do," he said to himself. But in that pub there would be the stagehands, and probably James, and he'd lose contact with her. He'd become a *journalist* again. He took her firmly out of danger around two corners, into a pub he picked at random. A quick look around—no, they weren't there. At least, if there were people from the theatre, she showed no sign. She asked for a beer. He ordered her a double Scotch, which she accepted. Then, having won a dozen preliminary rounds already, he took time to think. Something was bothering him—what? Yes, it was what he had observed backstage, Barbara and James Poynter. Was she having an affair with him? Because if so, it would all be much more difficult. He made himself see the two of them together, and thought with a jealousy surprisingly strong: *Yes, that's it*. Meantime he sat looking at her, seeing himself look at her, *a man gazing in calm appreciation at a woman:* waiting for her to feel it and respond. She was examining the pub. Her white woollen suit was belted, and had a not unprovocative suggestion of being a uniform. Her flat yellow hair, hastily pushed back after work, was untidy. Her clear white skin, without any colour, made her look tired. Not very exciting, at the moment, thought Graham, but maintaining his appreciative pose for when she would turn and see it. He knew what she would see: he was relying not only on the "warm kindly" beam of his gaze, for this was merely a reinforcement of the impression he knew he made. He had black hair, a little greyed. His clothes were loose and bulky—

masculine. His eyes were humorous and appreciative. He was not, never had been, concerned to lessen the impression of being settled, dependable: the husband and father. On the contrary, he knew women found it reassuring.

When she at last turned she said, almost apologetic: "Would you mind if we sat down? I've been lugging great things around all day." She had spotted two empty chairs in a corner. So had he, but rejected them, because there were other people at the table. "But my dear, of course!" They took the chairs, and then Barbara said: "If you'll excuse me a moment." She had remembered she needed make-up. He watched her go off, annoyed with himself. She was tired; and he could have understood, protected, sheltered. He realised that in the other pub, with the people she had worked with all day, she would not have thought: "I must make myself up, I must be on show." That was for outsiders. She had not, until now, considered Graham an outsider, because of his taking his chance to seem one of the working group in the theatre; but now he had thrown his opportunity away. She returned armoured. Her hair was sleek, no longer defenceless. And she had made up her eyes. Her eyebrows were untouched, pale gold streaks above the brilliant green eyes whose lashes were blackened. Rather good, he thought, the contrast. Yes, but the moment had gone when he could say: Did you know you had a smudge on your cheek? Or—my dear girl!—pushing her hair back with the edge of a brotherly hand. In fact, unless he was careful, he'd be back at starting point.

He remarked: "That emerald is very cunning"—smiling into her eyes.

She smiled politely, and said: "It's not cunning, it's an accident, it was my grandmother's." She flirted her hand lightly by her face, though, smiling. But that was something she had done before, to a compliment she had had before, and often. It was all social, she had become social entirely. She remarked: "Didn't you say it was half past nine we had to record?"

"My dear Barbara, we've got two hours. We'll have another drink or two, then I'll ask you a couple of questions, then we'll drop down to the studio and get it over, and then we'll have a comfortable supper."

"I'd rather eat now, if you don't mind. I had no lunch, and I'm really hungry."

"But my dear, of course." He was angry. Just as he had been surprised by his real jealousy over James, so now he was thrown off balance by his anger: he had been counting on the long quiet dinner afterwards to establish intimacy. "Finish your drink and I'll take you to Nott's." Nott's was expensive. He glanced at her assessingly as he mentioned it. She said: "I wonder if you know Butler's? It's good and it's rather close." Butler's was good, and it was cheap, and he gave her a good mark for liking it. But Nott's it was going to be. "My dear, we'll get into a taxi and be at Nott's in a moment, don't worry."

She obediently got to her feet: the way she did it made him understand how badly he had slipped. She was saying to herself: Very well, he's like that, then all right, I'll do what he wants and get it over with. . . .

Swallowing his own drink he followed her, and took her arm in the pub doorway. It was polite within his. Outside it drizzled. No taxi. He was having bad luck now. They walked in silence to the end of the street. There Barbara glanced into a side street where a sign said: BUTLER'S. Not to remind him of it, on the contrary, she concealed the glance. And here she was, entirely at his disposal, they might never have shared the comradely moment in the theatre.

They walked half a mile to Nott's. No taxis. She made conversation: this was, he saw, to cover any embarrassment he might feel because of a half-mile walk through rain when she was tired. She was talking about some theory to do with the theatre, with designs for theatre building. He heard himself saying, and repeatedly: Yes, yes, yes. He thought about Nott's, how to get things right when they reached Nott's. There he took the head-waiter aside, gave him a pound, and instructions. They were put in a corner. Large Scotches appeared. The menus were spread. "And now, my dear," he said, "I apologise for dragging you here, but I hope you'll think it's worth it."

"Oh, it's charming, I've always liked it. It's just that . . ." She stopped herself saying: it's such a long way. She smiled at him, raising her glass, and said: "It's one of my very favorite places, and I'm glad you dragged me here." Her voice was flat with tiredness. All this was appalling; he knew it; and he sat thinking how to retrieve his position. Meanwhile she fingered the menu. The headwaiter took the order, but Graham made a gesture which said: Wait a moment. He wanted the Scotch to take effect before she ate. But she saw his silent order; and, without annoyance or reproach, leaned forward to say, sounding patient: "Graham, please, I've got to eat, you don't want me drunk when you interview me, do you?"

"They are bringing it as fast as they can," he said, making it sound as if she were greedy. He looked neither at the headwaiter nor at Barbara. He noted in himself, as he slipped further and further away from contact with her, a cold determination growing in him; one apart from, apparently, any conscious act of will, that come what may, if it took all night, he'd be in her bed before morning. And now, seeing the small pale face, with the enormous green eyes, it was for the first time that he imagined her in his arms. Although he had said: *Yes, that one,* weeks ago, it was only now that he imagined her as a sensual experience. Now he did, so strongly that he could only glance at her, and then away towards the waiters who were bringing food.

"Thank the Lord," said Barbara, and all at once her voice was gay and intimate. "Thank heavens. Thank every power that is. . . ." She was making fun of her own exaggeration; and, as he saw, because she wanted to put him at his ease after his boorishness over delaying the food. (She hadn't been taken in, he saw, humiliated, disliking her.) "Thank all the gods of Nott's," she went on, "because if I hadn't eaten inside five minutes I'd have died, I tell you." With which she picked up her knife and fork and began on her steak. He poured wine, smiling with her, thinking that *this* moment of closeness he would not throw away. He watched her frank hunger as she ate, and thought: Sensual—it's strange I hadn't wondered whether she would be or not.

"Now," she said, sitting back, having taken the edge off her hunger: "Let's get to work."

He said: "I've thought it over very carefully—how to present you. The first thing seems to me, we must get away from that old chestnut: Miss Coles, how extraordinary for a woman to be so versatile in her work . . . I hope you agree?" This was his trump card. He had noted, when he had seen her on television, her polite smile when this note was struck. (The smile he had seen so often tonight.) This smile said: All right, if you *have* to be stupid, what can I do?

Now she laughed and said: "What a relief. I was afraid you were going to do the same thing."

"Good, now you eat and I'll talk."

In his carefully prepared monologue he spoke of the different styles of theatre she had shown herself mistress of, but not directly: he was flattering her on the breadth of her experience; the complexity of her character, as shown in her work. She ate, steadily, her face showing nothing. At last she asked: "And how did you plan to introduce this?"

He had meant to spring that on her as a surprise, something like: Miss Coles, a surprisingly young woman for what she has accomplished (she was thirty? thirty-two?) and a very attractive one. . . . "Perhaps I can give you an idea of what she's like if I say she could be taken for the film star Marie Carletta. . . ." The Carletta was a strong earthy blonde, known to be intellectual. He now saw he could not possibly say this: he could imagine her cool look if he did. She said: "Do you mind if we get away from all that—my manifold talents, et cetera. . . ." He felt himself stiffen with annoyance; particularly because this was not an accusation, he saw she did not think him worth one. She had assessed him: This is the kind of man who uses this kind of flattery and therefore. . . . It made him angrier that she did not even trouble to say: Why did you do exactly what you promised you wouldn't? She was being invincibly polite, trying to conceal her patience with his stupidity.

"After all," she was saying, "it is a stage designer's job to design what comes up. Would anyone take, let's say Johnnie Cranmore" (another stage designer) "onto the air or television and say: How very versatile you are because you did that musical about Java last month and a modern play about Irish labourers this?"

He battened down his anger. "My dear Barbara, I'm sorry. I didn't realise that what I said would sound just like the mixture as before. So what shall we talk about?"

"What I was saying as we walked to the restaurant: can we get away from the personal stuff?"

Now he almost panicked. Then, thank God, he laughed from nervousness, for she laughed and said: "You didn't hear one word I said."

"No, I didn't. I was frightened you were going to be furious because I made you walk so far when you were tired."

They laughed together, back to where they had been in the theatre. He leaned over, took her hand, kissed it. He said: "Tell me again." He thought: Damn, now she's going to be earnest and intellectual.

But he understood he had been stupid. He had forgotten himself at twenty—or, for that matter, at thirty; forgotten one could live inside an idea, a set of ideas, with enthusiasm. For in talking about her ideas (also the ideas of the people she worked with) for a new theatre, a new style of theatre, she was as she had been with her colleagues over the sketches or the blue material. She was easy, informal, almost chattering. This was how, he remembered, one talked about ideas that were a breath of life. The ideas, he thought, were intelligent enough; and he would agree with them, with her, if he believed it mattered a damn one way or another, if any of these enthusiasms mattered a damn. But at least he now had the key, he knew what to do. At the end of not more than half an hour, they were again two professionals, talking about ideas they shared, for he remembered caring about all this himself once. *When? How many years ago was it that he had been able to care?*

At last he said: "My dear Barbara, do you realise the impossible position you're putting me in? Margaret Ruyen who runs this programme is determined to do you personally, the poor woman hasn't got a serious thought in her head."

Barbara frowned. He put his hand on hers, teasing her for the frown: "No, wait, trust me, we'll circumvent her." She smiled. In fact Margaret Ruyen had left it all to him, had said nothing about Miss Coles.

"They aren't very bright—the brass," he said. "Well, never mind: we'll work out what we want, do it, and it'll be a *fait accompli*."

"Thank you, what a relief. How lucky I was to be given you to interview me." She was relaxed now, because of the whisky, the food, the wine, above all because of this new complicity against Margaret Ruyen. It would all be easy. They worked out five or six questions, over coffee, and took a taxi through rain to the studios. He noted that the cold necessity to have her, to make her, to beat her down, had left him. He was even seeing himself, as the evening ended, kissing her on the cheek and going home to his wife. This comradeship was extraordinarily pleasant. It was balm to the wound he had not known he carried until that evening, when he had had to accept the justice of the word *journalist*. He felt he could talk forever about the state of the theatre, its finances, the stupidity of the government, the philistinism of . . .

At the studios he was careful to make a joke so that they walked in on the laugh. He was careful that the interview began at once, without conversation with Margaret Ruyen; and that from the moment the green light went on, his voice lost its easy familiarity. He made sure that not one personal note was struck during the interview. Afterwards, Margaret Ruyen, who was pleased, came forward to say so; but he took her aside to say that Miss Coles was tired and needed to be taken home at once: for he knew this must look to Barbara as if he were squaring a producer who had been expecting a different interview. He led Barbara off, her hand held tight in his against his side. "Well," he said, "we've done it, and I don't think she knows what hit her."

"Thank you," she said, "it really was pleasant to talk about something sensible for once."

He kissed her lightly on the mouth. She returned it, smiling. By now he felt sure that the mood need not slip again, he could hold it.

"There are two things we can do," he said. "You can come to my club and have a drink. Or I can drive you home and you can give me a drink. I have to go past you."

"Where do you live?"

"Wimbledon." He lived, in fact, at Highgate; but she lived in Fulham. He was taking another chance, but by the time she found out, they would be in a position to laugh over his ruse.

"Good," she said. "You can drop me home then. I have to get up early." He made no comment. In the taxi he took her hand; it was heavy in his, and he asked: "Does James slave-drive you?"

"I didn't realize you knew him—no, he doesn't."

"Well I don't know him intimately. What's he like to work with?"

"Wonderful," she said at once. "There's no one I enjoy working with more."

Jealousy spurted in him. He could not help himself: "Are you having an affair with him?"

She looked: what's it to do with you? but said: "No, I'm not."

"He's very attractive," he said, with a chuckle of worldly complicity. She said nothing, and he insisted: "If I were a woman I'd have an affair with James."

It seemed she might very well say nothing. But she remarked: ""He's married."

His spirits rose in a swoop. It was the first stupid remark she had made. It was a remark of such staggering stupidity that . . . he let out a humoring snort of laughter, put his arm around her, kissed her, said: "My dear little Babs."

She said: "Why Babs?"

"Is that the prerogative of James. And of the stagehands?" he could not prevent himself adding.

"I'm only called that at work." She was stiff inside his arm.

"My dear Barbara, then . . ." He waited for her to enlighten and explain, but she said nothing. Soon she moved out of his arm, on the pretext of lighting a cigarette. He lit it for her. He noted that his determination to lay her and at all costs, had come back. They were outside her house. He said quickly: "And now, Barbara, you can make me a cup of coffee and give me a brandy." She hesitated; but he was out of the taxi, paying, opening the door for her. The house had no lights on, he noted. He said: "We'll be very quiet so as not to wake the children."

She turned her head slowly to look at him. She said, flat, replying to his real question: "My husband is away. As for the children, they are visiting friends tonight." She now went ahead of him to the door of the house. It was a small house, in a terrace of small and not very pretty houses. Inside a little, bright, intimate hall, she said: "I'll go and make some coffee. Then, my friend, you must go home because I'm very tired."

The *my friend* struck him deep, because he had become vulnerable during their comradeship. He said gabbling: "You're annoyed with me— oh, please don't, I'm sorry."

She smiled, from a cool distance. He saw, in the small light from the ceiling, her extraordinary eyes. "Green" eyes are hazel, are brown with green flecks, are even blue. Eyes are chequered, flawed, changing. Hers were solid green, but really, he had never seen anything like them before. They were like very deep water. They were like—well, emeralds; or the absolute clarity of green in the depths of a tree in summer. And now, as she smiled almost perpendicularly up at him, he saw a darkness come over them. Darkness swallowed the clear green. She said: "I'm not in the least annoyed." It was as if she had yawned with boredom. "And now I'll get the things . . . in there." She nodded at a white door and left him. He went into a long, very tidy white room, that had a narrow bed in one corner, a table covered with drawings, sketches, pencils. Tacked to the walls with drawing pins were swatches of coloured stuffs. Two small chairs stood near a low round table: an area of comfort in the working room. He was thinking: I wouldn't like it if my wife had a room like this. I wonder what Barbara's husband . . .? He had not thought of her till now in relation to her husband, or to her children. Hard to imagine her with a frying pan in her hand, or for that matter, cosy in the double bed.

A noise outside: he hastily arranged himself, leaning with one arm on the mantelpiece. She came in with a small tray that had cups, glasses, brandy, coffeepot. She looked abstracted. Graham was on the whole flattered by this: it probably meant she was at ease in his presence. He realised he was a little tight and rather tired. Of course, she was tired too, that was why she was vague. He remembered that earlier that evening he had lost a chance by not using her tiredness. Well now, if he were intelligent . . . She was about to pour coffee. He firmly took the coffeepot out of her hand, and nodded at a chair. Smiling, she obeyed him. "That's better," he said. He poured coffee, poured brandy, and pulled the table towards her. She watched him. Then he took her hand, kissed it, patted it, laid it down gently. Yes, he thought, I did that well.

Now, a problem. He wanted to be closer to her, but she was fitted into a damned silly little chair that had arms. If he were to sit by her on the floor . . .? But no, for him, the big bulky reassuring man, there could be no casual gestures, no informal postures. Suppose I scoop her out of the chair onto the bed? He drank his coffee as he plotted. Yes, he'd carry her to the bed, but not yet.

"Graham," she said, setting down her cup. She was, he saw with annoyance, looking tolerant. "Graham, in about half an hour I want to be in bed and asleep."

As she said this, she offered him a smile of amusement at this situation—man and woman maneuvering, the great comic situation. And with part of himself he could have shared it. Almost, he smiled with her, laughed. (Not till days later he exclaimed to himself: Lord what a mistake I made, not to share the joke with her then: that was where I went seriously wrong.) But he could not smile. His face was frozen, with a stiff pride. Not because she had been watching him plot; the amusement she now offered him took the sting out of that; but because of his revived determination that he was going to have his own way, he was going to have her. He was not going home. But he felt that he held a bunch of keys, and did not know which one to choose.

He lifted the second small chair opposite to Barbara, moving aside the coffee table for this purpose. He sat in this chair, leaned forward, took her two hands, and said: "My dear, don't make me go home yet, don't, I beg you." The trouble was, nothing had happened all evening that could be felt to lead up to these words and his tone—simple, dignified, human being pleading with human being for surcease. He saw himself leaning forward, his big hands swallowing her small ones; he saw his face, warm with the appeal. And he realised he had meant the words he used. They were nothing more than what he felt. He wanted to stay with her because she wanted him to, because he was her colleague, a fellow worker in the arts. He needed this desperately. But she was examining him, curious rather than surprised, and from a critical distance. He heard himself saying: "If James were here, I wonder what you'd do?" His voice was aggrieved; he saw the sudden dark descend over her eyes, and she said: "Graham, would you like some more coffee before you go?"

He said: "I've been wanting to meet you for years. I know a good many people who know you."

She leaned forward, poured herself a little more brandy, sat back, holding the glass between her two palms on her chest. An odd gesture: Graham felt that this vessel she was cherishing between her hands was herself. A patient, long-suffering gesture. He thought of various men who had mentioned her. He thought of Jack Kennaway, wavered, panicked, said: "For instance, Jack Kennaway."

And now, at the name, an emotion lit her eyes—what was it? He went on, deliberately testing this emotion, adding to it: "I had dinner with him last week—oh, quite by chance!—and he was talking about you."

"Was he?"

He remembered he had thought her sullen, all those years ago. Now she seemed defensive, and she frowned. He said: "In fact he spent most of the evening talking about you."

She said in short, breathless sentences, which he realised were due to anger: "I can very well imagine what he says. But surely you can't think I enjoy being reminded that . . ." She broke off, resenting him, he saw, because he forced her down onto a level she despised. But it was not his level either: it was all her fault, all hers! He couldn't remember not being in control of a situation with a woman for years. Again he felt like a man teetering on a tightrope. He said, trying to make good use of Jack Kennaway, even at this late hour: "Of course, he's a charming boy, but not a man at all."

She looked at him, silent, guarding her brandy glass against her breasts.

"Unless appearances are totally deceptive, of course." He could not resist probing, even though he knew it was fatal.

She said nothing.

"Do you know you are supposed to have had the great affair with Jack Kennaway?" he exclaimed, making this an amused expostulation against the fools who could believe it.

"So I am told." She set down her glass. "And now," she said, standing up, dismissing him. He lost his head, took a step forward, grabbed her in his arms, and groaned: "Barbara!"

She turned her face this way and that under his kisses. He snatched a diagnostic look at her expression—it was still patient. He placed his lips against her neck, groaned "Barbara" again, and waited. She would have to do something. Fight free, respond, something. She did nothing at all. At last she said: "For the Lord's sake, Graham!" She sounded amused: he was again being offered amusement. But if he shared it with her, it would be the end of his chance to have her. He clamped his mouth over hers, silencing her. She did not fight him off so much as blow him off. Her mouth treated his attacking mouth as a woman blows and laughs in water, puffing off waves or spray with a laugh, turning aside her head. It was a gesture half annoyance, half humour. He continued to kiss her while she moved her head and face about under the kisses as if they were small attacking waves.

And so began what, when he looked back on it afterwards, was the most embarrassing experience of his life. Even at the time he hated her for his ineptitude. For he held her there for what must have been nearly half an hour. She was much shorter than he, he had to bend, and his neck ached. He held her rigid, his thighs on either side of hers, her arms clamped to her side in a bear's hug. She was unable to move, except for her head. When his mouth ground hers open and his tongue moved and writhed inside it, she still remained passive. And he could not stop himself. While with his intelligence he watched this ridiculous scene, he was determined to go on, because sooner or later her body must soften in wanting his. And he could not stop because he could not face the horror of the moment when he set her free and she looked at him. And he hated her more, every moment. Catching glimpses of her great green eyes, open and dismal beneath his, he knew he had never disliked anything more than those "jewelled" eyes. They were repulsive to him. It occurred to him at last that even if by now she wanted him, he wouldn't know it, because she was not able to move at all. He cautiously loosened his hold so that she had an inch or so leeway. She remained quite passive. As if, he thought derisively, she had read or been told that the way to incite men maddened by lust was to fight them. He found he was thinking: Stupid cow, so you imagine I find you attractive, do you? You've got the conceit to think that!

The sheer, raving insanity of this thought hit him, opened his arms, his thighs, and lifted his tongue out of her mouth. She stepped back, wiping her mouth with the back of her hand, and stood dazed with incredulity. The embarrassment that lay in wait for him nearly engulfed him, but he let anger postpone it. She said positively apologetic, even, at this moment, humorous: "You're crazy, Graham. What's the matter, are you drunk? You don't seem drunk. You don't even find me attractive."

The blood of hatred went to his head and he gripped her again. Now she had got her face firmly twisted away so that he could not reach her mouth, and she repeated steadily as he kissed the parts of her cheeks and neck that were available to him: "Graham, let me go, do let me go, Graham." She went on saying this; he went on squeezing, grinding, kissing and licking. It might go on all night: it was a sheer contest of wills, nothing else. He thought: It's only a really masculine woman who wouldn't have given in by now out of sheer decency of the flesh! One thing he knew, however: that she would be in that bed, in his arms, and very soon. He let her go, but said: "I'm going to sleep with you tonight, you know that, don't you?"

She leaned with hand on the mantelpiece to steady herself. Her face was colourless, since he had licked all the makeup off. She seemed quite different: small and defenceless with her large mouth pale now, her smudged green eyes fringed with gold. And now, for the first time, he felt what it might have been supposed (certainly by her) he felt hours ago. Seeing the small damp flesh of her face, he felt kinship, intimacy with her, he felt intimacy of the flesh, the affection and good humour of sensuality. He felt she was flesh of his flesh, his sister in the flesh. He felt

DORIS LESSING

desire for her, instead of the will to have her; and because of this, was ashamed of the farce he had been playing. Now he desired simply to take her into bed in the affection of his senses.

She said: "What on earth am I supposed to do? Telephone for the police, or what?" He was hurt that she still addressed the man who had ground her into sulky apathy; she was not addressing *him* at all.

She said: "Or scream for the neighbours, is that what you want?"

The gold-fringed eyes were almost black, because of the depth of the shadow of boredom over them. She was bored and weary to the point of falling to the floor, he could see that.

He said: "I'm going to sleep with you."

"But how can you possibly want to?"—a reasonable, a civilised demand addressed to a man who (he could see) she believed would respond to it. She said: "You know I don't want to, and I know you don't really give a damn one way or the other."

He was stung back into being the boor because she had not the intelligence to see that the boor no longer existed; because she could not see that this was a man who wanted her in a way which she must respond to.

There she stood, supporting herself with one hand, looking small and white and exhausted, and utterly incredulous. She was going to turn and walk off out of simple incredulity, he could see that. "Do you think I don't mean it?" he demanded, grinding this out between his teeth. She made a movement—she was on the point of going away. His hand shot out on its own volition and grasped her wrist. She frowned. His other hand grasped her other wrist. His body hove up against hers to start the pressure of a new embrace. Before it could, she said: "Oh Lord, no, I'm not going through all that again. Right, then."

"What do you mean—right, then?" he demanded.

She said: "You're going to sleep with me. O.K. Anything rather than go through that again. Shall we get it over with?"

He grinned, saying in silence: "No darling, oh no you don't, I don't care what words you use, I'm going to have you now and that's all there is to it."

She shrugged. The contempt, the weariness of it, had no effect on him, because he was now again hating her so much that wanting her was like needing to kill something or someone.

She took her clothes off, as if she were going to bed by herself: her jacket, skirt, petticoat. She stood in white bra and panties, a rather solid girl, brown-skinned still from the summer. He felt a flash of affection for the brown girl with her loose yellow hair as she stood naked. She got into bed and lay there, while the green eyes looked at him in civilised appeal: Are you really going through with this? Do you have to? Yes, his eyes said back: I do have to. She shifted her gaze aside, to the wall, saying silently: Well, if you want to take me without any desire at all on my part, then go ahead, if you're not ashamed. He was not ashamed, because he was maintaining the flame of hate for her which he knew quite well was all that stood between him and shame. He took off his clothes, and got into bed beside her. As he did so, knowing he was putting himself in the position of raping a woman who was making it elaborately clear he bored her, his flesh subsided completely, sad, and full of reproach because a few moments ago it was reaching out for his sister whom he could have made happy. He lay on his side by her, secretly at work on himself, while he supported himself across her body on his elbow, using the free hand to manipulate her breasts. He saw that she gritted her teeth against his touch. At least she could not know that after all this fuss he was not potent.

In order to incite himself, he clasped her again. She felt his smallness, writhed free of him, sat up and said: "Lie down."

While she had been lying there, she had been thinking: The only way to get this over with is to make him big again, otherwise I've got to put up with him all night. His hatred of her was giving him a clairvoyance: he knew very well what went on through her mind. She had switched on, with the determination to *get it all over with,* a sensual good humour, a patience. He lay down. She squatted beside him, the light from the ceiling blooming on her brown shoulders, her flat fair hair falling over her face. But she would not look at his face. Like a bored, skilled wife, she was: or like a prostitute. She administered to him, she was setting herself to please him. Yes, he thought, she's sensual, or she could be. Meanwhile she was succeeding in defeating the reluctance of his flesh, which was the tender token of a possible desire for her, by using a cold skill that was the result of her contempt for him. Just as he decided: Right, it's enough, now I shall have her properly, she made him come. It was not a trick, to hurry or cheat him, what defeated him was her transparent thought: Yes, that's what he's worth.

Then, having succeeded, and waited for a moment or two, she stood up, naked, the fringes of gold at her loins and in her armpits speaking to him a language quite different from that of her green, bored eyes. She looked at him and thought, showing it plainly: What sort of man is it who . . .? He watched the slight movement of her shoulders: a just-checked shrug. She went out of the room: then the sound of running water. Soon she came back in a white dressing gown, carrying a yellow towel. She handed him the towel, looking away in politeness as he used it. "Are you going home now?" she enquired hopefully, at this point.

"No, I'm not." He believed that now he would have to start fighting her again, but she lay down beside him, not touching him (he could feel the distaste of her flesh for his) and he thought: Very well, my dear, but there's a lot of the night left yet. He said aloud: "I'm going to have you properly tonight." She said nothing, lay silent, yawned. Then she remarked consolingly, and he could have laughed outright from sheer surprise: "Those were hardly conducive circumstances for making love." She was *consoling* him. He hated her for it. A proper little slut: I force her into bed, she doesn't want me, but she still has to make me feel good, like a prostitute. But even while he hated her he responded in kind, from the habit of sexual generosity. "It's because of my admiration for you, because . . . after all, I was holding in my arms one of the thousand women."

A pause. "The thousand?" she enquired, carefully.

"The thousand especial women."

"In Britain or in the world? You choose them for their brains, their beauty—what?"

"Whatever it is that makes them outstanding," he said, offering her a compliment.

"Well," she remarked at last, inciting him to be amused again: "I hope that at least there's a short list you can say I am on, for politeness' sake."

He did not reply for he understood he was sleepy. He was still telling himself that he must stay awake when he was slowly waking and it was morning. It was about eight. Barbara was not there. He thought: My God! What on earth shall I tell my wife? Where was Barbara? He remembered the ridiculous scenes of last night and nearly succumbed to shame. Then he thought, reviving anger: If she didn't sleep beside me here I'll never forgive her. . . . He sat up, quietly, determined to go through the house until he found her and, having found her, to possess her, when the door opened and she came in. She was fully dressed in a green suit, her hair done, her eyes made up. She carried a tray of coffee, which she set down beside the bed. He was conscious of his big loose hairy body, half uncovered. He said to himself that he was not going to lie in bed, naked, while she was dressed. He said: "Have you got a gown of some kind?" She handed him, without speaking, a towel, and said: "The bathroom's second on the left." She went out. He followed, the towel around him. Everything in this house was gay, intimate—not at all like her efficient working room. He wanted to find out where she had slept, and opened the first door. It was the kitchen, and she was in it, putting a brown earthenware dish into the oven. "The next door," said Barbara. He went hastily past the second door, and opened (he hoped quietly) the third. It was a cupboard full of linen. "This door," said Barbara, behind him.

"So all right then, where did you sleep?"

"What's it to do with you? Upstairs, in my own bed. Now, if you have everything, I'll say goodbye, I want to get to the theatre."

"I'll take you," he said at once.

He saw again the movement of her eyes, the dark swallowing the light in deadly boredom. "I'll take you," he insisted.

"I'd prefer to go by myself," she remarked. Then she smiled: "However, you'll take me. Then you'll make a point of coming right in, so that James and everyone can see—that's what you want to take me for, isn't it?"

He hated her, finally, and quite simply, for her intelligence; that not once had he got away with anything, that she had been watching, since they

THE SEX OBJECT

338

had met yesterday, every movement of his campaign for her. However, some fate or inner urge over which he had no control made him say sentimentally: "My dear, you must see that I'd like at least to take you to your work."

"Not at all, have it on me," she said, giving him the lie direct. She went past him to the room he had slept in. "I shall be leaving in ten minutes," she said.

He took a shower, fast. When he returned, the workroom was already tidied, the bed made, all signs of the night gone. Also, there were no signs of the coffee she had brought in for him. He did not like to ask for it, for fear of an outright refusal. Besides, she was ready, her coat on, her handbag under her arm. He went, without a word, to the front door, and she came after him, silent.

He could see that every fibre of her body signalled a simple message: Oh God, for the moment when I can be rid of this boor! She was nothing but a slut, he thought.

A taxi came. In it she sat as far away from him as she could. He thought of what he should say to his wife.

Outside the theatre she remarked: "You could drop me here, if you liked." It was not a plea, she was too proud for that. "I'll take you in," he said, and saw her thinking: Very well, I'll go through with it to shame him. He was determined to take her in and hand her over to her colleagues, he was afraid she would give him the slip. But far from playing it down, she seemed determined to play it his way. At the stage door, she said to the doorman: "This is Mr. Spence, Tom—do you remember, Mr. Spence from last night?" "Good morning Babs," said the man, examining Graham, politely, as he had been ordered to do.

Barbara went to the door to the stage, opened it, held it open for him. He went in first, then held it open for her. Together they walked into the cavernous, littered, badly lit place and she called out: "James, James!" A man's voice called out from the front of the house: "Here, Babs, why are you so late?"

The auditorium opened before them, darkish, silent, save for an early-morning busyness of charwomen. A vacuum cleaner roared, smally, somewhere close. A couple of stagehands stood looking up at a drop which had a design of blue and green spirals. James stood with his back to the auditorium, smoking. "You're late, Babs," he said again. He saw Graham behind her, and nodded. Barbara and James kissed. Barbara said, giving allowance to every syllable: "You remember Mr. Spence from last night?" James nodded: How do you do? Barbara stood beside him, and they looked together up at the blue-and-green backdrop. Then Barbara looked again at Graham, asking silently: All right now, isn't that enough? He could see her eyes, sullen with boredom.

He said: "Bye, Babs. Bye, James. I'll ring you, Babs." No response, she ignored him. He walked off slowly, listening for what might be said.

For instance: "Babs, for God's sake, what are you doing with him?" Or she might say: "Are you wondering about Graham Spence? Let me explain."

Graham passed the stagehands who, he could have sworn, didn't recognise him. Then at last he heard James's voice to Barbara: "It's no good, Babs, I know you're enamoured of that particular shade of blue, but do have another look at it, there's a good girl. . . ." Graham left the stage, went past the office where the stage doorman sat reading a newspaper. He looked up, nodded, went back to his paper. Graham went to find a taxi, thinking: I'd better think up something convincing, then I'll telephone my wife.

Luckily he had an excuse not to be at home that day, for this evening he had to interview a young man (for television) about his new novel.

Women
Without Men

Women without men are usually assumed to be so involuntarily. Both in life and in literature they are generally considered to be odd, pitiable, or laughable—and sometimes all three. Edna O'Brien in "The Call" evokes the stereotype of a woman alone, waiting for a man to take the initiative. Being passive as her lover and our society expect her to be, she can only accept the pain his rejection has caused her. O'Brien does not emphasize her heroine's situation as ludicrous; she leaves her with dignity, though fully aware of her weakness and vulnerability. O'Brien's persona learns from her experience that she can start over. As readers we hope that she will not simply repeat her experience with another man. As long as women accept society's verdict that they have no status except through their relationships with men, they will continue to put themselves into the position of being victims. Women will see their need for men without perceiving men's equal need for them, a need calling for free communication instead of the pretense of waiting to be asked. Because of society's heavy condemnation of women without men, resisting the traditional courtship role of the coy lady waiting to be swept off her feet will be difficult; self-assertion and self-definition will be elusive goals for women.

Women who have never "belonged" to a man—old maids—are perceived as ahuman, peculiar beings outside the world of human relations. W. H. Auden's Miss Gee and Mary E. Wilkins Freeman's Louisa Ellis in "A New England Nun" are perceived as having missed out on life; they are observers, not participants. Miss Gee turns her head away as she passes "loving couples" who do not ask her to stay; Louisa turns with relief from the prospect of marriage, happy to see her fiancé in love with a younger woman. The cancer that consumes Miss Gee and the dog that Louisa keeps chained up and feeds only "corn-mush and cakes" symbolize these women's "foiled creative fire" and invite the reader's pity. Yet the reader is also asked to see these women as absurd. The images of Miss Gee bicycling through a field pursued by a bull and of Louisa sweeping up after Joe are ludicrous as well as pathetic. They seem beyond human charity. The Oxford Groupers, members of a religious organization teaching the original Christian doctrine of charity, dissect the body of Miss Gee. Images of narrowness and waste—sewing and resewing a seam—invite us to see Louisa's decision to live alone as a refusal really to live. Yet Louisa's choice can be viewed as the beginning of a richer life. Though she "dies to the world" as a nun does upon taking her vows, it is arrogant to conclude that being herself and living on her own terms in a world she has created for herself are a diminishment of life. Many an overworked wife living with a demanding mother-in-law, as Louisa's successor will have to do, would envy her her freedom. One could hardly envy Miss Gee; yet to imply that a childless woman is comparable to a retired man—both are subject to cancer—is to assert that motherhood is the only means for a woman to achieve humanity, that to be flat-chested, sterile, and unwanted by men is not to live at all. Auden's poem is a clear statement that, for women, anatomy is destiny.

Sarah Orne Jewett lets us see in "Aunt Cynthy Dallet" the kind of life Louisa might achieve if she lives to be old. Aunt Cynthy enjoys keeping up the tradition of gift-giving on New Year's Day, as she has enjoyed living most of her life alone, isolated on a mountain. An elderly niece, perceiving Aunt Cynthy's need for some help in her extreme old age, saves her aunt's pride by making the proposal to move in with her seem to stem only from the niece's needs. The other characters in the story feel nothing but admiration for Aunt Cynthy. Since the niece's need for a place to stay is very genuine and Aunt Cynthy sees herself as helping her niece, the story ends happily for both women, though both give up their solitude with regret. The persona of Denise Levertov's three-part poem "Living Alone" admits in the second part to moods of depression when solitude oppresses her. But depression gives way to the feeling that being alone and able to hear silence is like a return to childhood when the idea that anything can happen is exhilarating. Levertov's solitary person shares in the general human sense of renewal symbolized by the return of life in the spring; one feels that her solitude is an epitome of the true human condition.

Colette's story "The Other Wife" shows that, from a woman's perspective, life without a man can indeed be attractive. Alice cannot feel pity for or superiority toward her husband's divorced first wife, whom they see sitting alone in a busy restaurant. Though the first wife is not "having a madly gay time," as Alice is, Alice sees her as a "superior woman" because she has left a husband she disliked living with. Alice begins to doubt her own good fortune in having married him; she sees the first wife's freedom as desirable and her own position as "dubious." Similarly, in Kate Chopin's "The Story of an Hour," the stereotype of the widow as a pitiful, inadequate woman is reversed when we see the protagonist fully happy during the hour when she accepts as true an erroneous report of her husband's death. She and the bride of Colette's story glimpse tantalizingly the attractiveness of life without men.

James Tiptree, Jr. (Alice Sheldon) goes further and gives us an image of women choosing to live completely away from men as a welcome alternative to their mundane lives as the workers who keep the world going but remain invisible to the men who are their bosses. The mother and daughter prefer an unknown destiny on a distant planet to playing their secondary role on earth. The male narrator finds such a choice incredible, though he marveled at the self-sufficiency and competence of the women when their plane crashed. This story expresses a major fear about women's liberation: that if they become independent, women will desert men. The fear seems well grounded if women are limited to their traditional roles.

Another fear that has become the source of powerful opposition to women's autonomy is that they will prefer women to men. Several of the works in this section show that such a preference can exist without necessarily being a threat to men. For example, older women are likely to be without men simply because they outlive them. The deep sense of unity experienced by the two older women in May Sarton's "Joy in Provence" transcends gender; their love goes beyond the physical to a sense of shared wisdom, of a communication that enables both of them to hear a voice that tells them to rejoice in life itself.

Jane Rule's "Middle Children" presents the choice of two women to live together as lovers as being the perfectly natural and logical outcome of their early life situations. Coming from large families where they had little parental attention and many responsibilities, they both know too much about the wife-mother role to want it for themselves. Discovering their common attitudes as college roommates, they continue to live together, "falling in love . . . gradually," and coming to the full expression of their sexuality. All of this is done "so tactfully that no one ever noticed it." And with compassion for friends caught in the marriage trap, they act as an "extended family" for them. The lovers' private happiness enables them to reach out to help others, including college boys and gay male couples.

In Judy Grahn's poem, the life Carol has chosen is viewed as shocking, even alarming by the speakers; they see her lesbian sexual preference as one they are thankful not to have made. The focus of the poem is on Carol's inner feelings, however; competent at work and in tasks at home, she harbors a dream of a freedom to live up to her full potential, to survive passivity and the need for any material support. Not yet being free, she keeps her anger "inside a passive form," ready to explode as if in a thunderstorm. Carol, like Rule's couple, is naturally what she is; but she is made to falsify her feelings because of attitudes like those held by the speakers.

In "Artemis," Olga Broumas openly expresses the joy of a lesbian relationship, emphasizing the special quality of loving a body that has "twin / chromosome ribbons" like one's own. Responding to her lover's body, the speaker, like Sarton's, feels in touch with a mystery "that defies / decoding." The clue to the mystery is the initial of her own name, which she perceives as significant, as part of the "curviform alphabet" of the two female bodies.

All of these works resist the stereotype that women without men are deprived. Here we see individual human beings, capable of meeting life on their own terms. That other individual women may have different experiences is exemplified in William Carlos Williams's poem "The Widow's Lament in Springtime." A woman who has shared her life with a man for thirty-five years may well feel as does this widow, for whom the return of spring brings the same mood as it does to Levertov's persona in the second part of "Living Alone." But for most widows—or for anyone who suffers the loss of a loved companion—this mood does pass; recognizing grief as a process enables us to reject the stereotype of the useless, dependent elderly widow as we do that of the old maid. Being alone is part of the human condition, and women seem more likely to experience it than men, either through choice or longevity. This likelihood merely confirms the humanity of women.

The capacity of woman to be fully human is also revealed in "The Burning," Estela Portillo Trambley's story of cruelty, based on fear, shown by a group of women to an old dying woman who has lived beneficently among them since girlhood. Because she came from a different tribe, she had always been alone, even though among them. She herself chose solitude when young, like Levertov's persona, who admits that "[s]olitude within multitude seduced me early." Trambley is drawing on myth to remind us that groups of women, like groups of men, can seek scapegoats for their own feelings. Her story is a reminder that power corrupts without respect to gender. It is a *system* of dominance that is the common enemy of women and men.

THE CALL

by

EDNA O'BRIEN

(b. 1932)

Born in County Clare, Ireland, Edna O'Brien studied pharmacy in Dublin. After moving to London she began to write fiction. Since 1960, a novel, play, or collection of short stories has appeared about every other year. Some of these have been filmed, and she has also written movie and television scripts. Known at first for her comic bawdiness, she has become increasingly concerned about women's dilemmas, both sexual and personal. She has written a play about the life of Virginia Woolf (1980) and James and Nora: A Portrait of Joyce's Marriage *(1981).*

She would be, or so she thought, over it—over the need and over the hope and over the certainty of that invisible bond that linked them—when suddenly it would come back. It was like a storm. She would start to shake. One morning, this frenzy made her almost blind, so that she could hardly see the design on the teacup she was washing, and even the simple suds in the aluminum sink seemed to enclose a vast pool of woe. When she saw two pigeons in the plane tree outside, it smote her heart because they were cooing and because they were close. Then her telephone rang in the other room. Going to answer it, with the tea cloth in her hand, she prayed, "Oh, God, let it be him," and in a sense her prayers were answered, though she could not be sure, because by the time she got to it whoever it was had rung off. She waited, trembling. It—he—would ring again.

There was sun on the trees in the garden outside, and the varying greenness of each tree was singled out and emphasized in the brightness. There was a dark green, which emitted a gloom that seemed to come from its very interior; there was a pale green, which spoke of happiness and limes; and there was the holly leaf so shiny it might have just been polished. There was the lilac, shedding and rusted because of the recent heavy rain, and the hanging mauve blooms gave the effect of having dropsy. And all of these greens seemed to tell her of her condition—of how it varied, of how sometimes she was not rallying and then again sometimes she would pass to another state, a relatively bright and buoyant state, and sometimes, indeed, she had dropsy. Yet he was not ringing back. But why? Ah, yes. She knew why. He did not care to lose face, and by ringing immediately it would be evident that it had been him. So she busied herself with little chores. She drained the dishes and then dried them thoroughly. Her face on their shining surfaces looked distorted. Just as well he was not coming! She took the loose fallen petals of sweet pea from a vase on the window ledge and squeezed them as if to squeeze the last bit of color and juice out of them. After twenty minutes of devoting herself to pointless trivia, to errands into which she read talismanic import, she decided that he was not going to ring, and so to put herself out of her misery she must ring him. He had lately given her the number. He had repeated it twice and when last leaving he had said it again. For six months he had kept it a secret. It was his work number. He would not, of course, give her his home number, since it was also his wife's. So why not ring? Why not? Because she found herself shaking before even attempting to dial. She foresaw how she would speak rapidly and hurriedly and ask him to lunch, and suppose he said no. She would wait for half an hour and then she would ring.

In that half hour, her whole body seemed to lose its poise and its strength. She felt sick and ashamed, as if she had done some terrible wrong— some childish wrong like wetting or soiling her bed—and she sought to find the root of this pointless notion of wrongdoing that was connected with an excruciating wait. She thought of previous times when she had been spurned by others and tried to marshal in herself the pride, the fury, the common sense that would cause her not to lay herself at his feet. She thought of the day when she would learn to get by—maybe learn to swim—and for an instant she saw herself thrashing through a pool and kicking and conquering. She said, "If I ring, does it not make me the stronger one?" Her words were hollow to herself. The sun shone, yet her house had a coldness—the coldness of a vault, the coldness when you press yourself on the tiled floor of an empty dark country chapel and beg your Maker to help you in these straits—and for no reason there crowded in on her mind images of a wedding, a slow procession down the aisle, a baptismal font with a rim of rust on its marble base, religious booklets about keeping company, and in the chapel porch an umbrella with one spoke protruding. In imagination she went out the gravelled path under the yew trees and smelled their solemn, permeating perfume. She thought, Yesterday I could do without him, today I can't. And then she remonstrated, You can.

She was going on a train that afternoon, to the country, and once on the train, no matter how great her unhappiness, she could not succumb to a frenzy. She thought, too, that if she rang him once she might ring him at all hours, she might make a habit of it. If only he would sit opposite her, take her hand, and tell her that he had no interest in her, then she believed that she would be free to let him go. . . . Or was he going? Was she herself becoming narked? She saw him once a fortnight, but that was not enough. These clandestine visits were the crumbs of the marriage table. The making do with nearly nothing. Where was the bounty of it? Where the abandon?

"You are what you are," she said. But did others have to suffer so? Did others lie down and almost expire under such longing? No. Others swam; others went far out to sea, others dived, others put oxygen flagons on their backs and went down into the depths of the ocean and saw the life there—the teeming, impersonal life—and detached themselves from the life up above. She feared that her love of nature—her love of woodland, her love of sun on hillside and meadow, her love of wild flowers and dog roses and cow parsley, her love of the tangled hedgerows—was only an excuse, a solace. Mortal love was what she craved.

She imagined how he would come and pass her by in the hall, being too shy to shake hands, and walk around the room inhaling her while also trying to observe by the jug of fresh flowers or the letters on her desk who had been here recently, and if perhaps she had found a lover. He had commanded her to, and had also commanded her not to. Always when he lay above her, about to possess her, he seemed to be surveying his pasture, to sniff like a bloodhound, making sure that no other would pass through to his burrow, making sure that she would be secret and sweet, and solely for him.

Ah, would that they were out on a hillside, or in the orchards of her youth, away from telephone calls or no telephone calls, away from suspicions, where he believed she wore perfume deliberately so his wife would guess his guilty secret. She was watching the face of her telephone, following with her eye the circle of congealed dust about the digits, where fingernail never reached nor duster ever strove; watching and praying. She heard a letter being pushed through her box and she ran to get it. Any errand was a mercy, a distraction, a slender way of postponing what she would do but must not do.

The letter was from a stranger. It bore a scape of a blue sea, a high craggy cliff, and a flying bird. The message said, "I thought this to be the bluebird of happiness but fear it might only be a common pigeon." It wished her happiness and to be well. It was signed, "A WELL-WISHER, MALE." She thought, Oh, Christ, the whole world knows of my stew, and she wondered calmly if this union she craved was something that others, wiser ones, had forgone—had left behind at their mothers' breasts, never to be retasted—and she thought of her dead mother with her hair tautly pinned up and of the wall of unvoiced but palpable hostility that had grown between them. She hoped then that she would be the same toward her man one day, withdrawn, cut off from him. Her mother's visage brought tears to her eyes. They were different tears from the ones she had been shedding earlier. They were a hot burst of uncontrolled grief that within minutes had sluiced her face and streamed over into her temples and wet her hair.

The half hour had passed in which she promised herself that she would ring him, and now she was talking to herself as to an addict, saying could she not wait a bit longer, could her longing not be diverted by work or a walk, could she not assuage the lump inside her throat by swallowing warmed honey on it, so that the syrup would slide down and soothe her. The needless pain there seemed to be intensified, as if a sharp current were passing through her. Could she not put it off until the morrow?

There is no stopping a galloping horse.

She went toward the telephone, and, as she did, it began to ring. It rang loudly. It rang like some tutelary ogre, telling her to pick it up quickly, telling her that it was the master of her fate, of her every moment, of the privacy of her room, of the tangle of her thoughts, of the weight of her desire, and of the enormity of her hope. She did not answer it. She did not know why she did not answer it. She simply knew that she could not answer it, and that she waited for its ringing to die down the way one waits for the ambulance siren to move out of one's hearing, to pass to the next street.

"Is this love?" she asked herself, admitting that she had wanted so much to answer it. The longing to see him, communicate with him, clasp her fingers in his, feed him, humor him, and watch him while he ran a comb through his hair was as strong and as candescent as it had ever been.

"You had better go out now," she said aloud, and quickly, but with a certain ceremony, she put an embroidered shawl over the phone, to muffle its sound.

It would be three days before she came back, and she saw a strip of water that would get wider and wider. Green and turbulent it was, and in time, she knew, it would swell into a vast sea, impassable and with no shore in sight. Time would sever them, but as yet it was love, and hard to banish.

MISS GEE

by

W. H. AUDEN

(1907–1973)

Born in England, W. H. Auden became a U.S. citizen in 1939 and divided his time between the two countries and a summer home in Austria. A major American poet, Auden turned from his early interest in Marxism to a deep commitment to Christianity; his long poem For the Time Being *(1941) expresses his belief in the need for faith in our time. His poems, many of which are light in tone, reflect a wide interest in politics, literature, and music. His last poems,* Thank You, Fog, *were published posthumously in 1975.*

Let me tell you a little story
    About Miss Edith Gee;
She lived in Clevedon Terrace
    At Number 83.

She'd a slight squint in her left eye,
    Her lips they were thin and small,
She had narrow sloping shoulders
    And she had no bust at all.

She'd a velvet hat with trimmings,
    And a dark-grey serge costume;
She lived in Clevedon Terrace
    In a small bed-sitting room.

She'd a purple mac for wet days,
    A green umbrella too to take,
She'd a bicycle with shopping basket
    And a harsh back-pedal brake.

The Church of Saint Aloysius
    Was not so very far;
She did a lot of knitting,
    Knitting for that Church Bazaar.

Miss Gee looked up at the starlight
    And said: 'Does anyone care
That I live in Clevedon Terrace
    On one hundred pounds a year?'

She dreamed a dream one evening
    That she was the Queen of France
And the Vicar of Saint Aloysius
    Asked Her Majesty to dance.

But a storm blew down the palace,
    She was biking through a field of corn,
And a bull with the face of the Vicar
    Was charging with lowered horn.

She could feel his hot breath behind her,
    He was going to overtake;
And the bicycle went slower and slower
    Because of that back-pedal brake.

Summer made the trees a picture,
    Winter made them a wreck;
She bicycled to the evening service
    With her clothes buttoned up to her neck.

She passed by the loving couples,
    She turned her head away;
She passed by the loving couples
    And they didn't ask her to stay.

Miss Gee sat down in the side-aisle,
    She heard the organ play;
And the choir it sang so sweetly
    At the ending of the day,

Miss Gee knelt down in the side-aisle,
    She knelt down on her knees;
'Lead me not into temptation
    But make me a good girl, please.'

The days and nights went by her
    Like waves round a Cornish wreck;
She bicycled down to the doctor
    With her clothes buttoned up to her neck.

She bicycled down to the doctor,
    And rang the surgery bell;
'O, doctor, I've a pain inside me,
    And I don't feel very well.'

Doctor Thomas looked her over,
    And then he looked some more;
Walked over to his wash-basin,
    Said, 'Why didn't you come before?'

Doctor Thomas sat over his dinner,
    Though his wife was waiting to ring;
Rolling his bread into pellets,
    Said, 'Cancer's a funny thing.

'Nobody knows what the cause is,
    Though some pretend they do;
It's like some hidden assassin
    Waiting to strike at you.

'Childless women get it,
    And men when they retire;
It's as if there had to be some outlet
    For their foiled creative fire.'

His wife she rang for the servant,
    Said, 'Don't be so morbid, dear,'
He said; 'I saw Miss Gee this evening
    And she's a goner, I fear.'

W. H. AUDEN

They took Miss Gee to the hospital,
    She lay there a total wreck,
Lay in the ward for women
    With the bedclothes right up to her neck.

They laid her on the table,
    The students began to laugh;
And Mr. Rose the surgeon
    He cut Miss Gee in half.

Mr. Rose he turned to his students,
    Said; 'Gentlemen, if you please,
We seldom see a sarcoma
    As far advanced as this.'

They took her off the table,
    They wheeled away Miss Gee
Down to another department
    Where they study Anatomy.

They hung her from the ceiling,
    Yes, they hung up Miss Gee;
And a couple of Oxford Groupers
    Carefully dissected her knee.

A NEW ENGLAND NUN

by

MARY E. WILKINS FREEMAN

(1852–1930)

Mary E. Wilkins Freeman wrote many novels and short stories about the frustrations of life in New England small towns, a subject she knew firsthand. Her short-story collections include A Humble Romance and Other Stories *(1887)*, A New England Nun and Other Stories *(1891)*, and The Wind in the Rose Bush *(1903)*. Many of these and several of her novels, such as* Jane Field *(1893), depict realistically the everyday life of women. Her works have recently been seriously studied by feminist critics.*

•────────────────────────────•

It was late in the afternoon, and the light was waning. There was a difference in the look of the tree shadows out in the yard. Somewhere in the distance cows were lowing and a little bell was tinkling; now and then a farm-wagon tilted by, and the dust flew; some blue-shirted laborers with shovels over their shoulders plodded past; little swarms of flies were dancing up and down before the people's faces in the soft air. There seemed to be a gentle stir arising over everything for the mere sake of subsidence— a very premonition of rest and hush and night.

This soft diurnal commotion was over Louisa Ellis also. She had been peacefully sewing at her sitting-room window all the afternoon. Now she quilted her needle carefully into her work, which she folded precisely, and laid in a basket with her thimble and thread and scissors. Louisa Ellis could not remember that ever in her life she had mislaid one of these little feminine appurtenances, which had become, from long use and constant association, a very part of her personality.

Louisa tied a green apron round her waist, and got out a flat straw hat with a green ribbon. Then she went into the garden with a little blue crockery bowl, to pick some currants for her tea. After the currants were picked she sat on the back door-step and stemmed them, collecting the stems carefully in her apron, and afterward throwing them into the hen-coop. She looked sharply at the grass beside the step to see if any had fallen there.

Louisa was slow and still in her movements; it took her a long time to prepare her tea; but when ready it was set forth with as much grace as if she had been a veritable guest to her own self. The little square table stood exactly in the centre of the kitchen, and was covered with a starched linen cloth whose border pattern of flowers glistened. Louisa had a damask napkin on her tea-tray, where were arranged a cut-glass tumbler full of teaspoons, a silver cream-pitcher, a china sugar-bowl, and one pink china cup and saucer. Louisa used china every day—something which none of her neighbors did. They whispered about it among themselves. Their daily tables were laid with common crockery, their sets of best china stayed in the parlor closet, and Louisa Ellis was no richer nor better bred than they. Still she would use the china. She had for her supper a glass dish full of sugared currants, a plate of little cakes, and one of light white biscuits. Also a leaf or two of lettuce, which she cut up daintily. Louisa was very fond of lettuce, which she raised to perfection in her little garden. She ate quite heartily, though in a delicate, pecking way; it seemed almost surprising that any considerable bulk of the food should vanish.

After tea she filled a plate with nicely baked thin corn-cakes, and carried them out into the back-yard.

"Caesar!" she called. "Caesar! Caesar!"

There was a little rush, and the clank of a chain, and a large yellow-and-white dog appeared at the door of his tiny hut, which was half hidden among the tall grasses and flowers. Louisa patted him and gave him the corn-cakes. Then she returned to the house and washed the tea-things, polishing the china carefully. The twilight had deepened; the chorus of the frogs floated in at the open window wonderfully loud and shrill, and once in a while a long sharp drone from a tree-toad pierced it. Louisa took off her green gingham apron, disclosing a shorter one of pink-and-white print. She lighted her lamp, and sat down again with her sewing.

In about half an hour Joe Dagget came. She heard his heavy step on the walk, and rose and took off her pink-and-white apron. Under that was still another—white linen with a little cambric edging on the bottom; that was Louisa's company apron. She never wore it without her calico sewing apron over it unless she had a guest. She had barely folded the pink and white one with methodical haste and laid it in a table-drawer when the door opened and Joe Dagget entered.

He seemed to fill up the whole room. A little yellow canary that had been asleep in his green cage at the south window woke up and fluttered wildly, beating his little yellow wings against the wires. He always did so when Joe Dagget came into the room.

"Good-evening," said Louisa. She extended her hand with a kind of solemn cordiality.

"Good-evening, Louisa," returned the man, in a loud voice.

She placed a chair for him, and they sat facing each other, with the table between them. He sat bolt-upright, toeing out his heavy feet squarely, glancing with a good-humored uneasiness around the room. She sat gently erect, folding her slender hands in her white-linen lap.

"Been a pleasant day," remarked Dagget.

"Real pleasant," Louisa assented softly. "Have you been haying?" she asked, after a little while.

"Yes, I've been haying all day, down in the ten-acre lot. Pretty hot work."

"It must be."

"Yes, it's pretty hot work in the sun."

"Is your mother well to-day?"

"Yes, mother's pretty well."

"I suppose Lily Dyer's with her now?"

Dagget colored. "Yes, she's with her," he answered slowly.

He was not very young, but there was a boyish look about his large face. Louisa was not quite as old as he, her face was fairer and smoother, but she gave people the impression of being older.

"I suppose she's a good deal of help to your mother," she said, further.

"I guess she is; I don't know how mother'd get along without her," said Dagget, with a sort of embarrassed warmth.

"She looks like a real capable girl. She's pretty-looking too," remarked Louisa.

"Yes, she is pretty fair looking."

Presently Dagget began fingering the books on the table. There was a square red autograph album, and a Young Lady's Gift-Book which had belonged to Louisa's mother. He took them up one after the other and opened them; then laid them down again, the album on the Gift-Book.

Louisa kept eying them with mild uneasiness. Finally she rose and changed the position of the books, putting the album underneath. That was the way they had been arranged in the first place.

Dagget gave an awkward little laugh. "Now what difference did it make which book was on top?" said he.

Louisa looked at him with a deprecating smile. "I always keep them that way," murmured she.

"You do beat everything," said Dagget, trying to laugh again. His large face was flushed.

He remained about an hour longer, then rose to take leave. Going out, he stumbled over a rug, and trying to recover himself, hit Louisa's work-basket on the table, and knocked it on the floor.

He looked at Louisa, then at the rolling spools; he ducked himself awkwardly toward them, but she stopped him. "Never mind," said she; "I'll pick them up after you're gone."

She spoke with a mild stiffness. Either she was a little disturbed, or his nervousness affected her, and made her seem constrained in her effort to reassure him.

When Joe Dagget was outside he drew in the sweet evening air with a sigh, and felt much as an innocent and perfectly well-intentioned bear might after his exit from a china shop.

Louisa, on her part, felt much as the kind-hearted, long-suffering owner of the china shop might have done after the exit of the bear.

She tied on the pink, then the green apron, picked up all the scattered treasures and replaced them in her work-basket, and straightened the rug. Then she set the lamp on the floor, and began sharply examining the carpet. She even rubbed her fingers over it, and looked at them.

"He's tracked in a good deal of dust," she murmured. "I thought he must have."

Louisa got a dust-pan and brush, and swept Joe Dagget's track carefully.

If he could have known it, it would have increased his perplexity and uneasiness, although it would not have disturbed his loyalty in the least. He came twice a week to see Louisa Ellis, and every time, sitting there in her delicately sweet room, he felt as if surrounded by a hedge of lace. He was afraid to stir lest he should put a clumsy foot or hand through the fairy web, and he had always the consciousness that Louisa was watching fearfully lest he should.

Still the lace and Louisa commanded perforce his perfect respect and patience and loyalty. They were to be married in a month, after a singular courtship which had lasted for a matter of fifteen years. For fourteen out of the fifteen years the two had not once seen each other, and they had seldom exchanged letters. Joe had been all those years in Australia, where he had gone to make his fortune, and where he had stayed until he made it. He would have stayed fifty years if it had taken so long, and come home feeble and tottering, or never come home at all, to marry Louisa.

But the fortune had been made in the fourteen years, and he had come home now to marry the woman who had been patiently and unquestioningly waiting for him all that time.

Shortly after they were engaged he had announced to Louisa his determination to strike out into new fields, and secure a competency before they should be married. She had listened and assented with the sweet serenity which never failed her, not even when her lover set forth on that long and uncertain journey. Joe, buoyed up as he was by his sturdy determination, broke down a little at the last, but Louisa kissed him with a mild blush, and said good-by.

"It won't be for long," poor Joe had said, huskily; but it was for fourteen years.

In that length of time much had happened. Louisa's mother and brother had died, and she was all alone in the world. But greatest happening of all—a subtle happening which both were too simple to understand—Louisa's feet had turned into a path, smooth maybe under a calm, serene sky, but so straight and unswerving that it could only meet a check at the grave, and so narrow that there was no room for any one at her side.

Louisa's first emotion when Joe Dagget came home (he had not apprised her of his coming) was consternation, although she would not admit it to herself, and he never dreamed of it. Fifteen years ago she had been in love with him—at least she considered herself to be. Just at that time, gently acquiescing with and falling into the natural drift of girlhood, she had seen marriage ahead as a reasonable future and a probable desirability of life. She had listened with calm docility to her mother's views upon the subject. Her mother was remarkable for her cool sense and sweet, even temperament. She talked wisely to her daughter when Joe Dagget presented himself, and Louisa accepted him with no hesitation. He was the first lover she had ever had.

She had been faithful to him all these years. She had never dreamed of the possibility of marrying any one else. Her life, especially for the last seven years, had been full of a pleasant peace, she had never felt discontented nor impatient over her lover's absence; still she had always looked forward to his return and their marriage as the inevitable conclusion of things. However, she had fallen into a way of placing it so far in the future that it was almost equal to placing it over the boundaries of another life.

When Joe came she had been expecting him, and expecting to be married for fourteen years, but she was as much surprised and taken aback as if she had never thought of it.

Joe's consternation came later. He eyed Louisa with an instant confirmation of his old admiration. She had changed but little. She still kept her pretty manner and soft grace, and was, he considered, every whit as attractive as ever. As for himself, his stint was done; he had his face turned away from fortune-seeking, and the old winds of romance whistled as loud and sweet as ever through his ears. All the song which he had been wont to hear in them was Louisa; he had for a long time a loyal belief that he heard it still, but finally it seemed to him that although the winds sang always that one song, it had another name. But for Louisa the wind had never more than murmured; now it had gone down, and everything was still. She listened for a little while with half-wistful attention; then she turned quietly away and went to work on her wedding clothes.

Joe had made some extensive and quite magnificent alterations in his house. It was the old homestead; the newly-married couple would live there, for Joe could not desert his mother, who refused to leave her old home. So Louisa must leave hers. Every morning, rising and going about among her neat maidenly possessions, she felt as one looking her last upon the faces of dear friends. It was true that in a measure she could take them with her, but, robbed of their old environments, they would appear in such new guises that they would almost cease to be themselves. Then there were some peculiar features of her happy solitary life which she would probably be obliged to relinquish altogether. Sterner tasks than these graceful but half-needless ones would probably devolve upon her. There would be a large house to care for; there would be company to entertain; there would be Joe's rigorous and feeble old mother to wait upon; and it would be contrary to all thrifty village traditions for her to keep more than one servant. Louisa had a little still, and she used to occupy herself pleasantly in summer weather with distilling the sweet aromatic essences from roses and peppermint and spearmint. By-and-by her still must be laid away. Her store of essences was already considerable, and there would be no time for her to distil for the mere pleasure of it. Then Joe's mother would think it foolishness; she had already hinted her opinion in the matter. Louisa dearly loved to sew a linen seam, not always for use, but for the simple, mild pleasure which she took in it. She would have been loath to confess how more than once she had ripped a seam for the mere delight of sewing it together again. Sitting at her window during long sweet afternoons, drawing her needle gently through the dainty fabric, she was peace itself. But there was small chance of such foolish comfort in the future. Joe's mother, domineering, shrewd old matron that she was even in her old age, and very likely even Joe himself, with his honest masculine rudeness, would laugh and frown down all these pretty but senseless old maiden ways.

Louisa had almost the enthusiasm of an artist over the mere order and cleanliness of her solitary home. She had throbs of genuine triumph at the sight of the window-panes which she had polished until they shone like jewels. She gloated gently over her orderly bureau-drawers, with their exquisitely folded contents redolent with lavender and sweet clover and very purity. Could she be sure of the endurance of even this? She had visions, so startling that she half repudiated them as indelicate, of coarse masculine belongings strewn about in endless litter; of dust and disorder arising necessarily from a coarse masculine presence in the midst of all this delicate harmony.

Among her forebodings of disturbance, not the least was with regard to Caesar. Caesar was a veritable hermit of a dog. For the greater part of his life he had dwelt in his secluded hut, shut out from the society of his kind and all innocent canine joys. Never had Caesar since his early youth watched at a woodchuck's hole; never had he known the delights of a stray bone at a neighbor's kitchen door. And it was all on account of a sin committed when hardly out of his puppyhood. No one knew the possible depth of remorse of which this mild-visaged, altogether innocent-looking old dog might be capable; but whether or not he had encountered remorse, he had encountered a full measure of righteous retribution. Old Caesar seldom lifted up his voice in a growl or a bark; he was fat and sleepy; there were yellow rings which looked like spectacles around his dim old eyes; but there was a neighbor who bore on his hand the imprint of several of Caesar's sharp white youthful teeth, and for that he had lived at the end of a chain, all alone in a little hut, for fourteen years. The neighbor, who was choleric and smarting with the pain of his wound, had demanded either Caesar's death or complete ostracism. So Louisa's brother, to whom the dog had belonged, had built him his little kennel and tied him up. It was now fourteen years since, in a flood of youthful spirits, he had inflicted that memorable bite, and with the exception of short excursions, always at the end of the chain, under the strict guardianship of his master or Louisa, the old dog had remained a close prisoner. It is doubtful if, with his limited ambition, he took much pride in the fact, but it is certain that he was possessed of considerable cheap fame. He was regarded by all the children in the village and by many adults as a very monster of ferocity. St. George's dragon could hardly have surpassed in evil repute Louisa Ellis's old yellow dog. Mothers charged their children with solemn emphasis not to go too near to him, and the children listened and believed greedily, with a fascinated appetite for terror, and ran by Louisa's house stealthily, with many sidelong glances at the terrible dog. If perchance he sounded a hoarse bark, there was a panic. Wayfarers chancing into Louisa's yard eyed him with respect, and inquired if the chain were stout. Caesar at large might have seemed a very ordinary dog, and excited no comment whatever; chained, his reputation overshadowed him, so that he lost his own proper outlines and looked darkly vague and enormous. Joe Dagget, however, with his good-humored sense and shrewdness, saw him as he was. He strode valiantly up to him and patted him on the head, in spite of Louisa's soft clamor of warning, and even attempted to set him loose. Louisa grew so alarmed that he desisted, but kept announcing his opinion in the matter quite forcibly at intervals. "There ain't a better-natured dog in town," he would say, "and it's down-right cruel to keep him tied up there. Some day I'm going to take him out."

Louisa had very little hope that he would not, one of these days, when their interests and possessions should be more completely fused in one. She pictured to herself Caesar on the rampage through the quiet and unguarded village. She saw innocent children bleeding in his path. She was herself very fond of the old dog, because he had belonged to her dead brother, and he was always very gentle with her; still she had great faith in his ferocity. She always warned people not to go too near him. She fed him on ascetic fare of corn-mush and cakes, and never fired his dangerous temper with heating and sanguinary diet of flesh and bones. Louisa looked at the old dog munching his simple fare, and thought of her approaching marriage and trembled. Still no anticipation of disorder and confusion in lieu of sweet peace and harmony, no forebodings of Caesar on the rampage, no wild fluttering of her little yellow canary, were sufficient to turn her a hair's breadth. Joe Dagget had been fond of her and working for her all these years. It was not for her, whatever came to pass, to prove untrue and break his heart. She put the exquisite little stitches into her wedding-garments, and the time went on till it was only a week before her wedding-day. It was a Tuesday evening, and the wedding was to be a week from Wednesday.

There was a full moon that night. About nine o'clock Louisa strolled down the road a little way. There were harvest-fields on either hand, bordered by low stone walls. Luxuriant clumps of bushes grew beside the wall, and trees—wild cherry and old apple trees—at intervals. Presently Louisa sat down on the wall and looked about her with mildly sorrowful reflectiveness. Tall shrubs of blueberry and meadowsweet, all woven together and tangled with blackberry vines and horse-briers, shut her in on either side. She had a little clear space between them. Opposite her, on the other side of the road, was a spreading tree; the moon shone between its boughs, and the leaves twinkled like silver. The road was bespread with a beautiful shifting dapple of silver and shadow; the air was full of a mysterious sweetness. "I wonder if it's wild grapes?" murmured Louisa. She sat there some time. She was just thinking of rising, when she heard footsteps and low voices, and remained quiet. It was a lonely place, and she felt a little timid. She thought she would keep still in the shadow and let the persons, whoever they might be, pass her.

But just before they reached her the voices ceased, and the footsteps. She understood that their owners had also found seats upon the stone wall. She was wondering if she could not steal away unobserved, when the voice broke the stillness. It was Joe Dagget's. She sat still and listened.

The voice was announced by a loud sigh, which was as familiar as itself. "Well," said Dagget, "you've made up your mind, then, I suppose?"

"Yes," returned another voice; "I'm going day after to-morrow."

"That's Lily Dyer," thought Louisa to herself. The voice embodied itself in her mind. She saw a girl tall and full-figured, with a firm, fair face, looking fairer and firmer in the moonlight, her strong yellow hair braided in a close knot. A girl full of calm rustic strength and bloom, with a masterful way which might have beseemed a princess. Lily Dyer was a favorite with the village folk; she had just the qualities to arouse the admiration. She was good and handsome and smart. Louisa had often heard her praises sounded.

"Well," said Joe Dagget, "I ain't got a word to say."

"I don't know what you could say," returned Lily Dyer.

"Not a word to say," repeated Joe, drawing out the words heavily. Then there was a silence. "I ain't sorry," he began at last, "that that happened yesterday—that we kind of let on how we felt to each other. I guess it's just as well we knew. Of course I can't do anything any different. I'm going right on an' get married next week. I ain't going back on a woman that's waited for me fourteen years, an' break her heart."

"If you should jilt her to-morrow, I wouldn't have you," spoke up the girl, with sudden vehemence.

"Well, I ain't going to give you the chance," said he; "but I don't believe you would, either."

"You'd see I wouldn't. Honor's honor, an' right's right. An' I'd never think anything of any man that went against 'em for me or any other girl; you'd find that out, Joe Dagget."

"Well, you'll find out fast enough that I ain't going against 'em for you or any other girl," returned he. Their voices sounded almost as if they were angry with each other. Louisa was listening eagerly.

"I'm sorry you feel as if you must go away," said Joe, "but I don't know but it's best."

"Of course it's best. I hope you and I have got common-sense."

"Well, I suppose you're right." Suddenly Joe's voice got an undertone of tenderness. "Say, Lily," he said, "I'll get along well enough myself, but I can't bear to think—You don't suppose you're going to fret much about it?"

"I guess you'll find out I sha'n't fret much over a married man."

"Well, I hope you won't—I hope you won't, Lily. God knows I do. And —I hope—one of these days—you'll—come across somebody else—"

"I don't see any reason why I shouldn't." Suddenly her tone changed. She spoke in a sweet, clear voice, so loud that she could have been heard across the street. "No, Joe Dagget," said she, "I'll never marry any other man as long as I live. I've got good sense, an' I ain't going to break my heart nor make a fool of myself; but I'm never going to be married, you can be sure of that. I ain't that sort of a girl to feel this way twice."

Louisa heard an exclamation and a soft commotion behind the bushes; then Lily spoke again—the voice sounded as if she had risen. "This must be put a stop to," said she. "We've stayed here long enough. I'm going home."

Louisa sat there in a daze, listening to their retreating steps. After a while she got up and slunk softly home herself. The next day she did her housework methodically; that was as much a matter of course as breathing; but she did not sew on her wedding-clothes. She sat at her window and meditated. In the evening Joe came. Louisa Ellis had never known that she had any diplomacy in her, but when she came to look for it that night she found it, although meek of its kind, among her little feminine weapons. Even now she could hardly believe that she had heard aright, and that she would not do Joe a terrible injury should she break her troth-plight. She wanted to sound him without betraying too soon her own inclinations in the matter. She did it successfully, and they finally came to an understanding; but it was a difficult thing, for he was as afraid of betraying himself as she.

She never mentioned Lily Dyer. She simply said that while she had no cause of complaint against him, she had lived so long in one way that she shrank from making a change.

"Well, I never shrank, Louisa," said Dagget. "I'm going to be honest enough to say that I think maybe it's better this way; but if you'd wanted to keep on, I'd have stuck to you till my dying day. I hope you know that."

"Yes, I do," said she.

That night she and Joe parted more tenderly than they had done for a long time. Standing in the door, holding each other's hands, a last great wave of regretful memory swept over them.

"Well, this ain't the way we've thought it was all going to end, is it, Louisa?" said Joe.

She shook her head. There was a little quiver on her placid face.

"You let me know if there's ever anything I can do for you," said he. "I ain't ever going to forget you, Louisa." Then he kissed her, and went down the path.

Louisa, all alone by herself that night, wept a little, she hardly knew why; but the next morning, on waking, she felt like a queen who, after fearing lest her domain be wrested away from her, sees it firmly insured in her possession.

Now the tall weeds and grasses might cluster around Caesar's little hermit hut, the snow might fall on its roof year in and year out, but he never would go on a rampage through the unguarded village. Now the little canary might turn itself into a peaceful yellow ball night after night, and have no need to wake and flutter with wild terror against its bars. Louisa could sew linen seams, and distil roses, and dust and polish and fold away in lavender, as long as she listed. That afternoon she sat with her needle-work at the window, and felt fairly steeped in peace. Lily Dyer, tall and erect and blooming, went past; but she felt no qualm. If Louisa Ellis had sold her birthright she did not know it, the taste of the pottage was so delicious, and had been her sole satisfaction for so long. Serenity and placid narrowness had become to her as the birthright itself. She gazed ahead through a long reach of future days strung together like pearls in a rosary, every one like the others, and all smooth and flawless and innocent, and her heart went up in thankfulness. Outside was the fervid summer afternoon; the air was filled with the sounds of the busy harvest of men and birds and bees; there were halloos, metallic clatterings, sweet calls, and long hummings. Louisa sat, prayerfully numbering her days, like an uncloistered nun.

AUNT CYNTHY DALLETT

by

SARAH ORNE JEWETT

(1849–1909)

A lifelong resident of Maine, Sarah Orne Jewett accompanied her physician father on his rounds and often wrote in her fiction about women herb healers, as well as about others she knew well in her own locale. Honored even in her lifetime as a regional writer, she has more recently been viewed as an important contributor to American literature. Jewett lived with women friends and maintained extensive correspondence with many women artists and writers; her letters were published in 1911 and 1967. The Country of the Pointed Firs *(1896) and* Deephaven *(1877) are still in print, and the story "A White Heron" was made into a movie in 1978.*

• ———————————————————— •

I

"No," said Mrs. Hand, speaking wistfully,—"no, we never were in the habit of keeping Christmas at our house. Mother died when we were all young; she would have been the one to keep up with all new ideas, but father and grandmother were old-fashioned folks, and—well, you know how 't was then, Miss Pendexter: nobody took much notice of the day except to wish you a Merry Christmas."

"They didn't do much to make it merry, certain," answered Miss Pendexter. "Sometimes nowadays I hear folks complainin' o' bein' overtaxed with all the Christmas work they have to do."

"Well, others think that it makes a lovely chance for all that really enjoys givin'; you get an opportunity to speak your kind feelin' right out," answered Mrs. Hand, with a bright smile. "But there! I shall always keep New Year's Day, too; it won't do no hurt to have an extra day kept an' made pleasant. And there's many of the real old folks have got pretty things to remember about New Year's Day."

"Aunt Cynthy Dallett's just one of 'em," said Miss Pendexter. "She's always very reproachful if I don't get up to see her. Last year I missed it, on account of a light fall o' snow that seemed to make the walkin' too bad, an' she sent a neighbor's boy 'way down from the mount'in to see if I was sick. Her lameness confines her to the house altogether now, an' I have her on my mind a good deal. How anybody does get thinkin' of those that lives alone, as they get older! I waked up only last night with a start, thinkin' if Aunt Cynthy's house should get afire or anything, what she would do, 'way up there all alone. I was half dreamin', I s'pose, but I couldn't seem to settle down until I got up an' went upstairs to the north garret window to see if I could see any light; but the mountains was all dark an' safe, same's usual. I remember noticin' last time I was there that her chimney needed pointin', and I spoke to her about it,—the bricks looked poor in some places."

"Can you see the house from your north gable window?" asked Mrs. Hand, a little absently.

"Yes'm; it's a great comfort that I can," answered her companion. "I have often wished we were near enough to have her make me some sort o' signal in case she needed help. I used to plead with her to come down and spend the winters with me, but she told me one day I might as well try to fetch down one o' the old hemlocks, an' I believe 't was true."

"Your aunt Dallett is a very self-contained person," observed Mrs. Hand.

"Oh, very!" exclaimed the elderly niece, with a pleased look. "Aunt Cynthy laughs, an' says she expects the time will come when age'll compel her to have me move up an' take care of her; and last time I was there she looked up real funny, an' says, 'I do' know, Abby; I'm most afeard sometimes that I feel myself beginnin' to look for'ard to it!' 'T was a good deal, comin' from Aunt Cynthy, an' I so esteemed it."

"She ought to have you there now," said Mrs. Hand. "You'd both make a savin' by doin' it; but I don't expect she needs to save as much as some. There! I know just how you both feel. I like to have my own home an' do everything just my way too." And the friends laughed, and looked at each other affectionately.

"There was old Mr. Nathan Dunn,—left no debts an' no money when he died," said Mrs. Hand. " 'T was over to his niece's last summer. He had a little money in his wallet, an' when the bill for funeral expenses come in there was just exactly enough; some item or other made it come to so many dollars an' eighty-four cents, and, lo an' behold! there was eighty-four cents in a little separate pocket beside the neat fold o' bills, as if the old gentleman had known beforehand. His niece couldn't help laughin', to save her; she said the old gentleman died as methodical as he lived. She didn't expect he had any money, an' was prepared to pay for everything herself; she's very well off."

" 'T was funny, certain," said Miss Pendexter. "I expect he felt comfortable, knowin' he had that money by him. 'T is a comfort, when all's said and done, 'specially to folks that's gettin' old."

A sad look shadowed her face for an instant, and then she smiled and rose to take leave, looking expectantly at her hostess to see if there were anything more to be said.

"I hope to come out square myself," she said, by way of farewell pleasantry; "but there are times when I feel doubtful."

Mrs. Hand was evidently considering something, and waited a moment or two before she spoke. "Suppose we both walk up to see your aunt Dallett, New Year's Day, if it ain't too windy and the snow keeps off?" she proposed. "I couldn't rise the hill if 't was a windy day. We could take a hearty breakfast an' start in good season; I'd rather walk than ride, the road's so rough this time o' year."

"Oh, what a person you are to think o' things! I did so dread goin' 'way up there all alone," said Abby Pendexter. "I'm no hand to go off alone, an' I had it before me, so I really got to dread it. I do so enjoy it after I get there, seein' Aunt Cynthy, an' she's always so much better than I expect to find her."

"Well, we'll start early," said Mrs. Hand cheerfully; and so they parted. As Miss Pendexter went down the foot-path to the gate, she sent grateful thoughts back to the little sitting-room she had just left.

"How doors are opened!" she exclaimed to herself. "Here I've been so poor an' distressed at beginnin' the year with nothin', as it were, that I couldn't think o' even goin' to make poor old Aunt Cynthy a friendly call. I'll manage to make some kind of a little pleasure too, an' somethin' for dear Mis' Hand. 'Use what you've got,' mother always used to say when every sort of an emergency come up, an' I may only have wishes to give, but I'll make 'em good ones!"

2

The first day of the year was clear and bright, as if it were a New Year's pattern of what winter can be at its very best. The two friends were prepared for changes of weather, and met each other well wrapped in their winter cloaks and shawls, with sufficient brown barége veils tied securely over their bonnets. They ignored for some time the plain truth that each carried something under her arm; the shawls were rounded out suspiciously, especially Miss Pendexter's, but each respected the other's air of secrecy. The narrow road was frozen in deep ruts, but a smooth-trodden little foot-path that ran along its edge was very inviting to the wayfarers. Mrs. Hand walked first and Miss Pendexter followed, and they were talking busily nearly all the way, so that they had to stop for breath now and then at the tops of the little hills. It was not a hard walk; there were a good many almost level stretches through the woods, in spite of the fact that they should be a very great deal higher when they reached Mrs. Dallett's door.

"I do declare, what a nice day 't is, an' such pretty footin'!" said Mrs. Hand, with satisfaction. "Seems to me as if my feet went o' themselves; gener'lly I have to toil so when I walk that I can't enjoy nothin' when I get to a place."

"It's partly this beautiful bracin' air," said Abby Pendexter. "Sometimes such nice air comes just before a fall of snow. Don't it seem to make anybody feel young again and to take all your troubles away?"

Mrs. Hand was a comfortable, well-to-do soul, who seldom worried about anything, but something in her companion's tone touched her heart, and she glanced sidewise and saw a pained look in Abby Pendexter's thin face. It was a moment for confidence.

"Why, you speak as if something distressed your mind, Abby," said the elder woman kindly.

"I ain't one that has myself on my mind as a usual thing, but it does seem now as if I was goin' to have it very hard," said Abby. "Well, I've been anxious before."

"Is it anything wrong about your property?" Mrs. Hand ventured to ask.

"Only that I ain't got any," answered Abby, trying to speak gayly. "'T was all I could do to pay my last quarter's rent, twelve dollars. I sold my hens, all but this one that had run away at the time, an' now I'm carryin' her up to Aunt Cynthy, roasted just as nice as I know how."

"I thought you was carrying somethin'," said Mrs. Hand, in her usual tone. "For me, I've got a couple o' my mince pies. I thought the old lady might like 'em; one we can eat for our dinner, and one she shall have to keep. But weren't you unwise to sacrifice your poultry, Abby? You always need eggs, and hens don't cost much to keep."

"Why, yes, I shall miss 'em," said Abby; "but, you see, I had to do every way to get my rent-money. Now the shop's shut down I haven't got any way of earnin' anything, and I spent what little I've saved through the summer."

"Your aunt Cynthy ought to know it an' ought to help you," said Mrs. Hand. "You're a real foolish person, I must say. I expect you do for her when she ought to do for you."

"She's old, an' she's all the near relation I've got," said the little woman. "I've always felt the time would come when she'd need me, but it's been her great pleasure to live alone an' feel free. I shall get along somehow, but I shall have it hard. Somebody may want help for a spell this winter, but I'm afraid I shall have to give up my house. 'T ain't as if I owned it. I don't know just what to do, but there'll be a way."

Mrs. Hand shifted her two pies to the other arm, and stepped across to the other side of the road where the ground looked a little smoother.

"No, I wouldn't worry if I was you, Abby," she said. "There, I suppose if 't was me I should worry a good deal more! I expect I should lay awake nights." But Abby answered nothing, and they came to a steep place in the road and found another subject for conversation at the top.

"Your aunt don't know we're coming?" asked the chief guest of the occasion.

"Oh, no, I never send her word," said Miss Pendexter. "She'd be so desirous to get everything ready, just as she used to."

"She never seemed to make any trouble o' havin' company; she always appeared so easy and pleasant, and let you set with her while she made her preparations," said Mrs. Hand, with great approval. "Some has such a dreadful way of making you feel inopportune, and you can't always send word you're comin'. I did have a visit once that's always been a lesson to me; 't was years ago; I don't know's I ever told you?"

"I don't believe you ever did," responded the listener to this somewhat indefinite prelude.

"Well, 't was one hot summer afternoon. I set forth an' took a great long walk 'way over to Mis' Eben Fulham's, on the crossroad between the cranberry ma'sh and Staples's Corner. The doctor was drivin' that way, an' he give me a lift that shortened it some at the last; but I never should have started, if I'd known 't was so far. I had been promisin' all summer to go, and every time I saw Mis' Fulham, Sundays, she'd say somethin' about it. We wa'n't very well acquainted, but always friendly. She moved here from Bedford Hill."

"Oh, yes; I used to know her," said Abby, with interest.

"Well, now, she did give me a beautiful welcome when I got there," continued Mrs. Hand. " 'T was about four o'clock in the afternoon, an' I told her I'd come to accept her invitation if 't was convenient, an' the doctor had been called several miles beyond and expected to be detained, but he was goin' to pick me up as he returned about seven; 't was very kind of him. She took me right in, and she did appear so pleased, an' I must go right into the best room where 't was cool, and then she said she'd have tea early, and I should have to excuse her a short time. I asked her not to make any difference, and if I couldn't assist her; but she said no, I must just take her as I found her; and she give me a large fan, and off she went.

"There. I was glad to be still and rest where 't was cool, an' I set there in the rockin'-chair an' enjoyed it for a while, an' I heard her clacking at the oven door out beyond, an' gittin' out some dishes. She was a brisk-actin' little woman, an' I thought I'd caution her when she come back not to make up a great fire, only for a cup o' tea, perhaps. I started to go right out in the kitchen, an' then somethin' told me I'd better not, we never'd been so free together as that; I didn't know how she'd take it, an' there I set an' set. 'T was sort of a greenish light in the best room, an' it begun to feel a little damp to me,—the s'rubs outside grew close up to the windows. Oh, it did seem dreadful long! I could hear her busy with the dishes an' beatin' eggs an' stirrin', an' I knew she was puttin' herself out to get up a great supper, and I kind o' fidgeted about a little an' even stepped to the door, but I thought she'd expect me to remain where I was. I saw everything in that room forty times over, an' I did divert myself killin' off a brood o' moths that was in a worsted-work mat on the table. It all fell to pieces. I never saw such a sight o' moths to once. But occupation failed after that, an' I begun to feel sort o' tired an' numb. There was one o' them late crickets got into the room an' begun to chirp, an' it sounded kind o' fallish. I couldn't help sayin' to myself that Mis' Fulham had forgot all about my bein' there. I thought of all the beauties of hospitality that ever I see!"—

"Didn't she ever come back at all, not whilst things was in the oven, nor nothin'?" inquired Miss Pendexter, with awe.

"I never see her again till she come beamin' to the parlor door an' invited me to walk out to tea," said Mrs. Hand. " 'T was 'most a quarter past six by the clock; I thought 't was seven. I'd thought o' everything, an' I'd counted, an' I'd trotted my foot, an' I'd looked more'n twenty times to see if there was any more moth-millers."

"I s'pose you did have a very nice tea?" suggested Abby, with interest.

"Oh, a beautiful tea! She couldn't have done more if I'd been the Queen," said Mrs. Hand. "I don't know how she could ever have done it all in the time, I'm sure. The table was loaded down; there was cup-custards and custard pie, an' cream pie, an' two kinds o' hot biscuits, an' black tea as well as green, an' elegant cake,—one kind she'd just made new, and called it quick cake; I've often made it since—an' she'd opened her best preserves, two kinds. We set down together, an' I'm sure I appreciated what she'd done; but 't wa'n't no time for real conversation whilst we was to the table, and before we got quite through the doctor come hurryin' along, an' I had to leave. He asked us if we'd had a good talk, as we come out, an' I couldn't help laughing to myself; but she said quite hearty that she'd had a nice visit from me. She appeared well satisfied, Mis' Fulham did; but for me, I was disappointed; an' early that fall she died."

Abby Pendexter was laughing like a girl; the speaker's tone had grown more and more complaining. "I do call that a funny experience," she said. "'Better a dinner o' herbs.' I guess that text must ha' risen to your mind in connection. You must tell that to Aunt Cynthy, if conversation seems to fail." And she laughed again, but Mrs. Hand still looked solemn and reproachful.

"Here we are; there's Aunt Cynthy's lane right ahead, there by the great yellow birch," said Abby. "I must say, you've made the way seem very short, Mis' Hand."

3

Old Aunt Cynthia Dallett sat in her high-backed rocking-chair by the little north window, which was her favorite dwelling-place.

"New Year's Day again," she said, aloud,—"New Year's Day again!" And she folded her old bent hands, and looked out at the great woodland view and the hills without really seeing them, she was lost in so deep a reverie. "I'm gittin' to be very old," she added, after a little while.

It was perfectly still in the small gray house. Outside in the apple-trees there were some blue-jays flitting about and calling noisily, like schoolboys fighting at their games. The kitchen was full of pale winter sunshine. It was more like late October than the first of January, and the plain little room seemed to smile back into the sun's face. The outer door was standing open into the green dooryard, and a fat small dog lay asleep on the step. A capacious cupboard stood behind Mrs. Dallett's chair and kept the wind away from her corner. Its doors and drawers were painted a clean lead-color, and there were places round the knobs and buttons where the touch of hands had worn deep into the wood. Every braided rug was straight on the floor. The square clock on its shelf between the front windows looked as if it had just had its face washed and been wound up for a whole year to come. If Mrs. Dallett turned her head she could look into the bedroom, where her plump feather bed was covered with its dark blue homespun winter quilt. It was all very peaceful and comfortable, but it was very lonely. By her side, on a light-stand, lay the religious newspaper of her denomination, and a pair of spectacles whose jointed silver bows looked like a funny two-legged beetle cast helplessly upon its back.

"New Year's Day again," said old Cynthia Dallett. Time had left nobody in her house to wish her a Happy New Year,—she was the last one left in the old nest. "I'm gittin' to be very old," she said for the second time; it seemed to be all there was to say.

She was keeping a careful eye on her friendly clock, but it was hardly past the middle of the morning, and there was no excuse for moving; it was the long hour between the end of her slow morning work and the appointed time for beginning to get dinner. She was so stiff and lame that this hour's rest was usually most welcome, but to-day she sat as if it were Sunday, and did not take up her old shallow splint basket of braiding-rags from the side of her footstool.

"I do hope Abby Pendexter'll make out to git up to see me this afternoon as usual," she continued. "I know 't ain't so easy for her to get up the hill as it used to be, but I do seem to want to see some o' my own folks. I wish 't I'd thought to send her word I expected her when Jabez Hooper went back after he came up here with the flour. I'd like to have had her come prepared to stop two or three days."

A little chickadee perched on the window-sill outside and bobbed his head sideways to look in, and then pecked impatiently at the glass. The old woman laughed at him with childish pleasure and felt companioned; it was pleasant at that moment to see the life in even a bird's bright eye.

"Sign of a stranger," she said, as he whisked his wings and flew away in a hurry. "I must throw out some crumbs for 'em; it's getting to be hard pickin' for the stayin'-birds." She looked past the trees of her little orchard now with seeing eyes, and followed the long forest slopes that led downward to the lowland country. She could see the two white steeples of Fairfield Village, and the map of fields and pastures along the valley beyond, and the great hills across the valley to the westward. The scattered houses looked like toys that had been scattered by children. She knew their lights by night, and watched the smoke of their chimneys by day. Far to the northward were higher mountains, and these were already white with snow. Winter was already in sight, but to-day the wind was in the south, and the snow seemed only part of a great picture.

"I do hope the cold'll keep off a while longer," thought Mrs. Dallett. "I don't know how I'm going to get along after the deep snow comes."

The little dog suddenly waked, as if he had had a bad dream, and after giving a few anxious whines he began to bark outrageously. His mistress tried, as usual, to appeal to his better feelings.

"'T ain't nobody, Tiger," she said. "Can't you have some patience? Maybe it's some foolish boys that's rangin' about with their guns." But Tiger kept on, and even took the trouble to waddle in on his short legs, barking all the way. He looked warningly at her, and then turned and ran out again. Then she saw him go hurrying down to the bars, as if it were an occasion of unusual interest.

"I guess somebody is comin'; he don't act as if 't were a vagrant kind o' noise; must really be somebody in our lane." And Mrs. Dallett smoothed her apron and gave an anxious housekeeper's glance round the kitchen. None of her state visitors, the minister or the deacons, ever came in the morning. Country people are usually too busy to go visiting in the forenoons.

Presently two figures appeared where the road came out of the woods,— the two women already known to the story, but very surprising to Mrs. Dallett; the short, thin one was easily recognized as Abby Pendexter, and the taller, stout one was soon discovered to be Mrs. Hand. Their old friend's heart was in a glow. As the guests approached they could see her pale face with its thin white hair framed under the close black silk handkerchief.

"There she is at her window smilin' away!" exclaimed Mrs. Hand; but by the time they reached the doorstep she stood waiting to meet them.

"Why, you two dear creatur's!" she said, with a beaming smile. "I don't know when I've ever been so glad to see folks comin'. I had a kind of left-all-alone feelin' this mornin', an' I didn't even make bold to be certain o' you, Abby, though it looked so pleasant. Come right in an' set down. You're all out o' breath, ain't you, Mis' Hand?"

Mrs. Dallett led the way with eager hospitality. She was the tiniest little bent old creature, her handkerchiefed head was quick and alert, and her eyes were bright with excitement and feeling, but the rest of her was much the worse for age; she could hardly move, poor soul, as if she had only a make-believe framework of a body under a shoulder-shawl and thick petticoats. She got back to her chair again, and the guests took off their bonnets in the bedroom, and returned discreet and sedate in their black woolen dresses. The lonely kitchen was blest with society at last, to its mistress's heart's content. They talked as fast as possible about the weather, and how warm it had been walking up the mountain, and how cold it had been a year ago, that day when Abby Pendexter had been kept at home by a snowstorm and missed her visit. "And I ain't seen you now, aunt, since the twenty-eighth of September, but I've thought of you a great deal, and looked forward to comin' more'n usual," she ended, with an affectionate glance at the pleased old face by the window.

"I've been wantin' to see you, dear, and wonderin' how you was gettin' on," said Aunt Cynthy kindly. "And I take it as a great attention to have you come to-day, Mis' Hand," she added, turning again towards the more distinguished guest. "We have to put one thing against another. I should hate dreadfully to live anywhere except on a high hill farm, 'cordin' as I was born an' raised. But there ain't the chance to neighbor that townfolks has, an' I do seem to have more lonely hours than I used to when I was younger. I don't know but I shall soon be gittin' too old to live alone." And she turned to her niece with an expectant, lovely look, and Abby smiled back.

"I often wish I could run in an' see you every day, aunt," she answered. "I have been sayin' so to Mrs. Hand."

"There, how anybody does relish company when they don't have but a little of it!" exclaimed Aunt Cynthia. "I am all alone to-day; there is going to be a shootin'-match somewhere the other side o' the mountain, an' Johnny Foss, that does my chores, begged off to go when he brought the milk unusual early this mornin'. Gener'lly he's about here all the fore part of the day; but he don't go off with the boys very often, and I like to have him have a little sport; 't was New Year's Day, anyway; he's a good, stiddy boy for my wants."

"Why, I wish you Happy New Year, aunt!" said Abby, springing up with unusual spirit. "Why, that's just what we come to say, and we like to have forgot all about it!" She kissed her aunt, and stood a minute holding her hand with a soft, affectionate touch. Mrs. Hand rose and kissed Mrs. Dallett too, and it was a moment of ceremony and deep feeling.

"I always like to keep the day," said the old hostess, as they seated themselves and drew their splint-bottomed chairs a little nearer together than before. "You see, I was brought up to it, and father made a good deal of it; he said he liked to make it pleasant and give the year a fair start. I can see him now, how he used to be standing there by the fireplace when we came out o' the two bedrooms early in the morning, an' he always made out, poor 's he was, to give us some little present, and he'd heap 'em up on the corner o' the mantelpiece, an' we'd stand front of him in a row, and mother be bustling about gettin' breakfast. One year he give me a beautiful copy o' the 'Life o' General Lafayette,' in a green cover,—I've got it now, but we child'n 'bout read it to pieces,—an' one year a nice piece o' blue ribbon, an' Abby—that was your mother, Abby—had a pink one. Father was real kind to his child'n. I thought o' them early days when I first waked up this mornin', and I couldn't help lookin' up then to the corner o' the shelf just as I used to look."

"There's nothin' so beautiful as to have a bright childhood to look back to," said Mrs. Hand. "Sometimes I think child'n has too hard a time now,— all the responsibility is put on to 'em, since they take the lead o' what to do an' what they want, and get to be so toppin' an' knowin'. 'T was happier in the old days, when the fathers an' mothers done the rulin'."

"They say things have changed," said Aunt Cynthy; "but staying right here, I don't know much of any world but my own world."

Abby Pendexter did not join in this conversation, but sat in her straight-backed chair with folded hands and the air of a good child. The little old dog had followed her in, and now lay sound asleep again at her feet. The front breadth of her black dress looked rusty and old in the sunshine that slanted across it, and the aunt's sharp eyes saw this and saw the careful darns. Abby was as neat as wax, but she looked as if the frost had struck her. "I declare, she's gittin' along in years," thought Aunt Cynthia compassionately. "She begins to look sort o' set and dried up, Abby does. She oughtn't to live all alone; she's one that needs company."

SARAH ORNE JEWETT

At this moment Abby looked up with new interest. "Now, aunt," she said, in her pleasant voice, "I don't want you to forget to tell me if there ain't some sewin' or mendin' I can do whilst I'm here. I know your hands trouble you some, an' I may 's well tell you we're bent on stayin' all day an' makin' a good visit, Mis' Hand an' me."

"Thank ye kindly," said the old woman; "I do want a little sewin' done before long, but 't ain't no use to spile a good holiday." Her face took a resolved expression. "I'm goin' to make other arrangements," she said. "No, you needn't come up here to pass New Year's Day an' be put right down to sewin'. I make out to do what mendin' I need, an' to sew on my hooks an' eyes. I get Johnny Foss to thread me up a good lot o' needles every little while, an' that helps me a good deal. Abby, why can't you step into the best room an' bring out the rockin'-chair? I seem to want Mis' Hand to have it."

"I opened the window to let the sun in awhile," said the niece, as she returned. "It felt cool in there an' shut up."

"I thought of doin' it not long before you come," said Mrs. Dallett, looking gratified. Once the taking of such a liberty would have been very provoking to her. "Why, it does seem good to have somebody think o' things an' take right hold like that!"

"I'm sure you would, if you were down at my house," said Abby, blushing. "Aunt Cynthy, I don't suppose you could feel as if 't would be best to come down an' pass the winter with me,—just durin' the cold weather, I mean. You'd see more folks to amuse you, an'—I do think of you so anxious these long winter nights."

There was a terrible silence in the room, and Miss Pendexter felt her heart begin to beat very fast. She did not dare to look at her aunt at first.

Presently the silence was broken. Aunt Cynthia had been gazing out of the window, and she turned towards them a little paler and older than before, and smiling sadly.

"Well, dear, I'll do just as you say," she answered. "I'm beat by age at last, but I've had my own way for eighty-five years, come the month o' March, an' last winter I did use to lay awake an' worry in the long storms. I'm kind o' humble now about livin' alone to what I was once." At this moment a new light shone in her face. "I don't expect you'd be willin' to come up here an' stay till spring,—not if I had Foss's folks stop for you to ride to meetin' every pleasant Sunday, an' take you down to the Corners plenty o' other times besides?" she said beseechingly. "No, Abby, I'm too old to move now; I should be homesick down to the village. If you'll come an' stay with me, all I have shall be yours. Mis' Hand hears me say it."

"Oh, don't you think o' that; you're all I've got near to me in the world, an' I'll come an' welcome," said Abby, though the thought of her own little home gave a hard tug at her heart. "Yes, Aunt Cynthy, I'll come, an' we'll be real comfortable together. I've been lonesome sometimes"—

" 'T will be best for both," said Mrs. Hand judicially. And so the great question was settled, and suddenly, without too much excitement, it became a thing of the past.

"We must be thinkin' o' dinner," said Aunt Cynthia gayly. "I wish I was better prepared; but there's nice eggs an' pork an' potatoes, an' you girls can take hold an' help." At this moment the roast chicken and the best mince pies were offered and kindly accepted, and before another hour had gone they were sitting at their New Year feast, which Mrs. Dallett decided to be quite proper for the Queen.

Before the guests departed, when the sun was getting low, Aunt Cynthia called her niece to her side and took hold of her hand.

"Don't you make it too long now, Abby," said she. "I shall be wantin' ye every day till you come; but you mustn't forget what a set old thing I be."

Abby had the kindest of hearts, and was always longing for somebody to love and care for; her aunt's very age and helplessness seemed to beg for pity.

"This is Saturday; you may expect me the early part of the week; and thank you, too, aunt," said Abby.

Mrs. Hand stood by with deep sympathy. "It's the proper thing," she announced calmly. "You'd both of you be a sight happier; and truth is, Abby's wild an' reckless, an' needs somebody to stand right over her, Mis' Dallett. I guess she'll try an' behave, but there—there's no knowin'!" And they all laughed. Then the New Year guests said farewell and started off down the mountain road. They looked back more than once to see Aunt Cynthia's face at the window as she watched them out of sight. Miss Abby Pendexter was full of excitement; she looked as happy as a child.

"I feel as if we'd gained the battle of Waterloo," said Mrs. Hand. "I've really had a most beautiful time. You an' your aunt mustn't forget to invite me up some time again to spend another day."

LIVING ALONE

by

DENISE LEVERTOV

(b. 1923)

Born in England, Denise Levertov had her first book of poetry published before coming to the United States with her husband in 1948. Since then she has written many volumes of poetry. An antiwar activist during the Vietnam War, she frequently read her poems to raise money for antiwar groups. Her works include Relearning the Alphabet *(1970),* The Poet in the World *(1973),* The Freeing of the Dust *(1975),* Light Up the Cave *(1981), and* Oblique Prayers *(1984).*

• —————————————————— •

I

In this silvery now of living alone,
doesn't it seem, I ponder,
anything can happen?
On the flat roof of a factory
at eye level from my window,
starling naiads dip in tremulous rainpools
where the sky floats, and is no smaller
than long ago.
Any strange staircase, as if I were twenty-one—
any hand drawing me up it,
could lead me to my life.
Some days.

And if I coast, down toward home, spring evenings, silently,
a kind of song rising in me to encompass
Davis Square and the all-night
cafeteria and the pool hall,
it is childhood's song, surely no note is changed,
sung in Valentines Park or on steep streets in the map of my mind
in the hush of suppertime, everyone gone indoors.
Solitude within multitude seduced me early.

II

Some days, though,
living alone,
there's only knowledge of silence,
clutter of bells cobwebbed
in crumbling belfry,
words jaggéd,
in midutterance broken.

Starlings, as before,
whistle wondering at themselves,
crescendo, diminuendo.
My heart pounds away,
confident as a clock.
Yet there is silence.

New leafed, the neighbor trees
round out. There's one,
near my window,
seems to have no buds, though.

III

I said, the summer garden I planted
bears only leaves—leaves in abundance—
but no flowers.
And then the flowers,
    many colors and forms,
    subtle, mysterious,
came forth.

I said, the tree has no buds.
And then the leaves,
    shyly, sparse, as if reluctant,
in less than two days appeared,
and the tree, now,
    is flying on green wings.

What magic denial
shall my life utter
to bring itself forth?

THE OTHER WIFE

by

COLETTE

(1873–1954)

*Colette is the pen name of the French novelist Sidonie Gabrielle
Claudine Colette, who collaborated with her husband under the pen
name Colette Willy in writing the* Claudine *books. She is best
known for her novels about women, especially* Chéri *(translated
1951) and* Gigi *(translated 1953).*

———————————————

'For two? This way, Monsieur and Madame, there's still a table by the
bay window, if Madame and Monsieur would like to enjoy the view.'

Alice followed the *maître d'hôtel*.

'Oh, yes, come on Marc, we'll feel we're having lunch on a boat at
sea . . .'

Her husband restrained her, passing his arm through hers.

'We'll be more comfortable there.'

'There? In the middle of all those people? I'd much prefer . . .'

'Please, Alice.'

He tightened his grip in so emphatic a way that she turned round.

'What's the matter with you?'

He said 'sh' very quietly, looking at her intently, and drew her towards
the table in the middle.

'What is it, Marc?'

'I'll tell you, darling. Let me order lunch. Would you like shrimps? Or
eggs in aspic?'

'Whatever *you* like, as you know.'

They smiled at each other, wasting the precious moments of an overworked, perspiring *maître d'hôtel* who stood near to them, suffering from
a kind of St. Vitus's dance.

'Shrimps,' ordered Marc. 'And then eggs and bacon. And cold chicken
with cos lettuce salad. Cream cheese? *Spécialité de la maison?* We'll settle

for the *spécialité*. Two very strong coffees. Please give lunch to my chauffeur, we'll be leaving again at two o'clock. Cider? I don't trust it. . . . Dry champagne.'

He sighed as though he had been moving a wardrobe, gazed at the pale noonday sea, the nearly white sky, then at his wife, finding her pretty in her little Mercury-type hat with its long hanging veil.

'You're looking well, darling. And all this sea-blue colour gives you green eyes, just imagine! And you put on weight when you travel. . . . It's nice, up to a point, but only up to a point!'

Her rounded bosom swelled proudly as she leant over the table.

'Why did you stop me taking that place by the bay window?'

It did not occur to Marc Séguy to tell a lie.

'Because you'd have sat next to someone I know.'

'And whom I don't know?'

'My ex-wife.'

She could not find a word to say and opened her blue eyes wider.

'What of it, darling? It'll happen again. It's not important.'

Alice found her tongue again and asked the inevitable questions in their logical sequence.

'Did she see you? Did she know that you'd seen her? Point her out to me.'

'Don't turn round at once, I beg you, she must be looking at us. A lady with dark hair, without a hat, she must be staying at this hotel. . . . On her own, behind those children in red . . .'

'Yes, I see.'

Sheltered behind broad-brimmed seaside hats, Alice was able to look at the woman who fifteen months earlier had still been her husband's wife. 'Incompatibility,' Marc told her. 'Oh, it was total incompatibility! We divorced like well-brought-up people, almost like friends, quietly and quickly. And I began to love you, and you were able to be happy with me. How lucky we are that in our happiness there haven't been any guilty parties or victims!'

The woman in white, with her smooth, lustrous hair over which the seaside light played in blue patches, was smoking a cigarette, her eyes half closed. Alice turned back to her husband, took some shrimps and butter and ate composedly.

'Why didn't you ever tell me,' she said after a moment's silence, 'that she had blue eyes too?'

'But I'd never thought about it!'

He kissed the hand that she stretched out to the bread basket and she blushed with pleasure. Dark-skinned and plump, she might have seemed slightly earthy, but the changing blue of her eyes, and her wavy golden hair, disguised her as a fragile and soulful blonde. She showed overwhelming gratitude to her husband. She was immodest without knowing it and her entire person revealed over-conspicuous signs of extreme happiness.

They ate and drank with good appetite and each thought that the other had forgotten the woman in white. However, Alice sometimes laughed too loudly and Marc was careful of his posture, putting his shoulders back and holding his head up. They waited some time for coffee, in silence. An incandescent stream, a narrow reflection of the high and invisible sun, moved slowly over the sea and shone with unbearable brilliance.

'She's still there, you know,' Alice whispered suddenly.

'Does she embarrass you? Would you like to have coffee somewhere else?'

'Not at all! It's she who ought to be embarrassed! And she doesn't look as though she's having a madly gay time, if you could see her . . .'

'It's not necessary. I know that look of hers.'

'Oh, was she like that?'

He breathed smoke through his nostrils and wrinkled his brows.

'Was she like that? No. To be frank, she wasn't happy with me.'

'Well, my goodness!'

'You're delightfully generous, darling, madly generous. . . . You're an angel, you're. . . . You love me . . . I'm so proud, when I see that look in your eyes . . . yes, the look you have now. . . . She. . . . No doubt I didn't succeed in making her happy. That's all there is to it, I didn't succeed.'

'She's hard to please!'

Alice fanned herself irritably, and cast brief glances at the woman in white who was smoking, her head leaning against the back of the cane chair, her eyes closed with an expression of satisfied lassitude.

Marc shrugged his shoulders modestly.

'That's it,' he admitted. 'What can one do? We have to be sorry for people who are never happy. As for us, we're so happy. . . . Aren't we, darling?

She didn't reply. She was looking with furtive attention at her husband's face, with its good colour and regular shape, at his thick hair, with its occasional thread of white silk, at his small, well-cared-for hands. She felt dubious for the first time, and asked herself: 'What more did she want, then?'

And until they left, while Marc was paying the bill, asking about the chauffeur and the route, she continued to watch, with envious curiosity, the lady in white, that discontented, hard-to-please, superior woman. . . .

THE STORY OF AN HOUR

by

KATE CHOPIN

(1850–1904)

In the past few years Kate Chopin has been rediscovered. Her novel The Awakening (1899) *has had several editions, and Per Seyersted edited her collected works and a selection,* The Storm and Other Stories (1974), *for the Feminist Press. Chopin shows the difficulties a woman trying to be herself faces in a traditional society such as New Orleans. She wrote most of her works as a widow with six children.*

· ———————————————— ·

Knowing that Mrs. Mallard was afflicted with a heart trouble, great care was taken to break to her as gently as possible the news of her husband's death.

It was her sister Josephine who told her, in broken sentences; veiled hints that revealed in half concealing. Her husband's friend Richards was there, too, near her. It was he who had been in the newspaper office when intelligence of the railroad disaster was received, with Brently Mallard's name leading the list of "killed." He had only taken the time to assure himself of its truth by a second telegram, and had hastened to forestall any less careful, less tender friend in bearing the sad message.

She did not hear the story as many women have heard the same, with a paralyzed inability to accept its significance. She wept at once, with sudden, wild abandonment, in her sister's arms. When the storm of grief had spent itself she went away to her room alone. She would have no one follow her.

There stood, facing the open window, a comfortable, roomy armchair. Into this she sank, pressed down by a physical exhaustion that haunted her body and seemed to reach into her soul.

She could see in the open square before her house the tops of trees that were all aquiver with the new spring life. The delicious breath of rain was in the air. In the street below a peddler was crying his wares. The notes of a distant song which some one was singing reached her faintly, and countless sparrows were twittering in the eaves.

There were patches of blue sky showing here and there through the clouds that had met and piled one above the other in the west facing her window.

She sat with her head thrown back upon the cushion of the chair, quite motionless, except when a sob came up into her throat and shook her, as a child who has cried itself to sleep continues to sob in its dreams.

She was young, with a fair, calm face, whose lines bespoke repression and even a certain strength. But now there was a dull stare in her eyes, whose gaze was fixed away off yonder on one of those patches of blue sky. It was not a glance of reflection, but rather indicated a suspension of intelligent thought.

There was something coming to her and she was waiting for it, fearfully. What was it? She did not know; it was too subtle and elusive to name. But she felt it, creeping out of the sky, reaching toward her through the sounds, the scents, the color that filled the air.

Now her bosom rose and fell tumultuously. She was beginning to recognize this thing that was approaching to possess her, and she was striving to beat it back with her will—as powerless as her two white slender hands would have been.

When she abandoned herself a little whispered word escaped her slightly parted lips. She said it over and over under her breath: "free, free, free!" The vacant stare and the look of terror that had followed it went from her eyes. They stayed keen and bright. Her pulses beat fast, and the coursing blood warmed and relaxed every inch of her body.

She did not stop to ask if it were or were not a monstrous joy that held her. A clear and exalted perception enabled her to dismiss the suggestion as trivial.

She knew that she would weep again when she saw the kind, tender hands folded in death; the face that had never looked save with love upon her, fixed and gray and dead. But she saw beyond that bitter moment a long procession of years to come that would belong to her absolutely. And she opened and spread her arms out to them in welcome.

There would be no one to live for her during those coming years; she would live for herself. There would be no powerful will bending hers in that blind persistence with which men and women believe they have a right to impose a private will upon a fellow-creature. A kind intention or a cruel intention made the act seem no less a crime as she looked upon it in that brief moment of illumination.

And yet she had loved him—sometimes. Often she had not. What did it matter! What could love, the unsolved mystery, count for in face of this possession of self-assertion which she suddenly recognized as the strongest impulse of her being!

"Free! Body and soul free!" she kept whispering.

KATE CHOPIN

381

Josephine was kneeling before the closed door with her lips to the keyhole, imploring for admission. "Louise, open the door! I beg; open the door—you will make yourself ill. What are you doing, Louise? For heaven's sake open the door."

"Go away. I am not making myself ill." No; she was drinking in a very elixir of life through that open window.

Her fancy was running riot along those days ahead of her. Spring days, and summer days, and all sorts of days that would be her own. She breathed a quick prayer that life might be long. It was only yesterday she had thought with a shudder that life might be long.

She rose at length and opened the door to her sister's importunities. There was a feverish triumph in her eyes, and she carried herself unwittingly like a goddess of Victory. She clasped her sister's waist, and together they descended the stairs. Richards stood waiting for them at the bottom.

Some one was opening the front door with a latchkey. It was Brently Mallard who entered, a little travel-stained, composedly carrying his grip-sack and umbrella. He had been far from the scene of the accident, and did not even know there had been one. He stood amazed at Josephine's piercing cry; at Richards' quick motion to screen him from the view of his wife.

But Richards was too late.

When the doctors came they said she had died of heart disease—of joy that kills.

THE WOMEN MEN DON'T SEE

by

JAMES TIPTREE, JR.

(b. 1918?)

Embarrassed by the praise for "The Women Men Don't See" as an example of how well a man could write about women, Alice Sheldon disclosed in 1974 that she is James Tiptree, Jr. A semi-retired psychologist, Sheldon has received four prizes since 1968 for science fiction writing. Widely traveled, she lives—or at least receives her mail—at McLean, Virginia. Sheldon's collection, Star Songs of an Old Primate *(1978), has an introduction by Ursula Le Guin; her most recent work is* Brightness Falls from the Air *(1985).*

• ——————————————— •

I see her first while the Mexicana 727 is barreling down to Cozumel Island. I come out of the can and lurch into her seat, saying "Sorry," at a double female blur. The near blur nods quietly. The younger one in the window seat goes on looking out. I continue down the aisle, registering nothing. Zero. I never would have looked at them or thought of them again.

Cozumel airport is the usual mix of panicky Yanks dressed for the sand pile and calm Mexicans dressed for lunch at the Presidente. I am a used-up Yank dressed for serious fishing; I extract my rods and duffel from the riot and hike across the field to find my charter pilot. One Captain Estéban has contracted to deliver me to the bonefish flats of Belize three hundred kilometers down the coast.

Captain Estéban turns out to be four-feet nine of mahogany Mayan *puro.* He is also in a somber Maya snit. He tells me my Cessna is grounded somewhere and his Bonanza is booked to take a party to Chetumal.

Well, Chetumal is south; can he take me along and go on to Belize after he drops them off? Gloomily he concedes the possibility—*if* the other party permits, and *if* there are not too many *equipajes.*

The Chetumal party approaches. It's the woman and her young companion—daughter?—neatly picking their way across the gravel and yucca apron. Their Ventura two-suiters, like themselves, are small, plain and neutral-colored. No problem. When the captain asks if I may ride along, the mother says mildly "Of course," without looking at me.

I think that's when my inner tilt-detector sends up its first faint click. How come this woman has already looked me over carefully enough to accept me on her plane? I disregard it. Paranoia hasn't been useful in my business for years, but the habit is hard to break.

As we clamber into the Bonanza, I see the girl has what could be an attractive body if there was any spark at all. There isn't. Captain Estéban folds a serape to sit on so he can see over the cowling and runs a meticulous check-down. And then we're up and trundling over the turquoise Jello of the Caribbean into a stiff south wind.

The coast on our right is the territory of Quintana Roo. If you haven't seen Yucatán, imagine the world's biggest absolutely flat green-gray rug. An empty-looking land. We pass the white ruin of Tulum and the gash of the road to Chichén Itzá, a half-dozen coconut plantations, and then nothing but reef and low scrub jungle all the way to the horizon, just about the way the conquistadors saw it four centuries back.

Long strings of cumulus are racing at us, shadowing the coast. I have gathered that part of our pilot's gloom concerns the weather. A cold front is dying on the henequen fields of Mérida to the west, and the south wind has piled up a string of coastal storms: what they call *llovisnos*. Estéban detours methodically around a couple of small thunderheads. The Bonanza jinks, and I look back with a vague notion of reassuring the women. They are calmly intent on what can be seen of Yucatán. Well, they were offered the copilot's view, but they turned it down. Too shy?

Another *llovisno* puffs up ahead. Estéban takes the Bonanza upstairs, rising in his seat to sight his course. I relax for the first time in too long, savoring the latitudes between me and my desk, the week of fishing ahead. Our captain's classic Maya profile attracts my gaze: forehead sloping back from his predatory nose, lips and jaw stepping back below it. If his slant eyes had been any more crossed, he couldn't have made his license. That's a handsome combination, believe it or not. On the little Maya chicks in their minishifts with iridescent gloop on those cockeyes, it's also highly erotic. Nothing like the oriental doll thing; these people have stone bones. Captain Estéban's old grandmother could probably tow the Bonanza . . .

I'm snapped awake by the cabin hitting my ear. Estéban is barking into his headset over a drumming racket of hail; the windows are dark gray.

One important noise is missing—the motor. I realize Estéban is fighting a dead plane. Thirty-six hundred; we've lost two thousand feet!

He slaps tank switches as the storm throws us around; I catch something about *gasolina* in a snarl that shows his big teeth. The Bonanza reels down. As he reaches for an overhead toggle, I see the fuel gauges are high. Maybe a clogged gravity feed line; I've heard of dirty gas down here. He drops the set; it's a million to one nobody can read us through the storm at this range anyway. Twenty-five hundred—going down.

His electric feed pump seems to have cut in: the motor explodes—quits—explodes—and quits again for good. We are suddenly out of the bottom of the clouds. Below us is a long white line almost hidden by rain: the reef. But there isn't any beach behind it, only a big meandering bay with a few mangrove flats—and it's coming up at us fast.

This is going to be bad, I tell myself with great unoriginality. The women behind me haven't made a sound. I look back and see they've braced down with their coats by their heads. With a stalling speed around eighty, all this isn't much use, but I wedge myself in.

Estéban yells some more into his set, flying a falling plane. He is doing one jesus job, too—as the water rushes up at us he dives into a hair-raising turn and hangs us into the wind—with a long pale ridge of sandbar in front of our nose.

Where in hell he found it I never know. The Bonanza mushes down, and we belly-hit with a tremendous tearing crash—bounce—hit again—and everything slews wildly as we flat-spin into the mangroves at the end of the bar. Crash! Clang! The plane is wrapping itself into a mound of strangler fig with one wing up. The crashing quits with us all in one piece. And no fire. Fantastic.

Captain Estéban pries open his door, which is now in the roof. Behind me a woman is repeating quietly, "Mother. Mother." I climb up the floor and find the girl trying to free herself from her mother's embrace. The woman's eyes are closed. Then she opens them and suddenly lets go, sane as soap. Estéban starts hauling them out. I grab the Bonanza's aid kit and scramble out after them into brilliant sun and wind. The storm that hit us is already vanishing up the coast.

"Great landing, Captain."

"Oh, yes! It was beautiful." The women are shaky, but no hysteria. Estéban is surveying the scenery with the expression his ancestors used on the Spaniards.

If you've been in one of these things, you know the slow-motion inanity that goes on. Euphoria, first. We straggle down the fig tree and out onto the sandbar in the roaring hot wind, noting without alarm that there's nothing but miles of crystalline water on all sides. It's only a foot or so deep, and the bottom is the olive color of silt. The distant shore around us is all flat mangrove swamp, totally uninhabitable.

"Bahía Espiritu Santo." Estéban confirms my guess that we're down in that huge water wilderness. I always wanted to fish it.

"What's all that smoke?" The girl is pointing at the plumes blowing around the horizon.

"Alligator hunters," says Estéban. Maya poachers have left burn-offs in the swamps. It occurs to me that any signal fires we make aren't going to be too conspicuous. And I now note that our plane is well-buried in the mound of fig. Hard to see it from the air.

Just as the question of how the hell we get out of here surfaces in my mind, the older woman asks composedly, "If they didn't hear you, Captain, when will they start looking for us? Tomorrow?"

"Correct," Estéban agrees dourly. I recall that air-sea rescue is fairly informal here. Like, keep an eye open for Mario, his mother says he hasn't been home all week.

It dawns on me we may be here quite some while.

Furthermore, the diesel-truck noise on our left is the Caribbean piling back into the mouth of the bay. The wind is pushing it at us, and the bare bottoms on the mangroves show that our bar is covered at high tide. I recall seeing a full moon this morning in—believe it, St. Louis—which means maximal tides. Well, we can climb up in the plane. But what about drinking water?

There's a small splat! behind me. The older woman has sampled the bay. She shakes her head, smiling ruefully. It's the first real expression on either of them; I take it as the signal for introductions. When I say I'm Don Fenton from St. Louis, she tells me their name is Parsons, from Bethesda, Maryland. She says it so nicely I don't at first notice we aren't being given first names. We all compliment Captain Estéban again.

His left eye is swelled shut, an inconvenience beneath his attention as a Maya, but Mrs. Parsons spots the way he's bracing his elbow in his ribs.

"You're hurt, Captain."

"*Roto*—I think is broken." He's embarrassed at being in pain. We get him to peel off his Jaime shirt, revealing a nasty bruise in his superb dark-bay torso.

"Is there tape in that kit, Mr. Fenton? I've had a little first-aid training."

She begins to deal competently and very impersonally with the tape. Miss Parsons and I wander to the end of the bar and have a conversation which I am later to recall acutely.

"Roseate spoonbills," I tell her as three pink birds flap away.

"They're beautiful," she says in her tiny voice. They both have tiny voices. "He's a Mayan Indian, isn't he? The pilot, I mean."

"Right. The real thing, straight out of the Bonampak murals. Have you seen Chichén and Uxmal?"

"Yes. We were in Mérida. We're going to Tikal in Guatemala . . . I mean, we were."

"You'll get there." It occurs to me the girl needs cheering up. "Have they told you that Maya mothers used to tie a board on the infant's forehead to get that slant? They also hung a ball of tallow over its nose to make the eyes cross. It was considered aristocratic."

She smiles and takes another peek at Estéban. "People seem different in Yucatán," she says thoughtfully. "Not like the Indians around Mexico City. More, I don't know, independent."

"Comes from never having been conquered. Mayas got massacred and chased a lot, but nobody ever really flattened them. I bet you didn't know that the last Mexican-Maya war ended with a negotiated truce in nineteen thirty-five?"

"No!" Then she says seriously, "I like that."

"So do I."

"The water is really rising very fast," says Mrs. Parsons gently from behind us.

It is, and so is another *llovisno*. We climb back into the Bonanza. I try to rig my parka for a rain catcher, which blows loose as the storm hits fast and furious. We sort a couple of malt bars and my bottle of Jack Daniels out of the jumble in the cabin and make ourselves reasonably comfortable. The Parsons take a sip of whiskey each, Estéban and I considerably more. The Bonanza begins to bump soggily. Estéban makes an ancient one-eyed Mayan face at the water seeping into his cabin and goes to sleep. We all nap.

When the water goes down, the euphoria has gone with it, and we're very, very thirsty. It's also damn near sunset. I get to work with a bait-casting rod and some treble hooks and manage to foul-hook four small mullets. Estéban and the women tie the Bonanza's midget life raft out in the mangroves to catch rain. The wind is parching hot. No planes go by.

Finally another shower comes over and yields us six ounces of water apiece. When the sunset envelops the world in golden smoke, we squat on the sandbar to eat wet raw mullet and Instant Breakfast crumbs. The women are now in shorts, neat but definitely not sexy.

"I never realized how refreshing raw fish is," Mrs. Parsons says pleasantly. Her daughter chuckles, also pleasantly. She's on Mamma's far side away from Estéban and me. I have Mrs. Parsons figured now; Mother Hen protecting only chick from male predators. That's all right with me. I came here to fish.

But something is irritating me. The damn women haven't complained once, you understand. Not a peep, not a quaver, no personal manifestations whatever. They're like something out of a manual.

"You really seem at home in the wilderness, Mrs. Parsons. You do much camping?"

"Oh goodness no." Diffident laugh. "Not since my girl scout days. Oh, look—are those man-of-war birds?"

Answer a question with a question. I wait while the frigate birds sail nobly into the sunset.

"Bethesda . . . Would I be wrong in guessing you work for Uncle Sam?"

"Why yes. You must be very familiar with Washington, Mr. Fenton. Does your work bring you there often?"

Anywhere but on our sandbar the little ploy would have worked. My hunter's gene twitches.

"Which agency are you with?"

She gives up gracefully. "Oh, just GSA records. I'm a librarian."

Of course. I know her now, all the Mrs. Parsonses in records divisions, accounting sections, research branches, personnel and administration offices. Tell Mrs. Parsons we need a recap on the external service contracts for fiscal '73. So Yucatán is on the tours now? Pity . . . I offer her the tired little joke. "You know where the bodies are buried."

She smiles deprecatingly and stands up. "It does get dark quickly, doesn't it?"

Time to get back into the plane.

A flock of ibis are circling us, evidently accustomed to roosting in our fig tree. Estéban produces a machete and a Mayan string hammock. He proceeds to sling it between tree and plane, refusing help. His machete stroke is noticeably tentative.

The Parsons are taking a pee behind the tail vane. I hear one of them slip and squeal faintly. When they come back over the hull, Mrs. Parsons asks, "Might we sleep in the hammock, Captain?"

Estéban splits an unbelieving grin. I protest about rain and mosquitoes.

"Oh, we have insect repellent and we do enjoy fresh air."

The air is rushing by about force five and colder by the minute.

"We have our raincoats," the girl adds cheerfully.

Well, okay, ladies. We dangerous males retire inside the damp cabin. Through the wind I hear the women laugh softly now and then, apparently cosy in their chilly ibis roost. A private insanity, I decide. I know myself for the least threatening of men; my non-charisma has been in fact an asset jobwise, over the years. Are they having fantasies about Estéban? Or maybe they really are fresh-air nuts . . . Sleep comes for me in invisible diesels roaring by on the reef outside.

We emerge dry-mouthed into a vast windy salmon sunrise. A diamond chip of sun breaks out of the sea and promptly submerges in cloud. I go to work with the rod and some mullet bait while two showers detour around us. Breakfast is a strip of wet barracuda apiece.

The Parsons continue stoic and helpful. Under Estéban's direction they set up a section of cowling for a gasoline flare in case we hear a plane, but nothing goes over except one unseen jet droning toward Panama. The wind howls, hot and dry and full of coral dust. So are we.

"They look first in the sea." Estéban remarks. His aristocratic frontal slope is beaded with sweat; Mrs. Parsons watches him concernedly. I watch the cloud blanket tearing by above, getting higher and dryer and thicker. While that lasts nobody is going to find us, and the water business is now unfunny.

Finally I borrow Estéban's machete and hack a long light pole. "There's a stream coming in back there, I saw it from the plane. Can't be more than two, three miles."

"I'm afraid the raft's torn." Mrs. Parsons shows me the cracks in the orange plastic; irritatingly, it's a Delaware label.

"All right," I hear myself announce. "The tide's going down. If we cut the good end of that air tube, I can haul water back in it. I've waded flats before."

Even to me it sounds crazy.

"Stay by plane," Estéban says. He's right, of course. He's also clearly running a fever. I look at the overcast and taste grit and old barracuda. The hell with the manual.

When I start cutting up the raft, Estéban tells me to take the serape. "You stay one night." He's right about that, too; I'll have to wait out the tide.

"I'll come with you," says Mrs. Parsons calmly.

I simply stare at her. What new madness has got into Mother Hen? Does she imagine Estéban is too battered to be functional? While I'm being astounded, my eyes take in the fact that Mrs. Parsons is now quite rosy around the knees, with her hair loose and a sunburn starting on her nose. A trim, in fact a very neat shading-forty.

"Look, that stuff is horrible going. Mud up to your ears and water over your head."

"I'm really quite fit and I swim a great deal. I'll try to keep up. Two would be much safer, Mr. Fenton, and we can bring more water."

She's serious. Well, I'm about as fit as a marshmallow at this time of winter, and I can't pretend I'm depressed by the idea of company. So be it.

"Let me show Miss Parsons how to work this rod."

Miss Parsons is even rosier and more windblown, and she's not clumsy with my tackle. A good girl, Miss Parsons, in her nothing way. We cut another staff and get some gear together. At the last minute Estéban shows how sick he feels: he offers me the machete. I thank him, but, no; I'm used to my Wirkkala knife. We tie some air into the plastic tube for a float and set out along the sandiest looking line.

Estéban raises one dark palm. *"Buen viaje."* Miss Parsons has hugged her mother and gone to cast from the mangrove. She waves. We wave.

An hour later we're barely out of waving distance. The going is surely god-awful. The sand keeps dissolving into silt you can't walk on or swim through, and the bottom is spiked with dead mangrove spears. We flounder from one pothole to the next, scaring up rays and turtles and hoping to god we don't kick a moray eel. Where we're not soaked in slime, we're desiccated, and we smell like the Old Cretaceous.

Mrs. Parsons keeps up doggedly. I only have to pull her out once. When I do so, I notice the sandbar is now out of sight.

Finally we reach the gap in the mangrove line I thought was the creek. It turns out to open into another arm of the bay, with more mangroves ahead. And the tide is coming in.

"I've had the world's lousiest idea."

Mrs. Parsons only says mildly, "It's so different from the view from the plane."

I revise my opinion of the girl scouts, and we plow on past the mangroves toward the smoky haze that has to be shore. The sun is setting in our faces, making it hard to see. Ibises and herons fly up around us, and once a big permit spooks ahead, his fin cutting a rooster tail. We fall into more potholes. The flashlights get soaked. I am having fantasies of the mangrove as universal obstacle; it's hard to recall I ever walked down a street, for instance, without stumbling over or under or through mangrove roots. And the sun is dropping down, down.

Suddenly we hit a ledge and fall over it into a cold flow.

"The stream! It's fresh water!"

We guzzle and garble and douse our heads; it's the best drink I remember. "Oh my, oh my—!" Mrs. Parsons is laughing right out loud.

"That dark place over to the right looks like real land."

We flounder across the flow and follow a hard shelf, which turns into solid bank and rises over our heads. Shortly there's a break beside a clump of spiny bromels, and we scramble up and flop down at the top, dripping and stinking. Out of sheer reflex my arm goes around my companion's shoulder—but Mrs. Parsons isn't there; she's up on her knees peering at the burnt-over plain around us.

"It's so good to see land one can walk on!" The tone is too innocent. *Noli me tangere.*

"Don't try it." I'm exasperated; the muddy little woman, what does she think? "That ground out there is a crush of ashes over muck, and it's full of stubs. You can go in over your knees."

"It seems firm here."

"We're in an alligator nursery. That was the slide we came up. Don't worry, by now the old lady's doubtless on her way to be made into handbags."

"What a shame."

"I better set a line down in the stream while I can still see."

I slide back down and rig a string of hooks that may get us breakfast. When I get back Mrs. Parsons is wringing muck out of the serape.

"I'm glad you warned me, Mr. Fenton. It *is* treacherous."

"Yeah." I'm over my irritation; god knows I don't want to *tangere* Mrs. Parsons, even if I weren't beat down to mush. "In its quiet way, Yucatán is a tough place to get around in. You can see why the Mayas built roads. Speaking of which—look!"

The last of the sunset is silhouetting a small square shape a couple of kilometers inland; a Maya *ruina* with a fig tree growing out of it.

"Lot of those around. People think they were guard towers."

"What a deserted-feeling land."

"Let's hope it's deserted by mosquitoes."

We slump down in the 'gator nursery and share the last malt bar, watching the stars slide in and out of the blowing clouds. The bugs aren't too bad; maybe the burn did them in. And it isn't hot any more, either—

in fact, it's not even warm, wet as we are. Mrs. Parsons continues tranquilly interested in Yucatán and unmistakably uninterested in togetherness.

Just as I'm beginning to get aggressive notions about how we're going to spend the night if she expects me to give her the serape, she stands up, scuffs at a couple of hummocks and says, "I expect this is as good a place as any, isn't it, Mr. Fenton?"

With which she spreads out the raft bag for a pillow and lies down on her side in the dirt with exactly half the serape over her and the other corner folded neatly open. Her small back is toward me.

The demonstration is so convincing that I'm halfway under my share of serape before the preposterousness of it stops me.

"By the way. My name is Don."

"Oh, of course." Her voice is graciousness itself, "I'm Ruth."

I get in not quite touching her, and we lie there like two fish on a plate, exposed to the stars and smelling the smoke in the wind and feeling things underneath us. It is absolutely the most intimately awkward moment I've had in years.

The woman doesn't mean one thing to me, but the obtrusive recessiveness of her, the defiance of her little rump eight inches from my fly— for two pesos I'd have those shorts down and introduce myself. If I were twenty years younger. If I wasn't so bushed . . . But the twenty years and the exhaustion are there, and it comes to me wryly that Mrs. Ruth Parsons has judged things to a nicety. If I *were* twenty years younger, she wouldn't be here. Like the butterfish that float around a sated barracuda, only to vanish away the instant his intent changes, Mrs. Parsons knows her little shorts are safe. Those firmly filled little shorts, so close . . .

A warm nerve stirs in my groin—and just as it does I become aware of a silent emptiness beside me. Mrs. Parsons is imperceptibly inching away. Did my breathing change? Whatever, I'm perfectly sure that if my hand reached, she'd be elsewhere—probably announcing her intention to take a dip. The twenty years bring a chuckle to my throat, and I relax.

"Good night, Ruth."

"Good night, Don."

And believe it or not, we sleep, while the armadas of the wind roar overhead.

Light wakes me—a cold white glare.

My first thought is 'gator hunters. Best to manifest ourselves as *turistas* as fast as possible. I scramble up, noting that Ruth has dived under the bromel clump.

"*Quién estás? A secorro!* Help, *señores!*"

No answer except the light goes out, leaving me blind.

I yell some more in a couple of languages. It stays dark. There's a vague scrabbling, whistling sound somewhere in the burn-off. Liking everything less by the minute, I try a speech about our plane having crashed and we need help.

A very narrow pencil of light flicks over us and snaps off.

"Eh-ep," says a blurry voice and something metallic twitters. They for sure aren't locals. I'm getting unpleasant ideas.

"Yes, help!"

Something goes *crackle-crackle whish-whish,* and all sounds fade away.

"What the holy hell!" I stumble toward where they were.

"Look." Ruth whispers behind me. "Over by the ruin."

I look and catch a multiple flicker which winks out fast.

"A camp?"

And I take two more blind strides. My leg goes down through the crust, and a spike spears me just where you stick the knife in to unjoint a drumstick. By the pain that goes through my bladder I recognize that my trick kneecap has caught it.

For instant basket-case you can't beat kneecaps. First you discover your knee doesn't bend any more, so you try putting some weight on it, and a bayonet goes up your spine and unhinges your jaw. Little grains of gristle have got into the sensitive bearing surface. The knee tries to buckle and can't, and mercifully you fall down.

Ruth helps me back to the serape.

"What a fool, what a god-forgotten imbecile—"

"Not at all, Don. It was perfectly natural." We strike matches; her fingers push mine aside, exploring. "I think it's in place, but it's swelling fast. I'll lay a wet handkerchief on it. We'll have to wait for morning to check the cut. Were they poachers, do you think?"

"Probably," I lie. What I think they were is smugglers.

She comes back with a soaked bandanna and drapes it on. "We must have frightened them. That light . . . it seemed so bright."

"Some hunting party. People do crazy things around here."

"Perhaps they'll come back in the morning."

"Could be."

Ruth pulls up the wet serape, and we say goodnight again. Neither of us are mentioning how we're going to get back to the plane without help.

I lie staring south where Alpha Centauri is blinking in and out of the overcast and cursing myself for the sweet mess I've made. My first idea is giving way to an even less pleasing one.

Smuggling, around here, is a couple of guys in an outboard meeting a shrimp boat by the reef. They don't light up the sky or have some kind of swamp buggy that goes whoosh. Plus a big camp . . . paramilitary-type equipment?

I've seen a report of Guevarista infiltrators operating on the British Honduran border, which is about a hundred kilometers—sixty miles—south of here. Right under those clouds. If that's what looked us over, I'll be more than happy if they don't come back . . .

I wake up in pelting rain, alone. My first move confirms that my leg is as expected—a giant misplaced erection bulging out of my shorts. I raise up painfully to see Ruth standing by the bromels, looking over the bay. Solid wet nimbus is pouring out of the south.

"No planes today."

"Oh, good morning, Don. Should we look at that cut now?"

"It's minimal." In fact the skin is hardly broken, and no deep puncture. Totally out of proportion to the havoc inside.

"Well, they have water to drink," Ruth says tranquilly. "Maybe those hunters will come back. I'll go see if we have a fish—that is, can I help you in any way, Don?"

Very tactful. I emit an ungracious negative, and she goes off about her private concerns.

They certainly are private, too; when I recover from my own sanitary efforts, she's still away. Finally I hear splashing.

"It's a big fish!" More splashing. Then she climbs up the bank with a three-pound mangrove snapper—and something else.

It isn't until after the messy work of filleting the fish that I begin to notice.

She's making a smudge of chaff and twigs to singe the fillets, small hands very quick, tension in that female upper lip. The rain has eased off for the moment; we're sluicing wet but warm enough. Ruth brings me my fish on a mangrove skewer and sits back on her heels with an odd breathy sigh.

"Aren't you joining me?"

"Oh, of course." She gets a strip and picks at it, saying quickly, "We either have too much salt or too little, don't we? I should fetch some brine." Her eyes are roving from nothing to noplace.

"Good thought." I hear another sigh and decide the girl scouts need an assist. "Your daughter mentioned you've come from Mérida. Have you seen much of Mexico?"

"Not really. Last year we went to Mazatlán and Cuernavaca . . ." She puts the fish down, frowning.

"And you're going to see Tikal. Going to Bonampak too?"

"No." Suddenly she jumps up brushing rain off her face. "I'll bring you some water, Don."

She ducks down the slide, and after a fair while comes back with a full bromel stalk.

"Thanks." She's standing above me, staring restlessly round the horizon.

"Ruth, I hate to say it, but those guys are not coming back and it's probably just as well. Whatever they were up to, we looked like trouble. The most they'll do is tell someone we're here. That'll take a day or two to get around, we'll be back at the plane by then."

"I'm sure you're right, Don." She wanders over to the smudge fire.

"And quit fretting about your daughter. She's a big girl."

"Oh, I'm sure Althea's all right . . . They have plenty of water now." Her fingers drum on her thigh. It's raining again.

"Come on, Ruth. Sit down. Tell me about Althea. Is she still in college?"

She gives that sighing little laugh and sits. "Althea got her degree last year. She's in computer programming."

"Good for her. And what about you, what do you do in GSA records?"

"I'm in Foreign Procurement Archives." She smiles mechanically, but her breathing is shallow. "It's very interesting."

"I know a Jack Wittig in Contracts, maybe you know him?"

It sounds pretty absurd, there in the 'gator slide.

"Oh, I've met Mr. Wittig. I'm sure he wouldn't remember me."

"Why not?"

"I'm not very memorable."

Her voice is factual. She's perfectly right, of course. Who was that woman, Mrs. Jannings, Janny, who coped with my per diem for years? Competent, agreeable, impersonal. She had a sick father or something. But dammit, Ruth is a lot younger and better-looking. Comparatively speaking.

"Maybe Mrs. Parsons doesn't want to be memorable."

She makes a vague sound, and I suddenly realize Ruth isn't listening to me at all. Her hands are clenched around her knees, she's staring inland at the ruin.

"Ruth. I tell you our friends with the light are in the next country by now. Forget it, we don't need them."

Her eyes come back to me as if she'd forgotten I was there, and she nods slowly. It seems to be too much effort to speak. Suddenly she cocks her head and jumps up again.

"I'll go look at the line, Don. I thought I heard something—" She's gone like a rabbit.

While she's away I try getting up onto my good leg and the staff. The pain is sickening; knees seem to have some kind of hot line to the stomach. I take a couple of hops to test whether the Demerol I have in my belt would get me walking. As I do so, Ruth comes up the bank with a fish flapping in her hands.

"Oh, no, Don! *No!*" She actually clasps the snapper to her breast.

"The water will take some of my weight. I'd like to give it a try."

"You mustn't!" Ruth says quite violently and instantly modulates down. "Look at the bay, Don. One can't see a thing."

I teeter there, tasting bile and looking at the mingled curtains of sun and rain driving across the water. She's right, thank god. Even with two good legs we could get into trouble out there.

"I guess one more night won't kill us."

I let her collapse me back onto the gritty plastic, and she positively bustles around, finding me a chunk to lean on, stretching the serape on both staffs to keep rain off me, bringing another drink, grubbing for dry tinder.

"I'll make us a real bonfire as soon as it lets up, Don. They'll see our smoke, they'll know we're all right. We just have to wait." Cheery smile. "Is there any way we can make you more comfortable?"

Holy Saint Sterculius: playing house in a mud puddle. For a fatuous moment I wonder if Mrs. Parsons has designs on me. And then she lets out another sigh and sinks back onto her heels with that listening look. Unconsciously her rump wiggles a little. My ear picks up the operative word: *wait*.

Ruth Parsons is waiting. In fact, she acts as if she's waiting so hard it's killing her. For what? For someone to get us out of here, what else? . . . But why was she so horrified when I got up to try to leave? Why all this tension?

My paranoia stirs. I grab it by the collar and start idly checking back. Up to when whoever it was showed up last night, Mrs. Parsons was, I guess, normal. Calm and sensible, anyway. Now she's humming like a high wire. And she seems to want to stay here and wait. Just as an intellectual pastime, why?

Could she have intended to come here? No way. Where she planned to be was Chetumal, which is on the border. Come to think, Chetumal is an odd way round to Tikal. Let's say the scenario was that she's meeting somebody in Chetumal. Somebody who's part of an organization. So now her contact in Chetumal knows she's overdue. And when those types appeared last night, something suggests to her that they're part of the same organization. And she hopes they'll put one and one together and come back for her?

"May I have the knife, Don? I'll clean the fish."

Rather slowly I pass the knife, kicking my subconscious. Such a decent ordinary little woman, a good girl scout. My trouble is that I've bumped into too many professional agilities under the careful stereotypes. *I'm not very memorable* . . .

What's in Foreign Procurement Archives? Wittig handles classified contracts. Lots of money stuff; foreign currency negotiations, commodity price schedules, some industrial technology. Or—just as a hypothesis—it could be as simple as a wad of bills back in that modest beige Ventura, to be exchanged for a packet from say, Costa Rica. If she were a courier, they'd want to get at the plane. And then what about me and maybe Estéban? Even hypothetically, not good.

I watch her hacking at the fish, forehead knotted with effort, teeth in her lip. Mrs. Parsons of Bethesda, this thrumming, private woman. How crazy can I get? *They'll see our smoke* . . .

"Here's your knife, Don. I washed it. Does the leg hurt very badly?"

I blink away the fantasies and see a scared little woman in a mangrove swamp.

"Sit down, rest. You've been going all out."

She sits obediently, like a kid in a dentist chair.

"You're stewing about Althea. And she's probably worried about you. We'll get back tomorrow under our own steam, Ruth."

"Honestly I'm not worried at all, Don." The smile fades; she nibbles her lip, frowning out at the bay.

"You know, Ruth, you surprised me when you offered to come along. Not that I don't appreciate it. But I rather thought you'd be concerned about leaving Althea alone with our good pilot. Or was it only me?"

This gets her attention at last.

"I believe Captain Estéban is a very fine type of man."

The words surprise me a little. Isn't the correct line more like "I trust Althea," or even, indignantly, "Althea is a good girl?"

"He's a man. Althea seemed to think he was interesting."

She goes on staring at the bay. And then I notice her tongue flick out and lick that prehensile upper lip. There's a flush that isn't sunburn around her ears and throat too, and one hand is gently rubbing her thigh. What's she seeing, out there in the flats?

Oho.

Captain Estéban's mahogany arms clasping Miss Althea Parsons' pearly body. Captain Estéban's archaic nostrils snuffling in Miss Parsons' tender neck. Captain Estéban's copper buttocks pumping into Althea's creamy upturned bottom . . . The hammock, very bouncy. Mayas know all about it.

Well, well. So Mother Hen has her little quirks.

I feel fairly silly and more than a little irritated. *Now* I find out . . . But even vicarious lust has much to recommend it, here in the mud and rain. I settle back, recalling that Miss Althea the computer programmer had waved good-bye very composedly. Was she sending her mother to flounder across the bay with me so she can get programmed in Maya? The memory of Honduran mahogany logs drifting in and out of the opalescent sand comes to me. Just as I am about to suggest that Mrs. Parsons might care to share my rain shelter, she remarks serenely, "The Mayas seem to be a very fine type of people. I believe you said so to Althea."

The implications fall on me with the rain. *Type.* As in breeding, bloodline, sire. Am I supposed to have certified Estéban not only as a stud but as a genetic donor?

"Ruth, are you telling me you're prepared to accept a half-Indian grandchild?"

"Why, Don, that's up to Althea, you know."

Looking at the mother, I guess it is. Oh, for mahogany gonads.

Ruth has gone back to listening to the wind, but I'm not about to let her off that easy. Not after all that *noli me tangere* jazz.

"What will Althea's father think?"

Her face snaps around at me, genuinely startled.

"Althea's father?" Complicated semismile. "He won't mind."

"He'll accept it too, eh?" I see her shake her head as if a fly were bothering her, and add with a cripple's malice: "Your husband must be a very fine type of a man."

Ruth looks at me, pushing her wet hair back abruptly. I have the impression that mousy Mrs. Parsons is roaring out of control, but her voice is quiet.

"There isn't any Mr. Parsons, Don. There never was. Althea's father was a Danish medical student . . . I believe he has gained considerable prominence."

"Oh." Something warns me not to say I'm sorry. "You mean he doesn't know about Althea?"

"No." She smiles, her eyes bright and cuckoo.

"Seems like rather a rough deal for her."

"I grew up quite happily under the same circumstances."

Bang, I'm dead. Well, well, well. A mad image blooms in my mind: generations of solitary Parsons women selecting sires, making impregnation trips. Well, I hear the world is moving their way.

"I better look at the fish line."

She leaves. The glow fades. *No.* Just no, no contact. Good-bye, Captain Estéban. My leg is very uncomfortable. The hell with Mrs. Parsons' long-distance orgasm.

We don't talk much after that, which seems to suit Ruth. The odd day drags by. Squall after squall blows over us. Ruth singes up some more fillets, but the rain drowns her smudge; it seems to pour hardest just as the sun's about to show.

Finally she comes to sit under my sagging serape, but there's no warmth there. I doze, aware of her getting up now and then to look around. My subconscious notes that she's still twitchy. I tell my subconscious to knock it off.

Presently I wake up to find her penciling on the water-soaked pages of a little notepad.

"What's that, a shopping list for alligators?"

Automatic polite laugh. "Oh, just an address. In case we—I'm being silly, Don."

"Hey," I sit up, wincing, "Ruth, quit fretting. I mean it. We'll all be out of this soon. You'll have a great story to tell."

She doesn't look up. "Yes . . . I guess we will."

"Come on, we're doing fine. There isn't any real danger here, you know. Unless you're allergic to fish?"

Another good-little-girl laugh, but there's a shiver in it.

"Sometimes I think I'd like to go . . . really far away."

To keep her talking I say the first thing in my head.

"Tell me, Ruth. I'm curious why you would settle for that kind of lonely life, there in Washington? I mean, a woman like you—"

"Should get married?" She gives a shaky sigh, pushing the notebook back in her wet pocket.

"Why not? It's the normal source of companionship. Don't tell me you're trying to be some kind of professional man-hater."

"Lesbian, you mean?" Her laugh sounds better. "With my security rating? No, I'm not."

"Well, then. Whatever trauma you went through, these things don't last forever. You can't hate all men."

The smile is back. "Oh, there wasn't any trauma, Don, and I *don't* hate men. That would be as silly as—as hating the weather." She glances wryly at the blowing rain.

"I think you have a grudge. You're even spooky of me."

Smooth as a mouse bite she says, "I'd love to hear about your family, Don?"

Touché. I give her the edited version of how I don't have one any more, and she says she's sorry, how sad. And we chat about what a good life a single person really has, and how she and her friends enjoy plays and concerts and travel, and one of them is head cashier for Ringling Brothers, how about that?

But it's coming out jerkier and jerkier like a bad tape, with her eyes going round the horizon in the pauses and her face listening for something that isn't my voice. What's wrong with her? Well, what's wrong with any furtively unconventional middle-aged woman with an empty bed. And a security clearance. An old habit of mind remarks unkindly that Mrs. Parsons represents what is known as the classic penetration target.

"—so much more opportunity now." Her voice trails off.

"Hurrah for women's lib, eh?"

"The lib?" Impatiently she leans forward and tugs the serape straight. "Oh, that's doomed."

The apocalyptic word jars my attention.

"What do you mean, doomed?"

She glances at me as if I weren't hanging straight either and says vaguely, "Oh . . ."

"Come on, why doomed? Didn't they get that equal rights bill?"

Long hesitation. When she speaks again her voice is different.

"Women have no rights, Don, except what men allow us. Men are more aggressive and powerful, and they run the world. When the next real crisis upsets them, our so-called rights will vanish like—like that smoke. We'll be back where we always were: property. And whatever has gone wrong will be blamed on our freedom, like the fall of Rome was. You'll see."

Now all this is delivered in a gray tone of total conviction. The last time I heard that tone, the speaker was explaining why he had to keep his file drawers full of dead pigeons.

"Oh, come on. You and your friends are the backbone of the system; if you quit, the country would come to a screeching halt before lunch."

No answering smile.

"That's fantasy." Her voice is still quiet. "Women don't work that way.

We're a—a toothless world." She looks around as if she wanted to stop talking. "What women do is survive. We live by ones and twos in the chinks of your world-machine."

"Sounds like a guerrilla operation." I'm not really joking, here in the 'gator den. In fact, I'm wondering if I spent too much thought on mahogany logs.

"Guerrillas have something to hope for." Suddenly she switches on a jolly smile. "Think of us as opossums, Don. Did you know there are opossums living all over? Even in New York City."

I smile back with my neck prickling. I thought I was the paranoid one.

"Men and women aren't different species, Ruth. Women do everything men do."

"Do they?" Our eyes meet, but she seems to be seeing ghosts between us in the rain. She mutters something that could be "My Lai" and looks away. "All the endless wars . . ." Her voice is a whisper. "All the huge authoritarian organizations for doing unreal things. Men live to struggle against each other; we're just part of the battlefields. It'll never change unless you change the whole world. I dream sometimes of—of going away—" She checks and abruptly changes voice. "Forgive me, Don, it's so stupid saying all this."

"Men hate wars too, Ruth," I say as gently as I can.

"I know." She shrugs and climbs to her feet. "But that's your problem, isn't it?"

End of communication. Mrs. Ruth Parsons isn't even living in the same world with me.

I watch her move around restlessly, head turning toward the ruins. Alienation like that can add up to dead pigeons, which would be GSA's problem. It could also lead to believing some joker who's promising to change the whole world. Which could just probably be my problem if one of them was over in that camp last night, where she keeps looking. *Guerrillas have something to hope for . . .?*

Nonsense. I try another position and see that the sky seems to be clearing as the sun sets. The wind is quieting down at last too. Insane to think this little woman is acting out some fantasy in this swamp. But that equipment last night was no fantasy; if those lads have some connection with her, I'll be in the way. You couldn't find a handier spot to dispose of the body . . . Maybe some Guevarista is a fine type of man?

Absurd. Sure . . . The only thing more absurd would be to come through the wars and get myself terminated by a mad librarian's boyfriend on a fishing trip.

A fish flops in the stream below us. Ruth spins around so fast she hits the serape. "I better start the fire," she says, her eyes still on the plain and her head cocked, listening.

All right, let's test.

"Expecting company?"

It rocks her. She freezes, and her eyes come swiveling around at me like a film take captioned Fright. I can see her decide to smile.

"Oh, one never can tell!" She laughs weirdly, the eyes not changed. "I'll get the—the kindling." She fairly scuttles into the brush.

Nobody, paranoid or not, could call *that* a normal reaction.

Ruth Parsons is either psycho or she's expecting something to happen—and it has nothing to do with me; I scared her pissless.

Well, she could be nuts. And I could be wrong, but there are some mistakes you only make once.

Reluctantly I unzip my body belt, telling myself that if I think what I think, my only course is to take something for my leg and get as far as possible from Mrs. Ruth Parsons before whoever she's waiting for arrives.

In my belt also is a .32 caliber asset Ruth doesn't know about—and it's going to stay there. My longevity program leaves the shoot-outs to TV and stresses being somewhere else when the roof falls in. I can spend a perfectly safe and also perfectly horrible night out in one of those mangrove flats . . . Am I insane?

At this moment Ruth stands up and stares blatantly inland with her hand shading her eyes. Then she tucks something into her pocket, buttons up and tightens her belt.

That does it.

I dry-swallow two 100 mg tabs, which should get me ambulatory and still leave me wits to hide. Give it a few minutes. I make sure my compass and some hooks are in my own pocket and sit waiting while Ruth fusses with her smudge fire, sneaking looks away when she thinks I'm not watching.

The flat world around us is turning into an unearthly amber and violet light show as the first numbness sweeps into my leg. Ruth has crawled under the bromels for more dry stuff; I can see her foot. Okay. I reach for my staff.

Suddenly the foot jerks, and Ruth yells—or rather, her throat makes that *Uh-uh-hhh* that means pure horror. The foot disappears in a rattle of bromel stalks.

I lunge upright on the crutch and look over the bank at a frozen scene.

Ruth is crouching sideways on the ledge, clutching her stomach. They are about a yard below, floating on the river in a skiff. While I was making up my stupid mind, her friends have glided right under my ass. There are three of them.

They are tall and white. I try to see them as men in some kind of white jumpsuits. The one nearest the bank is stretching out a long white arm toward Ruth. She jerks and scuttles further away.

The arm stretches after her. It stretches and stretches. It stretches two yards and stays hanging in the air. Small black things are wiggling from its tip.

I look where their faces should be and see black hollow dishes with vertical stripes. The stripes move slowly . . .

There is no more possibility of their being human—or anything else I've ever seen. What has Ruth conjured up?

The scene is totally silent. I blink, blink—this cannot be real. The two in the far end of the skiff are writhing those arms around an apparatus on a tripod. A weapon? Suddenly I hear the same blurry voice I heard in the night.

"Guh-give," it groans. "G-give . . ."

Dear god, it's real, whatever it is. I'm terrified. My mind is trying not to form a word.

And Ruth—Jesus, of course—Ruth is terrified too; she's edging along the bank away from them, gaping at the monsters in the skiff, who are obviously nobody's friends. She's hugging something to her body. Why doesn't she get over the bank and circle back behind me?

"G-g-give." That wheeze is coming from the tripod. "Pee-eeze give." The skiff is moving upstream below Ruth, following her. The arm undulates out at her again, its black digits looping. Ruth scrambles to the top of the bank.

"Ruth!" My voice cracks. "Ruth, get over here behind me!"

She doesn't look at me, only keeps sidling farther away. My terror detonates into anger.

"Come back here!" With my free hand I'm working the .32 out of my belt. The sun has gone down.

She doesn't turn but straightens up warily, still hugging the thing. I see her mouth working. Is she actually trying to *talk* to them?

"Please . . ." She swallows. "Please speak to me. I need your help."

"RUTH!!"

At this moment the nearest white monster whips into a great S-curve and sails right onto the bank at her, eight feet of snowy rippling horror.

And I shoot Ruth.

I don't know that for a moment—I've yanked the gun up so fast that my staff slips and dumps me as I fire. I stagger up, hearing Ruth scream "No! No! No!"

The creature is back down by his boat, and Ruth is still farther away, clutching herself. Blood is running down her elbow.

"Stop it, Don! They aren't attacking you!"

"For god's sake! Don't be a fool, I can't help you if you won't get away from them!"

No reply. Nobody moves. No sound except the drone of a jet passing far above. In the darkening stream below me the three white figures shift uneasily; I get the impression of radar dishes focusing. The word spells itself in my head: *Aliens.*

Extraterrestrials.

What do I do, call the President? Capture them single-handed with my peashooter? . . . I'm alone in the arse end of nowhere with one leg and my brain cuddled in meperidine hydrochloride.

"Prrr-eese," their machine blurs again. "Wa-wat hep . . ."

"Our plane fell down," Ruth says in a very distinct, eerie voice. She points up at the jet, out towards the bay. "My—my child is there. Please take us *there* in your boat."

Dear god. While she's gesturing, I get a look at the thing she's hugging in her wounded arm. It's metallic, like a big glimmering distributor head. What—?

Wait a minute. This morning: when she was gone so long, she could have found that thing. Something they left behind. Or dropped. And she hid it, not telling me. That's why she kept going under that bromel clump—she was peeking at it. Waiting. And the owners came back and caught her. They want it. She's trying to bargain, by god.

"—Water," Ruth is pointing again. "Take us. Me. And him."

The black faces turn toward me, blind and horrible. Later on I may be grateful for that "us." Not now.

"Throw your gun away, Don. They'll take us back." Her voice is weak.

"Like hell I will. You—who are you? What are you doing here?"

"Oh god, does it matter? He's frightened," she cries to them. "Can you understand?"

She's as alien as they, there in the twilight. The beings in the skiff are twittering among themselves. Their box starts to moan.

"Ss-stu-dens," I make out. "S-stu-ding . . . not—huh-arm-ing . . . w-we . . . buh . . ." It fades into garble and then says "G-give . . . we . . . g-go . . ."

Peace-loving cultural-exchange students—on the interstellar level now. Oh, no.

"Bring that thing here, Ruth—right now!"

But she's starting down the bank toward them saying, "Take me."

"Wait! You need a tourniquet on that arm."

"I know. Please put the gun down, Don."

She's actually at the skiff, right by them. They aren't moving.

"Jesus Christ." Slowly, reluctantly, I drop the .32. When I start down the slide, I find I'm floating; adrenaline and Demerol are a bad mix.

The skiff comes gliding toward me, Ruth in the bow clutching the thing and her arm. The aliens stay in the stern behind their tripod, away from me. I note the skiff is camouflaged tan and green. The world around us is deep shadowy blue.

"Don, bring the water bag!"

As I'm dragging down the plastic bag, it occurs to me that Ruth really is cracking up, the water isn't needed now. But my own brain seems to have gone into overload. All I can focus on is a long white rubbery arm

with black worms clutching the far end of the orange tube, helping me
fill it. This isn't happening.

"Can you get in, Don?" As I hoist my numb legs up, two long white
pipes reach for me. *No you don't.* I kick and tumble in beside Ruth.
She moves away.

A creaky hum starts up, it's coming from a wedge in the center of the
skiff. And we're in motion, sliding toward dark mangrove files.

I stare mindlessly at the wedge. Alien technological secrets? I can't see
any, the power source is under that triangular cover, about two feet long.
The gadgets on the tripod are equally cryptic, except that one has a big
lens. Their light?

As we hit the open bay, the hum rises and we start planing faster and
faster still. Thirty knots? Hard to judge in the dark. Their hull seems
to be a modified trihedral much like ours, with a remarkable absence of
slap. Say twenty-two feet. Schemes of capturing it swirl in my mind. I'll
need Estéban.

Suddenly a huge flood of white light fans out over us from the tripod,
blotting out the aliens in the stern. I see Ruth pulling at a belt around
her arm still hugging the gizmo.

"I'll tie that for you."

"It's all right."

The alien device is twinkling or phosphorescing slightly. I lean over to
look, whispering, "Give that to me, I'll pass it to Estéban."

"No!" She scoots away, almost over the side. "It's theirs, they need it!"

"What? Are you crazy?" I'm so taken aback by this idiocy I literally
stammer. "We have to, we—"

"They haven't hurt us. I'm sure they could." Her eyes are watching
me with feral intensity; in the light her face has a lunatic look. Numb as
I am, I realize that the wretched woman is poised to throw herself over
the side if I move. With the alien thing.

"I think they're gentle," she mutters.

"For Christ's sake, Ruth, they're *aliens!*"

"I'm used to it," she says absently. "There's the island! Stop! Stop here!"

The skiff slows, turning. A mound of foliage is tiny in the light. Metal
glints—the plane.

"Althea! Althea! Are you all right?"

Yells, movement on the plane. The water is high, we're floating over
the bar. The aliens are keeping us in the lead with the light hiding them.
I see one pale figure splashing toward us and a dark one behind, coming
more slowly. Estéban must be puzzled by that light.

"Mr. Fenton is hurt, Althea. These people brought us back with the
water. Are you all right?"

"A-okay." Althea flounders up, peering excitedly. "You all right?
Whew, that light!" Automatically I start handing her the idiotic water bag.

"Leave that for the captain," Ruth says sharply. "Althea, can you climb in the boat? Quickly, it's important."

"Coming."

"No, no!" I protest, but the skiff tilts as Althea swarms in. The aliens twitter, and their voice box starts groaning. "Gu-give . . . now . . . give . . ."

"*Que llega?*" Estéban's face appears beside me, squinting fiercely into the light.

"Grab it, get it from her—that thing she has—" but Ruth's voice rides over mine. "Captain, lift Mr. Fenton out of the boat. He's hurt his leg. Hurry, please."

"Goddamn it, wait!" I shout, but an arm has grabbed my middle. When a Maya boosts you, you go. I hear Althea saying, "Mother, your arm!" and fall onto Estéban. We stagger around in water up to my waist; I can't feel my feet at all.

When I get steady, the boat is yards away. The two women are head-to-head, murmuring.

"Get them!" I tug loose from Estéban and flounder forward. Ruth stands up in the boat facing the invisible aliens.

"Take us with you. Please. We want to go with you, away from here."

"Ruth! Estéban, get that boat!" I lunge and lose my feet again. The aliens are chirruping madly behind their light.

"Please take us. We don't mind what your planet is like; we'll learn—we'll do anything! We won't cause any trouble. Please. Oh *please*." The skiff is drifting farther away.

"Ruth! Althea! Are you crazy? Wait—" But I can only shuffle night-marelike in the ooze, hearing that damn voice box wheeze, "N-not come . . . more . . . not come . . ." Althea's face turns to it, open-mouthed grin.

"Yes, we understand," Ruth cries. "We don't want to come back. Please take us with you!"

I shout and Estéban splashes past me shouting too, something about radio.

"Yes-s-s" groans the voice.

Ruth sits down suddenly, clutching Althea. At that moment Estéban grabs the edge of the skiff beside her.

"Hold them, Estéban! Don't let her go."

He gives me one slit-eyed glance over his shoulder, and I recognize his total uninvolvement. He's had a good look at that camouflage paint and the absence of fishing gear. I make a desperate rush and slip again. When I come up Ruth is saying, "We're going with these people, Captain. Please take your money out of my purse, it's in the plane. And give this to Mr. Fenton."

She passes him something small; the notebook. He takes it slowly.

"Estéban! No!"

He has released the skiff.

"Thank you so much," Ruth says as they float apart. Her voice is shaky; she raises it. "There won't be any trouble, Don. Please send this cable. It's to a friend of mine, she'll take care of everything." Then she adds the craziest touch of the entire night. "She's a grand person; she's director of nursing training at N.I.H."

As the skiff drifts, I hear Althea add something that sounds like "Right on."

Sweet Jesus . . . Next minute the humming has started; the light is receding fast. The last I see of Mrs. Ruth Parsons and Miss Althea Parsons is two small shadows against that light, like two opossums. The light snaps off, the hum deepens—and they're going, going, gone away.

In the dark water beside me Estéban is instructing everybody in general to *chingarse* themselves.

"Friends, or something," I tell him lamely. "She seemed to want to go with them."

He is pointedly silent, hauling me back to the plane. He knows what could be around here better than I do, and Mayas have their own longevity program. His condition seems improved. As we get in I notice the hammock has been repositioned.

In the night—of which I remember little—the wind changes. And at seven thirty next morning a Cessna buzzes the sandbar under cloudless skies.

By noon we're back in Cozumel, Captain Estéban accepts his fees and departs laconically for his insurance wars. I leave the Parsons' bags with the Caribe agent, who couldn't care less. The cable goes to a Mrs. Priscilla Hayes Smith, also of Bethesda. I take myself to a medico and by three PM I'm sitting on the Cabañas terrace with a fat leg and a double margharita, trying to believe the whole thing.

The cable said, *Althea and I taking extraordinary opportunity for travel. Gone several years. Please take charge our affairs. Love, Ruth.*

She'd written it that afternoon, you understand.

I order another double, wishing to hell I'd gotten a good look at that gizmo. Did it have a label. Made by Betelgeusians? No matter how weird it was, *how* could a person be crazy enough to imagine—?

Not only that but to hope, to plan? *If I could only go away* . . . That's what she was doing, all day. Waiting, hoping, figuring how to get Althea. To go sight unseen to an alien world . . .

With the third margharita I try a joke about alienated women, but my heart's not in it. And I'm certain there won't be any bother, any trouble at all. Two human women, one of them possibly pregnant, have departed for, I guess, the stars; and the fabric of society will never show a ripple. I brood: do all Mrs. Parsons' friends hold themselves in readiness for any eventuality, including leaving Earth? And will Mrs. Parsons somehow one day contrive to send for Mrs. Priscilla Hayes Smith, that grand person?

I can only send for another cold one, musing on Althea. What suns will Captain Estéban's sloe-eyed offspring, if any, look upon? "Get in, Althea, we're taking off for Orion." "A-okay, Mother." Is that some system of upbringing? *We survive by ones and twos in the chinks of your world-machine . . . I'm used to aliens . . .* She'd meant every word. Insane. How could a woman choose to live among unknown monsters, to say good-bye to her home, her world?

As the margharitas take hold, the whole mad scenario melts down to the image of those two small shapes sitting side by side in the receding alien glare.

Two of our opossums are missing.

JOY IN PROVENCE

by

MAY SARTON

(b. 1912)

Born in Belgium, May Sarton came to Cambridge, Massachusetts, in 1916 and was educated there before going to New York to study acting. She left the theater in 1937 to teach creative writing and has since lectured and taught at many colleges. Her first volume of poetry appeared in 1937, her first novel in 1938. She has published several volumes of autobiography since 1959. She has received prestigious awards and grants and several honorary doctorates, and is a fellow of the American Academy of Arts and Sciences. At Seventy: A Journal *appeared in 1984.*

•————————————————————•

(for Camille Mayran)

I found her, rich loser of all,
Whom two wars have stripped to the bone,
High up on her terrace wall
Over vineyards asleep in the sun—
Her riches, that ample scene
Composed in the barn's round door;
Her riches, rough cliff and pine,
Aromatic air—and no more.
Here, seasoned and sweetened by loss,
She thrives like thyme in the grass.

This woman's feet are so light,
So light the weight of her eyes
When she walks her battlements late
To harvest her thoughts as they rise,
She is never caught, only wise.
She rests on the round earth's turning
And follows the radiant skies,
Then reads Pascal in the morning.

And, walking beside her, I learned
How those dazzling silences burned.

On the longest day of June,
When summer wanes as it flowers
And dusk folds itself into dawn,
We shared the light-drenched hours.
We lay on rough rock in the sun,
Conversing till words were rare,
Conversing till words were done,
High up in the pungent air,
Then silently paced while the moon
Rose to dance her slow pavane.

The wine from a meditation
Was mine to drink deeply that night,
O vintage severe, and elation,
To be pressed out of loss, and from light!

Alive to her thought, yet alone,
As I lay in my bed, close to prayer,
A whisper came and was gone:
"Rejoice" was the word in the air.
But when the silence was broken,
Not by me, not by her, who had spoken?

MIDDLE CHILDREN

by

JANE RULE

(b. 1931)

Born in New Jersey, Jane Rule studied at Mills College in California. She has held many jobs, some taken to gain background material for her writing; she has been a teacher—of handicapped children, in a preparatory school, and at the University of British Columbia in Vancouver. She also operates her own printing press. Her first novel, The Desert of the Heart, *appeared in 1964; she has published several other novels, including* Against the Season *(1984) and* The Young in One Another's Arms *(1984), and many short stories, as well as a critical survey entitled* Lesbian Images *(1976). Her most recent works include* Inland Passage *(1985), a collection of short stories, and* A Hot-Eyed Moderate *(1985), a collection of essays.*

•————————————————————•

Clare and I both come from big families, a bossy, loving line of voices stretching away above us to the final authority of our parents, a chorus of squawling, needy voices beneath us coming from crib or play pen or notch in tree. We share, therefore, the middle child syndrome: we are both over earnest, independent, inclined to claustrophobia in crowds. The dreams of our adolescent friends for babies and homes of their own we privately considered nightmares. Boys were irredeemably brothers who took up more physical and psychic space than was ever fair. Clare and I, in cities across the continent from each other, had the same dream: scholarships for college where we would have single rooms, jobs after that with our own apartments. But scholarship students aren't given single rooms; and the matchmakers, following that old cliche that opposites attract, put us, east and west, into the same room.

Without needing to discuss the matter, we immediately arranged the furniture as we had arranged furniture with sisters all our lives, mine along one wall, hers along the other, an invisible line drawn down the center of the room, over which no sock or book or tennis racket should ever stray. Each expected the other to be hopelessly untidy; our sisters were. By the end of the first week, ours was the only room on the corridor that looked like a military barracks. Neither of us really liked it, used to the posters and rotting corsages and dirty clothes of our siblings, but neither of us could bring herself to contribute any clutter of her own. "Maybe a painting?" Clare suggested. I did not know where we could get one. Clare turned out to be a painter. I, a botanist, who could never grow things in my own room before where they might be watered with Coke or broken by a thrown magazine or sweater, brought in a plant stand, the first object to straddle the line because it needed to be under the window. The friends each of us made began to straddle that line, too, since we seemed to be interchangeably good listeners, attracting the same sort of flamboyant, needy first or last or only children.

"Sandra thinks she may be pregnant," I would say about Clare's friend who had told me simply because Clare wasn't around.

"Aren't they all hopeless?" Clare would reply, and we middle children would shake our wise, cautious heads.

We attracted the same brotherly boys as well who took us to football games and fraternity drunks and sexual wrestling matches on the beach. We used the same cool defenses, gleaned not from the advice of our brothers but from observing their behavior.

"Bobby always told me not to take the 'respect' bit too seriously if I wanted to have any fun," Clare said, "but I sometimes wonder why I'd want 'respect' or 'fun.' Doesn't it all seem to you too much trouble? This Saturday there's a marvelous exhibit. Then we could just go out to dinner and come home."

We had moved our desks by then. Shoved together, they could share one set of reference books conveniently and frugally for us both. We asked to have one chest of drawers taken out of the room. Neither of us had many clothes, and, since we wore the same size, we had begun to share our underwear and blouses to keep laundry day to once a week. I can't remember what excuse we had for moving the beds. Perhaps by the time we did, we didn't need an excuse, for ourselves anyway.

I have often felt sorry for people who can't have the experience of falling in love like that, gradually, without knowing it, touching first because pearls have to be fastened or a collar straightened, then more casually because you are standing close together looking at the same assignment sheet or photograph, then more purposefully because you know that there is comfort and reassurance for an exam coming up or trouble in the family. So many people reach out to each other before there is any sympathy or affection. When Clare turned into my arms, or I into hers—neither of us knows just how it was—the surprise was like coming upon the right answer to a question we did not even know we had asked.

Through the years of college, while our friends suffered all the uncertainties of sexual encounter, of falling into and out of love, of being too young and then perhaps too old in a matter of months, of worrying about how to finance graduate school marriages, our only problem was the clutter of theirs. We would have liked to clear all of them out earlier in order to enjoy the brief domestic sweetness of our own sexual life. But we were from large families. We knew how to maintain privacy, a space of our own, so tactfully that no one ever noticed it. Our longing for our own apartment, like the trips we would take to Europe, was an easy game. Nothing important to us had to be put off until then.

Putting off what was unimportant sometimes did take ingenuity. The boys had no objection to being given up, but our corridor friends were continually trying to arrange dates for us. We decided to come back from one Christmas holiday engaged to boys back home. That they didn't exist was never discovered. We gave each other rings and photographs of brothers. Actually I was very fond of Bobby, and Clare got on just as well with my large and boisterous family. Our first trip to Europe, between college and graduate school, taught us harder lessons. It seemed harmless enough to drink and dance with the football team traveling with us on the ship, but, when they turned up, drunken and disorderly at our London hotel, none of our own outrage would convince the night porter that we were not at fault. Only when we got to graduate school did we find the social answer: two young men as in need of protection as we were, who cared about paintings and concerts and growing things and going home to their own bed as much as we did.

When Clare was appointed assistant professor in art history and I got a job with the parks board, we had been living together in dormitories and student digs for eight years. We could finally leave the clutter of other lives behind us for an apartment of our own. Just at a time when we saw other relationships begin to grow stale or burdened with the continual demands of children, we were discovering the new privacy of making love on our own living room carpet at five o'clock in the afternoon, too hungry then to bother with cocktails or dressing for dinner. Soon we got quite out of the habit of wearing clothes except when we went out or invited people in. We woke making love, ate breakfast and made love again before we went to work, spent three or four long evenings a week in the same new delight until I saw in Clare's face that bruised, ripe look of a new, young wife, and she said at the same moment, "You don't look safe to go out."

In guilt we didn't really discuss, we arranged more evenings with friends, but, used to the casual interruptions of college life, we found such entertainment often too formal and contrived. Then for a week or two we would return to our honeymoon, for alone together we could find no reason not to make love. It is simply not true to say such things don't improve with practice.

"It's a good thing we never knew how bad we were at it," Clare said, one particularly marvelous morning.

When we didn't know, however, we had had more sympathy for those around us, accommodating themselves to back seats of cars or gritty blankets on the beach. Now our friends, either newly wed in student digs where quarreling was the only acceptable—that is, unavoidable—noise, or exhausted by babies, made wry jokes about missing the privacy of drive-in movies or about the merits of longer bathtubs. They were even more avid readers of pornography than they had been in college. We were not the good listeners we had been. I heard Clare being positively high minded about what a waste of time all those dirty books were.

"You never used to be a prude," Sandra said in surprise.

That remark, which should have made Clare laugh, kept her weeping half the night instead. I had never heard her so distressed, but then perhaps she hadn't had the freedom to be. "We're too different," she said, and "We're not kind any more."

"Maybe we should offer to baby sit for Sandra and lend them the apartment," I suggested, not meaning it.

We are both very good with babies. It would be odd if we weren't. Any middle child knows as much about colic and croup as there is to know by the time she's eight or nine. The initial squeamishness about changing diapers is conquered at about the same age. Sandra, like all our other friends, had it all to learn at twenty-three. Sometimes we did just as I had suggested, sitting primly across from each other like maiden aunts, Clare marking papers, I thumbing through books that could help me to imagine what was going on in our apartment. Or sometimes Sandra would call late at night, saying, "You're fond of this kid, aren't you? Well, come and get him before we kill him." Then we'd take the baby for a midnight ride over the rough back roads that are better for gas pains than any pacing. I didn't mind that assignment, but I was increasingly restless with the evenings we spent in somebody else's house.

"You know, if we had a house of our own," I said, "we could take the baby for the night, and they could just stay home."

I realize that there is nothing really immoral about lending your apartment to a legally married couple for the evening so that you can spend a kind and moral night out with their baby, but it seemed to me faintly and unpleasantly obscene: our bed . . . perhaps even our living room rug. I was back to the middle child syndrome. I wanted to draw invisible lines.

"They're awfully tidy and considerate," Clare said, "and they always leave us a bottle of scotch."

"Well, we leave them a bottle of scotch as well."

"We drink more of it than they do."

I didn't want to sound mean.

"If we had a house, we could have a garden."

"You'd like that," Clare decided.

Sandra's husband said we could never get a mortgage, but our combined income was simply too impressive to ignore. We didn't really need a large house, just the two of us, though I wanted a studio for Clare, and she wanted a green house and work shop for me. The difficulty was that neither of us could think of a house that was our size. We weren't used to them. The large, old houses that felt like home were really no more expensive than the new, compact and efficient boxes the agent thought suitable to our career centered lives. Once we had wandered through the snarled, old garden and up into the ample rooms of the sort of house we had grown up in, we could not think about anything else.

"Well, why not?" I asked.

"It has five bedrooms."

"We don't have to use them all."

"We might take a student," Clare said.

We weren't surprised at the amount of work involved in owning an old house. Middle children aren't. Our friends, most of whom were still cooped up in apartments, liked to come out in those early days for painting and repair parties, which ended with barbecue suppers on the back lawn, fenced in and safe for toddlers. Our current couple of boys were very good at the heavy work of making drapes and curtains. They even enjoyed helping me dig out old raspberry canes. It was two years before Clare had time to paint in the studio, and my green house turned out to be a very modest affair since I had so many other things to do, cooking mostly.

We have only one room left now for stray children. The rest are filled with students, boys we decided, which is probably a bit prudish, and it's quite true that they take up more physical and psychic space than is ever fair. Still, they're only kids, and, though it takes our saintly cleaning woman half a day a week just to dig out their rooms, they're not bad about the rest of the house.

Harry is a real help to me with the wine making, inclined to be more careful about the chemical details than I am. Pete doesn't leave his room except to eat unless we've got some of the children around; then he's even willing to stay with them in the evening if we have to go out. Carl, who's never slept a night alone in his life since he discovered it wasn't necessary, doesn't change girls so often that we don't get to know them, and he has a knack for finding people who fit in: take a turn at the dishes, walk the dogs, check to see that we have enough cream for breakfast.

Clare and I have drawn one very careful line across the door of our bedroom, and, though it's not as people proof as our brief apartment, it's a good deal better than a dormitory. We even occasionally have what we explain as our cocktail there before dinner when one of Carl's girls is minding the vegetables; and, if we don't get involved in too interesting a political or philosophical discussion, we sometimes go upstairs for what we call the late news. Both of us are still early to wake, and, since Pete will get up with any visiting child, the first of the day is always our own.

"Pete's a middle child," Clare said the other morning, hearing him sing a soft song to Sandra's youngest as he carried her down the stairs to give her an early bottle. "I hope he finds a middle child for himself one day."

"I'd worry about him if he were mine," I said.

"Oh, well, I'd worry about any of them if they were mine. I simply couldn't cope."

"I just wouldn't want to."

"There's a boy in my graduate seminar . . ." Clare began.

I was tempted to say that, if we had a family of our own, we'd always be worrying and talking about them even when we had time to ourselves, but there was still an hour before we had to get up, and I've always felt generous in the early morning, even when I was a kid in a house cluttered with kids from which I dreamed that old dream of escape.

CAROL, IN THE PARK, CHEWING ON STRAWS

by

JUDY GRAHN

(b. 1940)

Judy Grahn teaches writing and gay culture at Mama Bear's Coffee House in Oakland, California. She was a founder of the Women's Press collective, now merged with Diana Press, and has published five volumes of poetry, a collection of essays exploring lesbian poetry, and a history of gay culture. Recent works include The Work of a Common Woman *(1978) and* The Queen of Wands *(1982). She often reads with other women poets as a demonstration of her belief that noncompetitive sharing expresses feminist ideals.*

• —————————————————— •

She has taken a woman lover
whatever shall we do
she has taken a woman lover
how lucky it wasnt you.
And all the day through she smiles and lies
and grits her teeth and pretends to be shy,
or weak, or busy. Then she goes home
and pounds her own nails, makes her own
bets, and fixes her own car, with her friend.
She goes as far
as women can go without protection
from men.
On weekends, she dreams of becoming a tree;
a tree that dreams it is ground up
and sent to the paper factory, where it
lies helpless in sheets, until it dreams
of becoming a paper airplane, and rises
on its own current; where it turns into a
bird, a great coasting bird that dreams of becoming
more free, even, than that—a feather, finally, or
a piece of air with lightning in it.

She has taken a woman lover
whatever can we say.
She walks around all day
quietly, but underneath it
she's electric;
angry energy inside a passive form.
The common woman is as common
as a thunderstorm.

ARTEMIS

by

OLGA BROUMAS

(b. 1949)

Daughter of an officer in the Greek diplomatic corps, Olga Broumas came to the United States when she was ten. She speaks several languages, has studied linguistics, and earned her M.F.A. from the University of Oregon. She has taught in colleges and has given many poetry readings. Her first book of poetry, Beginning with O *(1977), won the Yale Younger Poets Award, and in 1980 she won a Guggenheim fellowship.* Soie Sauvage *(1980) and* Pastoral Jazz *(1983) are collections of her poems. She lives in Provincetown on Cape Cod.*

Let's not have tea.   White wine
eases the mind along
the slopes
of the faithful body, helps

any memory once engraved
on the twin
chromosome ribbons, emerge, tentative
from the archaeology of an excised past.

I am a woman
who understands
the necessity of an impulse whose goal or origin
still lie beyond me.   I keep the goat

for more
than the pastoral reasons.   I work
in silver the tongue-like forms
that curve round a throat

an arm-pit, the upper
thigh, whose significance stirs in me
like a curviform alphabet
that defies

decoding, appears
to consist of vowels, beginning with O, the O-
mega, horseshoe, the cave of sound.
What tiny fragments

survive, mangled into our language.
I am a woman committed to
a politics
of transliteration, the methodology

of a mind
stunned at the suddenly
possible shifts of meaning—for which
like amnesiacs

in a ward on fire, we must
find words
or burn.

THE WIDOW'S LAMENT
IN SPRINGTIME

by

WILLIAM CARLOS WILLIAMS

(1883–1963)

Even though he was a hard-working New Jersey physician, William Carlos Williams managed to write more than twenty-five volumes of poetry and fiction. His epic poem Paterson *(1946–1958) reflects his knowledge of and compassion for people, his sense of history, and his use of the language and rhythms of speech.*

•───────────────────────────•

Sorrow is my own yard
where the new grass
flames as it has flamed
often before but not
with the cold fire
that closes round me this year.
Thirtyfive years
I lived with my husband.
The plumtree is white today
with masses of flowers.
Masses of flowers
load the cherry branches
and color some bushes
yellow and some red
but the grief in my heart
is stronger than they
for though they were my joy
formerly, today I notice them
and turned away forgetting.

WILLIAM CARLOS WILLIAMS

Today my son told me
that in the meadows,
at the edge of the heavy woods
in the distance, he saw
trees of white flowers.
I feel that I would like
to go there
and fall into those flowers
and sink into the marsh near them.

THE BURNING

by

ESTELA PORTILLO TRAMBLEY

(b. 1936)

Estela Portillo Trambley teaches theatre arts in a community college in her native city of El Paso. She is the author of a play, Days of the Swallow *(1972), which has been frequently anthologized, and of a collection of short stories,* Rain of Scorpions *(1975). Her writing expresses her sense of unity with other Chicanas.*

— • ——————————————— •

The women of the barrio, the ones pock-marked by life, sat in council. Existence in dark cubicles of wounds had withered the spirit. Now, all as one, had found a heart. One tired soul stood up to speak. "Many times I see the light she makes of darkness, and that light is a greater blackness, still."

There was some skepticism from the timid. "Are you sure?"

"In those caves outside the town, she lives for days away from everybody. At night, when she is in the caves, small blinking lights appear, like fireflies. Where do they come from? I say, the blackness of her drowns the life in me."

Another woman with a strange wildness in her eyes nodded her head in affirmation. "Yes, she drinks the bitterness of good and swallows, like the devil-wolf, the red honey milk of evil."

A cadaverous one looked up into a darkened sky. "I hear thunder; lightning is not far." In unison they agreed, "We could use some rain."

The oldest one among them, one with dirty claws, stood up with arms outstretched and stood menacingly against the first lightning bolt that cleaved the darkness. Her voice was harsh and came from ages past. "She must burn!"

The finality was a cloud, black and tortured. Each looked into another's eyes to find assent or protest. There was only frenzy, tight and straining. The thunder was riding the lightning now, directly over their heads. It was a blazing canopy that urged them on to deeds of fear. There was still no rain. They found blistering words to justify the deed to come. One woman, heavy with anger, crouched to pour out further accusations. "She is the devil's pawn. On nights like this, when the air is heavy like thick blood, she sings among the dead, preferring them to the living. You know why she does it . . . eh? I'll tell you! She chases the dead back to their graves."

"Yes, yes. She stays and stays when death comes. Never a whimper, nor a tear, but I sense she feels the death as life like one possessed. They say she catches the flitting souls of the dead and turns them into flies. That way the soul never finds heaven."

"Flies! Flies! She is a plague!"

A clap of thunder reaffirmed. The old one with nervous, clutching claws made the most grievous charge, the cause for this meeting of the judgment. She shaped with bony gestures the anger of the heart. "She is the enemy of God! She put obscenities on our doorsteps to make us her accomplices. Sacrilege against the holy church!"

There was a fervor now, rising like a tide. They were for her burning now. All the council howled that Lela must burn that night. The sentence belonged to night alone. The hurricane could feed in darkness. Fear could be disguised as outrage at night. There were currents now that wanted sacrifice. Sacrifice is the umbilical cord of superstition. It would devastate before finding a calm. Lela was the eye of the storm, the artery that must flow to make them whole when the earth turned to light. To catch an evil when it bounced as shadow in their lives, to find it trapped in human body, this was an effective stimulant to some; to others it was a natural depressant to cut the fear, the dam of frustration. This would be their method of revelation. The doubt of themselves would dissolve.

But women know mercy! Mercy? It was swallowed whole by chasms of desire and fear of the unknown. Tempests grow in narrow margins that want a freedom they don't understand. Slaves always punish the free.

But who was Lela? She had come across the mountain to their pueblo many years before. She had crossed la Barranca del Cobre alone. She had walked into the pueblo one day, a bloody, ragged, half-starved young girl. In an apron she carried some shining sand. She stood there, like a frightened fawn, at the edge of the village. As the people of the pueblo gathered around her strangeness, she smiled, putting out her hand for touch. They drew back and she fell to the ground in exhaustion.

They took her in, but she remained a stranger the rest of her life in the pueblo upon which she had stumbled. At the beginning, she seemed but a harmless child. But, as time passed and she resisted their pattern of life, she was left alone. The people knew she was a Tarahumara from Batopilas. Part of her strangeness was the rooted depth of her own religion. She did not convert to Christianity. People grew hostile and suspicious of her.

But she had also brought with her the miracle sand. It had strange curative powers. In no time, she began to cure those in the pueblo who suffered from skin disease, from sores, or open wounds.

"Is it the magic of her devil gods?" the people asked themselves. Still, they came for the miracle cure that was swift and clean. She became their *curandera* outside their Christian faith.

The people in her new home needed her, and she loved them in silence and from a distance. She forgave them for not accepting her strangeness and learned to find adventure in the Oneness of herself.

Many times she wanted to go back to Batopilas, but too many people needed her here. She learned the use of medicinal herbs and learned to set broken bones. This was what she was meant to do in life. This purpose would not let her return to Batopilas. Still, she did not convert to Christianity. The people, begrudgingly, believed in her curative powers, but did not believe in her. Many years had passed and Lela was now an old woman, and the council of women this night of impending storm had decided her fate.

Lela lay dying in her one room hut. There was a fire with teeth that consumed her body. She only knew that her time was near an end as she lay in her small cot. Above the bed was a long shelf she had built herself that held rows of clay figurines. These were painted in gay colors and the expression on the tiny faces measured the seasons of the heart. They were live little faces showing the full circle of human joy and pain, doubt and fear, humor and sobriety. In all expressions there was a fierceness for life.

Lela had molded them through the years, and now they stood over her head like guardians over their maker. . . . Clay figurines, an act of love learned early in her childhood of long ago. In Batopilas, each home had its own rural god. He was a friend and a comforter. The little rural gods were like any other people. They did not rule or demand allegiance. The little rural gods of river, sky, fire, seed, birds, all were chosen members of each family. Because they sanctified all human acts, they were the actions of the living, like an aura. They were a shrine to creation.

Lela's mother had taught the little girl to mold the clay figures that represented the rural gods. This was her work and that of Lela's in the village, to provide clay little gods for each home and for festive occasions. This is why Lela never gave them up in her new home. She had molded them with her hands, but they dwelled boundless in the center of her being. The little gods had always been very real, very important, in her reverence for life.

There had been in Batopilas a stone image of the greater god, Tecuat. He was an impressive god of power that commanded silence and obedience. People did not get close to Tecuat except in ritual. As a girl, Lela would tiptoe respectfully around the figure of Tecuat, then she would breathe a sigh of relief and run off to find the little gods.

This was her game, god-hunting. One day, she had walked too far towards the pines, too far towards a roar that spoke of rushing life. She followed a yellow butterfly that also heard a command of dreams. She followed the butterfly that flitted towards a lake. As she followed, she looked for little gods in the glint of the sun, and in the open branches that pierced the absoluteness of the sky. The soft breath of wind was the breath of little gods, and the crystal shine of rocks close to the lake was a winking language that spoke of peace and the wildness of all joy.

When she had reached the lake, she stepped into the water without hesi-

ESTELA PORTILLO TRAMBLEY

423

tation. She felt the cool wet mud against her open toes. She walked into the water, touching the ripple of its broken surface with her finger tips. After a while, there was no more bottom. She began to cut the water with smooth, clean strokes, swimming out towards the pearl-green rocks that hid the roar. She floated for a while looking up at the light filtering through eternal trees. The silence spoke of something other than itself. It spoke in colors born of water and sun. She began to swim more rapidly towards the turn that led to the cradle of the roar, the waterfall. . . .

This is what Lela, the old Lela dying on her bed, was remembering . . . the waterfall. It helped to ease the pain that came in waves that broke against her soul and blackened the world. Then, there was the calm, the calm into which the experience machine brought back the yesterdays that were now soft, kind memories. She opened her eyes and looked up at the row of clay figures. She was not alone. "The waterfall . . ." she whispered to herself. She remembered the grotto behind the waterfall. It had been her hermitage of dreams, of wonder. Here her Oneness had knitted all the little gods unto herself until she felt the whole of earth—things within her being. Suddenly, the pain cut her body in two. She gripped the edge of the cot. There were blurs of throbbing white that whirled into black, and all her body trembled until another interval of peace returned for a little while.

There was no thought; there was no dream in the quiet body. She was a simple calm that would not last. The calm was a gift from the little gods. She slept. It was a fitful, brief sleep that ended with the next crash of pain. The pain found gradual absorption. She could feel the bed sheet clinging to her body, wet with perspiration. She asked herself in a half-moan, "When will the body give way?" Give way . . . give way, for so long, Lela had given way and had found ways to open herself and the world she understood. It had been a vital force in her. She could have been content in Batopilas. The simple truths of Nature might have fulfilled her to the end of her days if she had remained in Batopilas. But there was always that reach in her for a larger self. Nature was a greatness, but she felt a different hunger and a different thirst.

There was a world beyond Batopilas; there were people beyond Batopilas. She was no longer a child. It was easy to find little gods in Nature, but as she grew older, it became a child's game. There was time to be a child, but there was now time for something more. That is why, one day, she had walked away from Batopilas.

Beyond the desert, she would find another pueblo. She knew there were many pueblos and many deserts. There was nothing to fear because her little gods were with her. On the first day of her journey, she walked all day. The piercing sun beat down on her and the world, as she scanned the horizon for signs of a way. Something at a distance would be a hope, would be a way to something new, a way to the larger self. At dusk, she felt great hunger and great thirst. Her body ached and her skin felt parched and dry. The night wind felt cold, so she looked for a shelter against the wind. She found a clump of mesquite behind some giant sahuaros. This was not the greenness she knew so well, but a garden of stars in the night sky comforted her until she fell asleep.

At first light she awakened refreshed and quickly resumed her journey. She knew she must make the best out of the early hours before the sun rose. By late morning, the desert yielded a mountain at a distance. She reached the mountain in time to rest from the sun and the physical effort of her journey. When the sun began to fall, she started up a path made narrow by a blanket of desert brush. It tore the flesh of her feet and legs as she made her way up the path. In a little while, it was hard to find sure footing. The path had lost itself in a cleavage of rocks. Night had fallen. She was not afraid, for the night sky, again, was full of blinking little gods.

Then it happened. She lost her footing and fell down, down over a crevice between two huge boulders. As she fell, her lungs filled with air. Her body hit soft sand, but the edge of her foot felt the sharpness of a stone. She lay there stunned for a few minutes until she felt a sharp pain at the side of her foot. Somewhat dizzy, she sat up and noticed that the side of her foot was bleeding profusely. She sat there and watched the blood-flow that found its way into the soft sand. She looked up at the boulders that silently rebuked her helplessness; then she began to cry softly. She had to stanch the blood. She wiped away her tears with the side of her sleeve and tore off a piece of skirt to use as a bandage. As she looked down at the wound again, she noticed that the sand where she had fallen was extremely crystalline and loose. It shone against a rising moon. She scooped up a handful and looked at it with fascination. "The sand of little gods," she whispered to herself. She took some sand and rubbed it on the wound before she applied the bandage. By now, she felt a burning fever. She wrapped the strip of skirt around the wound now covered with the fine, shining sand. Then she slept. But it was a fitful sleep, for her body burned with fever. Half awake and half in a dream, she saw the sands take the shapes of happy, little gods. Then, at other times, the pain told her she was going to die. After a long time, her exhausted body slept until the dawn passed over her head.

When she finally awakened, she felt extremely well. Her body was rested and her temperature, to her great surprise, was normal. She looked down at the wound. The blood was caked on the bandage. She took it off to look at the wound. She could hardly believe her eyes. There was no longer any open wound. There was a healthy scab, and the area around the wound had no infection. It was a healing that normally would have taken weeks. She stood on her foot and felt no pain. "My little gods!" she thought. She fell down on her knees and kissed the shining sand. After a while, she removed her apron and filled it with the shining sand. She secured it carefully before she set off on her climb. As she made her way out of the crevice, she marked the path leading to the shining sand to find her way to it again. It was hard making marks with a sharp stone, and it seemed to take forever. At last, she reached the top of the crevice and noticed, to her great joy, that it led down to a pueblo at a distance. She made her way to strangers that day. Now, at the end of a lifetime, Lela felt the pain roll, roll, roll itself into a blindness. She struggled through the blackness until she gasped back the beginning of the calm. With the new calm came a ringing memory from her childhood. She saw the kindly face of the goddess, Ta Te. She who was born of the union of clean rock, she who was eternal. Yes, Ta Te understood all the verdant things . . . the verdant things.

And who were these women who sat in council? They were one full sweep of hate; they were one full wave of fear. Now these village women were outlined against a greyish sky where a storm refused to break. Spider-like, apelike, toadlike was the ferocity of their deadness. These were creatures of the earth who mingled with mankind. But they were minions to torture because the twist of littleness bound them to condemn all things unknown, all things untried. The infernal army could not be stopped now. The scurrying creatures began to gather firewood in the gloom. With antlike obedience they hurried back and forth carrying wood to Lela's hut. They piled it in a circle around her little house. The rhythm of their feet sang, "We'll do! We'll do!"
"The circle of fire will drain her powers!" claimed the old one with claws.
"Show me! Show me! Show me!" Voices lost as one.
As the old one with claws ordered more wood, the parish priest came running from his church. With raised arms he shouted as he ran, "Stop! Do you hear? Stop this madness!"
It can be argued that evil is not the reversal of good, but the vacuum of good. Thus, the emptiness is a standing still, a being dead, an infinite pain . . . like dead wood. No one listened to him.
"Burn! Burn! Burn!"
Life? The wood? The emptiness? The labor pains were that of something already lost, something left to the indefinite in life. The priest went from one woman to another begging, pleading, taking the wood from their hands.
"Burn! Burn! Burn!"
The old priest reasoned. "All is forgiven, my children. She only made some figurines of clay!"
There was a hush. The one woman with the claws approached the priest and spit out the condemnation, "She took our holy saints, Mary, Joseph, and many others and made them obscene. How can you defend the right hand of the devil? Drinking saints! Winking saints! Who can forgive the hideous suggestions of her clay devils? Who?"
The priest said simply, "You."
But if there is only darkness in a narrow belief, who can believe beyond the belief, or even understand the belief itself? The women could not forgive because they did not believe beyond a belief that did not go beyond symbol and law. Somehow, symbol and law, without love, leaves no opening. The clay figures in the church with sweet, painted faces lifted to heaven were much more than figures of clay to these women. Their still postures with praying hands were a security. Now, the priest who had blessed them

with holy water said they were not a sanctuary of God. Why did he contradict himself?

The old one with the claws felt triumphant. "She has made our saints into pagan gods!"

The priest shook his head sadly. "It is not a sin, what she did!"

No one listened. The piling of wood continued until the match was lit. Happy . . . Happy fire . . . it would burn the sin and the sinner.

Something in Lela told her this was the last struggle now. She looked up at her clay figurines one last time. Her eyes had lost their focus. The little gods had melted into one another; all colors were mixed. They grew into silver strands of light that crossed and mingled and found new forms that pulled away from one center. In half consciousness, she whispered, "Yes, yes, pull away. Find other ways, other selves, grow. . . ."

She smiled; the last calm had taken her back to the caves outside the pueblo. The caves were not like the grotto behind the waterfall, but they were a place for Oneness, where one could look for the larger self. Here the solitude of the heart was a bird in space. Here, in the silence of aloneness, she had looked for the little gods in the townspeople. In her mind, she had molded their smiles, their tears, their embraces, their seeking, their *just being*. Her larger self told her that the miracle of the living act was supreme, the giving, the receiving, the stumbling, and the getting up.

In the caves she had sadly thought of how she had failed to reach them as a friend. Her silences and her strangeness had kept them apart. But, she would find a way of communicating, a way of letting them know that she loved them. "If I give shape and form to their beauty," she thought. "If I cannot tell them I love them with words. . . ."

The light of the moving, mixing little gods was becoming a darkness. Her body would give in now. Yet, she still wished for Batopilas and the old ways with her last breath, "If only . . . if only I could be buried in the tradition of my fathers . . . a clean burning for new life . . . but here, here, there is a dark hole for the dead body. . . . Oh, little gods, take me back to my fathers. . . ."

The little gods were racing to the waterfall.

ESTELA PORTILLO TRAMBLEY

427

WOMAN
BECOMING

But every contradiction
Has the condition of resolving
Itself through the process
Through the process
Through the process of
Becoming, becoming, becoming,
Becoming, BECOMING!
                          —Megan Terry,
                       Approaching Simone

Women writers have taken three major approaches to show that their characters may transcend social roles to become fully human beings who respond with joy and anguish to their experience of the world. Many writers realistically record their experience as women to show its commonality with that of other women and to validate it. Such writing helps women overcome their feelings of isolation and encourages them to stop internalizing their failures as purely individual. It promotes sisterhood, and it offers male readers a basis for comparing their experience. Other writers concentrate on frank explorations of the "problem that has no name"—Betty Friedan's words for women's unease about their socially imposed roles. These writers describe women's feelings, often realistically, and suggest that the very act of describing and recognizing the problem will lead to its solution. And, realizing the deep emotional grounding of women's roles, many writers are rewriting old myths from a feminine perspective. All three of these approaches emphasize *process* more than achievement. Women are seen finding ways to be self-creators, distinguishing between themselves as objects of others' perceptions and as perceiving, imagining individuals capable of making their own worlds.

   The various literary genres lend themselves to these different approaches in different ways. The novel, traditionally close to realism, most frequently records daily life over a period of time for a multitude of characters. Through stream of consciousness and symbolism, it reveals attitudes and feelings toward experience and assesses the significance of these reactions. Unfortunately, some novelists' revelations about female sexuality prove to be so titillating that critics fail to see their revelations about the need for personal liberation. Erica Jong's *Fear of Flying* (1973), for instance, was greeted excitedly as an exposé of female lust; most critics failed to comment on its exposé of the heroine Isadora's desperation in her roles as submissive wife, amateur poet, incomplete human being. Jong, like other contemporary women novelists, has employed novelistic forms traditionally used to show masculine quests for identity. The picaresque novel of adventure and the novel of development (*Bildungsroman*) are used to show women as agents in their own fate, as individuals with their own life stories and need for autonomy. But successful users of these forms adapt them to the reality of female situations and psychological needs. In a more recent novel, *Fanny* (1980), Jong turns the male quest for self-identity into a mother's search for her kidnapped daughter, and the mother is rescued by her own lost mother. Tillie Olsen in *Yonnondio* (1974) links a mother's walk with her children into a different neighborhood where trees are in blossom to the depths of mother-daughter emotions. Margaret Atwood in *Surfacing* (1972) turns a daughter's real trip to solve the mystery of her father's death into a mythical journey into the depths of the self, made possible only after she recognizes her bond with both father and mother. Lisa Alther in *Kinflicks* (1974) combines the picaresque and the *Bildungsroman* in linking, with great wit, a daughter's sexual and psychic adventures with her need to receive her mother's blessing before she can become fully herself. These and many other novels undergird a convincing surface realism with insights into the center of personality.

Representative drama and "confessional" poetry also record women's experience realistically. Lorraine Hansberry's *A Raisin in the Sun* (1959), for example, explodes stereotypes about the superhuman black mother. Sylvia Plath's poetry makes totally understandable the suicide she recorded in her novel *The Bell Jar* (1963) and acted out in her own life. But both the drama and the poetry of the 1970s have emphasized women's symbolic inner journey and their need to rewrite myth.

Women dramatists, historically rare because of the public nature of theater and its need for establishment support and capital not usually available to women, have been turning to the remote origins of drama to find new modes of expression. Poetic ritual, song, and ceremony appear in such works as Ntozake Shange's *For Colored Girls Who Have Considered Suicide / When the Rainbow is Enuf* (1975) and Megan Terry's *Approaching Simone* (1970). Choral recitation and the assumption of many roles by one actor are characteristic techniques in these and the more than two hundred plays by women published since the 1960s and in the many others that have been presented in semiprofessional and amateur productions without being published. Eve Merriam's *Out of Our Father's House* (1977) brings together authentic voices from the diaries and letters of women separated in time and space. Susan Griffin's *Voices* (1975) shows women who are a community because of their shared experience. These techniques are dramatically effective; they are also political statements of women's need to share in history. Today feminist theater is one of the most vibrant art forms; because drama is the most public of literary genres, it promises to maintain the vitality of the feminist perspective.

Contemporary lyric poetry shares some of the characteristics of drama; both published and unpublished poets read their work in libraries and coffee houses as well as in public halls. Poets' voices are also embodied in print through the proliferation of small publishing houses and magazines that welcome experimentation. The contemporary movement away from established verse forms toward the rhythms of speech has been hospitable to women poets; their central concern is for a language capable of expressing their insights. An excerpt from Denise Levertov's *Relearning the Alphabet* (1970) emphasizes this need:

> Relearn the alphabet,
> relearn the world, the world
> understood anew only in doing, under-
> stood only as
> looked-up-into out of earth,
> the heart of an eye looking,
> the heart of a root
> planted in earth.
> Transmutation is not
> under the will's rule.

In order to communicate a sense of self, a woman poet must present herself as a subject, as active, as in process. To communicate her deep knowledge of the world, perceived with the heart's eye "planted in earth"— or, as another of Levertov's titles indicates, *With Eyes at the Back of Her Head*—she needs to find words free of connotations relating to male knowledge of the world. In "Unlearning to Not Speak" Marge Piercy emphasizes that women must learn to speak in the first person, singular and plural, to express "her own true hunger / and pleasure / and rage." In "Artemis" Olga Broumas speaks of trying to decode a "curviform alphabet" to describe joy in the body; vowels have new depths of meaning, "beginning with O, the O- / mega, horseshoe, the cave of sound"—and, significantly, the first initial of the poet who is speaking through the goddess-persona. Like fiction and drama, feminist poetry emphasizes through realism, expression of emotion, and new myths the need of women for a sense of identity, of community, of full humanity.

The selections that follow supplement those in earlier sections, which both described and went beyond the major stereotypes of women. The selections in this part show women undergoing change, in the process of self-creation. Though honestly showing the pain that accompanies such change, these works share a sense of women's autonomy and of their joy in discovering their humanity. The selections are arranged to parallel both an individual's emerging awareness of feminine possibility and the group experience of the women's movement.

Emily Dickinson wrote "A Prison Gets to Be a Friend" in 1862 after she withdrew from society to discover her own voice. The range of interpretation, for this and Dickinson's work in general, indicates how her feminine response to the human condition has expanded tradition. Her profound understanding of the subtle appeal of captivity explains not only why women have accepted their secondary status but also why victims in general so often cooperate in their own oppression. Psychological factors— the appeal of safety, the comfort of the familiar, the illusory nature of freedom—seduce the adult from the memory of joy as a reality, a possibility. Long before Freud, Dickinson perceived the submergence of our deepest consciousness during adult life. The "Phantasm Steel" is as immovable as the stereotypes and archetypes buried in the unconscious. This poem vividly conveys the need for liberation; it offers no solutions, but in doubting that "Heaven" will compensate for the earthly fate, it encourages us to explore human alternatives. Its consciousness of reality is the first step in the process of change, a step necessary for each individual as well as for society.

In Tillie Olsen's "Tell Me a Riddle" a dying old woman, bitter about the discontinuity forced upon her by her roles of wife and mother, experiences a deep sense of continuity with her younger and inner self. Olsen's poetic prose evokes feelings of anguish and waste, not only for Eva but for her husband and children, who are also limited by their socially imposed roles. "Tell Me a Riddle" eloquently underlines a frequent theme of feminist writing: that liberation of women is part of the liberation of all human beings. It exemplifies the expansion of human experience that is possible through focusing on the neglected experience of half the human race. The poignancy of having one's consciousness raised only when close to death makes the tone of "Tell Me a Riddle" almost elegiac. The story commemorates women in generations past and present to whom the possibility of liberation has not even occurred. Other works show women in more hopeful stages of liberation. Michele Murray's little poem "Coming to Self" asserts the normality of self-discovery for a woman. Marge Piercy's "Unlearning to Not Speak," a call for a sense of community, implies that it can be achieved.

The play *Three Women* by Charlotte Perkins Gilman dramatizes a young woman's refusal to be either wife and mother *or* worker and old maid; she rejects the sacrifice inherent in choosing one of the roles, in rejecting either love or work. Significantly, the alternative Gilman suggests is based on economic freedom; by paying for housework, women may find it possible to combine love and work. One wishes that Olsen's Eva had had such an option—that of freedom from the drudgery and isolation of house-work and child care. Even though Eva resists going to a home for the elderly, she might have welcomed communal child care and meal prepara-tion when raising a family.

The camaraderie suggested in *Three Women* is between mother, aunt, and daughter. Sharon Olds's poem "Best Friends" stresses female bonding between young friends; writing in memory of a childhood friend who died at nine and for whom she has named her daughter, Olds eloquently testifies to the enduring strength of early bonds between young girls. Such early memories also sustain the speaker of Lucille Clifton's poem, who re-mains able to see "the best looking gal in Georgia" in the aged "wet brown bag of a woman" now confronting her. With Susan Griffin's help in "I Like to Think of Harriet Tubman," readers can see heroines from far back in our communal memory. Though we may have long felt resistant to the truism that women have been absent from history, we need vivid images like Griffin's to enable us to know the power of our foremothers.

Susan Glaspell's play *Trifles,* which she later rewrote as the short story "A Jury of Her Peers," adds to our sense that women have had power. Glaspell's realistic details make it entirely credible that a sheriff's wife and the neighbor of a woman accused of murdering her husband would combine their powers of observation and deduction in order to protect the woman. Though they deduce her guilt, they refuse to share this knowledge with their husbands, who have openly showed contempt for the trivia of the accused woman's life, so apparent in her empty house. Annoyed by the men's dismissal of what they know to be significant clues, the women join together to see that justice, as they see it, is done; they judge the crime to be justified by the dead husband's cruelty to his wife. Such cooperation among women belies the stereotype of cattiness and rivalry as the dominant mode of women's relationships among themselves.

Glaspell's "jury" works like detectives in recognizing the significance of trifles and reconstructing a crime. In Adrienne Rich's poem "Diving into the Wreck," the persona is like an adventurer as she prepares herself for her dangerous quest. She has the knowledge, skills, and tools needed to succeed. Fully aware of the danger, the diver sets out, as did epic heroes, to complete herself. Her lonely voyage to watery depths symbolizes a search for origins, beyond history; a "book of myths" is a poor guide at best, especially since in it "our names do not appear." The diver must learn to accept the support of the water instead of trying to overcome it; the decision to accept the universe proves to be an effective strategy and allows the in-spection of the wreck. Searching for reality rather than its story, the diver, away from earthly limitations and familiar environment, becomes an-drogynous, a representative of all humanity, present and past; the wreck is the wreck of time, the sum of all human experience. Whether the motive is "cowardice or courage," what matters is the confrontation with reality, which the camera may record; the images it catches may revise the book of myths and the diver's name may become part of history when she surfaces. The dive may become a new myth. Whatever the results, the poem implies that the quest is worthwhile, necessary; there is hope of change.

Martha Collins in "Homecoming" subtly rewrites the myth of Odysseus' twenty-year-long quest, during which his wife Penelope stayed at home, weaving and unweaving as a device to ward off suitors who wished to use her power as the wife of a leader. Collins's persona asserts her independence. Though willing to share some space with a man, she must have her own space in which she can continue to make herself "at home." Though such a need for privacy may seem selfish, it is clearly a need of all human beings; the woman who has remained at home asserts her humanity. Similarly, those who are the "We" of Alice Walker's poem "Beyond What" assert their refusal to be defined by stereotypical roles. Like Rich's diver, they "reach for destinies," that is, seek their identity on an abstract level; but in doing so they "swing [their] eyes around / as well as side to side / to see the world." In rejecting the old stereotype of love as two lovers "melting" or "squeezing / into One," they refuse to consider themselves as halves of a whole; they see themselves instead as two wholes, two fully human beings, joined by love in "a council between equals." Walker's image calls for transcendence of racial barriers as well as those of traditional romance. The context of "separate *and* equal," as opposed to the more limited "separate *but* equal," is clearly implied. The image also transcends gender; Plato's conceptualization of the two halves to be united by love is not limited to heterosexual unions. These meanings, which underlie Walker's abstract "destinies," not only emphasize the particular situation of black women—who must free themselves from oppression based on race, gender, and sexual preference, who must rise above being "the mules of the universe," in Zora Neale Hurston's phrase—but also point toward the feminist ideal that liberation from sexist stereotyping will benefit all who have been limited by the restrictions that go with polaristic thinking.

Many female characters in the selections in Part II occupy a space in which they can actively become themselves. We see striking images of women who are acting, doing, achieving; they counteract the old image of women as passive, as acted upon. Dickinson's view of comfortable acceptance of traditional roles—"The narrow Round"—as the avoidance of liberty, of natural childlike joy, places the responsibility for diminished life upon the prisoner and rejects the hope of miraculous escape. The poem implies that only autonomous action—toward which self-awareness is the first step—can resist the lure of familiar bonds. In other works some images explicitly deny old role expectations. "Unlearning to not speak," "No melting. No squeezing / into One," and "Never again to be forced to move to the rhythms of others" express such denial. The emphasis is not on reaction but action. "These things shall be," asserts Eva in "Tell Me a Riddle"; "Still she believed," her husband marvels as she gasps "Lift high banner of reason justice freedom light." Perceiving heroism in a seemingly destroyed old woman, a speaker is inspired to "stand up"; thinking of Harriet Tubman, who "led an army / and won a battle / and defied the laws," a speaker gains courage for a battle for justice that she sees as "beginning." We hear women speaking admiringly of other women: "She was nothing if not enterprising"; "She taught me to read"; "she was going to knot it"; "seasoned and sweetened by loss, / She thrives." We hear them speak of their closeness to each other: "I like to think of Harriet Tubman"; "We shared the sun-drenched hours"; "She felt sorry for me. With someone on my side, I felt new courage. . . ."; "I remember . . . my own sense of love returned."

But whether denying old restrictions or celebrating newfound female community, most authors stress the need for, the anguish of, and the joy in self-discovery. In "Coming to Self" Michele Murray's metaphor "as iron comes by fire / from the ore" expresses the difficulty of the process and "as gold washes clean in the stream" affirms its value; both metaphors are of human processes that come close to the inevitability of natural processes. The simplicity of the poem's assertion underlines the certainty of "Coming to Self." Equal assurance comes through in the wit of Martha Collins's final line, "I am making myself at home"; the process of self-creation happens, appropriately enough for a woman, at home, but the persona will feel at home in a new way now that she has claimed her space.

The women who wrote the works in this section demonstrate through literature their skill and will to share with others their experience, their fantasies, their hopes. Our response should be to participate actively in making their texts live through our sympathetic reading.

A PRISON GETS TO BE
A FRIEND

by

EMILY DICKINSON

(1830–1886)

Famous for being a recluse, Emily Dickinson spent her entire life in Amherst, Massachusetts, except for a year at Mount Holyoke Female Seminary. At her death, over 900 poems were found in manuscript, only 7 of which had been published. An additional 900 poems have since been discovered, many not published until 1945. Now recognized as a major poet, Dickinson wrote of love, death, God, and nature. Unconventional both in form and content, her work seems very modern. Her letters were published in three volumes in 1958.

A Prison gets to be a friend–
Between its Ponderous face
And Ours–a Kinsmanship express–
And in its narrow Eyes–

We come to look with gratitude
For the appointed Beam
It deal us–stated as our food–
And hungered for–the same–

We learn to know the Planks–
That answer to Our feet–
So miserable a sound–at first–
Nor ever now–so sweet–

As plashing in the Pools–
When Memory was a Boy–
But a Demurer Circuit–
A Geometric Joy–

The Posture of the Key
That interrupt the Day
To Our Endeavor–Not so real
The Cheek of Liberty–

As this Phantasm Steel–
Whose features–Day and Night–
Are present to us–as Our Own–
And as escapeless–quite–

The narrow Round–the Stint–
The slow exchange of Hope–
For something passiver–Content
Too steep for looking up–

The Liberty we knew
Avoided–like a Dream–
Too wide for any Night but Heaven–
If That–indeed–redeem–

TELL ME A RIDDLE

"These Things Shall Be"

by

TILLIE OLSEN

(b. 1913)

*Born in Nebraska, Tillie Olsen has lived most of her adult life in
San Francisco. A Depression-era high-school dropout self-taught in
public libraries, she wrote and published when young, but the necessity of raising and supporting four children silenced her for twenty
years.* Tell Me a Riddle, *a collection of short stories first published
in 1962, is now regarded as a classic. Her novel* Yonnondio: From
the Thirties, *"lost" for forty years, was published in 1974, and* Silences, *a collection of essays on human creativity, appeared in 1978.*
Mother of a Daughter, Daughter of a Mother *(1984) is a collection
of poems published by the Feminist Press. In recent years Tillie
Olsen has received many awards and honors and has taught and
lectured widely.*

• ——————————————————————— •

I

For forty-seven years they had been married. How deep back the stubborn,
gnarled roots of the quarrel reached, no one could say—but only now,
when tending to the needs of others no longer shackled them together,
the roots swelled up visible, split the earth between them, and the tearing
shook even to the children, long since grown.

Why now, why now? wailed Hannah.

As if when we grew up weren't enough, said Paul.

Poor Ma. Poor Dad. It hurts so for both of them, said Vivi. They never
had very much; at least in old age they should be happy.

Knock their heads together, insisted Sammy; tell 'em: you're too old
for this kind of thing; no reason not to get along now.

Lennie wrote to Clara: They've lived over so much together; what
could possibly tear them apart?

Something tangible enough.

Arthritic hands, and such work as he got, occasional. Poverty all his life, and there was little breath left for running. He could not, could not turn away from this desire: to have the troubling of responsibility, the fretting with money, over and done with; to be free, to be *care*free where success was not measured by accumulation, and there was use for the vitality still in him.

There was a way. They could sell the house, and with the money join his lodge's Haven, cooperative for the aged. Happy communal life, and was he not already an official; had he not helped organize it, raise funds, served as a trustee?

But she—would not consider it.

"What do we need all this for?" he would ask loudly, for her hearing aid was turned down and the vacuum was shrilling. "Five rooms" (pushing the sofa so she could get into the corner) "furniture" (smoothing down the rug) "floors and surfaces to make work. Tell me, why do we need it?" And he was glad he could ask in a scream.

"Because I'm use't."

"Because you're use't. This is a reason, Mrs. Word Miser? Used to can get unused!"

"Enough unused I have to get used to already. . . . Not enough words?" turning off the vacuum a moment to hear herself answer. "Because soon enough we'll need only a little closet, no windows, no furniture, nothing to make work, but for worms. Because now I want room. . . . Screech and blow like you're doing, you'll need that closet even sooner. . . . Ha, again!" for the vacuum bag wailed, puffed half up, hung stubbornly limp. "This time fix it so it stays; quick before the phone rings and you get too important busy."

But while he struggled with the motor, it seethed in him. Why fix it? Why have to bother? And if it can't be fixed, have to wring the mind with how to pay the repair? At the Haven they come in with their own machines to clean your room or your cottage; you fish, or play cards, or make jokes in the sun, not with knotty fingers fight to mend vacuums.

Over the dishes, coaxingly: "For once in your life, to be free, to have everything done for you, like a queen."

"I never liked queens."

"No dishes, no garbage, no towel to sop, no worry what to buy, what to eat."

"And what else would I do with my empty hands? Better to eat at my own table when I want, and to cook and eat how I want."

"In the cottages they buy what you ask, and cook it how you like. *You* are the one who always used to say: better mankind born without mouths and stomachs than always to worry for money to buy, to shop, to fix, to cook, to wash, to clean."

"How cleverly you hid that you heard. I said it then because eighteen hours a day I ran. And you never scraped a carrot or knew a dish towel sops. Now—for you and me—who cares? A herring out of a jar is enough. But when *I* want, and nobody to bother." And she turned off her ear button, so she would not have to hear.

But as *he* had no peace, juggling and rejuggling the money to figure: how will I pay for this now?; prying out the storm windows (there they take care of this); jolting in the streetcar on errands (there I would not have to ride to take care of this or that); fending the patronizing relatives just back from Florida (at the Haven it matters what one is, not what one can afford), he gave *her* no peace.

"Look! In their bulletin. A reading circle. Twice a week it meets."

"Haumm," her answer of not listening.

"A reading circle. Chekhov they read that you like, and Peretz. Cultured people at the Haven that you would enjoy."

"Enjoy!" She tasted the word. "Now, when it pleases you, you find a reading circle for me. And forty years ago when the children were morsels and there was a Circle, did you stay home with them once so I could go? Even once? You trained me well. I do not need others to enjoy. Others!" Her voice trembled. "Because *you* want to be there with others. Already it makes me sick to think of you always around others. Clown, grimacer, floormat, yesman, entertainer, whatever they want of you."

And now it was he who turned on the television loud so he need not hear.

Old scar tissue ruptured and the wounds festered anew. Chekhov indeed. She thought without softness of that young wife, who in the deep night hours while she nursed the current baby, and perhaps held another in her lap, would try to stay awake for the only time there was to read. She would feel again the weather of the outside on his cheek when, coming late from a meeting, he would find her so, and stimulated and ardent, sniffing her skin, coax: "I'll put the baby to bed, and you—put the book away, don't read, don't read."

That had been the most beguiling of all the "don't read, put your book away" her life had been. Chekhov indeed!

"Money?" She shrugged him off. "Could we get poorer than once we were? And in America, who starves?"

But as still he pressed:

"Let me alone about money. Was there ever enough? Seven little ones— for every penny I had to ask—and sometimes, remember, there was nothing. But always *I* had to manage. Now *you* manage. Rub your nose in it good."

But from those years she had had to manage, old humiliations and terrors rose up, lived again, and forced her to relive them. The children's needings; that grocer's face or this merchant's wife she had had to beg credit from when credit was a disgrace; the scenery of the long blocks walked around when she could not pay; school coming, and the desperate going over the old to see what could yet be remade; the soups of meat bones begged "for-the-dog" one winter. . . .

Enough. Now they had no children. Let *him* wrack his head for how they would live. She would not exchange her solitude for anything. *Never again to be forced to move to the rhythms of others.*

For in this solitude she had won to a reconciled peace.

Tranquillity from having the empty house no longer an enemy, for it stayed clean—not as in the days when it was her family, the life in it, that had seemed the enemy: tracking, smudging, littering, dirtying, engaging her in endless defeating battle—and on whom her endless defeat had been spewed.

The few old books, memorized from rereading; the pictures to ponder (the magnifying glass superimposed on her heavy eyeglasses). Or if she wishes, when he is gone, the phonograph, that if she turns up very loud and strains, she can hear: the ordered sounds and the struggling.

Out in the garden, growing things to nurture. Birds to be kept out of the pear tree, and when the pears are heavy and ripe, the old fury of work, for all must be canned, nothing wasted.

And her one social duty (for she will not go to luncheons or meetings) the boxes of old clothes left with her, as with a life-practised eye for finding what is still wearable within the worn (again the magnifying glass superimposed on the heavy glasses) she scans and sorts—this for rag or rummage, that for mending and cleaning, and this for sending away.

Being able at last to live within, and not move to the rhythms of others, as life had forced her to: denying; removing; isolating; taking the children one by one; then deafening, half-blinding—and at last, presenting her solitude.

And in it she had won to a reconciled peace.

Now he was violating it with his constant campaigning: *Sell the house and move to the Haven.* (You sit, you sit—there too you could sit like a stone.) He was making of her a battleground where old grievances tore. (Turn on your ear button—I am talking.) And stubbornly she resisted —so that from wheedling, reasoning, manipulation, it was bitterness he now started with.

And it came to where every happening lashed up a quarrel.

"I will sell the house anyway," he flung at her one night. "I am putting it up for sale. There will be a way to make you sign."

The television blared, as always it did on the evenings he stayed home, and as always it reached her only as noise. She did not know if the tumult was in her or outside. Snap! she turned the sound off. "Shadows," she whispered to him, pointing to the screen, "look, it is only shadows." And in a scream: "Did you say that you will sell the house? Look at me, not at that. I am no shadow. You cannot sell without me."

"Leave on the television. I am watching."

"Like Paulie, like Jenny, a four-year-old. Staring at shadows. *You cannot sell the house.*"

"I will. We are going to the Haven. There you would not hear the television when you do not want it. I could sit in the social room and watch. You could lock yourself up to smell your unpleasantness in a room by yourself—for who would want to come near you?"

"No, no selling." A whisper now.

"The television is shadows. Mrs. Enlightened! Mrs. Cultured! A world comes into your house—and it is shadows. People you would never meet in a thousand lifetimes. Wonders. When you were four years old, yes, like Paulie, like Jenny, did you know of Indian dances, alligators, how they use bamboo in Malaya? No, you scratched in your dirt with the chickens and thought Olshana was the world. Yes, Mrs. Unpleasant, I will sell the house, for there better can we be rid of each other than here."

She did not know if the tumult was outside, or in her. Always a ravening inside, a pull to the bed, to lie down, to succumb.

"Have you thought maybe Ma should let a doctor have a look at her?" asked their son Paul after Sunday dinner, regarding his mother crumpled on the couch, instead of, as was her custom, busying herself in Nancy's kitchen.

"Why not the President too?"

"Seriously, Dad. This is the third Sunday she's lain down like that after dinner. Is she that way at home?"

"A regular love affair with the bed. Every time I start to talk to her."

Good protective reaction, observed Nancy to herself. The workings of hos-til-ity.

"Nancy could take her. I just don't like how she looks. Let's have Nancy arrange an appointment."

"You think she'll go?" regarding his wife gloomily. "All right, we have to have doctor bills, we have to have doctor bills." Loudly: "Something hurts you?"

She startled, looked to his lips. He repeated: "Mrs. Take It Easy, something hurts?"

"Nothing. . . . Only you."

"A woman of honey. That's why you're lying down?"

"Soon I'll get up to do the dishes, Nancy."

"Leave them, Mother, I like it better this way."

"Mrs. Take It Easy, Paul says you should start ballet. You should go to see a doctor and ask: how soon can you start ballet?"

"A doctor?" she begged. "Ballet?"

"We were talking, Ma," explained Paul, "you don't seem any too well. It would be a good idea for you to see a doctor for a checkup."

"I get up now to do the kitchen. Doctors are bills and foolishness, my son. I need no doctors."

"At the Haven," he could not resist pointing out, "a doctor is *not* bills. He lives beside you. You start to sneeze, he is there before you open up a Kleenex. You can be sick there for free, all you want."

"Diarrhea of the mouth, is there a doctor to make you dumb?"

"Ma. Promise me you'll go. Nancy will arrange it."

"It's all of a piece when you think of it," said Nancy, "the way she attacks my kitchen, scrubbing under every cup hook, doing the inside of the oven so I can't enjoy Sunday dinner, knowing that half-blind or not, she's going to find every speck of dirt. . . ."

"Don't, Nancy, I've told you—it's the only way she knows to be useful. What did the *doctor* say?"

"A real fatherly lecture. Sixty-nine is young these days. Go out, enjoy life, find interests. Get a new hearing aid, this one is antiquated. Old age is sickness only if one makes it so. Geriatrics, Inc."

"So there was nothing physical."

"Of course there was. How can you live to yourself like she does without there being? Evidence of a kidney disorder, and her blood count is low. He gave her a diet, and she's to come back for follow-up and lab work. . . . But he was clear enough: Number One prescription—start living like a human being. . . . When I think of your dad, who could really play the invalid with that arthritis of his, as active as a teenager, and twice as much fun. . . ."

"You didn't tell me the doctor says your sickness is in you, how you live." He pushed his advantage. "Life and enjoyments you need better than medicine. And this diet, how can you keep it? To weigh each morsel and scrape away each bit of fat, to make this soup, that pudding. There, at the Haven, they have a dietician, they would do it for you."

She is silent.

"You would feel better there, I know it," he says gently. "There there is life and enjoyments all around."

"What is the matter, Mr. Importantbusy, you have no card game or meeting you can go to?"—turning her face to the pillow.

For a while he cut his meetings and going out, fussed over her diet, tried to wheedle her into leaving the house, brought in visitors:

"I should come to a fashion tea. I should sit and look at pretty babies in clothes I cannot buy. This is pleasure?"

"Always you are better than everyone else. The doctor said you should go out. Mrs. Brem comes to you with goodness and you turn her away."

"Because *you* asked her to, she asked me."

"They won't come back. People you need, the doctor said. Your own cousins I asked; they were willing to come and make peace as if nothing had happened. . . ."

"No more crushers of people, pushers, hypocrites, around me. No more in *my* house. You go to them if you like."

"Kind he is to visit. And you, like ice."
"A babbler. All my life around babblers. Enough!"

"She's even worse, Dad? Then let her stew a while," advised Nancy. "You can't let it destroy you; it's a psychological thing, maybe too far gone for any of us to help."

So he let her stew. More and more she lay silent in bed, and sometimes did not even get up to make the meals. No longer was the tongue-lashing inevitable if he left the coffee cup where it did not belong, or forgot to take out the garbage or mislaid the broom. The birds grew bold that summer and for once pocked the pears, undisturbed.

A bellyfull of bitterness and every day the same quarrel in a new way and a different old grievance the quarrel forced her to enter and relive. And the new torment: I am not really sick, the doctor said it, then why do I feel so sick?

One night she asked him: "You have a meeting tonight? Do not go. Stay . . . with me."

He had planned to watch "This Is Your Life," but half sick himself from the heavy heat, and sickening therefore the more after the brooks and woods of the Haven, with satisfaction he grated:

"Hah, Mrs. Live Alone And Like It wants company all of a sudden. It doesn't seem so good the time of solitary when she was a girl exile in Siberia. 'Do not go. Stay with me.' A new song for Mrs. Free As A Bird. Yes, I am going out, and while I am gone chew this aloneness good, and think how you keep us both from where if you want people, you do not need to be alone."

"Go, go. All your life you have gone without me."

After him she sobbed curses he had not heard in years, old-country curses from their childhood: Grow, oh shall you grow like an onion, with your head in the ground. Like the hide of a drum shall you be, beaten in life, beaten in death. Oh shall you be like a chandelier, to hang, and to burn. . . .

She was not in their bed when he came back. She lay on the cot on the sun porch. All week she did not speak or come near him; nor did he try to make peace or care for her.

He slept badly, so used to her next to him. After all the years, old harmonies and dependencies deep in their bodies; she curled to him, or he coiled to her, each warmed, warming, turning as the other turned, the nights a long embrace.

It was not the empty bed or the storm that woke him, but a faint singing.

She was singing. Shaking off the drops of rain, the lightning riving her lifted face, he saw her so; the cot covers on the floor.

"This is a private concert?" he asked. "Come in, you are wet."

"I can breathe now," she answered; "my lungs are rich." Though indeed the sound was hardly a breath.

"Come in, come in." Loosing the bamboo shades. "Look how wet you are." Half helping, half carrying her, still faint-breathing her song.

A Russian love song of fifty years ago.

He had found a buyer, but before he told her, he called together those children who were close enough to come. Paul, of course, Sammy from New Jersey, Hannah from Connecticut, Vivi from Ohio.

With a kindling of energy for her beloved visitors, she arrayed the house, cooked and baked. She was not prepared for the solemn after-dinner conclave, they too probing in and tearing. Her frightened eyes watched from mouth to mouth as each spoke.

His stories were eloquent and funny of her refusal to go back to the doctor; of the scorned invitations; of her stubborn silence or the bile "like a Niagara"; of her contrariness: "If I clean it's no good how I cleaned; if I don't clean, I'm still a master who thinks he has a slave."

(Vinegar he poured on me all his life; I am well marinated; how can I be honey now?)

Deftly he marched in the rightness for moving to the Haven; their money from social security free for visiting the children, not sucked into daily needs and into the house; the activities in the Haven for him; but mostly the Haven for *her:* her health, her need of care, distraction, amusement, friends who shared her interests.

"This does offer an outlet for Dad," said Paul; "he's always been an active person. And economic peace of mind isn't to be sneezed at, either. I could use a little of that myself."

But when they asked: "And you, Ma, how do you feel about it?" could only whisper:

"For him it is good. It is not for me. I can no longer live between people."

"You lived all your life *for* people," Vivi cried.

"Not with." Suffering doubly for the unhappiness on her children's faces.

"You have to find some compromise," Sammy insisted. "Maybe sell the house and buy a trailer. After forty-seven years there's surely some way you can find to live in peace."

"There is no help, my children. Different things we need."

"Then live alone!" He could control himself no longer. "I have a buyer for the house. Half the money for you, half for me. Either alone or with me to the Haven. You think I can live any longer as we are doing now?"

"Ma doesn't have to make a decision this minute, however you feel,

Dad," Paul said quickly, "and you wouldn't want her to. Let's let it lay a few months, and then talk some more."

"I think I can work it out to take Mother home with me for a while," Hannah said. "You both look terrible, but especially you, Mother. I'm going to ask Phil to have a look at you."

"Sure," cracked Sammy. "What's the use of a doctor husband if you can't get free service out of him once in a while for the family? And absence might make the heart . . . you know."

"There was something after all," Paul told Nancy in a colorless voice. "That was Hannah's Phil calling. Her gall bladder. . . . Surgery."

"Her *gall* bladder. If that isn't classic. 'Bitter as gall'—talk of psychosom——"

He stepped closer, put his hand over her mouth, and said in the same colorless, plodding voice. "We have to get Dad. They operated at once. The cancer was everywhere, surrounding the liver, everywhere. They did what they could . . . at best she has a year. Dad . . . we have to tell him."

2

Honest in his weakness when they told him, and that she was not to know. "I'm not an actor. She'll know right away by how I am. Oh that poor woman. I am old too, it will break me into pieces. Oh that poor woman. She will spit on me: 'So my sickness was how I live.' Oh Paulie, how she will be, that poor woman. Only she should not suffer. . . . I can't stand sickness, Paulie, I can't go with you."

But went. And play-acted.

"A grand opening and you did not even wait for me. . . . A good thing Hannah took you with her."

"Fashion teas I needed. They cut out what tore in me; just in my throat something hurts yet. . . . Look! so many flowers, like a funeral. Vivi called, did Hannah tell you? And Lennie from San Francisco, and Clara; and Sammy is coming." Her gnome's face pressed happily into the flowers.

It is impossible to predict in these cases, but once over the immediate effects of the operation, she should have several months of comparative well-being.

The money, where will come the money?

Travel with her, Dad. Don't take her home to the old associations. The other children will want to see her.

The money, where will I wring the money?

Whatever happens, she is not to know. No, you can't ask her to sign papers to sell the house; nothing to upset her. Borrow instead, then after. . . .

I had wanted to leave you each a few dollars to make life easier, as other fathers do. There will be nothing left now. (Failure! you and your "business is exploitation." Why didn't you make it when it could be made?——Is that what you're thinking, Sammy?)

Sure she's unreasonable, Dad——but you have to stay with her; if there's to be any happiness in what's left of her life, it depends on you.

Prop me up, children, think of me, too. Shuffled, chained with her, bitter woman. No Haven, and the little money going. . . . How happy she looks, poor creature.

The look of excitement. The straining to hear everything (the new hearing aid turned full). Why are you so happy, dying woman?

How the petals are, fold on fold, and the gladioli color. The autumn air.

Stranger grandsons, tall above the little gnome grandmother, the little spry grandfather. Paul in a frenzy of picture-taking before going.

She, wandering the great house. Feeling the books; laughing at the maple shoemaker's bench of a hundred years ago used as a table. The ear turned to music.

"Let us go home. See how good I walk now." "One step from the hospital," he answers, "and she wants to fly. Wait till Doctor Phil says."

"Look—the birds too are flying home. Very good Phil is and will not show it, but he is sick of sickness by the time he comes home."

"Mrs. Telepathy, to read minds," he answers; "read mine what it says: when the trunks of medicines become a suitcase, then we will go."

The grandboys, they do not know what to say to us. . . . Hannah, she runs around here, there, when is there time for herself?

Let us go home. Let us go home.

Musing; gentleness—*but for the incidents of the rabbi in the hospital, and of the candles of benediction.*

Of the rabbi in the hospital:

Now tell me what happened, Mother.

From the sleep I awoke, Hannah's Phil, and he stands there like a devil in a dream and calls me by name. I cannot hear. I think he prays. Go away, please, I tell him, I am not a believer. Still he stands, while my heart knocks with fright.

You scared *him,* Mother. He thought you were delirious.

Who sent him? Why did he come to me?

It is a custom. The men of God come to visit those of their religion they might help. The hospital makes up the list for them—race, religion— and you are on the Jewish list.

Not for rabbis. At once go and make them change. Tell them to write: Race, human; Religion, none.

And of the candles of benediction:

Look how you have upset yourself, Mrs. Excited Over Nothing. Pleasant memories you should leave.

Go in, go back to Hannah and the lights. Two weeks I saw candles and said nothing. But she asked me.

So what was so terrible? She forgets you never did, she asks you to light the Friday candles and say the benediction like Phil's mother when she visits. If the candles give her pleasure, why shouldn't she have the pleasure?

Not for pleasure she does it. For emptiness. Because his family does. Because all around her do.

That is not a good reason too? But you did not hear her. For heritage, she told you. For the boys, from the past they should have tradition.

Superstition! From our ancestors, savages, afraid of the dark, of themselves: mumbo words and magic lights to scare away ghosts.

She told you: how it started does not take away the goodness. For centuries, peace in the house it means.

Swindler! does she look back on the dark centuries? Candles bought instead of bread and stuck into a potato for a candlestick? Religion that stifled and said: in Paradise, woman, you will be the footstool of your husband, and in life—poor chosen Jew—ground under, despised, trembling in cellars. And cremated. And cremated.

This is religion's fault? You think you are still an orator of the 1905 revolution? Where are the pills for quieting? Which are they?

Heritage. How have we come from our savage past, how no longer to be savages—this to teach. To look back and learn what humanizes— this to teach. To smash all ghettos that divide us—not to go back, not to go back—this to teach. Learned books in the house, will humankind live or die, and she gives to her boys—superstition.

Hannah that is so good to you. Take your pill, Mrs. Excited For Nothing, swallow.

Heritage! But when did I have time to teach? Of Hannah I asked only hands to help.

Swallow.

Otherwise—musing; gentleness.

Not to travel. To go home.

The children want to see you. We have to show them you are as thorny a flower as ever.

Not to travel.

Vivi wants you should see her new baby. She sent the tickets—airplane tickets—a Mrs. Roosevelt she wants to make of you. To Vivi's we have to go.

A new baby. How many warm, seductive babies. She holds him stiffly, *away* from her, so that he wails. And a long shudder begins, and the sweat beads on her forehead.

"Hush, shush," croons the grandfather, lifting him back. "You should forgive your grandmamma, little prince, she has never held a baby before, only seen them in glass cases. Hush, shush."

"You're tired, Ma," says Vivi. "The travel and the noisy dinner. I'll take you to lie down."

(A long travel from, to, what the feel of a baby evokes.)

In the airplane, cunningly designed to encase from motion (no wind, no feel of flight), she had sat severely and still, her face turned to the sky through which they cleaved and left no scar.

So this was how it looked, the determining, the crucial sky, and this was how man moved through it, remote above the dwindled earth, the concealed human life. Vulnerable life, that could scar.

There was a steerage ship of memory that shook across a great, circular sea: clustered, ill human beings; and through the thick-stained air, tiny fretting waters in a window round like the airplane's—sun round, moon round. (The round thatched roofs of Olshana.) Eye round—like the smaller window that framed distance the solitary year of exile when only her eyes could travel, and no voice spoke. And the polar winds hurled themselves across snows trackless and endless and white—like the clouds which had closed together below and hidden the earth.

Now they put a baby in her lap. Do not ask me, she would have liked to beg. Enough the worn face of Vivi, the remembered grandchildren. I cannot, cannot. . . .

Cannot what? Unnatural grandmother, not able to make herself embrace a baby.

She lay there in the bed of the two little girls, her new hearing aid turned full, listening to the sound of the children going to sleep, the baby's fretful crying and hushing, the clatter of dishes being washed and put away. They thought she slept. Still she rode on.

It was not that she had not loved her babies, her children. The love— the passion of tending—had risen with the need like a torrent; and like a torrent drowned and immolated all else. But when the need was done— oh the power that was lost in the painful damming back and drying up of what still surged, but had nowhere to go. Only the thin pulsing left that could not quiet, suffering over lives one felt, but could no longer hold nor help.

On that torrent she had borne them to their own lives, and the riverbed was desert long years now. Not there would she dwell, a memoried wraith. Surely that was not all, surely there was more. Still the springs, the springs were in her seeking. Somewhere an older power that beat for life. Somewhere coherence, transport, meaning. If they would but leave her in the air now stilled of clamor, in the reconciled solitude, to journey on.

TILLIE OLSEN

451

And they put a baby in her lap. Immediacy to embrace, and the breath
of *that* past: warm flesh like this that had claims and nuzzled away all
else and with lovely mouths devoured; hot-living like an animal—
intensely and now; the turning maze; the long drunkenness; the drowning
into needing and being needed. Severely she looked back—and the shudder
seized her again, and the sweat. Not that way. Not there, not now could
she, not yet. . . .

And all that visit, she could not touch the baby.

"Daddy, is it the . . . sickness she's like that?" asked Vivi. "I was so
glad to be having the baby—for her. I told Tim, it'll give her more happiness
than anything, being around a baby again. And she hasn't played with
him once."

He was not listening, "Aahh little seed of life, little charmer," he
crooned, "Hollywood should see you. A heart of ice you would melt. Kick,
kick. The future you'll have for a ball. In 2050 still kick. Kick for your
grandaddy then."

Attentive with the older children; sat through their performances (command performance; we command you to be the audience); helped Ann
sort autumn leaves to find the best for a school program; listened gravely
to Richard tell about his rock collection, while her lips mutely formed
the words to remember: *igneous, sedimentary, metamorphic;* looked for
missing socks, books, and bus tickets; watched the children whoop after
their grandfather who knew how to tickle, chuck, lift, toss, do tricks, tell
secrets, make jokes, match riddle for riddle. (Tell me a riddle, Grammy.
I know no riddles, child.) Scrubbed sills and woodwork and furniture in
every room; folded the laundry; straightened drawers; emptied the
heaped baskets waiting for ironing (while he or Vivi or Tim nagged:
You're supposed to rest here, you've been sick) but to none tended or gave
food—and could not touch the baby.

After a week she said: "Let us go home. Today call about the tickets."

"You have important business, Mrs. Inahurry? The President waits
to consult with you?" He shouted, for the fear of the future raced in him.
"The clothes are still warm from the suitcase, your children cannot show
enough how glad they are to see you, and you want home. There is plenty
of time for home. We cannot be with the children at home."

"Blind to around you as always: the little ones sleep four in a room
because we take their bed. We are two more people in a house with a
new baby, and no help."

"Vivi is happy so. The children should have their grandparents a while,
she told to me. I should have my mommy and daddy. . . ."

"Babbler and blind. Do you look at her so tired? How she starts to talk and she cries? I am not strong enough yet to help. Let us go home."
(To reconciled solitude.)

For it seemed to her the crowded noisy house was listening to her, listening for her. She could feel it like a great ear pressed under her heart. And everything knocked: quick constant raps: let me in, let me in.
How was it that soft reaching tendrils also became blows that knocked?

C'mon, Grandma, I want to show you. . . .
Tell me a riddle, Grandma. (*I know no riddles.*)
Look, Grammy, he's so dumb he can't even find his hands. (Dody and the baby on a blanket over the fermenting autumn mould.)
I made them—for you. (Ann) (Flat paper dolls with aprons that lifted on scalloped skirts that lifted on flowered pants; hair of yarn and great ringed questioning eyes.)
Watch me, Grandma. (Richard snaking up the tree, hanging exultant, free, with one hand at the top. Below Dody hunching over in pretend-cooking.) (*Climb too, Dody, climb and look.*)
Be my nap bed, Grammy. (The "No!" too late.) Morty's abandoned heaviness, while his fingers ladder up and down her hearing-aid cord to his drowsy chant: eentsiebeentsiespider. (*Children trust.*)
It's to start off your own rock collection, Grandma. That's a trilobite fossil, 200 million years old (millions of years on a boy's mouth) and that one's obsidian, black glass.

Knocked and knocked.
Mother, I *told* you the teacher said we had to bring it back all filled out this morning. Didn't you even ask Daddy? Then tell *me* which plan and I'll check it: evacuate or stay in the city or wait for you to come and take me away. (Seeing the look of straining to hear.) It's for Disaster, Grandma. (*Children trust.*)
Vivi in the maze of the long, the lovely drunkenness. The old old noises: baby sounds; screaming of a mother flayed to exasperation; children quarreling; children playing; singing; laughter.

And Vivi's tears and memories, spilling so fast, half the words not understood.
She had started remembering out loud deliberately, so her mother would know the past was cherished, still lived in her.
Nursing the baby: My friends marvel, and I tell them, oh it's easy to be such a cow. I remember how beautiful my mother seemed nursing my brother, and the milk just flows. . . . Was that Davy? It must have been Davy. . . .

Lowering a hem: How did you ever . . . when I think how you made everything we wore . . . Tim, just think, seven kids and Mommy sewed everything . . . do I remember you sang while you sewed? That white dress with the red apples on the skirt you fixed over for me, was it Hannah's or Clara's before it was mine?

Washing sweaters: Ma, I'll never forget, one of those days so nice you washed clothes outside; one of the first spring days it must have been. The bubbles just danced while you scrubbed, and we chased after, and you stopped to show us how to blow our own bubbles with green onion stalks . . . you always. . . .

"Strong onion, to still make you cry after so many years," her father said, to turn the tears into laughter.

While Richard bent over his homework: Where is it now, do we still have it, the Book of the Martyrs? It always seemed so, well—exalted, when you'd put it on the round table and we'd all look at it together; there was even a halo from the lamp. The lamp with the beaded fringe you could move up and down; they're in style again, pulley lamps like that, but without the fringe. You know the book I'm talking about, Daddy, the Book of the Martyrs, the first picture was a bust of Spartacus . . . Socrates? I wish there was something like that for the children, Mommy, to give them what you. . . . (And the tears splashed again.)

(What I intended and did not? Stop it, daughter, stop it, leave that time. And he, the hypocrite, sitting there with tears in his eyes—it was nothing to you then, nothing.)

. . . The time you came to school and I almost died of shame because of your accent and because I knew you knew I was ashamed; how could I? . . . Sammy's harmonica and you danced to it once, yes you did, you and Davy squealing in your arms. . . . That time you bundled us up and walked us down to the railway station to stay the night 'cause it was heated and we didn't have any coal, that winter of the strike, you didn't think I remembered that, did you, Mommy? . . . How you'd call us out to see the sunsets. . . .

Day after day, the spilling memories. Worse now, questions, too. Even the grandchildren: Grandma, in the olden days, when you were little. . . .

It was the afternoons that saved.

While they thought she napped, she would leave the mosaic on the wall (of children's drawings, maps, calendars, pictures, Ann's cardboard dolls with their great ringed questioning eyes) and hunch in the girls' closet on the low shelf where the shoes stood, and the girls' dresses covered.

For that while she would painfully sheathe against the listening house, the tendrils and noises that knocked, and Vivi's spilling memories. Sometimes it helped to braid and unbraid the sashes that dangled, or to trace the pattern on the hoop slips.

Today she had jacks and children under jet trails to forget. Last night, Ann and Dody silhouetted in the window against a sunset of flaming man-made clouds of jet trail, their jacks ball accenting the peaceful noise of dinner being made. Had she told them, yes she had told them of how they played jacks in her village though there was no ball, no jacks. Six stones, round and flat, toss them out, the seventh on the back of the hand, toss, catch and swoop up as many as possible, toss again. . . .

Of stones (repeating Richard) there are three kinds: earth's fire jetting; rock of layered centuries; crucibled new out of the old (*igneous, sedimentary, metamorphic*). But there was that other—frozen to black glass, never to transform or hold the fossil memory . . . (let not my seed fall on stone). There was an ancient man who fought to heights a great rock that crashed back down eternally—eternal labor, freedom, labor . . . (stone will perish, but the word remain). And you, David, who with a stone slew, screaming: Lord, take my heart of stone and give me flesh.

Who was screaming? Why was she back in the common room of the prison, the sun motes dancing in the shafts of light, and the informer being brought in, a prisoner now, like themselves. And Lisa leaping, yes, Lisa, the gentle and tender, biting at the betrayer's jugular. Screaming and screaming.

No, it is the children screaming. Another of Paul and Sammy's terrible fights?

In Vivi's house. Severely: you are in Vivi's house.

Blows, screams, a call: "Grandma!" For her? Oh please not for her. Hide, hunch behind the dresses deeper. But a trembling little body hurls itself beside her—surprised, smothered laughter, arms surround her neck, tears rub dry on her cheek, and words too soft to understand whisper into her ear (Is this where you hide too, Grammy? It's my secret place, we have a secret now).

And the sweat beads, and the long shudder seizes.

It seemed the great ear pressed inside now, and the knocking. "We have to go home," she told him, "I grow ill here."

"It's your own fault, Mrs. Bodybusy, you do not rest, you do too much." He raged, but the fear was in his eyes. "It was a serious operation, they told you to take care. . . . All right, we will go to where you can rest."

But where? Not home to death, not yet. He had thought to Lennie's, to Clara's; beautiful visits with each of the children. She would have to rest first, be stronger. If they could but go to Florida—it glittered before him, the never-realized promise of Florida. California: of course. (The money, the money, dwindling!) Los Angeles first for sun and rest, then to Lennie's in San Francisco.

He told her the next day. "You saw what Nancy wrote: snow and wind back home, a terrible winter. And look at you—all bones and a swollen belly. I called Phil: he said: 'A prescription, Los Angeles sun and rest.'"

TILLIE OLSEN

455

She watched the words on his lips. "You have sold the house," she cried, "that is why we do not go home. That is why you talk no more of the Haven, why there is money for travel. After the children you will drag me to the Haven."

"The Haven! Who thinks of the Haven any more? Tell her, Vivi, tell Mrs. Suspicious: a prescription, sun and rest, to make you healthy. . . . And how could I sell the house without *you?*"

At the place of farewells and greetings, of winds of coming and winds of going, they say their good-byes.

They look back at her with the eyes of others before them: Richard with her own blue blaze; Ann with the nordic eyes of Tim; Morty's dreaming brown of a great-grandmother he will never know; Dody with the laughing eyes of him who had been her springtide love (who stands beside her now); Vivi's, all tears.

The baby's eyes are closed in sleep.

Good-bye, my children.

3

It is to the back of the great city he brought her, to the dwelling places of the cast-off old. Bounded by two lines of amusement piers to the north and to the south, and between a long straight paving rimmed with black benches facing the sand—sands so wide the ocean is only a far fluting.

In the brief vacation season, some of the boarded stores fronting the sands open, and families, young people and children, may be seen. A little tasselled tram shuttles between the piers, and the lights of roller coasters prink and tweak over those who come to have sensation made in them.

The rest of the year it is abandoned to the old, all else boarded up and still; seemingly empty, except the occasional days and hours when the sun, like a tide, sucks them out of the low rooming houses, casts them onto the benches and sandy rim of the walk—and sweeps them into decaying enclosures once again.

A few newer apartments glint among the low bleached squares. It is in one of these Lennie's Jeannie has arranged their rooms. "Only a few miles north and south people pay hundreds of dollars a month for just this gorgeous air, Grandaddy, just this ocean closeness."

She had been ill on the plane, lay ill for days in the unfamiliar room. Several times the doctor came by—left medicine she would not take. Several times Jeannie drove in the twenty miles from work, still in her Visiting Nurse uniform, the lightness and brightness of her like a healing.

"Who can believe it is winter?" he asked one morning. "Beautiful it is outside like an ad. Come, Mrs. Invalid, come to taste it. You are well enough to sit in here, you are well enough to sit outside. The doctor said it too."

But the benches were encrusted with people, and the sands at the sidewalk's edge. Besides, she had seen the far ruffle of the sea: "there take me," and though she leaned against him, it was she who led.

Plodding and plodding, sitting often to rest, he grumbling. Patting the sand so warm. Once she scooped up a handful, cradling it close to her better eye; peered, and flung it back. And as they came almost to the brink and she could see the glistening wet, she sat down, pulled off her shoes and stockings, left him and began to run. "You'll catch cold," he screamed, but the sand in his shoes weighed him down—he who had always been the agile one—and already the white spray creamed her feet.

He pulled her back, took a handkerchief to wipe off the wet and the sand. "Oh no," she said, "the sun will dry," seized the square and smoothed it flat, dropped on it a mound of sand, knotted the kerchief corners and tied it to a bag—"to look at with the strong glass" (for the first time in years explaining an action of hers)—and lay down with the little bag against her cheek, looking toward the shore that nurtured life as it first crawled toward consciousness the millions of years ago.

He took her one Sunday in the evil-smelling bus, past flat miles of blister houses, to the home of relatives. Oh what is this? she cried as the light began to smoke and the houses to dim and recede. Smog, he said, everyone knows but you. . . . Outside he kept his arms about her, but she walked with hands pushing the heavy air as if to open it, whispered: who has done this? sat down suddenly to vomit at the curb and for a long while refused to rise.

One's age as seen on the altered face of those known in youth. Is this they he has come to visit? This Max and Rose, smooth and pleasant, introducing them to polite children, disinterested grandchildren, "the whole family, once a month on Sundays. And why not? We have the room, the help, the food."

Talk of cars, of houses, of success: this son that, that daughter this. And *your* children? Hastily skimped over, the intermarriages, the obscure work—"my doctor son-in-law, Phil"—all he has to offer. She silent in a corner. (Car-sick like a baby, he explains.) Years since he has taken her to visit anyone but the children, and old apprehensions prickle: "no incidents," he silently begs, "no incidents." He itched to tell them. "A very sick woman," significantly, indicating her with his eyes, "a very sick woman." Their restricted faces did not react. "Have you thought maybe she'd do better at Palm Springs?" Rose asked. "Or at least a nicer section of the beach, nicer people, a pool." Not to have to say "money" he said instead: "would she have sand to look at through a magnifying glass?" and went on, detail after detail, the old habit betraying of parading the queerness of her for laughter.

After dinner—the others into the living room in men- or women-clusters, or into the den to watch TV—the four of them alone. She sat close to him, and did not speak. Jokes, stories, people they had known, beginning of

TILLIE OLSEN

457

reminiscence, Russia fifty-sixty years ago. Strange words across the Duncan Phyfe table: *hunger; secret meetings; human rights; spies; betrayals; prison; escape*—interrupted by one of the grandchildren: "Commercial's on; any Coke left? Gee, you're missing a real hair-raiser." And then a granddaughter (Max proudly: "look at her, an American queen") drove them home on her way back to U.C.L.A. No incident—except there had been no incidents.

The first few mornings she had taken with her the magnifying glass, but he would sit only on the benches, so she rested at the foot, where slatted bench shadows fell, and unless she turned her hearing aid down, other voices invaded.

Now on the days when the sun shone and she felt well enough, he took her on the tram to where the benches ranged in oblongs, some with tables for checkers or cards. Again the blanket on the sand in the striped shadows, but she no longer brought the magnifying glass. He played cards, and she lay in the sun and looked towards the waters; or they walked—two blocks down to the scaling hotel, two blocks back—past chili-hamburger stands, open-doored bars, Next -to- New and perpetual rummage sale stores.

Once, out of the aimless walkers, slow and shuffling like themselves, someone ran unevenly towards them, embraced, kissed, wept: "dear friends, old friends." A friend of *hers,* not his: Mrs. Mays who had lived next door to them in Denver when the children were small.

Thirty years are compressed into a dozen sentences; and the present, not even in three. All is told: the children scattered; the husband dead; she lives in a room two blocks up from the sing hall—and points to the domed auditorium jutting before the pier. The leg? phlebitis; the heavy breathing? that, one does not ask. She, too, comes to the benches each day to sit. And tomorrow, tomorrow, are they going to the community sing? Of course he would have heard of it, everybody goes—the big doings they wait for all week. They have never been? She will come to them for dinner tomorrow and they will all go together.

So it is that she sits in the wind of the singing, among the thousand various faces of age.

She had turned off her hearing aid at once they came into the auditorium. —as she would have wished to turn off sight.

One by one they streamed by and imprinted on her—and though the savage zest of their singing came voicelessly soft and distant, the faces still roared—the faces densened the air—chorded into

> children-chants, mother-croons, singing of the chained
> love serenades, Beethoven storms, mad Lucia's scream
> drunken joy-songs, keens for the dead, work-singing

while from floor to balcony to dome a bare-footed sore-covered little
girl threaded the sound-thronged tumult, danced her ecstasy
of grimace to flutes that scratched at a cross-roads village wedding

Yes, faces became sound, and the sound became faces; and faces and sound
became weight—pushed, pressed

"Air"—her hands claw his.

"Whenever I enjoy myself. . . ." Then he saw the gray sweat on her face. "Here. Up. Help me, Mrs. Mays," and they support her out to where she can gulp the air in sob after sob.

"A doctor, we should get for her a doctor."

"Tch, it's nothing," says Ellen Mays, "I get it all the time. You've missed the tram; come to my place. Fix your hearing aid, honey . . . close . . . tea. My view. See, she *wants* to come. Steady now, that's how." Adding mysteriously: "Remember your advice, easy to keep your head above water, empty things float. Float."

The singing a fading march for them, tall woman with a swollen leg, weaving little man, and the swollen thinness they help between.

The stench in the hall: mildew? decay? "We sit and rest then climb. My gorgeous view. We help each other and here we are."

The stench along into the slab of room. A washstand for a sink, a box with oilcloth tacked around for a cupboard, a three-burner gas plate. Artificial flowers, colorless with dust. Everywhere pictures foaming: wedding, baby, party, vacation, graduation, family pictures. From the narrow couch under a slit of window, sure enough the view: lurching rooftops and a scallop of ocean heaving, preening, twitching under the moon.

"While the water heats. Excuse me . . . down the hall." Ellen Mays has gone.

"You'll live?" he asks mechanically, sat down to feel his fright; tried to pull her alongside.

She pushed him away. "For air," she said; stood clinging to the dresser. Then, in a terrible voice:

After a lifetime of room. Of many rooms.

Shhh.

You remember how she lived. Eight children. And now one room like a coffin.

She pays rent!

Shrinking the life of her into one room like a coffin Rooms and rooms like this I lie on the quilt and hear them talk

Please, Mrs. Orator-without-Breath.

Once you went for coffee I walked I saw A Balzac a Chekhov to write it Rummage Alone On scraps

Better old here than in the old country!

TILLIE OLSEN

459

On scraps Yet they sang like like Wondrous! *Humankind one has to believe* So strong for what? To rot not grow?

Your poor lungs beg you. They sob between each word.

Singing. Unused the life in them. She in this poor room with her pictures Max You The children Everywhere unused the life And who has meaning? Century after century still all in us not to grow?

Coffins, rummage, plants: sick woman. Oh lay down. We will get for you the doctor.

"And when will it end. Oh, *the end." That* nightmare thought, and this time she writhed, crumpled against him, seized his hand (for a moment again the weight, the soft distant roaring of humanity) and on the strangled-for breath, begged: "Man . . . we'll destroy ourselves?"

And looking for answer—in the helpless pity and fear for her (for *her*) that distorted his face—she understood the last months, and knew that she was dying.

4

"Let us go home," she said after several days.

"You are in training for a cross-country race? That is why you do not even walk across the room? Here, like a prescription Phil said, till you are stronger from the operation. You want to break doctor's orders?"

She saw the fiction was necessary to him, was silent; then: "At home I will get better. If the doctor here says?"

"And winter? And the visits to Lennie and to Clara? All right," for he saw the tears in her eyes, "I will write Phil, and talk to the doctor."

Days passed. He reported nothing. Jeannie came and took her out for air, past the boarded concessions, the hooded and tented amusement rides, to the end of the pier. They watched the spent waves feeding the new, the gulls in the clouded sky; even up where they sat, the wind-blown sand stung.

She did not ask to go down the crooked steps to the sea.

Back in her bed, while he was gone to the store, she said: "Jeannie, this doctor, he is not one I can ask questions. Ask him for me, can I go home?"

Jeannie looked at her, said quickly: "Of course, poor Granny. You want your own things around you, don't you? I'll call him tonight. . . . Look, I've something to show you," and from her purse unwrapped a large cookie, intricately shaped like a little girl. "Look at the curls—can you hear me well, Granny?—and the darling eyelashes. I just came from a house where they were baking them."

"The dimples, there in the knees," she marveled, holding it to the better light, turning, studying, "like art. Each singly they cut, or a mold?"

"Singly," said Jeannie, "and if it is a child only the mother can make them. Oh Granny, it's the likeness of a real little girl who died yesterday—Rosita. She was three years old. *Pan del Muerto,* the Bread of the Dead. It was the custom in the part of Mexico they came from."

Still she turned and inspected. "Look, the hollow in the throat, the little cross necklace. . . . I think for the mother it is a good thing to be busy with such bread. You know the family?"

Jeannie nodded. "On my rounds. I nursed. . . . Oh Granny, it is like a party; they play songs she liked to dance to. The coffin is lined with pink velvet and she wears a white dress. There are candles. . . ."

"In the house?" Surprised, "They keep her in the house?"

"Yes," said Jeannie, "and it is against the health law. The father said it will be sad to bury her in this country; in Oaxaca they have a feast night with candles each year; everyone picnics on the graves of those they loved until dawn."

"Yes, Jeannie, the living must comfort themselves." And closed her eyes.

"You want to sleep, Granny?"

"Yes, tired from the pleasure of you. I may keep the Rosita? There stand it, on the dresser, where I can see; something of my own around me."

In the kitchenette, helping her grandfather unpack the groceries, Jeannie said in her light voice:

"I'm resigning my job, Grandaddy."

"Ah, the lucky young man. Which one is he?"

"Too late. You're spoken for." She made a pyramid of cans, unstacked, and built again.

"Something is wrong with the job?"

"With me. I can't be"—she searched for the word—"What they call professional enough. I let myself feel things. And tomorrow I have to report a family. . . ." The cans clicked again. "It's not that, either. I just don't know what I want to do, maybe go back to school, maybe go to art school. I thought if you went to San Francisco I'd come along and talk it over with Momma and Daddy. But I don't see how you can go. She wants to go home. She asked me to ask the doctor."

The doctor told her himself. "Next week you may travel, when you are a little stronger." But next week there was the fever of an infection, and by the time that was over, she could not leave the bed—a rented hospital bed that stood beside the double bed he slept in alone now.

Outwardly the days repeated themselves. Every other afternoon and evening he went out to his newfound cronies, to talk and play cards. Twice a week, Mrs. Mays came. And the rest of the time, Jeannie was there.

By the sickbed stood Jeannie's FM radio. Often into the room the shapes of music came. She would lie curled on her side, her knees drawn up, intense in listening (Jeannie sketched her so, coiled, convoluted like an ear), then thresh her hand out and abruptly snap the radio mute—still to lie in her attitude of listening, concealing tears.

Once Jeannie brought in a young Marine to visit, a friend from high-school days she had found wandering near the empty pier. Because Jeannie asked him to, gravely, without self-consciousness, he sat himself cross-legged on the floor and performed for them a dance of his native Samoa.

Long after they left, a tiny thrumming sound could be heard where, in her bed, she strove to repeat the beckon, flight, surrender of his hands, the fluttering footbeats, and his low plaintive calls.

Hannah and Phil sent flowers. To deepen her pleasure, he placed one in her hair. "Like a girl," he said, and brought the hand mirror so she could see. She looked at the pulsing red flower, the yellow skull face; a desolate, excited laugh shuddered from her, and she pushed the mirror away—but let the flower burn.

The week Lennie and Helen came, the fever returned. With it the excited laugh, and incessant words. She, who in her life had spoken but seldom and then only when necessary (never having learned the easy, social uses of words), now in dying, spoke incessantly.

In a half-whisper: "Like Lisa she is, your Jeannie. Have I told you of Lisa who taught me to read? Of the highborn she was, but noble in herself. I was sixteen; they beat me; my father beat me so I would not go to her. It was forbidden, she was a Tolstoyan. At night, past dogs that howled, terrible dogs, my son, in the snows of winter to the road, I to ride in her carriage like a lady, to books. To her, life was holy, knowledge was holy, and she taught me to read. They hung her. Everything that happens one must try to understand. She killed one who betrayed many. Because of betrayal, betrayed all she lived and believed. In one minute she killed, before my eyes (there is so much blood in a human being, my son), in prison with me. All that happens, one must try to understand.

"The name?" Her lips would work. "The name that was their pole star; the doors of the death houses fixed to open on it; I read of it my year of penal servitude. Thuban!" very excited, "Thuban, in ancient Egypt the pole star. Can you see, look out to see it, Jeannie, if it swings around *our* pole star that seems to *us* not to move.

"Yes, Jeannie, at your age my mother and grandmother had already buried children . . . yes, Jeannie, it is more than oceans between Olshana and you . . . yes, Jeannie, they danced, and for all the bodies they had they might as well be chickens, and indeed, they scratched and flapped their arms and hopped.

"And Andrei Yefimitch, who for twenty years had never known of it and never wanted to know, said as if he wanted to cry: but why my dear friend this malicious laughter?" Telling to herself half-memorized phrases from her few books. "Pain I answer with tears and cries, baseness with indignation, meanness with repulsion . . . for life may be hated or wearied of, but never despised."

Delirious: "Tell me, my neighbor, Mrs. Mays, the pictures never lived, but what of the flowers? Tell them who ask: no rabbis, no ministers, no priests, no speeches, no ceremonies: ah, false—let the living comfort themselves. Tell Sammy's boy, he who flies, tell him to go to Stuttgart and see where Davy has no grave. And what? . . . And what? where millions have no graves—save air."

In delirium or not, wanting the radio on; not seeming to listen, the words still jetting, wanting the music on. Once, silencing it abruptly as of old, she began to cry, unconcealed tears this time. "You have pain, Granny?" Jeannie asked.

"The music," she said, "still it is there and we do not hear; knocks, and our poor human ears too weak. What else, what else we do not hear?"

Once she knocked his hand aside as he gave her a pill, swept the bottles from her bedside table: "no pills, let me feel what I feel," and laughed as on his hands and knees he groped to pick them up.

Nighttimes her hand reached across the bed to hold his.

A constant retching began. Her breath was too faint for sustained speech now, but still the lips moved:

> *When no longer necessary to injure others*
> *Pick pick pick Blind chicken*
> *As a human being responsibility*

"David!" imperious, "Basin!" and she would vomit, rinse her mouth, the wasted throat working to swallow, and begin the chant again.

She will be better off in the hospital now, the doctor said.

He sent the telegrams to the children, was packing her suitcase, when her hoarse voice startled. She had roused, was pulling herself to sitting.

"Where now?" she asked. "Where now do you drag me?"

"You do not even have to have a baby to go this time," he soothed, looking for the brush to pack. "Remember, after Davy you told me—worthy to have a baby for the pleasure of the ten day rest in the hospital?"

"Where now? Not home yet?" Her voice mourned. "Where *is* my home?"

He rose to ease her back. "The doctor, the hospital," he started to explain, but deftly, like a snake, she had slithered out of bed and stood swaying, propped behind the night table.

"Coward," she hissed, "runner."

"You stand," he said senselessly.

"To take me there and run. Afraid of a little vomit."

He reached her as she fell. She struggled against him, half slipped from his arms, pulled herself up again.

"Weakling," she taunted, "to leave me there and run. Betrayer. All your life you have run."

He sobbed, telling Jeannie. "A Marilyn Monroe to run for her virtue. Fifty-nine pounds she weighs, the doctor said, and she beats at me like a Dempsey. Betrayer, she cries, and I running like a dog when she calls; day and night, running to her, her vomit, the bedpan. . . ."

"She needs you, Grandaddy," said Jeannie. "Isn't that what they call love? I'll see if she sleeps, and if she does, poor worn-out darling, we'll have a party, you and I: I brought us rum babas."

They did not move her. By her bed now stood the tall hooked pillar that held the solutions—blood and dextrose—to feed her veins. Jeannie moved down the hall to take over the sickroom, her face so radiant, her grandfather asked her once: "you are in love?" (Shameful the joy, the pure overwhelming joy from being with her grandmother; the peace, the serenity that breathed.) "My darling escape," she answered incoherently, "my darling Granny"—as if that explained.

Now one by one the children came, those that were able. Hannah, Paul, Sammy. Too late to ask: and what did you learn with your living, Mother, and what do we need to know?

Clara, the eldest, clenched:

Pay me back, Mother, pay me back for all you took from me. Those others you crowded into your heart. The hands I needed to be for you, the heaviness, the responsibility.

Is this she? Noises the dying make, the crablike hands crawling over the covers. The ethereal singing.

She hears that music, that singing from childhood; forgotten sound— not heard since, since. . . . And the hardness breaks like a cry: Where did we lose each other, first mother, singing mother?

Annulled: the quarrels, the gibing, the harshness between; the fall into silence and the withdrawal.

I do not know you, Mother. Mother, I never knew you.

Lennie, suffering not alone for her who was dying, but for that in her which never lived (for that which in him might never live). From him too, unspoken words: *good-bye Mother who taught me to mother myself.*

Not Vivi, who must stay with her children; not Davy, but he is already here, having to die again with *her* this time, for the living take their dead with them when they die.

Light she grew, like a bird, and, like a bird, sound bubbled in her throat while the body fluttered in agony. Night and day, asleep or awake (though indeed there was no difference now) the songs and the phrases leaping.

And he, who had once dreaded a long dying (from fear of himself, from horror of the dwindling money) now desired her quick death profoundly, for *her* sake. He no longer went out, except when Jeannie forced him; no longer laughed, except when, in the bright kitchenette, Jeannie coaxed his laughter (and she, who seemed to hear nothing else, would laugh too, conspiratorial wisps of laughter).

Light, like a bird, the fluttering body, the little claw hands, the beaked shadow on her face; and the throat, bubbling, straining.

He tried not to listen, as he tried not to look on the face in which only the forehead remained familiar, but trapped with her the long nights in that little room, the sounds worked themselves into his consciousness, with their punctuation of death swallows, whimpers, gurglings.

Even in reality (swallow) *life's lack of it*
Slaveships deathtrains clubs eeenough
The bell summon what enobles
   78,000 in one minute (whisper of a scream) *78,000*
human beings we'll destroy ourselves?

"Aah, Mrs. Miserable," he said, as if she could hear, "all your life working, and now in bed you lie, servants to tend, you do not even need to call to be tended, and still you work. Such hard work it is to die? Such hard work?"

The body threshed, her hand clung in his. A melody, ghost-thin, hovered on her lips, and like a guilty ghost, the vision of her bent in listening to it, silencing the record instantly he was near. Now, heedless of his presence, she floated the melody on and on.

"Hid it from me," he complained, "how many times you listened to remember it so?" And tried to think when she had first played it, or first begun to silence her few records when he came near—but could reconstruct nothing. There was only this room with its tall hooked pillar and its swarm of sounds.

No man one except through others
Strong with the not yet in the now
Dogma dead war dead one country

"It helps, Mrs. Philosopher, words from books? It helps?" And it seemed to him that for seventy years she had hidden a tape recorder, infinitely microscopic, within her, that it had coiled infinite mile on mile, trapping every song, every melody, every word read, heard, and spoken— and that maliciously she was playing back only what said nothing of him, of the children, of their intimate life together.

"Left us indeed, Mrs. Babbler," he reproached, "you who called others babbler and cunningly saved your words. A lifetime you tended and loved, and now not a word of us, for us. Left us indeed? Left me."

And he took out his solitaire deck, shuffled the cards loudly, slapped them down.

Lift high   banner of reason (tatter of an orator's voice)
justice   freedom   light
Humankind   life   worthy   capacities
Seeks (blur of shudder) *belong   human being*
"Words, words," he accused, "and what human beings did *you* seek around you, Mrs. Live Alone, and what humankind think worthy?"

Though even as he spoke, he remembered she had not always been isolated, had not always wanted to be alone (as he knew there had been a voice before this gossamer one; before the hoarse voice that broke from silence to lash, make incidents, shame him—a girl's voice of eloquence that spoke their holiest dreams). But again he could reconstruct, image, nothing of what had been before, or when, or how, it had changed.

Ace, queen, jack. The pillar shadow fell, so, in two tracks; in the mirror depths glistened a moonlike blob, the empty solution bottle. And it worked in him: *of reason and justice and freedom . . . Dogma dead:* he remembered the full quotation, laughed bitterly. "Hah, good you do not know what you say; good Victor Hugo died and did not see it, his twentieth century."

Deuce, ten, five. Dauntlessly she began a song of their youth of belief:

> *These things shall be, a loftier race*
> *than e'er the world hath known shall rise*
> *with flame of freedom in their souls*
> *and light of knowledge in their eyes*

King, four, jack "In the twentieth century, hah!"

> *They shall be gentle, brave and strong*
> *to spill no drop of blood, but dare*
> *all . . .*
>
> *on earth and fire and sea and air*

"To spill no drop of blood, hah! So, cadaver, and you too, cadaver Hugo, 'in the twentieth century ignorance will be dead, dogma will be dead, war will be dead, and for all mankind one country—of fulfilment?' Hah!"

> *And every life* (long strangling cough) *shall*
> *be a song*

The cards fell from his fingers. Without warning, the bereavement and betrayal he had sheltered—compounded through the years—hidden even from himself—revealed itself,

uncoiled,
released,
sprung

and with it the monstrous shapes of what had actually happened in the century.

A ravening hunger or thirst seized him. He groped into the kitchenette, switched on all three lights, piled a tray—"you have finished your night snack, Mrs. Cadaver, now I will have mine." And he was shocked at the tears that splashed on the tray.

"Salt tears. For free. I forgot to shake on salt?"

Whispered: "Lost, how much I lost."

Escaped to the grandchildren whose childhoods were childish, who had never hungered, who lived unravaged by disease in warm houses of many rooms, had all the school for which they cared, could walk on any street, stood a head taller than their grandparents, towered above—beautiful skins, straight backs, clear straightforward eyes. "Yes, you in Olshana," he said to the town of sixty years ago, "they would be nobility to you."

And was this not the dream then, come true in ways undreamed? he asked.

And are there no other children in the world? he answered, as if in her harsh voice.

And the flame of freedom, the light of knowledge?

And the drop, to spill no drop of blood?

And he thought that at six Jeannie would get up and it would be his turn to go to her room and sleep, that he could press the buzzer and she would come now; that in the afternoon Ellen Mays was coming, and this time they would play cards and he could marvel at how rouge can stand half an inch on the cheek; that in the evening the doctor would come, and he could beg him to be merciful, to stop the feeding solutions, to let her die.

To let her die, and with her their youth of belief out of which her bright, betrayed words foamed; stained words, that on her working lips came stainless.

Hours yet before Jeannie's turn. He could press the buzzer and wake her to come now; he could take a pill, and with it sleep; he could pour more brandy into his milk glass, though what he had poured was not yet touched.

Instead he went back, checked her pulse, gently tended with his knotty fingers as Jeannie had taught.

She was whimpering; her hand crawled across the covers for his. Compassionately he enfolded it, and with his free hand gathered up the cards again. Still was there thirst or hunger ravening in him.

That world of their youth—dark, ignorant, terrible with hate and disease—how was it that living in it, in the midst of corruption, filth,

treachery, degradation, they had not mistrusted man nor themselves; had
believed so beautifully, so . . . falsely?

"Aaah, children," he said out loud, "how we believed, how we belonged." And he yearned to package for each of the children, the
grandchildren, for everyone, *that joyous certainty, that sense of mattering,
of moving and being moved, of being one and indivisible with the great
of the past, with all that freed, ennobled.* Package it, stand on corners, in
front of stadiums and on crowded beaches, knock on doors, give it as a
fabled gift.

"And why not in cereal boxes, in soap packages?" he mocked himself.
"Aah. You have taken my senses, cadaver."

Words foamed, died unsounded. Her body writhed; she made kissing
motions with her mouth. (Her lips moving as she read, poring over the
Book of the Martyrs, the magnifying glass superimposed over the heavy
eyeglasses.) *Still she believed?* "Eva!" he whispered. "Still you believed?
You lived by it? These Things Shall Be?"

"One pound soup meat," she answered distinctly, "one soup bone."

"My ears heard you. Ellen Mays was witness: 'Humankind . . . one
has to believe.'" Imploringly: "Eva!"

"Bread, day-old." She was mumbling. "Please, in a wooden box . . . for
kindling. The thread, hah, the thread breaks. Cheap thread"—and a
gurgling, enormously loud, began in her throat.

"I ask for stone; she gives me bread—day-old." He pulled his hand
away, shouted: "Who wanted questions? Everything you have to wake?"
Then dully, "Ah, let me help you turn, poor creature."

Words jumbled, cleared. In a voice of crowded terror:

"Paul, Sammy, don't fight.

"Hannah, have I ten hands?

"How can I give it, Clara, how can I give it if I don't have?"

"You lie," he said sturdily, "there was joy too." Bitterly: "Ah how cheap
you speak of us at the last."

As if to rebuke him, as if her voice had no relationship with her
flailing body, she sang clearly, beautifully, a school song the children had
taught her when they were little; begged:

"Not look my hair where they cut. . . ."

(The crown of braids shorn.) And instantly he left the mute old woman
poring over the Book of the Martyrs; went past the mother treading at the
sewing machine, singing with the children; past the girl in her wrinkled
prison dress, hiding her hair with scarred hands, lifting to him her
awkward, shamed, imploring eyes of love; and took her in his arms,
dear, personal, fleshed, in all the heavy passion he had loved to rouse from
her.

"Eva!"

Her little claw hand beat the covers. How much, how much can a
man stand? He took up the cards, put them down, circled the beds,

walked to the dresser, opened, shut drawers, brushed his hair, moved his hand bit by bit over the mirror to see what of the reflection he could blot out with each move, and felt that at any moment he would die of what was unendurable. Went to press the buzzer to wake Jeannie, looked down, saw on Jeannie's sketch pad the hospital bed, with *her;* the double bed alongside, with him; the tall pillar feeding into her veins, and their hands, his and hers, clasped, feeding each other. And as if he had been instructed he went to his bed, lay down, holding the sketch (as if it could shield against the monstrous shapes of loss, of betrayal, of death) and with his free hand took hers back into his.

So Jeannie found them in the morning.

That last day the agony was perpetual. Time after time it lifted her almost off the bed, so they had to fight to hold her down. He could not endure and left the room; wept as if there never would be tears enough.

Jeannie came to comfort him. In her light voice she said: Grandaddy, Grandaddy don't cry. She is not there, she promised me. On the last day, she said she would go back to when she first heard music, a little girl on the road of the village where she was born. She promised me. It is a wedding and they dance, while the flutes so joyous and vibrant tremble in the air. Leave her there. Grandaddy, it is all right. She promised me. Come back, come back and help her poor body to die.

For two of that generation
Seevya and Genya
Infinite, dauntless, incorruptible

Death deepens the wonder

COMING TO SELF

by

MICHELE MURRAY

(1934–1974)

Born in Brooklyn, Michele Murray grew up in New York City and earned degrees from the New School for Social Research and the University of Connecticut. She was a college teacher and for many years a book reviewer for major journals; she published two novels for children and edited an anthology on images of women. Her poems appeared in many journals before being collected in The Great Mother and Other Poems *(1974), published after her untimely death from cancer.*

after these years
as iron comes by fire
from the ore
as gold washes clean in the stream
the dross
sifted and sifted
falling away
into the clear water

UNLEARNING TO NOT SPEAK

by

MARGE PIERCY

(b. 1936)

Marge Piercy was born in Detroit and was the first in her family to attend college. She has published several volumes of poetry, in-cluding Breaking Camp *(1968),* Hard Loving *(1969),* Living in the Open *(1976), and* Circles in the Water *(1982), and five novels, in-cluding* Woman on the Edge of Time *(1976),* Vida *(1980), and* Braided Lives *(1982). An ardent feminist, Piercy presents her women characters realistically yet tenderly.*

Blizzards of paper
in slow motion
sift through her.
In nightmares she suddenly recalls
a class she signed up for
but forgot to attend.
Now it is too late.
Now it is time for finals:
losers will be shot.
Phrases of men who lectured her
drift and rustle in piles:
Why don't you speak up?
Why are you shouting?
You have the wrong answer,
wrong line, wrong face.
They tell her she is womb-man,
babymachine, mirror image, toy,
earth mother and penis-poor,
a dish of synthetic strawberry icecream
rapidly melting.

She grunts to a halt.
She must learn again to speak
starting with *I*
starting with *We*
starting as the infant does
with her own true hunger
and pleasure
and rage.

THREE WOMEN

A One Act Play

by

CHARLOTTE PERKINS GILMAN

(1860–1935)

Born in Hartford, Connecticut, Charlotte Perkins Gilman was the niece of Harriet Beecher Stowe and shared her aunt's zeal for reforming society nearer to women's values of loving relationships. A prolific lifelong writer, Gilman's two major works, rediscovered by feminist scholars, are Women and Economics *(1898), the original title of which was* Economic Relation of the Sexes as a Factor in Social Development, *and "The Yellow Wallpaper," a short story about a wife's descent into madness when her husband confines her to her room. First published in a journal in 1892, the story has been separately republished by the Feminist Press.*

• ———————————————— •

Characters

ALINE MORROW   A kindergartner of about twenty-five, at first plainly dressed; a good-looking, pleasant, friendly girl; kind, strong, reliable. Later, blossoms out into an ultra-feminine and attractive gown, coiffure, manner, etc.

MRS. MORROW   Her mother. A quiet, rather sad-faced, very domestic, elderly-looking woman of about fifty, somewhat old-fashioned, dressed in black.

MISS UPTON   Her aunt. Some ten years younger than Mrs. Morrow, vivacious, handsome, richly dressed, successful and popular.

MRS. ELLIS   Mother of some of Aline's pupils. Excitable, staccato little woman, devoted to Aline and her work.

DR. RUSSELL   A physician. Wishes to marry Aline.

A MAID

Scene

Parlor in Mrs. Morrow's home. Evening. Center table with shaded light. Mrs. Morrow discovered rocking in a low chair and darning stockings, humming a little hymn tune, as "Abide With Me."

(Bell heard. Enter maid.)

MAID Mrs. Ellis.

MRS. MORROW Show her right in.

(Enter Mrs. Ellis.)

MRS. MORROW Glad to see you, Mrs. Ellis. Won't you sit down—and lay off your things?

MRS. ELLIS Oh, no, thank you! I can't stop but a *moment*—just a *moment!* *Excuse* my intruding, but I just couldn't wait to show her the babies' pictures! Where is she?

MRS. MORROW She's at Mrs. Anderson's. More of her babies there, you know. But she'll be here directly, I'm sure. Won't you show them to me?

MRS. ELLIS Why, yes, of course! Do *you* care for children as she does? Now, Mrs. Morrow, I wonder if you *appreciate* that daughter of yours! The children simply *worship* her!

MRS. MORROW And she seems to worship them, Mrs. Ellis.

MRS. ELLIS—Oh, she does! She *does!* If ever there was a world-mother it's that girl! She has genius—absolute *genius!*

(Enter Miss Upton. She is in evening dress and carries an evening wrap over her arm.)

MISS UPTON What genius have you discovered now, Mrs. Ellis?

MRS. ELLIS Oh, good *evening*, Miss Upton! I'm so *glad* to see you. It's that *wonderful* niece of yours, Miss Upton. She has such a genius for her work, her *beautiful* work—the kindergarten, you know.

MISS UPTON Yes, Aline's an artist in her line—a real one.

MRS. ELLIS Of course, it's not like yours—not like *Art!* We hear *wonderful* things about you, Miss Upton.

MISS UPTON Thank you, Mrs. Ellis. I wish I *were* doing wonderful things.

MRS. ELLIS Oh, you *are!* You *are!* Why, that article about you in the Centurion quite staggered me, Miss Upton. To think that I really knew a woman who could paint such marvelous pictures!

MISS UPTON I see you've brought us some marvelous pictures, Mrs. Ellis. *(Takes photos.)* These are excellent—excellent.

MRS. MORROW Clara is very fond of children's pictures, Mrs. Ellis.

MRS. ELLIS Yes, I know. What was it the great critic said? That you not only painted mothers and children—you painted motherhood!

(Enter Aline.)

ALINE Well, mother. Good evening, all. *(All rise to welcome her. She greets Mrs. Ellis cordially, puts an arm about both mother and aunt, kisses each affectionately. Sees photos.)* Ah, my babies! *(Takes pictures and looks at them with evident delight.)*

MRS. ELLIS *(Admiringly.)* I do believe you love our babies as well as we mothers do!

MISS UPTON Better than some mothers I've seen, Mrs. Ellis. I believe that mothers are born and not made.

MRS. MORROW You're right, Clara.

MRS. ELLIS I'm so glad you like them, Miss Morrow! These are for you. I couldn't wait to show them. *Good* evening, all! I have to go back and put the children to bed. *Good* night, Miss Upton. *Good* night, Mrs. Morrow. *Good* night, *dear* Miss Morrow! *(Exit Mrs. Ellis.)*

MRS. MORROW How fond those children's mothers are of you, Aline!

ALINE They are very kind indeed—most of them. Aren't you rather unusually gorgeous, Aunt Clara? Going out, of course!

MISS UPTON Yes—later. It's the Jainville's reception.

ALINE And which of your forty adorers is coming for you, Auntie?

MISS UPTON A woman of forty needs forty adorers, Aline. But, speaking of gorgeousness—aren't you going to change *your* dress?

ALINE What for? I don't have forty adorers.

MISS UPTON No, but you have *one,* and that's much more important. *(Bell heard. Maid appears.)*

MAID Dr. Russell.

MISS UPTON Come, now, run along and put on a pretty frock, child—do!

ALINE Why should I? *(Looks in mirror.)* This is a perfectly good dress.

MISS UPTON *(Kissing her.)* You are a perfectly good—goose, Aline Morrow. *(Enter Dr. Russell. Coat on, gloves in hand. Greets them all most politely.)*

DR. RUSSELL Good evening, Mrs. Morrow—Miss Upton. Good evening, Miss Morrow.

MRS. MORROW Sit down, Dr. Russell, sit down. Take your coat off, won't you?

DR. RUSSELL Thank you, Mrs. Morrow. I've only a moment. *(Looks at watch.)* On my way to a patient. *(Miss Upton rises, gathers cloak about her.)*

DR. RUSSELL Allow me. *(Offers to [help.])*

MISS UPTON No, thank you. I need a practiced hand for a few moments. Sister, you'll have to come and help me.

MRS. MORROW Yes, certainly, Clara. *(Exit both.)*

DR. RUSSELL Your aunt is a very popular lady.

ALINE Isn't she! She's like a young girl! Everybody likes her. It's a beautiful life. Don't you admire her work, Dr. Russell?

DR. RUSSELL I do, indeed. And yet—even with all her friends, and her successes—it is a pity that so lovely a woman is not married. Don't you think so, Miss Morrow?

ALINE Oh—I don't know! I've seen many married women that couldn't compare with Aunt Clara for happiness. Look at the last addition to my family. *(Shows him the photographs.)*

DR. RUSSELL Very pretty, very pretty.

ALINE Did I ever show you my jewels—a la Cornelia? *(Brings out a great array of photos of children and sets them up.)*

DR. RUSSELL You are very fond of children, aren't you?

ALINE Fond of children! Of course. What are women for?

DR. RUSSELL I thought you held they were for many other purposes.

ALINE Oh, yes—as *persons*—for any kind of work they like. You always forget that women are persons. But as *women*—they are for children.

DR. RUSSELL I can't see the difference—I see only the woman. *(Looks at her admiringly. She is looking at the photos. He rises. Comes to her, takes the pictures from her hands, seizes her hands.)*

DR. RUSSELL I cannot wait another day, Aline! When will you marry me?

ALINE Marry you! Why, I did not know— *(Laughs softly.)* I can't lie to save me. I did know you wanted me to—at least, I hoped so.

DR. RUSSELL Hoped? Oh, Aline! My Aline! *(She holds him at arm's length.)*

ALINE Wait! Wait! I haven't said I would yet.

DR. RUSSELL You said you loved me. At least, you said you hoped I— Aline! You do love me?

ALINE *(Soberly.)* I do love you, Gordon. I've loved you—ever so long. *(He tries to embrace her.)* No! No! We've got to talk a little first.

DR. RUSSELL What is there to talk about? If you love me that's all there is to it. *(He takes one hand and kisses it over and over. She withdraws it with a little breathless sob.)*

ALINE Don't do that—yet! I can't think—and I've got to think now! *(She stands away from him, puts a chair before her and confronts him.)*

DR. RUSSELL What do you mean, Aline? *(Half seriously.)* Is there A Past between us?

ALINE No—but there is a Future!

DR. RUSSELL *(Puzzled.)* The future will be ours together, surely.

ALINE *(Slowly.)* Some of it will—and some of it won't. We may have a beautiful future together— *(She drops her voice lovingly at the word, then lifts her head and goes on clearly.)* but we also want a beautiful future separately.

DR. RUSSELL Separately? What do you mean?

ALINE Didn't you have a big, bright future before you knew me—hopes of advancement in your profession—ambition to do great work—to serve humanity?

DR. RUSSELL Of course I had—and have yet. But that is not *separate,* dear. My whole life will be yours. All that I have—all that I do—all my hope and ambition and success—it is all for you. You shall share it.

ALINE That is true, I hope. I should, gladly, share in your professional ambition and success—but would you also share in mine?

DR. RUSSELL *(Looks puzzled.)* In yours?

ALINE *(Watches him eagerly, gives a little disappointed cry.)* Oh, haven't you even *thought* that my work was dear to me—as dear as yours to you? *(Comes a little toward him.)*

DR. RUSSELL *(Regarding her confusedly.)* Do you mean that you would wish to go on teaching school—after we were married?

ALINE Yes.

DR. RUSSELL For a while, you mean.

ALINE All my life.

DR. RUSSELL You never mentioned this before.

ALINE How could I?

DR. RUSSELL *(Turns, walks up and down. He crosses to her suddenly.)* You love me? Say it again!

ALINE *(Solemnly.)* I love you.

DR. RUSSELL Do you not love me well enough to give up teaching school?

ALINE Do you love me well enough to give up practicing medicine?

DR. RUSSELL *(Hotly.)* Aline! It is not the same thing.

ALINE   Why not?

DR. RUSSELL   A man does not have to give up his work to marry.

ALINE   Neither does a woman, nowadays.

DR. RUSSELL   Nowadays! Women haven't left off being women nowadays, have they?

ALINE   No—but they have begun to be something more.

DR. RUSSELL   *(Coming closer, holding her hand. Draws her to a sofa.)* Come, dear. Let us sit and talk it over. I love you too well to deny you anything in reason, but surely—the duties of the wife and mother come first in a woman's life. You believe that, don't you?

ALINE   No honestly—I don't agree with you. I think the first duty of anybody—man or woman—is to do their best work for the world. Oh, my dear, don't make it so—hard! See—I am willing to be your wife. I should hope to be *(her voice drops reverently)* a mother. But I am by nature, by habit, by seven years' training, a *teacher*—and I cannot give it up.

DR. RUSSELL   *(Takes both her hands and leans nearer.)* Not for love's sake? *(She hesitates. He slips his arm around her, draws her to him.)* Look at me, Aline! Ah, my dearest! Only marry me and I will engage to make you forget your school-teaching. *(She starts up; he follows her.)* Trust me, Aline. You love me; that is enough. I have not had one kiss yet—not one. And I've been wanting it so—ever since I first saw you—for two years. *(He tries to turn her face to his, but she breaks from him breathlessly.)*

ALINE   No! No! Gordon—not yet! You—move me so—I find it hard to be wise. *(He comes nearer.)* Don't touch me—go and sit over there. *(He sits.)* Don't look at me—please. Look at the table. *(He looks at it, smiling. They sit opposite.)* We must be perfectly agreed about this before it is too late.

DR. RUSSELL   It is too late already, Aline. If a woman gives her heart to a man—

ALINE   She may still refuse to marry him if she so choose—even if it breaks her heart.

DR. RUSSELL   And his?

ALINE   Yes—even that. Two broken hearts are better than one broken marriage.

DR. RUSSELL   *(Drumming on the table—trying to be patient.)* I wish you would consider this thing practically, dear.

ALINE   *(Eagerly.)* That is just what I am trying to do. Now, see. You know how we live here—you know how good the food is—and how cheap—and how little service is required, or management. If we had a house this way—with meals and service from outside—I could be as free as I am now.

DR. RUSSELL *(Rising.)* You forget Aline. A girl does. There is more than housekeeping to consider. The best use of all your kindergartening will be to help you when your own little ones demand your care. Can you not foresee?

ALINE *(Rising, facing him squarely, standing tall and pale.)* Can I not foresee? You, a man, ask me, a woman, if I cannot foresee motherhood! I have foreseen it since I was a child. Since I was a girl of fifteen I have planned and worked and tried to live my best, in the hope that some day— I tell you I am not a girl. I am a woman.

DR. RUSSELL You glorious woman! I knew your heart would guide you. I knew the Teacher would give way to the Mother. *(Approaches her, tries to embrace her, she holding him off.)*

ALINE *(Pleadingly.)* Don't misunderstand me, Gordon. I should still be a teacher—and a better mother because of it.

DR. RUSSELL *(Angry, disappointed, hurt, stands by, folds his arms.)* You propose, then, that my home shall be the adjunct of a boarding-house—and that I rent an office as I do now, and live as the husband of a school-teacher?

ALINE I propose nothing, Dr. Russell. I understood you to propose marriage. Do you withdraw the proposal?

(They stand facing one another. Both take a step forward. He holds out his arms to her.)

DR. RUSSELL I love you better than anything else in life! Aline!

ALINE Except your prejudices!

DR. RUSSELL *(Clock strikes. Starts and looks at his watch.)* Please do not decide now! Please wait a little. I must keep my appointment. I will be back as soon as I can. Let me beg you to consider—ask your own heart. Consult your mother.

ALINE I will—and my aunt.

DR. RUSSELL And don't forget that we love each other! *(Exit Dr. Russell.)*

(Aline, left alone, gradually loses her determined air, runs to window and looks after him. The curtains partly conceal her. Re-enter Mrs. Morrow. Takes her chair again, looks for thimble, wets her finger and slips it on. Seats herself and begins to rock and hum and darn again. Aline turns and comes to her. Kisses her daintily, affectionately.)

ALINE There's a dear little curl in the back of your neck, Motherkin. It's so pretty. *(Mrs. Morrow kisses her warmly.)* Now you go right on being a picture of contented domesticity—I want to ask you something. *(Brings low stool or cushion and sits at her mother's feet. Lays her arm on her mother's knees, chin on hands and looks at her. Mother strokes her hair lovingly.)* Can you darn stockings and give advice at the same time, Motherkin?

MRS. MORROW *(Darning.)* What do you want advice about? I thought you never took any.

ALINE I may not take this. Asking advice and taking it are two quite different things. *(Plays with darning cotton.)* It's about marrying—or not marrying. Or, rather, it's about giving up my profession—or not giving it up.

MRS. MORROW Dr. Russell? *(Aline nods.)* And he wants you to give up your work—insists upon it?

ALINE Yes. It amounts to that. I thought he knew how I felt about it. It is rather difficult, you see—to tell a man your views on post-matrimonial industry before he proposes!

MRS. MORROW *(With sudden change of feeling.)* Of course it's difficult! Whatever the girl does is difficult! She's supposed to be blankly innocent and unsuspecting, and to say "This is so sudden!" else she's unwomanly. On the other hand, "a true woman" always knows if a man loves her! If she does not foresee it all and stave him off in what they call "a thousand delicate ways"—then she's accused of leading him on. So there you are! *(Nods defiantly.)*

ALINE *(Gently.)* Well—I've often said what I thought about a woman's working after she was married, but he seemed as surprised as if he'd never met the idea.

MRS. MORROW Did you put it to him at once?

ALINE Yes. That is *(a little embarrassed)* we discussed it. He's coming back for an answer.

MRS. MORROW Seems to me, in your case, there's no difficulty at all. Here's this blessed "Dunham" answers all the housekeeping problem. Delicious and cheap. Meals sent in hot. Service by the hour. He knows about that.

ALINE Yes, of course. And he's often eaten with us, and knows how nice it is; but he says he wants a home of his own.

MRS. MORROW That is—a cook of his own. And he doesn't even know what he would escape. *(Lays down her work.)* Look here, child. You could manage perfectly. He could rent our lower floor. Clara would be glad to get her a studio down town; she only stays here to help me out—bless her! The rooms would be better for him than where he is now, and on the same block. He wouldn't lose anything.

ALINE I wish he thought so.

MRS. MORROW Why, what does the man want? I'd rent you the house and we'd all go into The Dunham. He *couldn't* live as cheaply any other way.

ALINE He doesn't like the idea.

MRS. MORROW Then when the children come you could substitute for a while—and go right on teaching. I could supervise, you know, till they are big enough for the kindergarten—and there you are.

ALINE I'd have to be out mornings—

MRS. MORROW Well? He'd have to be *in* mornings, wouldn't he? Office hours! And in case children were in mortal peril I guess a grandmother and a doctor-father—with a trained nurse—could keep 'em alive until you were telephoned for. Why it's ideal!

ALINE But, Mother—he won't see it. He—he's a man. It's feeling. You can't reason against feeling. *(She meditates, smiling softly. Her mother watches her anxiously.)*

MRS. MORROW I know—I know, dear. It is delicious—at first. It is hard—very hard—to decide. *(Pause.)* You ask my advice, Aline. I know you won't take it. *(She rises, stands upright with clenched hands.) DON'T GIVE UP YOUR PROFESSION FOR THE BEST MAN ON EARTH!*

ALINE Why, Mother! Why, *Mother! (Mrs. Morrow drops limply into a chair again and buries her face in the pile of stockings and sobs despairingly. Aline kneels by her, puts her arms around her, caresses, tries to soothe her.)* Mother! Mother, dear! Don't cry so! Oh, Mother, I'd no idea that you felt this way! You have me—isn't that something?

MRS. MORROW Something? *(Turns and embraces her with intense fervor.)* Something! You are everything. You are *all*—all there is.

ALINE *(Holding her close.)* Dearest Mother! I wouldn't leave you in any case. Whoever takes me has got to take you, too.

MRS. MORROW *(Draws away sharply, almost angrily.)* It's not that! I never even thought of *that.* Did I object to your going to college, or to Germany to study? I'm not a common pig-mother! It's your *work* I'm thinking of. My own life has gone—gone forever—except as it is in you. I can't lose yours, too.

ALINE *(Puzzled, grieved, asks softly.)* Weren't you happy with Father?

MRS. MORROW *(Trying to speak composedly.)* Yes. Yes, I was. I loved him dearly. I loved him enough to give up my work to please him. But, my child, do not believe Eros himself if he tells you that "love is enough." It isn't. We have other interests—other powers and desires. I had a Voice—once.

ALINE Why, Mother! I never heard you sing.

MRS. MORROW No. You never heard me sing.

ALINE And you gave it up—for him?

MRS. MORROW Yes—for love. And I had love—until he died. He didn't intend to die—but the Voice went first. You see, dear, he didn't care for music at all—especially vocal music. He didn't like the people who did care for it. He hated to have me go out without him. There was no money for lessons, no time for practice. It is all gone.

ALINE You had the home—the children.

MRS. MORROW Yes, thank God! I loved my home, and I loved my children dearly. But even while I had them—even while my heart and my hands were full—there was always this great empty place. You have grown up. It's ten years since I lost your father. I am fifty now. I may live ten—twenty—thirty years more, and, except for you, my life is empty. *(She rises, puts all her work neatly into basket. Aline watches her, silent.)* If you do care for my advice, if the loss of my life can be of any use to save yours, you will stick to your work as your aunt did. She was wiser than I. She refuses to give up. Now she is a happy woman—successful, popular, known, honored, well paid. She has *lived*. Yours is real mother-work, too. You can love and help more children than you ever could have of your own. Oh, you'll be hungry, of course! You'll be hungry for love—for your own babies. But I tell you, if you have them, and don't have your work, you'll starve!

(Re-enter Miss Upton. Mrs. Morrow controls herself and gathers up her darning.)

ALINE *(With an effort.)* Carriage not come yet, Aunt Clara?

MISS UPTON *(Looks at clock.)* No, it's really not time yet. *(To Mrs. Morrow.)* Why will you waste time darning stockings, Molly? *I* can't afford it. I can earn a dozen pair—silk ones—in the time it would take me to darn six.

MRS. MORROW My time isn't as valuable as yours, Clara. I've left my cotton upstairs— *(Rises.)*

ALINE Let me get it, Mother. *(Her mother kisses her and whispers to her, Aline nods understandingly. Mrs. Morrow goes out. Aline goes and stands by the fire. Miss Upton looks at papers on table, walks about a bit, hangs her cloak over the back of a tall carved chair by table, sits on arm, swings one dainty foot, picks up silver cigarette case.)*

MISS UPTON You don't mind if I have a cigarette, Aline? *(Takes one.)*

ALINE *(Turning and coming to her.)* I think you're entitled to whatever you want, Aunt Clara. You certainly are a successful woman.

MISS UPTON I'm doing very well.

ALINE Your free, happy life! And your beautiful work—your own real work! I congratulate you with all my heart. *(Her aunt puts an arm around her, kisses her, goes on smoking, and looking about, swinging her foot a little, airy, successful, complacent.)*

ALINE But, Auntie, can you talk to me a little? Can you give me some sagacious advice on a very solemn question?

MISS UPTON Of course I will. Giving advice is a pleasure to all of us—more especially to women—most especially to unmarried women. Is it whom you shall marry? Marry Dr. Russell, by all means. I'd like to marry him myself.

ALINE Neither you nor Mother seems to have been in any doubt as to Dr. Russell's intentions.

MISS UPTON Why, no. Were you? He's all right, Aline. You've spoken to your mother, then. Has he asked you?

ALINE Yes. He's coming back for his answer.

MISS UPTON You say "yes." If that's the question, I wonder you want advice.

ALINE No; that's not the question. The question is, shall I drop my work, give up my profession, to be his wife?

MISS UPTON *(Stops smiling and sits up straight.)* Does he make it a condition?

ALINE I'm afraid he does.

MISS UPTON *(Fiercely, intensely, starting to her feet.)* Then do it! Do it in a minute! Drop it once and for all. Forswear it; forget it—and thank God for a good man's love.

ALINE Why, Aunt Clara! I—thought—you—I thought you were—

MISS UPTON You thought I was happy in my work, no doubt. Everyone does. I mean they shall. I had my chance of happiness once—and lost it. But I made my choice and I stand by it. I'm a good loser. We Uptons are. I never let even your mother know. She had her happiness. She thought I had mine. *(Aline listens. Miss Upton walks about much excited. Turns to Aline.)* But you are young, Aline. You have your best years all before you. You have the crown and glory and blessing of your life in your hands. Take it, Aline! Take it. *(Aline stares, amazed.)* I've never spoken of this to a living soul, but I love you, Aline. You are a splendid girl, and I don't want you to spoil your life as I have spoiled mine.

ALINE Don't, Aunt Clara—don't speak of it if it hurts you. I understand—

MISS UPTON *(Interrupting.)* Understand? You don't understand. No woman could understand unless she had lived twenty years without love—and knew she had thrown it away.

ALINE *(Earnestly.)* Isn't the work a comfort, Aunt Clara? Your success, your wide, free life?

MISS UPTON *(Fiercely.)* Of course it is—and my clothes are a comfort—and my dinner! But they do not, unfortunately, meet the same want. You need not say a word, Aline. I know. I stood in your shoes, I had the same ideas, and I chose the work. Well—I can make money. I can do as I please, but— *(She stretches out empty arms and snatches them back, empty, to her heart.)* I've never held my baby in my arms. *(She stands silent. Aline goes to her, tries to comfort her. She waves her away.)* It's not only babies, though that's ache enough—just the physical ache for them, for their little blundering, crumpling fingers on your face; their foolish, delicious curly feet; the down on their heads; the sweetness of the backs of their necks; the hugableness of them! It's not only the babies, Aline. It's the husband! Women are not supposed to care— They do—!

ALINE   You have so many friends, Aunt Clara.

MISS UPTON   Oh, you make me angry! You girl! You child! How can I make you see? Ten thousand friends are not the same as the man you love! Haven't you a heart, child, in your body?

ALINE   Yes—I have. But I have a head, too, and I thought—

MISS UPTON   Stop thinking. Feel. Just make sure that you love—plain *love* him—and then marry him.

ALINE   But I'm not sure. I do love him, but after loving him, after marrying him, there remain the years of a lifetime.

MISS UPTON   They do, indeed. I was twenty when I refused my lover—for my work. Twenty years have gone by. I suppose there may be thirty more—I'm a strong woman. Fifty years—without any one of my own! *(She throws up her arms in a wild gesture, sinks on a seat by the table, buries her face, and bursts into heavy sobs—strained agonizing sobs. Aline stands, trying to soothe her.)*

MISS UPTON   Go away. It's only a little hysteria. I'll be quieter when I'm alone. I'm used to being alone. Go away. *But take my advice.*
(Aline goes out.)
(Mrs. Morrow re-enters.)

MRS. MORROW   Tired of waiting, Clara?

MISS UPTON   *(Raises her head.)* Yes, I am. *(Rises, walks about, looks at clock. Mrs. Morrow is gathering up her work.)* Well, Molly, I guess you and I are going to lose a daughter soon.

MRS. MORROW   I hope not! Oh, I hope not!

MISS UPTON   Hope not? I'd like to know why! She'll never get a finer man than Gordon Russell—nor one more devoted to her. You don't want her to live single, do you?

MRS. MORROW   No, but she'd much better do that than give up her profession.

MISS UPTON   Why, Molly Morrow! *You* talk that way! *You* have been happy with your husband and children. You certainly do not want her to miss all that?

MRS. MORROW That sounds well from you, *Clara*. After all your success! Actions speak louder than words. *(Miss Upton looks at her, hesitates.)* Just remember that Aline was fairly *born* a kindergartner as you were a painter. Think of all her years of study and training—and how she loves it—and how useful she is to all those little children, and their mothers!

MISS UPTON And what are all those little children and their mothers—and all those years of study and training—and all her love of it, to the love of one little child of her own, in her own arms?

MRS. MORROW Why, Clara! *Clara!* Do you mean—?

MISS UPTON Do I mean—what? And what do you mean?

MRS. MORROW Why, I always thought—that you—oh, Clara! You don't mean to tell me that you've been—sorry—all these years?

MISS UPTON I did not mean to tell you, but it seems I have. You were happy. Why should I distress you with my unhappiness?

MRS. MORROW Happy? *I—*

MISS UPTON *(Whirling upon her.)* You were *NOT?* Molly!

MRS. MORROW I have been wretched all my life, Clara, because I gave up my work for love.

MISS UPTON And I because I didn't.

MRS. MORROW Two lives ruined! But Aline shan't waste hers. I have told her.

MISS UPTON So have I.

MRS. MORROW You haven't advised her to give up?

MISS UPTON I certainly have. *(They stand opposed. Bell heard. They do not notice it. Dr. Russell appears at the door.)*

DR. RUSSELL I beg pardon. *(Both turn upon him.)*

MRS. MORROW Come in, Dr. Russell.

MISS UPTON Yes. Come in. *(He enters.)*

DR. RUSSELL Is Miss Morrow—?

MRS. MORROW Yes, she's here. She'll be in presently. She—Dr. Russell—

DR. RUSSELL Yes, Mrs. Morrow.

MRS. MORROW Why can't you be willing for Aline to keep on with her work? She'll never be happy without it.

MISS UPTON She'll never be happy with it—and without love.

MRS. MORROW Clara, stop! She is *my* child, Dr. Russell. I am her mother. But not even motherhood makes up for losing one's own work. I know what it costs to give up all one's personal life for love!

MISS UPTON And I know what it costs *not to*. Dr. Russell, don't let her refuse you. If she loves you—and I'm pretty sure she does—you marry her.

DR. RUSSELL I wish for her happiness—

MRS. MORROW Then let her keep her work.

MISS UPTON Then marry her.

DR. RUSSELL After all, she must decide. Believe me, Mrs. Morrow, all my life shall be given to make her happy—if she will take it. But a woman must choose between her career and marriage. She must choose.

MISS UPTON Well, Molly, he's right. You chose—I chose—now she must choose. Come. We must leave it to her. *(They go out much depressed.)*
(Dr. Russell proceeds to walk up and down the room, sits, tries to read, plays with flowers, gets very impatient. Rings. Maid appears.)

DR. RUSSELL Does Miss Morrow know I'm here?

MAID I'll see, sir. *(Exit maid. Reappears after a bit.)* Miss Morrow will be down presently, sir.

DR. RUSSELL *(Continuing to show great strain and impatience.)* She never kept me waiting before—I wonder if it means—
(Finally she enters. He is standing with his back to the door; does not see her. She is exquisitely dressed in a white, misty, clinging, shimmering gown with an elusive sparkle in it. Her hair is beautifully done, much more softly and richly than her usual method. A red and white rose are tucked in her hair, and she carries one of each in her hand. She comes softly behind him, stands a moment, looks mischievously at him, reaches out a rose and touches his hand with it. He starts, turns, holds out his arms to her.)

DR. RUSSELL My darling! *(She shakes her head, smiling, retreating, looking up at him archly.)*

ALINE I don't know yet whether I'm your darling or not. That remains to be decided. This is a very serious matter, Dr. Russell.

DR. RUSSELL I don't know you tonight, Aline. You are another woman, somehow.

ALINE Well, do you like the other woman?

DR. RUSSELL *(Starts toward her.)* Like her? Oh, my dear! I knew you were lovely, but I never knew you so enchanting.

ALINE Thank you. I'm glad you're pleased with me. No—no—be patient a little yet. If we marry we have a lifetime before us to be happy in. If we don't—

DR. RUSSELL   If we don't! Aline! Have you not decided—yet?

ALINE   I? Oh, yes. *I* have decided, but you haven't.

DR. RUSSELL   I am too desperately in earnest to guess riddles, Aline. Please answer me. Will you be my wife?

ALINE   I cannot bear to give up my work, Gordon.

DR. RUSSELL   You mean—? Aline! You will not let that keep us apart?

ALINE   *(Fervently.)* Indeed I will not. It shall never come between us nor interfere with my love and duty to you.

DR. RUSSELL   *(Stands, his hands gripped together looking at her.)* Then you will—

ALINE   Listen, now. Let me say all I have to say, and then *you* may decide, if you please, whether to abide by *your* choice or not. You asked me to marry you—then made conditions. I am willing to marry you. *I* make no conditions. I do not say, "You must give up smoking," or "You must be a total abstainer," or "You must choose between me and something else you love." I love you, Gordon, unconditionally. *(He tries to embrace her, but she checks him.)* I love a man who is a doctor, a splendid doctor. I would marry the man and be proud of the doctor. You love a woman who is a teacher, a devoted one. You would marry the woman; she would be your wife. You wouldn't marry the teacher. She would go on teaching.

DR. RUSSELL   This is all sophistry, Aline. You expect the impossible. Oh, why not trust your heart—

ALINE   I expect nothing impossible, Gordon—only what I know to be practicable. You must leave the arrangements of the housework and the care of—the family—to me. That is plainly the woman's duty. I am no child, you know. *(Looks up at him, rose at lips, smiling.)*

DR. RUSSELL   You look about sixteen to-night! You are deliciously beautiful! And puzzling beyond words! You say you love me. I feel that you love me. You do, don't you, dear? Yet you sit there talking like a judge. If I shut my eyes I seem to hear the New Woman laying down the law. If I open them—Lilith couldn't be lovelier. *(She looks at him with such mischievous sweetness, such tremor of soft withdrawal, that he comes to her. She lets him sit on the sofa beside her, and then faces him so calmly that he feels more remote than before.)*

DR. RUSSELL   You are being very cruel, Aline. Don't you know it? You are holding my heart in your hands. Tell me, dear; give me your answer. Will you be my wife?

ALINE   *(Very coldly and without interest.)* Yes.

CHARLOTTE PERKINS GILMAN

DR. RUSSELL You will give up your work?

ALINE (*Gently, warmly, tenderly, with her heart in her eyes.*) No.

DR. RUSSELL What *do* you mean, Aline? You torture me. Tell me your decision. You have had time to consider. You have advised with your family. (*Rises.*) You must have made up your mind.

ALINE (*Rising, also.*) Yes, I have considered. I have advised with my family. I have seen the effects of this choice you require—the choice between living and loving. I have seen what it means to a woman to have love—and lose life. And what it means to have life—and lose love.

DR. RUSSELL It is the woman's problem, and must be faced. You have your Life. I offer you—Love. Which will you choose?

ALINE Both, if you please. (*He stands checked, astonished, angry, and hurt. She sinks down on the cushions, hides her face, sobs—or laughs. He sees a tear shine between her fingers, is beside her, his arms around her. She pushes him away. Then she turns her face and smiles up at him entrancingly, her head back on the velvet cushions, her two great roses lifted to her chin.*) If I were a man—and a lover—and the woman I loved was willing to marry me, I don't *think* I'd let a thing like this stand between us. (*He drops beside her, draws her to him, his voice quite shaken.*)

DR. RUSSELL I *thought* I knew best about this, Aline. But you may be right.

ALINE My dear—you must take me as a teacher or not take me at all!

DR. RUSSELL We will try it together, Aline. Only love me!
(*She comes to him.*)

(*Curtain*)

BEST FRIENDS

by

SHARON OLDS

(b. 1942)

Born in San Francisco and educated at Stanford University and Columbia University, Sharon Olds now lives in New York City. She has published many poems in major journals such as The New Yorker, The Atlantic Monthly, *and* The Paris Review, *and has received fellowships from both the National Endowment for the Arts and the Guggenheim Foundation. Her poems have been collected in* Satan Says *(1980) and* The Dead and the Living *(1984).*

•——————————————————•

(for Elizabeth Ewer, 1942–51)

The day my daughter turned ten, I thought of the
lank, glittering, greenish cap of your
gold hair. The last week of
your life, when I came each day after school,
I'd study the path to your front door,
the bricks laid close as your hairs. I'd try to
read the pattern, frowning down
for a sign.
        The last day—there was not
a mark on that walk, not a stone out of place—
the nurses would not let me in.

We were nine. We had never mentioned death
or growing up. I had no more imagined
you dead
than you imagined me
a mother. But when I had a daughter
I named her for you, as if pulling you back
through a crack between the bricks.
                She is ten now, Liddy.
She has outlived you, her dark hair gleaming like
the earth into which the path was pressed,
the path to you.

MISS ROSIE

by

LUCILLE CLIFTON

(b. 1936)

Born in New York State, Lucille Clifton attended Howard University and Fredonia State Teachers College. The mother of six children, she has written several children's books. She is best known for her collections of poetry Good Times *(1969) and* Good News About the Earth *(1972). Her autobiography,* An Ordinary Woman, *appeared in 1974. Recent works include* Amifika *(1977),* Two-Headed Woman *(1980), and* Source Beautiful *(1981).*

When I watch you
wrapped up like garbage
sitting, surrounded by the smell
of too old potato peels
or
when I watch you
in your old man's shoes
with the little toe cut out
sitting, waiting for your mind
like next week's grocery
I say
when I watch you
you wet brown bag of a woman
who used to be the best looking gal in Georgia
used to be called the Georgia Rose
I stand up
through your destruction
I stand up

I LIKE TO THINK OF
HARRIET TUBMAN

by

SUSAN GRIFFIN

(b. 1943)

*Susan Griffin has an A.B. in English and experience in many differ-
ent jobs usually filled by women: waitress, teacher, and artist's
model. A divorcée and single parent, she lives in San Francisco
with other women. She has published two collections of poems; a
play,* Voices *(1975); and two philosophical works,* Women and Nature *(1979) and* Pornography and Silence *(1981).*

• ———————————————— •

I like to think of Harriet Tubman.
Harriet Tubman who carried a revolver,
who had a scar on her head from a rock thrown
by a slave-master (because she
talked back), and who
had a ransom on her head
of thousands of dollars and who
was never caught, and who
had no use for the law
when the law was wrong,
who defied the law. I like
to think of her.
I like to think of her especially
when I think of the problem of
feeding children.

The legal answer
to the problem of feeding children
is ten free lunches every month,
being equal, in the child's real life,

to eating lunch every other day.
Monday but not Tuesday.
I like to think of the President
eating lunch Monday, but not
Tuesday.
And when I think of the President
and the law, and the problem of
feeding children, I like to
think of Harriet Tubman
and her revolver.

And then sometimes
I think of the President
and other men,
men who practice the law,
who revere the law,
who make the law,
who enforce the law
who live behind
and operate through
and feed themselves
at the expense of
starving children
because of the law,
men who sit in paneled offices
and think about vacations
and tell women
whose care it is
to feed children
not to be hysterical
not to be hysterical as in the word
hysterikos, the greek for
womb suffering,
not to suffer in their
wombs,
not to care,
not to bother the men
because they want to think
of other things
and do not want
to take the women seriously.
I want them

to take women seriously.
I want them to think about Harriet Tubman,
and remember,
remember she was beat by a white man
and she lived
and she lived to redress her grievances,
and she lived in swamps
and wore the clothes of a man
bringing hundreds of fugitives from
slavery, and was never caught,
and led an army,
and won a battle,
and defied the laws
because the laws were wrong, I want men
to take us seriously.
I am tired wanting them to think
about right and wrong.
I want them to fear.
I want them to feel fear now
as I have felt suffering in the womb, and
I want them
to know
that there is always a time
there is always a time to make right
what is wrong,
there is always a time
for retribution
and that time
is beginning.

TRIFLES

by

SUSAN GLASPELL

(1882–1948)

Perhaps best known as a dramatist and a founder of the Province-town Players, Susan Glaspell won a Pulitzer Prize in 1930 for her play Alison's House, *based on the life of Emily Dickinson. She wrote several novels and short stories, of which* "A Jury of Her Peers" *is the most famous; it was reprinted in* The Best Short Stories of 1917. Trifles *is Glaspell's earlier dramatic version of that story.*

•————————————————————•

Scene

The kitchen in the now abandoned farm-house of John Wright, a gloomy kitchen, and left without having been put in order—unwashed pans under the sink, a loaf of bread outside the bread-box, a dish-towel on the table—other signs of incompleted work. At the rear the outer door opens and the SHERIFF *comes in followed by the* COUNTY ATTORNEY *and* HALE. *The* SHERIFF *and* HALE *are men in middle life, the* COUNTY ATTORNEY *is a young man; all are much bundled up and go at once to the stove. They are followed by the two women—the Sheriff's wife first; she is a slight wiry woman, with a thin nervous face.* MRS. HALE *is larger and would ordinarily be called more comfortable looking, but she is disturbed now and looks fearfully about as she enters. The women have come in slowly, and stand close together near the door.*

COUNTY ATTORNEY *(rubbing his hands)* This feels good. Come up to the fire, ladies.

MRS. PETERS *(after taking a step forward)* I'm not—cold.

SHERIFF *(unbuttoning his overcoat and stepping away from the stove as if to mark the beginning of official business)* Now, Mr. Hale, before we move things about, you explain to Mr. Henderson just what you saw when you came here yesterday morning.

COUNTY ATTORNEY   By the way, has anything been moved? Are things just as you left them yesterday?

SHERIFF *(looking about)*   It's just the same. When it dropped below zero last night I thought I'd better send Frank out this morning to make a fire for us—no use getting pneumonia with a big case on, but I told him not to touch anything except the stove—and you know Frank.

COUNTY ATTORNEY   Somebody should have been left here yesterday.

SHERIFF   Oh—yesterday. When I had to send Frank to Morris Center for that man who went crazy—I want you to know I had my hands full yesterday. I knew you could get back from Omaha by to-day and as long as I went over everything here myself—

COUNTY ATTORNEY   Well, Mr. Hale, tell just what happened when you came here yesterday morning.

HALE   Harry and I had started to town with a load of potatoes. We came along the road from my place and as I got here I said, "I'm going to see if I can't get John Wright to go in with me on a party telephone." I spoke to Wright about it once before and he put me off, saying folks talked too much anyway, and all he asked was peace and quiet—I guess you know about how much he talked himself; but I thought maybe if I went to the house and talked about it before his wife, though I said to Harry that I didn't know as what his wife wanted made much difference to John—

COUNTY ATTORNEY   Let's talk about that later, Mr. Hale. I do want to talk about that, but tell now just what happened when you got to the house.

HALE   I didn't hear or see anything; I knocked at the door, and still it was all quiet inside. I knew they must be up, it was past eight o'clock. So I knocked again, and I thought I heard somebody say "Come in." I wasn't sure, I'm not sure yet, but I opened the door—this door *(indicating the door by which the two women are still standing)* and there in that rocker— *(pointing to it)* sat Mrs. Wright.
(They all look at the rocker.)

COUNTY ATTORNEY   What—was she doing?

HALE   She was rockin' back and forth. She had her apron in her hand and was kind of—pleating it.

COUNTY ATTORNEY   And how did she—look?

HALE   Well, she looked queer.

COUNTY ATTORNEY   How do you mean—queer?

HALE   Well, as if she didn't know what she was going to do next. And kind of done up.

COUNTY ATTORNEY   How did she seem to feel about your coming?

HALE   Why, I don't think she minded—one way or other. She didn't pay much attention. I said, "How do, Mrs. Wright, it's cold, ain't it?" And she said "Is it?"—and went on kind of pleating at her apron. Well, I was surprised; she didn't ask me to come up to the stove, or to set down, but just sat there, not even looking at me, so I said, "I want to see John." And then she—laughed. I guess you would call it a laugh. I thought of Harry and the team outside, so I said a little sharp: "Can't I see John?" "No," she says, kind o' dull like. "Ain't he home?" says I. "Yes," says she, "he's home." "Then why can't I see him?" I asked her out of patience. " 'Cause he's dead," says she. *"Dead?"* says I. She just nodded her head, not getting a bit excited, but rockin' back and forth. "Why—where is he?" says I, not knowing what to say. She just pointed upstairs—like that *(himself pointing to the room above)*. I got up, with the idea of going up there. I walked from there to here—then I says, "Why, what did he die of?" "He died of a rope round his neck," says she, and just went on pleatin' at her apron. Well, I went out and called Harry. I thought I might—need help. We went upstairs and there he was lyin'—

COUNTY ATTORNEY   I think I'd rather have you go into that upstairs, where you can point it all out. Just go on now with the rest of the story.

HALE   Well, my first thought was to get that rope off. It looked . . . *(Stops, his face twitches.)* . . . but Harry, he went up to him, and he said, "No, he's dead all right, and we'd better not touch anything." So we went back down stairs. She was still sitting that same way. "Has anybody been notified?" I asked. "No," says she, unconcerned. "Who did this, Mrs. Wright?" said Harry. He said it business-like—and she stopped pleatin' of her apron. "I don't know," she says. "You don't *know?*" says Harry. "No," says she. "Weren't you sleepin' in the bed with him?" says Harry. "Yes," says she, "but I was on the inside." "Somebody slipped a rope round his neck and strangled him and you didn't wake up?" says Harry. "I didn't wake up," she said after him. We must 'a looked as if we didn't see how that could be, for after a minute she said, "I sleep sound." Harry was going to ask her more questions, but I said maybe we ought to let her tell her story first to the coroner, or the sheriff, so Harry went fast as he could to Rivers' place, where there's a telephone.

COUNTY ATTORNEY   And what did Mrs. Wright do when she knew that you had gone for the coroner?

HALE   She moved from that chair to this over here . . . *(Pointing to a small chair in the corner.)* . . . and just sat there with her hands held together and looking down. I got a feeling that I ought to make some conversation, so I said I had come in to see if John wanted to put in a telephone, and at that she started to laugh, and then she stopped and looked at me—scared. *(The* COUNTY ATTORNEY, *who has had his notebook out, makes a note.)* I dunno, maybe it wasn't scared. I wouldn't like to say it was. Soon Harry got back, and then Dr. Lloyd came, and you, Mr. Peters, and so I guess that's all I know that you don't.

COUNTY ATTORNEY *(looking around)* I guess we'll go upstairs first—and then out to the barn and around there. *(To the* SHERIFF.*)* You're convinced that there was nothing important here—nothing that would point to any motive?

SHERIFF Nothing here but kitchen things.
(The COUNTY ATTORNEY, *after again looking around the kitchen, opens the door of a cupboard closet. He gets up on a chair and looks on a shelf. Pulls his hand away, sticky.)*

COUNTY ATTORNEY Here's a nice mess.
(The women draw nearer.)

MRS. PETERS *(to the other woman)* Oh, her fruit; it did freeze. *(To the Lawyer.)* She worried about that when it turned so cold. She said the fire'd go out and her jars would break.

SHERIFF Well, can you beat the women! Held for murder and worryin' about her preserves.

COUNTY ATTORNEY I guess before we're through she may have something more serious than preserves to worry about.

HALE Well, women are used to worrying over trifles.
(The two women move a little closer together.)

COUNTY ATTORNEY *(with the gallantry of a young politician)* And yet, for all their worries, what would we do without the ladies? *(The women do not unbend. He goes to the sink, takes a dipperful of water from the pail and, pouring it into a basin, washes his hands. Starts to wipe them on the roller-towel, turns it for a cleaner place.)* Dirty towels! *(Kicks his foot against the pans under the sink.)* Not much of a housekeeper, would you say, ladies?

MRS. HALE *(stiffly)* There's a great deal of work to be done on a farm.

COUNTY ATTORNEY To be sure. And yet . . . *(With a little bow to her.)* . . . I know there are some Dickson county farmhouses which do not have such roller towels.
(He gives it a pull to expose its full length again.)

MRS. HALE Those towels get dirty awful quick. Men's hands aren't always as clean as they might be.

COUNTY ATTORNEY Ah, loyal to your sex, I see. But you and Mrs. Wright were neighbors. I suppose you were friends, too.

MRS. HALE (*shaking her head*) I've not seen much of her of late years. I've not been in this house—it's more than a year.

COUNTY ATTORNEY And why was that? You didn't like her?

MRS. HALE I like her all well enough. Farmers' wives have their hands full, Mr. Henderson. And then—

COUNTY ATTORNEY Yes—?

MRS. HALE (*looking about*) It never seemed a very cheerful place.

COUNTY ATTORNEY No—it's not cheerful. I shouldn't say she had the homemaking instinct.

MRS. HALE Well, I don't know as Wright had, either.

COUNTY ATTORNEY You mean that they didn't get on very well?

MRS. HALE No, I don't mean anything. But I don't think a place'd be any cheerful for John Wright's being in it.

COUNTY ATTORNEY I'd like to talk more of that a little later. I want to get the lay of things upstairs now.
(*He goes to the left, where three steps lead to a stair door.*)

SHERIFF I suppose anything Mrs. Peters does'll be all right. She was to take in some clothes for her, you know, and a few little things. We left in such a hurry yesterday.

COUNTY ATTORNEY Yes, but I would like to see what you take, Mrs. Peters, and keep an eye out for anything that might be of use to us.

MRS. PETERS Yes, Mr. Henderson.
(*The women listen to the men's steps on the stairs, then look about the kitchen.*)

MRS. HALE I'd hate to have men coming into my kitchen, snooping around and criticizing.
(*She arranges the pans under sink which the Lawyer had shoved out of place.*)

MRS. PETERS Of course it's no more than their duty.

MRS. HALE Duty's all right, but I guess that deputy sheriff that came out to make the fire might have got a little of this on. (*Gives the roller towel a pull.*) Wish I'd thought of that sooner. Seems mean to talk about her for not having things slicked up when she had to come away in such a hurry.

MRS. PETERS (who has gone to a small table in the left rear corner of the room, and lifted one end of a towel that covers a pan) She had bread set. (Stands still.)

MRS. HALE (eyes fixed on a loaf of bread beside the bread-box, which is on a low shelf at the other side of the room. Moves slowly toward it.) She was going to put this in there. (Picks up loaf, then abruptly drops it. In a manner of returning to familiar things.) It's a shame about her fruit. I wonder if it's all gone. (Gets up on the chair and looks.) I think there's some here that's all right, Mrs. Peters. Yes—here; (Holding it toward the window.) this is cherries, too. (Looking again.) I declare I believe that's the only one. (Gets down, bottle in her hand. Goes to the sink and wipes it off on the outside.) She'll feel awful bad after all her hard work in the hot weather. I remember the afternoon I put up my cherries last summer. (She puts the bottle on the big kitchen table, center of the room, front table. With a sigh, is about to sit down in the rocking-chair. Before she is seated realizes what chair it is: with a slow look at it, steps back. The chair which she has touched rocks back and forth.)

MRS. PETERS Well, I must get those things from the front room closet. (She goes to the door at the right, but after looking into the other room, steps back.) You coming with me, Mrs. Hale? You could help me carry them.
(They go in the other room: reappear, MRS. PETERS carrying a dress and skirt, MRS. HALE following with a pair of shoes.)

MRS. PETERS My, it's cold in there.
(She puts the clothes on the big table, and hurries to the stove.)

MRS. HALE (examining the skirt) Wright was close. I think maybe that's why she kept so much to herself. She didn't even belong to the Ladies' Aid. I suppose she felt she couldn't do her part, and then you don't enjoy things when you feel shabby. She used to wear pretty clothes and be lively, when she was Minnie Foster, one of the town girls singing in the choir. But that—oh, that was thirty years ago. This all you was to take in?

MRS. PETERS She said she wanted an apron. Funny thing to want, for there isn't much to get you dirty in jail, goodness knows. But I suppose just to make her feel more natural. She said they was in the top drawer in this cupboard. Yes, here. And then her little shawl that always hung behind the door. (Opens stair door and looks.) Yes, here it is.
(Quickly shuts door leading upstairs.)

MRS. HALE (abruptly moving toward her) Mrs. Peters?

MRS. PETERS Yes, Mrs. Hale?

MRS. HALE Do you think she did it?

MRS. PETERS *(in a frightened voice)* Oh, I don't know.

MRS. HALE Well, I don't think she did. Asking for an apron and her little shawl. Worrying about her fruit.

MRS. PETERS *(starts to speak, glances up, where footsteps are heard in the room above. In a low voice)* Mr. Peters says it looks bad for her. Mr. Henderson is awful sarcastic in a speech and he'll make fun of her sayin' she didn't wake up.

MRS. HALE Well, I guess John Wright didn't wake when they was slipping that rope under his neck.

MRS PETERS No, it's strange. It must have been done awful crafty and still. They say it was such a—funny way to kill a man, rigging it all up like that.

MRS. HALE That's just what Mr. Hale said. There was a gun in the house. He says that's what he can't understand.

MRS. PETERS Mr. Henderson said coming out that what was needed for the case was a motive; something to show anger, or—sudden feeling.

MRS. HALE *(who is standing by the table)* Well, I don't see any signs of anger around here. *(She puts her hand on the dish towel which lies on the table, stands looking down at table, one half of which is clean, the other half messy.)* It's wiped here. *(Makes a move as if to finish work, then turns and looks at loaf of bread outside the bread-box. Drops towel. In that voice of coming back to familiar things.)* Wonder how they are finding things upstairs? I hope she had it a little more red-up up there. You know, it seems kind of *sneaking*. Locking her up in town and then coming out here and trying to get her own house to turn against her!

MRS. PETERS But, Mrs. Hale, the law is the law.

MRS. HALE I s'pose 'tis. *(Unbuttoning her coat.)* Better loosen up your things, Mrs. Peters. You won't feel them when you go out.

(MRS. PETERS takes off her fur tippet, goes to hang it on hook at back of room, stands looking at the under part of the small corner table.)

MRS. PETERS She was piecing a quilt. *(She brings the large sewing basket and they look at the bright pieces.)*

MRS. HALE It's log cabin pattern. Pretty, isn't it? I wonder if she was goin' to quilt it or just knot it?
(Footsteps have been heard coming down the stairs. The SHERIFF enters, followed by HALE and the COUNTY ATTORNEY.)

SHERIFF They wonder if she was going to quilt it or just knot it.
(The men laugh, the women look abashed.)

COUNTY ATTORNEY (*rubbing his hands over the stove*) Frank's fire didn't do much up there, did it? Well, let's go out to the barn and get that cleared up.
(*The men go outside.*)

MRS. HALE (*resentfully*) I don't know as there's anything so strange, our takin' up our time with little things while we're waiting for them to get the evidence. (*She sits down at the big table smoothing out a block with decision.*) I don't see as it's anything to laugh about.

MRS. PETERS (*apologetically*) Of course they've got awful important things on their minds.
(*Pulls up a chair and joins* MRS. HALE *at the table.*)

MRS. HALE (*examining another block*) Mrs. Peters, look at this one. Here, this is the one she was working on, and look at the sewing! All the rest of it has been so nice and even. And look at this! It's all over the place! Why, it looks as if she didn't know what she was about!
(*After she has said this they look at each other, then start to glance back at the door. After an instant* MRS. HALE *has pulled at a knot and ripped the sewing.*)

MRS. PETERS Oh, what are you doing, Mrs. Hale?

MRS. HALE (*mildly*) Just pulling out a stitch or two that's not sewed very good. (*Threading a needle.*) Bad sewing always made me fidgety.

MRS. PETERS (*nervously*) I don't think we ought to touch things.

MRS. HALE I'll just finish up this end. (*Suddenly stopping and leaning forward.*) Mrs. Peters?

MRS. PETERS Yes, Mrs. Hale?

MRS. HALE What do you suppose she was so nervous about?

MRS. PETERS Oh—I don't know. I don't know as she was nervous. I sometimes sew awful queer when I'm just tired. (MRS. HALE *starts to say something, looks at* MRS. PETERS, *then goes on sewing.*) Well, I must get these things wrapped up. They may be through sooner than we think. (*Putting apron and other things together.*) I wonder where I can find a piece of paper, and string.

MRS. HALE In that cupboard, maybe.

MRS. PETERS (*looking in cupboard*) Why, here's a bird-cage. (*Holds it up.*) Did she have a bird, Mrs. Hale?

MRS. HALE Why, I don't know whether she did or not—I've not been here for so long. There was a man around last year selling canaries cheap, but I don't know as she took one; maybe she did. She used to sing real pretty herself.

MRS. PETERS (*glancing around*) Seems funny to think of a bird here. But she must have had one, or why should she have a cage? I wonder what happened to it?

MRS. HALE I s'pose maybe the cat got it.

MRS. PETERS No, she didn't have a cat. She's got that feeling some people have about cats—being afraid of them. My cat got in her room and she was real upset and asked me to take it out.

MRS. HALE My sister Bessie was like that. Queer, ain't it?

MRS. PETERS (*examining the cage*) Why, look at this door. It's broke. One hinge is pulled apart.

MRS. HALE (*looking too*) Looks as if some one must have been rough with it.

MRS. PETERS Why, yes.
(*She brings the cage forward and puts it on the table.*)

MRS. HALE I wish if they're going to find any evidence they'd be about it. I don't like this place.

MRS. PETERS But I'm awful glad you came with me, Mrs. Hale. It would be lonesome for me sitting here alone.

MRS. HALE It would, wouldn't it? (*Dropping her sewing.*) But I tell you what I do wish, Mrs. Peters. I wish I had come over some times when *she* was here. I (*Looking around the room.*)—wish I had.

MRS. PETERS But of course you were awful busy, Mrs. Hale—your house and your children.

MRS. HALE I could've come. I stayed away because it weren't cheerful—and that's why I ought to have come. I—I've never liked this place. Maybe because it's down in a hollow and you don't see the road. I dunno what it is, but it's a lonesome place and always was. I wish I had come over to see Minnie Foster sometimes. I can see now—
(*Shakes her head.*)

MRS. PETERS Well, you mustn't reproach yourself, Mrs. Hale. Somehow we just don't see how it is with other folks until—something comes up.

MRS. HALE Not having children makes less work—but it makes a quiet house, and Wright out to work all day, and no company when he did come in. Did you know John Wright, Mrs. Peters?

MRS. PETERS Not to know him; I've seen him in town. They say he was a good man.

MRS. HALE Yes—good; he didn't drink, and kept his word as well as most,

I guess, and paid his debts. But he was a hard man, Mrs. Peters. Just to pass the time of day with him. *(Shivers.)* Like a raw wind that gets to the bone. *(Pauses, her eye falling on the cage.)* I should think she would 'a wanted a bird. But what do you suppose went with it?

MRS. PETERS   I don't know, unless it got sick and died.
(She reaches over and swings the broken door, swings it again, both women watch it.)

MRS. HALE   You weren't raised round here, were you? (MRS. PETERS *shakes her head.)* You didn't know—her?

MRS. PETERS   Not till they brought her yesterday.

MRS. HALE   She—come to think of it, she was kind of like a bird herself—real sweet and pretty, but kind of timid and—fluttery. How—she—did—change. *(Silence; then as if struck by a happy thought and relieved to get back to every day things.)* Tell you what, Mrs. Peters, why don't you take the quilt in with you? It might take up her mind.

MRS. PETERS   Why, I think that's a real nice idea, Mrs. Hale. There couldn't possibly be any objection to it, could there? Now, just what would I take? I wonder if her patches are in here—and her things. *(They look in the sewing basket.)*

MRS. HALE   Here's some red. I expect this has got sewing things in it. *(Brings out a fancy box.)* What a pretty box. Looks like something somebody would give you. Maybe her scissors are in here. *(Opens box. Suddenly puts her hand to her nose.)* Why—(MRS. PETERS *bends nearer, then turns her face away.)* There's something wrapped up in this piece of silk.

MRS. PETERS   Why, this isn't her scissors.

MRS. HALE *(lifting the silk)*   Oh, Mrs. Peters—it's—
(MRS. PETERS bends closer.)

MRS. PETERS   It's the bird.

MRS. HALE *(jumping up)*   But, Mrs. Peters—look at it. Its neck! Look at its neck! It's all—other side *to.*

MRS. PETERS   Somebody—wrung—its neck.
(Their eyes meet. A look of growing comprehension, of horror. Steps are heard outside. MRS. HALE slips box under quilt pieces, and sinks into her chair. Enter SHERIFF and COUNTY ATTORNEY. MRS. PETERS rises.)

COUNTY ATTORNEY *(as one turning from serious things to little pleasantries)* Well, ladies, have you decided whether she was going to quilt it or knot it?

MRS. PETERS   We think she was going to—knot it.

SUSAN GLASPELL

503

COUNTY ATTORNEY   Well, that's interesting, I'm sure. *(Seeing the bird-cage.)* Has the bird flown?

MRS. HALE *(putting more quilt pieces over the box)*   We think the—cat got it.

COUNTY ATTORNEY *(preoccupied)*   Is there a cat?
(MRS. HALE glances in a quick covert way at MRS. PETERS.)

MRS. PETERS   Well, not now. They're superstitious, you know. They leave.

COUNTY ATTORNEY *(to SHERIFF PETERS, continuing an interrupted conversation)*   No sign at all of any one having come from the outside. Their own rope. Now let's go up again and go over it piece by piece. *(They start upstairs.)* It would have to have been some one who knew just the—
(MRS. PETERS sits down. The two women sit there not looking at one another, but as if peering into something and at the same time holding back. When they talk now it is in the manner of feeling their way over strange ground, as if afraid of what they are saying, but as if they can not help saying it.)

MRS. HALE   She liked the bird. She was going to bury it in that pretty box.

MRS. PETERS *(in a whisper)*   When I was a girl—my kitten—there was a boy took a hatchet, and before my eyes—and before I could get there—*(Covers her face an instant.)* If they hadn't held me back I would have—*(Catches herself, looks upstairs where steps are heard, falters weakly)*—hurt him.

MRS. HALE *(with a slow look around her)*   I wonder how it would seem never to have had any children around. *(Pause.)* No, Wright wouldn't like the bird—a thing that sang. She used to sing. He killed that, too.

MRS. PETERS *(moving uneasily)*   We don't know who killed the bird.

MRS. HALE   I knew John Wright.

MRS. PETERS   It was an awful thing was done in this house that night, Mrs. Hale. Killing a man while he slept, slipping a rope around his neck that choked the life out of him.

MRS. HALE   His neck. Choked the life out of him.
(Her hand goes out and rests on the bird-cage.)

MRS. PETERS *(with rising voice)*   We don't know who killed him. We don't know.

MRS. HALE *(her own feeling not interrupted)*   If there'd been years and years of nothing, then a bird to sing to you, it would be awful—still, after the bird was still.

MRS. PETERS *(something within her speaking)*   I know what stillness is.

When we homesteaded in Dakota, and my first baby died—after he was two years old, and me with no other then—

MRS. HALE *(moving)* How soon do you suppose they'll be through, looking for the evidence?

MRS. PETERS I know what stillness is. *(Pulling herself back.)* The law has got to punish crime, Mrs. Hale.

MRS. HALE *(not as if answering that)* I wish you'd seen Minnie Foster when she wore a white dress with blue ribbons and stood up there in the choir and sang. *(A look around the room.)* Oh, I *wish* I'd come over here once in a while. That was a crime! That was a crime! Who's going to punish that?

MRS. PETERS *(looking upstairs)* We mustn't—take on.

MRS. HALE I might have known she needed help! I know how things can be—for women. I tell you, it's queer, Mrs. Peters. We live close together and we live far apart. We all go through the same things—it's all just a different kind of the same thing. *(Brushes her eyes, noticing the bottle of fruit, reaches out for it.)* If I was you I wouldn't tell her her fruit was gone. Tell her it *ain't*. Tell her it's all right. Take this in to prove it to her. She—she may never know whether it was broke or not.

MRS. PETERS *(takes the bottle, looks about for something to wrap it in; takes petticoat from the clothes brought from the other room, very nervously begins winding this around the bottle. In a false voice)* My, it's a good thing the men couldn't hear us. Wouldn't they just laugh. Getting all stirred up over a little thing like a—dead canary. As if that could have anything to do with—with—wouldn't they *laugh!*
(The men are heard coming down stairs.)

MRS. HALE *(under her breath)* Maybe they would—maybe they wouldn't.

COUNTY ATTORNEY No, Peters, it's all perfectly clear except a reason for doing it. But you know juries when it comes to women. If there was some definite thing. Something to show—something to make a story about—a thing that would connect up with this strange way of doing it.
(The women's eyes meet for an instant. Enter HALE *from outer door.)*

HALE Well, I've got the team around. Pretty cold out there.

COUNTY ATTORNEY I'm going to stay here a while by myself. *(To the* SHERIFF.*)* You can send Frank out for me, can't you? I want to go over everything. I'm not satisfied that we can't do better.

SHERIFF Do you want to see what Mrs. Peters is going to take in?
(The Lawyer goes to the table, picks up the apron, laughs.)

COUNTY ATTORNEY Oh, I guess they're not very dangerous things the ladies have picked out. *(Moves a few things about, disturbing the quilt pieces which cover the box. Steps back.)* No, Mrs. Peters doesn't need supervising. For that matter, a sheriff's wife is married to the law. Ever think of it that way, Mrs. Peters?

MRS. PETERS Not—just that way.

SHERIFF *(chuckling)* Married to the law. *(Moves toward the other room.)* I just want you to come in here a minute, George. We ought to take a look at these windows.

COUNTY ATTORNEY *(scoffingly)* Oh, windows!

SHERIFF We'll be right out, Mr. Hale.
(HALE goes outside. The SHERIFF follows the COUNTY ATTORNEY into the other room. Then MRS. HALE rises, hands tight together, looking intensely at MRS. PETERS, whose eyes make a slow turn, finally meeting MRS. HALE's. A moment MRS. HALE holds her, then her own eyes point the way to where the box is concealed. Suddenly MRS. PETERS throws back quilt pieces and tries to put the box in the bag she is wearing. It is too big. She opens box, starts to take bird out, cannot touch it, goes to pieces, stands there helpless. Sound of a knob turning in the other room. MRS. HALE snatches the box and puts it in the pocket of her big coat. Enter COUNTY ATTORNEY and SHERIFF.)

COUNTY ATTORNEY *(facetiously)* Well, Henry, at least we found out that she was not going to quilt it. She was going to—what is it you call it, ladies?

MRS. HALE *(her hand against her pocket)* We call it—knot it, Mr. Henderson.

(Curtain)

DIVING INTO THE WRECK

by

ADRIENNE RICH

(b. 1929)

A graduate of Radcliffe College, Adrienne Rich has described her life as one of privilege. Her early poems reflect the anguish of her role conflict as wife, mother, and writer. More recently she has written of the lesbian experience. In addition to writing many volumes of poetry, including The Dream of a Common Language *(1978), Rich has become a leader in feminist thought and literary theory. A book on motherhood appeared in 1976 and a collection of essays,* On Lies, Secrets, and Silences, *in 1979. Recent collections of poetry include* The Fact of a Doorframe: Poems Selected and New, 1950–84 *(1984) and* A Wild Patience Has Taken Me This Far *(1981).*

• ——————————————————— •

First having read the book of myths,
and loaded the camera,
and checked the edge of the knife-blade,
I put on
the body-armor of black rubber
the absurd flippers
the grave and awkward mask.
I am having to do this
not like Cousteau with his
assiduous team
aboard the sun-flooded schooner
but here alone.

There is a ladder.
The ladder is always there
hanging innocently
close to the side of the schooner.
We know what it is for,
we who have used it.

Otherwise
it's a piece of maritime floss
some sundry equipment.

I go down.
Rung after rung and still
the oxygen immerses me
the blue light
the clear atoms
of our human air.
I go down.
My flippers cripple me,
I crawl like an insect down the ladder
and there is no one
to tell me when the ocean
will begin.

First the air is blue and then
it is bluer and then green and then
black I am blacking out and yet
my mask is powerful
it pumps my blood with power
the sea is another story
the sea is not a question of power
I have to learn alone
to turn my body without force
in the deep element.

And now: it is easy to forget
what I came for
among so many who have always
lived here
swaying their crenellated fans
between the reefs
and besides
you breathe differently down here.

I came to explore the wreck.
The words are purposes.
The words are maps.
I came to see the damage that was done
and the treasures that prevail.

I stroke the beam of my lamp
slowly along the flank
of something more permanent
than fish or weed
the thing I came for:
the wreck and not the story of the wreck
the thing itself and not the myth
the drowned face always staring
toward the sun
the evidence of damage
worn by salt and sway into this threadbare beauty
the ribs of the disaster
curving their assertion
among the tentative haunters.

This is the place.
And I am here, the mermaid whose dark hair
streams black, the merman in his armored body
We circle silently
about the wreck
we dive into the hold.
I am she: I am he

whose drowned face sleeps with open eyes
whose breasts still bear the stress
whose silver, copper, vermeil cargo lies
obscurely inside barrels
half-wedged and left to rot
we are the half-destroyed instruments
that once held to a course
the water-eaten log
the fouled compass

We are, I am, you are
by cowardice or courage
the one who find our way
back to this scene
carrying a knife, a camera
a book of myths
in which
our names do not appear.

HOMECOMING

by

MARTHA COLLINS

(b. 1940)

Born in Nebraska, Martha Collins was raised in Iowa and educated at Stanford University and the University of Iowa. A professor of English at the University of Massachusetts at Boston, she has published her poems widely in periodicals. Her first collection, A Catastrophe of Rainbows, *appeared in 1985.*

So you're home from the wars,
or at least a summer
facsimile of them.
You're welcome, but
please don't rush.
There are some things
to be seen.

First you'll notice
these guests. You'll call
them suitors, and be
mistaken: they've
not cluttered
the hearth or changed
the order of things.

You'll find the bed
in the same quiet place,
neatly spread as before.
But you should know
I've grown accustomed

to sleeping in all
its spaces.

The sun-colored table
sits in the kitchen, prepared
for the usual
feasts, you'll think.
But I'm not quite ready
to serve your dinners,
to pour your wines.

I'd rather sit by the big
bay window, the one we saved
for special times.
There's an extra chair,
but please be still,
for it's here I've come
to reflect.

Perhaps you'll resent
the uncommon manner
in which I've come
to possess our rooms.
But you can't conceive
of the more extreme measures
I've thought of taking,

like pounding stakes
in the floor and stretching
ropes to inform you
this or that is mine,
stamping my name
on favorite walls,
carving initials

on window sills,
or merely breathing
autograph spaces
on panes of glass.
But of course
we're bound
to share, and it's more

than a neat
arrangement
of tables and chairs and beds.
And perhaps it's as
simple as getting familiar,
accepting
the common places again.

But please
understand,
and try to find
your own space
where you can see beyond
these ceilings and floors
and windows and walls.

It shouldn't be hard:
you have been miles
away, after all,
while I have been
making myself at home.

BEYOND WHAT

by

ALICE WALKER

(b. 1944)

*Born in Georgia, Alice Walker was educated at Spelman College
and Sarah Lawrence College. She spent many years in Mississippi
but currently lives in San Francisco. She has been a fellow of the
Radcliffe Institute and has taught and read her poetry in many colleges. She has published three novels, a collection of short stories,* In
Love and Trouble: Stories of Black Women *(1973), and two volumes of poetry. An influential essay, "In Our Mothers' Gardens"*
(Ms. *magazine, 1972), explores the problems of women as artists,
and is the title essay of* In Search of Our Mothers' Gardens:
Womanist Prose *(1983). Her novel* The Color Purple *(1983) won
a Pulitzer Prize.*

We reach for destinies beyond
what we have come to know
and in the romantic hush
of promises
perceive each
the other's life
as known mystery.
Shared. But inviolate.
No melting. No squeezing
into One.
We swing our eyes around
as well as side to side
to see the world.

To choose, renounce,
this, or that—
call it a council between equals
call it love.

PART
III

SELF-IMAGES

In the last fifteen years a flood of diaries and letters written by women has been published; manuscripts found in attics or languishing unpublished in libraries have been discovered by feminist scholars or by descendants of the writers, and several anthologies of excerpts from such writings have appeared. Feminist critics and theorists have begun to formulate ways of looking at and evaluating these writings, of differentiating their significance from that of similar writings by men, which have for centuries been widely published and criticized. Though personal writings collectively may seem to be very different from fiction in that they profess to be telling the truth, it is clear that the truth told as a writer sees it shares many features with fiction. For this reason, along with excerpts from writings presented as truth, a fictional work in diary form ("The Thousand Springs") is included; seeing the resemblances and differences makes clearer the methods and effects of both.

It is hard to describe the variety of women's diaries, journals, and letters; they resist categorization and comparison to such a degree that evaluation seems almost impossible. But we can at least attempt a definition. The terms *diary* and *journal* denote dailiness, but a more descriptive label in recent use has been *discontinuous prose,* or writing that is done intermittently, whether daily or regularly or not. Under this heading we can also include letters, which differ from diaries and journals in having an addressee. But even this difference is not entirely a dividing feature, since many diaries are addressed to an alter ego or an imaginary friend and many others were written with publication in mind. Indeed, however secretly a journal is kept, it is hard not to think that a reader has been imagined, at least unconsciously.

Dailiness may characterize the expected frequency of the writing of a diary, but it is often also applicable to the content. We expect a diary to be a record of daily life, of the experiences that are repeated from day to day, including, perhaps, the experience of keeping a diary! But diarists may also record the unusual, the events and thoughts that made a day memorable. Journal-keepers often focus on just a few aspects of events or on special parts of their lives, such as relationships with parents, education, development of tastes, or decisions about their work. Women writers have often chosen to focus in their personal writings on their spiritual quests and development. Even though first-person writing must be selective, its principles of selection allow revelations about women's inner thoughts that we seldom see elsewhere. As Estelle Jellinek has pointed out in *Women's Autobiography,* women's discontinuous writings have differed from men's both in content and form; women focus more than men on personal life and on relationships with family and friends, and their forms, as Jellinek says, "are analogous to the fragmented, interrupted, and formless nature of their lives." The rediscovery of women diarists from the past and the flood of new autobiographical writings enable us to recover a perspective on life that has been hidden and that can now be used to correct earlier conclusions about human priorities and values.

Diaries and journals might also be categorized by their duration: some are lifelong, starting in childhood; others start and stop, reflecting the very human trait of procrastination, as well as the fact that sustained writing is a difficult activity. Diaries also, of course, vary widely in writing style, an echo of the wide range of talent, education, and class among their authors. Of course, self-selection is inevitable; those deprived of literacy, of materials for writing, or of time and privacy must be silent. Because of their traditional roles, even women of education and talent have been almost as silent as the men and women denied literacy by race and economic circumstances.

In the twentieth century we are accustomed to attempts at self-definition, but we should not project such motives anachronistically onto diaries and other personal writings from earlier times. It seems clear that the dominant motive behind personal writings before our century was to keep a semipublic record of family and community life, a document that would become a part of history, a record of what might otherwise escape recording. To write one's religious autobiography has since St. Augustine's *Confessions* been viewed as a way of testifying to the greatness of the object of religious quest, not to that of the subject—the seeker. Even modern diaries may have a public purpose; Anaïs Nin, whose six published volumes of diaries represent only a fraction of what she actually wrote, has said that she wanted to record, especially for other women, experiences that she saw as unique opportunities for understanding women's psychology and position in the world. But that purpose is superimposed on her intention in her early diaries—to win back a father who had abandoned the family. Motives for writing are often very mixed, and readers will find material in most women's diaries that they can use to measure their own experiences.

The overall effect of reading diaries is to marvel at the human spirit and what it can endure and accomplish. Against the intimate record of another's life, readers can place their own in perspective. And seeing the variety of styles, content, and degrees of intermittency may well inspire a reader of diaries to become a writer of one.

Selections in This Section

The personal writings have been selected to serve as an epitome of the variety that exists in the genre; in each excerpt is included the writer's statement of what keeping a journal or writing letters has meant to her. In view of the diversity of content and the range of chronology, the selections are grouped by form. Readers will see other ways of grouping them and of comparing them with selections in earlier sections of this anthology.

Diaries/Journals The distinguishing mark of these selections is that activities and thoughts of a particular day are usually recorded either on the day or soon after. The first selection, "The Thousand Springs," by Mary Gray Hughes, is a fictional journal; only days of the week, not dates, are specified and no place is named, so that even the ostensible purpose of recording history is absent. Almost a satire of the most humdrum of journals, which record such mundane events as the weather and daily tasks, the entries are unified by the topic announced in the first entry: "raining." But underlying the trivia is a story that the reader is asked to create: a woman who longs to be a writer is frustrated by her duties as wife and mother; her care and solicitude for her children leads to their escape from the effects of a flood, but she receives no care and dies. The drive to write, to find expression, leads only to this short record of her life, "found," as so many other personal journals have been, after her death.

Hughes uses the unifying devices, the subtle conflict, and the drama that we expect of fiction; yet she is true to the diary form. Readers of Käthe Kollwitz's diary can supply knowledge that lends unity to the daily entries; we know that Kollwitz was a great artist. Like Hughes's protagonist, she felt the conflict between her need for artistic expression and the claims of husband, sons, and mother. Both these diarists suffer from forces they cannot control—flood in one case, war in the other. A reader can both admire the valor with which these women meet such forces and pity them for what they have to endure; both works have some of the capacity of great tragedies for drawing the reader into the subjects' perspectives. Kollwitz in her entry for New Year's Eve, 1925, reports being a reader of her own diary; she records her depression in reliving past times through her diary as well as her discovery of "what a half-truth a diary presents." She recognizes that she has written "only when there were obstacles and halts to the flow of life, seldom when everything was smooth and even." This perception gives us a clue as to how we should approach all such writing: there is a story—as in Hughes's work—but it is seldom the whole story. A reader of diaries should be alert to such self-conscious moments as Kollwitz's, moments seldom found in fiction.

Joanna Field, a distinguished psychoanalyst, kept a diary specifically in order to gain insights into her own selectivity, to let what she chose to write about daily events present clues to her subconscious motivations. It is interesting that this very intellectual and thoughtful woman suffered from problems we may think unique to ourselves; like so many others, she says,

"I was always expecting things to be difficult, distrusting my own ability, fearing the criticisms of others." Her quest into her own mind, to find the causes of these feelings, transcends her scientific knowledge and study. It is self-examination that reveals to her that she is capable of the kind of thought that brings with it "a quality of delight" totally unknown in the kind of thought involved in "going about daily practical affairs." Reading Field's journal is like waching "Woman Thinking," making fine distinctions and reaching important conclusions about the nature of thought, such as have been associated with the "Man Thinking" of Emerson's essays or Rodin's famous statue "The Thinker." Field's self-revelation enables us to perceive thinking as a gender-free activity.

Anaïs Nin wrote about the diary she kept from the age of eleven: "What I have to say is really distinct from the artist and art. *It is the woman who has to speak*. And it is not only the woman Anaïs who has to speak, but I who have to speak for many women. As I discover myself, I feel I am merely one of many. . . . I begin to understand women of yesterday and today. The mute ones of the past, the inarticulate, and the women of today, all action, and copies of men. And I, in between . . ." (*Diary I,* p. 289). As a student of the new science of psychoanalysis, as a woman artist among famous men, as one who experienced the life of her time in the great cultural centers of Paris and New York, Nin had much to say, much that is meaningful to other women. She recognized in herself the duality especially common in women: "There were always in me, two women at least, one woman desperate and bewildered, who felt she was drowning, and another who would leap into a scene, as upon a stage, conceal her true emotions because they were weaknesses, helplessness, despair, and present to the world only a smile, and eagerness, curiosity, enthusiasm, interest" (*Diary I,* p. 270). The reader of Nin's diary will often find the second woman represented and be somewhat repulsed by what seems like egocentrism, even snobbism; but reading extensive parts of the diary wins the reader's sympathy and recognition of herself in Nin's experience. The excerpts here focus on Nin's attempts through psychoanalysis to understand her basic conflict between herself as artist and herself as woman; with Dr. Otto Rank, the author of several works on the creative person, she reached a level of self-understanding, but it was only in working with a woman analyst that she was able to reconcile her basic conflict. Significantly, she was able to realize that her obsessive daily need to write long excerpts in her diary prevented her from rising above dailiness to perceive an order in her life; she perceived and imposed order through editing her diary. Though not many diarists have, as Nin does, made readers wonder if she conducted her life so as to record it, her diary clearly served as a defense against the true implications of her actions.

These excerpts from Nin do not show the many portraits she drew of people and places and her responses to art and literature, which are important aspects of her diary. If they had been included here, even those sections would have seemed very different from the journal kept by Zora

Neale Hurston, a black woman who studied anthropology at Columbia University under a famous professor, Frank Boas, and then returned to her native Florida to write about her own people—an outsider with an insider's knowledge. Like Nin, Hurston transformed some of her insights into fiction; her novel *Their Eyes Were Watching God* vividly shows her world from the perspective of a young uneducated black woman. Hurston's book *Tell My Horse,* from which the selection here is taken, belongs to a popular kind of journal, the travel record. In it Hurston uses narrative and first-person commentary to make understandable to American readers the complex Haitian concept of a female voodoo goddess, Erzulie Freida.

Marie Noël's journal, like Nin's, reveals her self-conflict as writer, as woman, and as dutiful daughter; but it also reveals an even more profound conflict, her fight against doubting God. These two conflicts interlock, and we see Noël in dialogue with God and with herself as she struggles to understand her life. She does not proceed chronologically; we learn of her present life early in her journal and later of her decisive experience at nine when she went to mass with her grandmother. Her journal makes clear that memory cuts into chronology to transcend the limitations of dailiness.

Like Noël, Rebecca Jackson writes of a religious struggle, but a more joyous one than Noël's. Jackson taught herself to read and write at thirty-five in order to record the "gifts of power" she had received through direct communication with God. Unlike Nin, who abhorred activism, and Noël, who remained in her native village for most of her life, Jackson became a preacher about the revelation she had received, traveling widely with another woman in days when such a venture was remarkable. The excerpts included here tell of Jackson's receiving the "gift" of reading, of insights gained through dreams, of a song "given" to her by the Lord. Jackson felt no conflict between being herself and creating this song, unlike Nin and Noël; she relied on a concept of poetic inspiration common in many cultures. But Jackson's life was not without conflict; she struggled in vain to persuade her husband to live a life of Shaker chastity.

Like Rebecca Jackson, Arozina Perkins practiced her faith, which was both in God and in the powers of education by action. Having begun to teach soon after completing her own education at sixteen, Perkins was an experienced teacher when she went west in 1850 with a group of other young women trained by a religious group in Hartford, Connecticut. Her diary tells of her idealism about teaching, about the ardors of her journey, and about the difficulties she encountered in a pioneer town in Iowa, then at the frontier. Though disillusioned, she did not lose her ideals. Her career was tragically short, known to us only through her brief diary (kept from November of 1848 to August of 1851) and a few letters. However, the record of her life is a corrective to the myth that the frontier woman was simply wife and mother; Perkins was one of over seven hundred young women sent out as teachers by a single organization.

Letters Our sample of letters comes from a series written over a period of years; since we have only half the correspondence, the letters read very much like a diary.

In Maimie Pinzer's letters to her benefactor and mentor, Mrs. Fanny Quincy Howe, a prominent Bostonian, only the honesty with which Maimie reveals her lapses into prostitution makes credible a life story that fiction would be hard-pressed to match. Born into a middle-class family, Pinzer had the bitter childhood experience of being repeatedly molested by an uncle. When she was thirteen, her father was murdered, leaving her mother to provide for five children. As the oldest, Pinzer resented becoming the household drudge and tried to earn spending money as a department store sales clerk. Tempted by the goods she sold, she became a prostitute and was totally cast off by her family; her mother even had her imprisoned. She met Herbert Welsh, a social worker who persuaded Mrs. Howe to help by writing to her; Pinzer wrote that her letters to these two people became for her "a sort of diary." Through writing them, she says, "I found that which is the reason people keep diaries. It records these thoughts and once they are carefully taken apart and written, you can follow the lines of your thoughts more clearly; and then it is a clearinghouse, and from one writing to the next, one's brain is cleared, ready to follow out the line of thought or perhaps start a new line of thought" (p. 12). Letters written to her do not survive, but it is clear that Pinzer made constant efforts to change her way of life because of the encouragement in them and the financial help she received from the writers. We cannot be sure of her ultimate fate: after a correspondence from 1910 to 1922, the letters ended abruptly; and nothing further is known of Maimie Pinzer.

Autobiographies Maimie Pinzer's letters hint at the ways in which a correspondence can reveal intimate details if the letters of both contributors are preserved. Augmented by diaries from one or both of the writers, letters are a major source of information about people's lives, and thus are valuable to biographers and autobiographers. A diarist who pauses to review her writing and finds a meaningful pattern may well write her life story in the first person, becoming both the narrator and the persona of a work that in many ways resembles fiction. Diaries may be viewed as modes of discovering the significance of one's life; autobiographies may be seen as the product of such a discovery.

No autobiographies are excerpted here. It is even more difficult to do them justice in selections than it is to do so for novels and other literary forms; their integral discontinuity cannot be perceived in excerpts. But reading these personal narratives, seeing their principles of selection, gives valuable insights not only into women's other writings but into the reality of women's lives as they perceive it. Fortunately, feminist scholars have provided helpful resources for finding the wealth of autobiographies, as well as related diaries, journals, and letters. In the Suggestions for Further Reading at the end of this book, many of these aids—bibliographies, collections of critical articles, anthologies of original writings—are listed. Mary Louise Briscoe's *A Bibliography of American Autobiography, 1945–1980* is the first to identify those by women in a list of some five thousand works; carefully and fully annotated, it can serve as a guide to reading. Margo Cully's anthology *A Day at a Time* includes many selections as well as an extensive bibliography; other anthologies of the experience of black, native American, ethnic American and lesbian women are now available.

In her book *Silences,* Tillie Olsen identifies the circumstances of race, economic and social class, and gender as deterrents to writing literature. Newly available writings reveal voices traditionally unheard; collectively they expand our knowledge of the world, of history, and of ourselves.

THE THOUSAND SPRINGS

by

MARY GRAY HUGHES

(b. 1930)

Born in Brownsville, Texas, Mary Gray Hughes studied at the University of Texas, Columbia University, and Oxford University. She won a National Endowment for the Arts fellowship in 1978 and has been writer-in-residence at the University of Illinois since 1977. In addition to several children's books, she has published three collections of short stories: The Calling *(1980),* My Wisdom *(1982), and* Little Face and Other Stories *(1984).*

•————————————————•

raining.

Sun.

No church this day due to river flooding. Fields sodden. All the animals affected, but none so skittish as the horses. Unable to comb ("curry," R. would say) them, and can ride only on the few high paths.

Michael says he has never seen such rains, nor the water so high, and this in 71 years! Which is the more astounding, that he has never seen such a thing, or that anyone could survive so many years in this . . . place?

Read Poe last night as had resolved to do. Truly an inferior writer. Nothing to compare with H. S. Harrison. His (Poe's) resuscitated fame of the modish, or critical, and transitory sort, of that I am sure.

Tues.

Birds I have heretofore not seen are found in all our trees and even along the eaves of the outbuildings. Yesterday the sun shone! We rushed blankets and bedding and oh boots boots boots outside to dry. Blessed dryness; blessed absence of the horrid wet. The walls of our bedroom (2nd storey!) are damp. Kendra has persistent cough, but, D.V., the sun will have restored her. R. spent *entire* day trying to dry milch cows. I baking, ironing, separating milk. Try to think of literature each day. And read each evening: Poe again; and the great, great Harrison.

Secret: I would like to write a story. Not just little sketch this time, but a real story. About the sea. Or ocean. And its long dry white beach. Someday!

Michael sits inside all day. Is in foul humor and will do nothing useful. Says there will be more rain. So sure. How can *he* know? Trying man. Even, yes I will write it—disgusting. Stood shredding the last, so difficultly obtained, newspaper while studying the western sky and using against its neutral face (surely it is neutral, is it not?) the most abusive language. Foul-mouthed abusive old man. My Father once said, "Adjustment to nature is love of God." Wise words. Shall try to observe them. Adjust and accept.

Wed.

Hardest rains yet! River over all the banks, and crest not yet arrived at County Dip! Men out all night driving, half-swimming stock to McDermott's Ridge. Floor damp under our feet. Water oozing up through cracks. Heretofore I had not known there were cracks in floor.

Day spent baking (flour damp!), cooking, separating milk, ironing clothes dry.

Michael inside by stove ALL day. Says he has the 'flu. Won't bathe. Smells. Disgusting. Andrew brings him sacks of piñon nuts which he roasts and they share by the stove—cracking, spitting, muttering together. Laughing. A. kind, I am glad to say, as I would wish in my son, but is he overly docile? Yet where in this land can/could he wrest any spirit? Any true determination? Any PRIDE? In a house that smells? Must stop. ACCEPT.

I am truly grateful, truly, for my children. Kendra better, thank God. She is not a strong child, but TRIES. Andrew quite different. Strong as a man, *he* says. Gulps his soup at dinner from his own childhood's handleless mug, won't use another, yet sits by Michael and teases, yes *teases,* him about the weather, and makes all laugh. True. Yet he, A., is no trouble to me, and in truth does the work of a man grown, though he is turned only twelve. In feature he is unlike me, I think, in all but nose. My mind wanders—shameful! Remember: CONCENTRATE. So are ALL things done.

Friday

It rains. Rain standing deep on the ground and it still rains. Rain on rain. Can see no mts. now, just rain. Rain, and rain seen through rain; rain become our windows, and our walls. We all sit, sleep, eat downstairs. No protection against the damp—the lot of us together steaming and close.

Stop. Must concentrate! Day spent baking, drying bedding over stove, separating milk. Continue to read novels of Henry Sydnor Harrison each night. Determined to better my mind and soul under and against all circumstances. Read Bible, too. No more Poe, for A. has removed all the vols., even the poems (Poe's I mean), to his bunk. Wants them for his.

AND, I begin a story. It is to be set, that is the setting of the story is to be, on a vast, dry strip of beach, and the seagulls spinning like motes in the sunlight overhead. I work fifteen min. each night. At the table.

Sat.

All the bedding wet, cannot dry it, and still it rains. Intermittent and drizzling, but rain. R. says the stock suffer in the feet. I am meant to feel concern for them. The truth is, I will write it here—I hate the stock.

I confess to yelling at R. this night. Must not do so again.

Paper I write on here is damp. Wood damp. Sputters and gives off poor heat. We all shiver. What sort of land is this with rain, when it does rain, that wounds, and mountains like hands raised against us.

Must set bread to rise. ACCEPT.

Monday

This morning I opened out the closets and found my last, only velvet gown . . . mildewed. Like a dead child I cradled it in my arms.

I iron clothes dry, bake, iron again. No hope of washing. Neither ourselves nor our clothes. Wood very damp; fires sputter and are slow. I make soup and nurse M., who is better. Kendra sits with him.

River to crest at week's end. R. and A. out constantly raising banks around the stock in the low pastures. I try to prepare warming meals. Make bread pudding. Raisins already plumped out from the damp! Heretofore I have never seen such a thing. Amazing. Seasonings also (Cinnamon and allspice are all I use; I never put nutmeg in my bread pudding) swelled and packed from damp.

Read 15 min. each night. Always my dear Harrison. PERSEVERE.

Monday
(Got yesterday's day wrong.)

M. better. Truly, he did have the influenza. Sleeps now; eats soup. Pray rest of us remain well and do not take it. I make strong soup for us all as well, and set bread, separate milk, clean kitchen THOROUGHLY. Good demeanor all day; no reading.

Tuesday

I add to the wet by weeping.

Thursday, Feb. 24

Praise God all my life, my son is restored to me. He had stayed and sheltered two days and the night on the high meadow caring for two of the stock. R. said he never worried, and it is true that he slept (exhaustion?) the entire night through, and when A. came in leading the heifer and calf R. but went out to him, saying no criticism, but helped to rub the animals dry. Now A. sleeps by stove, clothes, mud, and all, and I let him be. Wood sputters with damp, and the light therefore flickers over him. I think he has never been happier than he is in these man-imitating days. I hate this land, God forgive me, but I do. This child-stealing land. How shall they have *time* to grow, such children? Even Kendra, ten, sits up late to rub the horses' feet. None step on her. Her cough is much improved, thank God.

Must build up fire, iron clothes dry.

Tomorrow, I promise self, shall read. Must separate milk, too.

But, praise God, I must, for A.'s return.

Sunday

The river lowers.

There is mud everywhere. On the table legs, the sides of the stove. Everywhere. We all wear boots in the house, to the delight of the children. We all smell. Like the stock. We are disgusting.

I bake, make soup, iron clothes dry. Iron sheets. All of them dirty as we cannot wash, yet I iron them. Iron over mud. Disgusting.

Andrew reads Poe all evening, and holds his calf for its warmth. His calf, now, as R. gave it to him. I clean kitchen and read. Reread the third, great chapter of Harrison's *V V'S EYES*. Surely one of the most beautiful (sustained) passages in all lit. I admit my own feeble efforts fall far short. But, I *keep* trying. The beach I write about, it is to be covered with the palest (whitest? most golden? Exact word important, certainly.) sand, very clean and dry and fine. This, the sandy beach, rises gently to large flat stones, or rocks, and on them a woman walks from the direction of the town. This is but the beginning, of course. There is to be more. I think it is not unpromising.

Monday

Andrew goes camping. CAMPING! R. lets him. He, A., says the mud smells rich. RICH. R. laughs. Says it will indeed make us richer for the land will be better than ever. From the river silt, which is valuable for crops, is what he means.

I wash clothes, table and legs, stove. I bathe. Wood difficult and house cold yet, but I manage. Will NOT be dirty even if must bathe cold. Set bread now, cut bones for soup, find old cloth for teat for calf, and mend.

The night is mine.

That is just a line I wrote here.

MARY GRAY HUGHES

527

Several days' lapse. All as usual. I bake. Read Harrison while bread rises. Joy. Joy. So weepy, however, I am become.

Worked two hours on story. TWO HOURS. Time fled. True. I was not aware of it. Feel story is not without some merit. But the ending . . . that is something of a problem, I admit. Cannot think how to end. PERSEVERE.

Throat scratchy.

Friday

Sunshine. True. Perfectly clear day with sunshine. Blue sky everywhere, clear as clear and the mountains sharp as shells against it. It dazes my eyes. The truth is, my eyes pain me. Even reading hurts. And I am drowsy as well. Fell off to sleep over table last night (night before? no matter) to be awakened by kind touch of A. on my arm. Kind, kind boy. No teasing for all the pages, half-pages, and bits of note-paper with my story on. Kind boy. Such a pity he did not, nor did Kendra, get my eyebrows. Strange. I thought one of them surely would.

CONCENTRATE. Must. Head strange. Confess that this, this writing, these actual lines here I mean, being written in bed. Heretofore I have never done such a thing. R. sent me up early. Said he would prepare noon meal, and clean kitchen. Also separate milk. True. Urged extra sweaters and blanket on me. Tea, too, to come later. Even watched me up the stairs. True. Imagine!

The above are the last fourteen and only known surviving entries, on sixteen and one-third bound quarto pages, comprising in its entirety the final and sole remaining section of the recently discovered, self-titled "Personal Journals" of Bertha Hudson Little, mother of Andrew Little, the writer.

From DIARIES AND LETTERS

by

KÄTHE KOLLWITZ

(1867–1945)

Though forced to work alone in patriarchal Germany and oppressed by the Nazis, Käthe Kollwitz became a great artist, famous for her stark black and white drawings, her lithographs, and her sculpture. Using her own aging face as a model, she focused on expressing the anguish caused by poverty and war, especially for women and children. Having lost a son and a grandson in the two world wars, she wanted her art to be a political statement. Two volumes of her diaries and letters were published in 1955; they elucidate the process underlying the more than one thousand drawings that were published in 1972.

• ——————————————————————— •

April 1910

I am gradually approaching the period in my life when work comes first. When both the boys went away for Easter, I hardly did anything but work. Worked, slept, ate and went for short walks. But above all I worked. And yet I wonder whether the "blessing" is not missing from such work. No longer diverted by other emotions, I work the way a cow grazes. . . .

April 1910

This period in my life seems to me very fine. Great piercing sorrows have not yet struck me; my darling boys are growing more independent. I can already see the time when they will break loose from me, and at the moment I look forward to it without sorrow. For then they will be mature enough for a life wholly their own, and I shall still be young enough for my own life.

May 15, 1910

How strongly I feel that this is a dividing period in their lives. How soon now something very real and definite will emerge out of the boys' lovelorn enthusiasms. Sensuality is burgeoning . . . it shows up in every one

KÄTHE KOLLWITZ

529

of their movements, in everything, everything. It is only a matter of opening a door and then they will *understand* it too, then the veil will be gone and the struggle with the most powerful of instincts begin . . . often they will feel it their enemy, and sometimes they will almost suffocate for the joy it brings. . . . I feel at once grave, ill at ease and happy as I watch our children—our *children*—growing to meet the greatest of instincts. May it have mercy on them!

September 29, 1910

My wish is to die after Karl. I could endure living alone better than he could. I am also closer to the children. But if I should die Karl could not manage alone. If I die, Karl would find it unbearable by himself. He loves the children enough to die for them, and yet there is alienation between them . . . I know no person who can love as he can, with his whole soul. Often this love has oppressed me; I wanted to be free. But often too it has made me so terribly happy. . . . Only a year ago I thought that once Hans was out of the house—but in any case as soon as both boys were out of the house—I should like to go away for a long time. To Paris. Now I desire this much less strongly. I get working nowadays as often as I need. That is what counts.

September 1, 1911

I imagine the following sculpture as utterly beautiful: a pregnant woman chiseled out of stone. Carved only down to the knees so that she looks the way Lise said she did the time she was pregnant with Maria: "As if I am rooted to the ground." The immobility, restraint, introspection. The arms and hands dangling heavily, the head lowered, all attention directed inward. And the whole thing in heavy, heavy stone. Title: *Pregnancy*.

New Year's Day, 1912

. . . No progress in my relationship with Karl. What he always speaks of, what seems to him still the sole worthwhile goal of our long living together—that we should grow together in the deepest intimacy—I still do not feel and probably never will learn to feel.

Are not the ties with the boys also growing slacker? I almost think so. For the last third of life there remains only work. It alone is always stimulating, rejuvenating, exciting and satisfying. . . .

August 27, 1914

A piece by Gabriele Reuter in the *Tag* on the tasks of women today. She spoke of the joy of sacrificing—a phrase that struck me hard. Where do all the women who have watched so carefully over the lives of their beloved ones get the heroism to send them to face the cannon? . . .

Cold, cloudy autumnal weather. The grave mood that comes over one when one knows: there is war, and one cannot hold on to any illusions any more. Nothing is real but the frightfulness of this state, which we almost grow used to. In such times it seems so stupid that the boys must go to war. The whole thing is so ghastly and insane. Occasionally there comes the foolish thought: how can they possibly take part in such madness? And at once the cold shower: they *must, must!* All is leveled by death; down with all the youth! Then one is ready to despair.

Only one state of mind makes it at all bearable: to receive the sacrifice into one's will. But how can one maintain such a state?

December 9, 1914
[after the death of her son
in the war]

My boy! On your memorial I want to have your figure on top, *above* the parents. You will lie outstretched, holding out your hands in answer to the call for sacrifice: "Here I am." Your eyes—perhaps—open wide, so that you see the blue sky above you, and the clouds and birds. Your mouth smiling. And at your breast the pink I gave you.

January 17, 1916

. . . Where are my children now? What is left to their mother? One boy to the right and one to the left, my right son and my left son, as they called themselves. One dead and one so far away, and I cannot help him . . . My whole life as a mother is really behind me now. I often have a terrible longing to have it back again—to have children, my boys, one to the right and one to the left; to dance with them as formerly when spring arrived and Peter came with flowers and we danced a springtide dance.

August 22, 1916

Stagnation in my work.
When I feel so parched, I almost long for the sorrow again. And then when it comes back I feel it stripping me physically of all the strength I need for work.
Made a drawing: the mother letting her dead son slide into her arms. I might make a hundred such drawings and yet I do not get any closer to him. I am seeking him. As if I had to find him in the work. . . .

December 26, 1919

There are days when Mother sleeps most of the time, murmuring softly in her dreams and daydreaming when she is awake. Always about children . . . It is really so sweet to see how the dreams and visions and fantasies of so old a mother always return to her children. So after all they were the strongest emotion in her life.

February 26, 1920

I want to do a drawing of a man *who sees the suffering of the world.* That can only be Jesus, I suppose. In the drawing where Death seizes the children there is also a woman in the background who sees the suffering of the world. The children being seized by death are not hers; she is too old for that. Nor is she looking; she does not stir, but she knows about the world's suffering. . . .

End of October, 1921

A lovely, happy period of work. The *Mothers* is making progress day by day. How wonderful life is at such times.

December 1922

. . . [My grandson] on the high chair, also at the table, with his back to me. All around his head the fine white hair, shot through with light. It so reminded me of our own children. Afterwards, when I held him on my lap, he kept pointing at me and saying, "Here, Gandmother." A pause between "Gand" and "mother," and then the word "mother" slipping out quickly, carelessly.

June 1924

The first day of Whitsun, a joyous and happy day for me. I went out to spend it with the children. Magnificent weather. . . . The twins are precious. Sturdy, droll, innocent little white heads. Babbling their own language. When Ottilie sits between them to feed them and gives each in turn a spoonful of pap, the one who doesn't have her turn clenches her fists and her face turns red at having to wait, while the other opens her mouth for the spoon with the smuggest air of contentment. It is wonderful to see. Happy Ottilie, who is so thoroughly maternal. Whatever comes later on, these three years of work with the babies will always give her a kind of satiated feeling. She is a mother through and through, much as she sometimes rants against being one.

Little Peter has given me a pink.

When I entered Mother's room today to bring her down to supper, I saw a strange scene. Like something out of a fairy tale. Mother sat at the table, under the lamp, in Grandfather's easy chair. In front of her were snapshots she was looking through. Diagonally across her shoulders sat Frau Klingelhof's big cat.

Mother used to be unable to stand cats. But now she likes to have the cat on her lap. The cat warms her hands. Sometimes it seems to me that Mother thinks the cat is a baby. When it wants to get down, Mother clasps it anxiously, as if she were afraid the baby will fall. Then her face is full of concern. She actually struggles with the cat.

In the picture Helmy Hart took of Mother, which shows only the head, Mother has a strange expression. The wisdom of great age is there. But it is not the wisdom that thinks in thoughts; rather it operates through dim feelings. These are not the "thoughts hitherto inconceivable" that Goethe had, but the summation of eighty-seven years of living, which are now unclearly felt. Mother muses. Yet even that is not quite it, for musing implies, after all, thinking. It is hard to say what the picture expresses. The features themselves do not definitely express one thing or another. Precisely because Mother no longer thinks, there is a unity about her. A very old woman who lives within herself in undifferentiated perception. Yes, that is right; but in addition: who lives within herself according to an order that is pure and harmonious. As Mother's nature always was.

It seems more and more evident to me that Mother does not recognize the cat for what it is, but thinks it is a baby. Often she wraps it up in a blanket and holds it just like a child. It is touching and sweet to see my old mother doing this.

Recently I began reading my old diaries. Back to before the war. Gradually I became very depressed. The reason for that is probably that I wrote only when there were obstacles and halts to the flow of life, seldom when everything was smooth and even . . . I distinctly felt what a half-truth a diary presents . . . I put the diaries away with a feeling of relief that I am safely out of those times. Yet they were times which I always think of as the best in my life, the decade from my mid-thirties to my mid-forties. . . .

Karl has died, July 19, 1940.

Recently I dreamed that I was together with the others in a room. I knew that Karl lay in the adjoining room. Both rooms opened out into an unlit hallway. I went out of my room into the hall and saw the door to Karl's room being opened, and then I heard him say in his kind, loving voice: "Aren't you going to say good night to me?" Then he came out and leaned against the wall, and I stood before him and leaned my body against his, and we held each other's hands and asked each other again and again: "How are you? Is everything all right?" And we were so happy being able to feel one another.

December 1941

My days pass, and if anyone asks me how things are I usually answer, "Not so good," or something of the sort.

Today I thought it over and decided that I am really not badly off. Naturally I cannot say that things are good—no one could say that. For we are at war and millions of human beings are suffering from it, and I along with them. Moreover, I am old and infirm. And yet I am often amazed at how I endure it without feeling altogether unhappy. For there are moments on most days when I feel a deep and sincere gratitude. Not only when we hear from Peter . . . but also when I sit at the open window and there is a blue sky or there are moving clouds. And also when I stretch out in bed at night, dog-tired. . . .

. . . I am afraid of dying—but being dead, oh yes, that to me is often an appealing prospect. If it were only not for the necessity of parting from the few who are dear to me here.

October 1942

Hans has been here. On Wednesday October 14. When he came into my room very silently, I understood that Peter was dead. He fell on September 22.

May 1943

Hans has reached the age of 51. Air-raid alarm the night of May 14. It was the loveliest of May nights. Hans and Ottilie did not go to sleep until very late. They sat in the garden and listened to a nightingale.

After work Hans came, then Ottilie and finally Lise. The four of us sat together. On his birthday table, below the grave relief, I had placed the lithograph *Death Calls,* the print of which I worked over. Then there was a drawing I had made of Karl one time when he was reading aloud to me. We were sitting around the living room table at the time. This drawing is a favorite of Hans'. And there was also the small etching, *Greeting,* which is closely connected with his birthday. . . .

Early next morning, Hans came again and brought a great bouquet of lilies from the garden. What happiness it is for me that I still have my boy whom I love so deeply and who is so fond of me.

Goethe to Lavater, 1779: "But let us stop worrying our particular religions like a dog its bone. *I have gone beyond purely sensual truth.*"

From A LIFE OF ONE'S OWN

by

JOANNA FIELD

(b. 1900)

Marion Milner, who uses the pseudonym Joanna Field, is a distinguished English painter, writer, and psychoanalyst; she trained to become an analyst after keeping and meditating on a journal she started in her twenties. She has had one-woman shows of her paintings in London and has published five books about psychological processes and creativity.

• ——————————————————— •

[*1926–1933*]

I had now discovered certain facts about the way my mind behaved. I had come to the conclusion that what mattered most to me seemed to depend on my powers of perceiving, and that these were, to some extent, under my own control. But the greatest obstacle in the way which was continually preventing me from being fully responsive to my surroundings seemed to be fear of difficulty. I thought then that my next task must be to look for reasons why I was always expecting things to be difficult, distrusting my own ability, fearing the criticisms of others. . . .

At first I did not find any more help in scientific explanations than I had done before. I had of course heard a lot of talk which purported to explain such attitudes in terms of current psychological doctrine—unconscious guilt feelings, inferiority complex, and the like. But though I understood that it was all supposed to be due to situations of my early childhood, I did not see how to apply such explanations to the particular problem which I had in hand. So I had floundered on, still blindly, until several years after I had begun to keep a diary—until, in fact, I was introduced to some experimental studies which eventually shed a flood of light on all my observations, although it took me many years to grasp their full implications.

The experiments dealt with the question of how children think. As far as I could understand it, the central discovery seemed to be that a most crucial step in the mental development of a child is learning how to distinguish between thoughts and things. It appeared that, at first, mental happenings must be indistinguishable from physical ones, for a child is not born knowing that what goes on in his own mind has not the same sort of independent existence as what goes on around him. He does not know that a feeling in his own mind is only his feeling, he has no means of telling, for instance, that the whole world is not darkened with his misery; for he cannot know, until he has laboriously experimented, which of the things he is aware of is part of himself, which is independent. Neither does he know that his feeling, a momentary boredom or pang of hunger, will not go on forever like a table or a chair, for he has not yet learned that feelings and ideas are things which pass. It follows that any discomfort is utterly overwhelming, for he cannot see it against the background of his past experience, and look forward knowing that it will soon be over. When his mother leaves him she has gone forever, the misery of loneliness is all there is. . . .

I gathered then that the psychologists made a very important distinction between the kind of childish thinking which results from the fact that thought is not aware of its own private and personal nature, and the common-sense reasoning which recognizes the existence of an external world independent of ideas and wishes. The transition from one kind of thinking to the other seemed to occur as a result of opposition. A child gradually discovers both that the physical world opposes his desires, that it cannot be wheedled into obeying him, and also that what is in his mind is not necessarily in other people's, so that in order to make other people do what he wants he must express his thoughts in words and produce reasons for his demands. By this means he is gradually led to look at his own thought and see it for what it is.

Although these experiments dealt only with children, I felt certain that they had a very important bearing upon my own problems. But since the main characteristic of the first kind of thought was that it was unconscious, it followed that if by any chance one had failed to grow out of it completely one would still not be directly aware of the fact. This suggested that it might be interesting to try to explore further the part of my thought of which I was not generally aware and find out how it behaved.

I decided that I would begin by a study of my wandering thought. I knew that I was much given to daydreaming, that my mind was always slipping away to irrelevant subjects when it should have been upon my work, that I was often preoccupied when people were talking and did not listen properly to what they said. I knew also that I felt vaguely guilty about this, and was afraid that it was a habit which would eventually catch me out in some critical situation. I was always falling back exhausted from the effort to concentrate, slipping into that state of blind submergence in which I passively followed my nosing thought in its wanderings. This seemed to be a state of peculiar blindness, for although I had the feeling that I could have said at any moment more or less what I was thinking if I had been asked, yet I did not ask it of myself, so did not in fact know. And when I did begin to try and find where my wandering attention had been to, I found it none too easy, for this free-drifting thought was a shy creature. If I did try to watch it too obviously it would scuttle away into its hole only to appear again as soon as I turned my head the other way. Finally I found that it was only by observing out of the corner of my eye and then immediately trying to fix what I had seen in words, that I could gain any clear idea of what was there. Even then I felt that the effort to put the idea into words somehow distorted its shape. . . .

Another trick that I discovered was to keep myself particularly alert to any little movements going on in the back of my mind, passing ideas which were often quite irrelevant to my task of the moment and which I would never have noticed in the ordinary way. I called these "butterflies," for they silently fluttered in from nowhere and were gone in a moment. A typical instance was when, in the middle of an emotional crisis, a "scene" with someone, I would be aware of a little faraway voice hinting at the back of my mind that my tears were not quite uncontrollable, that I was really staging the emotion in order to prove something to myself—or perhaps in order to get something from the other person. Once or twice even I was able to turn round upon myself quickly enough to catch the real intention and fix it in words. . . .

One of my next observations was that I seemed very liable to assume that because something was said it must therefore be true. I would listen to one person's story of a quarrel and believe it as absolute fact, never remembering that thought is relative, that I was listening only to one view of the situation and that when I met the partner to the quarrel I would hear quite a different version. I would read a book review, accepting the judgment given as the final truth, and then, when I happened on a second review of the same book giving a different opinion, I would feel quite lost and confused. The same thing happened when I read the newspapers. I would believe implicitly whatever I read in any paper about political affairs, finding it almost impossible to remember to withhold my acceptance of what was said until I had also heard other opinions.

All this certainly seemed very like the child's mistake which I had read about, the tendency to assume that whatever idea was in my mind at the moment must be real, must be fact in the same sense that tables and chairs are facts. Even when two opposing opinions were presented to me simultaneously I did not learn to judge between them. I merely felt lost, confusedly swaying from one to the other, quite unable to realize each as a partial and individual view, each contributing something from which I might draw in order to create a third opinion. It also occurred to me now that this might explain why I was so desperately dependent upon what people thought of me. For to childish thinking, the fact that something had been said made it true.

Then I began to observe that not only opinions but moods also had an absolute quality. Sometimes I found that in my happy moments I could not believe that I had ever been miserable, I planned for the future as if happiness were all there was; while in my moments of despair I could not even remember what happiness felt like, and the whole future was black.

I found also that this kind of thinking did really believe in its own power to alter fact. Several times when I had made some stupid mistake I caught my mind going over the incident again and again, as if by thinking hard enough what I ought to have done I could undo the mistake and make it as though it had not happened.

I then began to catch "butterflies" which showed me quite clearly that this kind of thinking also takes it for granted that oneself is something absolute and special, as if it could never really remember to take into account the existence of other minds. When troubles came to me I heard part of myself saying incredulously: "That this should have happened to ME! To think that *I* should have to find my life not as I would have chosen!" although I knew perfectly well that things of the same sort happen to everyone. And certainly my thought was quite oblivious of the private character of its ideas. It mistook them for things of such absolute importance that it was often filled with incredulous indignation when other people did not adapt themselves to suit it. Just as a child says, "Naughty table!" when it bumps its head, and thinks the wind is blowing "on purpose," so when my affairs were going badly I was constantly catching butterflies of resentment, attempts to make out that it was all So-and-so's *fault*. . . .

By now, therefore, I had sufficient experience of the workings of my own mind, backed up by whatever theoretical knowledge I had been able to absorb, to convince me of the necessity of continually admitting to myself in words those thoughts I was ashamed of. But being convinced that it was necessary did not mean that it was easy to do. I did learn very soon how to know the signs that would tell me when I was evading an unadmitted thought—worry, depression, headache, feelings of rush and over-busyness— but it took me much longer to learn ways of finding the thought that was causing the trouble. Part of my mind seemed in fact quite determined that I should not discover what the trouble was. [It] put up endless excuses and deceits; it would feign all manner of urgencies to distract my attention, like a bird pretending to trail a broken wing in order that intruders may be drawn away from her nest. Chief of these tricks of distraction was the making of most reasonable reasons to explain my own actions or desires, and the making of further reasons to explain why it was not necessary to look for any hidden thought, since the reason I was giving was so obviously adequate.

As a result of these observations I made myself two rules:

1. The cause of any overshadowing burden of worry or resentment is never what it seems to be.

Whenever it hangs over me like a cloud and refuses to disperse, then I must know that it comes from the area of blind thought and the real thing I am worrying about is hidden from me.

2. To reason about such feelings, either in oneself or others, is futile.

I now began to understand why it was no good arguing against obsessive fears or worries, for the source of them was beyond the reach both of reason and common sense. They flourished in the no man's land of mind where a thing could be both itself and something else at the same time, and the only way to deal with them was to stop all attemps to be reasonable and to give the thoughts free rein. In dealing with other people this meant just listening while they talked out whatever was in their minds; in dealing with myself it usually meant letting my thoughts write themselves.

Even when I had made this rule, however, the resistance against writing my thoughts at these times was still very strong. I would even occasionally have a vague sense of what absurdity was the real cause of my worry, but I would refuse to admit it, saying to myself: "There can't be anything un-reasonable in what I am doing, I know exactly why I am doing it; there's no earthly need to write, to look for a hidden reason, I *know* it's not that, I know exactly what it is"—and always the more certain I felt, the more certainly I was wrong.

My next task was, then, to find out what sort of ideas these were which it was such an urgent matter to keep hidden from myself, and how they came to be there.

From DIARY

by

ANAÏS NIN

(1903–1977)

Born in Paris in 1903, Anaïs Nin began her diary in the form of letters to her father, who had abandoned the family when she was eleven; it expanded to many volumes, of which five have been published. Nin also wrote short stories and literary criticism; she practiced briefly as a lay psychoanalyst in New York City in 1933 and lectured widely in this country, where she lived for the last years of her life.

• ─────────────────────────── •

[November 1933]

Rank had begun to consider the neurotic as a failed artist, as a creative personality gone wrong. Neurosis was a *malfunction of the imagination*. Rank did not treat neurotics with the contempt that some doctors did, as the old doctors treated insanity. . . .

First, he seized upon the diary as a shell, and as a defense. Then he asked me not to write it any more, and this was as difficult as asking a drug addict to do without his drugs. Not content with that, he asked me to live alone for a while, to disentangle my real self from all my "roles," to free myself of the constellation of relationships and identifications. . . . he took the image of today, the pattern of my life in the present. To come close to others I had surrendered many of my beliefs and attitudes. But closeness achieved by such compromises and abdications is not genuine.

When my father [a famous concert musician] appeared, I realized how many things I had been in rebellion against, in open mutiny, I should say, which had been merely a way to blaspheme, to desecrate, to repudiate his values, order, harmony, balance, and classical lucidity.

Dr. Rank immediately clarified my relationship to June. It was not Lesbianism. I was imitating my father, courting women.

"You replace the lost object of your love by imitating him. It was also an act of fear of man's sensuality which had caused you so much sorrow as a child." (I knew all the storms and wars at home were due to my father's interest in women.)

ANAÏS NIN

541

I *became* my father. I was the intellectual adviser of my mother. I wrote. I read books.

"And what about music?" asked Rank.

"No, music I repudiated. I don't know why. I love it, I have a strong emotional response to it, but I refused to become a musician."

Mental surgery, liberation of the instincts, the pure knowledge of deformation is not sufficient, as Allendy [her former analyst] carried it out. It is a process of creation. The analyst has to communicate, to impart the capacity to create, and for self-creation. He has in his favor the power to arouse faith, but no matter how profound his perception, the final effort had to be made by me.

Now, with Allendy, I felt that certain definite categorizations, overlooking the creative, the metaphysical, were reductions, in order to fit me into a general pattern.

Dr. Rank, on the contrary, expanded his insight.

With Allendy, I was an ordinary woman, a full human being, a simple and naïve one; and he would exorcise my disquietudes, vague aspirations, my creations which sent me out into dangerous realms.

Allendy took pains to delineate my character, my true nature, my human attitudes, but it was by a process of oversimplification. The mold into which he tried to fit me came to a climax the day he suggested I should take love more lightly, give it less importance, to evade tragedy. That I should take a playful attitude towards it. It should be sweet and casual, easygoing and interchangeable. "I will teach you to play, not to take it tragically, not to pay too heavy a price for it, to make it pleasant."

This was the natural conclusion to the formation of my human self, to normalcy; and if he was right about overcoming tragedy, *par contre,* he overlooked the deeper cravings of an artist, for whom deep full love is the only possible form, no simmering life but a boiling one, no small compromise with reality. He saw me as a Creole in a white negligee, New Orleans style, sitting on a rocking chair with a fan, feminine, awaiting light-footed lovers.

This conclusion put an end to my faith in Allendy. Whatever magic I had been able to find in analysis, whatever beneficial influence, was defeated by the kind of Anaïs this naturalness was leading me into. Rather than enter this ordinary life, which was death to my imagination (my grandmother's life!) and my creativity, I chose to retrogress into my neurosis and obsessions. Disease was, in this case, more inspiring and more fertile to poetry.

Dr. Rank agreed with me.

"You sought to preserve your creative instincts and what would nourish them. But neurosis itself does not nourish the artist, you know; he creates in spite of it, out of anything, any material given to him." . . .

He has understood the role of the diary. Playing so many roles, dutiful daughter, devoted sister, mistress, protector, my father's newfound illusion,

Henry's [novelist Henry Miller, a close friend] needed all-purpose friend, I had to find one place of truth, one dialogue without falsity.

When others asked the truth of me, I was convinced it was not the truth they wanted, but an illusion they could bear to live with. I was convinced of people's need of illusion. My father had to believe that, after rediscovering each other, we would abandon all our other relationships and devote our lives to each other. When he returned to Paris after the relaxation of the summer, his social life began, and he began to try and fit me into it. He wanted me to dress conventionally and discreetly, at the best of the *couturiers,* as Maruca did . . . neutral colors, English tailored suits in the morning, neatly cut and trimmed hair, every hair in place . . . and appear at his house, where the life resembled that of Jeanne, completely artificial, insincere, snobbish. My artist life was just the opposite. My artist friends liked slovenliness, even shabbiness. They were at ease, and would have been more so if *I* could have dressed indifferently, sloppily, casually, if my hair had been in disorder, my skirt pinned up, etc.

Somewhere in between lies Anaïs, who wants a free life but not a shabby one.

Rank immediately touched upon a vital point, the connection between the diary and my father. . . .

"You are right when you feel your father was trying to stress and reinforce the resemblances so that you would become duplicates, and then he could love his feminine self in you as you could love your male self in him. He was also the one who dared to be Don Juan. Didn't you tell me that he set out to possess more women than Don Juan, to surpass the legendary figure of a thousand mistresses? This, your double was doing for *you,* while you were loved by the men he might have wanted to be loved by, and so you could have been the perfect Androgyne.

"There is so much more in all this than the simple fact of incestuous longings. It is only one of the many variations upon the effort we make to unite with others; and when, for one reason or another, fusion with others has become difficult, one falls back again into the easiest one, the ready-made one, of blood affinities. It is only one of the millions of ways to palliate loneliness." . . .

. . . I felt Rank's influence, his sureness that the diary was bad for me. I knew immediately that I would show him all this, that everything is transparent to him because I wish it to be so. This is my fourth attempt at a truthful relationship. It failed with Henry because there is so much he does not understand; it failed with my father because he wants a world of illusion; it failed with Allendy because he lost his objectivity. . . . then Rank began to show me how my concept of woman was *mother*. To protect, serve, mother, care for. So it was the mother in me which found uses for her talents, but the woman? It was being such a mother that made me feel I was a woman.

[Martha] Jaeger, by being a woman, by her particular intuition as a woman, has caught a truth not known to any male analyst: the guilt for creating which is strong in woman. Creation linked with femininity and a threat to it. A threat to relation with man.

In a woman who loves man as much as I do, it becomes paralyzing. The feminine and the maternal having developed protection and nourishment, not war, destruction, or revolution for the sake of new worlds. I had guilt for writing about those I loved, exposing the character of the father. Henry never weighed the consequences of his portraits. I feel them as a danger to love.

Secrets. Need to disguise. The novel was born of this. If I used myself as a character it was because it was an experiment with the suitable object, as in chemistry. It is easy to work in one's own mine, to dig for oil or gold on one's own property. I never met any character but Henry capable of living out so much. The desire to know intimately drives one back into the only honest "I" who tested and lived out what it describes. . . .

I tried to efface my creation with a sponge, to drown my creation because my concept of devotion and the roles I had to play clashed with my creative self.

I opposed creation, its sincerity and revelation, to the disguised self. Creation and revelation threaten my loves; threatened the roles my love forced me to play. In love I played a role to give each man whatever he needed or wanted at the cost of my life. . . .

But Jaeger smiles. Guilt. Guilt everywhere.

I did not want to rival man. Man was my brothers, younger than I, Joaquin and Thorvald. I must protect them, not outshine them. I did not want to be a man. Djuna Barnes was masculine. George Sand.

I did not want to steal man's creation, his thunder.

Creation and femininity seemed incompatible. The *aggressive* act of creation.

"Not aggressive," said Jaeger, "*active.*"

I have a horror of the masculine "career" woman.

To create seemed to me such an assertion of the strongest part of me that I would no longer be able to give all those I love the feeling of their being stronger, and they would love me less.

An act of independence would be punished by desertion. I would be abandoned by all those I loved.

Men fear woman's strength. I have been deeply aware of men's weakness, the need to guard them from my strength.

I have made myself less powerful, have concealed my powers.

At the press, I make Gonzalo [a fellow artist] believe he has discovered this, he has suggested that improvement, that he is cleverer, stronger. I have concealed my abilities like an evil force that would overwhelm, hurt, or weaken others.

I have crippled myself.

Dreams of Chinese woman with bound feet.

I have bound myself spiritually.

I have associated creation with ruthlessness, absence of scruples, indifference to consequences as I see it in Henry. (His story about his father and mother, a cruel caricature.)

I see strongly creative women crush their men. I fear this. I have feared all aggressiveness, all attacks, all destruction. Above all, self-assertion.

Jaeger said: "All you are trying to do is to throw off this mother role imposed on you. You want a give-and-take relationship."

Jaeger, by being true to the woman, creating the woman in me, by her particular intuition as a woman, has penetrated truths not observed by either Allendy or Rank. The creator's guilt in me has to do with my femininity, my subjection to man.

Also with my maternal self in conflict with my creative self. A negative form of creation.

Also the content of my work is related to the demon in me, the adventure-loving, and I do feel this adventurousness a danger to my loves.

Guilt about exposing the father.

Secrets.

Need of disguises.

Fear of consequences.

Great conflict here. Division.

If only I could invent, invent other characters. Objective work which would not involve guilt. Rank said woman could not invent. Will begin to describe others minutely. I was more at ease with myself as a character because it is easier to excavate on one's own property. I could be used for all experiences, was protean, unlimited.

When I started out with an invented character, based always on someone I knew, and then sought to expand, I found myself inside restricted forms, limited outlines, characters who could not go far enough into experience. I felt in a tight mold, and returned to my experience which I tried to transpose into other women.

But this was a misconception. You do not get rid of the self by giving it away, by annihilation. When a child is uprooted it seeks to make a center from which it cannot be uprooted. That was a safety island, but now I must relinquish this too. . . .

Friday morning I went to Jaeger with all my notes on creation. My material is novel, and in a sense adds to an unsolved problem. Jaeger is concerned with this. It was more than analysis, I feel we are beginning to create together. She is my guide, but I can see that I am a good subject. I feel elated and strong because something is being created, and I feel something is being discovered which baffled men analysts. Rank always admitted that man-made psychology might not apply to woman. He honestly threw up his hands at Jaeger's problems.

What I consider my weaknesses are feminine traits: incapacity to destroy, ineffectualness in battle.

"I am the same," said Jaeger.

It is strange and wonderful that the analysis was conducted this time by way of the emotions. It was her feminine compassion, her feminine intuition which discovered the maternal complex, and the conflict before creation.

I represent, for other women too, the one who wanted to create with, by, and through her femininity.

I am a good subject because I have lived out everything, and because contrary to most creative women of our time I have not imitated man, or become man.

It is the creative self which will rescue me. Constitutionally I am more or less doomed to suffer, and I have had little relief from anxiety and doubts, but the displacement is taking place harmoniously and I am entering a larger realm.

Jaeger quoted the legend of the woman who was ordered to cross the river and would not, because she did not want to leave love behind. But when she finally crossed she found love on the other side. I brought up the fear of disconnection and solitude.

The evolution of woman. I am living it and suffering it for all women. I have loved as woman loves.

The process which takes place with Jaeger is one of flights into great depths and discoveries. She is helped by my articulateness, I am guided by her objectivity. She is inspired by the richness of my material, I am calmed and strengthened by her clairvoyance.

ERZULIE FREIDA

by

ZORA NEALE HURSTON

(1891?–1960)

*Born in Eatonville, Florida, an all-black town, Zora Neale Hurston
returned there after training as an anthropologist at Columbia University; her famous novel,* Their Eyes Were Watching God *(1937),
is set in Eatonville.* Mules and Men *(1935) is a record of her studies
of folklore in the Caribbean, and* Dust Tracks on the Road *(1942)
is her autobiography. A collection of other works,* I Love Myself
When I Am Laughing *(1979), was edited by Alice Walker. "Erzulie Freida" is from* Tell My Horse *(1938), a travel journal.*

•————————————————————•

[*1930?*]

Nobody in Haiti ever really told me who Erzulie Freida was, but they told
me what she was like and what she did. From all of that it is plain that she
is the pagan goddess of love. In Greece and Rome the goddesses of love
had husbands and bore children, Erzulie has no children and her husband
is all the men of Haiti. That is, anyone of them that she chooses for herself.
But so far, no one in Haiti has formulated her. As the perfect female she
must be loved and obeyed. She whose love is so strong and binding that it
cannot tolerate a rival. She is the female counterpart of Damballah [the
chief male god]. But high and low they serve her, dream of her, have visions
of her as of the Holy Grail. Every Thursday and every Saturday millions of
candles are lighted in her honor. Thousands of beds, pure in their snowy
whiteness and perfumed are spread for her. Desserts, sweet drinks, perfumes and flowers are offered to her and hundreds of thousands of men of
all ages and classes enter those pagan bowers to devote themselves to this
spirit. On that day, no mortal woman may lay possessive hands upon these
men claimed by Erzulie. They will not permit themselves to be caressed or
fondled even in the slightest manner, even if they are married. No woman
may enter the chamber set aside for her worship except to clean it and
prepare it for the "service." For Erzulie Freida is a most jealous female
spirit. Hundreds of wives have been forced to step aside entirely by her
demands.

She has been identified as the Blessed Virgin, but this is far from true.

Here again the use of the pictures of the Catholic saints have confused observers who do not listen long enough. Erzulie is not the passive queen of heaven and mother of anybody. She is the ideal of the love bed. She is so perfect that all other women are a distortion as compared to her. The Virgin Mary and all of the female saints of the Church have been elevated, and celebrated for their abstinence. Erzulie is worshipped for her perfection in giving herself to mortal man. To be chosen by a goddess is an exaltation for men to live for. The most popular Voodoo song in all Haiti, outside of the invocation to Legba [the god of the gate], is the love song to Erzulie.

Erzulie is said to be a beautiful young woman of lush appearance. She is a mulatto and so when she is impersonated by the blacks, they powder their faces with talcum. She is represented as having firm, full breasts and other perfect female attributes. She is a rich young woman and wears a gold ring on her finger with a stone in it. She also wears a gold chain about her neck, attires herself in beautiful, expensive raiment and sheds intoxicating odors from her person. To men she is gorgeous, gracious and beneficent. She promotes the advancement of her devotees and looks after their welfare generally. She comes to them in radiant ecstasy every Thursday and Saturday night and claims them.

Toward womankind, Erzulie is implacable. It is said that no girl will gain a husband if an altar to Erzulie is in the house. Her jealousy delights in frustrating all the plans and hopes of the young woman in love. Women do not "give her food" unless they tend toward the hermaphrodite or are elderly women who are widows or have already abandoned the hope of mating. To women and their desires, she is all but maliciously cruel, for not only does she choose and set aside for herself, young and handsome men and thus bar them from marriage, she frequently chooses married men and thrusts herself between the woman and her happiness. From the time that the man concludes that he has been called by her, there is a room in her house that the wife may not enter except to prepare it for her spiritual rival. There is a bed that she must make spotless, but may never rest upon. It is said that the most terrible consequences would follow such an act of sacrilege and no woman could escape the vengeance of the enraged Erzulie should she be bold enough to do it. But it is almost certain that no male devotee of the goddess would allow it to occur.

How does a man know that he has been called? It usually begins in troubled dreams. At first his dreams are vague. He is visited by a strange being which he cannot identify. He cannot make out at first what is wanted of him. He touches rich fabrics momentarily but they flit away from his grasp. Strange perfumes wisp across his face, but he cannot know where they came from nor find a name out of his memory for them. The dream visitations become more frequent and definite and sometimes Erzulie identifies herself definitely. But more often, the matter is more elusive. He falls ill, other unhappy things befall him. Finally his friends urge him to visit a houngan for a consultation. Quickly then, the visitor is identified as the goddess of love and the young man is told that he has been having bad luck because the goddess is angry at his neglect. She behaves like any other female when she is spurned. A baptism is advised and a "service" is instituted for the offended loa and she is placated and the young man's ill fortune ceases.

But things are not always so simply arranged. Sometimes the man chosen is in love with a mortal woman and it is a terrible renunciation he is called upon to make. There are tales of men who have fought against it valiantly as long as they could. They fought until ill luck and ill health finally broke their wills before they bowed to the inexorable goddess. Death would have ensued had they not finally given in, and terrible misfortune for his earthly inamorata also. However, numerous men in Haiti do not wait to be called. They attach themselves to the cult voluntarily. It is more or less a vow of chastity certainly binding for specified times, and if the man is not married then he can never do so. If he is married his life with his wife will become so difficult that separation and divorce follows. So there are two ways of becoming an adept of Erzulie Freida—as a "reclamé" meaning, one called by her, and the other way of voluntary attachment through inclination. . . .

The "baptism" or initiation into the cult of Erzulie is perhaps the most simple of all the voodoo rites. All gods and goddesses must be fed, of course, and so the first thing that the supplicant must do is to "give food" to Erzulie. There must be prepared a special bread and Madeira wine, rice-flour, eggs, a liqueur, a pair of white pigeons, a pair of chickens. There must be a white pot with a cover to it. This food is needed at the ceremony during which the applicant's head is "washed."

This washing of the head is necessary in most of their ceremonies. In this case the candidate must have made a natte (mat made of banana leaf-stems) or a couch made of fragrant branches of trees. He must dress himself in a long white night shirt. The houngan places him upon the leafy couch and recites three Ave Maria's, three Credos and the Confiteor three times. Then he sprinkles the couch with flour and a little syrup. The houngan then takes some leafy branches and dips them in the water in the white pot which has been provided for washing the head of the candidate. While the priest is sprinkling the head with this, the hounci and the Canzos are singing:

"Erzulie Tocan Freida Dahomey, Ce ou qui faut ce' ou qui bon
Erzulie Freida Tocan Maitresse m'ap mouter
Ce' ou min qui Maitresse."

["Erzulie Tocan Freida Dahomey, you are strong and you are good
Mistress Erzulie Tocan, I am going up
Yes, you are my mistress."]

ZORA NEALE HURSTON

549

The hounci and the adepts continue to sing all during the consecration of the candidate unassisted by the drums. The drums play *after* a ceremony to Erzulie, *never during* the service. While the attendants are chanting, the houngan very carefully parts the hair of the candidate who is stretched upon the couch. After the parted hair is perfumed, an egg is broken on the head, some Madeira wine, cooked rice placed thereon, and then the head is wrapped in a white handkerchief large enough to hold everything that has been heaped upon the head. The singing keeps up all the while. A chicken is then killed on the candidate's head and some of the blood is allowed to mingle with the other symbols already there. The candidate is now commanded to rise. This is the last act of the initiation. Sometimes a spirit enters the head of the new-made adept immediately. He is "mounted" by the spirit of Erzulie who sometimes talks at great length, giving advice and making recommendations. While this is going on a quantity of plain white rice is cooked—a portion sufficient for one person only, and he eats some of it. What he does not eat is buried before the door of his house.

The candidate now produces the ring of silver, because silver is a metal that has wisdom in it, and hands it to the houngan who takes it and blesses it and places it upon the young man's finger as in a marriage ceremony. Now, for the first time since the beginning of the ceremony, the priest makes the libation. The five wines are elevated and offered to the spirits at the four cardinal points and finally poured in three places on the earth for the dead, for in this as in everything else in Haiti, the thirst of the dead must be relieved. The financial condition of the applicant gauges the amount and the variety of the wines served on this occasion. It is the wish of all concerned to make it a resplendent occasion and there is no limit to the amount of money spent if it can be obtained by the applicant. Enormous sums have been spent on these initiations into the cult of Erzulie Freida. It is such a moment in the life of a man! More care and talent have gone into the songs for this occasion than any other music in Haiti. Haiti's greatest musician, Ludoric Lamotte, has worked upon these folk songs. From the evidence, the services to Erzulie are the most idealistic occasions in Haiti. It is a beautiful thing. Visualize a large group of upper class Haitians all in white, their singing voices muted by exaltation doing service to man's eternal quest, a pure life, the perfect woman, and all in a setting as beautiful and idyllic as money and imagination available can make it. "Erzulie, Nin Nin, Oh'!" is Haiti's favorite folk song.

I

"Erzulie ninnin, oh! hey! Erzulie ninnim oh, hey!
Moin senti ma pe' monte', ce moin minn yagaza.

["Godmother Erzulie, oh! hey! Godmother Erzulie, oh, hey!
I feel that I am going up, this is your godchild."]

"General Jean-Baptiste, oh ti parrain
Ou t'entre' lan caille la, oui parrain
Toutes mesdames yo a genoux, chapelette you
Lan main yo, yo pe' roule' mise' yo
Ti mouns yo a' genoux, chapelette you
Erzulie ninninm oh, Hey gran Erzulie Freida
Dague, Tocan, Mirorize, nan nan ninnin oh, hey
Movin senti ma pe' monte' ce' moin minn yagaza."

["General Jean-Baptiste, oh little godfather
You entered the house, yes godfather
All the women on their knees, their rosary beads
In their hands, calling their misery
The children on their knees, with their rosaries
Godmother Erzulie oh, Hey Grandma Erzulie Freida
Dague, Tocan, Mirorize, Godmother oh, hey
I feel that I am going up, this is your godchild."]

3

(Spoken in "Langage" recitative)

"Oh Aziblo, qui dit qui dit ce' bo yo
Ba houn bloco ita ona yo, Damballah Ouedo
Tocan, Syhrinise o Agoue', Ouedo, Pap Ogoun oh,
Dambala, O Legba Hypolite, Oh
Ah Brozacaine, Azaca, Neque, nago, nago pique cocur yo
Oh Loco, co loco, bel loco Ouedo, Loco guinea
Ta Manibo, Docu, Doca, D agoue' moinminn
Negue, candilica calicassague, ata, couine des
Oh mogue', Clemezie, Clemeille, papa mare' yo.

[Untranslatable African ritualistic terms]

4

"Erzulie, Ninninm oh, hey grann' Erzulie
Freida dague, Tocan Miroize, maman, ninninm oh, hey!
Moun senti ma pe' mouti', ce moin mimm yagaza, Hey!"

ZORA NEALE HURSTON

["Godmother, Erzulie oh, hey grandma Erzulie
Freida dague, Tocan Miroize, mother, godmother oh, hey!
I feel that I am going up, this is your godchild, Hey!"]

More upper class Haitians "make food" for Erzulie Freida than for any other loa in Haiti. Forever after the consecration, they wear a gold chain about their necks under their shirts and a ring on the finger with the initials E. F. cut inside of it. I have examined several of these rings. I know one man who has combined the two things. He has a ring made of a bit of gold chain. And there is a whole library of tales of how this man and that was "reclamé" by the goddess Erzulie, or how that one came to attach himself to the Cult. I have stood in one of the bedrooms, decorated and furnished for a visit from the invisible perfection. I looked at the little government employee standing there amid the cut flowers, the cakes, the perfumes and the lace covered bed and with the spur of imagination, saw his common clay glow with some borrowed light and his earthiness transfigured as he mated with a goddess that night—with Erzulie, the lady upon the rock whose toes are pretty and flowery.

From NOTES FOR MYSELF

by

MARIE NOËL

(1883–1967)

Marie Noël was the pseudonym of Marie-Melanie Rouget, who lived all her life in the provincial town of Auxerre, France. The oldest of four children and the only daughter, she assumed many house-hold responsibilities, which interfered with her writing time; how-ever, she wrote several volumes of poetry as well as keeping a jour-nal in which she recorded her lifelong struggle with religious doubts. She is respected in France as a poet, and the translation of her journal into English has increased her reputation in the United States as well.

• ——————————————————— •

[I] *1920–1933*

How often poetry has welled up in me like bubbling water wanting to break through the stones of a walled-up fountain!

Alas! in the hour of grace, everything stood in its way: the house which, at that precise moment, needed attention, my elderly mother who needed my presence, brothers and sisters who asked for counsel, a child who asked for music and pictures, and all the other people in the neighbor-hood, each of whom asked for something in turn.

My poetry called for leisure.—I pushed it aside.—It has had only what others left.

Except when I was ill, the best time of all, for no one could take that from me. . . .

Eternal life? Yes. Life can only be eternal.

But individual immortality?

The mere fact of passing outside time so modifies the soul that it is no longer recognizable. If time and space—the two essential modes of our thinking—are removed from us, what will remain?

What is eternity, life without time or place? Nonexistence, perhaps.

Relative, not total, nonexistence. (There is something other than this conscious, definite, limited self. There is Being.)

Nonexistence comparable to the "Night" of ecstasy, in which all the faculties—memory, imagination, thought, reason—have disappeared; outside time, outside space, the breath of God, the impalpable soul which reaches God because it first comes from God, returns to God, is fused with God.

Ecstasy enables me to understand death, beatitude. It is accompanied by the momentary destruction of the person. In ecstasy there is no more time or place, man has crossed over, gone outside himself.

Perhaps death is an eternal ecstasy.

Or the total rejection by the soul of all that was not God . . . into "outer darkness."

The smaller our souls, the more completely we will disappear.

The greater our souls, the more completely we will be saved. . . .

The family . . . great peril for strong souls. It bends them to its prejudices, its interests, its affections; it asphyxiates them, sterilizes them for its benefit. The great Saints broke with all.

And Christ?

"Why were you looking for me? Know you not that I must be about my father's business? . . ."

"Those who hear my word are my father, my mother, my brothers, my sisters. . . ."

"Lord, permit me first to go bury my father." "Let the dead bury the dead."

Through the family, for the family and those around me, I have endangered—perhaps lost—my soul and my work.

Forgive me, Lord! Save me still. Consider that my greatest weakness was pity.

July 1930.

Death of a little girl. Her agony. The desperate appeal of her eyes, of her breathing.

After that, look at God. . . .

God. I have given our little girl back to Him. She had eyes that were afraid, a heart that fluttered. It is better to gather in early children like her in order to shelter them from their tears.

Weeping, the heart assents. The mind blinds itself, tramples on itself, and accepts. But there is further on, deeper down, an ageless soul, as devoid of faith as the first animal on the earth, before the Testaments and the revelations, a mother's cry, flesh which laments because this other bit of flesh has been pursued, tracked down, seized, strangled without pity.

She begged for mercy! There was no mercy. She called for her father. There was no father.

What is God? . . . What is God? . . .

Hindrances to writing, thinking, or even praying, this is my daily life.

More and more I am the victim of a disorderly situation which I am powerless to remedy: my elderly mother ill all winter, a neurotic servant, a big old-fashioned house—Twelve bedrooms!—And we have twelve tenants in several other houses. I am the sole manager. A very poor one. The houses are very old and shabby. I am always having to run after the mason or the plumber. . . . And then there are the legal documents and tax forms that take so much time.

If I were alone, I would get rid of a part of this burdensome heritage, but, deprived of "that which alone is needful to me," I live like a poor servant beneath the weight of the family possessions. . . .

[III]   *1934–1936*

My name, my place among men: Surplus.

"Surplus in the flock."
Surplus in the household.
Surplus in friendship.

Never "first in some heart," never essential, never alone needful for some being, some soul, some life . . . whatever betide . . . on earth or in heaven. . . .

Surplus.

Nearly all the people of my age and class—especially those who write—have traveled, seen the world, visited cities, met people, attended theaters, gone to museums, heard the wonderful music of which I am always dreaming: Salzburg . . . Mozart . . . *Figaro* . . . *The Magic Flute*. . . .

And *Pelléas!*

But I, as long as I was young, spent Sunday after Sunday at the Church Club, and now that I am older, every Sunday for many years I have gone and gone with mamma to visit my aunt.

In seclusion in a good, faithful country house, tied down by duties, closely watched by the old people, cut off from the universe and even from nearby places. . . .

I have had only God for space.

In Him I have secured my liberty, my highways, I have dared my mountains and my precipices, I have risked like others, more than any other, my adventures and my perils. . . .

MARIE NOËL

When I was fifteen, I often prayed at night. I kneeled down, and God sometimes spoke to me.

One night when I had found Him prepared to grant me anything, I asked Him for three things all at once:

> To suffer greatly,
> To be a poet,
> To be a saint,

because at that time it seemed to me that nothing could be nobler.

Forthwith it appeared to me that He placed in my hands the three seeds of the three kinds of greatness.

Suffer greatly. This he gave to me. I did not know what it was! He gave it to me. I had only to say "yes." I have said "yes." Always.

Be a poet. This he gave to me. I have half lost it.

Oh! He has not been niggardly in his Grace. All my life, continually, He has sown in me the seeds of poetry. Some have sprouted and borne fruit. But the greater part died, choked by thorns . . . thorns? no! vegetables! Good vegetables, good useful plants, good works in the family, in the household, in society, all the innumerable duties that have crowded out my duty to myself.

I have always feared that what was *me* and *mine* was less God's will than what belonged to others.

Be a saint. This God gave to me. I have lost it.

I have not given up everything for Him, ardently, madly, as, ardent and mad, I might have done.

Perhaps I have loved Him above all things, but I have not loved Him alone. I have loved all things. And I have lost the grace of being a saint, unless there be a beginning of saintliness in the perpetually wounded submission, the continual surrender of myself that, out of love for Christ, I have accorded to what in others was so "different," so alien to me!

Thus God's two gifts of poetry and saintliness, which He so marvellously bestowed on my youth, have opposed each other all my life: as if there were, in every vocation, one God who cheats and foils the other.

I have not known to which God, to which form of God, I should dedicate myself. And I do not know which God will condemn me, will pardon me, on the last day, when my only defense will be to give back a single one of the three gifts: suffering.

Old wives' moral. . . . You can't chase two hares—you can't climb two mountains—at the same time.

NOTES ON MY WORK

Inspiration

In the beginning, the meeting.
Fresh delight, like finding a mushroom in a meadow.
Sudden birth. A song comes to me. . . .
This usually happens to me when, after a troubled period, I am laden
with anguish or disquietude. As if suffering gave to my inmost recesses a
blow of a pickax that rends me, tears me, scars me, and causes to well
up in me the living spring of poetry.
A song is born in me. . . . It knows and says nothing of the birth
pangs . . . it is ignorant of my sorrow today . . . it is full of another hurt
which, underneath life, one does not see, as one does not see, under the
ground, the roots of plants.
A song is born in me, song of all ages, as it was doubtless born in the
girls and women of old who sang of their life while they spun—sweetheart,
betrothed, deserted, mismarried, widow, mother bereaved of her child—
who sang of their life without telling it in songs which were for a moment
songs about them, belonging to them, before they were nobody's, everybody's songs.

> Mon père m'y a marié'
> Il est temps de nous en aller . . .

> [My father has given me away
> It is time to go away . . .]

I should like for a tender or sorrowful girl, long after me, to remember
one of my songs without knowing who composed it, as if it were she
herself. . . .

1951.

Someone asked me recently with what religious Order I had drunk so
deeply from liturgical sources.
Until recent years I had never spoken to a monk or a nun, never set
foot in the parlor of an abbey.
But my grandmother was one of those old Frenchwomen who sang
Vespers every Sunday, Complin on feast days, and who followed scrupu-
lously in their big old yellow-leaved missals the Tenebrae of Holy Week
and the High Matins of Christmas and Allhallows.
I was not more than nine. She took me with her. It was for me the

MARIE NOËL

557

entrance into a sublime world, outside the other world, where God and man exchanged unheard-of words that had no meaning in other lands.

On the evening of Allhallows, at six o'clock, we both penetrated into the fathomless Night of the Cathedral, which at this hour, under the soaring vaults, had neither beginning nor end.

There were few worshipers on the chairs. From the portal to the altar, the entire church was hung with the black of state funerals, dimly lit in the choir by a few frightened candles flickering in the semi-darkness.

In the tower, the knell tolled . . . the wonderful knell of the Cathedral of Auxerre, tragic group of deep-throated bells that suddenly burst into sobs—five or six heart-rending notes—then relapsed into silence, from which they again emerged, after a few anguished moments, with the dark tears they had gone to draw from some hidden well of grief and fear.

I tremblingly awaited the return of these poignant bells. . . . Meanwhile, we chanted with the priests the psalms of David and the lamentations of Job. I heard there—at the age of nine—the inconsolable cry of man. It entered me then and has never since left me. . . .

From GIFTS OF POWER

by

REBECCA JACKSON

(17??–1871)

*A religious visionary in the Shaker tradition, Rebecca Jackson was
born in Philadelphia; though her diary was not known until this
century, she made her mark in her lifetime as an independent
itinerant preacher. Her spiritual awakening at thirty-five, which lead
her to learn to read so that she could understand the Bible on her
own, was met with disapproval by many. However, she won many
followers and left behind a black Shaker community she had
founded.*

•———————————————————•

. . . I can truly say that my prayers have been answered again and again,
for which I give the glory to that God to whom it belongs. I am only a pen
in His hand. Oh, that I may prove faithful to the end.

[*1831?*]

The Gift of Reading

A remarkable providence of God's love for me. After I received the blessing
of God, I had a great desire to read the Bible. I am the only child of my
mother that had not learning. And now, having the charge of my brother
and his six children to see to, and my husband, and taking in sewing for
a living, I saw no way that I could now get learning without my brother
would give me one hour's lesson at night after supper or before he went to
bed. His time was taken up as well as mine. So I spoke to him about it. He
said he would give me one or two lessons, I being so desirous to learn.
(He was a tolerable scholar, so that he was able to teach his own children
at home, without sending them to school. For a time, he fulfilled the offices
of seven men in the Methodist church. And when he ceased from this, he
worked hard and earned his bread by the sweat of his brow.) And my
brother so tired when he would come home that he had not power so to do,
and it would grieve me. Then I would pray to God to give me power over
my feelings that I might not think hard of my brother. Then I would be
comforted.

So I went to get my brother to write my letters and to read them. So he was awriting a letter in answer to one he had just read. I told him what to put in. Then I asked him to read. He did. I said, "Thee has put in more than I told thee." This he done several times. I then said, "I don't want thee to *word* my letter. I only want thee to *write* it." Then he said, "Sister, thee is the hardest one I ever wrote for!" These words, together with the manner that he had wrote my letter, pierced my soul like a sword. (As there was nothing I could do for him or his children that I thought was too hard for me to do for their comfort, I felt hurt, when he refused me these little things. And at this time,) I could not keep from crying. And these words were spoken in my heart, "Be faithful, and the time shall come when you can write." These words were spoken in my heart as though a tender father spoke them. My tears were gone in a moment.

One day I was sitting finishing a dress in haste and in prayer. This word was spoken in my mind, "Who learned the first man on earth?" "Why, God." "He is unchangeable, and if He learned the first man to read, He can learn you." I laid down my dress, picked up my Bible, ran upstairs, opened it, and kneeled down with it pressed to my breast, prayed earnestly to Almighty God if it was consisting to His holy will, to learn me to read His holy word. And when I looked on the word, I began to read. And when I found I was reading, I was frightened—then I could not read one word. I closed my eyes again in prayer and then opened my eyes, began to read. So I done, until I read the chapter. I came down. "Samuel, I can read the Bible." "Woman, you are agoing crazy!" "Praise the God of heaven and of earth, I can read His holy word!" Down I sat and read through. And it was in James. So Samuel praised the Lord with me. When my brother came to dinner I told him, "I can read the Bible! I have read a whole chapter!" "One thee has heard the children read, till thee has got it by heart." What a wound that was to me, to think he would make so light of a gift of God! But I did not speak. Samuel reproved him and told him all about it. He sat down very sorrowful. I then told him, "I had a promise, the day thee wrote my letter to sister Diges, that if I was faithful I would see the day when I can write." (I repeated this conditional promise to him at the time and said then "I will write thee a letter." He said, he had no doubt of it. This soon after took place.) So I tried, took my Bible daily and praying and read until I could read anywhere. The first chapter that I read I never could know it after that day. I only knowed it was in James, but what chapter I never can tell.

Oh how thankful I feel for this unspeakable gift of Almighty God to me! Oh may I make a good use of it all the days of my life!

[*1843*]

Then I woke and found the burden of my people heavy upon me. I had borne a burden of my people for twelve years, but now it was double, and I cried unto the Lord and prayed this prayer, "Oh, Lord God of Hosts, if

Thou art going to make me useful to my people, either temporal or spiritual,—for temporally they are held by their white brethren in bondage, not as bound man and bound woman, but as bought beasts, and spiritually they are held by their ministers, by the world, the flesh, and the devil. And if these are not a people in bondage, where are there any on the earth?—Oh, my Father and my God, make me faithful in this Thy work and give me wisdom that I may comply with Thy whole will."

This was March the 12th, 1843, in [a house in] Albany, New York State.

March 13th, I laid down and slept. When I woke the wind was blowing as if it would seize the house into the air. And I was afraid of the suffering of my body under the moving of the house. And in this feeling, I prayed to the Lord to give me strength. And in a few minutes, I was brought into the shower of flowers. And as I looked through, I seen the blessed saints come through the flowers. And I was in the house that I was, in the dream the night before. So it pleased the Lord to show me in a dream and prepare me for this heavenly interview.

These saints came until they filled the house, and the wind was ablowing as if it would destroy everything on the earth. They told me that they came to comfort me, and to give me understanding. The wind, they told me, this was the way God made known his power to his little ones in these last days. For this wind could not hurt his saints, for the Holy Ghost carried them over all danger. And if the house was lifted into the air, I would be carried over all and be made happy (in the wind as they were in it coming to me. While they were talking I was made happy). And the wind was to me like a shower of glory. And they carried me away with them. And when I found myself again, I woke out of a sweet sleep. It was morning, and the wind was not unusual for a high wind. And oh, the blessed instruction that them blessed saints gave me! May I never forget it, but live to the glory of God in all things!

March 24, 1843, at supper, it pleased the Lord to give me the following lines.

The Lord is good to them that serve Him.
Oh how good, oh how good.
He will save us from all danger,
Oh how good, oh how good.

The Lord will save the soul that serves Him,
Oh how good, oh how good.
He will give them peace forever,
Oh how good, oh how good.

He will clear the way before them,
Oh how good, oh how good.

REBECCA JACKSON

561

He will give them strength and wisdom,
For to conquer, for to conquer.

Let us hasten then to serve Him,
Oh how sweet, oh how sweet.
He has filled me like a bottle,
With new wine, with new wine.

For to empty unto others,
Oh how precious, oh how precious.
Oh that I may be so faithful,
As to finish, as to finish.

And then soar away into Heaven,
Into glory, into glory,
There to see my Blessed Savior,
Whom I love here, oh how I love here.

This is the first spiritual song given to me, that I have been permitted to write, and when I received it, I was forty-eight years, one month, and nine days old. Though I had often received heavenly songs and sung them in the spirit, they were taken away, and then given me again as was needful. . . .

From THE DIARY OF
AROZINA PERKINS

by

AROZINA PERKINS

(1826–1854)

Arozina Perkins's love of her native Vermont mountains gave her a longing for freedom and beauty; her decision at twenty-five to go west to teach resulted from that longing and from a missionary faith in teaching and strong religious feelings. Though often homesick and discouraged in the pioneer community she served in Iowa, she achieved success as a teacher. She died at twenty-eight, having been rejected by her fiancé after her brother was jailed for a crime that was not named in her writings.

·———————————————·

[*S. Marshfield, Mass. Sept. 1850.*]

Remembrances of long ago.

"Look at that child's bare feet and tattered garments! How *could* you kiss the little vagrant? That is a new coin for charity, methinks!" Hush, hush, friend, you forget that we ourselves were once children. Think of the guilelessness of your own heart then, and how the fount of your warm affections was stirred up by a kindly look or a loving word, and chilled by harshness and neglect. That child has a *soul* struggling within that humbly clad form, and beaming from her bright, blue eyes—we may not know the richness and beauty of the gem—the delicate "shading of its ever varying lustre: its fleeting lines lie all too deep for mortal gaze, but, dim it by unkindness, and you leave a rust that will forever mar its shape and clearness."

Has the memory of a look never haunted you thro' long years, and as the same brow may beam upon you now, will not the remembrance of the cloud of long ago not cast a shadow over it? Oh, childhood's heart is deep, and impressions made at that early period, when the judgment is not strong enough to suggest reasons and weigh appearances, will often endure, and mould the character to coldness and distrust when all else, save the careless eye that gave the glance of scorn and the tongue that uttered the bitter word, is forgotten. Could we recall all the incidents of our childish years, the little wounds our sensitive natures then received, traced from these seemingly trivial causes thro' long years of tho't and action and feeling, might perhaps teach us the vastness of their effects upon our past and present conduct and sentiments. Would parents think of the delicate workings of their own spirits in childhood, how cautious would they be in word and example, and how prayerfully would they strive to lead their young charge aright. And *teachers* too, would *they* but sometimes smile upon the child of poverty, 'twould wake to life a host of affection's flowers, and cast a sunbeam far into the future.— —

You have often chided me for my reserve. Do you know any of the causes of it? I could tell you a little tale that might bring a smile to your lip, perhaps, you would deem it so insignificant, but the results have been too grave and lasting to myself to raise a tho't of merriment.— — You remember Mr. [E. M.] T[oo]f, who was preceptor in our little village Academy. He was, no doubt, a good teacher, and his sternness might have had a salutary effect upon the minds of some of his pupils, but upon mine it had a fearful influence.

I was a child, and had been told by partial friends that I was a *grand reader,* and consequently, my first day under his tuition, I went confidently through my sentence in the class—did my best—and looked to him for his approbation. But instead of bestowing one word of praise upon my childish endeavors he turned them into ridicule, and provokingly said I "read like a rabbit eating beans," which caused such a laugh among the grown up young ladies and gentlemen around me that I bent my head to the desk and wept.

I know I read rapidly, and should have been corrected, but in a very different manner; and had he told me so kindly, and shewed me how to improve, I would have strained every nerve to have complied, but I was from that time a changed being. As reading was the first exercise in the afternoon I ever after had an excuse for being tardy till the forty minutes devoted to it had expired. Had I not possessed a perfect mania for study, this circumstance might have made me hate the sight of a teacher, or school-house. As it was, I went in determined however *never* to *read* again, and if I happened accidentally a few minutes too early, I always waited in the hall, till the rattle of slates, and steps of the teacher assured me that the dreaded task was over. No doubt Mr. T[oof] wondered, but I was invariably so punctual in the morning, and conned my lessons all so diligently that he ceased to reprove me for my tardiness. If he suspected the cause, he never mentioned it. Oh had he done so kindly, how much after suffering it might have prevented. For it was not till months, yes, years after, when, as that teacher was succeeded by others, that I overcame my fearful timidity sufficiently to get up in school and read a sentence without trembling. And, you may smile, but it was even the burthen of my childish prayers that this dreaded fearfulness might be removed. My friends were surprised that I, who had even been so fond of reading them stories heretofore, should so suddenly refuse to articulate a sentence to them from a book.

Do you think this strange? yet 'tis true, and may, perhaps, account for some of my oddities, for, tho' I eventually overcame my bashfulness in this respect, yet reserve and timidity cling to me, and ever will, and the want of confidence it occasioned in my own abilities; has been *the bane of my life*.

This little incident caused me almost to dislike that teacher, and when, a few days after, I placed my hand so as to conceal a bright, new *patch* on my old, faded calico dress, as I passed his desk coming in from recess, it was thro' fear of him, and not shame of my poverty.

— I could have loved Mrs. T.———for I always idolized my teachers, but the glance of her grey eye was cold and proud, and a dread came over me as the hour came around for reciting my daily lesson to her. And tho' she often praised my diligence and progress, I know she loved me less than my classmate, Alma, for the world's cruel distinction was between us. *Her* parents were wealthy—*mine* poor. But in the simplicity of our young hearts, *we* loved each other fondly. How shameful that republicans should attempt to play the aristocratic. (Mrs. T.'s mother was a washerwoman report said, yet the daughter, who if she behaved properly, would have derived honor therefrom, in my opinion, inasmuch as she had been able amid many difficulties to gain an education sufficient to place her in the responsible position of preceptress, still chose to act the lofty and dignified, and said "there should be two *classes* in *society*." Which class she would place herself in, or me either, I did not inquire then, for I was a child.) *Now* I can only laugh at her airs, but then I was too young to perceive the ridiculous in it, and was only impressed with the *awe* her presence inspired. Perhaps my organ of reverence was developed earlier than that of mirthfulness, which may account for it.

Well, to proceed: among the poor, economy is a virtue that springs from necessity, and as I was the youngest born, the *mantle* of my elder sisters sometimes fell in my direction, and about this time a white dress had been made over for me. It was a bright, smiling morning in summer and the Phebe sang merrily in the tree that grew on the little island near the bridge in the middle of the stream as I took my Grammar and Fables and danced gaily to recitation: for I studied at home that I might have more time to assist my mother. I had on the simple, snowy robe, remade in modern style, low, and with short sleeves, but the *material* was antique, and the skirt, which had been cut in *gores,* remained the same. Now I should have positively forgotten whether I had on a bark blanket, or a princess' purple, when I sat down to my lesson, had I not caught the eye of Mrs. T. roving in a curious expression over my new dress—and noticed a haughty curl on her proud lip which I shall never forget. With the lofty air of a martyr I went through the lesson while Mrs. T. smiled, and Alma wondered "how I could spell and pronounce those many syllabled, accented French words" which she missed, and was "sure she never could get thro' with."

My step homeward was rather more measured than it had been an hour before, and I made some resolutions in my little head which have extended to this day. One was, to *despise arrogance;* and another was to wear what I pleased, if it corresponded with my circumstances, and never to censure others for doing the same. Another was, to consider the adorning of the person nothing in comparison with the importance of improving the mind. And this last decision carried me thro' years of study in some old, worn out, faded calico, or the remains of a once handsome gingham, *fitted* to myself by my own unskillful hands, without a thought of discontent or envy of those whose fathers' means enabled them to appear in better garments; happy if I could only carry out the plan I had formed to get knowledge.— —

Faint, yet pursuing.

How much is comprehended in these three words. A volume of meaning, sufficient for the motto of a lifetime, lies folded up in them. That was a cheering discourse that Rev. Mr. Newcomb gave us from this text, and I tho't the speaker himself must have been actuated by the same active principles that he labored to imbue others with.

Faint, yet pursuing, faint with exertion, toil, faint with the view of difficulties before and about us, faint with the strife to overcome our own sinful natures, faint with the reproaches of the wordling, yet should we press onward, heeding no discouragements, yielding not to our feelings of depression but continue steadily and unremittingly, if slowly, to follow the great line of duty that is marked out to us.

Faint, yes, I am often faint, and feel my utter weakness and incapacity to accomplish aught that is good. I am faint, and falter in my efforts to discountenance slander, faint in attempting to explain my motives to the understanding of others. I am faint, wandering homeless in this cold world, often alone and without sympathy. Faint, when I look around and see the vice that is prevalent in all places, and *faint* when I consider the deceitfulness of my own heart. Still ought I to proceed, still speak and act for truth, still wander on and murmur not, for the orphan's God is mine. *Israel's* Guide will lead *me* too, if I trust in Him, faint yet pursuing, thro' every trial, every danger. Then shall this [be] my device, and when, wearied, and sick and faint, and almost ready to sink by the way, I'll struggle on— yet pursuing.— —

The sunset. Most winning and beautiful did our pastor delineate the charactor of Christ tonight, and never seemed these words more full of meaning—Except Ye have the *Spirit* of *Christ* ye are none of his. And then, with holy fervor he told us of that Spirit of humility, of meekness and forbearance, of benevolence, of *Love,* till his cheek glowed and his eye beamed with the greatness of his theme, and tears sprang into my own eyes as I traced the contrast with my own wicked spirit. Thoughtfully I walked homeward—the sun was just declining from the edge of the horizon, and a dark, purple cloud was heaving above it and stretched far away into the clear cerulean of heaven. It was edged with a fringe of the brightest silver light, and, as the orb of day rolled his car out of sight, there remained in his track a massy wreath of the most gorgeously colored hues that I ever beheld, and, as gradually those golden billows changed and mingled into one, they assumed the form of a large, most intensely brilliant T, pictured out in fine relief from its richly tinted ground. Long, broad streaks, of pure, pearly white, centred, like the spirit of Love and Union, in that far, western point, and the sky above was dashed with tiny touches, delicately shaded as the inner surface of the sea shell. I never witnessed a more beautiful scene, and I fancied that immense, cloud wreathed T the very embodyment of *Truth*, high, sublime, glorious TRUTH!

As this evening drapery faded, the moon gained lustre, and threw fair light and soft shadows round, and the sad toned Whip-poor-will repeated his mournful song with unvarying monotony.

— — L. A. Tilden has been with us a day or two, and we were busy in remembrances of the summer we spent together.

— — I have just been thinking of the *West,* and, unconsciously, I confess that a moment of weakness came over me, and for the first time a shudder spread thro' my frame at the idea of going *alone.* But it was soon passed, and altho' it would be pleasant to have friends accompany me, yet we cannot expect to have all we wish for here—and *faint* yet pursuing I'll go on.

— — Jane saw a rainbow last night made by the *moon* against a very dark cloud, and *white* in its curve: it must have been beautiful. It was about eight or nine o'clock in the evening. Don't know that I ever heard before that the moon *could* make rainbows.

Finished my drawing class. They have seemed very much interested, and progressed finely.

— — Every day proves to me that there is nothing of an earthly nature worth living for—hopes and anticipations—all what are they? but the shadow of the sunset cloud, bright and beautiful, but passing away.

Partings again—how can I endure them? Here I have just learned to love some whose acquaintance I commenced the first few months I spent in Marshfield, and now is to be broken off again abruptly, and perhaps never again be resumed. My life seems like a strange, bewildered dream. 'Tis like the zephyr's harp. I just begin a strain of low, sweet music, when a sudden blast will sweep the chords, and, ere the echo dies away, 'tis broken by the tones of many high and lofty strains that tremble, blend, then die. My harp is waked by every breath, stirred by the tones and words that scarce could move the vibrations of other strings. There seems a struggling to express the music of the spirits and if some gentle hand calls forth an answering strain, a rougher one will drown the harmony and cause a discord there.

— Now, the time to which I have been looking forward is come. I go to meet the class at Hartford, preparatory to labors in the West.—A fond farewell to friends, and prayers for their happiness.

[*Enroute to Iowa, Nov. 8, 1850*]

. . . I was deeply impressed with the stillness and solitude that pervaded the whole vast expanse. *Here* was grandeur—sublimity even; and, amid the luxuriance of Spring and Summer, there must be the strange, wild beauty too, I gazed and gazed upon the "circling vastness." It seemed

> "As if an ocean, in its gentlest swell
> Stood still, with all its rounded billows fixed,
> And motionless forever."

I was in the centre of a wide Western Prairie, and one of the many dreams of my early days was being realized; and for a time I was happy. I tho't how often, when a schoolgirl, I had traced out on the map the very spot upon which I now stood, while my mind was filled with imaginings of its wildness, and tho'ts of future devotedness to the cause of Truth and Education here. I was *happy* in the exercise of that foreshadowed *devotedness now*, and prayed that *it* might be *pure* and *holy*.

[*Fort Des Moines, Iowa, November 13, 1850.*]

About eight o'clock in the evening I reached my destination. C. McK[ay] Esq. was at the tavern and accompanied me to his brother's [Judge McKay]. I must have been *unexpected*, for I fancied there was much coolness in my reception; but *that* I did not heed much, for tho' I had been six long weeks on the way, and was wearied and worn with fatigue, and the warmth of kindness *would* have seemed cheering, yet I was not in a sensitive mood just then. I had been sped in the swift moving car, tossed upon the heaving, tumultuous bosom of Erie, threaded the windings of the Ohio and ascended awhile the broad stream of the Mississippi; I had been racked and *churned* nearly 200 miles in mud wagons and hacks, and *now,* as I was at the end of the race there were obligations of gratitude in my heart for my safe preservation too great to admit one tho't of murmuring because strangers did not *immediately* regard me with the love and affection of my friends at home. God has been exceedingly good and merciful to me; and when I reflect upon *all* His providences, and how many dear and kind friends, have been formed to me from strangers, hitherto, I'll not distrust him now.

The next morning C. McKay, called, and we went out upon a hill whence was a fine view of the town and surrounding country.

Mr. McKay lives in a brick house, pretty comfortable, too, for this region. It has three rooms, while the majority of dwellings here have but one. We had, for breakfast, wild turkey, cold, and warm. For dinner, turkey and squirrels. Next day a dish of venison.

Saturday, I wrote all day to B[arnabas].

Sabbath, attended Rev. Mr. Bird's meeting holden at the Court House. The room was filled. There is but one church here, and that belongs to the Methodists.

Monday evening.

Felt *lonely,* extremely so.

Tuesday.

A fine day, walked with Judge McK. to town.

Wednesday.

Commenced a cloak for Mrs. McK.

Thursday.

C—— called; very kindly offered me his services.

Friday afternoon.

Judge McK. has just returned from hunting, with two, great wide-eyed *owls.* I wondered if they were going to make us *eat them,* too. *Guess* I could *see* into *dark* things *then;* perhaps be able to disentangle the snarl of my *school* prospects! Oh, yes, I might then be *visionary* in reality.

I have found matters here very different from my expectations with regard to the *wants* of the people. Mrs. Bird has a new schoolhouse just completed, and the only one in town, and a school of about forty children. Of this I was totally ignorant until since I came here. There is a district school three months in the year, usually during the winter, and one of the trustees commenced it at the Court House, but the other two objecting to his terms, and, determined to have a school on a cheap scale, hired another man, and turned Mr. G. out of the house. Upon examining their teacher, however, he proved a complete ignoramus, and they had to look about for another. The school where I expected, in case of emergency, to find *"certain"* employment, was engaged: by some mistake, or misunderstanding, *two* teachers were employed; one of whom, learning the fact, gave up, and offered his services here. The other had been dismissed unknown to the other, and thus *that* school was *teacherless. This* I did not learn however until *I* commenced. Well, the gentleman was examined, and Y. says he knew no more than the first one, only that he knew enough to keep his ignorance from the other two of the trustees. *He* would not sign his certificate, and if he persists in refusing to do so, I do not know as it can be considered that he is lawfully employed. Mr. Y[oung] called on me the day he was "unhoused," spoke very discouragingly of my commencing a school, and, certainly, I never have been so puzzled to determine what is duty. Had I known the state of things here I think I would have taken Mr. Williams' and R.'s kind advice, and remained [in Keokuk], or gone to Montebello.

But I was here now, and it wo'd be silly as well as impractical to get back; and after thinking and praying over the subject, I finally concluded to begin and teach this winter, at least, tho' tuition is so low, and board and all necessary expenses so high, that I may not even clear *them*. I went to Mr. Bird's on purpose to get his advice. He and his wife were very kind to me, but I could perceive that my coming had troubled them. They need not fear that *I* shall undermine *their* school. It seems that their friends have tho't this was my object, or the object of some one in getting me here. Oh Sectarianism! when will your votaries cease their dissensions?

I have almost been tempted to believe there is *no* regard for *truth* among the western people; and now, shall never expect when I am told a thing here, to find it *is* so, and I have almost come to the conclusion to place confidence in *no one* again, except in Him in whom all Truth dwells. I told Mr. B[ird] my circumstances, and that necessity alone compelled me to do something, yet if I should in the least interfere with Mrs. B. I would sooner return to Montebello (for I tho't I might perhaps *borrow* the means.) I wished that friend C[andee] who was instrumental alone in getting me here knew all the trouble I was in. I can blame no one but myself for coming so far with no other assurance than that contained in Judge McK.'s letter to Gov. S[lade] that, "if she will come I will see that she *does* want for anything while she remains." The omission was accidental, of course; but the class had quite a laugh over it, and I tho't very probably that it might be verified, tho' not in the sense in which it has been. That is, I did not expect to "want" for a *school*.

Yet it *may* be all for the best that I am here—the dealings of Providence are mysterious, and

> "There's a Divinity that shapes our ends,
> Rough-hew them how we will."

The morning after my arrival, I overheard the people in the kitchen talking of my prospects, and so forth, and some one remarked "She wishes she was at home, I reckon." No, I did not; I tho't there was a wise purpose, hidden to us, in it all, and resolved to go forward trustingly and meekly, and I knew that the Lord would sustain me.

I think Gov. S. and Mrs. Grosvenor would have been interested, and my Eastern friends, who tried to dissuade me from the "wild notion" of coming out here, would have laughed, to have witnessed the scene that morning of Monday the 25th of Nov. at the little Methodist church of Fort Des Moines.

Judge McK. was industriously *kindling a fire* in a tall coal stove, and I, after *sweeping out,* sat down patiently *waiting* for *scholars. My* appearance then, I think, would have formed a grand subject for friend Bakewell's pencil; for if the countenance is an index of the mind and heart, every variety of curious & anxious and ludicrous expression must have characterized mine, *then.* He must picture me, too, *far from friends,* nearly 2000 miles from my Eastern ones, and make it appear *real* to give the true effect.

The first day, I had nine scholars. At noon I went to Mr. H. Everley's to board. I have found them to be *very* pleasant and friendly. He and wife were formerly baptists, and are still so in principle, tho' they have united with the Methodists rather than lose all church privileges. They have but two children, Joseph and Mary, the first six, the other nine years old. I have a nice, comfortable room, with a bed, stove, sofa and carpet. I do love the quiet piety of this family, and am thankful that my lot has been cast with them.

Fort Des Moines, Nov. 28th.

Went out this morning to school with only a hood & shawl, entirely innocent of how the wind blows here, and came home at night much wiser. Found the presiding elder here.

29.

Wrote to S[ullivan]. Have been severely tried all the week about my fire at school. The coal is so dirty, and it is so cold here, I tho't this is but a *beginning,* and I *must* have patience. More trials than this are doubtless in store for me. Wrote to Mrs. Wood [of Keokuk], today. Monday, eight more scholars, wrote to sister Eliza.

Dec. 6th. Friday Evening.

This, then, is the ultimatum of all my hopes and desires to do good at the west! Were I sensible that I am *needed* here, I should rejoice, even amid all difficulties. But Mrs. B[ird]'s school renders mine unnecessary now, and people consider it a *favor* to *me* to send their children to school. It certainly *cannot* be a *very great* favor to the poor children to revolve around that stove, trying to keep themselves from freezing by a fire that is so high and hot as to burn one side while the other is shaking with the ague. I claim the merit of having discovered a new law of attraction, not mentioned in any philosophy I ever studied—that of *heat,* which proves here completely irrisistible when exerted upon *certain bodies* coming within the sphere, of its influence. Very important, truly!

It is certainly sadly interesting to witness half my pupils suffering all the different stages of the ague and fever every other day. It almost gives *me* the shakes to see them. The little fellows seem to bear it with great resignation. I have been troubled with a severely sore throat—the result of my initiatory process, but think I shall, after this, become toughened to it. My *toes* too have been *frozen,* but will get well.

Fairfield, Iowa, June 2 [*1851*].

Have been here since May 14, and it has rained every day but two or three. Mr. and Mrs. Bell met me very cordially and the teacher of the primary department Miss S. Weir, occupies the room with me, opening upon the porch above, a nice cosey little place and I have charge of all the advanced pupils who are so pleasant thus far that I have promised myself contentment, if not happiness this summer. Miss Weir has about 25, and I nearly the same number; and there are now six boarding scholars.

The buildings are pleasantly located, and where the grounds are covered with shrubbery, as they will be as soon as it can grow, it will be a delightful and healthful location. This is the first Seminary upon the plan of a Young Ladies' boarding school as yet started in the state. It has been in operation only three sessions, but is quite popular, and thriving. Mr. B. is an old gentleman who has been very useful in the causes of education and church extension, and has undergone many privations and trials in his efforts for the West. He has only two children at home—Miss Mary, a curious, original (pleasant?) girl, and her sister Caroline, a sweet yet proud looking young lady. Her manners may, upon further acquaintance, prove to be merely the result of natural reserve. I like them all very much, and only fear they will not like me as well.

Last night the sudden news of the death of her father came to Miss W[eir] and she, with her sister, one of the boarding scholars, has gone home. Oh, how I feel for her in her distress; but there lies a weight of agony upon *my* spirit that I must bear *alone;* worse, oh how *much* worse than the news of the departure of the dearest friend, were the contents of that letter to me. Oh, my brother! if you knew what anguish I have suffered on your account the past winter, how guarded would you have been to avoid a second fall! But it is not for *my own* sake that I deplore it, deeply as I feel the disgrace. Father in Heaven watch over and reclaim him! He never could have received my letter, or he would have been on his way to me, by this time instead of that horrid place again. I fear that I may be blamed for accepting the responsible station I now occupy. Can it be that S.'s misconduct does not affect me? O may I be taught the way of duty, and nerves to perform it however onerous.

From THE MAIMIE PAPERS

by

MAIMIE PINZER

(1885–19??)

Born in Philadelphia of immigrant Polish and Russian parents, Maimie Pinzer left school at thirteen when the murder of her father plunged the family into poverty. Rejected by her mother and other relatives for her sexual activity, she became a prostitute. She was befriended by certain benefactors, including Fanny Howe, a prominent Bostonian. Her letters to Mrs. Howe show that she was capable of real friendship, which helped her in her struggles to leave "the life." Her whereabouts after 1922, when her letters ceased, remains a mystery.

• ——————————————————— •

Philadelphia, January 12, 1911

. . . And yet I could not buckle down to cutting out entirely all the things I had summed up while in the hospital as being empty and not worthwhile. At times, I would go all over the thoughts that passed through my mind while in the various hospitals and would decide that I would keep my word to myself and cut it out. Of course, the attending luxuries that go with loose living I did not want to give up. But, summed all up, it is anything but a pleasant road to travel; and I saw how the few luxuries did not make up for the indignities offered me and the cautious way I had to live. As, for instance, I love women—that is, I would like to have women friends—but I can't have; or rather, I couldn't have. I avoided them, even though very often I would meet one who would want to be friendly, and even now, the habit is so strong in me that I never encourage any advances from them—much as I should like to—for I couldn't find any enjoyment in being on friendly terms with a woman who lived a sporting sort of life, and the others, I dreaded would find out, perhaps inadvertently, something about me, and perhaps cut me, and I couldn't stand that; so I always repel any advances they make—so much so, that Mr. Jones thinks I am rude about it. When we lived in Enid, Oklahoma, a small town of 12,000 people, I had an occasion to look up a lady who owned a Boston Terrier, and I took quite a fancy to her and she did to me. She had a very beautiful home and was very wealthy. For once, I permitted myself the luxury of accepting her invitations to little luncheons to be partaken only with her. She seemed to enjoy talking with me, and although everything I talked about was superficial and mostly lies, I too enjoyed going to her home. As we had been there almost six months when I met her, and I had never done anything wrong in the town, I hadn't much to fear, although I used to go to Oklahoma City about once a month to meet a man I knew there. So for six months I was very friendly with her and two other younger girls— the daughters of the local banker—when one day, like a bolt out of a clear sky, this lady's father (she was unmarried and about thirty-five years old— she kept house for her father) called to see me and in very terse language told me I must not continue my friendship with his daughter. It afterwards developed that a young man who called on one of these younger girls knew something ugly about me and told it to their father, who in turn told it to Mr. Kemble, who told his daughter. But she would not believe it at first, but must have later—for when her dog saw me on the street some time later and came to me, she called him away and cut me direct. At any rate, we left town the following week—although Mr. Jones was business agent for the carpenter's Union, receiving $25.00 a week without having to do any manual labor. I could not stand living there longer; and since then, with the exception of being "charming" to some friends of Mr. Welsh's who knew all about me, I haven't ventured to know any women except you—and that's different, of course.

When I was in the hospital in St. Louis in 1909, again I came to the conclusion that I would live right and perhaps be happy. I thought my mode of life explained why I was lying there all alone, without the visits of a human being other than the general nurse and no word from anyone— besides the letters from my husband, which are always the very kindest and affectionate. I would see all about me at the visiting hour people hurrying and scurrying to the various beds to see the other patients, bringing them fruit and flowers and magazines. I don't think I ever wanted anything in my life so much as I did some grapes while I was there, but I had no friends to bring or send them to me. Then the conviction was strong in me again that it was surely my fault that I was so friendless and that I would surely try living straight and start to make friends that were real. But, while I had that thought in my brain, I tucked it conveniently out of my road— and hadn't been out of the hospital three weeks before I went to San Antonio, Texas, with a circuit attorney of St. Louis who too had been ill in the St. Agnes Hospital when I was, and who had the same doctor. The doctor ordered the trip for his health and I went along, writing my husband some absurd story about my uncle Louis who lives thirty miles out of San Antonio sending me the ticket to go there. (Fact of the matter was, when I did go to this small town to visit my uncle whom I hadn't seen in ten years, he treated me as one would an acquaintance and never even asked me to stop for a meal.) At any rate, when I returned from San Antonio, went to Oklahoma City to join Mr. Jones, I was again thoroughly and heartily weary of my precarious way of living, for I had another belittling experience in San Antonio. And then I just sat down and waited. For what, I didn't know, but I had an idea that I wasn't going to meet anyone and would just cut it all out. Then came Mr. Welsh's first letter; and no sooner was that correspondence started than I knew why, before that, I could only *think* to live decent. For I found that which is the reason people keep diaries. It records these thoughts, and once they are carefully taken apart and written, you can follow the lines of your thoughts more clearly; and then it is a clearing-house, and from one writing to the next, one's brain is cleared, ready to follow out the line of thought or perhaps start a new line of thought. In that way, Mr. Welsh helped me most, for I kept a sort of diary in my letters to him of my thoughts as they came to me each day. And then, when I felt I was responsible to a real live father for my actions, I was very careful as to what I did. And I never did anything (even the most ridiculous detail) that I didn't write to him of it; and I was happier than ever before in my life. And because I believed in him, he readily convinced me that I had a Father in Heaven; and when I think back to the first few weeks I was in the hospital last spring, I doubt whether it was really I who had such childlike faith in prayers. I haven't even the slightest atom of that left, but I wish I had. It was very comforting. In a measure I'm like a child for I love to show off, provided I have the right sort of an audience. I know when I procured the work at the *North American,* it was because I wanted to show everyone how clever I was; and then when Mr. Welsh left and I had no one to applaud, I quit being clever. You know, I've told you how hard I've looked for work. Well I have, in a halfhearted sort of a way and with the feeling: "Oh! What's the use— for I don't propose to get up at 6:30 to be at work at 8 and work in a close, stuffy room with people I despise, until dark, for $6.00 or $7.00 a week! When I could, just by phoning, spend an afternoon with some congenial person and in the end have more than a week's work could pay me." Doesn't that sound ugly—and it feels ugly—but they are my thoughts. I had them very persistently when I ceased writing regularly to Mr. Welsh, and you don't know how I miss writing my thoughts to him. I feel perhaps that is why I wrote you the day I was so very despondent. As yet, they are still thoughts— . . .

Montreal, August 20, 1915

I know you are worrying as to how I intend to manage this winter. And though I will tell you not to let it worry you, I know that isn't easy. You will probably think I've thought it all out as to how I will do—but really, I haven't, because I just can't. . . . Conditions are bad enough— couldn't be worse—but if any person knew that they were going to exist for a given period, they would act, knowing there was no recourse. But as it is, "hope springs eternal." And in my case, hardly a day—two at the most—but something seems to clear the way for a change in the near future, but unfortunately so far hasn't materialized. Here, as everywhere, I've

MAIMIE PINZER

no doubt, everyone hangs on to the hopes that at the end of each season, the war will be over, and with it the hard times.

In my letter to Mr. Welsh, I wrote that according to what I see and read, no one should expect or even accept, in these days, more than their mere keep. There is so much suffering and misery from need and other causes that I don't expect, and wouldn't accept, more than just enough to keep alive. Yet even that seems difficult to accomplish.

Attempting to think it all out clearly seems impossible; all sorts of thoughts crowd in, chasing out the original problem of how I intend to manage. But by putting it all down, I can see it, even if I cannot arrive at any solution. So if you don't mind, I will write it all out here, and you, too, can see where I stand—for I know you do think for me and worry not a little. I can't help but feel sure of this. Your kindness to me makes it very evident.

If these were normal times, and after considering everything, I should make an attempt to interest people in starting a mission of some sort, for friendless girls, with me at the head; and for my labors I should expect my keep and a tiny sum over it to put away so that I could feel I had some sort of assurance that I wouldn't end my days in a poorhouse or old ladies home.

In order to do this, I'd want to—and feel sure I could—interest Montreal people who could give something toward its support. Just now that is out of the question.

My own intelligence, aside from several experiences I've had, tells me that it is not possible to enlist the sympathies of Canadians in any enterprise that doesn't in some way affect the soldiers or, missing that, their families. Truly I don't blame them. Not that I think they should be so anxious for the soldier above every other consideration, but because they are beseiged on all sides for money to aid all sorts of causes that are military, I don't blame them for feeling no other consideration counts. As an instance: nearly every building that has heretofore been used for charitable purposes, of various natures, has been taken over for military purposes—barracks, recruiting offices, this or that league—but all for military purposes. What of those who benefited thru these other and original lines? They must manage as I will have to. Miss Rothwell, a probation officer, had some interest in Stella Phillips—due to her mother's having reported her to the police courts and she having been placed under Miss Rothwell's eyes. On my return from Phila., I called up Miss Rothwell to ask for an appointment to tell her what had been done for Stella Phillips. She informed me that her services (at the city's cost) had been turned over to the Patriotic Society and she had no time for Stella Phillips, her business being now with *Tommy Atkins*. I asked her what woman had been put in her place—and she said all were now working for the Patriotic Society. What of the many girls she looked after—for I knew personally at least eight—whom she encouraged, watched over in a measure, gave little lifts to when they were without food, etc.? These girls still exist—and more of them, due to conditions worse than existed formerly—but they are not connected with this war, so must shift for themselves.

I tell you all this to show you my opinion of what chances there are for raising money thru Montreal people for a new mission. . . . It is accepted then that I couldn't expect a livelihood—not now anyway—thru conducting a mission.

It is an old story, that the way is blocked for me to take up many of the situations that I am mentally fitted for—and which now also there are few of. Aside from these where mental ability is necessary, it is absolutely impossible for me to get those of the other sort. Salesperson, waitress, worker (physical) of any sort in a shop (due to insurance which prevents their employing anyone who has defective eyesight)—and sifted down, there is nothing else but housework. Which, since living here, I am fitted for—but can you think of any house that is fairly well kept that would have me? . . . Figured down, and logically, there doesn't seem much chance for me unless I happen on the proper place and I have no doubt there is such a place, provided I could wait long enough for it.

In the various agencies where I have applied, that are maintained by the city or otherwise to cope with this "unemployed problem," I was given a blank to fill out, and that I never heard from them is because they no doubt find others whose plight is worse, and leave me to find help elsewhere. You think (perhaps) how could anything I wrote make my plight seem less pitiful than others? Well I'll tell you. One question was: "Should you not find work, would you starve unless you resorted to unlawful acts." (I suppose they meant stealing, or adultery, etc.) I answered in the negative, for could I say truthfully that I would starve when I know that you, Miss Huntington, Miss Payson, Mr. Welsh, Miss Outerbridge and one or two more, would not let me do that? Now bear in mind that I do not keep in mind that I can depend on any of these friends, and were these not abnormal times, I am sure I'd not have to put them to the test. But just the same, when a point-blank question of that sort is put before me, how else can I answer it and stick to my determination to be above deceit?

Other questions, such as, "Have you received an education? (which no doubt is asked to determine one's ability) made me appear less needy than others; for though in the strict sense of the word I did not recieve [*sic*] an education, yet I am not to be classed as "uneducated":

"How many languages can you speak?"
"How many languages can you read?"
"How many languages can you write?"

And I answered "five" to the first (German, French, English, Yiddish and Russian); "four" to the second question, and "two" to the last. All this, I am sure, made me seem less hopeless than some of the others who, at the most (French Canadians), are only bi-lingual.

I bring all this out to show you, then, why I can expect no help from such sources. Though I did write in the proper classification that I was unable to cope with conditions mainly because of my impaired sight, and even more defective appearance, I received not a word from them—though Stella (who also registered) did. Though in her case she was referred to the Catholic Church—who recommended that she leave all worldly cares and enter the Sacred Heart Convent as a penitent. Sweet outlook! That means for life. So, you see—here I am, right where I started and no nearer to the solution than when I started.

Suppose I had not these friends,—that's the thought that comes next—what should I do? That's the worst of it—one can't really know what they would do unless they just had to do it. And always the thought comes back—"But you have those friends." You see, I am writing to you as I would *think*, and I hope you will understand that I am not so brutally frank to make my case seem better: it is just because it is all *so*, as far as I can see.

I picture myself in another girl's place, and I eliminate friends who can, or do, help. Then comes the thought "Well, she could sew (perhaps), or nurse, do housework—or even go in a factory of some sort." Yet all that is closed to me. So I can't really and fairly, do what another girl would do.

When every other consideration fails, there comes a thought which I can't eliminate any more than I can that I have friends who will not let me starve—and that is Mr. Benjamin. We have never discussed this phase of the situation—but I know he realizes it as I do, that if I have no means, and work of some sort isn't available, I will have to return to live with him.

Just now he hasn't a dollar in the world. I mean just that. On Tuesday, he bought me a strip of war tax stamps; and when he got his change, he said, "This is my all," (and it was 20 cents) "until I put something over"—meaning selling some stock. The only reason that the plan of living with him comes to my mind is because, for the same rent he pays, I could live; and though food for two costs more than food for one—eaten together, and with care, I could live on what his food costs him in the restaurants (for he eats only in absolutely clean places, and they are always expensive). I haven't discussed this probability with him; and I believe—if it were necessary—I'd have to suggest it, because he never has in any way referred to this possibility ever occurring again. . . .

When I think about the possibility of returning to that life again, I feel more puzzled at what the girls would think of me, and the fact that my brother James's prophecy would come true (for he says I am a prostitute at heart—he didn't tell me that, but I saw it in writing to my oldest brother, who scarcely knows me, and whom I wouldn't know if I met him) than I do about the actual wrong I should be committing. For I have the knowledge that I don't want to be bad. But I don't see what else I shall do, if I don't soon find some way of earning my keep. When writing to Mr. Welsh several days ago, I didn't mention this possibility. I hope you won't consider this deceit. I couldn't do it—it would pain him, and I hadn't the courage to inflict it on him. I know too that you won't welcome the thought; so I say, don't let it fret you, for perhaps it may not come to that.

I cast about in my mind for excuses for myself, and I can think of many. So a new thought comes to me: "Suppose this was some other girl's plight. Not a young girl who, just because she came to you," (I am addressing myself) "would make you want to shield her, but some girl you heard of. And as you are always able to criticise girls generally—except those whom you interest yourself in—what would you say she should do?" I'd say, first off—"Oh! she can't tell me she can't find work—I'd find work for her!" But really I am not lazy. There isn't a moment I'm not active. I'm too much so, if anything—so I won't admit laziness as a fault. Then I'd say, "If she isn't lazy, perhaps she's super-sensitive and imagines she wouldn't be desirable." There may be some truth in that. But I can offset that, by saying I always answer the ads by letter, and almost invariably get an audience—because I do know how to answer ads to command attention—and then when I go in answer to them, I am let down hard by the first or second question. Further I might say: "Well, she surely could sell something from door to door." Yet in my case, that is not possible. Here (and in Phila., and perhaps everywhere) any person who thru any affliction goes from door to door, to canvass, is liable to fine, imprisonment, or both. . . .

"Then what do girls do, who not only haven't a good appearance, thru a like affliction, and who aren't able to see as well as others, yet who haven't been gifted with intelligence enough to pick up an education sufficiently good to get positions such as you have had?" I don't know exactly what they do, unless they resort to living as I did formerly; or perhaps marry; or if they do work, are laundresses, potato peelers, scrubwomen. And perhaps, instead of feeling any pride because I have been able to pick up a little knowledge, I should regard it as "a dangerous thing," since it takes me out of the class that I've every reason to believe I should be in.

Montreal, December 19, 1917

What explanation can I offer? My silence puzzles me equally as it does you. In trying to understand it, I've reached some of these conclusions.

I used to love to write, and when I had spare time, or even when I should be sleeping, I rushed to ink. Now I despise to; and I even feel annoyed when I am asked to "do" letters for Yiddish, Russian, Polish, or French people. Of course, I do them, but I hate to. And I gave up writing for . . . families of men in German prisons—though with this work I used to earn money.

My only reason, as I can make it out, is because I am always so troubled. And if I thought I'd always remain so, I'd write anyway; but it always seems as if I were to find it better "shortly." And I always hope to write "shortly"; for in writing to you and to Miss Huntington, I would have to write everything—troubles and all—as I felt we were so intimate. But when the "shortly" did come, I was head and ears in trouble again, and I did hate to admit it.

You recall I used to write you when I was troubled. I think this was because when I had these troubles, I'd find on going to bed that I couldn't sleep. I'd feel so outraged; and when I wrote to you, I got relief. And I believe now I tell it to Ira, and he always advises that I wait, and, I'll see, everything works out right. And in that way I hesitate to write, and I wait for what Ira calls "shortly."

I know I could and should write short letters or postals, to let my friends know I am all right. Poor Mr. Welsh, I treated him to a siege of silence, and he writes—advising me as if I were ten years old—that I should learn to write short letters, often. As if I didn't know this! Of course I do. And don't think I don't suffer—I do. For Miss Huntington's picture hangs directly *en face* the chair in which I sit when I am in my room, and I always see her eyes reproaching me. Though your picture is there, too, it is not so large, nor so distinct; and it is she who reproaches me daily. But I just shift my eye and feel uncomfortable.

I suppose by this time you imagine all sorts of dire things have happened. Perhaps they weren't so bad—but, to me, seemed terrible. And I feel I have been a failure.

SUGGESTIONS FOR FURTHER READING

·————————————————·

In recent years, the proliferation of works relevant to the study of images of women in literature has been so great that no one reader can begin to keep up. For this edition, the editor has, with regret, eliminated references to interdisciplinary works, although feminist literary criticism and theory still draw heavily from works in psychology, anthropology, history, philosophy, and linguistics. Fortunately, many of the bibliographical aids listed below cover all fields, including literature. Also, review articles in periodicals and anthologies of essays often have bibliographies of works from allied fields.

Major works are listed below, in four categories: Bibliographies; Periodicals; Literary Criticism (subdivided into separate works and anthologies); and Anthologies of Literature by Women. The editor has seen each of the works listed and has supplied some annotations for collective works. Bibliographies and works about individual authors have not been listed; many are included not only in some of the sources listed here but in more general bibliographies such as that of the Modern Language Association of America. Readers are reminded that the first frame of reference for any author included in this anthology is the author's other works; information in the biographical sketches and in the list of acknowledgments should be helpful.

The editor wishes to acknowledge her debt to many of the works cited in this bibliography. Especially significant in establishing the basic concept of organization were works by Mary Ellman and Katharine Rogers; more recently, the views of Elaine Showalter, Sandra Gilbert, Susan Gubar, Jane Tompkins, and my colleague Mary Helen Washington have influenced my selections.

Bibliographies

Bakerman, Jane S., and Mary Jean DeMarr. *Adolescent Female Portraits in the Novel, 1961–81: An Annotated Bibliography.* New York: Garland, 1983.

Annotations include a brief plot summary and an analysis of the function of the adolescent female characters; a checklist of important images is included.

Ballou, Patricia K. *Women: A Bibliography of Bibliographies* (1970–79). Boston: G. K. Hall, 1980.

Even though 557 titles are included, the list is selective. Items 162–199 are on literature and literary criticism; most items are extensively annotated. Both bibliographies separately published as books and those included as parts of books or in periodical articles are listed.

Bergman, Len V., and Marie B. Rosenberg. *Women and Society: A Critical Review of the Literature with a Selected Bibliography.* Beverly Hills, Calif.: Sage Publications, 1975; 2d ed., 1978.

Although it does not aim at completeness, this impressive 3-volume bibliography is very thorough. Two categories are important: women in literature and the arts, and women in biographies, autobiographies, and memoirs.

Borenstein, Audrey. *Older Women in 20th-Century America: A Selected Annotated Bibliography.* New York: Garland, 1982.

Chapters 8, 10, 11, and 12 list literary works, literary criticism, oral histories, and diaries and letters of older women; the work is liberally annotated.

Briscoe, Mary Louise, with Barbara Tobias and Lynn Z. Bloom. *American Autobiography, 1945–1980: A Bibliography.* Madison: University of Wisconsin Press, 1982.

More than five thousand autobiographies are listed. Those by women are identified with an asterisk. Annotations give the main features of each work. This work includes the list of women's autobiographies, *First Person Female, American,* published in 1980 as a special supplement to the journal *American Notes & Queries.*

Cardinale, Susan. *Anthologies By and About Women: An Analytical Index.* Westport, Conn.: Greenwood Press, 1982.

This 822-page index reproduces the tables of contents of 375 anthologies in various fields, with cross-indexes to individual authors, to the titles of the separate works anthologized, and to forty subject headings. Subjects include biography and autobiography, literary criticism, drama, poetry, fiction, science fiction, black women, older women, and lesbianism. A keyword index includes image, self-image, lesbian, myth, and stereotype.

Coven, Brenda. *American Women Dramatists of the Twentieth Century: A Bibliography.* Metuchen, N.J.: Scarecrow Press, 1982.

This work lists 133 individual women, with a separate bibliography of primary and secondary sources for each; it has a section on works about women dramatists and lists other bibliographies, including those in books and articles.

Daims, Diva, and Janet Grimes. *Toward a Feminist Tradition: An Annotated Bibliography of Novels in English by Women, 1891–1920.* New York: Garland, 1981.

This work supersedes an earlier compilation by the same editors, *Novels in English by Women: A Checklist*. More than 3400 titles by 1723 authors of novels were selected to exemplify the feminist tradition of nonconventional heroines, who assume responsibility for their own lives. Annotations include reviews of the works.

Haber, Barbara. *The Women's Annual: 1980; The Year in Review*. Boston: G. K. Hall, 1981.
This continuing bibliography (with different editors in other years) furnishes annually "timely information about women [in America]." Organized topically, each section has a review of scholarship and a bibliography; one topic is "Women, Scholarship, and the Humanities."

———. *Women in America: A Guide to Books, 1963–75*. Boston: G. K. Hall, 1978.
A chapter titled "Literature, the Fine Arts, and Popular Culture" (pp. 95–123) includes biographies and literary criticism; it is heavily annotated.

Hulme, Marylin A., and Olin Ferris. *Fair Play: A Bibliography of Non-stereotyped Materials*. Rutgers, N.J.: Rutgers University, Douglass College, 1977.
Volume 2 of a bibliography compiled at the Training Institute for Sex Desegregation of the Public Schools, this pamphlet furnishes a list for kindergarten through twelfth grade of materials in print that counteract sexual stereotypes; many works listed are also widely taught in college courses.

Kessler, Carol, and Gail Rudenstein. "Mothers and Daughters in Literature: A Preliminary Bibliography," in *Women's Studies: An Interdisciplinary Journal* 6 (1979), 223–234.
An expanded list appeared in Davidson, Cathy N., and E. M. Broner, *The Lost Tradition: Mothers and Daughters in Literature* (New York: F. Ungar, 1980).

Myers, Carol Fairbanks, ed. *Women in Literature: Criticism of the Seventies* (1976) and *More Women in Literature: Criticism of the Seventies* (1979). Metuchen, N.J.: Scarecrow Press.
List, by author, books and articles about women writers and about images of women by men and women; include general bibliographies of literary criticism.

Reardon, Joan, and Kristine A. Thorsen, eds. *Poetry by American Women, 1900–1975: A Bibliography*. Metuchen, N.J.: Scarecrow Press, 1979.
Both a primary bibliography of works by poets and a secondary one of works about poets. It aims at completeness.

Ritchie, Maureen. *Women's Studies: A Checklist of Bibliographies*. London: Mansell, 1980.
This list has a section on literature, which includes twenty-four bibliographies published in the 1970s.

Roberts, J. R. *Black Lesbians: An Annotated Bibliography*. Foreword by
Barbara Smith. Tallahassee, Fla.: Naiad Press, 1981.
Items 1–42 list biographical materials; items 151–240 list fiction, poetry, and
criticism by and/or about black lesbians.

Rosenfelt, Deborah Silverton. *Strong Women: An Annotated Bibliography
of Literature for the High School Classroom*. Old Westbury, N.Y.:
Feminist Press, 1976.
A selected list of anthologies as well as individual works of autobiography,
biography, fiction, poetry, and drama.

Williamson, Jane, ed. *New Feminist Scholarship: A Guide to Bibliographies*.
Old Westbury, N.Y.: The Feminist Press Clearinghouse on Women's
Studies, 1979.
Lists 391 bibliographies published before 1979 in books or periodicals in
English. Fifty-two percent of the entries are annotated. Items 192–210
(pp. 62–67) are under the category of literature; bibliographies of
individual women writers are *not* included. A detailed index of titles
augments the thirty subject categories. A useful list of publishers and
addresses includes small feminist presses.

Periodicals

Annotated Guide to Women's Periodicals in the United States. Richmond,
Ind. Vol. 1, 1982. This promises to be an ongoing publication; it is
annotated and attempts to be comprehensive.

Chrysalis: A Magazine of Women's Culture (1977). Nos. 8 and 9 have a
catalogue of feminist publishers; nos. 10 and 11 contain annotated lists of
feminist plays, published and unpublished.

Concerns (1974). A quarterly newsletter published by the Women's Caucus
for the Modern Languages of the Modern Language Association of
America. It lists works in progress on feminist criticism and literary theory.

Conditions (1977). This magazine emphasizes lesbian writing. Issue no. 5
was a special issue on black women.

Feminist Studies (1972). This quarterly, interdisciplinary in scope, has
frequent literary articles.

Frontiers: A Journal of Women Studies (1975). Frequent articles and
reviews on literary topics; the Spring 1979 issue contains a review of
feminist poetry for the last ten years and an article on using literary
criticism in the classroom. Beginning with the Spring 1980 issue, this
journal publishes abstracts of the proceedings of the National Women's
Studies Association's annual convention.

Ladder, The (1966). A lesbian publication of literary works and book
reviews, as well as occasional theoretical articles. Several anthologies of
works from this journal are listed in later sections of this bibliography.

Legacy (1984). Begun as a newsletter on nineteenth-century American women writers, this publication is expanding to become a quarterly in 1985.

National Women's Studies Association. *Newsletter* (1983). Originally published by the Feminist Press, this publication has announcements of national and regional meetings and occasional reviews.

Sage: A Scholarly Journal on Black Women (1984). Includes some literary articles and book reviews, as well as autobiographical and biographical pieces. Vol. 1 (Fall 1984) was a special issue on mothers and daughters.

Signs: Journal of Women in Culture and Society (1975). This interdisciplinary scholarly journal has frequent issues and articles pertinent to the study of literature. Vol. 7 (Autumn 1981) has a review essay on mothers and daughters as well as a section of several articles on French feminist theory, including translations of important texts. Volume 9 has a special issue on lesbianism and writing by lesbians.

Sinister Wisdom (1976). This journal, published in Rockland, Me., appears three times a year and focuses on lesbian concerns.

Women's Review of Books (1984). Published monthly by the Wellesley Center for Research on Women, this journal has in-depth reviews by prominent scholars in all disciplines of women's scholarship.

Women's Studies: An Interdisciplinary Journal (1972). This long-established journal is broad in scope and has had many distinguished articles and reviews of literary importance. Vol. V (1977) and vol. VII (1980) had special issues on women's poetry; vol. VI, no. 2 (1979) focuses on mothers and daughters in literature.

Women's Studies International Forum (1985) is a continuation of the *Women's Studies International Quarterly* (1978). Published in England, it aims at the "rapid publication" of research findings and review articles in all fields.

Women's Studies Quarterly (1972). A continuation of the *Women's Studies Newsletter* originally published by the Feminist Press, this publication often focuses on teaching; vol. XI (Winter 1983) was devoted to teaching about mothering. An index to the *Quarterly*, the *Newsletter*, and to *Women's Studies International Quarterly* for 1972–1982 is available from the Feminist Press.

Literary Criticism

This list is divided into one section of separate works of criticism by individual authors and a second section of anthologies of essays by several authors. In this edition, for the first time, it has been necessary to exclude the many interdisciplinary works that have been important to literary theorists, in order to be as inclusive as possible of the strictly literary works.

Works that focus on analysis of male writers' images of women still appear, but the majority of recent works focus on women writers. Though not exhaustive, the lists below include the major works published through mid-1985.

Separate Works

Agress, Lynne. *The Feminine Irony: Women on Women in Early-Nineteenth-Century English Literature*. Rutherford, N.J.: Associated University Presses, 1978.

Allen, Mary. *The Necessary Blankness: Women in Major American Fiction of the Sixties*. Bloomington: Indiana University Press, 1976.

Auerbach, Nina. *Woman and the Demon: The Life of a Victorian Myth*. Cambridge: Harvard University Press, 1982.

Baym, Nina. *Woman's Fiction: A Guide to Novels by and about Women in America, 1820–1870*. Ithaca, N.Y.: Cornell University Press, 1978.

Beer, Patricia. *Reader, I Married Him: A Study of the Women Characters of Jane Austen, Charlotte Brontë, Elizabeth Gaskell, and George Eliot*. London: Macmillan Press, 1974.

Christ, Carol P. *Diving Deep and Surfacing: Women Writers on Spiritual Quest*. Boston: Beacon Press, 1980.

Christian, Barbara. *Black Women Novelists: The Development of a Tradition, 1892–1976*. Westport, Conn.: Greenwood Press, 1980.

Dash, Irene. *Wooing, Wedding, and Power: Women in Shakespeare's Plays*. New York: Columbia University Press, 1981.

de Beauvoir, Simone. *The Second Sex*. New York: Knopf, 1953.

Deegan, Dorothy. *The Stereotype of the Single Woman in the American Novel*. 1919; reprint, New York: Octagon Books, 1969.

de Rougemont, Denis. *Love in the Western World*. New York: Pantheon, 1956.

DuBois, Ellen Carol, et al. *Feminist Scholarship: Kindling in the Groves of Academe*. Urbana: University of Illinois Press, 1985.

DuPlessis, Rachel Blau. *Writing Beyond the Ending: Narrative Strategies of Twentieth-Century Women Writers*. Bloomington: Indiana University Press, 1985.

Edwards, Lee R. *Psyche as Hero: Female Heroism and Fictional Form*. Middletown, Conn.: Wesleyan University Press, 1984.

Ellman, Mary. *Thinking about Women*. New York: Harcourt Brace Jovanovich, 1968.

Ferrante, Joan M. *Woman as Image in Medieval Literature, From the Twelfth Century to Dante*. New York: Columbia University Press, 1975.

Fetterly, Judith. *The Resisting Reader: A Feminist Approach to American Literature*. Bloomington: Indiana University Press, 1978.

Fiedler, Leslie A. *Love and Death in the American Novel*. Rev. ed. New York: Stein and Day, 1966.

Foster, Jeanette. *Sex Variant Women in Literature*. 1956; reprint, Baltimore: Diana Press, 1975.

Friedan, Betty. *The Feminine Mystique*. New York: Norton, 1963.

——. *The Second Stage*. New York: Summit Books, 1982.

Fryer, Judith. *The Faces of Eve: Women in the Nineteenth Century American Novel*. New York: Oxford University Press, 1976.

Gelfant, Blanche. *Women Writing in America: Voices in Collage*. Hanover, N.H.: University Press of New England, 1985.

Gilbert, Sandra M., and Susan Gubar. *The Madwoman in the Attic: The Woman Writer and the Nineteenth-Century Literary Imagination*. New Haven: Yale University Press, 1979.

Gould, Jean. *American Women Poets: Pioneers of Modern Poetry*. New York: Dodd Mead, 1980.

Grahn, Judy. *The Highest Apple: Sappho and the Lesbian Poetic Tradition*. San Francisco: Spinsters Ink, 1985.

Hall, Nor. *The Moon and the Virgin: Reflections on the Archetypal Feminine*. New York: Harper & Row, 1980.

Heilbrun, Carolyn. *Toward a Recognition of Androgyny*. New York: Knopf, 1973.

——. *Reinventing Womanhood*. New York: Norton, 1979.

Homans, Margaret. *Women Writers and Poetic Identity: Dorothy Wordsworth, Emily Brontë, and Emily Dickinson*. Princeton: Princeton University Press, 1981.

Huf, Linda. *A Portrait of the Artist as a Young Woman*. New York: Frederick Ungar, 1983.

Juhasz, Susan. *Naked and Fiery Forms: Modern American Poetry by Women, A New Tradition*. New York: Harper & Row, 1976.

Kolbenschlag, Madonna. *Kiss Sleeping Beauty Good-Bye*. New York: Doubleday, 1979.

Kolodny, Annette. *The Lay of the Land: Metaphor as Experience and History in American Life and Letters*. Chapel Hill: University of North Carolina Press, 1976.

——. *The Land Before Her: Fantasy and Experience of the American Frontiers, 1630–1860*. Chapel Hill: University of North Carolina Press, 1984.

McNall, Sally Allen. *Who Is in the House? A Psychological Study of Two Centuries of Women's Fiction in America, 1795 to the Present*. New York: Elsevier Science, 1981.

McNaron, Toni A. H. *The Sister Bond: A Feminist View of a Timeless Connection*. New York: Pergamon Press, 1985.

Miller, Nancy K. *The Heroine's Text: Readings in the French and English Novel, 1722–1782*. New York: Columbia University Press, 1980.

Millett, Kate. *Sexual Politics*. New York: Doubleday, 1970.

Modleski, Tania. *Loving with a Vengeance: Mass-Produced Fantasies for Women*. Hamden, Conn.: Archon Books, 1982.

Moers, Ellen. *Literary Women: The Great Writers*. New York: Doubleday, 1976.

Myres, Sandra L. *Westering Women and the Frontier Experience, 1800–1915*. Albuquerque: University of New Mexico Press, 1982.

Olauson, Judith. *The American Woman Playwright: A View of Criticism and Character*. Troy, N.Y.: Whitston, 1981.

Olsen, Tillie. *Silences: Why Writers Don't Write*. New York: Delacorte, 1978.

Pearson, Carol, and Katherine Pope. *The Female Hero in American and British Literature*. Ann Arbor, Mi.: R. R. Bowker, 1981.

Pomeroy, Sarah B. *Goddesses, Whores, Wives, and Slaves: Women in Classical Antiquity*. New York: Schocken, 1975.

Poovey, Mary. *The Proper Lady and the Woman Writer: Ideology as Style in the Works of Mary Wollstonecraft, Mary Shelley, and Jane Austen*. Chicago: University of Chicago Press, 1984.

Pratt, Annis. *Archetypal Patterns in Women's Fiction*. Bloomington: Indiana University Press, 1981.

Radway, Janet. *Reading the Romance: Women, Patriarchy, and Popular Literature*. Chapel Hill: University of North Carolina Press, 1984.

Rogers, Katharine M. *The Troublesome Helpmate: A History of Misogyny in Literature*. Seattle: University of Washington Press, 1966.

Rule, Jane. *Lesbian Images*. New York: Doubleday, 1975.

———. *A Hot-Eyed Moderate*. Tallahassee, Fla.: Naiad Press, 1985.

Showalter, Elain. *A Literature of Their Own: British Women Novelists from Brontë to Lessing*. Princeton: Princeton University Press, 1977.

Spacks, Patricia. *The Female Imagination*. New York: Knopf, 1975.

Stewart, Grace. *A New Mythos: The Novel of the Artist as Heroine, 1877–1977*. Montreal: Eden Press, 1979.

Taylor, Anne Robinson. *Male Novelists and Their Female Voices: Literary Masquerades*. Troy, N.Y.: Whitston, 1981.

Todd, Janet M. *Women's Friendship in Literature: The Eighteenth Century Novel in England and France*. New York: Columbia University Press, 1980.

Tompkins, Jane. *Sensational Designs: The Cultural Work of American Fiction, 1790–1860*. New York: Oxford University Press, 1985.

Wade-Gayles, Gloria. *No Crystal Stair: Visions of Race and Sex in Black Women's Fiction*. New York: Pilgrim Press, 1984.

Walker, Alice. *In Search of Our Mothers' Gardens: Womanist Prose.*
San Diego: Harcourt Brace Jovanovich, 1983.

Walker, Cheryl. *The Nightingale's Burden: Women Poets and American
Culture Before 1900.* Bloomington: Indiana University Press, 1982.

Watts, Emily Stipes. *The Poetry of American Women from 1632 to 1945.*
Austin: University of Texas Press, 1977.

Williams, Merryn. *Women in the English Novel, 1800–1900.* London:
Macmillan, 1984.

Woodbridge, Linda. *Women and the English Renaissance: Literature and
the Nature of Womankind.* Urbana: University of Illinois Press, 1984.

Anthologies of Literary Criticism

Abel, Elizabeth, ed. *Writing and Sexual Difference.* Chicago: University of
Chicago Press, 1982.
Essays from the periodical *Critical Inquiry* (1980–1982), by such critics as
Sandra Gilbert, Elaine Showalter, Mary Jacobus, Susan Gubar, Annette
Kolodny, Judith Gardiner, and Catherine Stimpson.

Abel, Elizabeth, Marianne Hirsch, and Elizabeth Langland, eds. *The
Voyage In: Fictions of Female Development.* Hanover, N.H.: University
Press of New England, 1983.
Essays discuss the *Bildungsroman* by women in the nineteenth and
twentieth centuries and in contemporary fiction. French, English, and
American writers are discussed.

Ascher, Carol, Louise DeSalvo, and Sara Ruddick, eds. *Between Women:
Biographers, Novelists, Critics, Teachers, and Artists Write about Their
Work on Women.* Boston: Beacon Press, 1984.
Twenty-five women write on the experience of writing about women
writers.

Barr, Marleen S., ed. *Future Females: A Critical Anthology.* Bowling Green,
Ohio: Bowling Green State University Popular Press, 1981.
Essays on women in science fiction.

Barr, Marleen S., and Nicholas D. Smith. *Women and Utopia: Critical
Interpretations.* Hanover, N.H.: University Press of New England, 1984.
Ten essays on utopian works by nineteenth and twentieth century writers,
including Ursula Le Guin, Doris Lessing, Suzy Charnas, and Elizabeth
Stuart Phelps.

Brown, Cheryl, and Karen Olson, eds. *Feminist Criticism: Essays on Theory,
Poetry, and Prose.* Metuchen, N.J.: Scarecrow Press, 1978.
Most of the twenty-six essays have been previously published; some are
papers presented at academic conventions. Four are theoretical essays
on the relationship between feminism and literary criticism; twelve are
theoretical/historical essays on prose writers, including Doris Lessing,

Anaïs Nin, and Jean Rhys; ten are practical criticism of women poets, including Emily Dickinson, H.D., Sylvia Plath, Anne Sexton, and Adrienne Rich.

Christian, Barbara., ed. *Black Feminist Criticism: Perspectives on Black Women Writers.* New York: Pergamon Press, 1985.
Sixteen essays study the work of such writers as Alice Walker, Toni Morrison, Gwendolyn Brooks, Paule Marshall, Audre Lorde, and Gloria Naylor. Themes examined include "Black Women Artists as Wayward," "The Dynamics of Difference," lesbianism, and Afro-American women.

Cornillon, Susan Koppelman, ed. *Images of Women in Literature: Feminist Perspectives.* Bowling Green, Ohio: Bowling Green State University Popular Press, 1972.
Contains twenty-three critical essays organized thematically: woman as heroine, the invisible woman, woman as hero, feminist aesthetics. Includes lists of works considered feminist, works by black women, and works portraying lesbian relationships.

Davidson, Cathy N., and E. M. Broner, eds. *The Lost Tradition: Mothers and Daughters in Literature.* New York: Frederick Ungar, 1980.
Twenty-four essays discuss mothers and daughters in literature from ancient times to modern, including in works by writers such as Cather, Colette, Woolf, Lessing, and Plath. There is an extensive bibliography.

Diamond, Arlyn, and Lee R. Edwards, eds. *The Authority of Experience: Essays in Feminist Criticism.* Amherst: University of Massachusetts Press, 1977.
Three theoretical essays of feminist criticism and thirteen applications of it to works of English and American literature, most of which are considered classics. No attempt is made to define the term *feminist criticism,* but all the essays operate on the assumption that art is a part of a larger social context, which it embodies and/or challenges. Works examined include *Troilus and Criseyde, The Taming of the Shrew, Moll Flanders, Jane Eyre, Mrs. Dalloway, The Golden Notebook, The Awakening,* and *A Farewell to Arms.*

Donovan, Josephine, ed. *Feminist Literary Criticism: Explorations in Theory.* Lexington: University of Kentucky Press, 1975.
Five essays and a conclusion by the editor identify male-dominated literary criticism with patriarchal ideology. Together the essays move toward a definition of feminist criticism as explicit rejection of male norms and a conscious attempt to apply a feminist perspective, with Virginia Woolf as a model.

Edwards, Lee R., Mary Heath, and Lisa Baskin. *Woman: An Issue.* Boston: Little, Brown, 1972.
This work (which was first published as vol. 13 of *The Massachusetts Review*) includes essays, poems, fiction, documents, and pictures. Three important essays of feminist criticism appear: one on stereotypes by

Cynthia Wolff; one on feminist theater by Joan Goulianos; and one on the feminist ideas in George Eliot's *Middlemarch*.

Eisenstein, Hester, and Alice Jardine, eds., *The Future of Difference*. Boston: G. K. Hall, 1980.
Papers of a conference held at Barnard College in 1979; this work includes twenty-one essays, which discuss differences among women and among feminists as well as between men and women with respect to power relationships. Authors include Nancy Chodorow, Domna C. Stanton, Jane Gallop, Carolyn Heilbrun, Carol Gilligan, Elizabeth Janeway, and Barbara Omolade.

Evans, Mari, ed. *Black Women Writers (1950–1980): A Critical Evaluation*. New York: Anchor Books, 1984.
Fifteen writers and thirty critics critique the writers' work.

Ferguson, Margaret W., Maureen Quilligan, and Nancy Vickers, eds. *Rewriting the Renaissance: The Discourses of Sexual Difference in Early Modern Europe*. Chicago: University of Chicago Press, forthcoming.
Eighteen essays consider both women writers and the representation of women in literature.

Fleishmann, Fritz, ed. *American Novelists Revisited: Essays in Feminist Criticism*. Boston: G. K. Hall, 1982.
Eighteen essays on "classic" American writers, male and female; women writers discussed are Cather, Wharton, Stein, and Stowe.

Gaudin, Colette, et al., eds. *Feminist Readings: French Texts/American Contexts. Yale French Studies*, no. 62, 1981.
Ten essays are grouped under three headings: Literary and Sexual Difference: Practical Criticism/Practical Critique; Rethinking Literary History; and The Politics of Theory, The Theory of Politics. Though most of the texts studied are French, this is an important link between French psychoanalytical and literary theory and American "gynocriticism," which is Elaine Showalter's term for the study of women writers rather than of theory *per se*. Translations of and essays on major French feminist critics also appeared in *Signs*, 7 (Autumn 1981).

Gilbert, Sandra M., and Susan Gubar, eds. *Shakespeare's Sisters: Feminist Essays on Women Poets*. Bloomington: University of Indiana Press, 1979.
Twenty-one scholarly and critical essays written especially for this volume consider British and American women poets in the context of the male-dominated environment of their personal life and/or of the literary world of their time. Includes two important theoretical essays about gender and creativity and about stages of development for women poets, a survey of Afro-American women poets, and essays on individual authors (Jane Lead, Anne Bradstreet, Anne Finch, Emily Brontë, Elizabeth Barrett Browning, Christina Rossetti, Emily Dickinson, Marianne Moore, H.D., Edna St. Vincent Millay, May Swenson, Gwendolyn Brooks,

Sylvia Plath, Anne Sexton, and others). Also has a fourteen-page bibliography of feminist criticism.

Grier, Barbara, ed. *Lesbiana: Book Reviews from The Ladder, 1966–72.* Tallahassee, Fla.: Naiad Press, 1976.
Reprints the columns in which books were reviewed as they appeared; reviews of plays, fiction, history, biography, and autobiography.

Heilbrun, Carolyn, and Margaret Higonnet, eds. *The Representation of Women in Fiction: Selected Papers from the English Institute, 1981.* Baltimore: Johns Hopkins University Press, 1983.
Essays from the first English Institute session on women offer varied perspectives on feminist theory and criticism of fiction. Authors are Elizabeth Ermarth, Susan Gubar, Jane Marcus, J. Hillis Miller, Nancy K. Miller, and Mary Poovey.

Hiller, Dana V., and Robin A. Sheets. *Women and Men: The Consequences of Power: A Collection of New Essays.* Cincinnati, Ohio: Office of Women's Studies, University of Cincinnati, 1977.
Contains conference papers on feminist literary theory by Judith Gardiner, Nina Auerbach, Catherine Stimpson, Barbara Tenenbaum, Sandra Gilbert, and Susan Gubar.

Horn, Pierre L., and Mary Beth Pringle, eds. *The Image of the Prostitute in Modern Literature.* New York: Frederick Ungar, 1984.
Ten essays written especially for this volume represent interdisciplinary viewpoints.

Hull, Gloria T., Patricia Bell Scott, and Barbara Smith, eds. *But Some of Us Are Brave: All the Women are White, and All the Blacks are Men: Black Women's Studies.* Old Westbury, N.Y.: Feminist Press, 1982.
Chapter 5 contains five essays on literature, criticism, and teaching; chapter 6 is a bibliographical essay on black women writers.

Jelinek, Estelle C., ed. *Women's Autobiography: Essays in Criticism.* Bloomington: Indiana University Press, 1980.
Critical essays about the theory and practice of women's autobiography and its difference from men's autobiography. Includes essays on Lillian Hellman, Gertrude Stein, Maya Angelou, Anaïs Nin, and Kate Millett, among others.

Juhasz, Suzanne, ed. *Feminist Critics Read Emily Dickinson.* Bloomington: Indiana University Press, 1983.
This is an example of an anthology of criticism on a single author. Nine essays, by the editor, Sandra Gilbert, Joanne A. Dobson, Margaret Homans, and Joanne Feit Diehl, among others, discuss Dickinson from a feminist perspective.

Keohane, Nanerl O., Michelle Z. Rosaldo, and Barbara C. Gelpi, eds. *Feminist Theory: A Critique of Ideology.* Chicago: University of Chicago Press, 1982.
Among other interdisciplinary essays, all of which originally appeared in

Signs, are two influential literary essays: Myra Jehlen, "Archimedes and the Paradox of Feminist Criticism"; and Jane Marcus, "Storming the Tool Shed."

Lee, L. L., and Merrill Lewis. *Women, Women Writers, and the West.* Troy, N.Y.: Whitston, 1979.
A collection of essays about various genres of writing by women: biographies, diaries, letters, fiction, and poetry; also contains essays about images of women by men writers.

Lenz, Carolyn Ruth Swift, Gayle Green, and Carol Thomas Neely, eds. *The Woman's Part: Feminist Criticism of Shakespeare.* Urbana: University of Illinois Press, 1980.
Seventeen essays and a twenty-page bibliography entitled "Women and Men in Shakespeare"; includes both general discussions and analyses of specific plays. The general essays are by Madelon Gohlke, Marianne Novy, Charles Frey, Paula Berggen, Catherine Stimpson, Carole McKewin, Clara Claiborne Park, and the editors.

Marks, Elaine, and Isabelle de Courtivron, eds. *New French Feminisms: An Anthology.* Amherst: University of Massachusetts Press, 1980.
Three introductory essays give perspectives on contemporary French psychoanalytic, linguistic, and Marxist approaches to literature, which appear in translation.

McGonnell-Ginet, Sally, Ruth Borker, and Nelly Furman, eds. *Women and Language in Literature and Society.* New York: Praeger, 1980.
Nelly Furman's essay "Textual Feminism" and seven essays in part IV ("Reading Women Writing") are important for literature students. The essays are by Bonnie Costello, Paula A. Treichler, Nancy K. Miller, Jane Gallop, Peggy Kamus, Caren Greenberg, and Gayatri Spivak.

Middlebrook, Diane Wood, and Marilyn Yalom, eds. *Coming to Light: American Women Poets in the Twentieth Century.* Ann Arbor: University of Michigan Press, 1985.
Sixteen essays about Sylvia Plath, H.D., Gertrude Stein, Louise Bogan, Adrienne Rich, and Anne Sexton, among others.

Miller, Beth, ed. *Women in Hispanic Literature: Icons and Fallen Idols.* Berkeley: University of California Press, 1983.
Seventeen essays, mostly on writers in Spain, but some are on Chicana, Argentine, Chilean, and Mexican writers.

Murray, Meg McGavran, ed. *Face to Face: Fathers, Mothers, Masters, Monsters—Essays for a Nonsexist Future.* Foreword by Florence Howe. Westport, Conn.: Greenwood Press, 1983.
Contains essays on women's attempts to deal with their internalized images, from sociological and psychological perspectives; two essays on literary topics by Kittye Delle Robbins and Mary Anne Ferguson are included.

Nyquist, Mary, and Margaret W. Ferguson. *Milton and Literary Theory.*
New York: Methuen, forthcoming.
Five of the essays are feminist.

Prenshaw, Peggy Whitman, ed. *Women Writers of the Contemporary South.*
Jackson: University Press of Mississippi, 1984.
Essays about seventeen women writers from the South whose works
appeared between 1945 and 1982 are included; they appeared earlier in
two special issues of *The Southern Quarterly.*

Showalter, Elaine, ed. *The New Feminist Criticism: Essays on Women,
Literature, and Theory.* New York: Pantheon Books, 1985.
Eighteen essays, previously published except for the introductory overview
by the editor, discuss topics such as feminist effects on the literary canon,
the relation of feminist criticism to women's culture, and the various
feminist theories about women's writings. These essays constitute almost a
history of feminist criticism.

Spender, Dale, ed. *Feminist Theorists: Three Centuries of Key Women
Thinkers.* New York: Pantheon Books, 1983.
Twenty-one contributors review the life and thought of women thinkers;
literary artists included are Mary Astell, Mary Wollstonecraft, Charlotte
Perkins Gilman, Olive Schreiner, and Virginia Woolf.

Squier, Susan Merrill, ed. *Women Writers and the City: Essays in Feminist
Literary Criticism.* Knoxville: University of Tennessee Press, 1984.
Essays on French, British, American, and Canadian writers' views of the
city and women. Authors considered include Virginia Woolf, George
Eliot, Doris Lessing, Margaret Atwood, Willa Cather, and Ntozake
Shange. An extensive bibliography is included.

Sternburg, Janet, ed. *The Writer on Her Work.* New York: Norton, 1980.
Sixteen American women writers discuss their writing habits and their
works; authors included are Anne Tyler, Joan Didion, Mary Gordon,
Nancy Milford, Honor Moore, Michele Murray, Margaret Walker, Susan
Griffin, Alice Walker, Ingrid Bengis, Toni Cade Bambara, Erica Jong,
Maxine Hong Kingston, Janet Burroway, Muriel Rukeyser, and Gail
Godwin.

Tate, Claudia, ed. *Black Women Writers at Work.* New York: Continuum
Press, 1983.
In interviews with feminist critics, fifteen writers discuss their views on
writing; among those included are Toni Morrison, Gwendolyn Brooks,
Gayle Jones, and Alice Walker.

Todd, Janet M. *Gender and Literary Voice.* New York: Holmes & Meier,
1980.
Contains a review of feminist literary criticism by Nina Auerbach and
seventeen other essays on specific authors from Christine de Pisan to Lisa
Alther.

Todd, Janet M., ed. *Be Good, Sweet Maid: An Anthology of Women &
Literature.* New York: Holmes & Meier, 1981.

Fifteen essays written in the 1970s, which appeared in *The Mary Wollstonecraft Newsletter,* which later became the journal *Women & Literature.*

———. *Men by Women.* New York: Holmes & Meier, 1981.
A collection of essays on male characters and maleness by women writers such as Jane Austen, the Brontës, George Eliot, Dorothy Richardson, and Sylvia Plath.

———. *Women Writers Talking.* New York: Holmes & Meier, 1983.
In interviews with feminist critics, fifteen French, British, and American women writers talk about their craft; among those included are Grace Paley, May Sarton, Maya Angelou, Marilyn French, and Germaine Greer.

Toth, Emily, ed. *Regionalism and the Female Imagination.* New York: Human Sciences Press, 1984.
The regions considered include New England, the South, Mormon country, the Midwest, and Louisiana. Authors considered include Harriette Arnow, Rose Terry Cooke, Doris Lessing, Edith Summers Kelley, Mary E. Wilkins Freeman, and Alice Dunbar-Nelson.

Anthologies of Literature by Women

Listed here are collections of short works (or occasionally of excerpts from long works) by women writers. Since many such anthologies appear as paperbacks or as textbooks, even fairly recent ones may not be in print by the time this book is published. But since many of them may be in some library collections and available on interlibrary loan, as many as possible are listed here; the emphasis is on works published since 1979.

Bankier, Joanna, and Deidre Lashgari. *Women Poets of the World.* London: Macmillan, 1983.
Poems from many countries, in translation, from early times to the present.

Barnstone, Aliki, and Willis Barnstone, eds. *A Book of Women Poets from Antiquity to Now.* New York: Schocken Books, 1980.
Contains the works of more than 275 poets from more than 75 different cultures and spanning four thousand years. Arranged chronologically, this book includes English language poetry as well as translations from many diverse languages; many twentieth-century works are included.

Bataille, Gretchen, and Kathleen Sands, eds. *American Indian Women: Telling Their Lives.* Lincoln: University of Nebraska Press, 1984.
This study of American Indian women's autobiographies, often oral, includes many excerpts and an extensive bibliography.

Beck, Evelyn T., ed. *Nice Jewish Girls: A Lesbian Anthology.* Watertown, Mass.: Persephone Press, 1982; reprint, New York: Crossing Press, 1984.
A collection of essays, poems, journal excerpts, fiction, letters, and a bibliography by and about Jewish lesbians. Most of the authors are lesser known; an essay by Adrienne Rich is included.

Bell, Roseann P., et al., eds. *Visions of Black Women in Literature*. New York: Anchor Press, 1979.
By juxtaposing stereotypes of black women with the varied reality presented by black women and men writers, this collection undercuts the stereotypes of black women. It includes works by critics as well as selections by such writers as Paule Marshall, Mari Evans, Margaret Walker, Sonia Sanchez, and Audre Lorde.

Bendixen, Alfred, ed. *Haunted Women: The Best Supernatural Stories by American Women Writers*. New York: Frederick Ungar, 1984.
Thirteen stories by nineteenth-century writers, plus one each by Edith Wharton and Gertrude Atherton.

Blicksilver, Edith, ed. *The Ethnic American Woman: Problems, Protests, Lifestyle*. Dubuque, Iowa: Kendall Hunt, 1979.
A collection of writings by and about twenty-three American ethnic groups, organized thematically around the chronology of women's lives, education, work, religion, and search for identity and love. Works of several genres, including historical and critical essays. There are tables of contents by ethnic group and by genre.

Brant, Beth, ed. *A Gathering of Spirit Writing and Art by North American Indian Women*. Watertown, Mass.: Sinister Wisdom Books, 1984.
More than two hundred poems and narratives by many authors; this work was a double issue of *Sinister Wisdom* (nos. 22/23).

Bulkin, Elly, and Joan Larkin, eds. *Amazon Poetry: An Anthology of Lesbian Poetry*. Brooklyn, N.Y.: Out and Out Books, 1975.
Works of thirty-eight poets, selected to "show the scope and intensity of lesbian experience."

———. *Lesbian Poetry*. Watertown, Mass.: Persephone Press, 1981.
Poems written by sixty-four poets who define themselves as lesbians.

Chinoy, Helen C., and Linda W. Jenkins, eds. *Women in the American Theater, Careers, Images, Movements: An Illustrated Anthology and Sourcebook*. New York: Crown, 1981.
Not strictly an anthology, this "sourcebook" indexes about seven hundred women playwrights and describes images of women in their plays.

Cochran, Jo, J. T. Stewart, and Mayumi Tsutakawa, eds. *Gathering Ground: New Writing and Art by Northwest Women of Color*. Seattle: The Seal Press, 1984.
A collection of fiction, poetry, letters, interviews, essays, and artwork by women of color in the Pacific Northwest.

Cosman, Carol, Joan Keefe, and Kathleen Weaver, eds. *The Penguin Book of Women Poets*. New York: Penguin, 1979.
Aimed at showing the timelessness and universality of women's concerns and talent, this collection spans 3,500 years and 40 literary traditions. It is organized chronologically and includes many twentieth-century works.

Covina, Gina, and Laurel Galan, eds. *The Lesbian Reader: An Amazon*

Quarterly Anthology. Guernville, Calif.: Amazon Press, 1975.
Poems, stories, essays, and a bibliography about lesbian erotic experience.

Cruikshank, Margaret, ed. *New Lesbian Writing: An Anthology.* San Francisco: Grey Fox Press, 1984.
A collection of poems, sketches, stories, and essays by lesbian writers. It includes a bibliography of recent lesbian literature (1980–1983).

Cully, Margo, ed. *A Day at a Time: Being the Diary Literature of American Women from 1766 to the Present.* Old Westbury, N.Y.: Feminist Press, 1985.
The subtitle, continued, explains the contents: "Including the Triumphs and Tragedies of Women of All Ages, from Diverse Classes and Cultures, Writing About Love, Work, Travel, War, Adventure, Politics, etc., in Their Own Words; to Which is Added an Essay on Diary Literature and a Bibliography of Many Hundreds of Published Diaries and Other Items of Interest."

Dorenkamp, Angela, et al., eds. *Images of Women in American Popular Culture.* New York: Harcourt Brace Jovanovich, 1985.
Excerpts from newspapers, periodicals, and books as well as some essays are organized around stereotypes of women.

Fairbairns, Zoe, et al., eds. *Tales I Tell My Mother: A Collection of Feminist Short Stories.* West Nyack, N.Y., and London: Journeyman Press, 1978; 2nd ed., 1980.
Fifteen short stories and five essays by five British women writers with a Socialist perspective appear in three categories: feminist fiction and language, feminist fiction and politics, and feminist fiction and aesthetics.

Fannin, Alice, Rebecca Lukens, and Catherine Hoyser Mann, eds. *Woman: An Affirmation.* Lexington, Mass.: D. C. Heath, 1979.
Contains works from many genres (autobiography, short story, folk tale, poetry, drama) to illustrate such themes as reawakening, self-definition, tensions caused by social expectations, autonomy, women's life experience. Two male authors and many women authors, mostly contemporary.

Ferguson, Moira, ed. *First Feminists: British Women Writers, 1578–1799.* Bloomington: Indiana University Press, 1985.
Twenty-eight writers including Aphra Behn and Mary Wollstonecraft.

Fetterly, Judith, ed. *Provisions: A Reader from 19th Century American Women.* Bloomington: Indiana University Press, 1985.
Stories or excerpts from books by sixteen writers are included, with explanatory essays by the editor on the context of their writing.

Fisher, Dexter, ed. *The Third Woman: Minority Women Writers of the United States.* Boston: Houghton Mifflin, 1980.
Contains essays on and writings by third-world women: American Indian, black, Chicana, and Asian-American writers. Many of the selections are recent and most have not been previously anthologized.

Flores, Angel, and Kate Flores, eds. *Feminist Poems from the Middle Ages*

to the Present: Four Bilingual Anthologies. Old Westbury, N.Y.:
Feminist Press, 1985.
Poems from four languages are represented, each edited separately:
Hispanic, Angel and Kate Flores; French, Domna Stanton; Italian, Muriel
Kittel et al.; German, Susan Cocalis.

France, Rachel, ed. *A Century of Plays by American Women.* New York:
Richard Rosen Press, 1979.
Includes twenty-three short plays by Rachel Crothers, Susan Glaspell,
Djuna Barnes, Gertrude Stein, Megan Terry, and others.

Freibert, Lucy M., and Barbara A. White, eds. *Hidden Hands: An
Anthology of American Women Writers, 1790–1870.* New Brunswick,
N.J.: Rutgers University Press, 1985.
Organized thematically under such subjects as didacticism, the novel of
seduction, melodrama, and frontier romance, this work includes excerpts
from many women novelists, most of whose works were popular in their
time but disappeared soon afterwards.

Gilbert, Sandra M., and Susan Gubar, eds. *The Norton Anthology of
Literature by Women: The Tradition in English.* New York: Norton,
1985.
Organized chronologically, this massive anthology of writing by women
in English from the fourteenth to the twentieth century includes a wide
selection of works. Four complete novels are included: *Jane Eyre, The
Awakening, The Bluest Eye,* and an early novel by Jane Austen in
epistolary form, *Love and Freindship.*

Godfrey, Kenneth, Audrey Godfrey, and Jill Mulvay Derr, eds. *Women's
Voices.* Salt Lake City: Deseret Books, 1982.
A compilation of diary excerpts from the writings of Mormon pioneer
women (1830–1900).

Gómez, Alma, Cherríe Moraga, and Mariana Romo-Carmona, eds. *Cuentos:
Stories by Latinas.* New York: Kitchen Table: Women of Color Press,
1983.
A collection of twenty-nine stories, in Spanish and English, by Latina
women.

Grier, Barbara, and Coletta Reid, eds. *The Lavender Herring: Lesbian
Essays from The Ladder.* Baltimore: Diana Press, 1976.
The essays include a group on the lesbian image in art, dealing with the
visual arts.

———. *Lesbian Lives: Biographies of Women from The Ladder.* Baltimore:
Diana Press, 1976.
Written by the editors and others, the biographies include ones about
writers Sappho, H.D., Sara Teasdale, Dorothy Thompson, Margaret
Fuller, Vernon Lee, Mary Wollstonecraft, and Edith Hamilton.

———. *The Lesbians Home Journal: Stories from The Ladder.* Baltimore:
Diana Press, 1976.

Twenty stories and two brief essays on the realistic lesbian novel and on available lesbian paperbacks.

Hampsten, Elizabeth. *Read This Only to Yourself: The Private Writings of Midwestern Women, 1880–1910*. Bloomington: Indiana University Press, 1982.
Excerpts from the manuscript diaries and letters of many obscure North Dakota women are included in a running explanatory commentary.

Hargrove, Anne C., and Maurine Magliocco, eds. *Portraits of Marriage in Literature*. Macomb, Ill.: Western Illinois University, 1984.
Thirteen essays examine the varied images of marriage both in fiction and in letters (between Thomas and Jane Carlyle, for example). Authors range from Chaucer to Diane Johnson.

Hedges, Elaine, and Ingrid Wendt, eds. *In Her Own Image: Women Working in the Arts*. Old Westbury, N.Y.: Feminist Press, 1980.
Essays, poetry, fiction, autobiographical excerpts, letters, as well as visual and other arts are presented in four sections: Household Work and Women's Art; Obstacles and Challenges; Definitions and Discoveries; Women's Art and Social Change.

Holmes, Kenneth L., ed. *Covered Wagon Women: Diaries and Letters from the Western Trails, 1840–90* (vol. 1). Glendale, Calif.: Arthur H. Clark, 1983.
This promises to be the first of ten volumes of unpublished works. The editor of this anthology has not seen this volume.

Kessler, Carol Farley, ed. *Daring to Dream: Utopian Stories by United States Women, 1836–1919*. Boston: Pandora Press, 1984.
Fifteen stories culled from out-of-print sources show utopias from a feminist perspective; an extensive annotated bibliography of 137 utopias is included.

Koppelmann, Susan, ed. *Between Mothers and Daughters: Stories Across a Generation*. Old Westbury, N.Y.: Feminist Press, 1984.
Eighteen stories from nineteenth- and twentieth-century American writers, including Fannie Hurst, Tess Slesinger, Tillie Olsen, and Joanna Russ.

———. *Old Maids: Short Stories by Nineteenth Century U.S. Women Writers*. Boston: Pandora Press, 1984.
Thirteen short stories by some little-known writers and by Elizabeth Stuart Phelps, Catherine Sedgwick, Alice Cary, Frances E. W. Harper, and Rebecca Harding Davis.

———. *The Other Woman: Stories of Two Women and a Man*. Old Westbury, N.Y.: Feminist Press, 1984.
Eighteen stories written between 1840 and 1980 by such writers as Charlotte Perkins Gilman, Ellen Glasgow, Marjorie Kinnan Rawlings, and Alice Walker.

Lifshin, Lyn, ed. *Ariadne's Thread: A Collection of Contemporary Women's Journals*. New York: Harper & Row, 1982.
Short excerpts were submitted in response to the editor's request for a

journal entry on themes important to women, such as work, self, love and friendship, and family. Some of the authors are comparatively unknown; prominent ones include Maxine Kumin, Alix Kates Shulman, Marge Piercy, Gail Godwin, Linda Hogan, Rita Mae Brown, Linda Pastan, and Denise Levertov.

————. *Tangled Vines: A Collection of Mother and Daughter Poems.* Boston: Beacon Press, 1978.
Poems by Anne Sexton, Shirley Kaufman, Diane Wakoski, Erica Jong, Marge Piercy, Sandra Hochman, Adrienne Rich, and others express the complicated emotional relationships between mothers and daughters and daughters and mothers.

Mahl, Mary R., and Helene Koon, eds. *The Female Spectator: English Women Writers Before 1800.* Old Westbury, N.Y.: Feminist Press, 1977.
This volume includes selections from *The Female Spectator* (a journal) as well as from British women writers who lived and wrote before 1800, including Julian of Norwich, Margery Kemp, Queen Catharine Parr, Queen Elizabeth, Katherine Philips, Aphra Behn, and Eliza Haywood.

Mason, Mary Grimley, and Carol Hurd Green, eds. *Journeys: Autobiographical Writings by Women.* Boston: G. K. Hall, 1979.
Stories of personal liberation through involvement with a person or cause, from Anne Bradstreet to Susan Sontag.

Mazow, Julia Wolf, ed. *The Woman Who Lost Her Names: Selected Writings of American Jewish Women.* San Francisco: Harper & Row, 1979.
Short stories, memoirs, and excerpts from novels that counter the stereotypes of the Jewish mother and the Jewish "princess."

McNaron, Toni A. H., and Yarrow Morgan, eds. *Voices in the Night: Women Speaking about Incest.* Pittsburgh, Pa.: Cleis Press, 1982.
A collection of forty-two poems, letters, journal entries by "those [women] who have survived incest."

Moffatt, Mary Jane, and Charlotte Painter, eds. *Revelations: Diaries of Women.* New York: Vintage, 1975.
Under the headings Love, Work, and Power, appear selections from many writers, including Louisa May Alcott, Anne Frank, George Sand, Sophie Tolstoy, Alice James, Virginia Woolf, Joanna Field, and Käthe Kollwitz.

Moore, Honor, ed. *The New Women's Theater: Ten Plays by Contemporary American Women.* New York: Random House, 1977.
Recent plays that explore women's experience and focus on four recurring themes: mother-daughter relationships, rites of autonomy, conflicts with men, and the need for self-definition. Authors include Myrna Lamb, Eve Merriam, Joanna Russ, Ursula Molinaro, Corrinne Jacher, Tina Howe, Honor Moore, Ruth Wolff, and Joanna Krauss.

Moraga, Cherríe, and Gloria Anzaldúa, eds. *This Bridge Called My Back. Writings by Radical Women of Color.* Watertown, Mass.: Persephone

Press, 1981; 2nd ed., New York: Kitchen Table: Women of Color Press, 1983.

Varied writings—journal entries, essays, poems, and interviews—define Third World feminism and the experiences on which it is based. Includes a bibliography that is organized topically: Afro-American, Asian/Pacific, Latina, Native American, as well as a list of small presses.

Olsen, Tillie, ed. *Mother to Daughter, Daughter to Mother: A Feminist Press Daybook and Reader*. Old Westbury, N.Y.: Feminist Press, 1984.

Organized for reading from month to month, this selection of some of Tillie Olsen's favorite poems on this topic includes short poems by some one hundred women authors, mostly contemporary; some are well known, some are published here for the first time.

Payne, Karen, ed. *Between Ourselves: Letters Between Mothers and Daughters, 1750–1982*. Boston: Houghton Mifflin, 1984.

Organized thematically, the majority of these letters are from little known twentieth-century writers. Among the better-known writers are Jessie Bernard, Robin Morgan, Sylvia Plath, Anne Sexton, Lady Mary Wortley Montagu, George Sand, and Louisa May Alcott.

Rogers, Katharine M., ed. *Before Their Time: Six Women Writers of the Eighteenth Century*. New York: Frederick Ungar, 1979.

Includes excerpts from British authors Anne Finch, Mary Astell, Mary Wortley Montagu, Charlotte Smith, Fanny Burney, and Mary Wollstonecraft.

Showalter, Elaine, ed. *These Modern Women: Autobiographical Essays from the Twenties*. Old Westbury, N.Y.: Feminist Press, 1978.

Seventeen essays by women whose works appeared in *The Nation* (1926–1927).

Spinner, Stephanie, ed. *Motherlove: Stories by Women about Motherhood*. New York: Dell, 1978.

Sixteen major contemporary American and British women writers break through old myths about motherhood and present varied, complex, and interesting characters who are mothers.

Stanley, Julia Penelope, and Susan Wolfe, eds. *The Coming Out Stories*. Watertown, Mass.: Persephone Press, 1980.

Contains forty-one autobiographical accounts of their coming out process by lesbians of different ages, habits, lifestyles, and beliefs. An introduction by Adrienne Rich places these diverse pieces in a historical context.

Stetson, Erlene, ed. *Black Sister: Poetry by Black American Women, 1746–1980*. Bloomington: Indiana University Press, 1981.

Nine pre-twentieth-century poets and forty-nine who wrote after 1900 are included. Stetson finds three unifying themes in these works: "a compelling quest for identity, a subversive perception of reality, and subterfuge and ambivalence as creative framework."

Walker, Barbara G. *The Women's Encyclopedia of Myths and Secrets*. San Francisco: Harper & Row, 1983.

This massive volume includes stories of female goddesses and concepts; the "secret" of the title is that of female goddesses as women's projective story of creation. Mostly scholarly sources are cited for the information given, but the work is heavily selective and relies on the work of Robert Graves.

Washburn, Penelope, ed. *Seasons of Woman: Song, Poetry, Ritual, Prayer, Myth, Story*. New York: Harper & Row, 1979.
Organized to follow a woman's life cycle, this anthology draws heavily on sources of great variety, for example, American Indian, Chinese, Indian, and Eskimo, along with many white American women writers.

Washington, Mary Helen, ed. *Black-Eyed Susans: Classic Stories by and About Black Women*. New York: Doubleday, 1975.
Contains ten stories by six black women writers with a critical and historical introduction by the editor. Authors included are Gwendolyn Brooks, Toni Morrison, Toni Cade Bambara, Alice Walker, Louise Meriwether, and Jean Wheeler Smith.

———. *Midnight Birds: Stories of Contemporary Black Women Writers*. New York: Anchor Press, 1980.
Contains twelve stories by nine authors, organized thematically, with critical comments for each category and a critical introduction by the editor. Authors represented are Paulette Childress White, Alexis DeVeaux, Alice Walker, Ntozake Shange, Frenchy Hodges, Gayl Jones, Toni Morrison, Toni Cade Bambara, and Sherley Anne Williams. All of the images combat the stereotype of the castrating black matriarch.

Woman Space: Future and Fantasy, Stories and Art by Women. Lebanon, N.H.: New Victoria, 1981.
Thirteen short stories, published collectively, by Joanna Russ, Carole Rosenthal, Josephine Saxton, and Lois Metzger, among others.

ACKNOWLEDGMENTS

•————————————————————•

SHERWOOD ANDERSON "Death in the Woods" reprinted by permission of Harold Ober Associates, Inc. Copyright © 1926 by The American Mercury, Inc. Copyright renewed 1953 by Eleanor Copenhaver Anderson.

MAX APPLE "Bridging" from *Free Agents* by Max Apple. Copyright © 1984 by Max Apple. Reprinted by permission of Harper & Row, Publishers, Inc.

W. H. AUDEN "Miss Gee" copyright 1940 and renewed 1968 by W. H. Auden. Reprinted from *W. H. Auden: Collected Poems,* edited by Edward Mendelson, by permission of Random House, Inc., and Faber & Faber.

JANE AUGUSTINE "Secretive" reprinted by permission of the author. First appeared in *Aphra, The Feminist Literary Magazine,* vol. 4, #4, Fall, 1973.

ANN BEATTIE "Tuesday Night" copyright © 1977 by Ann Beattie. Reprinted from *Secrets and Surprises,* by Ann Beattie, by permission of Random House, Inc. Originally appeared in *The New Yorker.*

SALLY BENSON "Little Woman" reprinted by permission; © 1938, 1966 The New Yorker Magazine, Inc.

RAY BRADBURY "I Sing the Body Electric!" from *I Sing the Body Electric!* © renewed 1969 by Ray Bradbury. Reprinted by permission of Harold Matson Company, Inc.

GWENDOLYN BROOKS "The Mother" from *The World of Gwendolyn Brooks* by Gwendolyn Brooks, copyright 1945 by Gwendolyn Brooks. Reprinted by permission of Harper & Row, Publishers, Inc.

OLGA BROUMAS "Artemis," from "Twelve Aspects of God," reprinted by permission of Yale University Press from *Beginning with O.* Copyright © 1977 by Olga Broumas.

HORTENSE CALISHER "The Middle Drawer" from *The Collected Stories of Hortense Calisher,* copyright © 1975 by Hortense Calisher. Reprinted by permission of Arbor House Publishing Company. All rights reserved.

JAN CLAUSEN "Daddy" from *Mother Sister Daughter Lover* by Jan Clausen, reprinted by permission of The Crossing Press.

LUCILLE CLIFTON "Miss Rosie" from *Good Times,* by Lucille Clifton. Copyright © 1969 by Lucille Clifton. Reprinted by permission of Random House, Inc.

COLETTE "The Other Woman" reprinted with permission of Macmillan Publishing Company from *The Other Woman* by Colette, translated by Margaret Crosland. Copyright © 1972 by Macmillan Publishing Company. By permission, Peter Owen, London.

MARTHA COLLINS "Homecoming" reprinted by permission of the author. Copyright © 1972 by Martha Collins. This poem originally appeared in *The Southern Review.*

MERIDEL LE SUEUR "Biography of My Daughter" from *Salute to Spring* reprinted by permission of the author.

DORIS LESSING "One off the Short List" from *A Man and Two Women* copyright © 1958, 1962, 1963 by Doris Lessing. Reprinted by permission of Simon & Schuster, Inc., and Jonathan Clowes Ltd.

DENISE LEVERTOV "Living Alone I, II, III" from Denise Levertov, *The Freeing of the Dust.* Copyright © 1975 by Denise Levertov. "Relearning the Alphabet" from Denise Levertov, *Relearning the Alphabet.* Copyright © 1970 by Denise Levertov Goodman. Both reprinted by permission of New Directions Publishing Corporation.

NORMAN MAILER "The Time of Her Time" reprinted by permission of the author and the author's agents, Scott Meredith Literary Agency, Inc., 845 Third Avenue, New York, NY 10022.

MICHELE MURRAY "Coming to Self" from *The Great Mother and Other Poems* reprinted by permission of James M. Murray, trustee under the will of Judith Michele Murray. © 1974 by Sheed & Ward, Inc.

ANAÏS NIN Excerpts from *The Diaries of Anaïs Nin,* Volumes I and III, copyright © 1966, 1969 by Anaïs Nin. Reprinted by permission of Harcourt Brace Jovanovich, Inc.

MARIE NOËL Excerpts reprinted from *Marie Noël: Notes for Myself.* Translated by Howard Sutton. Copyright © 1968 by Cornell University. Used by permission of the publisher, Cornell University Press.

JOYCE CAROL OATES "The Girl" reprinted from *The Goddess and Other Stories* by Joyce Carol Oates by permission of the publisher, Vanguard Press, Inc. Copyright © 1974, 1973, 1972, 1971, 1970, 1969, 1967, 1966 by Joyce Carol Oates.

EDNA O'BRIEN "The Call" copyright © 1979 by Edna O'Brien. Reprinted by permission of Lescher & Lescher, Ltd. Originally appeared in *The New Yorker.*

SHARON OLDS "Best Friends" from *The Dead and the Living,* by Sharon Olds. Copyright © 1983 by Sharon Olds. Reprinted by permission of Alfred A. Knopf, Inc.

TILLIE OLSEN "Tell Me a Riddle" excerpted from the book *Tell Me a Riddle* by Tillie Olsen. Copyright © 1956, 1957, 1960, 1961 by Tillie Olsen. Reprinted by permission of Delacorte Press/Seymour Lawrence.

EUGENE O'NEILL *Before Breakfast* from *The Plays of Eugene O'Neill,* by Eugene O'Neill. Copyright 1924 by Boni and Liveright, Inc. Reprinted by permission of Random House, Inc.

AROZINA PERKINS Excerpts from *Women Teachers on the Frontier,* Polly Kaufman, ed. © by Yale University 1984.

JAYNE ANNE PHILLIPS "Souvenir" excerpted from the book *Black Tickets* by Jayne Anne Phillips. Copyright © 1976, 1977, 1978, 1979 by Jayne Anne Phillips. Reprinted by permission of Delacorte Press/Seymour Lawrence.

MARGE PIERCY "Unlearning to Not Speak" from *Circles on the Water* by Marge Piercy. Copyright © 1969, 1971, 1973 by Marge Piercy. Reprinted by permission of Random House, Inc.

MAIMIE PINZER Excerpt from *The Maimie Papers* reprinted by permission of The Feminist Press and Indiana University Press.

ADRIENNE RICH "Diving into the Wreck" is reprinted from *Diving into the Wreck, Poems 1971–1972,* by Adrienne Rich, with the permission of W. W. Norton & Company, Inc. Copyright © 1973 by W. W. Norton & Company, Inc.

JANE RULE "Middle Children" from *Theme for Diverse Instruments,* copyright © 1975 by Jane Rule. Reprinted by permission of the author.

MAY SARTON "Joy in Provence" is reprinted from *A Private Mythology* by May Sarton, with the permission of W. W. Norton & Company, Inc. Copyright © 1966 by May Sarton.

NTOZAKE SHANGE "With no immediate cause" from *Nappy Edges* reprinted by permission of St. Martin's Press.

IRWIN SHAW "The Girls in Their Summer Dresses" excerpted from the book *Short Stories: Five Decades* by Irwin Shaw. Copyright © 1937, 1938, 1939, 1940, 1941, 1942,

1943, 1944, 1945, 1946, 1947, 1949, 1950, 1952, 1953, 1954, 1955, 1956, 1957, 1958, 1961, 1963, 1964, 1967, 1968, 1969, 1971, 1973, 1977, 1978 by Irwin Shaw. Reprinted by permission of Delacorte Press.

MAY SWENSON "Women" from *New and Selected Things Taking Place* by May Swenson. Copyright © 1968 by May Swenson. Originally appeared in *The New American Review*. By permission of Little, Brown and Company in association with The Atlantic Monthly Press.

MEGAN TERRY Lines from *Approaching Simone* reprinted by permission of Megan Terry.

JEAN THOMPSON "Driving to Oregon" from *The Gasoline Wars* © 1979 by Jean Thompson. "Driving to Oregon" originally appeared in *Carolina Quarterly* XXIX (Spring/ Summer 1977). By permission of the University of Illinois Press.

JAMES TIPTREE, JR. "The Women Men Don't See" copyright © 1974 by James Tiptree, Jr. Reprinted by permission of the author and the author's agent, Virginia Kidd.

JEAN TOOMER "Fern" is reprinted from *CANE* by Jean Toomer, with permission of Liveright Publishing Corporation. Copyright 1923 by Boni and Liveright.

ESTELA PORTILLO TRAMBLEY "The Burning" reprinted by permission of the author.

ALICE WALKER "Beyond What" from *Revolutionary Petunias & Other Poems,* copyright © 1973 by Alice Walker. Reprinted by permission of Harcourt Brace Jovanovich, Inc.

RUTH WHITMAN "Cutting the Jewish Bride's Hair" from *The Marriage and Other Poems,* copyright © 1968 by Ruth Whitman. Reprinted by permission of Harcourt Brace Jovanovich, Inc.

KATE WILHELM "Baby, You Were Great!" from *Orbit* 2 reprinted by permission of the author. Copyright © 1969 by Damon Knight.

SHERLEY ANNE WILLIAMS "Tell Martha Not to Moan" reprinted from *The Massachusetts Review.* © The Massachusetts Review, Inc.

WILLIAM CARLOS WILLIAMS "The Widow's Lament in Springtime" from William Carlos Williams, *Collected Earlier Poems.* Copyright 1938 by New Directions Publishing Corporation. Reprinted by permission of New Directions Publishing Corporation.